A PICTORIAL HISTORY OF THE
WORLD'S GREAT TRIALS

New, Enlarged Edition

A PICTORIAL HISTORY OF THE

FROM SOCRATES

WORLD'S GREAT TRIALS

BRANDT AYMAR
and
EDWARD SAGARIN

TO JEAN HARRIS

New, Enlarged Edition

BONANZA BOOKS · NEW YORK

Also by Brandt Aymar

CRUISING IS FUN
THE COMPLETE CRUISER
GUIDE TO BOATMANSHIP, SEAMANSHIP
AND SAFE BOAT HANDLING
CRUISING GUIDE
A PICTORIAL HISTORY OF THE MARINE
MUSEUMS OF THE WORLD
THE YOUNG MALE FIGURE
LAWS AND TRIALS THAT CREATED HISTORY
(with Edward Sagarin)

Edited by Brandt Aymar

TREASURY OF SNAKE LORE
THE PERSONALITY OF THE CAT
THE DECK CHAIR READER
THE PERSONALITY OF THE BIRD
THE PERSONALITY OF THE HORSE
THE PERSONALITY OF THE DOG

We appreciate permission to use certain excerpts and portions of actual trial testimony from the following: The Viking Press, Inc., for *Eichmann in Jerusalem* by Hannah Arendt, © 1963, by Hannah Arendt; Simon and Schuster, Inc., for *Attorney for the Damned* by Arthur Weinberg, © 1957, by Arthur Weinberg; Holt, Rinehart and Winston, Inc., for *The Sacco-Vanzetti Case: Transcript of the Record*, edited by Newton D. Baker, *et al.;* Alfred A. Knopf, Inc., for *The Era of Construction*, by Kenneth M. Stampp, and *The Record: The Trial of Adolf Eichmann for the Crimes Against the Jewish People and Against Humanity*, by Lord Russell of Liverpool; and a quotation from *The Legacy of Sacco and Vanzetti* by Louis Joughin and Edmund M. Morgan.

This 1985 edition is published by Bonanza Books,
distributed by Crown Publishers, Inc.
One Park Avenue, New York, New York 10016.

Printed and Bounded in the United States of America

Library of Congress Cataloging in Publication Data

Aymar, Brandt.
  A pictorial history of the world's great trials.

  Bibliography: p.
  Includes index.
  1. Trials.   I. Sagarin, Edward, 1913–
II. Title.   III. Title: World's great trials.
K540.A96   1985   345'.07   84-27413

ISBN 0-517-467933

h g f e d c b a

Contents

Introduction

THE HISTORY OF ALL SOCIETIES COULD BE WRITTEN AS A chronicle of wars and of trials, and indeed they have in common that they constitute two of the most dramatic occurrences where man faces his fellowman as adversary. In the courtroom, as on the battlefield, the struggle is often one of life and death, and out of each such battle there emerges not only a victor and a vanquished (or sometimes two sides that are vanquished), but a new world that is not quite what it had been before.

Trials are probably as old as *Homo sapiens,* or at least date back to the time when man began to live with other human beings in a community that was the prototype of what is today called a society. The guilt or innocence of an accused was once decided by his ability to withstand torture, and at other times by revelation from supernatural forces. The right to decide the fate of an accused has been vested in witch doctors, tribal chiefs, learned judges, and juries of one's peers. No matter the system, the miscarriages of justice were many, and their end is not in sight.

In trials are recorded the history of crime and of man's struggle against those who transgress, as well as the history of courtroom procedures and of the effort to protect the rights of the accused. And at the same time, through many historic trials man has left evidence of some of his noblest struggles: the fight for ever-widening freedom, from oppression of a state, from genocidal extermination and virulent racism.

The interest of men and women in courtroom procedures is unceasing; it is attested today by newspaper headlines of situations that will be forgotten tomorrow. But though forgotten, many of these trials will leave their mark on society, sometimes changing, if only slightly, man's outlook, attitudes, and procedures, and sometimes redirecting the course of a nation.

Hundreds of trials, criminal and civil, of significance in the life and development of nations could be named. Here we have dipped into a few, and of necessity overlooked many others. Here, in the thirty-one trials we have chosen, we have sought to find both the significant and the cross-sectional, that would capture both the spirit of courts and the spirits of many types of courts: those of many nations, civilian and military, and even of an unofficial or "rump" nature.

We start with Socrates, for some the man who never was, and end with Eichmann, the man who sought to efface himself and pretend that he was no more. Between them we have military trials: those of the Lincoln conspirators, who almost certainly should not have been tried by a military court; of Alfred Dreyfus, where the French military and France herself was on trial before world opinion; of Billy Mitchell, who sought court-martial as part of his effort to obtain a dialogue in which he could espouse his cause of greater air strength; of Edith Cavell, whose life and death were utilized by the Allies as part of the propaganda struggle against Germany.

Royalty has fallen and history has been changed through significant trials: those of Mary Queen of Scots and of Charles I, and then, on the other side of the Channel, that of Louis XIV, executed by the revolutionaries. Centuries earlier, Joan of Arc stood trial in France and was burned at the stake, accused of leading her people against the authorities; and in our own times, Jomo Kenyatta, facing a situation that might be called analogous, was adjudged guilty and went off to prison, only to emerge and become head of his liberated nation.

No chronicle of trials is complete without impeachment, and no impeachment trial matched the significance of that of Andrew Johnson, the President who, but for one vote, would have lost his job. Trials are often the story of man against government and of government against man; this will be seen in the cases of Zenger, Scopes, Ferrer, and others. They are the story of man's struggle for intellectual freedom, for the right of heresy, as will be seen in the stories of Socrates, Joan, Galileo, and Mindszenty.

Trials illustrate a variety of facts, situations, and circumstances. In Nuremberg and again in Israel, we have ex post facto law, with the defendants accused of crimes of such enormity that, even if they were not illegal, they were nevertheless criminal. The significance of these trials for the future of international relations can hardly be exaggerated. On the other hand, in the case of Trotsky we have a trial that was not a trial, in the sense that it was an unofficial hearing, set up by a group of illustrious intellectuals, to permit Trotsky to speak to the world and to vindicate himself of the charges that had been made against him by the Stalin régime. Again, this type of "court" with this type of "trial" could have repercussions in the future that are hardly foreseeable today.

We have narrated some trials that have been told many times before. That of Sacco and Vanzetti, it seems to us, is never told too often; and Scottsboro stands in grave danger of being forgotten by the younger generation today.

The trials have their lessons: in human liberty, in human error, and in the superhuman effort to bring to the courtroom an ever more precise method of judging the guilty and exonerating the innocent. It is a never-ending process, and we can only hope that great progress has been made. Such progress, we are confident, is enhanced by a knowledge and understanding of the past.

Ideally, the chronicler should be impartial, but this is an impossible requirement. Partiality is displayed by the choice of one fact rather than another to narrate, as well as by the manner in which the material is arranged. No reader of the Dreyfus case can be other than outraged at the crude frame-up, but in other cases sympathies may differ. We are more sympathetic to the managers who sought Johnson's impeachment than almost all other modern writers have been; we cannot, after reading the testimony, have doubt about the guilt of Hauptmann, but entertain many doubts about whether he received a fair trial; and find most unconvincing those who state not only that Sacco was guilty but also that he received a fair trial before an impartial judge!

We hope, however, that our views have not interfered with the task of presenting these events as we understood them and in some instances lived through them and that the reader will find not only the excitement and drama that these courtroom scenes inherently possess but will also see therein the many important lessons that history has to teach us.

Acknowledgments

WE DEEPLY APPRECIATE THE VERY VALUABLE HELP THAT so many people gave us in the preparation of this book: Daniel J. Foley; Virginia Daiker, Library of Congress; Lieutenant Colonel Gene Gurney; Lieutenant Colonel Robert Webb and Colonel Grover Heiman, Book and Magazine Division, United States Department of Defense; Dr. Hans Trefousse, professor of history, Brooklyn College, New York; D. E. J. MacNamara, criminologist, the City University of New York; Ezekiel Lifschitz, Yivo Institute for Jewish Research; Martin H. Bush, Carnegie Library, Syracuse University; Mary B. Gifford, Fall River Historical Society; Louis Torres, Federal Hall National Memorial, New York; Ellen Shaffer, the Free Library of Philadelphia; Rachel Minick, New-York Historical Society; Marion K. Conant, Dedham Historical Society; Dr. and Mrs. H. Ewing Bowmar; Kendall J. Cram, Tennessee State Library and Archives; Edith Gregor Halpert, Downtown Gallery, New York; Eugene D. Becker, Minnesota Historical Society; Treves di Bonfili; Will Edell, Wide World Photos; Maurice Davey, United Press International; and the invaluable reference sources of the New York Public Library, the Library of Congress, and the National Archives.

Many of the illustrations in this book are from famous contemporary periodicals: *Frank Leslie's Weekly, Harper's Weekly, Harper's Monthly, Illustrated London News, The Graphic, Police Gazette, Illustrated American, Vanity Fair,* and others.

We have made every effort to credit the illustrations and the text references to the proper sources. If we have inadvertently omitted any, we shall be happy to add this information in subsequent printings.

THE
TRIALS

SOCRATES SOPHRONISCI FILIVS: ATHENIESIS
Ex marmore antiquo.

P.P.Rubens delin.
P.Pontius sculpsit A°. 1638.

Cum priuilegiis Regis Christianiss.
Principum Belgarum et Ord. Belarum

"Socrates" by Paul Pontius.   *The New York Public Library*

Socrates

[399 B.C.]

THE ATHENIAN COURTS OF JUSTICE IN SOCRATES' DAY BORE little if any resemblance to our modern courts of justice. There were no judges, no prosecutors, no defense counsels. There was only a jury, but not of twelve good men and true. An Athenian jury might consist of 101 citizens of Athens, or 501, or 1,001. The odd number was a guarantee that there could not be a tie, for a simple majority was all that was needed to convict or acquit.

The court before which Socrates was tried was known as the Court of the Heliasts. It had jurisdiction over all public cases other than homicide. Any Athenian citizen of sound mind, age thirty or more and not afflicted with any disabilities, and a full citizen of Athens, could become a member of this court. At the beginning of each judicial year citizens offered themselves voluntarily, and a list was drawn up of all those who qualified. Perhaps 6,000 in all were accepted for the year. Each was paid a small sum of three obols (about nine cents a day); so it at once becomes obvious that only the lower strata of Athenian society were attracted to such duty, certainly not a jury of the peers of Socrates. These 6,000 were divided into ten sections known as dicasteries, and each dicastery consisted of some 500 or more citizens from every tribe and from every walk of life. Each day a case was tried before a dicastery, and all cases had to be concluded in the space of one day, and the verdict rendered, thus dispensing almost instant justice, compared to the long-drawn-out trials to which we are accustomed.

How did a person become a defendant before such a court? Any Athenian citizen who enjoyed the full rights of citizenship could bring an accusation against his neighbor and have him tried in this court of law. But there was a safeguard against unwarranted and purely malicious attacks. A plaintiff in such a private suit had to pay all court costs if he lost. Moreover, if one fifth of the jurors did not support his charge, he was fined heavily, as much as 1,000 drachmas (about $1,000). There was no appeal from the Court of the Heliasts, either for the prosecutor or for the defendant.

In his charge the accuser also named the penalty he wished imposed. Here again the defendant was not entirely at the mercy of his accuser. If he was declared guilty, and a bare majority of one was sufficient to bring this about, he could then propose an alternate penalty, which, if accepted by the jurors, would then be his punishment.

There were several procedures necessary for an accuser to bring a criminal charge against another person. First, he had to put the accusation in writing and bring it to the office of the king-archon, where he presented it to a magistrate, along with the name of the accused, his address, and a description of his person. If the magistrate considered the accusation trivial or involving no violation of the law, he then and there threw the case out. But if there seemed grounds for the complaint, he set a date for a preliminary hearing with accuser and accused. It was the accuser's duty to call up the accused, inform him before two witnesses of the charge, and advise him to appear at the preliminary hearing on a certain day. At this hearing both parties put in writing their declarations and supported such with evidence. Unless such evidence had been given at this hearing, it could not be introduced at the actual trial before the Court of the Heliasts. The magistrate then fixed the day upon which the case would be tried.

In the trial of Socrates in 399 B.C., the dicastery consisted of 501 judges, or jurors. Presiding over the court was the king-archon himself, who acted as a sort of traffic manager. He had no judicial duties to perform and nothing to say in regard to the case itself. He simply conducted the trial, and oversaw the voting procedure by which jurors dropped "guilty" or "not guilty" tokens into the proper receptacle. When all the judges, spectators, accusers, and accused had assembled on the appointed day, the king-archon solemnly opened the trial and informed the jurors that the case to be tried on this day was that of Meletus against Socrates. A clerk then read the indictment:

Meletus, the son of Meletus, of Pitthea, impeaches Socrates, the son of Sophroniscus of Alopece, to wit: Socrates is guilty on the ground that he does not recognize the gods recognized by the State, but introduces other new divinities; he is further guilty on the ground that he corrupts the youth. The penalty is death.

Thus Socrates was accused of the grave crimes of impiety and of corrupting Athenian youth. How did it happen that the greatest philosopher and thinker of his day, known throughout the civilized world for his wit and wisdom, found himself in the dire predicament of fighting for his life before those very fellow citizens among whom he had lived for all his seventy years? Partly it was due to his unfortunate past political alliances, and partly to his infuriating superiority in exposing the ignorance and lack of true knowledge on the part of all his contemporaries, whether they were senators or peasants. As the Delphic oracle had spoken: "No man is wiser than Socrates." The leading citizens of Athens resented it.

* * *

From the time he was a young man, Socrates' international fame as a person of outstanding intellectual power had been established. His insatiable curiosity had led him from student days to delve into the greatest thinking of the times, sometimes embracing one school briefly, questioning it, and then abandoning it as logically unsatisfactory. He was well known to the sophists of his day, and often tangled horns with Protagoras, their eminent leader. He distinguished himself as a brave fighter in the wars then being fought, in 431 B.C., at Potidaea, and in many other campaigns. About this time, influenced by the Delphic oracle's pronouncement that no man was wiser than Socrates, he felt a divine message sending him upon his lifelong mission to seek the supreme knowledge and also to recruit all who would listen to him to seek it.

In 415 B.C. the Athenian Army suffers a disastrous defeat at Sicily. The repeated reverses of the once impregnable Athenian forces toward the end of the century put fear into the hearts of the Athenians, so that those, like Socrates, who questioned the prevailing form of government were bound to incur the wrath of the inhabitants.

Alcibiades, once the darling of Athenian society, was banished for profaning the Eleusinian mysteries. But so desperate was Athens for leaders in the war against Sparta that he was recalled. As pictured here, in 407 B.C. he makes his triumphal return. Due to his arrogant attitude and to military reverses, he was forced to flee Athens in disgrace less than a year later. Alcibiades was in his youth one of Socrates' closest friends, an association that, for political and military reasons, weighed heavily against Socrates at his trial.

The New York Public Library

"Socrates y Alcibiades" by L. Lipparini. Alcibiades in his teens had formed a passionate attachment to Socrates, but later, at the time of this painting, he has become a dilettante, while Socrates has turned to the preaching of his moral philosophy.

Courtesy Raccolia Treves de Bonfili, Venice

At the outbreak of the great Peloponnesian War, Socrates had many friends in high circles, the most famous of whom was Alcibiades. Alcibiades was the darling of Athenian democracy, a beautiful youth who led his country to many victories, only to turn traitor, after being accused of burlesquing the sacred Eleusinian mysteries. Thereupon he had fled to Sparta, where he became the leader against his Athenian fellow citizens. Although he was many years younger than Socrates, the two formed a deep attachment for each other, one that in modern terminology would be termed homosexual, although the word has quite different connotations at this time. It is hinted that Anytus, one of Socrates' accusers at his trial,

was jealous of this relationship; coupled with the fact that Anytus' own son was one of the "pupils" of Socrates, this may have induced him to join the team of prosecutors.

The charge against Socrates of corrupting the Athenian youths had nothing whatever to do with sex relations, nor was any such accusation or evidence supporting it introduced at the trial. "Corrupting" in this sense meant influencing youths to question the wisdom of their parents and the leaders of Athenian society to a point where, however valid the questions, the elders deeply resented being made to look ridiculous to their sons and fellow citizens.

A statue of Socrates dressed in the typical Athenian attire that he was accustomed to wearing in his strolls about Athens. *British Museum*

For a number of years now, the once proud and invincible Athens had been fighting and losing wars. In 413 B.C. the Athenians fought with their backs to the wall against Syracuse. The war ended in the complete collapse of the old moral, political, and economic order of Athens. The following years were no less militarily unkind to the city-state, and she capitulated in 404 to Lysander. The Spartans, having no use for democracy, pressured Athens to replace her form of government with an oligarchy ruled by a Commission of Thirty. The rule of this body was marked by arbitrary executions and property confiscations so odious that in 403 the commission was summarily expelled, and Athens returned once again to democratic rule. Unfortunately for the reputation of Socrates, two of his close associates were prominent in the machinations of the Thirty: Critias, a cousin of Plato's mother, and Charmides, her brother. Thus it again appeared, as in the case of Alcibiades, that Socrates was educating traitors. It was also well known that Socrates was not in sympathy with the democratic form of government. As might be expected of an eminent philosopher, whose sole mission in life was the quest of knowledge, Socrates believed in a rule of the intellectuals. Those who qualified in knowledge should lead the citizens of Athens, not those elected by popular acclaim. Thus his political affiliations and philosophy alienated a large segment of influential Athenians, and led directly to the trial. These enemies wanted him banished from the country and out of their sight. They had no wish for his death, only for his removal from their society. But Socrates had other plans.

❊   ❊   ❊

"Socrates and His Friends" by John La Farge.
Minnesota Historical Society

"Socrates and His Disciples Mocked by Courtesans," by Jules Pascin,
shows the conflict between the search for knowledge and the
pleasures of Athenian life.
The Museum of Modern Art, New York

Shortly before Socrates is accused by
Meletus and brought to trial, he is
derided and laughed at by his fellow
Athenians as he goes for his daily
walks around the city.

At the opening of the trial, the accusers spoke first, each one of the three presenting his view and evidence of Socrates' apparent guilt. Since the charge was originated by Meletus, he naturally spoke first, and concerned himself with Socrates' speculations in physical science, which resulted, so he claimed, in the rejection of the recognized gods of the State. Since it was no crime in Athens at that time to worship any gods one wished, it is difficult to see how this constituted a crime of impiety. Nor was there any illegality in Socrates' "divine sign" or "divine voice," which Meletus accused him of obeying. The citizens of Athens were well aware of Socrates' self-proclaimed mission. Meletus hit closer to home when he charged that Socrates had ridiculed the poets, an unpopular pastime to say the least, since poets were regarded as divine seers and the true teachers of the people. While Meletus' charge was undoubtedly popular with the 501 judges, there was hardly a shred of legality to it.

The second accuser was Lycon, a rhetorician, who proceeded to entrance the jurors with his knowledge of the law. He cited previous cases where impiety had been the charge, and stressed the importance of enforcing the law. He ended with an implication, probably little understood by the jurors, that Socrates had continually ridiculed the rhetoricians.

It is hard to see why a respected leader such as Anytus could have become embroiled in the trial of Socrates, yet he probably was the prime instigator, a man intensely jealous of Socrates, whose name and opinions were forever cropping up to plague him. Socrates had caused Anytus' own son to question his father's wisdom and his qualifications. Stung to the quick by Socrates' many attacks on the politicians and statesmen, both present and past, Anytus stressed this antipathy in his charge. He made many telling points against the prisoner when accusing him of criticizing public life but refusing to partake in any public functions, which to an Athenian was the moral obligation of every citizen. (Socrates was to go to great lengths in the *Apology* to explain his reasons for leading a private, not a public, life.) And, of course, having been hit close to home, Anytus charged Socrates with teaching the younger to disrespect their parents and to criticize many of the democratic institutions, such as the use of the lot in appointing men to office. Because he had been instrumental in formulating the Amnesty of 404–403 for any criminal acts committed before its enactment, he referred only obscurely to Socrates' close friendships with such *personae non gratae* as Alcibiades and Critias. But even an obscure reference was clear enough to the jurors, who were very familiar with the former associates and "pupils" of Socrates.

The accusers ended their speeches, and now the philosopher was to answer their charges. If he made a brilliant defense, as given to us by Plato in the *Apology*, it was nevertheless far short of one calculated to influence the 501 jurors to acquit him. Socrates had refused the help of a professional to formulate his defense, preferring instead to go before the court and tell the truth in his own words. That he had little expectation of being acquitted is inherent in his casual manner of speaking, as if he were engaging in a private discourse, and in his apparent disregard of what the jurors thought, as long as he could, as usual, speak the truth.

Socrates defending himself before his judges.
From a relief by Antonio Canova.

A group of jurors
in a court
of Athens.

Socrates began his defense by asking his judges to forgive the way he spoke in court: "At the age of more than seventy years, I am now for the first time appearing before a court of justice, so that I am an utter stranger to the manner of speaking here." He then went on to say that the real reason for his being tried was not the two formal charges now being put against him by Meletus, Anytus, and Lycon, but the many enemies he had acquired over the years and the false rumors they had spread about him. "These I fear more than Anytus and his friends . . . those who getting hold of you for the most part while you were yet children, have persuaded you to believe this false accusation, that there is a certain Socrates, a wise man, who speculates on things in the heavens and searches into all things under the earth, and makes the worse appear the better reason."

He then told the court whence came the rumor of his being the wisest man in the world (the Delphic oracle) and how he set out to refute it by finding a man wiser than himself. One of those he questioned was a leading Athenian statesman: "It seemed to me that this man had the appearance of being wise in the eyes of many others, and most of all in his own, but in reality was not wise. Whereupon I tried to convince him that he only thought himself wise but was not really so, and consequently I became an object of hatred to him and to many of those who were present." No wonder!

Such, indeed, was the way Socrates had infuriated the leaders of Athenian society by mocking them in front of their contemporaries and exposing their foibles in front of their children. Could Socrates have believed that his jurors were any more sympathetic to such demonstrations, true as they might be, than the embarrassed victims?

Socrates then called Meletus to answer some questions in regard to his charge of impiety, and quickly tricked Meletus into accusing him of being an atheist: "But tell me, in the name of Zeus, do you really think that I believe there is no God?"

Meletus cried out, "By Zeus, I swear that you believe there is no God at all." It was a very clever twist on the part of Socrates, for Meletus' charge was that Socrates had introduced gods other than those recognized by the State, so how could he possibly have been an atheist?

Socrates countered, "Nobody will believe that, Meletus, and I doubt whether you do yourself." The entire charge of impiety was so nebulous that the accusers themselves did not know what it meant, and the jurors had even less notion of its meaning. Thus, on any legal basis, the first charge in the indictment was invalid.

Socrates told the court that by putting him to death they would only harm themselves. He referred to himself as God's gift to Athenian society:

Such a man, citizens, you will not easily find again, and if you take my advice you will spare me. . . . And that I am such a gift of God to the state you can see from this my conduct; for it is not in the ordinary course of human nature that I should have been thus neglectful of my own affairs, and have suffered my household interests to be uncared for these many years, while I was continually busying myself with yours, going about to each one of you individually, like a father or an elder brother, and trying to take thought for virtue.

He then went to some lengths to justify why he never gave his advice in public before the senate but only in private conversations. The one time he was in the senate he held out against all the others for law and order, even against a threat of prison or death:

Our tribe had chief direction of state affairs on that occasion when the ten generals who had not picked up the men after the naval combat were brought to trial. You wished to try them all in a body, which was contrary to law, as you all afterwards admitted; but I then alone, out of the whole body of fifty Prytanes, was opposed to doing anything against the laws and voted in opposition. . . . Do you really think, then, that I could have lived for so many years if I had led a public life, and, acting as an honest man, had stood by the right and held this, as I ought, above every other consideration?

Then Socrates turned to the charge against him of corrupting the youth of Athens:

I have never been a teacher to any man, but if any one, whether young or old, wished to hear me speak while carrying out my mission, I never grudged him the opportunity. Nor is it my habit to discourse when I am paid, and refuse to discourse when I am not; but I hold myself ready to be questioned alike by rich and poor; or if any one prefers that I should question him, I let him first answer me and then hear what I have to say. And whether any of my hearers become better or worse, for that I cannot justly be made answerable . . . if I am corrupting some of the young men, and have corrupted others, surely some of those who are now grown up, and have come to know that when young they received bad advice from me, ought now to appear in court in order to accuse me and have me punished. Or if they themselves were unwilling to do this, some of their kinsfolk, fathers or brothers, or others belonging to them, should, if members of their family had received any harm at my hands, remember it now against me and seek my punishment.

Socrates then brought his defense to a close: "Well, citizens, these facts and perhaps others of the same nature make up about all the defense I can offer." He stated that he would not ask his judges for mercy or implore them with many tears or bring his children to court to plead for him. Such would not be honorable and, the world knowing him to surpass most men, it would be unworthy.

It does not seem to me right either to owe one's escape to entreaties or to supplicate a judge rather than to enlighten and convince him. For the judge sits in court to give judgment, not to award justice by favor; and he has not sworn to grant favors to whomsoever he pleases, but to judge according to the laws. . . . For if I were to persuade you and by force of entreaties overpower your oaths, I should clearly be teaching you not to believe in gods, and accusing myself of not believing in them while in the very act of defending myself against this accusation. But far from this, O men of Athens, I do believe in them as does not one of my accusers; and to you and to God I leave it to judge my case as shall be best for me as well as for yourselves.

Thus spoke Socrates.

The judges now turned to voting on his guilt or innocence. Each of the 501 advanced to the urns and deposited his verdict. Upon counting, it was found that by sixty votes the majority was against the accused.

Since Meletus had proposed the death penalty, it was now Socrates' turn to make a counterproposal for penalty. All present expected Socrates to propose banishment for himself, which alternative would have been immediately accepted and his life spared. But they had not reckoned with the absolute integrity of the philosopher. He had no intention of outwitting the death penalty, and almost jokingly suggested that he be supported in the Prytaneum at public expense for the rest of his life. Then he continued discussing more serious alternatives, ending with a fine. Although very poor, he suggested: "I might possibly pay one mina of silver; therefore I propose that amount. But Plato here, O men of Athens, and Crito and Critobulus and Apollodorus bid me say thirty minas, and offer to be my sureties. This, then, I propose; and for the payment of the money they will be ample security to you."

The judges now voted on the two proposed penalties, and chose death.

Socrates took the remainder of his time, while the clerks were gathering up all their materials, to discourse on death as a good thing: "Death must be one of two things: either he who is dead becomes naught, and has no consciousness of anything; or else, as men say, there is a certain change and removal of the soul from this place to some other." If the former, it would be like the most wonderful dreamless sleep a man ever had. If the latter, what greater good than thus being set free from so-called judges and being able to face the true judges of Hades and meet all the great men of the past. Socrates told them that for him to die now was best. He looked forward to being released from worldly affairs. In farewell he said: "But now it is time for us to go away, I to die, you to live. Which of us is going to a better fate is unknown to all save God."

*   *   *

The custom in Athenian criminal law was for a condemned man to be turned over at once to a law body known as the "Eleven," whose duty it was to see that the execution took place within twenty-four hours. Socrates was an exception.

Each year a boat was dispatched, after a sacred ceremony, to the shrine of Apollo in Delos, in memory of the deliverance by Theseus from the annual tribute of seven lads and seven maidens to the Minos of Cnossus, from whence they never returned. Until this ship came back, no executions were allowed to be carried out. The religious ceremonies had begun the day before the trial of Socrates took place, so the Eleven were faced with the problem of what to do with him until the ship arrived. As it happened, contrary winds forced the ship's delay, and it was a month before it finally reached Athens. Socrates' wealthy friend Crito begged the court to let him remain free until that time, but his plea was refused. Consequently, the condemned philosopher was put in the prison of the Eleven, but was allowed a certain amount of freedom in receiving and passing the day with friends and admirers. Several friends from abroad came to Athens to be with him until the end. For the first time in his life, he took to writing poetry, composing a Paean to Apollo and putting into verse Aesop's fables.

During this month's wait Crito and some of his other friends raised enough money to bribe the proper officials and effect an escape. This would have met with the approval of the Athenians, who wanted only banishment, not death. But Socrates refused, seeing in such an escape a renunciation of all the principles he had advocated in his lifetime. However wrong Anytus and Meletus had been in accusing him, and however unfair the verdict against him, it was the legal finding of the court, and to escape would be a crime against the State. For Socrates to commit a crime after advocating a life of virtue and conduct according to the laws was unthinkable.

In reasoning with Crito on his entreaty to escape, Socrates argued:

Do we then hold that we ought in no way intentionally to commit injustice, or that we may commit it in one way, and not in another; or do we still, as in former times, admit that to act unjustly is in no case good and honorable? And all the principles which we have acknowledged within these last few days to be now thrown away, and have we, Crito, at our age, been thus long and earnestly reasoning among ourselves, unconscious all the while that we are no better than children? Or rather, whether the mass of men acknowledge it or not, and whether a sterner or milder fate is in store for us, is not what we said before still true, that to do injustice is in every way a disgrace and an evil to the doer of it? Do we admit this or not?

To which Crito replied, "We do."

Socrates then recited to Crito what he believed the State would logically say if he did escape. The State is speaking:

As it is now, if you depart hence [that is, take the hemlock], you go as one wronged, not by us, the laws, but by men; but if you take to flight, thus disgracefully rendering back injustice and injury by breaking the covenants and agreements which you yourself made with us, and working evil against those whom least of all you ought to injure,—your own self as well as your friends, your country and ourselves—we shall be angry with you here while you are yet alive, and our brothers, the laws in Hades, will not receive you kindly, knowing that you sought, so far as in you lay, to destroy us. So do not, we beg you, let Crito persuade you to follow his advice rather than ours.

Then, ending his argument, he urged Crito to accept his logic:

These, you must know, my dear friend Crito, are the words which I seem to hear, even as the Corybantes imagine that they hear the sound of flutes; and their echo resounding within me makes me unable to hear aught beside. Know, therefore, that if you say anything contrary to this, you will but speak in vain. Nevertheless, if you think that anything will be gained thereby, say on.

But Crito was now convinced: "No, Socrates, I have nothing more to say."

"Then so let it rest, Crito: and let us follow in this way, since in this way it is that God leads."

*　　*　　*

The ship had now arrived from Delos, and the Eleven had early the next morning informed Socrates to be ready for death that day. Phaedo and other friends of the philosopher learned of this early in the morning when they arrived at the prison. When they reached Socrates' cell they found that he had been freed from his shackles and that his wife Xanthippe, carrying their infant son, was with him. Seeing his friends enter, she burst into tears, and, at Socrates' request, was taken home.

The rest of the day was spent by Socrates answering many questions that were disturbing his friends:

To you, my judges, I want to declare my reason for thinking that a man who has really given up his life to the pursuit of philosophy should take courage when about to die, and be of good hope that, after leaving this life, he will attain to the greatest good yonder. And how this may be, Simmias and Cebes, I will try to tell you.

It is apt to escape the notice of others, that they who are rightly following philosophy are devoting themselves solely to the study of dying and death. Now, if this be true, and they have been their whole life long eagerly anticipating this one thing alone, it would surely be absurd for them to be distressed when that to which they had been looking forward with a devotion of a lifetime had at length arrived.

At this unassailable logic Simmias had to laugh. Socrates then continued with a discussion of how at death the soul was released from the body and at the same time purified of the unworthy desires and tendencies of living and endowed with courage, temperance, and wisdom. The subject of immortality itself consumed several hours.

Now the sun was almost setting, and Socrates left his friends to take a bath. After this, his children and the women of his household came to bid him farewell and hear his last directions. When they had gone, Socrates returned to his friends, where they all sat quietly, saying very little. Soon the servant of the Eleven arrived to inform him that it was time to drink the poison and to tearfully bid him goodbye. Socrates was ready: "Let the poison be brought if it is already mixed; if not, let the man mix it."

A servant standing nearby was sent to get the hemlock, and, when he returned with it, Socrates said, "Well, my friend, I must ask you, since you have had experience in these matters, what I ought to do."

"Nothing," replied the servant, "but walk about after drinking until you feel a heaviness in your legs, and then, if you lie down, the poison will take effect of itself."

With a prayer to the gods, Socrates then took the libation and lightly tossed it down. His friends could stand it no longer, and all broke into tears. Socrates was amazed: "What are you doing, you strange people? My chief reason for sending away the women was that we might be spared such discordance as this; for I have heard that a man ought to die in solemn stillness. So pray be composed, and restrain yourselves!"

Socrates rose and began his last walk around in his cell. Soon, feeling the heaviness coming on, he lay down and covered his face with the sheet. From time to time the man who had given him the poison felt his legs and pressed hard on them. Socrates said he could not feel anything. Higher and higher rose the numbness until it reached his waist. At this point he looked out from under the sheet and said to Crito: "'We owe a cock to Aesculapius. Pay the debt, and do not neglect it." Crito replied: "It shall be done, Socrates. But think if you have nothing else to say."

There was no answer, for the poison had reached the heart, and Socrates was dead.

* * *

The trial of Socrates was in a sense anticlimatic to his life as a philosopher. True, it hastened him to face death, the ultimate concern, in his own words, of all philosophers—if the word "hasten" can be used for a man over seventy. But Socrates during his life had made his philosophical principles well enough known to the world and intimately understood by his closest followers, especially Plato and Xenophon, that they would have been perpetuated, trial or no trial, just as were the teachings of Christ several hundred years later, crucifixion or no crucifixion. The trial did, however, serve to bring into dramatic focus the conflict of strict moral truths with rabble reasoning. From youth to old age Socrates sought to discover in true knowledge the meaning of life itself. He abhorred hypocrisy; he loathed opportunism; he embraced an orderly life lived according to immutable laws of nature, so far as they were known to mankind in the fifth and fourth centuries before Christ. Thus he spent his life in search of such truth as was arrived at by logical reasoning, starting from a rational hypothesis. As with many great men of his day, this was too stringent a philosophy to be a popular one. He irked and pricked the consciences of his fellow citizens to a point where he became intolerable. And so they condemned him to death.

Socrates sending away his family before drinking the poison.
From a relief by Antonio Canova.

"The Death of Socrates" by Jacques Louis David. He takes the fatal hemlock as his
friends break down weeping, for which he chides them, saying
that that is why he has sent away the womenfolk.
The Metropolitan Museum of Art, Wolfe Fund, 1931

The death of Socrates.
From a relief by Antonio Canova.

In the history of mankind, the meaning of morality differs according to time and place; and Athenian society was a far cry from Anglo-Saxon Puritanism. For Socrates, morality had a deeper meaning: living by established values without deviating from them for the sake of opportunism, as witness his refusal to escape from prison, even when it had been neatly and financially arranged.

What are these established values? Socrates was the first to create the concept of the *soul*, which has ever since dominated the thinking of the majority of people of the Western world. Man's supreme reason for being was to cultivate the soul, make the best of it, and finally answer for its state when at last upon death it went to Hades. It was this philosophy that was ready-made for the coming Christianity. Man was master of his own soul, and could shape its personality in any way he wished, wise or foolish, virtuous or vicious, according to how he wished to live. It was irrefutably bound up with an individual's personal intelligence and character. Socrates "brought philosophy down from heaven to earth," and taught that it was man's primary duty to tend his soul and make it as good as possible. Thus his "divine mission" was to make others realize how ignorant they were and how unjustified in doing and believing as they did. He admonished them to live, not by opinions or fancy assumptions, but by reason arrived at by logic and knowledge. A tyrant, for instance, thinking himself above the laws, might subjugate property and personal freedoms to his own whims, but this did not bring him the happiness he wanted because what he was doing was wrong; his soul was diseased. This is not to say that hedonism was wrong, that good and pleasure could not be the same thing. But the pleasure had to be real, and not the imagined results of evildoing.

Just as Athenians did not distinguish between public and private life, Socrates did not distinguish between the actions of private individuals and the State in the application of his moral philosophy. Here he came violently in conflict with the leaders of democratic Athens, from Themistocles to Pericles, whom he accused of lacking the knowledge of good and who were therefore unfit to rule. Even though they made Athens wealthy and powerful, they did nothing for the moral values of the people. Such chopping-down-to-size of national heroes was one of the chief reasons for Socrates' being prosecuted. His theory of rule by intellectuals was decidedly antidemocratic.

Socrates was the first man in the world consciously to question the relationship of scientific objects with their moral values. Today, we question the status of our scientific discoveries, and still wonder just what is a moral ideal. It is the heritage of Socrates that man in his intellectual pursuits questions, doubts, and demands answers.

* * *

It would be ironical if one were to discover overwhelming evidence that there was no Socrates, that he was a creation primarily of Plato, as a few have contended. This is unlikely; but though the evidence points to the man, much of his philosophy seems to be Plato's, and many events of his life may be apocryphal. Was he tried by the Athenians, and condemned? Was he offered an escape that he refused? These are matters that it is difficult today to state with certainty. One need only apply to the questions the Socratic method of skeptical challenging and searching.

But through his life and the trial (or Plato's version of it), there is a Socratic legacy. For Plato, Socrates was "truly the wisest, and justest, and best of all the men I have ever known." If one were to summarize the trial of Socrates in a few words, he was condemned, not for offering answers, but for posing questions. Into the minds of youth, he instilled doubt: this alone, Athenian power could not face.

"Jeanne d'Arc" by Barrios
Library of Congress

2

Joan of Arc

[1431]

ON MAY 7, 1429, THE FRENCH, UNDER THE LEADERSHIP OF a young girl of seventeen, drove the mighty English army out of the once impregnable fortress of Les Tourelles outside Orléans, and thus brought about a complete reversal of the military and political situation in France and reestablished the sagging morale of the French army. It was the culminating victory for Joan of Arc, known as La Pucelle (the maiden or the virgin), who had welded a wretched French army, whose only creed was greed, into a potent fighting force simply through her own belief in God's will and her own inspiring leadership in battle. It was her devout purpose, transmitted to her by God through His saints, Catherine and Margaret, abetted by St. Michael, to drive the English from France and restore the Dauphin, Charles VII, to his rightful throne.

On the morning of Sunday, July 16, 1429, at a colorful ceremony in the cathedral at Rheims, Joan of Arc had her fondest wish granted. In full armor, standing close to the king, she saw two of the ecclesiastical peers lift up the chair on which Charles sat, while others held the crown over his head. By this simple act, Charles VII was coronated. Joan knelt before him, embraced his knees, and with tears running down her cheeks said, "Gentle King, now has God's pleasure been accomplished Who willed that I should raise the siege of Orléans and lead you to this city of Rheims for your coronation, thus manifesting that you are the true King to whom this Realm of France by right belongs."

For her deeds of valor in restoring the monarchy of France to its rightful rule, she paid with her life, consumed in the flames of a monumental conspiracy between King Henry VI of England and the Church of Rome, and virtually abandoned by the very king she had set on the throne.

* * *

Once crowned, Charles ignored all her entreaties to march on Paris, take it, and thus forestall further effective action by his two enemies: the Burgundians under Philip and the English under the Duke of Bedford, Regent of France. Instead, Charles's advisers counseled the concluding of a peace treaty. Through their efforts a general truce, established the previous Christmas, was extended into April, 1430. This was just what the Duke of Burgundy and his English allies needed to get their military machine in readiness for a return campaign to retake Orléans. For months he had been urging Charles to take some concrete action to implement the truce, namely, the turning over to him of the city of Compiègne. The brave people of Compiègne adamantly refused to be a pawn in this maneuver, and wrote Charles that they were his loyal subjects and would serve only him. Inspired by their fortitude, Joan, unbeknown to the king, headed for that city, rallying around her the irregular forces in the area, who were constantly harassing the Burgundians and the English. By provoking quick clashes here and there with her mobile forces, she thus prevented the enemy from gaining any permanent footholds from which they might launch a successful attack on Compiègne, which in Joan's military strategy must be held as a springboard for an eventual attack on Paris. She was aware that the enemy was equally anxious to take Compiègne, the chief hurdle to their military objectives.

On Easter Sunday, April 17, four thousand Burgundians and fifteen hundred English, together with a strong force of artillery, siege engines, and sappers marched toward Compiègne. The truce was ended. For weeks now, using Compiègne as her base, Joan with her army of two thousand men had moved around the countryside, fighting the enemy in many places. On May 23 Joan with five hundred men rode out of Compiègne to launch a surprise attack on the town of Margny. There they took the Burgundians by surprise, but meanwhile they had been spotted by Jean de Luxembourg and his friends, who were approaching the town on horseback. Luxembourg dispatched a messenger to Clairoix, who returned with a large force of Flemings and Burgundians, intending to cut Joan's forces off from returning to Compiègne. In the ensuing battle most of Joan's forces succeeded in retreating into the fortress of Compiègne; but, unknown to Joan, the forces inside, fearing the entry of the enemy, had raised the bridge and lowered the portcullis. Joan was trapped ouside the fortification. She fought heroically to the end, until an enemy bowman grabbed hold of her and pulled her from her horse. She surrendered to an archer, a nobleman in the ranks of the Bastard of Wandomme. She was now the prisoner of its feudal overlord, Jean de Luxembourg.

The English now knew exactly what they wanted. Joan of Arc must at all costs be burned at the stake, if the English armies were ever to be effective again in their conquest of France. Joan's very presence at the head of the French forces made them almost supernaturally invincible. Never again could she be allowed to lead them.

"Joan of Arc" by Jules Bastien-Lepage. Here the Maid of Orléans is in the garden of her family's home in Domrémy.
The Metropolitan Museum of Art; gift of Erwin Davis, 1889

At the bidding of her "holy voices" Joan left home, resolved in her mission to set Charles VII on the throne as the rightful King of France. From out of the royal multitude assembled, Joan points a finger at the king, hitherto unknown to her.

But Bedford did not own the prisoner. She had been captured in the Bastard of Wandomme's territory and was a prisoner of Jean de Luxembourg, who in turn was a vassal to Philip of Burgundy. The English decided to buy Joan from her captor. In spite of the existing international law forbidding the sale of a prisoner-of-war to the enemy, Philip at last agreed to turn her over to the English for 10,000 gold pounds, plus an annuity to Jean de Luxembourg. Nor was there any reason for turning her over to the ecclesiastical forces of the Church. But Bedford knew the only way to get her burned at the stake was by ecclesiastical trial, conducted with every canonical guarantee. A trial was necessary if Joan was to be sentenced to death, and a Church trial as the best means of silencing criticism.

It was one of those bitter twists of history that Joan was captured within the diocese of Pierre Cauchon, Bishop of Beauvais, a greedy, power-hungry man whose eyes were set on the vacant Archbishopric of Rouen and eventually a cardinal's hat. He had already sold himself to the English, who had rewarded him admirably. He was, therefore, delighted to join with Bedford in his nefarious plans. Cauchon would claim Joan as a prisoner of the Church and condemn her; but, even better, he would get her to confess her league with the forces of evil and to denounce the very coronation of Charles VII she had fought so hard to achieve. But the confession must be made *of her own free will*, if anyone was to be-

lieve it. And the Church must be responsible for the foregone verdict of guilty. Accordingly, he would quickly call for judges to be drawn from the University of Paris, the Inquisition, and the Bench of Bishops.

Joan of Arc leads a newly aroused French army on toward Orléans and against the English and Burgundian enemies of Charles VII.

After her many victories in behalf of her king, Joan is finally captured at Compiègne, when the gates to the town were lowered, leaving her outside, at the mercy of the English.

Meanwhile Joan had been taken from Noyon to the castle of Beaulieu, where she made her first unsuccessful attempt at escape. From there she was transferred to Beaurevoir, where she was nearly killed after jumping from her seventy-foot tower. At Beaurevoir she was treated kindly by the wife and aunt of her captor, Jeanne de Béthune and Jeanne de Luxembourg, in whose charge she was placed. She was then moved about constantly—to Arras, to the castle of Drugy, to Le Crotoy, where she could look out over the English Channel. She was sustained in these days by two considerations: she was treated fairly and honorably as a prisoner of war, and her "voices" were still speaking to her and encouraging her. On November 24 she was transferred by barge and taken to Vinieu, thence to Saint-Valéry, to Eu, to Dieppe, and finally to Rouen. It was nearly Christmas, 1430, when she arrived at the castle of Rouen and was put in chains in its tower, attended now by boorish male guards who took every opportunity to attempt to rape her and abuse her. It was in this cell that she was visited by the Earls of Stafford and Warwick. To them she said: "I know well that these English will do me to death, thinking when I am dead to gain the kingdom of France, but if they were a thousand godons more than they are now, they shall not have the kingdom." This so enraged Stafford that he drew his sword to kill her, but was restrained by Warwick.

*　*　*

We need not go into all the devious machinations that Cauchon was masterminding during these months preceding the trial. While the University of Paris wanted Joan brought there for trial, Cauchon, at the bidding of the English, succeeded in having Rouen chosen as its locale. He had sent emissaries everywhere to unearth incriminating facts that he could use against Joan. He found few, and promptly suppressed all reports that tended to exonerate her. Thus he began her trial with very little legal evidence.

On January 3, 1431, Henry VI of England, having come to visit Warwick in the castle of Rouen, where Joan was imprisoned in one of its towers, had issued the letters patent necessary to start the proceedings against Joan. In them, he only "lent" her to the ecclesiastical judges for them to decide whether or not she was to be punished by death, but he made it clear that the English retained full authority over her.

The following copy of these letters patent, with the remarks that accompany them, is extracted from the work of M. Le Brun Charmettes:

A woman causing herself to be called La Pucelle, abandoning the habit and vestments of the female sex, against divine law, an abominable act in the sight of God, disproved and forbidden by all law, attired, dressed, and armed in the habit and state of a man, has committed and exercised cruel homicidal deeds, and, as it is said, has given the simple multitude to understand, to seduce and abuse them, that she was sent on the part of God, and had a knowledge of his divine secrets,

Visited in her prison cell at the castle of Rouen by the earls of Stafford and Warwick, she so enrages Stafford that he pulls out his sword and threatens to kill her, but is restrained by Warwick.

King Henry VI of England, who arrived in
France on January 3, 1431, and went directly
to the castle of Rouen, where he
signed the necessary letters-patent for the
temporary transferral of Joan
to the ecclesiastical judges for trial.
*The Free Library of Philadelphia,
Carson Collection*

together with many other dogmas very perilous, prejudicial,
and scandalous to our holy Catholic faith; in following up
which abuses, and exercising hostility between us and our
people, she has been taken armed before Compiègne by certain of our loyal subjects, and since conducted a prisoner
before you." Being then desirous that the delivering up of
the captive to the ecclesiastical tribunal should not appear to
be the act of the English king, the following clause is added:
—"And on account of these superstitions, false dogmas, and
other crimes of leze Majesty divine, she has by many reputed
as suspect, noted, and defamed, who have required at our
hands forthwith, through the revered father in God our loved
and trusty counsellor the bishop of Beauvais, ecclesiastical
judge and ordinary of the said Jeanne on account of her being taken and apprehended within the confines and limits of
his diocese, and alike exhorted by our dear and most saintly
daughter the university of Paris, that it may please us to give
and deliver up to the said reverend father in God the said
Jeanne, to interrogate and examine her on the said counts."
It is somewhat singular that throughout this document the
English ministry did not make their youthful sovereign utter
a syllable respecting the inquisition; but a particular clause
leaves to the bishop appointed as judge, the power of acting
conjointly with that tribunal; "and to proceed against her
[Jeanne]," continue the letters patent, "according to the ordinances and dispositions of the divine and canonical rights:
to call such as ought to be summoned": an expression that
may as well apply to the inquisition as to the doctors in
theology, canon, and civil rights. Lastly, these letters order
that La Pucelle shall be delivered over to the bishop of
Beauvais, for the purpose of her being tried, "according to
God and reason"; and orders are issued to all to give to the

prelate "aid, defence, protection, and comfort." It is therein
also expressly reserved, at all events, that Jeanne shall still be
retained—"even in case she is not found guilty or attainted
with the acts above mentioned."

By the middle of February, Cauchon was ready to
proceed with the trial. On February 19 it was stated
that on the basis of preliminary investigations there
was good reason to try the Maid and convict her on religious grounds. To complete his court, Cauchon in-
veigled the Vicar of the Inquisition, Jean Lemaître, to
sit as co-judge. He was reluctant to serve, not believing
in Joan's guilt, and did so only on orders of his superior,
Graverend. He was there only for a small part of the
trial, but voted for her death in order to save his own
skin. He had been threatened with execution unless he
did. There were many other members of the court who
objected to the legality of the proceedings and to
Cauchon's fraudulent practices of tampering with the
evidence. They advised Joan to appeal directly to the
Pope, but they were of no avail against Cauchon's unrelenting fury and domination. The members of his
court either lived in terror of their lives and property
or followed meekly his every order. Cauchon had brought
in six members of the all-powerful University of Paris,
who had triumphed over kings and popes alike but
which in recent years had lost its men of stature. The
two younger ones, who still possessed a sense of justice,
took one look at the setup and returned to Paris for
good. Including judges, lawyers, and assessors, the
court consisted of 117 persons. Against this formidable
array, writes Lucien Fabre, "isolated, without anyone to
advise or support her, seated on a high stool, dressed in
black hose and a black tunic, with her dark hair cropped
to the shape of an inverted basin ending just above the
ears, her eyes bright with fever and fatigue, emaciated,
but burning with the fire of the spirit, and having God
within her—Joan." Her public trial, or more precisely,
her public questioning, began on Wednesday, February
21, 1431. The judges well knew what was expected of
them by the English.

*   *   *

The questioning lasted over three weeks, from February 21 to March 17. The first day the Bishop of Beauvais
stated his credentials for presiding at the trial, and, when
Joan was brought in, outlined to her why she was being
tried by this court for her unorthodox actions both in
this province and others throughout France. She was
urged to tell the truth and asked to take such an oath.
To this she agreed with one reservation. She would say
nothing of her secret communications with King Charles
VII, whom she had put on the rightful throne of France.
Cauchon forbade her to leave the prison, threatening to
convict her of heresy if she did. But Joan answered that
if she could possibly escape she would.

On Thursday, February 22, the interrogation took place in the Robing Room of the castle. After a few preliminary questions regarding her rituals of faith, such as going to confession, Joan told the court that when she was thirteen years old she had first heard a voice from God, which badly frightened her. The voice had told her to be good, to go to church often, and that she should leave Domrémy and go elsewhere in France. There she should free the city of Orléans from the siege by the English and Burgundians. The voice gave her explicit instructions: whom to see and what to do. As to putting on male clothes, she said it was her own idea. She told her judges of the letters she had sent to the English at Orléans telling them to withdraw and give up the siege.

Each day Joan was questioned for several hours, the questions coming at her from all directions, and often several questions at once. For a naïve peasant girl she handled them with what seemed to be the skill of an expert lawyer, but it was more a case of simple honesty and forthrightness. Her judges were amazed. The high point of the third trial session on Saturday, February 24, came when they asked her if she considered herself blessed with the grace of God, to which she answered: "If I am not, may God effect it: and if I am, may God retain me in it; for I should esteem myself the most unfortunate of women, I would rather die than know that I were without the pale of the grace and love of God."

At the fourth session, on Tuesday, February 27, she was closely questioned about her voices. Now she revealed their names; they were the voices of St. Catherine

Joan, in chains, stops to pray on her way to her first appearance before the ecclesiastical court.

"The Trial of Joan of Arc" by Louis Maurice Boutet de Monvel. Presiding over the court on his throne (*upper left*) is Pierre Cauchon, Bishop of Beauvais. *The Corcoran Gallery of Art, W. A. Clark Collection*

The trial continues in another room of the castle, with the Bishop of Beauvais still presiding and his hand-picked judges surrounding him.

and St. Margaret, and she recognized them "by their salutations and the manner of their performing reverence." But even before these saints had spoken to her, she had been comforted by St. Michael. She refused to elaborate further.

The fifth session was held on Thursday, March 1. It was here that Joan made one of her most famous predictions: Within seven years the English would lose everything they had gained in France. (They did.) Further questioning about her saints then took place. When asked if St. Margaret spoke English, she replied incredulously, "How should she speak English, seeing that she is not on their side?" With an unintentional bit of humor she answered their question as to whether St. Michael appeared to her in the nude: "Do you think that the Almighty has not wherewithal to clothe him?"

The sixth questioning period took place on Saturday, March 3, when the judges elicited testimony regarding the male clothes she wore. They exhorted her to put on female attire, but she refused. She also refused to say who had advised her to dress as a man. Further questioning went into the details of her armor and some of her actions in battle.

There now occurred a week's respite while Cauchon met with "many venerable doctors and masters versed in divine and canon law." Together they went over all of Joan's testimony to date and decided just where she should be questioned further. Cauchon decided that additional questioning would be conducted by only a small number of judges chosen by him for each session and that it would take place in Joan's prison cell. Because Joan was eliciting by far too much sympathy, he saw the dangers in further public trials. Thus the seventh session took place on Saturday, March 10, in the jail. Jean de La Fontaine (not the French poet and fabulist by the same name, who lived some two centuries later) asked about her actions in and around Compiègne, the armor she and her compatriots wore, and what riches her king had given her. Joan told him, "I require nothing for myself of my king but very good arms, good horses, and money to pay the people of my hôtel." La Fontaine wanted to know what sign confirming her holy mission she gave the king when she first picked him out from the assembly. On this score Joan was adamant in her refusal to answer.

The eighth and ninth sessions took place in the prison on Monday, March 12. In the morning Joan was asked about a breach-of-promise suit she was supposed to have brought against a youth from the town of Toul. This she denied, saying that she had consecrated her virginity to heaven as long as God wished it. In the afternoon she told her judges about her plans to go to England and release her hero, the Duke of Orléans, from his captivity there.

At this point in the trial the Inquisition entered the scene in the person of Jean Lemaître, vicar of the Inquisitor, sent by Paris to try Joan on matters of faith. He joined Cauchon in conducting the Court, and together they proceeded to question Joan in prison on Tuesday, March 13. The subject was the coronation of King Charles VII, and dealt with the angel who brought the crown and who had been seen by Joan doing reverence to the king by bowing before him. The angel, she stated, was seen and recognized by the clerics present.

On Wednesday, March 14, there were two sessions of questioning in prison. In the morning the judges wanted to know why she had jumped from her prison tower at Beaurevoir. It was, she stated, because she had heard that the people of Compiègne were all to be put to the fire and the sword because of their loyalty to the king, and she had wanted to save them. At this point she predicted that they would be liberated before the festival of St. Martin (a prediction that came true on November 1 when the English and Burgundians were roundly defeated and forced to give up the siege of the city). Turning on the Bishop of Beauvais, she admonished him: "You state that you are my judge. I am not aware that you are such; but I charge you take heed and do not judge me wrongfully, as in such case you will place your soul in great jeopardy; and I finally forewarn you that should it please the Almighty God to punish you, I have only fulfilled my duty in thus giving you timely notice." What incredible strength of simple faith must have bolstered her at that moment to turn the tables of the trial and threaten her powerful judge with eternal damnation. At the afternoon session they inquired if she did not believe she had committed mortal sins when she attacked Paris on a Feast Day, when she jumped from the tower of Beaurevoir, when she wore men's clothes. She denied these were sins; but, if they were, it was for God and her confessor to decide, not them.

On Thursday, March 15, in prison, a touchy subject, and one full of legal pitfalls, was presented to Joan.

The judges explained the difference between the Church Militant (meaning the pope, cardinals, prelates, clergy, and so forth) and the Church Triumphant (meaning God, the saints, and the souls). They demanded that she commit herself to the Church Militant. Confused by all this, she declared that she did not understand such questions of doctrine but that she knew of no remarks of hers that were contrary to the faith.

Further questioning on this subject continued during the morning session in prison on Saturday, March 17, to which she answered that she came to put the rightful King of France on the throne in God's name, and to the Church Triumphant she submitted all her deeds and actions, not to the Church Militant. It was a stand that, in the fifteenth century, constituted unforgivable heresy. On this occasion the questioning became so unorganized and malicious, jumping from those about her angels to her male attire, to her saints, to the love and hatred God might show toward the English or the French, that Joan admonished her interrogators, "Good brothers, do pray speak one after the other." In the afternoon questions concerning her virginity were put to her. She maintained that one of the reasons she wore male attire was better to protect herself from the attempted sexual attacks of her guards. In such clothes her chastity was more secure. Asked whether were she to lose her virginity, her saints would still visit her, Joan stated that no revelation had been made to her on that score.

Pierre Cauchon, with a recorder, continues the trial in Joan's prison cell.

Thus ended the weeks of interminable questioning. Had the die for the death sentence not already been cast, Joan, in any other age, might have gone free. Her innocence of the charges made against her was apparent even to many of her judges. Now it was necessary to turn her own testimony against her in such a way as to leave not a shadow of a doubt that the court was acting with irreproachable legality in condemning her to death. To this end, the court ordered that all the proceedings to date be condensed in a number of articles, legally verified. These were then read to Joan for her approval, which she gave with a few minor changes. Their reading took two days, Tuesday and Wednesday, March 27 and 28, at the end of which time Cauchon announced that a judgment would be rendered according to law and reason.

* * *

At this point Cauchon began to have grave doubts about the outcome of the trial should the verdict be based on the questions put to Joan and on her answers. He conceived the plan, which he persuaded his colleagues to accept, of suppressing all of Joan's answers by reducing the original seventy articles to twelve. These would be presented objectively as problems of law to eminent authorities who would be asked for their learned opinions. On April 5, the twelve articles were sent by Cauchon to the men selected, with the request to comment on them "in the interests of the Faith":

Articles of Accusation alleged against Jeanne d'Arc, and concerning which the University of Paris was consulted by the Tribunal instituted at Rouen.

ARTICLE I

A certain woman says and affirms, that being of the age of thirteen or thereabouts, she has beheld with her mortal eyes Saint Michael, who came to offer her consolation, and sometimes also Saint Gabriel, who appeared to her under a corporeal form; and at other times a great host of angels, and that then Saints Catherine and Margaret also presented themselves to her under corporeal forms; that she even beholds them daily, and has heard their voices; that sometimes she has embraced and kissed them, touching their bodies. She has also seen the heads of angels and of the two saints; but she would state nothing respecting the other parts of their bodies nor their habiliments.

That these two saints have sometimes spoken to her near a fountain situated contiguous to a great tree commonly called The Fairies' Tree, which fairies are said to frequent, and whither persons resort for the recovery of their health, although profane the spot; and that many times in this and other places she has worshipped, and performed reverence to them.

She further states, that these two saints appeared and showed themselves to her afterwards, adorned with beautiful and precious wreaths of flowers, and that they repeatedly stated to her, by the order of God, that it was necessary she should repair to a certain secular prince, and promise him, that by her assistance and labour he should recover, by force of arms, a very large temporal domain and great worldly honour; that he would prove victorious over his enemies; that he would receive her into his service, and would furnish her with arms and a body of armed men for the execution of her promises. And moreover, &c. (See Article V.)

She further states, that these two saints tolerated her conduct, when, without the knowledge and against the will of her father and mother, at the age of seventeen, or thereabouts, she quitted the paternal dwelling; and associating herself with a multitude of armed men, spent her days and nights with them, seldom having any female companion.

The saints said and commanded her to execute many other things, in consequence of which she styles herself the messenger of the God of heaven and of the church triumphant.

ARTICLE II

This same woman further states, that the sign which induced the prince to whom she was sent to place confidence in her revelations, and to allow her to carry on the war, was the descent of Saint Michael and a host of angels, some with wings, and some wearing crowns, among whom were Saints Catherine and Margaret; that having presented themselves to the prince, Saint Michael and his attendant saints and angels tarried for a long time upon the earth, parading the paths, ascending the steps, and appearing in his chamber; that one of these angels presented the prince with a crown of very pure and precious gold, and bowed in reverence to him. This woman once stated that she believed that the prince was alone when he received this sign, but it appears that many persons were near him; and at another time, that an archbishop received the sign, which was a crown, and gave the same to the prince, in presence of many temporal lords.

ARTICLE III

This woman knows and is certain, that he who visits her is Saint Michael, on account of the excellent advice and succours which he has afforded her, the good doctrine which he has instilled into her, and because he declared himself to be Saint Michael; that she in like manner distinguishes the two saints from each other, because they name themselves when saluting her; that on this account she believes him to be Saint Michael; and she believes that the conversations and actions of the said saint are true and good, as firmly as she believes that our Lord Jesus Christ suffered and died for our redemption.

ARTICLE IV

She moreover states, that she is certain of many acts that will come to pass in future, and professes to have had a foreknowledge, through the revelations made to her by the two saints, of certain profound secrets: for instance, *that she will be delivered from prison*, and that the French, *in her company*, will perform the grandest feats of arms ever yet achieved in Christendom; and still further, that by these revelations she was made acquainted with persons she had never seen before; and that she discovered and caused to be found a certain sword that was concealed under ground.

Joan identifies the voices that come to her as those of three saints: St. Michael, St. Catherine, and St. Margaret, all of whom she was familiar with from their statues in her local church.

dress, or that she would not do so unless by God's command; and that, if she wore the male costume with those in whose behalf she armed herself and so acted prior to her capture and detention, it was one of the most signal services which could occur to the kingdom of France; adding, that for all the world she would not make oath that she never again would wear man's clothing, or desist from bearing arms; and in saying thus much, she states, that she has acted well, and that she does right in obeying God and his orders.

ARTICLE VI

She avows and agrees that she has caused several letters to be written, in which were the words *"Jesus Maria,"* and the figure of a cross; that she sometimes subjoined a second cross, and that the latter signified that what she mentioned in her letter was not to be put into effect; that in other letters she stated, that she would cause those to be executed who should not obey her letters and ordinances; that she should be recognised by the feats she performed, having the best right, even the order of the God of heaven; and she frequently asserts that she has performed nothing but by virtue of the revelations and commands of God.

ARTICLE VII

She further says and avows, that when about seventeen years of age, she went, of her own accord, and by virtue of a revelation, to a certain esquire whom she had never seen, leaving the paternal roof against the will of her father and mother, who were almost bereft of their senses when made acquainted with her departure; that she entreated this esquire to conduct or cause her to be conveyed to the prince of whom we have previously spoken; that, in consequence, this captain, at her request, gave her a sword and the accoutrements of a man, and that he ordered a knight, a squire, and four valets, to escort her; that on arriving in the presence of the prince, she told him she was anxious to carry on the war against his adversaries, and at the same time promised to procure for him a vast territory and to overcome his enemies, for which purpose she was despatched by the God of heaven; adding, that in all this she has acted rightly by the order of God, and in virtue of revelation.

ARTICLE VIII

She says and declares, that of herself, and without being forced or engaged thereto by any one, she precipitated herself from a certain high tower, rather choosing to die than be delivered into the hands of her adversaries, and survive the destruction of the City of Compiègne. She further says, that she could not prevent thus precipitating herself to the earth, notwithstanding the two saints had ordered her to the contrary; and although she agrees that it was a weighty crime to offend these saints, yet she well knows that the sin was forgiven after she had confessed herself; and this she states was revealed to her.

ARTICLE V
(First, in reference to Article I)

She adds that the two saints commanded her, by order of God, to assume and to wear the dress of a man; that she adopted the same, and still retains it, obeying this injunction with such scrupulous perseverance, that she sometimes plainly states, she would rather die than relinquish these vestments, unless such a command was by the order of God; nay, she has even submitted to be debarred from attending mass, and from receiving the sacrament of the eucharist, at the periods prescribed to the faithful, rather than resume the female attire.

ARTICLE V

This same woman states and affirms, that by the command and with the good-will of God, she has adopted and uniformly worn the dress commonly assumed by men. She further states, that, having received the order of God to wear such apparel, it was requisite she should appear in a short robe, a petticoat, sleeves, and short clothes fastened with many tags; that her hair should be cropped round above the ears, and nothing appear upon her person indicating the female sex, save and except what nature had given her to distinguish the difference of the sexes. She confesses that she has frequently received the eucharist thus attired; and although several times charitably spoken to and advised to resume the vestments of a woman, she could never be prevailed upon to acquiesce, explicitly stating, that she would rather die than change her

ARTICLE IX
(First, in reference to Article I)

The two saints revealed to her that she should be saved in the glory of the blessed, and that she would ensure the salvation of her soul, if she preserved her virginity, which she had offered up the first time she saw and heard them; and in respect to this revelation she affirms, that she is as certain of her salvation, as if she was actually and in very deed enjoying the kingdom of heaven.

ARTICLE IX

This same woman affirms that these two saints promised to conduct her into paradise, if she faithfully preserved the virginity of her body and soul, which she had dedicated to them. She says that she is as sure of this as if she were already in the glory of the saints; and she does not think she has committed any deadly sin, or else it appears to her the two saints would not visit her daily, as they are wont to do.

ARTICLE X

This same woman states and affirms, that God loves certain persons, whom she designated and names, and who are still living; that he loves them better than herself; and that she knows this by means of the revelation of Saints Catherine and Margaret, who speak to her, not in English, but in French, because they are not on the English side; and that as soon as she had ascertained that the voices were in favour of the prince above adverted to, she did not love the Burgundians.

ARTICLE XI

She says and avows, that in respect to these voices and spirits, whom she denominates Michael, Gabriel, Catherine, and Margaret, she has worshipped them many times, by uncovering her head [*caput discoperiendo*], in bending her knees, in prostrating herself to the earth upon which they trod, and in offering up to them her virginity; that when embracing and kissing the two female saints, she corporeally and sensibly touched their persons; that she has frequently summoned them to her in order to demand their aid and advice, though they frequently appear without being called; that she acquiesces with and obeys their counsels, and has so continued to do from the commencement, without consulting any one, whether father or mother, whether curate, prelate, or any other ecclesiastic. Nevertheless she believes that voices, with male and female saints of this description, visit her from God, and by his orders, as firmly as she believes in the Christian religion, and that our Lord Jesus Christ has suffered death for our deliverance; and that if an evil spirit appeared feigning to be Saint Michael, she would well know how to discern whether it was himself or not.

This woman further adds, that of her own consent, and without being urged thereto, she has sworn to these two saints not to reveal the sign of the crown which was given to the prince to whom it was sent; and she also states that she could not reveal the same until she gained permission so to do.

ARTICLE XII

This woman avows and affirms, that if the church were desirous she should do any act contrary to what she says God has ordered her, she would not comply for any earthly thing, affirming that she knows what is contained in her process proceeds from the ordinance of God, and that it would be out of her power to act otherwise. Besides this she adds, that she will not refer to the decision of the church militant, or to that of any living man, but to our Lord God alone, more especially as regards the revelations, and the matters to which they relate, and to every thing she has done by virtue of those revelations; and she states that she has not uttered this and the other answers from her own head, but that she has spoken and delivered them by command of those voices, and by virtue of the revelations made to her; although the judges and other persons present declared to her several times the article of the faith—*I believe in the one Holy and Catholic Church,* explaining to her that every living follower of the faith is bound to obey and submit his words and actions to the church militant, particularly in matters of faith, and what concerns the sacred doctrine and ecclesiastical ordinances.

(And in reference to Article I)

She has hesitated and refused to submit herself, her words, and actions, to the church militant, although several times exhorted and required; stating that it is impossible for her to act contrary to what she has affirmed in her process to have done by the order of God; and that, in respect to those things, she does not refer to the decision or judgment of any living creature, but solely to the judgment of God.

When, on April 10, Cauchon had received virtually no replies, he was both surprised and worried. Sending his men to find out why the learned were so reluctant to give their opinions, he found that they were suspicious of the whole trial and all its aspects: Cauchon's competence in trying it, his partiality, the number of judges trying the case, the English riding herd on the court for a guilty verdict, Joan's not being allowed to appeal to the Pope or to the Council of Basel (a congregation of the whole universal Church), the accused having no one to represent her, and many other irregular procedures.

Cauchon was undaunted. Late as it was in the proceedings, he would call upon the University of Paris (made pliable to his purposes by a few well-placed bribes) to authenticate the findings of the court. On April 14, there being thirty members present, it was agreed to adjourn until the answers were received from the University of Paris concerning the twelve articles.

* * *

About this time Joan became seriously ill, and no wonder! For months she had been subjected to ill-treatment by her guards, to constant interrogation, to many sleepless nights, and to lack of any kind of activity. The English were worried. Would natural causes snatch their prey from them before they could have the satisfaction of burning her? The Earl of Warwick summoned two physicians, and warned them: "The King of England would not for the world that she should die a natural death; he has paid dearly for her, and her days must end by the hand of justice; he expects to have her burnt. See her, therefore, and adopt every precaution that she may recover."

On April 18 Cauchon visited her in her cell and, counting on her sick condition, tried to extract a complete recantation. He failed. Again, on May 2, in the presence of sixty-three assessors before whom a pale and weak Joan had been brought, he delivered a public admonition. She was warned that not to yield was tantamount to confessing herself a heretic. But she remained steadfast in her conviction that she had said all she was going to say and that she placed herself in the hands of God. Cauchon was at his wits' end. He was failing badly in his purpose to persuade her to place herself in the hands of the Church. On May 9 they threatened her with torture. She was taken to the torture chamber of the castle where insidious instruments were meticulously described to her. But she refused to say more. Reluctantly Cauchon gave up the idea that torture would make her recant.

On May 23 the answers arrived from the University of Paris. They were all that Cauchon could have hoped for. Their sanctimonious faculties announced her guilty of lying, blasphemy, consorting with the agents of the Devil, heresy, and many other crimes. Unless, after being duly warned, she admitted her errors to the satisfaction of her judges, she should be turned over to the secular arm for punishment, which, of course, meant the stake.

Pierre Morice, canon of the cathedral at Rouen, was given the task of reading the warning to her. He exhorted her to renounce her ways and give herself up to the Church. But steeled by the presence of her voices, Joan replied: "Even were the sentence put in force, did I behold the fire prepared, the faggots lighted, and the executioner on the point of throwing me into the flames, I would not in death utter a thing that was not pronounced during the process." Cauchon then decided for the next day on a mock trial and threat of execution.

Joan was taken in the prisoner's cart to the burial ground of the abbey, where two scaffolds were erected: one for the judges, and one for Joan and Guillaume Erard, doctor of theology, who was to deliver the sermon. He used as his text a passage from the Gospel According to John: "The branch cannot bear fruit of itself except it abide in the vine." A short distance away stood the executioner and nearby the faggots arranged around the stake. Joan was unaware that all this was merely playacting to frighten her into signing an abjuration. At the end of the sermon the articles of abjuration were read to her. It consisted of barely eight lines in which she agreed never again to carry arms, wear male clothes, or have her hair cut short. As Joan remained silent, Cauchon rose and read her the sentence of condemnation. Others threatened her, and some pleaded with her to sign: "Joan, do as you are advised: Will you be the cause of your own death?"

By now, thoroughly frightened and in mortal fear at the prospect of being burned to death, Joan was ready to comply: "Let this schedule be inspected by the clerks of the Church in whose hands I am to be placed; and if they advise me to sign it, and to perform the things that are told me, I am willing to do so." Triumphantly they placed the schedule before her to sign, but the crafty Cauchon, unseen, substituted another and much longer schedule for the short version. Thus Joan unwittingly affixed her X to a document of whose contents she knew nothing. Instead of the brief eight lines, she signed an illegal statement:

Every person who has erred and mistaken the Christian faith, and afterwards, by the grace of God, is returned to the light of truth and to the unity of our holy mother church, should have special care lest the enemy in hell should turn him back and cause him to relapse into error and damnation. On account of this, I Jeanne, commonly called La Pucelle, miserable sinner, after what I have thus seen of the error to which I was devoted, and that by the grace of God I am returned to our holy mother church, in order that it may be seen, that not feignedly, but of good heart and good will, I am returned to her: I confess that I have most grievously sinned, *in lying by pretending* to have heard revelations and apparitions from God, by the angels and Saint Catherine and Saint Margaret; in seducing souls; *in creating things foolishly and lightly* [the same contradiction appears in the sentence]; in uttering superstitious divinations; in blaspheming God, and

Worn down by the ordeal of the long trial and imprisonment, and threatened with burning at the stake, Joan finally agreed to sign an abjuration of barely eight lines. But Cauchon substitutes a lengthy and incriminating document, which she unknowingly signs instead.

his saints male and female; in trespassing against divine law, the holy Scriptures, and the canon laws; in adopting a dissolute and unbecoming dress, against the decency of nature, and hair cropped short round in disguise of a man, against the comeliness of the feminine sex; in also wearing armour, with great presumption, and cruelly desiring the effusion of human blood; in saying that I have performed all these things by the command of God, the angels, and the above-mentioned saints—and that in so acting I have done well, and not been mistaken; in despising God and his sacraments; in raising seditions; and in committing idolatry by adoring evil spirits and invoking them. Which crimes and errors, with good heart and without fiction, I, by the grace of our Lord God, returned to the path of truth, by the holy doctrine and the good counsel of you and the doctors and masters you have sent me, abjure detest, deny, and from all renounce and depart: and upon the several points abovesaid submit myself to the correction, disposition, amendment, and total determination of our holy mother church and your good justice. I equally swear, vow, and promise to my Lord Saint Peter, prince of apostles, to our holy father, the Pope of Rome, his vicar and his successors, and to you, my lords, the reverend father in God my lord bishop of Beauvais, and the religious personage master Jehan le Maître, vicar of my lord the inquisitor of the faith, as well as to my judges, that never by any exhortation, or other manner, I will return to the errors aforesaid, from which it has pleased our Lord to take and deliver me; but always remain in union with our holy mother church, and in obedience to our holy father the Pope of Rome. And this I say, attest, and swear, by the Almighty God and by the holy Evangelists. And in confirmation hereof, I have signed this schedule with my signature. JEHANNE, ☒

Immediately upon Joan's signature being affixed to the false schedule, Cauchon pulled from his sleeve a new sentence, one of mitigation in place of the death sentence, and read it to her:

"As you have sinned against God and Church, we condemn you, as a matter of grace and moderation, to pass the residue of your days in prison, to share the bread of bitterness and the water of agony, to weep for your sins, and to commit no more in the future."

Joan was now relieved, for at last, she thought, she would be out of the hands of the English and in ecclesiastical custody. But her relief was short lived, as Cauchon sternly commanded the guards, "Take her back whence you brought her." Warwick was stunned, not realizing Cauchon's guile. He was positive the English had lost their precious prisoner. But Cauchon reassured him: "Do not worry; we shall soon have our hands on her again."

Returned to the prison, Joan was ordered to change from her male clothes into female attire. She obeyed. Her jailors, however, did not remove the male garments from her cell but left them there in a sack. Several soldiers remained in her cell with her. They resumed their previous callous behavior and their attempts to attack her virginity. When these were of no avail, they beat her until she bled. Such tortures went on for two days. Then during the night her guards stole her female clothes. When she asked for them the next morning, they taunted her and told her to put on her male attire. This she refused to do, knowing that to do so would be a violation of her abjuration. But by noon she was forced to put on the male attire so that the guards would allow her to rise and relieve herself. Since these were the only garments her guards would allow her, she had no choice but to continue wearing them.

This news was not long in reaching the ears of the Bishop of Beauvais and his vice-inquisitor. Now was the moment for which they had been waiting. Along with eight assessors they hastened to the prison, saw that Joan was once again dressed as a man, and accused her on the spot of being a relapsed heretic. Joan was in tears. She explained that the soldiers had taken away her female attire, how the promises made to unshackle her and allow her to go to Mass and receive the sacrament had not been kept, how she was being kept in the English jail instead of being turned over to the Church prison. But Cauchon was deaf to the truth of her assertions. Closing in for the kill, he at once asked her about her saints and if she had heard from them recently. Knowing all was now lost, and wishing to die rather than endure further torture at the hands of the English soldiers, Joan admitted that she had talked with them: "Since Thursday they have declared to me that I was guilty of a great fault [signing the abjuration]. In short, everything which I have said or done since Thursday last has been performed under the dread of being burnt." Torn between her fear of the stake and her faith in her saints, she had finally chosen the latter.

On Tuesday, May 29, Beauvais called the judges together, along with doctors of theology and law, members of the clergy, and other important personages. He reviewed the case to date, then read Joan's last confessions of the previous day. In their considered opinion she was a heretic who, although recently abjured, had now obviously relapsed.

The next morning, May 30, 1431, Brother Martin L'Advenu was sent to tell her of her fate and to hear her confession. She was petrified with fear, but he managed to calm her down. Her request for the sacrament of the eucharist was granted. What had Cauchon to lose at this point? He went to her prison for the last time. She accused him reproachfully: "Bishop, it is owing to you that I die."

He answered, "Ah, Joan, you die because you have relapsed into your former errors." Resigned now, she replied:

"Alas, had you placed me in the prisons of the ecclesiastical court, this would not have happened. On this account I appeal from you to God."

* * *

An engraving by Florian after a
mural by J. E. Lenepveu.

It was nine in the morning when, dressed in women's clothes, Joan was put in the prison cart, which was then drawn to the Rouen marketplace. The square was packed with soldiers, church dignitaries, and nobles. Three scaffolds had been erected: one for the judges, including the secular judges who would pronounce Joan's sentence; one for the spectators; and the stake itself with faggots piled high around it.

Nicolas Midi addressed her: "Joan, go thy way in peace; the Church can no longer protect thee, and therefore yields thee to the secular arm."

Joan then fell on her knees and offered prayers to God. She asked forgiveness for anything she might have done to offend. She absolved the king of any blame. She asked all the clerics present, all her enemies as well as her friends, to pray for her soul.

The English soldiers were getting impatient. They resented the long-drawn-out rituals that always attended such executions. Finally Beauvais read the formal sentence casting her out from the Church. Immediately, at his last words, the soldiers, not waiting for the pronouncement of the death sentence by the secular judge, grabbed her and roughly dragged her to the stake. Somehow during this clamorous melee the secular judge apparently mumbled out the sentence and the authority by which she was to be burned. But since this formality was lost in the shouting and tumult, it was questionable whether any such sentence was uttered.

As she was being dragged to the stake, Joan pleaded that a crucifix be brought from the church so that she might keep looking at it until the end. This was done. Then she was tied to the stake, and the miter of the Inquisition, on which was written "Heretic, Relapse, Apostate, Idolatress," was placed above her brow.

Now the executioners lighted the faggots at several places, and the flames began to flicker up around her. Martin L'Advenu had helped her mount the scaffold and was still with her as the flames licked higher. Thinking of his safety, she warned him to climb down quickly. Once she asked for holy water. As the first flame touched her, she screamed. The crowd froze. A deathly silence ensued, broken only by the crackling of the flames. As the flames and smoke completely engulfed her, she looked up to heaven, and half imploring, half screaming, cried out her one last word: "Jesus!"

Some time later in the day, the executioner gathered up the ashes that had once been Joan, and threw them in the Seine.

*   *   *

The impact of the trial of Joan of Arc on the course of history was momentous. Joan's martyrdom had broken the morale of the English soldiers. They believed they had burned a saint and would be punished for it. In a sense they were. Philip of Burgundy, perhaps influenced by the resentful reactions to Joan's death, soon realized he was of French blood, and signed an alliance with Charles VII on December 21, 1435. This at last gave Paris to Charles. From then on, the English were defeated at almost every turn. On June 17, 1453 complete victory came to the French in the Battle of Castillon, when six thousand attacking Englishmen were repulsed and most of them annhilated. Joan had not sacrificed herself in vain. She had succeeded in laying the foundations for a united France, which soon became the reality for which she gave her life.

As to the memory of Joan herself, grave doubts concerning the validity of the trial began to assail those who took part in it, as well as men of learning all over France who had followed the proceedings. On February 15, 1449, King Charles VII declared that Joan had been unjustly put to death, and ordered an investigation into the facts. Its conclusions affirmed that the trial was invalid and was based on invidious assumptions.

In 1452 the then Archbishop of Rouen, who was an ardent admirer of Joan, apointed Jean Bréhal, an inquisitor, to make an official investigation. This was carried out. But it was obvious that if the work of so high a Church authority as the Bishop of Beauvais with the concurrence of the Inquisitor Lemaître were to be undone, only the Pope in Rome could do it. An appeal was made to Pope Nicholas V, but he showed no inclination to take interest. Upon his death, Calixtus II became Pope, and immediately, on June 1455, granted the apostolic letters needed. They allowed Isabelle Romée and Joan's brothers to bring suit to prove that the charges of heresy and others against Joan were false. Their tearful and moving plea was heard on November 17, 1455, at Notre-Dame in Paris. It was a great success. It aroused the interest of the entire Christian world, including the learned doctors of the university. It led to the opening of four separate investigations at Rouen, Domrémy, Orléans, and Paris. The minutes of the trial, the results of these investigations, a number of articles, all were placed before the judges who had heard Isabelle Romée at Notre-Dame. These judges then conducted seven hearings from December 12, 1455, to May 31, 1456, six in Paris and the last in Rome. It is not necessary to go into the reams of testimony (the ninety-one articles all aimed at showing a revision was necessary), nor the questioning of Manchon, the still-living clerk of the court at Joan's trial. Suffice it to say that Manchon shatteringly admitted that the final twelve articles on which Joan was judged were *not based on Joan's actual replies and that Joan had not even been read the twelve condemnatory articles.*

The iniquities of the Rouen trial were now self-evident to the judges. On July 7, 1456, they recapitulated the whole affair and declared that Isabelle Romée had won her case. They invalidated the proceedings of 1431. They restored Joan to the Church, declaring that she had never really been separated from it. Fittingly, their verdict was read publicly in Rouen. Hundreds of years later, on May 9, 1920, Joan of Arc was canonized as a saint by Pope Benedict XV in Rome.

In the annals of trials, the interrogation, condemnation, and execution of Joan are events in a long line, which began long before Socrates and did not end with Galileo, in which ideas went on trial in the form of people. Joan was tried for her heresies, and as long as there are dogmas, there will be heretics. When such people are tried and condemned by their contemporaries, it is often because their ideas are so vital; but, unfortunately for them—and for us—the moment for their ideas had not yet arrived in history.

The mother of Joan of Arc tearfully pleads for a posthumous revision of Joan's sentence on November 17, 1455, at Notre-Dame in Paris.

Mary, Queen of Scots.

3

Mary, Queen of Scots

[1586]

THE LAST HALF OF THE SIXTEENTH CENTURY SAW THE great European Renaissance flower into full bloom. The revival of the spirit of learning and of inquiry had taken hold in the British Isles, where Shakespeare and Marlowe and Bacon, among many others, were producing some of the greatest intellectual achievements in the history of mankind. But it was an age of intrigue, of constant civil war over religious and other issues, of murder and mayhem, conspiracy and execution, that gripped these same islands across the Channel. This was the atmosphere in which Mary, Queen of Scots, lived, plotted, married, divorced, loved and hated, and finally lost her head after a two-day trial dominated by her presence, and followed by a Star Chamber trial whose greatest significance was found in her absence.

In 1548 Mary Stuart, a child of six, sailed for France to become betrothed to the Dauphin of France, as a result of an alliance between the Scots and the French. In 1558, the year that marked the marriage of Mary to the dauphin, Elizabeth ascended the throne of England. To Catholic Europe, Elizabeth's birth was illegitimate, and Mary Stuart was the rightful Queen of England. Henry II of France ordered her to assume the royal arms of England. With this edict, the rivalry to death was brought to life between Protestant Elizabeth and Catholic Mary. After nineteen years of imprisonment, it culminated in Mary's two-day trial in Fotheringay Castle on October 14 and 15, 1586.

* * *

What chain of events had transpired to change a winning, gentlehearted girl with a level head on her shoulders into a coldly calculating, disillusioned, and revengeful queen?

On the death of Henry II, Francis and Mary became King and Queen of France. But Francis soon followed his father to the grave, and Mary sorrowfully left France for her native Scotland, arriving in August, 1561. It was

a Scotland dominated by the Protestants led by John Knox, sharply at odds with her Catholic subjects. Queen Mary was, however, given permission to hear Mass celebrated in her own private chapel. At this point in her reign the young queen ruled with skill and tact. The question soon arose as to Mary's second marriage. Elizabeth proposed one of her favorites, Lord Robert Dudley, but Mary, with a willfulness and determination of her own, had already secretly married her cousin, Henry, Lord Darnley. On July 29, 1565, they were remarried at Holyrood Castle. This aroused the Protestants, and a short civil war ensued. In October, 1565, the queen's army of 18,000 men defeated the Earl of Murray's forces and compelled him to flee to England. Darnley now became jealous of the intimacy betwen Mary and Rizzio, her secretary, and planned the latter's death. On March 9, 1566, Rizzio was dragged from the queen's presence and killed without trial. Mary was aware of her husband's part in the plot, but they were reconciled by the birth of their son, James, on June 19, 1566. But bitterness again erupted between them, and coincidentally Darnley was killed in a mysterious gunpowder explosion while at his Kirk O' Field residence. The murderer was Bothwell, who was the queen's lover, as revealed in the famous "Casket Letters." It was he who had led her forces against Murray and whom, barely more than three months later, she took as her third husband, even though he was a staunch Protestant. Mary's amorous intrigues often took precedence over her affairs of state. The new marriage was stormy, with only weak military actions against those who denounced Bothwell's crime (even though officially he had been vindicated). Their forces were quickly defeated, and under the terms of surrender Mary and Bothwell were forced to part. Queen Mary was imprisoned in Lochleven Castle, where on June 20, 1567, she was forced to abdicate the throne of Scotland in favor of her son James. Murray was appointed regent until James, a one-year-old infant, became of age.

After the death of her first husband, King Francis II of France, Mary returned to Scotland and soon secretly married her cousin, Henry, Lord Darnley. This portrait of Darnley depicts him shortly after their marriage.

Noted for her impetuous love affairs, Mary is shown here with her favorite and her secretary, David Rizzio. Her husband, Lord Darnley, was so enraged at their relationship that he had Rizzio murdered.

"Mary, Queen of Scots, and Henry, Lord Darnley" in a mezzotint after R. Elstrake. Because of her infatuation for Lord Bothwell, Mary soon shed Darnley, who was killed by a mysterious gunpowder explosion while at his Kirk-of-Field residence. *Museum of Fine Arts, Boston, Harvey D. Parker Collection*

Lord Bothwell, Mary's third husband.

"Mary, Queen of Scots, Signing Her Abdication" in an engraving after W. Allan. Scandalized at her love affairs and suspicious connection with the murder of Lord Darnley, the Scottish lords force her to sign her abdication of the Scottish throne in favor of her son James. She signs it on June 20, 1567, while imprisoned in Lochleven Castle. *Museum of Fine Arts, Boston, Harvey D. Parker Collection*

On May 2, 1568, on her second attempt, Mary escaped from Lochleven in a boat supplied by eighteen-year-old Willie Douglas and abetted by Elizabeth, who sent a letter and ring signifying her royal protection. It was this act that influenced Mary to flee to England for help when her forces, which had rallied to her at her escape, were again defeated. On May 16, 1568, she landed at Workington in Cumberland, believing that Elizabeth would help her regain her Scottish crown. She knew better than to count on France. On July 15 she was removed to Bolton Castle in Yorkshire.

Mary was now accused of complicity in the death of Darnley and warned to divorce Bothwell. On January 10, 1569, however, the Queen's Council judged that nothing had been proved against her.

Mary was now sent from one castle to another, which must not only have exasperated her but also given her qualms about Elizabeth's sincerity. On November 28, 1569, she was taken to Sheffield Castle and put in the care of the Earl of Shrewsbury. For the next fourteen years this was her home.

In 1581 there was a plot afoot by her kinsman, the Duke of Guise, to invade England and place Mary and her son James jointly on the throne held by Elizabeth. The plan failed when the Scottish accomplices were defeated. Mary then sent Elizabeth a torrent of letters in which she bewailed her years in prison and the way she was being treated by her cousin, and assured her she had no aspirations whatsoever to the throne of England.

On her second attempt, aided by Willie Douglas, the eighteen-year-old son of her royal jailor, Mary successfully escapes from Lochleven Castle.

Lochleven Castle, from which Mary made two attempts to escape.

Fleeing to England in the hope of gaining the support of Queen Elizabeth, her English cousin, Mary was imprisoned on July 15, 1568, in Bolton Castle in Yorkshire. She was then moved from one castle to another until she was finally taken to Sheffield Castle on November 28, 1569, and put in the care of the Earl of Shrewsbury. There she spent the next fourteen years.

Library of Congress

But by January, 1583, Elizabeth was losing patience with her royal charge. She remarked to Castelman: "If the Queen of Scotland had had anyone else to deal with she would have lost her head long ago. She has a correspondence with rebels in England, agents in Paris, Rome and Madrid, and carries on plots against me all over Christendom, the object of which (as messengers who have been taken confess) is to deprive me of my kingdom and my life."

Mary was now in rapid succession moved to Wingfield Manor in 1584, to Tutbury in January, 1585, and to Chartley Castle on December 24, 1585. It is from this castle that she carried on her fateful correspondence with Anthony Babington in the last-gasp hope that the wild plans of himself and his confederates would at least gain her the freedom she had sought during so many years of imprisonment.

* * *

By now—1586—the years in prison had taken their toll on Mary. She lived in constant dread of a sudden and violent death at the hands of Elizabeth's loyal subjects. Life now seemed hopeless and release from her captivity a jaded dream. Full of bitter hatred, desperate to a point of recklessness, she was ready to welcome and condone any plan, however audacious, that might liberate her. It was in this frame of mind that she gave her approval to the scheme of the Prince of Parma for Spain to invade England, free her from her captivity, and accept him as her husband. Mary wrote all her letters in cipher for her own safety's sake. Little did she realize that Elizabeth's loyal confidant, Sir Francis Walsingham, and his spies had broken her code, systematically intercepted her correspondence, and deciphered it.

In another incriminating letter written to Charles Paget, Mary referred to the Spanish invasion plan and said she would do her utmost to get her son James to join the enterprise. If he should refuse, she would recommend the Catholic nobility to give him up to the King of Spain until she wished him released. All of this she was to deny emphatically at her trial.

England at this period was honeycombed with spies: those loyal to Queen Elizabeth devoted their energies to gathering incriminating evidence against the Queen of Scots; those loyal to Mary constantly tried to open up paths of communication between the captive queen and her friends and backers on the outside. However innocent Mary was to appear at her trial, the facts were only too clear that she welcomed and abetted all efforts to free her, perhaps even at the expense of the murder of the Queen of England. The former she readily admitted; the latter she vehemently denied.

Thus it happened that at the same time the Prince of Parma in Spain was planning his invasion of England, a group of her loyal followers in England were plotting to murder Elizabeth. Known as the "Babington Conspiracy," it was doomed to failure because Walsingham, informed by his spies, was aware of almost every move that was being made. Not only was he aware; he also insidiously instigated his spies to help nurture the plot in order to implicate Mary in it, thus bringing about her destruction.

Anthony Babington was a young man of fashion who pitied the plight of the Queen of Scots. He was thus easily drawn into a plan, devised by Gilbert Gifford, one of Walsingham's Catholic spies (he had both Catholic and Protestant ones) to murder Elizabeth. Babington, anxious to free Mary, demurred at murdering Elizabeth until Gifford produced an English priest named Ballard who convinced him that it was a legal deed sanctioned by the Pope himself. Babington then enlisted five young men of his own age and station, to whom, with the consent of Gifford and Ballard, he disclosed the plans of the

conspiracy. These were Chidiock Titchbourne, Charles Tilney, Edward Abbington, John Charnock, and an Irishman named Barnwell. A number of others agreed to join in the freeing of Mary after Elizabeth was dead. They all met daily to discuss their plans. At each meeting at least three of Walsingham's spies were present. So far, Mary seemed to know nothing of this plot. She was cautioned by Morgan, who was still imprisoned in the Bastille in France, against corresponding with Ballard because he was engaged in matters that if discovered she must have knowledge of. But he did seem to recommend she correspond with Babington himself. Whether from true advice or forged advice, Mary did write a short letter to Babington declaring confidence in him, as proposed by Morgan, and thanking him for his good affection. Mary at this time was at Chartley Castle, in the custody of Sir Amias Paulet, who kept Walsingham informed of all that went on.

On July 12 Mary received a letter, allegedly from Babington, in which he wrote that "one Ballard, a man of virtue and learning, and of singular zeal to the Catholic cause and your majesty's service, informed me of great preparations by the Christian princes, your majesty's allies, for the deliverance of our country from the extreme and miserable estate wherein for a long time it hath remained." He went on to detail parts of the plan: "First, for the assuring of invasions, sufficient strength on the invaders' parts to arrive is appointed, with a strong party at every place to join them and warrant their landing, the deliverance of your majesty, *the despatch of the usurping competition.*" Had she been in doubt up to this point as to the intentions of Babington and his fellow conspirators to do away with Elizabeth, she now knew. Was this emphasized phrase written by Babington or inserted by Philipps? Mary's secretary, Nau, wrote a short note to Babington acknowledging receipt of the letter and telling him an answer would be sent in three days. This was, of course, intercepted.

On July 17 Mary wrote a long letter to Babington in reply. She was now desperate and more than willing to risk her life to regain her freedom. If the copy of this letter, produced at her trial, was a genuine reproduction of her original, then she indeed approved not only of the plan of invasion and of the rising of the Catholics but also of the murder of Elizabeth. While there are strong suspicions that the letter was tampered with, she had every reason at this point to turn her long-smoldering hatred for her cousin into active participation on behalf of her freedom, even to the extreme of condoning Elizabeth's murder.

She urged Babington: "The affairs being prepared, and forces in readiness both within and without the realm, *then shall it be time to set the gentlemen on work, taking good order upon the accomplishment of their design.*"

Truly incriminating evidence—if she truly wrote it. She ends her long letter: "Whatever issue the matter taketh, I do, and shall, think myself obliged, so long as I live, toward you for the offers you make to hazard yourself as you do for my deliverance; and by any means that I may have, I shall do my endeavor to recompense you as you deserve."

Was Mary a party to the conspiracy of Babington? Many have agreed with the French ambassador in London, M. de Châteauneuf, who stated at the time that the Queen of Scots was justified in doing all that was alleged against her to obtain her liberty. Whether she was or not, the conspiracy came to an abrupt end when Walsingham finally decided to pounce on his mouse. Ballard was arrested and unmercifully racked. The others were quickly apprehended. On September 13 Babington and six of his companions were arraigned in Westminster. Only Ballard had been tortured. All were persuaded to plead guilty. On September 20 they were taken to St. Giles's in the Fields where they were lingeringly and painfully put to death. The next day seven others were hanged with merciful speed. Thus ended the conspiracy, the consequences of which were to bring to trial Mary Queen of Scots.

*   *   *

Many years of Mary's life were spent in prison, but the prisons were usually large and spacious castles, and here she had at her disposal secretaries and servants, ample food and clothing, and all the conveniences, even luxuries, known to the aristocracy of Elizabethan England— all, that is, except freedom.

Mary, Queen of Scots, swearing that she had never sought to have Elizabeth killed. This scene takes place at Fotheringay Castle, to which she has been transferred to await trial.

On Sunday, September 25, 1586, Mary Stuart was brought to Fotheringay Castle. That she was taken here, now a state prison, left no doubt to her that she would at last be brought to trial. Shortly after her arrival, on October 1, Sir Amias Paulet, in whose charge she was, requested an interview. He told her that Queen Elizabeth was fully aware of her part in the Babington plot and was surprised that she should deny the charges brought against her, especially when Elizabeth had clear proof in her possession. He advised Mary to admit to these charges and beg Elizabeth's pardon. Immediately seeing through this deception, Mary replied: "As a sinner I am truly conscious of having often offended my Creator, and I beg Him to forgive me, but as Queen and Sovereign I am aware of no fault or offense for which I have to render account to any one here below, as I recognize no authority but God and His Church. As therefore I could not offend, I do not wish for pardon; I do not seek, nor would I accept it from any one living." Thus she reasserted the divine right of kings and queens, and in this she remained adamant to the end.

On October 8 the commissioners appointed to judge the Scottish queen met at Westminister where the chancellor, Sir Thomas Browley, reviewed the alleged conspiracy and read the letters addressed by Babington to Mary, her answers, and the testimony extracted from her two secretaries, Nau and Curle. Nearly all agreed that Mary should be brought to trial, as a result of which the commissioners were ordered to meet at Fotheringay, and the peers of the kingdom were invited to attend.

On Saturday, October 11, they arrived at Fotheringay. On Sunday they attended service in the castle chapel. Heading the list was the Primate of England, which also included Cecil, Lord Burleigh, Walsingham, the Earls of Leicester and Warwick, Elizabeth's secretary, Beale, and others. They now sent a message to Mary stating that since Elizabeth had proof of Mary's participation in the plot against her life, she was sending some of her peers and counselors to examine and judge her. To which Mary replied: "As a Queen I cannot submit to orders, nor can I submit to the laws of the land without injury to myself, the King my son and all other sovereign princes. . . . I decline my judges as being of a contrary faith to my own. . . . I am a Catholic, and have placed myself under the protection of those Catholic kings and princes who have offered me their services. If they have planned any attempt against Queen Elizabeth, I have not been cognisant of it, and therefore it is wrong to treat me as if I were guilty."

Time after time the commissioners urged, cajoled, and threatened in order to convince Mary to accept them as her judges. All her refusals were recorded and sent to Elizabeth. Finally, at Mary's request, they showed and explained to her their commission. It was based on two acts of Parliament passed two years previously. First, it

was declared to be high treason for anyone to speak of Mary's succession to the Crown of England while Elizabeth was alive. Second, it decreed that if anyone of any rank, in England or abroad, should conspire against the life of Elizabeth or connive at such conspiracy, it should be lawful for any extraordinary jury of twenty-four members to adjudge that case. It was obvious that these laws were directed solely at Mary to pave the way to try her legally, thus absolving Elizabeth of blame as to the consequences of her trial.

Asked if she would not proceed against a conspirator if she were peacefully ruling her own kingdom, Mary replied: "Never would I act in such a manner. . . . You frame your laws according to your own wishes. . . . I do not feel bound to submit to your laws. If you wish to proceed according to the common law of England, you must produce examples and precedents. If you follow common law, those only who framed it can interpret it. Roman Catholics alone have the right to explain and apply it." Then again on the legality of trying her, she said: "If you wish to try me by the true civil law, I demand that some members of the universities be allowed to judge my case, so that I may not be left to the judgment of such lawyers as are subservient to the laws of England alone."

These fruitless exchanges continued until Sir Christopher Hatton in a conciliatory manner explained that the commissioners were only trying to ascertain whether the Queen of Scots was, or was not, guilty of having participated in the plot against Elizabeth. If the queen refused to be examined, the people would believe that she was guilty; whereas if she consented to be questioned she could prove her innocence. This line of reasoning obviously moved Mary, so that she wavered in her determination. Finally, two other arguments broke her down. The commissioners said they would proceed whether she agreed or not, and Elizabeth sent her a scathing letter which nonetheless contained a hope of clemency:

You have planned in divers ways and manners to take my life and to ruin my kingdom by the shedding of blood. I never proceeded so harshly against you; on the contrary, I have maintained you and preserved your life with the same care which I use for myself. Your treacherous doings will be proved to you, and made manifest in the very place where you are. And it is my pleasure that you shall reply to my Nobles and to the Peers of my kingdom as you would to myself were I there present. I have heard of your arrogance, and therefore I demand, charge, and command you to reply to them. *But answer fully, and you may receive greater favour from us.*

ELIZABETH

On the morning of the 14th, at her request, a delegate of the commissioners, including her bitter foe Walsingham, waited on her. To them she conveyed her decision to appear for questioning before the commissioners and peers provided she could answer only to the accusation "which touches on the life of Queen Elizabeth, of which I swear and protest that I am innocent. I say nothing upon any other matter whatsoever as to any friendship or treaty with any other foreign princes." To this the commissioners agreed, and at last the die was cast.

* * *

The spacious room in which Mary Stuart was to be tried adjoined her apartment. At the upper end stood a dais with a throne carrying the arms of England. This represented Queen Elizabeth herself. In front of the dais was a seat prepared for Queen Mary with a cushion for her feet. Benches were placed on each side of the room: those on the right being occupied by Lord Chancellor Browley, the Lord Treasurer Burleigh and the earls; on the left the barons and knights of the Privy Council, Sir James Crofts, Sir Christopher Hatton, Sir Francis Walsingham, Sir Ralph Sadler, and Sir Walter Mildmay. Before the earls and barons sat two premier judges and the High Baron of the Exchequer, four other judges, and

two doctors of civil law. At a large table in front of the dais sat the representatives of the Crown: Popham, the attorney general; Egerton, solicitor general; Gawdy, the queen's sergeant; Barker, the notary; and two clerks to take down the official report of the proceedings. What documentary evidence there was lay on the table. At the far end of the room, as spectators, stood the gentlemen attendants and servants of the lords of commission.

At nine o'clock on October 14, 1586, Queen Mary made her entrance, supported on each side by Melville and Burgoing and followed by her surgeon, Jacques Gervais; her apothecary, Pierre Gorion, and three waiting women, Gillis Mowbray, Jane Kenedy, and Alice Curle. Owing to severe rheumatism she walked with difficulty but with commanding dignity. The commissioners did her the courtesy of uncovering their heads. She looked curiously around at the members of the court, then remarked mournfully to Melville, "Alas, here are many counsellors, but not one for me."

Mary, Queen of Scots, entering the courtroom at Fotheringay Castle at nine o'clock on the morning of October 14, 1586. The commissioners to try her were selected from the highest lords, earls, barons and knights of the realm. The evidence lies on the long table, and two clerks are ready to record the proceedings.

The lord chancellor opened the proceedings with a speech telling why Queen Elizabeth was impelled to call this court to hear the evidence against Mary. To which Mary replied: "I came into the kingdom under promise of assistance and aid against my enemies, and not as a subject, as I could prove to you had I my papers; instead of which I have been detained and imprisoned. I protest publicly that I am an independent sovereign and princess, and I recognize no superior but God alone. I therefore require that before I proceed further, it be recorded that whatever I may say in replying here to the Commissioners of my good sister, the Queen of England (who, I consider, has been wrongly and falsely prejudiced against me), shall not be to my prejudice, nor that of the princes of my allies, nor the King my son, nor any of those who may succeed me." In reply, Bromley denied that Mary had come into England under a promise of assistance from Elizabeth. They would, however, record Mary's protest without accepting or approving it.

Gawdy, the queen's sergeant, rose and explained the commission, then touched on the seizure of Babington, the suspected correspondence between him and Queen Mary, the details of the plot and the six men who had conspired to murder Queen Elizabeth. Mary denied that she had ever spoken to Babington and that she knew anything of the six men alluded to. At that point another lawyer rose and recited from memory certain letters which were alleged to have been dictated by Babington of his own free will before being put to death, and copies of other letters said to have been signed by Babington and the other plotters. Mary demanded they produce all the original letters to compare them with the copies:

Till then I must content myself with affirming solemnly that I am guiltless of the crimes imputed to me. I do not deny that I have earnestly wished for liberty and done my utmost to procure it for myself. . . . I have written to my friends, I confess; I appealed to them to assist me escape from these miserable prisons in which I have languished for nearly nineteen years. I have also, I confess, often pleaded the cause of the Catholics with the Kings of Europe, and for their deliverance from the oppression under which they lie, I would willingly have shed my blood. But I declare formally that I never wrote the letters that are produced against me. Can I be responsible for the criminal projects of a few desperate men, which they planned without my knowledge or participation?

About one o'clock the queen retired for her dinner, and upon her return the reading of the letters, depositions, and confessions continued. They were read at random, and so answered true or false by the queen. They all were directed at convincing the lords of her guilt. In spite of the confusion of the questioning, Mary remained calm and determined. She then repeated much of the talks she had had in her own room with the commissioners who interviewed her, emphasizing once again the illegality of this court to try her.

Burleigh interrupted her and accused her of assuming the name and arms of England, and of having aspired to the Crown. Mary replied: "What I did at that time was in obedience to the commands of Henry the Second, my father-in-law, and you well know the reason."

"But," protested Burleigh, "you did not give up these practices even after we signed the peace with King Henry."

Mary answered: "'You made the arrangements to your own interest and advantage. I was not thereby bound to renounce my rights, or to abandon them to my own great prejudice and that of my successors, receiving nothing in return, I owed you nothing. I was not dependent on your Queen, nor am I now, and I was not obliged to cede to her rights so important. If I had shown such weakness I should have been always reproached with it as having acted to my own blame and dishonour."

"You have also," insisted Burleigh, "continued to assert your pretension to the English Crown."

"I have never given up my rights," answered the queen. "I do not now and never will. . . . God and you know whether I have the right or not to the Crown of England. I have offered myself to maintain the rights of my sister Queen Elizabeth as being the eldest, but I have no scruple of conscience in desiring the second rank, as being the legitimate and nearest heir. I am the daughter of Henry VII. This cannot be taken from me by any law, or council, assembly, or judgment, nor consequently can my rights."

Thus Mary stoutly maintained her right of succession to the English throne. The truth of this the lords knew full well. But they were protesting it on grounds entirely different from that of its legality. Mary was a Catholic, and no Catholic could be allowed to rule Protestant England. Backing Mary were the pope in Rome and the king in France. Backing Elizabeth was the entire Protestant cause. Mary's own son, James, was a Protestant, and with his mother out of the way another Protestant would succeed Elizabeth on the throne. On the surface of it, Mary was fighting for her life against charges of threatening Elizabeth. But the real charge was that she was a Catholic queen supported by the Catholic powers of Europe, and as such a threat to England itself as long as she lived. Removing her from the scene once for all would resolve the problem, and this the lords of the court intended to do—with as much apparent legality as possible.

In this respect Mary had played admirably into their hands. She was well aware of the Babington plot to assassinate Elizabeth, whether or not she gave her written approval. After all those years as prisoner, she was desperate to escape, and very appreciative of any lengths to which her friends and supporters would go to help her. But now, at her trial, she must at all costs deny any knowledge or complicity in the plot. As they read aloud the alleged correspondence between Babington and herself, she stoutly denied she had seen any letters of

Babington, much less replied to them. The judges produced ciphers, letters, and many dispositions, including those of her two secretaries, Curle and Nau, to prove their case.

The queen turned to Walsingham and said: "It is easy to imitate ciphers and handwriting. . . . I fear this is the work of Monsieur de Walsingham for my destruction: of him who I am certain has tried to deprive me of my life, and my son of his." She was now fully aware that her letters had been intercepted and deciphered.

Indignantly Walsingham rose and said: "I protest that my soul is free from all malice. God is my witness that, as a private person, I have done nothing unworthy of an honest man, and as Secretary of State, nothing unbefitting my duty." Both were indulging in double-talk, Walsingham even more than Mary. Both knew what a farce the trial had been.

Mary then admitted that some of the ciphers were hers, but claimed that they had been tampered with so that their meanings were distorted. Once again she reiterated that she had no hand in any of the many conspiracies against Elizabeth's life. Technically she was right: no hand in them, perhaps, but much heart.

The judges now introduced the confessions of her secretaries Nau and Curle, regarding certain letters Mary had received and to which she had dictated her replies. These confessions proved, said the judges, that Mary had actually directed the conspiracy. Grasping for any possible loophole, and well aware that this was secondary evidence, Mary indignantly demanded:

Why are not Nau and Curle examined in my presence? . . if they have written, be it what it may, concerning the enterprise, they have done it of themselves, and did not communicate it to me, and on this point I disavow them. Nau, as a servant of the King of France, may have undertaken things not according to my wishes; he had undertakings that I did not know of . . . I know that Nau had many peculiarities, likings, and intentions, that I cannot mention in public, but which I much regret, for he does me great injustice. For my part, I do not wish to accuse my secretaries, but I see plainly that what they have said is from fear of torture and death.

Then looking at one of the dispositions attributed to Nau, she said spiritedly: "And I see well that he has written it with his own hand; may it not be that while translating and putting my letters into cipher, my secretaries may have inserted things which I did not dictate to them? The majesty and safety of princes would be reduced to nought, if their reputation depended upon the writing and witnesses of their secretaries." The logic of this was unanswerable. In any fair trial, even for those days, the case would have been thrown out of court. But the judges were there to convict, not to try. Without letting her reply, they heaped a torrent of abuse on her, furiously repeating all the accusations and evidence, and all together declaring her to be guilty. Thus ended the first day of the trial.

According to one chronicler summing up the day's proceedings: "It cannot be denied that, even according to their own account, she had maintained throughout a decisive superiority over her opponents. Without counsel, or witnesses, or papers, and armed with nothing but her own clear intellect and heroic spirit, she had answered, point by point, all their allegations. Knowing the weakness of their proofs, they had artfully mixed up the charge of conspiracy with the scheme of invasion." Mary had, of course, seen through their pretensions, and time after time brought them back to the real issue.

* * *

The second and last day of the trial showed a departure from established procedure, unheard of in any other State trial of the period. Burleigh conducted the entire proceedings, with both the attorney general and the queen's sergeant remaining silent. The queen had been granted her request to address the assembly at the opening of the second day's proceedings. First she admonished them for the way she was being treated: "The manner in which I am treated appears to me very strange; not only am I brought to this place to be tried, contrary to the rights of persons of my quality, but my case is discussed by those who are not usually employed in the affairs of kings and princes. . . . Instead of this, I find myself overwhelmed under the importunity of a crowd of advocates and lawyers, who appear to be more versed in the formalities of petty courts of justice, in little towns, than in the investigation of questions such as the present."

She accused the judges of breaking their promise that she be tried solely on the charge of her alleged attempts on the life of Queen Elizabeth. She requested that she be permitted to reply to each person and each question separately. To this, Burleigh agreed, and the morning discussions proceeded along similar questions of the previous day.

A little later Burleigh accused her of forming many plans for her deliverance by outside help: "At the very moment that the last treaty for your freedom was concluded, Parry, one of your servants, was secretly sent by Morgan to assassinate the Queen."

"You are indeed my enemy," the queen exclaimed.

"Yes," answered Burleigh, "I am the enemy of the enemies of Queen Elizabeth."

At this point letters were read from Mary to Charles Paget discussing the projected invasion, one from Cardinal Allen to the queen addressing her as his sovereign. They presented further evidence purporting to show that the murder of the queen, her councilors, and principal noblemen had already been decided upon, that all Catholics were ready to rise up and place the Queen of Scots on the throne of England, and that in Rome prayers were offered for Mary as to the legitimate Queen of England.

In reply Mary denied knowledge of any plot, but firmly stated that her deliverance from her prison was promised by the foreign princes, that the Catholics would naturally help in this attempt as being to their own best interest, inasmuch as they were being wrongfully persecuted by the Protestant rulers, and that she had no desire to take the place of the queen. She concluded: "In short, you will find that I have no other desire than the overthrow of Protestantism and the deliverance of myself and the afflicted Catholics, for whom (as I have often said) I am ready to shed my blood."

At last the solicitor general asked her if she had anything more to say in her own defense. To which Mary replied: "I again demand to be heard in full Parliament, and to confer personally with Queen Elizabeth."

She then rose to leave, adding: "I am ready and willing to give pleasure and do service to the Queen, my good sister, and to employ myself for her and for the good of the kingdom in all that I can, for I love both." She said a few words in private to Walsingham, then addressed herself with dignity to the assembly: "My lords and gentlemen, my cause is in the hands of God."

With her departure the commissioners were ready to pass sentence, but Burleigh announced that Elizabeth had written from Windsor at midnight of the 14th that, even in the event she was found guilty, the sentence should be suspended until she could review their report. Accordingly the assembly was to wait ten days, then meet in the Star Chamber at Westminister.

Thus ended the trial of Mary Queen of Scots, one of the most unfair and illegal trials in history. It is not a question of how guilty, if at all, Mary was. On the basis of the evidence in the hands of the judges, much of it apparently falsified, she should never have been convicted of the charge for which she was tried. On the basis of a great deal of evidence of which the judges were *not* aware, Mary undoubtedly deserved her fate.

*   *   *

On October 25 the commissioners resumed their meeting in the Star Chamber at Westminister and with the accused absent found her guilty of having "contrived and imagined, since the 1st of June aforesaid, divers matters tending to the hurt, death and destruction of the Queen of England." Thereupon both Houses of Parliament, in order to secure her own safety, suggested to Elizabeth that Mary should be executed at once.

Privately Elizabeth was in full agreement, but publicly she deemed it expedient for her rule that Mary's death should not be attributed to her. Already rumors abounded that Philip of Spain was preparing a vast force at Lisbon to invade England. The Prince of Parma was expected to rescue the Queen of Scots and carry off Elizabeth herself. The Duke of Guise was actually landing in Sussex, and the Scots had marched across the border. Weird as these

Queen Elizabeth, herself is finally forced to sign Mary's death warrant, upon the completion of the trial declaring her guilty.

tales were, the people of England were aroused. But Elizabeth still delayed in signing the death warrant. What she wanted was for her lords to interpret her wishes and put Mary to death without the need for her signing any death warrant. In this way it would appear that her overeager subjects had exceeded their authority and acted against her own wish to save Mary's life. The lords were not so inclined, and resorted to other strategies. On the basis of the wild rumors circulating the country, they terrified her with dire prophecies.

On February 1 Elizabeth ordered Lord Howard, the lord high admiral, to send Davison, in whose charge the unsigned warrant was, to her. He immediately answered her call, bringing with him some papers for her to sign, among which was the warrant for Mary's execution. Elizabeth signed all the papers, feigning not to know that the warrant was among them. But she quickly changed her mind and explained to him that the reason she had waited so long to sign it was to indicate her reluctance to do so. She then instructed Davison to take the warrant to the lord chancellor for him to affix the great seal to it and send it on to those who would preside at its execution. Further she ordered that the execution must take place inside Fotheringay Castle as a matter of secrecy. She was deeply worried as to how resentfully France and Scotland might react to Mary's death.

The commissioners deliver the death warrant to Mary shortly after dinner on February 7, 1587 and instruct her to be ready for her execution early the following morning.

Again Elizabeth asked Davison to convince Sir Amias Paulet and other loyal subjects to do the deed themselves without using the warrant. Their own necks at stake, these loyal subjects were not *that* loyal. They begged off. Meanwhile, fearing that Elizabeth, as she had done before in the case of the Duke of Norfolk's execution, would cancel the warrant, Davison acquainted Burleigh and Sir Christopher Hatton with his suspicions. Burleigh quickly summoned the members of the council and obtained their agreement to all sharing the responsibility of the execution. The warrant was given to Beale, the clerk of the council, to take to the earls of Kent and Shrewsbury, who were appointed to see that it was executed. Beale reached Fotheringay on February 5, after informing Kent of his duty on the way, and then brought the news to Shrewsbury.

Shortly after dinner on February 7, the commissioners asked Mary for an audience, which, after getting up out of bed, she granted them. They then read her the death warrant signed by Elizabeth, to which she listened with her usual calmness and dignity. At the end of the reading she delivered a short speech to them in which she said: "I thank you for such welcome news. You will do me a great good in withdrawing me from this world,

out of which I am very glad to go, on account of the miseries I see in it, and of being myself in continual affliction. I am of no good and of no use to any one. I have long looked for this, and have expected it day by day for eighteen years."

Kent now urged Mary to think of her soul, and offered her the Dean of Peterborough to comfort her. She would have no part of this Protestant, and told Kent: "Having lived till now in the true faith, this is not the time to change, but on the contrary, it is the very moment when it is most needful that I should remain firm and constant, as I intend to do." That Kent would seek to convert Mary to Protestantism in her last hours instead of allowing her the solace of her own faith indicates the depth of bitterness between the adherents of the two religions. Mary asked to see her own priest, but this Elizabeth had harshly forbidden. Denying her request, the lords told her, "It is our duty to prevent such abominations which offend God."

The queen then asked when she was to die, to which in faltering tones Shrewbury answered, "Tomorrow morning at eight o'clock."

*   *   *

"Mary, Queen of Scots, on the Evening Preceding Her Execution" in an engraving by John Sartain. Having refused the offer for the Protestant Dean of Peterborough to comfort her on her last night, she prays alone in her own Catholic faith. *Museum of Fine Arts, Boston, Harvey D. Parker Collection*

"Mary, Queen of Scots, Parting with Her Friends" in an engraving after A. Colin. At six o'clock on the morning of her scheduled execution, Mary read her will to her friends and distributed small purses to her faithful attendants. *Museum of Fine Arts, Boston, Harvey D. Parker Collection*

At the striking of six o'clock on Tuesday morning, February 8, the queen awoke and dressed in the finest clothes she had left. She assembled her entire household, then asked Bourgoing to read aloud her will, which she had composed the night before. At the end of the reading she signed it and ordered that it be delivered to the Duke of Guise. She distributed little purses to her attendants. The last-minute details being attended to, she now passed into the antechamber to pray. While she was there, a messenger knocked loudly on the door and announced that the lords were waiting. Her request for a short extension to finish her prayers was rejected, it now being slightly after eight o'clock. Assisted by Bourgoing, she walked out of her room. Her servants pleaded that they could not bear to assist her and hand her over to the executioner, so Mary asked to be assisted, and two soldiers were ordered to do so. Now her servants were told they could proceed no further. Supported by the guards, the queen then calmly descended the great staircase. At this point in the procession the commissioners finally allowed Mary's two women, Jane Kenedy and Alice Curle, to accompany her. They then entered the great hall which was draped all in black. At the upper

end stood the twelve-foot-square scaffold, rising about two feet off the floor and covered with black serge. By the oak block stood the two executioners. In all, there were about three hundred spectators.

When Mary saw the scaffold, she raised the crucifix she was carrying above her head and walked to it with great dignity. Unable to step up onto it by herself, she was assisted by Paulet, to whom she said with ironic wit: "Thanks for your courtesy, Sir Amias; this will be the last trouble I shall give you, and the most agreeable service you have rendered me." Then seating herself on the stool that had been prepared for her, she asked that her chaplain be sent to her. To the end the Protestants would not allow a Catholic clergyman to attend her.

Beale stepped up on the scaffold and read the royal commission for her execution. By now Mary's thoughts, as reflected in almost joyous expression, were on heavenly matters. She seemed almost oblivious to still earthly ones. However, she delivered a short speech of forgiveness to those who had done her wrong, after which the Protestant Dean of Peterborough informed her that he had been appointed to prepare her for death.

Mary prepares to leave her room for her last walk to the scaffold on the floor below.

Regally she descends
the steps to the great hall
of the castle.

"Peace, Mr. Dean," Mary gently rebuked him, "I have nothing to do with you; I do not wish to hear you; you can be silent if you please and go from hence." She refused to listen to him, and, while the crowd of witnesses were chanting Protestant prayers, she prayed aloud in Latin. At last the time had arrived, and, refusing an offer to help her remove her dress, she called her two servants to her and, with their aid, disrobed. When she was ready and had sent her women from the scaffold, the executioners fell on their knees and begged to be forgiven for what they were about to do. "I forgive you with all my heart," Mary answered fervently, "for in this hour I hope you will bring an end to all my troubles." They then led her to the block and made her lie flat with her head on it. As Mary uttered her last words, *"In manus tuas Domine commendo,"* the now distraught executioner brought

Mary, seated on the stool provided for her, hears Beale read
the royal commission for her execution, while the
two executioners wait by the block.

down the ax. It was a clumsy swing that severely wounded the queen. He struck a second blow, as if chopping down a tree, and then a third. With this last blow, the Catholic cause in England died along with the Catholic Queen of Scots.

For six months the body, almost forgotten, lay in Fotheringay Castle. It was then taken to the Cathedral of Peterborough, where after an impressive ceremony it was buried. Sixteen years later, her son, now James I, King of England, as a result perhaps of a twinge of conscience, had the body brought to Westminster Abbey, where, in its beautiful tomb, it rests today.

*   *   *

It is all a story of suspicion and intrigue, conspiracy and murder. Yet the importance of the trial of Mary, Queen of Scots, may be found in the decision, after two days of open trial, to retire and conclude the case in her absence: that is, in executive session or the Star Chamber. The case of Mary has popularized the phrase "Star Chamber proceedings," with all that it implies: a closed court hidden from the searching eyes of the public, where corruption or despotism can dispose of the freedom or the lives of the accused. When, to this day, there are demands for secret trials for reasons of political expediency or national security, the public is suspicious and outraged, and hurls back at the judges the epithet Star Chamber! It is the heritage of many British trials, not the least of which was that of Mary; and it is ironical that she whose life was hardly placed at the disposal of the cause of liberty should have alerted us to a watchword that is a safeguard of that freedom.

The executioner raises the ax to behead the queen. So distraught was he that the first blow only severely wounded her. He then struck two more blows, thus ending the life of Mary, Queen of Scots.

4

Guy Fawkes

[1606]

Members of the conspiracy known as the "Gunpowder Plot."

HISTORY IS FILLED WITH CONSPIRACIES AGAINST ROYALTY and government leaders, but few stories are as daring, imaginative, and incredible as the Gunpowder Plot, for which Guy Fawkes and about a dozen others paid with their lives.

The early part of the seventeenth century saw Protestantism already established as the state Church in England, but many Catholics still hoped to recapture Crown and country, and a special target for their efforts was King James I.

Guy Fawkes was born into the new faith of the Reformation, but he changed his loyalties in his youth, and joined forces with those intent on the overthrow of James. Some of his colleagues hoped for aid from a Spanish invasion; others were bolder in their plans, but more self-reliant.

The Gunpowder Plot, as history has called it, was probably conceived in the spring of 1604, its originator a young man named Robert Catesby. He suggested to John Wright and then to Thomas Winter that, in one swoop, the king, the House of Lords and the House of Commons could all be blown up, and the Catholics could then seize power. To what extent any sections of the Catholic hierarchy cooperated with, or even had knowledge of, the conspiracy, is open to doubt; some names of a few Jesuit priests crop up in the proceedings, but none were actually implicated in any plot.

In April, 1604, Thomas Winter went to the Continent to recruit aid from British Catholics in exile, and his greatest success was in lining up Guy Fawkes, young, handsome, and adventurous, dedicated to the task before him. Soon to be recruited into the conspiracy was another ex-Protestant, Thomas Percy, a brother-in-law of Wright. After considerable maneuvering, Percy managed to rent a house immediately adjoining Parliament, obtained the ouster of the tenant, and proceeded to plan the great detonation.

Others were recruited and sworn to secrecy, while vigorous work proceeded in the cellar of the house. Great quantities of gunpowder were amassed, and over this there were placed iron bars and huge stones to increase the destructive impact of the explosion, all carefully concealed beneath ordinary-appearing coal and wood.

On October 26, 1605, a letter was delivered to Lord Monteagle, a parliamentary leader, warning him not to attend the forthcoming session of Parliament:

for god & man hath concurred to punish the wickedness of this tyme and thinke not slightlye of this advertisement but retyere youre selfe into youre countri . . .

Who sent the letter? Was there an agent of the king among the conspirators? It is significant that it was received by Monteagle, who was related to several of the conspirators. Perhaps it was only an effort to spare his life, and not to foil the plot.

But the jig was up. The conspirators fled; only Fawkes wanted to remain and to follow through with the plans. He had been assigned, or had volunteered for, the central task, to ignite the materials, and then to make a hurried escape in the few minutes before the explosion would take place.

On November 4, Fawkes was arrested; a few days later, Catesby and three conspirators were killed, several others arrested, and, except for Monteagle's brother-in-law, Francis Tresham (often suspected of writing the admonishing letter, and who died in jail), were tried and executed.

The trial of Guy Fawkes and seven others took place on January 27, 1606. The indictment spelled out the plot in full detail, and to this indictment, all pleaded not guilty. It is a curious document, this indictment, as seen by a twentieth-century reader. It opens with these words:

The matter that is now to be offered to you, my Lords the Commissioners, and to the trial of you, the Knights and

Gentlemen of the Jury, is matter of treason, but of such horror, and monstrous nature, that before now,

The Tongue of Man never delivered,

The Ear of Man never heard,

The Heart of Man never conceived,

Nor the Malice of Hellish or Earthly

Devil ever practised;

For, if it be abominable to murder the least,

If to touch God's Anointed be to oppose themselves against God,

If (by blood) to subvert Princes, States and Kingdoms, be hateful to God and Man, as all true Christians must acknowledge;

Then, how much more than too too monstrous shall all Christian hearts judge the horror of this treason, to murder and subvert

Such a King,

Such a Queen,

Such a Prince,

Such a Progeny,

Such a State,

Such a Government,

So complete and absolute,

That God approves:

The World admires:

All true English Hearts honour and reverence:

The Pope and his Disciples only envies and maligns.

The case for the Crown was offered by the attorney general, Sir Edward Coke. It was detailed and damning, although it went into flights of fantasy to implicate the Catholic Church. It was followed by the confessions of the accused, and then came the verdict. Of the defense,

there was none at all, as was customary in a treason trial. When the defendants were asked if they wished to be heard, two asked for mercy, one pleaded that he had been guilty of conspiracy that had been planned but not executed, and one asked that he be hanged both for himself and his brother. Of Fawkes, the record reads:

Guy Fawkes being asked why he pleaded "Not Guilty," having nothing to say for his excuse, answered that he had so done in respect of certain conferences mentioned in the indictment, which he said that he knew not of, which were answered to have been set down according to course of law, as necessarily pre-supposed before the resolution of such a design.

It was not an age of lengthy appeals; the trial was held on the 27th of January, and on the 30th four of the men were executed, and four more, this time including Guy Fawkes, the following day. Thus ended the most imaginative of all conspiracies.

Why Guy Fawkes came to be the legendary figure in the entire episode is not clear. He was not the most youthful, nor was he the only one reputed to be handsome and virile. He was certainly not the central conspirator, nor was he the originator of the plot. Perhaps he became a martyr-hero because he did not flee, and because he had volunteered for the most dangerous of the roles, the last to leave the scene. Even among villains, there is admiration for courage; the plot was never carried out, and the British folklore began to forget what might have been, and to admire the qualities of one of the men who lost his life in the effort.

Guy Fawkes interrogated, prior to his brief trial, by James I and his council in the king's bedchamber at Whitehall.

"Galileo Galilei" in an engraving by Pietro Bettelini.
The New York Public Library

5

Galileo Galilei

[1633]

WHEN THE POLISH SCIENTIST NICOLAUS COPERNICUS promulgated in the early years of the sixteenth century the theory, based on various findings that preceded him, that the earth revolves around the sun, it caused no earth-shaking reverberations. In spite of the accepted belief by both the Catholics and the newly rebellious Protestants in the Ptolemy-Aristotle theory that the earth was the center of the universe and that the sun and all the planets revolved around it, Copernicus incurred no wrath, no outcry, no great denunciations, although he did have many detractors, as could well be expected.

How was it, then, that nearly one hundred years later, the world's most eminent scientist, Galileo Galilei, espousing and advancing the Copernican theory, was to incite the papal wrath and ecclesiastical condemnation that was to shock both Catholic and non-Catholic worlds and saddle the Catholic Church with one of its most unwanted, thorniest problems?

The answer lies not in the similar scientific theories each man believed in and taught, but in the effort made by Galileo to impose his theories on the religious dogma of the Church; nay even to sway the Church away from its accepted dogma that the earth was the center of the universe and convert it to the opposite Copernican theory. As many a martyr before him, Galileo was to learn the fate of the heretic who questions the view of an existing religious hierarchy. Copernicus, on the other hand, had exercised caution, even to the point of reluctance to have his works published. While his followers knew of their contents, they were not published until after his death.

Galileo, while not the inventor of the telescope, put it to its best use, and was thus the first seriously to turn it on the heavens, searching for scientific facts that would explain the wonders of the universe. By it he increased the number of known planets and satellites from seven to eleven. Indeed, so astute were his scientific findings that he was soon elevated to fame in both lay and ecclesiastical circles, probably becoming the best-known man in Europe. His lectures were always crowded with enthusiastic followers. In 1610 the Grand Duke of Tuscany appointed him as first philosopher and mathematician at the University of Pisa at a yearly salary of 1,000 scudi for life. Lured by this offer from Venice, he left the only state in Italy that dared stand up against the power of Rome, little realizing that in moving he was putting his head between the jaws of the ecclesiastical lion.

Even more deluding, in March, 1611, he was triumphantly received at Rome by the Tuscan ambassador, Pope Paul V, and Cardinal Barberini (later to become Pope Urban VIII). To the latter two he not only showed his discoveries, but was delighted when they fully confirmed his observations. Up to this point he was receiving the sanctions of the Church itself!

In 1610 Galileo had published *Nuntius Siderius*, in which he gave the results of using his telescope to search the heavens: the planet Jupiter had satellites, Saturn had a ring, Venus passed through phases like the moon, the sun had spots. Galileo's triumphs were approaching their zenith. But at the time of his 1611 visit to Rome, opponents were already appearing who claimed that the Bible contradicted Galileo's theories. They even denied the existence of satellites of Jupiter that were readliy seen through Galileo's telescopes. Now Galileo, instead of keeping strictly to science, entered into the religious implications of his findings by protesting in an intemperate letter the interpretation of Scripture that one Father Cassini, a Dominican, used in attacking the Copernican doctrine as taught by Galileo. For the next several years Galileo, both in published works and personal teachings, argued his theories.

Copernicus, who, almost a hundred years
before Galileo, crystallized the findings
that the earth revolved around the sun.

"Galileo with a Young Scholar" by Cesare Cantagalli. In 1610 the Grand Duke of Tuscany
appointed him first philosopher and mathematician at the University of Pisa.
Institudo Statale d'Arte di Siena

On December 21, 1613, Galileo wrote an eloquent letter to his friend Father Castelli, professor of mathematics at Pisa, in which he stated:

It appears to me, therefore, that no effect of nature, which experience places before our eyes, or is the necessary conclusion derived from evidence, should be rendered doubtful by passages of Scripture which contains thousands of words admitting of various interpretations, for every sentence of Scripture is not bound by such rigid laws as is every effect of Nature. . . . Since two truths can obviously never contradict each other, it is the part of wise interpreters of Holy Scripture to take the pains to find out the real meaning of its statements in accordance with the conclusions regarding nature which are quite certain, either from the clear evidence of sense or from necessary demonstration.

Brilliant, haughty, filled with the power of success, and fortunate in his powerful patrons in both Church and State, here is Galileo expounding the independence of man's reason. Such a radical declaration of independence delighted his friends, enraged his enemies.

The controversy came to a head when Pope Paul V became thoroughly displeased with Galileo's brazen demands that the Church reinterpret the Scriptures in relation to the demonstrated laws of Nature. On February 19, 1616, the Congregation of the Inquisition received two propositions to censure: first, that the sun was the center of the world and consequently immovable locally; and second, that the earth was not the center of the world, nor immovable, but moved around itself by rotation. On February 23 they declared them both foolish and absurd, the first being heretical since it contradicted numerous texts of Holy Scripture, the second erroneous in point of faith. They ordered Galileo, through Cardinal

Bellarmine, on pain of imprisonment to abstain from teaching such a doctrine. Galileo promised to obey them, thinking that this whole matter was merely a question of discipline, not of doctrine.

In 1622 Pope Paul V died and was eventually followed by Galileo's friend Cardinal Barberini as Urban VIII. In April, 1624, he received Galileo cordially and pronounced that the Copernican theory had not been condemned by the Church as heretical but was considered "temerarious," or in other words a rash opinion. Galileo, encouraged by the temper of the times in his favor, decided to publish a new book, on which he had been working, which he hoped would influence the minds of both ecclesiastics and laymen toward Copernicanism. So in May, 1630, he went to Rome and sought permission of Pope Urban VIII to publish it. The pope turned the matter over to Father Visconti, who reported that some passages would have to be corrected to show that the question was being treated purely as a hypothesis.

Florence, where Galileo lived, was now hit by a plague, and correspondence between that city and Rome badly disrupted. However the Inquisitor of Florence received from Rome the power to approve officially of the *Dialogue* under certain conditions indicating that the work dealt only with the mathematical question connected with Copernicanism, that it would not assert Copernicanism to be a positive truth but merely a hypothesis, that there would be no alluding to the interpretation of the Scripture, and that it should be stated that by the decree of 1616 the authorities were aware of the reasons against it, and had enjoined Galileo from "teaching it."

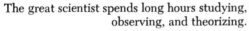

The great scientist spends long hours studying, observing, and theorizing.

Pope Paul V, who was so incensed at Galileo's demands that the Church accept the Copernican theory of the world, that in February, 1616, he ordered the Congregation of the Inquisition to censor Galileo's theories.
Bibliothèque Nationale, Paris

Title page drawn by Stefan Della Bella for Galileo's great work *Dialogue on the Two Greatest Systems in the World*, which was published in 1632 and immediately aroused a storm of protest from the Catholic world. The three figures depict Aristotle, Ptolemy, and Galileo in the guise of Copernicus.
The New York Public Library

Cardinal Roberto Bellarmine, who transmitted the Church's order to Galileo.
Bibliothèque Nationale, Paris

Besides the preface (probably written by Father Riccardi and amended by Galileo), *Dialogue* was divided into four parts, each being one day's discussions between three men. The three talkers were Salviati, a Florentine; Sagredo, a Venetian; and Simplicio, a simpleton who would express the true doctrine of the day as a foil for the others to tear it apart and project the true theories of Galileo. Many of the arguments of Simplicio were similar to those uttered by Pope Urban VIII, whether Galileo realized it or not, a fact that so incensed the pope against the book that he lost his best friend at court. The first day's conversations dealt with dimensions and motion of heavenly bodies, the moon's rough terrain as opposed to the contemporary polished-surface belief and the spots on the sun. The second day dealt with the revolution of the earth on it axis and how improbable it was that the whole celestial sphere should round the earth in twenty-four hours. The third day took up the matter of certain positions of known stars, followed by a refutation of the Aristotelean idea of the universe (a number of concentric hollow spheres with the earth in the center) and the basic arguments for the Copernican theory. The fourth day was devoted to the subject of tides, about which Galileo knew little and which was full of errors. The entire tenor of the *Dialogue* was to make the opponents of Galileo's theories look ridiculous in their arguments.

The printing of the *Dialogue on the Two Greatest Systems in the World* was completed in 1632, and Galileo sent some bound, gilt copies to Rome. It was dedicated to Ferdinand II, Grand Duke of Tuscany.

All over Europe the *Dialogue* was hailed as the most important book that had ever been printed. Owing to the plague in Florence, however, copies of the book were weeks late in reaching Rome, where the reaction was quite the opposite.

The followers of the Aristotelean school were incensed. The pope was highly displeased, saying that Galileo had entered upon ground he never should have touched. He was appalled that his ecclesiastics had been hoodwinked into giving the book an imprimatur. A special commission a month later reported that Galileo had disobeyed orders by affirming as an absolute truth the movement of the earth, instead of as a hypothesis, and by not even mentioning the order of 1616 to abandon the opinion that the earth revolved and that the sun was the center of the universe.

The Imprimatur of the Catholic Church on the work which was withdrawn by Pope Urban VIII. *The New York Public Library*

Pope Urban VIII, who was shocked and dismayed by the *Dialogue*, in which Galileo had put into the speeches of Simplicio (a simpleton) many of the arguments used by the pope in his friendly talks with Galileo on the Aristotelean versus the Copernican theory of the universe. *Fogg Art Museum, Harvard University*

Why was the Inquisition so upset and what was the justification for maintaining that Galileo's theory of the earth and all the satellites revolving around the sun contradicted the Scriptures? The answer to this question is inherent in a literal interpretation of both the Old and the New Testaments of the Holy Bible. Did not Moses say that God created the earth in five days and the rest of the universe in one? But Galileo claimed that the earth was but a speck in a vast and unexplained series of universes. How could God have possibly spent so much time on a speck and so little time creating these unending universes? Where was Heaven and where was Hell in such a vast complex? And how could God look down on His people on earth from His Heaven if the earth were traveling at the speed of one thousand miles a minute around the sun? Did not Moses say that God planted the sun, the moon, and the stars in the firmament and did he not say that the firmament was Heaven? And that "God came down from Heaven to see the tower which the children of men builded"? Was not Elijah carried upward in a whirlwind, and did not Jesus Christ ascend to Heaven? Further, how could the Deity keep track of the faithfulness and wickedness of his children with the earth in such an orbit?

If the scientific theories of Galileo were accepted, what would happen to the Church's interpretation of the Scriptures? Even the most faithful of true believers would begin to doubt their infallibility. Thus the Church of that day had no choice but to strike Galileo down and to silence him for the rest of his days. Arrogantly, although perhaps without deliberate intent, Galileo had forced his good friend Pope Urban VIII into a position from which Urban had no alternative—and this very reluctantly—to pushing the prosecution of Galileo, silencing him, and stopping the spread of his theories. Whatever Urban, the man, thought of the Copernican findings, as pope he could not condone any onslaught on the infallibility of the Holy Scriptures.

Another Church memorial drawn up at the time listed eight accusations against the philosopher:

1. Having, without leave, placed at the beginning of his work the permission for printing, delivered at Rome.
2. Having, in the body of the work, put the true doctrine in the mouth of a fool, and having approved it but feebly by the argument of another interlocutor.
3. Having quitted the region of hypothesis by affirming, in an absolute manner, the mobility of the Earth and the stability of the Sun, etc.

Galileo in prison in Rome during his trial before the Holy Court, which charged that he had defied the Church's orders of 1616 and was guilty of heresy in continuing to teach that the earth revolved around the sun.

4. Having treated the subject as one that was not already decided, and in the attitude of a person waiting for a definition, and supposing it to have not been yet promulgated.

5. Having despised the authors who were opposed to the above-mentioned opinion, though the Church uses them in preference to others.

6. Having affirmed (untruly) the equality supposed to exist, for understanding geometrical matters, between the divine and human intellect.

7. Having stated, as a truth, that the partisans of Ptolemy ought to range themselves with those of Copernicus, and denied the converse.

8. Having wrongly attributed the tides to the stability of the Sun and mobility of the Earth, which things do not exist.

An order was issued to the Inquisitor of Florence to ban the book in Italy and all foreign countries. It took effect in July, 1632, while the *Dialogue* was at the height of its popularity, and Galileo was drunk with success.

Galileo was forthwith summoned to Rome. He appealed to Cardinal Barberini and the Grand Duke of Tuscany that his advanced age (seventy years) and his ill health made it difficult to comply, but the pope countered with a threat, conveyed through the Inquisitor of Florence, to bring him to Rome, fettered as a prisoner, if he did not come at once. On January 20, 1633, Galileo set out on a slow trip to Rome, arriving on February 13. He was met by representatives of the Tuscan ambassador, Niccolini, and escorted to his palace, a gesture implying freedom and official welcome. However, after a short stay at the palace he was taken to the office of the Inquisition and put in prison. The charges against him were grave. "May God forgive him," said Pope Urban VIII, "for having involved himself in these questions. . . . There is one argument which nobody has been ever able to refute, which is that God is Almighty and may do as He sees fit. If He can do all, why question His works?" Galileo, by submitting Nature to laws, had questioned God's free will!

Because of his renowned position and his reputation throughout Europe as the world's leading man of science, he was given every consideration in jail, including the ambassador's servants to bring him special food and a valet who took care of him and slept in the next room.

"Galileo Devant Le Saint Office" by Robert-Fleury. Brushing aside his feeble defense, the court demands his abjuration.
Louvre, Paris

On April 12, 1633, Galileo appeared for the first time before the court. He admitted to the authorship of the *Dialogue*. He admitted that his opinion regarding the movement of the earth around a fixed sun had been formerly condemned in 1616 by the Congregation of the Index as contrary to the Holy Scriptures. But he maintained that Cardinal Bellarmine had told him it was possible to hold the Copernican doctrine as a hypothesis. He did not remember, after all these years, being told that he could not "teach it" in any manner. He did not mention these matters to the Master of the Vatican when asking for the imprimatur for the *Dialogue* because he felt, rather than upholding the theory of a mobile earth, he was proving that the ideas of Copernicus were *not* acceptable. He fooled no one, and only infuriated the Holy See all the more.

How much Galileo was tortured in order to wring a confession of heresy and make him repent no one knows. Like all prisoners questioned by the Inquisition, he was forced to take the vow of silence on threat of excommunication. And Galileo was a good Catholic as well as an able scientist.

At the second official inquiry on April 30, Galileo admitted to his judges: "I freely confess that on rereading my *Dialogue* it seems to me to have been so edited that to the reader unaware of my true intentions, the arguments for the Copernican systems which I meant to refute, are represented in such a way that they may have been *for* rather than *against*." He went on to say that vain ambition and pure ignorance had caused him to write in a way that could be misinterpreted. To what pitiful lengths Galileo resorted in order to escape from his predicament, for he believed strongly in his own theories and would never renounce them to himself, whatever he was forced to do in court! After this second session he was allowed to return to the ambassador's house.

On May 10, he was called to the Palace of the Holy See, where he was told he had eight days in which to prepare his defense. Having already prepared it, he immediately launched into it. He pleaded that he had done his best to avoid all fault in the book, which he had dutifully submitted to the Grand Inquisitor.

Galileo again before the Court of Inquisition
in an engraving after Cabasson.

Referring to the injunction of 1616, Galileo went on:

I say, then, that as at that time reports were spread abroad by evil-disposed persons, to the effect that I had been summoned by the Lord Cardinal Bellarmine to abjure certain of my opinions and doctrines, and that I had consented to abjure them, and also to submit to punishment for them, I was thus constrained to apply to His Eminence, and to solicit him to furnish me with a certificate explaining the cause for which I was summoned before him; which certificate I obtained, in his own handwriting, and it is the same that I now produce with the present document.

From this it clearly appears that it was merely announced to me that the doctrine attributed to Copernicus of the motions of the earth and the stability of the sun must not be held or defended and . . . beyond this general announcement affecting every one, any other injunction in particular was intimated to me, no trace thereof appears there.

But the court again refused to accept his reasonings. The *Dialogue* was turned over to the Index, and it was decided to question Galileo, under threat of torture, as to his basic meaning, devoid of such ambiguities.

On June 21 he was thus recalled before the Holy See and asked how long he had held the opinion that the sun, not the earth, was the center of the universe, Galileo replied: "For some time since. That is to say before the determination of the Sacred Congregation of the Index, I considered the two opinions, that of Ptolemy and that of Copernicus, were subject to discussion, because either of them might be correct according to Nature. But later . . . convinced by the wisdom of my superiors, my doubts ceased, and I have since held as I still do, that the opinion of Ptolemy is correct and cannot be doubted."

The court then read certain passages from the *Dialogue* which were irreconcilable with what he had just said. He protested that in the book he had stated the *pros* and *cons* of the case, but he himself did not agree with the condemned theory. "I do not hold, and have never held, the opinions of Copernicus since the order was given me to abandon them." Then in almost weary resignation: "In any case, I am here in your hands. Do as you think best."

After signing his forced confession Galileo was returned to prison. The next day, June 22, he was taken to the monastery of Santa Maria Sopra Minerva, where, before the cardinals and the prelates of the congregation he heard his sentence and read his abjuration.

First he was accused of openly violating the order given him not to maintain Copernicanism, of unfairly gaining permission to print his book without informing them of the prohibition of 1616, of still believing in the condemned opinion, although he left it undecided and perhaps probable—still a grave offense, since an opinion contrary to Scripture, of course, could not be probable.

A long sentence was then read, the essence of which was that the *Dialogue* was henceforth prohibited, he was to be condemned to the prison of the Holy Office for as long as the Holy Office decided, and he was to recite seven penitential psalms once a week for three years.

Then, on his knees, Galileo was forced to read his abjuration:

The Abjuration of Galileo

I, Galileo Galilei, son of the late Vincent Galileo, a Florentine, at the age of seventy, appearing personally in judgment, and being on my knees in the presence of you, most eminent and most reverend lords cardinal of the universal Christian commonwealth, inquisitors general against heretical depravity, having before my eyes the holy gospels, on which I now lay my hands, swear that I have always believed, and now believe, and God helping, that I shall for the future always believe whatever the holy catholic and apostolic Roman church holds, preaches, and teaches. But because this holy office had enjoined me by precept, entirely to relinquish the false dogma which maintains that the sun is the centre of the world, and immoveable, and that the earth is not the centre, and moves; not to hold, defend, or teach by any means, or by writing, the aforesaid false doctrine; and after it had been notified to me, that the aforesaid doctrine is repugnant to the holy scripture, I have written and printed a book, in which I treat of the same doctrine already condemned, and adduce reasons with great efficacy, in favor of it, not offering any solution of them; therefore I have been adjudged and vehemently suspected of heresy; namely, that I maintained and believed that the sun is the centre of the world, and immoveable, and that the earth is not the centre, and moves. Therefore, being willing to take out of the minds of your eminences, and of every catholic Christian, this vehement suspicion of right conceived against me, I, with sincere heart, and faith unfeigned, abjure, execrate, and detest, the above said errors and heresies, and generally every other error and sect contrary to the above said holy church; and I swear that I will never any more hereafter say or assert, by speech or writing, any thing through which the like suspicion may be had of me; but, if I shall know any one heretical, or suspected of heresy, I will denounce him to this holy office, or to the inquisitor and ordinary of the place in which I shall be. I moreover swear and promise that I will fulfil and observe entirely all the penitences which have been imposed upon me, or which shall be imposed by this holy office. But if it shall happen that I shall go contrary (which God avert) to any of my words, promises, protestations, and oaths, I subject myself to all the penalties and punishments which, by the holy canons, and other constitutions, general and particular, have been enacted and promulgated against such delinquents. So help me God, and his holy gospels, on which I now lay my hands.

I, the aforesaid Galileo Galilei, have abjured, sworn, promised, and have bound myself as above, and in the fidelity of those with my own hands, and have subscribed to this present writing of my abjuration, which I have recited word by word. At Rome, in the convent of Minerva, this 22d of June, of the year 1633.

I, Galileo Galilei, have abjured as above, with my own hand.

Ascanio Piccolomini, Archbishop of Siena, Galileo's good friend in whose house he stayed for five months after the trial.
Bibliothèque Nationale, Paris

Galileo's house in Florence, to which he was permitted to retire in 1638, after his health failed and he had lost his eyesight. Here he spent his final days, and here he died on January 8, 1642, at the age of seventy-eight.

Galileo's tomb in Santa Croce, Florence, designed by G. B. Foggini. Permission to build it was not given until March, 1737, nearly one hundred years after the scientist's death.

The Church's purpose in judging Galileo guilty was to check the spread of the Copernican doctrine among the faithful and to discredit the authority of the world's most famous scientist. The abjuration and notice of Galileo's punishment were sent on July 2, 1633, to all the vicars "so that it may come to the knowledge of all professors of philosophy and mathematics . . . that they may understand the gravity of the fault he has committed as well as the punishment they will have to undergo should they (likewise) fall into it."

*　　*　　*

Pope Urban VIII at once commuted Galileo's sentence to a secluded residence in the palace of the Tuscan ambassador. Shortly thereafter he was allowed to transfer to the palace of the Archbishop of Siena, Piccolomini, one of his dearest friends and admirers. However, when word reached Rome that Piccolomini was expressing opinions that Galileo had been unjustly condemned, they gave him permission to retire to his house at Arcetri near Florence, provided he would consider himself virtually under house arrest and receive no one but his family and relatives.

Age was now beginning to tell. Gradually he lost his sight and became almost totally blind. In 1638, after many pleas to Rome on the part of his friends and relatives, the Church was finally convinced that Galileo was now a very sick old man and had little time to live. They allowed him to return to Florence on condition that he would speak to no one regarding the movement of the earth. There, on January 8, 1642, one of the world's greatest scientists died at the age of seventy-eight, fortified by the last rites of the Church and "the benediction of Urban VIII."

*　　*　　*

Galileo's contributions to mankind were prodigious: his investigations into mechanics and physics, his discovery of the theory of the pendulum, the law of falling bodies, his invention of the thermometer and his advances in the uses of the telescope. Many leaders of the Church realized the value of the genius of Galileo. Pushed to the wall by his arrogant logic, the very foundations of their Holy Scriptures questioned, they still refrained from the final punishment which two hundred years previous they had meted out to Joan of Arc for a like foundation-shaking heresy.

If the trial of Galileo Galilei leaves one dismayed that even so great a mind can bend before the onslaught of his questioners and persecutors, it nevertheless stands as a landmark in the struggle of mankind to establish the right to challenge and reject timeworn dogmas that are accepted on faith, even when the challenger is labeled a heretic.

"Charles the First on Horseback" by Anthony Van Dyck.
National Gallery, London

6

Charles I of England

[1648]

WHEN CHARLES STUART WAS BORN IN 1600, THE CONCEPT of the divine rights of kings was not only firmly established but unquestioned in England. With the beheading of Charles I on January 30, 1649, the traditional monarchy in England died, never again to achieve the absolute state known to kings for centuries before that date. What had happened in those few short years to change the political destiny of a great world power so abruptly and throw it into a bitter civil war? Many things: temporal, religious, and social.

Under the rule of Charles's father, James I, England had been at peace for many years, a peace that brought prosperity and riches to the Protestant merchants and the landed gentry of England. English trade had flourished, and with it a new middle class had begun to emerge. Money breeds independence, so it was quite natural that in the only legislative body in which they could be represented, the knights and burgesses of the House of Commons began to assert themselves. While the real responsibility for the government was lawfully the king, he could and occasionally did call together his nobles and a delegation from the people to help him. But only on his own initiative. Otherwise the king, by virtue of tradition, considered himself responsible only to God. True, as a safeguard against such kingly prerogatives, Parliament had previously been granted by the Crown what is known as its privileges: the exclusive right to impose taxes of every kind and the right to petition the king for redress of grievances. These privileges the Parliament through successive reigns continually strove to extend. From the day of his ascension to the throne in 1625, King Charles, dedicated to the infallibility of the divine right of kings, waged a long and intense contest with his Parliament. It lasted a quarter of a century and ended with his losing his prerogatives and his head. In fact, at his coronation Charles put an important modification into his oath, swearing to respect the liberties of the people only insofar as they did not clash with the prerogative of the Crown, thus setting the stage for the disastrous years to follow. For the first four years Charles and Parliament sparred together without openly declaring war. Then suddenly Charles, deciding to rule the empire by himself, dissolved Parliament. For the next ten years he refused to convoke the legislature. Only when he became desperate for money did he finally call the Parliament. Little good did it do him. Instead of granting him funds, they argued interminably for further extension of the powers of Parliament and a lessening of the king's influence in government. This state of affairs lasted another ten years. Other events tended to alienate Charles from his people.

Shortly after the funeral of James I, Charles married Henrietta Maria, daughter of the King of France, a Catholic. This necessitated a special dispensation from the pope, which was obtained. To the people of England, anti-Roman, staunchly Protestant, this was an affront for which they never forgave him. Infuriated, they petitioned him to forbid any English Catholic to enter the queen's service, as being a great disservice to the Protestant cause in the realm; also, "that all Jesuit and Catholic priests, owing allegiance to the See of Rome, should be sent away from the country according to the laws already existing." To which the king evasively answered, "The laws on this subject shall be enforced." It soon became apparent, however, that Charles was something less than sincere. The reason for his apparent acquiescence was that he and the Duke of Buckingham (both his father's and now his own closest adviser) were very eager to get funds from the Commons to further their grandiose war plans. Buckingham, admiral of the fleet, was engaged in a bitter personal quarrel with Cardinal Richelieu, thus bringing England into war with France. Buckingham's naval ineptness resulted in the grand British Navy being disastrously cut down to one third its original size. Public indignation rose against Buckingham, and the king was blamed. The murder of Buckingham in 1628 came too late to restore the people's confidence in Charles.

Charles dissolved Parliament in March, 1629, and personally took over the government. He used his prodigious power of the court of Star Chamber, first to punish his enemies, then to fill up his treasury by imposing enormous fines on them. In this way he raised considerable sums to carry on his government without Parliament. At the same time he abused his legal power of taxing the maritime counties to raise funds to support his navy by levying the same taxes on the inland counties. Obviously the people subjected to this unlawful tax objected.

On the religious front, Charles made himself equally unpopular with the people. The ruling Church of England, presided over by the Archbishop of Canterbury, was in those days extremely wealthy, its bishops and clergy being supported by revenues derived from vast amounts of property. They were entirely independent of any control by their parishioners. They had their own laws, legislature, courts, judges, and capital. Over this vast realm within a realm Charles appointed a dedicated man named Laud as the Archbishop of Canterbury. Unfortunately, Laud applied himself far too vigorously to what he believed was his one great duty in life: supporting and confirming the authority of the king and the power and influence of the English episcopacy. In doing so, he clashed head on with the large and increasing English populace who hated the whole episcopal system. They were incensed at what they believed were Laud's

popish ceremonies of worship. They devotedly cherished Christianity in its pure, uncontaminated form, thus earning for themselves the designation of Puritans. Here, then, was another major element of contention between Charles and a large segment of his subjects. Not content with limiting this religious struggle to England, Laud attempted to extend the power of the Church of England to Scotland at the time when Charles went to Scotland to be crowned. Here he ran headlong into the stubborn resistance of the established Presbyterian Church. With typical Stuart arrogance, Charles took his army north to subdue the Scots by force. The army, however, was far more in sympathy with the Scots than with the king. Hence, upon the more practical advice of his council, he gave up his contest with Scotland. All that he had accomplished was to sow further seeds of discontent among the people of England, who themselves harbored strong fellow feelings with the Scots. And to add to the humiliation, Charles was again forced to call Parliament in November, 1640, in order to pay for sending the Scots home from their invasion of England.

This new Parliament was headed by John Pym, whose chief aim was to make the king dependent on Parliament. To this end he destroyed the king's only efficient advisers; first, the Earl of Strafford, whom Charles had appointed virtual king over the people of Ireland, then put in charge of the campaign against the Scots. Strafford became so

Thomas Wentworth, Earl of Strafford, who became so arrogant in his ruling of Ireland and his campaigns in Scotland on King Charles's behalf that the House of Commons finally managed to have him tried for treason.

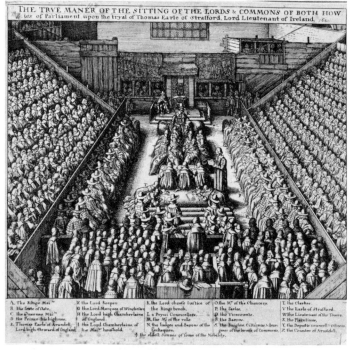

The trial of Thomas, Earl of Strafford.
The Free Library of Philadelphia,
Carson Collection

arrogant and so oblivious of the people's desires that Pym and the House of Commons finally succeeded in having him tried for treason and put to death. In this, by a series of intrigue and maneuvers, Charles was forced by Commons and his own House of Lords to agree. Laud soon followed on the chopping block. By now, their confidence greatly increased by these victories over Laud and Strafford, the members of Commons were demanding of Charles more and more concessions. To put an end to the king's authority to dissolve Parliament at will, they passed a bill providing that henceforth the Houses (both Lords and Commons) could not be prorogued (that is, discontinued) or dissolved without their own consent. The peers dared not reject it; the king, though violently opposed, was now aware of the dangers and intimidations besetting him, and was literally forced to sign the measure. Thus was established a major turning point in English political history. The Commons now became its own master.

As the year 1641 drew to a close, Charles decided he had made sufficient concessions to Commons. In January, 1642, he came to the House of Commons in person and demanded of that startled body that several of their leaders be given over to him to be tried for high treason. An indignant Commons refused. The long-coming civil war began in earnest when the king formally raised his standard at Nottingham in August, 1642. Sides were quickly aligned: the Episcopalians joined the king, along with the gentry and nobility; the mechanics, artisans, merchants, and common people backed the Parliament. Rural districts under the control of the wealthy landlords backed the king; the cities and towns sided with Parliament. England was divided as never before. The outcome, of course, is history. Charles lost at every turn.

By the spring of 1646 the king was utterly defeated in war. In an evasive action he surrendered to the Scottish army. In return for their protection and backing, the Scots demanded that he become a Presbyterian, but Charles would have no part of it. On January 30, 1647, they turned him over to the English Parliament.

Meanwhile a third force, and ultimately the ruling force, entered the picture: the army, headed by Lord General Fairfax, a leading member of the House of Commons, had refused to disband at the orders of Parliament after the end of hostilities, knowing full well that such a course would mean the end of its power. But the real power behind the army command at this time was Oliver Cromwell, a genius at combining long-range plans with daring and immediate actions to achieve his ultimate goal: he was determined to send Charles to the block and so put an end to the monarchy in England. But he was equally determined to do it legally. Cromwell remaining in the background, the House of Commons would decree the death penalty for Charles I of England.

* * *

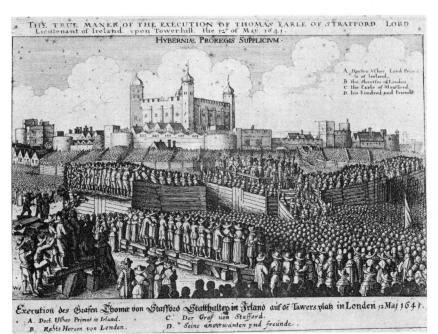

The execution of the Earl of Strafford.
*The Free Library of Philadelphia,
Carson Collection*

William Laud, Archbishop of Canterbury, who ruled the Church of England in such a way as to further the power of the monarchy and the Episcopal Church of England, thereby incurring the wrath of the Puritans and Presbyterians. He was tried, and followed Strafford on the block.

King Charles the First strides into the House
of Commons and demands that five leading
members be given over to his authority.
Commons haughtily refuses.
The Free Library of Philadelphia,
Carson Collection

Charles the First raises his standard at Nottingham on
August 25, 1642, thus opening the long-awaited Civil War.
An engraving from a fresco by C. W. Cope in the
Peers Corridor of the Houses of Parliament.
The Free Library of Philadelphia,
Carson Collection

Thomas, Lord Fairfax, the leader of the victorious army of the Roundheads and a leading member of the House of Commons.

"Oliver Cromwell" by Robert Walker.
National Portrait Gallery, London

At the time it received Charles as prisoner, Parliament was radically divided into two factions: a moderate group of Presbyterians and a group known as the Independents, whose leader was Oliver Cromwell. Thus this latter group was closely linked to the army, who had won the war for Parliament against the king. At this point the king saw in this serious legislative division a ray of hope. In May, 1648, a second civil war broke out with Royalist risings in South Wales, in Kent, Essex, and the North, followed by another invasion from Scotland. The army under Fairfax and Cromwell had no trouble defeating them. But while they were away in the field, the Presbyterians gained control of the House of Commons and reopened negotiations with the king, an action codified as the Treaty of Newport. It was, however, a vain gesture, for as soon as the war was over, the army at once repudiated the treaty. Meeting on November 16, 1648, the army council resolved to bring the king to justice for making war on the people.

To do this with at least some semblance of legality it was necessary to have a House of Commons composed entirely of those who backed the army. Accordingly, on December 6 and 7 a Colonel Pride and his men were stationed at the approaches to Westminster and refused to admit to Parliament any of those who had supported the proposed treaty with the king. A rump House of Commons, reduced to about 70 members (143 having been ejected), clearly (if not legally) opened the way to setting up a court to try Charles. The army, whose march on London was never effectively opposed, was now in complete charge both in Parliament and outside. Cromwell, who would never have endorsed such a militant seizure of Commons, was away at the time and did not return until the 8th of December. Faced with a fait accompli, he accepted it and said he was glad of it.

* * *

Meanwhile the king was a prisoner in Hurst Castle, well aware that he had not long to live. At midnight on the 17th of December he was awakened by the sound of troops in the castle yard. Although fearing assassination at any moment, he was not molested. Two days later, under heavy escort, he began his journey to Windsor Castle.

On the day that he reached his old castle, the 23rd of December, the House of Commons voted that he should be brought to trial, and appointed a committee to draw up the impeachment. An ordinance was adopted by which a high court was appointed to try him. It was to be composed of 150 commissioners, including peers, chief justices, baronets, knights, aldermen, and many other important personages. But when, on the 2nd of January, the ordinance was presented to the House of Lords, the latter would have none of it. "There is no Parliament without the King," declared Lord Manchester, "therefore the King cannot commit treason against Parliament." The Commons then instituted, by passing another ordinance, the High Court of Justice. They persuaded John Bradshaw, a fairly successful lawyer, but a somewhat ambitious fanatic, to take the chair of lord-presi-

Oliver Cromwell, the real power behind the army, who demanded that King Charles be executed.

John Bradshaw, president of the High Court of Justice that was set up to try King Charles.

dency of the court. On January 10 he accepted. The following few days were spent in organizing the court and setting up court procedures and functions, during which it was decided to move the king from Windsor Castle to St. James's Palace in London. On Friday, the 19th of January, a body of cavalry, again headed by Major Harrison, escorted the King to St. James's Palace, which was completely surrounded by guards. Even his bedroom had two guards outside. The only attendant he was now allowed to have was Sir Thomas Herbert, who slept by his bedside and was to stay with him to the end.

* * *

On the morning of January 20th the high court met privately in the Painted Chamber and settled the final details of the proceedings. Shortly after noon it was announced that the king was arriving, carried on a sedan chair, and was at that moment passing between the two files of soldiers. Cromwell ran to the window and returned pale and excited: "My masters, he is come! he is come! . . . I desire you to let us resolve here what answer we shall give the King when he comes before us; for the first question he will ask us will be, by what authority and commission do we try him." After a pause, Henry Martyn said, "In the name of the Commons and Parliament assembled, and all the good people of England." No objection was raised, and the court proceeded to Westminster Hall in solemn procession, led by Lord-President Bradshaw. The president took his place in a chair of crimson velvet. He had taken the precaution of lining his hat with iron, fearful of an attack by the Royalists who might have infiltrated the spectators' gallery. To his right and left were members of the court. Cromwell and Martyn seated themselves modestly out of the way in the rows behind the lord-president. Then the spectators were let into the galleries. When all noise and talk had subsided, the act of the House of Commons setting up and giving authority to the high court was read, along with the names of those appointed to serve. Of the 135 appointed, only sixty-nine were present. Notably absent was Lord Fairfax. When his name was called, a veiled woman (believed later to have been Lady Fairfax) called out from the gallery, "He has more wit than to be here." The roll call having been dispensed with, Bradshaw ordered, "Mr. Sergeant, bring in your prisoner."

* * *

The king appeared under the guard of Colonel Hacker and thirty-two officers. He was conducted to a chair of crimson velvet that faced the court and was directly opposite the chair of Lord-President Bradshaw. He looked hard and sternly around at the tribunal; then, without removing his high hat, sat down. But immediately he stood up again and surveyed first the spectators,

then the court, with an air of superiority that infuriated his enemies. He sat down again amid universal silence.

Bradshaw rose immediately and addressed the king:

Charles Stuart, King of England: The Commons of England being deeply sensible of the calamities that have been brought upon this nation, which are fixed upon you as the principal author of them, have resolved to make inquisition for blood; and, according to that debt and duty they owe to justice, to God, the kingdom, and themselves, they have resolved to bring you to trial and judgment, and for that purpose, have constituted this High Court of Justice, before which you are brought.

He then ordered Cooke, the solicitor general, to read the charges.

As Cooke rose, the king tapped him on the shoulder with his cane, saying "Hold! Silence!"—at which point the gold head of the cane dropped off. Having no servant to pick it up, the king retrieved it himself. When he sat back in his chair, his changed expression indicated perhaps that he had just realized the precarious status of his position. Cooke then read the indictment, which was as follows:

"THAT HE the said CHARLES STUART, being admitted King of England, and therein trusted with a limited power to govern by, and according to the Laws of the Land, and not otherwise; and by his trust, oath and office, being obliged to use the power committed to him, for the good and benefit of the People, and for the preservation of their rights and liberties; yet nevertheless, out of a wicked design to erect and uphold in himself an unlimited and tyrannical power to rule according to his will, and to overthrow the rights and liberties of the People, yea to take away and make void the foundations thereof, and of all redress and remedy of misgovernment, which by the fundamental constitutions of this kingdom, were reserved on the People's behalf, in the right and power of frequent and successive parliaments or national meetings in Councel, He the said CHARLES STUART, for accomplishment of such his designs, and for the protecting of himself and his adherents, in his and their wicked practices, to the same ends, hath traiterously and maliciously levied war against the present Parliament, and the People therein represented; particularly, upon or about the thirtieth day of June, in the year of our Lord 1642, at Beverley, in the county of York; and upon or about the thirtieth day of July, in the year aforesaid, in the county of the city of York; and upon or about the four and twentieth day of August in the same year, in the county of the Town of Nottingham, where, and when he set up his standard of war; and also on or about the twenty third day of October in the same year, at Edge-Hill and Keynton Field, in the county of Warwick; and upon or about the thirtieth day of November in the same year, at Brainford, in the county of Middlesex; and upon or about the thirtieth day of August, in the year of our Lord 1643, at Caversham-Bridge, near Reading, in the county of Berks; and upon or about the thirtieth day of October, in the year last mentioned, at or near the city of Gloucester; and upon or about the thirtieth day of November, in the year last mentioned, at Newbury, in the county of Berks; and upon or about the thirty first day of July, in the year of our Lord 1644, at Cropredy-

Bridge, in the county of Oxon; and upon or about the thirtieth day of September, in the last year mentioned, at Bodwyn and other Places near adjacent, in the county of Cornwall; and upon or about the thirtieth day of November, in the year last mentioned, at Newbury aforesaid; and upon or about the eighth day of June, in the year of our Lord 1645, at the Town of Leicester; and also upon the fourteenth day of the same month in the same year, at Nazeby-Field, in the county of Northampton. At which several times and places, or most of them, and at many other places in this Land, at several other times within the years afore-mentioned, and in the year of our Lord 1646, He the said CHARLES STUART hath caused and procured many thousands of the free people of this nation to be slain, and by divisions, parties, and insurrections within this Land, by invasions from foreign parts, endeavoured and procured by him, and by many other evil ways and means, He the said CHARLES STUART hath not only maintained and carried on the said war both by land and sea, during the year before mentioned, but also hath renewed or caused to be renewed the said war against the Parliament and good People of this nation, in this present year 1648, in the counties of Kent, Essex, Surrey, Sussex, Middlesex, and many other counties and places in England and Wales, and also by sea. And particularly He the said CHARLES STUART hath for that purpose given commission to his son the Prince, and others, whereby, besides multitudes of other persons, many such as were by the Parliament intrusted and employed for the safety of the nation (being by him or his agents corrupted to the betraying of their trust, and revolting from the Parliament) have had entertainment and commission for the continuing and renewing of war and hostility against the said Parliament and People, as aforesaid; by which cruel and unnatural wars by him the said CHARLES STUART levied, continued and renewed as aforesaid, much innocent blood of the free People of this nation hath been spilt, many families have been undone, the publick treasury wasted and exhausted, trade obstructed, and miserably decayed, vast expence and dammage

to the nation incurred, and many parts of this land spoiled, some of them even to desolation. And for further prosecution of his said evil designs, He the said CHARLES STUART doth still continue his commissions to the said Prince, and other rebels and revolters both English and foreigners, and to the E. of Ormond, and to the Irish rebels and revolters associated with him; from whom further invasions upon this land are threatened, upon the procurement and on the behalf of the said CHARLES STUART.

"All which wicked designs, wars and evil practices of him the said CHARLES STUART, have been, and are carried on for the advancement and upholding of a personal interest of will and power, and pretended prerogative to himself and his family, against the publick interest, common right, liberty, justice and peace of the People of this nation, by and for whom he was intrusted as aforesaid.

"By all which it appeareth, that He the said CHARLES STUART hath been, and is the occasioner, author, and continuer of the said unnatural, cruel and bloody wars, and therein guilty of all the treasons, murders, rapines, burnings, spoils, desolations, dammages and mischiefs to this nation acted and committed in the said wars, or occasioned thereby.

"And the said John Cooke, by protestation saving on the behalf of the said People of England, the liberty of exhibiting at any time hereafter any other charge against the said CHARLES STUART, and also of replying to the answers which the said CHARLES STUART shall make to the premises, or any of them, or any other charge that shall be so exhibited, doth for the said treasons and crimes, on the behalf of the said People of England, impeach the said CHARLES STUART, as a tyrant, traytor, murderer, and a publick and implacable enemy to the Commonwealth of England, and pray that the said CHARLES STUART, King of England, may be put to answer all and every the premises, and that such proceedings, examinations, tryals, sentences, and judgments may be thereupon had, as shall be agreable to justice.

"*Subscribed,* JOHN COOKE."

The Trial of Charles I. *Library of Congress*

King Charles at his trial before what he termed an "illegal Court." To the end he refused to recognize its authority to try him. An engraving after E. Bower.

The trial of Charles the First
in Westminster Hall.
From an old print.

"The Tryal of the King."
The Free Library of Philadelphia,
Carson Collection

During the reading of the indictment the king, as if uninterested, looked sternly around at the galleries, then at the court. He rose and looked around again, then sat down. At the words "Charles Stuart as a tyrant, traytor, murderer, and a publick and implacable enemy to the Commonwealth of England," he smiled, or even, as some chroniclers have it, laughed in the court's face.

BRADSHAW. Sir, you have now heard your charge. The Court expects your answer.

THE KING. I would know by what power I am called hither; I was, not long ago, in the Isle of Wight, and and there I entered into a treaty with both Houses of Parliament, with as much public faith as it is possible to be had of any people in the world; and we were upon the conclusion of the treaty. Now I would know by what authority, I mean lawful—there are many unlawful authorities in the world, thieves and robbers by the highway—but I would know by what authority I was brought from thence, and carried from place to place, and I know not what; and when I know what lawful authority, I shall answer.

Remember I am your King, your lawful King, and what sins you bring upon your heads and the judgment of God upon this land, think well upon it. I say, think well upon it before you go farther from one sin to a greater. Therefore let me know by what lawful authority I am seated here and I shall not be unwilling to answer. In the meantime I shall not betray my trust: I have a trust committed to me by God, by old and lawful descent. I will not betray it to answer to a new and unlawful authority; therefore resolve me that, and you shall hear more of me."

BRADSHAW. If you had been pleased to observe what was hinted to you by the Court at your first coming hither, you would have known by what authority; which authority requires you, in the name of the people of England, of which you are elected king, to answer.

THE KING. No, sir, I deny that.

BRADSHAW. If you acknowledge not the authority of the Court, they must proceed.

THE KING. I do tell them so; England was never an elective kingdom, but an hereditary kingdom, for near these thousand years: therefore let me know by what authority I am called hither. Here is a gentleman, Lieutenant-Colonel Cobbett, ask him if he did not bring me from the Isle of Wight by force. I will stand as much for the privilege of the House of Commons, rightly understood, as any man whatsoever. I see no House of Lords here, that may constitute a Parliament, and the King, too, should have been in it. Is this the bringing of a King to his Parliament?

BRADSHAW. The Court expects you should give them a final answer. If you do not satisfy yourself, though we tell you our authority, we are satisfied with our authority, and it is upon God's authority and the kingdom's.

THE KING. It is not my apprehension, nor your's either, that ought to decide it.

BRADSHAW. The Court hath heard you, and you are to be disposed of as they have commanded.

At this point Bradshaw saw that he was getting into serious trouble. If the king persisted in his refusal to recognize the court, and refused to answer to the charge, the trial was stymied. Until the prisoner pleaded one way or the other, the prosecution could not commence. Seeing he was geting nowhere with the king, Bradshaw adjourned the court until Monday, January 22nd. Amid conflicting shouts of "Justice! Justice!" and "God Save the King! God Save Your Majesty!" Charles was escorted back to St. James's Palace, where he was to ponder on the train of events over the weekend.

* * *

On Monday when the court resumed, sixty-two members were present. In spite of a strict order for silence, the king was greeted with loud acclamations from the galleries. As Bradshaw again tried to get Charles to plead on the indictment and recognize the authority of the court, the king remained obstinate:

BRADSHAW. Sir, you may remember at the last Court you were told the occasion of your being brought hither and you heard a Charge read against you, containing a Charge of High Treason, and other High Crimes against the Realm of England, and instead of answering, you interrogated the Court's authority and jurisdiction. Sir, the Authority is the Commons of England in Parliament assembled, who required your answer to the Charge, either by confessing or denying.

THE KING. When I was here last, it is very true I made that question. And truly if it were only in my particular case I would have satisfied myself with the protestation I made the last time I was here, against the legality of this Court, and that a King cannot be tried by any superior jurisdiction on Earth. But it is not my case alone, it is the freedom and liberty of England, and do you pretend what you will, I stand more for their liberties, for if power without Law may make laws, may alter the fundamental laws of the Kingdom, I do not know what subject he is in England can be sure of his life or anything he calls his own. . . .

BRADSHAW. Sir, you have offered something to the Court; I shall speak something to you, the sense of the Court. Sir, neither you nor any man are permitted to dispute that point: you are concluded [overruled]; you may not demur to the jurisdiction of the Court. They sit here by the authority of the Commons of England, and all your predecessors and you are responsible to them.

THE KING. I deny that, show me one precedent.

BRADSHAW. Sir, we sit not here to answer your questions. Plead to your charge—guilty, or not guilty?

THE KING.   You never heard my reasons yet.

BRADSHAW.   Sir, your reasons are not to be heard against the highest jurisdiction.

THE KING.   Show me that jurisdiction where reason is not to be heard.

BRADSHAW.   Sir, we show it you here—the Commons of of England. Sergeant, take away the prisoner.

THE KING.   Remember that the King of England suffers, being not permitted to give his reasons, for the liberty of the people. God save the King!

On this day the commissioners from Scotland had delivered some papers to the House of Commons expressing a distinct dislike for the current proceedings against the king and declaring their deep interest in his well-being and in peaceful settlements of all disputes. The Commons never looked at them. They had more important business at hand.

*   *   *

On Tuesday, January 23, 1649, the same wrangling went on. Finally Solicitor General Cooke stated that, according to law, if the prisoner refuses to plead "Guilty" or "Not Guilty," and thus opens the way to be fairly tried, it is an implicit confession (*pro confesso*) of guilt, and that he may be speedily judged. Bradshaw called this to the attention of the king, who ignored it and insisted he be allowed to speak on the subject of the liberties of the people of England. Bradshaw at last lost his temper: "Sir, this is the third time that you have publicly disowned this Court, and put an affront upon it. . . . Gentlemen, you that took charge of the prisoner, take him back again."

As the guards led him to Sir Robert Cottor's house, where he was then imprisoned, the crowds outside, now more than ever in sympathy with the king, lustily shouted, "God save the King!"

On Wednesday and Thursday, January 24th and 25th, the court examined witnesses in the Painted Chamber, in spite of the fact that the trial could not go into that stage until the king had pleaded. Charles, of course, was not in court. Late in the day of the 25th, the court, sitting in private, passed the resolutions that the court would proceed to a sentence of condemnation against the king and that the condemnation would be for being tyrant, traitor, and murderer, and for being a public enemy to the commonwealth of England.

On Friday, January 26, the court again sat in private, and resolved: "That the Court do agree to the Sentence now read" and "That the said Sentence shall be engrossed. That the King be brought to Westminster tomorrow to receive his Sentence."

*   *   *

The die was cast, and all that remained was to pass sentence. The court had held a two-hour session in the Painted Chamber, and now, at noon on the 27th, the roll was called in full court. Sixty-seven members were pres-

ent. Amid cries of "Execution," "Justice" from the soldiers present and a terrified silence from the civilian spectators, the king entered. Before sitting down, he turned to Bradshaw and said: "Sir, I desire a word to be heard a little, and I hope I shall give no occasion of interruption."

BRADSHAW.   You may answer in your turn; hear the Court first.

THE KING.   If it please you, sir, I desire to be heard. It is only in a word. A sudden judgment—

BRADSHAW.   Sir, you shall be heard in due time; but you are to hear the Court first.

THE KING.   Sir, I desire—it will be in order to what I believe the Court will say. A hasty judgment is not so soon recalled.

BRADSHAW.   Sir, you shall be heard before the judgment is passed. In the meantime you may forbear. . . . Gentlemen, it is well known to you all that the prisoner at the bar hath been several times convened and brought before this Court to make answer to a charge of treason and other high crimes, exhibited against him, in the name of the people of England.

"It's a lie! not one-half of them!" exclaimed the same voice that had answered to the name of Fairfax. "Where are they or their consent? Oliver Cromwell is a traitor!"

When the resultant clamor had died down, the king said: "I desire that I may be heard by the Lords and Commons in the Painted Chamber; for it is not my person that I look on alone—it is the kingdom's welfare and the kingdom's peace."

This was Charles's last brave attempt to get a fair and legal trial. It moved not only the spectators but also many members of the court itself. Colonel Downs rose to his feet and exclaimed: "Have we hearts of stone? Are we men?" He was quickly silenced by Cromwell, but he persisted, and addressed the president: "My Lord, I am not satisfied to give my consent to this sentence. I desire the Court to adjourn and to hear me, and deliberate." It being parliamentary procedure, the court had no choice. They all went into the adjoining room. It was but a temporary interlude. The doubts of Downs were no match for the determination of Cromwell. The court returned, and Bradshaw told the king his request had been denied. He then launched into his long speech summarizing the faults of which the king had been guilty, at the end of which he instructed the clerk to read the sentence:

CLERK.   Whereas the Commons of England in Parliament had appointed them a High Court of Justice for the trial of Charles Stuart, King of England, before whom he had been three times convened; and at the first time a charge of high-treason and other crimes and misdemeanors was read in behalf of the Kingdom of England, etc. [Here the charge was repeated and the king required to give an answer, which he refused to do.] For all which treasons and crimes, this

Court doth adjudge, that he, the said Charles Stuart, as a tyrant, traitor, murderer and public enemy to the good people of this nation, shall be put to death by severing of his head from his body.

BRADSHAW. The sentence now read and published is the act, sentence, judgment, and resolution of the whole Court.

THE KING. Sir, will you hear me a word?

BRADSHAW. Sir, you are not to be heard after sentence.

THE KING. No, sir?

BRADSHAW. No, sir; by your favour, sir. Guards, withdraw your prisoner!

THE KING. I may speak after sentence; by your favour, sir, I may speak after my sentence, ever. By your favour—

BRADSHAW. Hold!

THE KING. The sentence, sir—I say, sir, I do—I am not suffered to speak. Expect what justice other people will have!

Charles now spent the rest of that day and the following one by preparing for death. His request for the comfort and prayers of Dr. Juxon, Bishop of London, had been granted, and except to bid farewell to those two of his children who were still in England, he refused to see any others. He was still attended, however, by Sir Herbert.

Early on the morning of the 30th, Charles rose and began his toilet. The agitated Herbert could scarcely comb his hair. In jest Charles admonished him: "I pray you, though my head be not long to stand on my shoulders, take the same pains with it as you were wont to do." Shortly after daybreak Bishop Juxon arrived and began prayers. At about ten o'clock there was a knock on the door. It was Colonel Hacker come to summon the king to Whitehall, where the scaffold had been erected the day before. After a short while Charles turned to the bishop and took his hand. "Come," he said, "let us go."

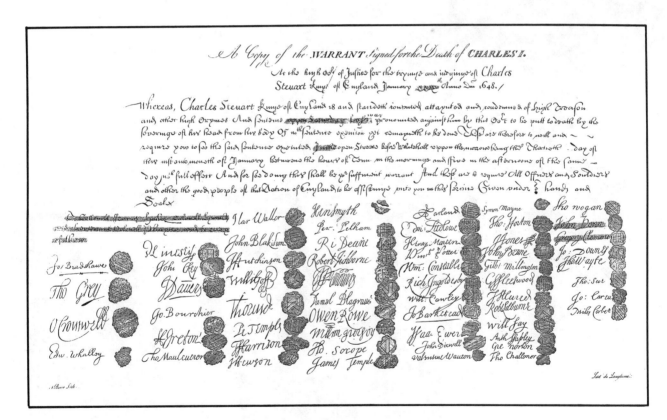

The Death Warrant:
Whereas, Charles Steuart King of England is and standeth convicted attainted and condemned of high treason and other high crimes And sentence upon Saturday last was pronounced against him by this Court, to be putt to death by the severing of his head from his body Of which sentence execution yet remaineth to be done These are therefore to will and require you to see the said sentence executed in the open street before Whitehall upon the morrow being the thirtieth day of this instant month of January between the hours of ten in the morning and five in the afternoon of the same day with full effect And for so doing this shall be your sufficient warrant And these are to require all officers and soldiers and others the good people of this Nation of England to be assisting unto you in this service Given under our hands and seals.

Charles the First saying goodbye
to his children prior
to his execution.

Charles the First on the scaffold bids goodbye to the Bishop of London while the
masked executioners wait on the side.

D. Juxon,
Bishop of London,
who administered to King Charles I
until the end.

They passed through the garden and into the park, where a double file of soldiers were drawn up. Amid the din of the drums, the king and his few close followers proceeded to the building and went up to the bedchamber. Here he spent his last few hours eating a bit of bread and taking a few sips of claret. Soon afterward, Colonel Hacker came for what was to be the last time. By now Charles was ready, and they walked through a passageway, broken through the wall for the occasion, onto the scaffold.

The scaffold was draped all in black, the ax and the block being located in the middle of it. Companies of soldiers surrounded it on all sides. In back of them, thousands of spectators were packed. The king delivered his last speech, but so great was the clamor that no one except Bishop Juxon and those few others near him heard it. While he was talking, someone touched the ax. In alarm Charles said: "Take heed of the ax! Pray, take heed of the ax!"

As Charles finished and parted his hair, the bishop said to him: "There is but one stage more. The stage is turbulent and troublesome; it is a short one; but you may consider it will soon carry you a very great way; it will carry you from earth to heaven."

The king replied: "I go from a corruptible to an incorruptible crown, where no disturbance can be." Then turning to the executioners he said: "When I put out my hands this way, then—."

After a few minutes in meditation Charles kneeled and placed his head on the block. "Stay for the sign," he told the executioner. After an instant, the king stretched out his hands, and the ax fell, severing his head with a single blow. A long, deep groan rose from the crowd.

The body was then placed in a cheap coffin. As a last gesture Cromwell went to the coffin, took the severed head in his hands, and raised it up. The coffin remained at Whitehall for seven days, and then, after much wrangling with Parliament by the king's friends and the lords, was finally buried in St. George's Hall in Windsor Castle.

* * *

"The Execution of Charles I" by Weesop.
Scottish National Portrait Gallery, Edinburgh

Oliver Cromwell, having achieved his goal of overthrowing the English monarchy,
gazes at the body of Charles I in its cheap coffin.

On October 13, 1660, Major General Harrison was hanged, drawn, and quartered, the first of the regicides to die in revenge of the murder of Charles I of England. During the first of those eleven short years, the Revolutionary Parliament ruled England, with Oliver Cromwell away fighting wars against the Catholics in Ireland, against the invaders from Scotland and the Royalist uprisings led by the son and heir presumptive of Charles I. Cromwell decisively won all three. Having finally annihilated the Royalist Army, Cromwell returned to his seat in the House of Commons. While away, he had become increasingly incensed at the way Commons had been ruling the country. Thus on April 20, 1653, as the day's session opened, he called in a handful of his soldiers and drove out the members and their Speaker. For the next five and a half years, until his death, he alone ruled

England. In those years England surpassed in power every nation in Europe, including her rival, Protestant Holland. But Cromwell died of ague fever on September 3, 1658. He was succeeded by his son Richard, a nondescript, who could not begin to keep in hand the army and the various parliamentary groups. He quickly abdicated. The resulting scramble for power simply threw the governing forces of England into turmoil. In the battle between two of Cromwell's loyal followers, General George Monk, Cromwell's military governor of Scotland, and the ambitious John Lambert, a lieutenant in the army, Monk roundly defeated his opponent. He then marched on and occupied London. With the assent of the city magistrates, he decided to recall the king, the self-proclaimed Charles II. Thus on May 29, 1660, on the occasion of his thirtieth birthday, Charles II returned to

London and the throne of England amid joyous acclaim. Monarchy had once again been restored to England.

While Charles II had no mind to be vindictive and, with a few exceptions, was willing to pardon the Regicides, the first Parliament of the new reign was overwhelmingly Royalist, and out for blood. Forty-one of the fifty-nine who had signed the death warrant were still alive. Of these, fifteen fled the country; four of them were subsequently tracked down and returned or gave themselves up. Many of the remaining were seized.

Their trials were as unfair as had been the trial of Charles I. Nine were condemned to the hideous death of being hanged until they were almost dead, then, while still conscious, disemboweled and quartered. As quickly as they had been dispatched, the Regicides, and, indeed, the trial and execution of Charles I itself, were soon forgotten. England returned to the monarchy that had for hundreds of years been her heritage. But with one difference: The king was no longer absolute. Royal absolutism had been severed from that heritage the instant Charles I's head had been severed from his body on that fateful day of January 30, 1649.

Drawings of the fates that befell the Regicides upon the restoration of the monarchy when Charles the Second came to England to assume the crown.

"The Trial of George Jacobs" by T. H. Matteson. The "afflicted girls" go into their tantrums when the prisoner they have named as a witch is brought into court. Jacobs was one of the nineteen people condemned and hanged in Salem in 1692.

Essex Institute Collection

7

Salem Witchcraft

[1692]

THE YEAR 1692 WAS PERHAPS THE MOST GLOOMY AND despondent period in the entire history of New England. Not so many years before, a group of courageous but somewhat bigoted colonists had migrated from Europe to Massachusetts, fleeing from almost inconceivable persecution and suffering in their own country. They settled in the midst of dark and unexplored forests. It is no wonder that their dour dispositions, in no way lightened by the hardships of their crossing and their incredible superstitions, were inevitably transmitted to their children. Indeed, owing to peculiar circumstances in the year 1692, this bleak philosophy of life was aggravated all the more, and none were more afflicted with it than the Puritans of Salem Township.

At this time it was common belief that the American Indians were the subjects and worshipers of the Devil. The very name Indian conjured up feelings of hostility and horror, and not without foundation. In 1689, John Bishop and Nicholas Reed, a servant of Edward Putnam, and in 1690 Godfrey Sheldon were killed by Indians. Consequently, in the latter part of 1691, about six months prior to the beginning of the witchcraft delusion, twenty-four scouts were constantly on duty in Essex County to guard against approaching Indians, the servants of the Devil.

On the political front these colonists had lost their charter and had thus been deprived of constitutional rights. Their future political destiny was left in doubt. Not only this, but, oppressed by excessive taxes, they were heavily in debt. Salem, alone, in 1691 was taxed £1,346.1.0, in addition to regular town taxes and the large amounts needed to support the ministry. Thus the people were poor; they enjoyed no luxuries. Pirates constantly raided their coasts, and a recent expedition against Canada had brought upon them the vengeance of France.

It was no wonder, then, that these simple and rustic people believed that the Devil himself had descended upon them with unabated fury.

* * *

During the seventeenth century, belief in witchcraft was neither new nor was it questioned. Trials and executions for witchcraft were carried out in all civilized countries. The English Church even granted licenses to certain ministers to cast out devils.

The leading Puritan minister of the day, and one who would play an important role in the Salem witchcraft trials and their aftermath, was Dr. Cotton Mather. The following excerpt from one of his sermons will make clear the prevailing belief in and fear of the Devil and his disciples. Like most Puritan sermons of that era, it was designed to scare the living daylights out of his parishioners and instill the fear of the Devil in them:

No place . . . that I know of, has got such a spell upon it as will always keep the Devil out. The meeting-house, wherein we assemble for the worship of God, is filled with many holy people and many holy concerns continually; but, if our eyes were so refined as the servant of the prophet had his of old, I suppose we should now see a throng of devils in this very place. The apostle has intimated that angels come in among us: there are angels, it seems, that hark how I preach, and how you hear, at this hour. And our own sad experience is enough to intimate that the devils are likewise rendezvousing here. It is reported in Job i. 5, "When the sons of God came to present themselves before the Lord, Satan came also among them." When we are in our church assemblies, oh, how many devils, do you imagine, crowd in among us! There is a devil that rocks one to sleep. There is a devil that makes another to be thinking of, he scarcely knows what himself. And there is a devil that makes another to be pleasing himself with wanton and wicked speculations. It is also possible, that we have our closets or our studies gloriously perfumed with devotions every day; but, alas! can we shut the Devil out of them? No: let us go where we will, we shall still find a devil nigh unto us. Only when we come to heaven, we shall be out of his reach for ever.

These Puritans believed devoutly in God, whom they feared and worshiped. They also believed just as strongly in the Devil, whom they hated and defied. In their minds a final, gigantic war was being waged by the Devil against God for the domination of the world and the ruin of all men's souls. This was not a technical creed, but a deep-seated conviction, and they willingly joined in the mammoth conflict on the side of God. "The humble hamlet of Salem Village was felt to be the great and final battleground."

* * *

The almost incredible happenings at Salem in 1692 originated with a West Indian servant of Sam Parris by the name of Tituba. She and her husband, John Indian, had brought with them many of the superstitions of the native tribes of these islands. During the winters of 1691 and 1692 a group of young girls, having little else to do and being typical frustrated teenagers, met at the Parris house for the purpose of learning and practicing Tituba's occult arts: palmistry, fortune-telling, necromancy, magic, and spiritualism. It began, innocently enough, as a game to pass the time. But the members of their group soon became so proficient in these arts that they began to show off before others in the community with strange action, exclamations, contortions, spasms, unnatural postures, wild gestures, incoherent and unintelligible sounds. They would drop insensible to the floor, writhe in agony,

suffer dreadful tortures, and utter loud and piercing outcries. Soon their antics were known to the whole community. As their conditions became worse and worse, the village doctor, Dr. Grigg, was called in to administer to the "afflicted girls." Diagnosis and medical treatment being sadly lacking at this time, Dr. Grigg resorted to the usual diagnosis of the day and declared the children "bewitched."

A handful of "bewitched" girls made up the motley lot: precocious nine-year-old Elizabeth, daughter of Mr. Parris; eleven-year-old Abigail Williams, his niece and member of the household; Ann Putnam, twelve-year-old daughter of the parish clerk, Sergeant Thomas Putnam, and the leading agent in the holocaust to follow; Mary Walcot, seventeen, daughter of Captain Jonathan Walcot, deacon of the parish prior to the formation of the Church; Mercy Lewis, also seventeen, and for a time previous in the family of the Reverend George Burroughs and now a servant in the family of Thomas Putnam; Elizabeth Hubbard, seventeen, a niece of the wife of Dr. Grigg, who lived with her; Elizabeth Booth and Susannah Sheldon, both eighteen; Mary Warren, twenty, a servant of John Procter; and Sarah Churchill, twenty, a servant of George Jacobs, Sr.

Abetted by three gossips (Mrs. Ann Putnam, mother of Ann Putnam, Mrs. Pope, and a woman named Bibber), the group soon spread alarm throughout the community.

"The Accusation of a Witch," a wood inlay. The arresting officer stands ready to handcuff the victim as one of the girls points an accusing finger at her, and Cotton Mather calls for divine help against the Devil inhabiting the suspect.
Essex Institute Collection

Little else was talked about except the terrible condition of the afflicted girls. They became objects of compassion and wonder, which served only to excite them to more extraordinary manifestations. They interrupted church services with incongruous questions and insolent remarks. Upon being told that there was present in church an old woman against whom a warrant for witchcraft had been issued the day before, Abigail Williams cried out, "Look where she sits upon the beam, sucking her yellow-bird betwixt her fingers." Ann Putnam joined in: "There is a yellow-bird sitting on the minister's hat, as it hangs on the pin in the pulpit." At other times the girls became so obstreperous that they broke up whole meetings. Since they were supposed to be under supernatural impulses, they were never punished, but looked upon with pity, awe, and even terror. Even the minister agreed that the Devil himself was working his wrath on these innocent victims. Since established doctrine had it that the Devil could not operate upon mortals himself but must do so through his intermediaries, namely, witches or wizards, the burning question in all minds was: "Who are these agents the Devil is using to afflict these girls?" They began to pressure the girls to name names. Reluctant at first to do so, when the urgings became insistent, one after another named three women in the community: "Good," "Osburn," "Tituba." So it followed, that on February 29, 1692, warrants charging witchcraft were issued against these three persons. Thus began a massive series of accusations by these "afflicted girls" against hundreds of innocent persons, which was to culminate in the hangings of twenty persons and the imprisonment of hundreds more.

* * *

These first three examinations for witchcraft set the stage for the many that were to follow. The complainants who procured the warrants in the cases of Sarah Good, Sarah Osburn, and Tituba were Joseph Hutchinson, Edward Putnam, Thomas Putnam, and Thomas Preston, all strong on common sense and unlikely to be carried away by popular enthusiasm—a fact that shows how nearly unanimous was the feeling that the girls actually were suffering as the result of witchcraft practices.

The prelude to these initial examinations was deliberately designed to give them the maximum publicity and notoriety. On March 1 the two leading magistrates of the neighborhood, members of the highest legislative and judicial body in the colony, assistants John Hathorne and Jonathan Corwin, entered Salem on horseback, followed by an imposing retinue of marshals, constables, and aids. The whole population was out to greet them, "excited to the highest pitch of indignation and abhorrence towards the prisoners." Adjourning to the meeting-house, the magistrates took seats at a long table in front of the pulpit, facing the assembly. After prayer, Constable George Locker produced Sarah Good, and Constable Joseph Herrick brought in Sarah Osburn and Tituba.

In designating Sarah Good as the first to be examined the clever prosecutors were on sound ground. She and her children were desperately poor, often without a house to shelter them. Her weak and ignorant husband had left her. Truly she was a welfare case in an age before such was conceived. No one could have more readily evoked popular suspicion. She was examined as follows:

The Examination of Sarah Good before the Worshipful Esqrs. John Hathorne and Jonathan Corwin

Sarah Good, what evil spirit have you familiarity with?
None.
Have you made no contracts with the Devil?
No.
Why do you hurt these children?
I do not hurt them. I scorn it.
Who do you employ then to do it?
I employ nobody.
What creature do you employ then?
No creature: but I am falsely accused.
Why did you go away muttering from Mr. Parris his house?
I did not mutter, but I thanked him for what he gave my child.
Have you made no contract with the Devil?
No. (Hathorne desired the children all of them to look upon her, and see if this were the person that hurt them; and so they all did look upon her, and said this was one of the persons that did torment them. Presently they were all tormented.)
Sarah Good, do you not see now what you have done? Why do you not tell us the truth? Why do you thus torment these poor children?
I do not torment them.
Who do you employ then?
I employ nobody. I scorn it.
How came they thus tormented?
What do I know? You bring others here, and now you charge me with it.
Why, who was it?
I do not know but it was some you brought into the meeting-house with you.
We brought you into the meeting-house.
But you brought in two more.
Who was it, then that tormented the children?
It was Osburn.
What is it you say when you go muttering away from persons' houses?
If I must tell, I will tell.
Do tell us then.
If I must tell, I will tell: it is the Commandments. I may say my Commandments, I hope.
What Commandment is it?
If I must tell you, I will tell: it is a psalm.
What psalm? Who do you serve?
I serve God.
What God do you serve?
The God that made heaven and earth. (Her answers were in a very wicked, spiteful manner, reflecting and retorting against the authority with base and abusive words; and many lies she was taken in. It was here said that her husband had said that he was afraid that she either was a witch or would be one very quickly.)

Once the girls have named a
member of the village a witch,
she is very quickly arrested and
thrown into jail.
Essex Institute Collection

Following her examination, John Hathorne then entered into the records a further report on the proceedings of that March 1:

Salem Village, March the 1st, 1692.—Sarah Good, upon examination, denied the matter of fact (viz.) that she ever used any witchcraft, or hurt the abovesaid children, or any of them.

The abovenamed children, being all present, positively accused her of hurting of them sundry times within this two months, and also that morning. Sarah Good denied that she had been at their houses in said time or near them, or had done them any hurt. All the abovesaid children then present accused her face to face; upon which they were all dreadfully tortured and tormented for a short space of time; and, the affliction and tortures being over, they charged said Sarah Good again that she had then so tortured them, and came to them and did it, although she was personally then kept at a considerable distance from them.

Sarah Good being asked if that she did not then hurt them, who did it; and the children being again tortured, she looked upon them, and said that it was one of them we brought into the house with us. We asked her who it was: she then answered, and said it was Sarah Osburn, and Sarah Osburn was then under custody, and not in the house; and the children, being quickly after recovered out of their fit, said that it was Sarah Good and also Sarah Osburn that then did hurt and torment or afflict them, although both of them at the same time at a distance or remote from them personally. There were also sundry other questions put to her, and answers given thereunto by her according as is also given in.

Note that the judge put the questions to Sarah Good and that these questions obviously presumed the guilt of the defendant. There was no lawyer to speak for her. All parties in the matter were prejudiced against her. Except for the accusations of the "bewitched" girls, the afflictions of whom even the prisoner never seemed to question as anything but genuine, there was not the slightest bit of evidence on which to convict her. But convict her they did, and eventually hanged her.

Sarah Good was removed, and Sarah Osburn brought in. Born Sarah Warren, she was married in 1622 to Robert Prince, a member of one of the leading families and owner of a valuable farm, and by whom she had two children, James and Joseph. Prince died, and Sarah married Alexander Osburn, who had come over from Ireland, and, to pay for his passage, sold himself, put himself under contract to his sponsor for fifteen pounds. Sarah bought out the balance due and hired him to manage her farm. Shortly after, she married him, thus incurring the censure and criticism of her townsfolk. The marriage proved to be an unhappy one, causing an upset in her mental state. She became bedridden, and as a result could not attend church regularly, as all godfearing Puritans must. As a woman of property who had remarried beneath her station, she became the object of scandalous remarks and malicious gossip. Envious neighbors were only too happy to find the afflicted girls pointing their accusing fingers at her. She was examined as follows, the record being entered in the handwriting of Ezekial Cheever:

SARAH OSBURN HER EXAMINATION

What evil spirit have you familiarity with?
None.
Have you made no contract with the Devil?
No: I never saw the Devil in my life.
Why do you hurt these children?
I do not hurt them.
Who do you employ, then, to hurt them?
I employ nobody.
What familiarity have you with Sarah Good?
None: I have not seen her these two years.
Where did you see her then?
One day, agoing to town.
What communications had you with her?
I had none, only "How do you do?" or so. I do not know her by name.
What did you call her, then? (Osburn made a stand at that; at last, said she called her Sarah.)
Sarah Good saith that it was you that hurt the children.
I do not know that the Devil goes about in my likeness to do any hurt. (Mr. Hathorne desired all the children to stand up, and look upon her, and see if they did know her, which they all did; and every one of them said that this was one of the women that did afflict them, and that they had constantly seen her in the very habit that she was now in. Three evidences declared that she said this morning, that she was more like to be bewitched than that she was a witch. Mr. Hathorne asked her what made her say so. She answered that she was frighted one time in her sleep, and either saw, or dreamed that she saw, a thing like an Indian all black, which did pinch her in her neck, and pulled her by the back part of her head to the door of the house.)
Did you never see any thing else?
No.
Hath the Devil ever deceived you, and been false to you?
I do not know the Devil. I never did see him.
What lying spirit was it then?
It was a voice that I thought I heard.
What did it propound to you?
That I should go no more to meeting; but I said I would, and did go the next sabbath-day.
Were you never tempted further?
No.
Why did you yield thus far to the Devil as never to go to meeting since?
Alas! I have been sick, and not able to go.

A further record of the proceedings was entered by John Hathorne:

Sarah Osburne, upon examination, denied the matter of fact, viz., that she ever understood or used any witchcraft, or hurt any of the abovesaid children.

The children above named, being all personally present, accused her face to face; which, being done, they were all hurt, afflicted, and tortured very much; which, being over, and they out of their fits, they said that said Sarah Osburne did then come to them, and hurt them, Sarah Osburne being then kept at a distance personally from them. Sarah Osburne was asked why she then hurt them. She denied it. It being asked of her how she could so pinch and hurt them, and yet she be at that distance personally from them, she answered she did not then hurt them, nor ever did. She was asked who, then, did it, or who she employed to do it. She answered she did not know that the Devil goes about in her likeness to do any hurt. Sarah Osburne, being told that Sarah Good, one of her companions, had, upon examination, accused her, she, notwithstanding, denied the same, according to her examination, which is more at large given in, as therein will appear.

Upon the completion of Sarah Osburn's examination, she was taken out of the meeting place and Tituba brought in for her examination, which proceeded as follows:

Tituba, what evil spirt have you familiarity with?
None.
Why do you hurt these children?
I do not hurt them.
Who is it then?
The Devil, for aught I know.
Did you never see the Devil?
The Devil came to me, and bid me serve him.
Who have you seen?
Four women sometimes hurt the children.
Who were they?
Goody Osburn and Sarah Good, and I do not know who the others were. Sarah Good and Osburn would have me hurt the children, but I would not. (She further saith there was a tall man of Boston that she did see.)
When did you see them?
Last night, at Boston.
What did they say to you?
They said, "Hurt the children."
And did you hurt them?
No: there is four women and one man, they hurt the children, and then they lay all upon me; and they tell me, if I will not hurt the children, they will hurt me.
But did you not hurt them?
Yes; but I will hurt them no more.
Are you not sorry that you did hurt them?
Yes.
And why, then, do you hurt them?
They say, "Hurt children, or we will do worse to you."
What have you seen?
A man come to me, and say, "Serve me."
What service?
Hurt the children: and last night there was an appearance that said, "Kill the children"; and, if I would not go on hurting the children, they would do worse to me.
What is this appearance you see?
Sometimes it is like a hog, and sometimes like a great dog.
What did it say to you?
The black dog said, "Serve me"; but I said, "I am afraid." He said, if I did not, he would do worse to me.
What did you say to it?
"I will serve you no longer." Then he said he would hurt me; and then he looks like a man, and threatens to hurt me. And he told me he had more pretty things that he would give me, if I would serve him.
What were these pretty things?
He did not show me them.
What else have you seen?

Two cats; a red cat, and a black cat.

What did they say to you?

They said, "Serve me."

When did you see them?

Last night; and they said, "Serve me"; but I said I would not.

What service?

Hurt the children.

Did you not pinch Elizabeth Hubbard this morning?

The man brought her to me, and made me pinch her.

Why did you go to Thomas Putnam's last night, and hurt his child?

They pull and haul me, and make go.

And what would they have you do?

Kill her with a knife.

How did you go?

We ride upon sticks, and are there presently.

Do you go through the trees or over them?

We see nothing, but are there presently.

Why did you not tell your master?

I was afraid: they said they would cut off my head if I told.

Would you not have hurt others, if you could?

They said they would hurt others, but they could not.

What attendants hath Sarah Good?

A yellow-bird, and she would have given me one.

What meat did she give it?

It did suck her between her fingers.

Did you not hurt Mr. Curren's child?

Goody Good and Goody Osburn told that they did hurt Mr. Curren's child, and would have had me hurt him too; but I did not.

What hath Sarah Osburn?

Yesterday she had a thing with a head like a woman, with two legs and wings.

What else have you seen with Osburn?

Another thing, hairy: it goes upright like a man, it hath only two legs.

Did you not see Sarah Good upon Elizabeth Hubbard, last Saturday?

I did see her set a wolf upon her to afflict her.

What clothes doth the man go in?

He goes in black clothes; a tall man, with white hair, I think.

How doth the woman go?

In a white hood, and a black hood with a top-knot.

Do you see who it is that torments these children now?

Yes: it is Goody Good; she hurts them in her own shape.

Who is it that hurts them now?

I am blind now: I cannot see.

Written by EZEKIEL CHEEVER.

SALEM VILLAGE, March the 1st, 1692.

Tituba, it should be pointed out, was well aware of the monstrous fancies of the day and, even with her retarded mentality, she had an inborn cunning and primitive imagination. Vividly she dressed up and embellished her lies, describing exactly what the witches she saw were wearing. One of them wore "a serge coat with a white hat." The Devil himself appeared "in black clothes sometimes, sometimes serge coat of other color.'" She described her wild witches' ride "upon a stick, or pole, and Good and Osburn behind me: we ride taking hold of one another." It was obvious that she had been well coached in the gossip of the moment and willfully used it as the basis of her answers.

Tituba was examined for several days, at the end of which time John Hathorne recorded this report:

Salem Village, March 1, 1692.—Tituba, an Indian woman, brought before us by Constable Jos. Herrick, of Salem, upon suspicion of witchcraft by her committed, according to the complaint of Jos. Hutchinson and Thomas Putnam, &c., of Salem Village, as appears per warrant granted, Salem, 29th February, 1692. Tituba, upon examination, and after some denial, acknowledged the matter of fact, as, according to her examination given in, more fully will appear, and who also charged Sarah Good and Sarah Osburn with the same.

Salem Village, March the 1st, 1692.—Sarah Good, Sarah Osburn, and Tituba, an Indian woman, all of Salem Village, being this day brought before us, upon suspicion of witchcraft, &c., by them and every one of them committed; Tituba, an Indian woman, acknowledging the matter of fact, and Sarah Osburn and Sarah Good denying the same before us; but there appearing, in all their examinations, sufficient ground to secure them all. And, in order to further examination, they were all *per mittimus* sent to the jails in the county of Essex.

Salem, March 2.—Sarah Osburn again examined, and also Tituba, as will appear in their examinations given in. Tituba again acknowledged the fact, and also accused the other two.

Salem, March 3.—Sarah Osburn, and Tituba, Indian, again examined. The examination now given in. Tituba again said the same.

Salem, March 5.—Sarah Good and Tituba again examined; and, in their examination, Tituba acknowledged the same she did formerly, and accused the other two above said.

John Hathorne
Jonathan Corwin

All three prisoners were brought from the jail in Ipswich about ten miles distant for daily questioning. Osburn and Good steadily maintained their innocence; Tituba reveled in professing her guilt and implicating the other two as having along with herself consorted with the Devil. On March 7 they were transferred to the jail in Boston.

In the examination of Tituba a pattern emerged that was to spell the difference between life and death of the poor souls pointed out as witches by the "afflicted" girls. Tituba began her testimony professing innocence. The girls immediately went into their torments and tantrums. As soon as Tituba began to confess, these spells subsided. She herself then became tormented before the very eyes of the magistrates and the awestruck crowd. With much writhing and contorting she broke loose from her compact with the Devil, thus ridding herself of the power to afflict. In the days to come, those who admitted they were witches and readily confessed their necromantic actions, while they remained in prison, were never brought to the gallows. Those who stoutheartedly maintained their innocence to the end were quickly brought to their end at the end of a rope.

*   *   *

As the accused professes her innocence, one of the bewitched girls falls screaming to the floor.
If the prisoner admitted to being a witch, the girls immediately ceased their convulsions.

Here is how Charles Upham in his book *Salem Witchcraft* summed up the feelings and sentiments of the people of Salem Village and surrounding countryside at the close of the first week in March, 1692:

The terrible sufferings of the girls in Mr. Parris's family and of their associates, for the two preceding months, had become known far and wide. A universal sympathy was awakened in their behalf; and a sentiment of horror sunk deep into all hearts, at the dread demonstration of the diabolical rage in their afflicted and tortured persons. A few, very few, distrusted; but the great majority, ninety-nine in a hundred of all the people, were completely swept into the torrent. Nathaniel Putnam and Nathaniel Ingersoll were entirely deluded, and continued so to the end. Even Joseph Hutchinson was, for a while, carried away. The physicians had all given their opinion that the girls were suffering from an "evil hand." The neighboring ministers, after a day's fasting and prayer, and a scrutinizing inspection of the condition of the afflicted children, had given it, as the result of their most solemn judgment, that it was a case of witchcraft. Persons from the neighboring towns had come to the place, and with their own eyes received demonstration of the same fact. Mr. Parris made it the topic of his public prayers and preaching. The girls, Sunday after Sunday, were under malign influence, to the disturbance and affrightment of the congregation. In all companies, in all families, all the day long, the sufferings and distraction occurring in the houses of Mr. Parris, Thomas Putnam, and others, and in the meeting-house, were topics of excited conversation; and every voice was loud in demanding, every mind earnest to ascertain, who were the persons, in confederacy with the Devil, thus torturing, pinching, convulsing, and bringing to the last extremities of mortal agony, these afflicted girls. Every one felt that, if the guilty authors of the mischief could not be discovered, and put out of the way, no one was safe for a moment.

* * *

These witch pins, now preserved among the files of the County Court at Salem, were used, so the girls affirmed, by the accused to torture and torment them. (*left*)
Essex Institute Collection

Witch cicatrix, not unlike the faces of witches, appear as leaf scars on certain trees in Salem when the leaves drop off in the late fall. (*right*)
Essex Institute Collection

Tituba, who has taught the girls some of her West Indian sorcery, asks Mary Wolcott what she sees in the mirror. Mary cries out, as Cotton Mather, Magistrate Hathorne, and Mary's brother enter, that it is Goodwife Corey coming to stab her with a spindle in her hand.

The trial of a witch.

At the trial of Martha Corey the accusing girls point to their victim and cry out, "There is a flock of yellow birds around her head."

Before the year 1692 was out, twenty persons would be hanged for the crime of witchcraft and hundreds accused and thrown into jail for the same reason. The pattern was set. The "bitch witches," as old George Jacobs, Sr., called the "afflicted" girls, would point their accusing fingers at whoever suited their fancy of the moment, then go into their fits. The unfortunate object of their spite would be arrested and brought before the magistrates for examination. Whether they denied or admitted the charge, they were thrown into jail to await trial.

The girls' next victim was Martha Corey, a very intelligent and devout woman, who discounted the whole witchcraft affair, thereby sealing her own doom. The girls well knew that if she were proceeded against, the public panic would be heightened. Gossip spread quickly, and by the time they came to arrest her, Martha Corey knew that the girls had identified her through her clothes as the one who had appeared to Ann Putnam and tortured her with pinching. On March 19 a warrant was issued for her arrest. Upon examination she angered the magistrates by her straightforward, sensible denials of her guilt, and her somewhat amused tolerance of the whole affair:

What did you strike the maid at Mr. Tho. Putnam's with?
I never struck her in my life.
There are two who saw you strike her with an iron rod.
I had no hand in it.
Who had? Do you believe these children are bewitched?
They may for ought I know: I have no hand in it.
Do not you believe there are witches in the country?
I do not know that there is any.

Martha had great confidence in her own innocence,

and was thus able to express herself in positive and forcible language. Her situation was complicated by the disagreement between herself and her husband, eighty-year-old Giles Corey, who was aghast at her disbelief in the sufferings of the girls. However, her courageous stand availed her nothing, and she was thrown into jail.

* * *

The next victim to be named was seventy-one-year-old Rebecca Nurse. She was the head of a large and prominent family, and a person of acknowledged worth. It was probably jealousy of her high standing and prosperity that goaded the girls into naming her as a witch. Rumor spread rapidly, and her friends rallied to her defense. The Porters visited her in her home, where they found her sick in bed and in a very frail condition. Perhaps mercifully, Rebecca Nurse was also deaf. They reported to the community her great sympathy for the afflicted girls and her hope that they would soon recover. Such sentiments meant less than nothing, and on March 23 a warrant for her arrest was issued. The next morning at eight she was brought to the house of Nathaniel Ingersoll for interrogation. Edward Putnam testified that he himself saw the shape of Rebecca Nurse torture his niece in his very presence. Here again, as in the identification of the clothes worn by Martha Corey, was a case of "spectral evidence," one on which so many were to be condemned to the gallows. It was the Reverend Mr. Samuel Parris himself who took down the examination of Rebecca Nurse and was instrumental in having this frail old woman committed to jail.

* * *

At the trial of Martha Corey, Mary Wolcott feigns illness and torment while accusing the prisoner. Even her husband, Giles, was convinced his wife was a witch.

The next complaints were brought against two eminently respectable women, Sarah Cloyse and Elizabeth Proctor, by John Indian:

John, who hurt you?
Goody Proctor first, and then Goody Cloyse.
What did she do to you?
She brought the book to me. (This is in reference to the belief that a witch brings the Devil's book to the afflicted so he will sign his soul away to the Devil.)
John, tell the truth: who hurt you?
The first was a gentlewoman I saw.
Who next?
Goody Cloyse.
But who hurt you next?
Goody Proctor.
What did she do to you?
She choked me and brought the book.
Where did she take hold of you?
Upon my throat, to stop my breath.

Shocked and amazed at these statements made by the Indian, Sarah Cloyse broke in, "When did I hurt thee?" He answered, "A great many times." She exclaimed, "Oh, you are a grievous liar." The court proceeded with the questioning, during which the witnesses accused Sarah Cloyse of having bitten the flesh of the Indian and drinking the blood of the accusers. All this was too much for poor Sarah, and she fainted dead away.

The pattern of questions and answers in the case of Elizabeth Proctor was the same. But in this instance she had comfort in her husband John's presence by her side and his strong and brave support of her during her terrible ordeal. He did not believe a word of what the girls said about his wife, with the result that, angered at his bold and unguarded language, the girls out of spite accused him of being a wizard. At this, many of the afflicted girls went into fits. Then some of the girls cried out, "There is Proctor going to take up Mrs. Pope's feet." Immediately Mrs. Pope's feet went up. Whomever the girls accused Proctor of attacking, the individual in question would go into a fit. Abigail Williams attempted to strike John Proctor, but, although her fist was doubled up, her hand opened before it only lightly touched him, and she cried out that her fingers burned.

The council adjourned to the next day, when they decreed that Sarah Cloyse, Elizabeth and John Proctor were all to be committed for trial. Along with Rebecca Nurse, Martha Corey, and Dorcas Good, they were sent to the jail in Boston in the custody of Marshal Herrick.

* * *

untill the 31 May 1692 at the same moment that I was hearing my
evidence read by the honoured Magistrats to take my Oath I was again
re-assaulted & tortured by my before mentioned Tormentor Rebekah Nurse
Sworne Salem Village May the 31
1692 Before us John Hathorne
Jonathan Corwin

The testimony of Ann Putnam junr witnesseth & saith that being in the
Room when her mother was afflicted she saw Martha Kory Sarah
& Rebekah Nurse on their apparition upon her mother

Testifyed to ye truth thereof
by Ann Putnam Salem
May. 31st. 1692
Before us John Hathorne
Jonathan Corwin Assists

Essex in the Province of the Massachusetts Bay in New England
Anno RRs & Reginae Gulielmi & Mariae Angliae &c. Quarto Annoqz Domini 1692
The Jurors for our Sov. Lord and Lady the King and Queen doe present That Abagaile Hobbs of Topsfeild in the County aforesaid Single Woman In the yeare of our Lord 1688 In Casco Bay In the Province of Mayne in New England Wickedly and felloniously a Covenant with the Evill Spirit the Devill did make Contrary to the peace of our Sov. Lord and Lady the King & Queen their Crowne and Dignity, and the forme of ... In that case made and Provided

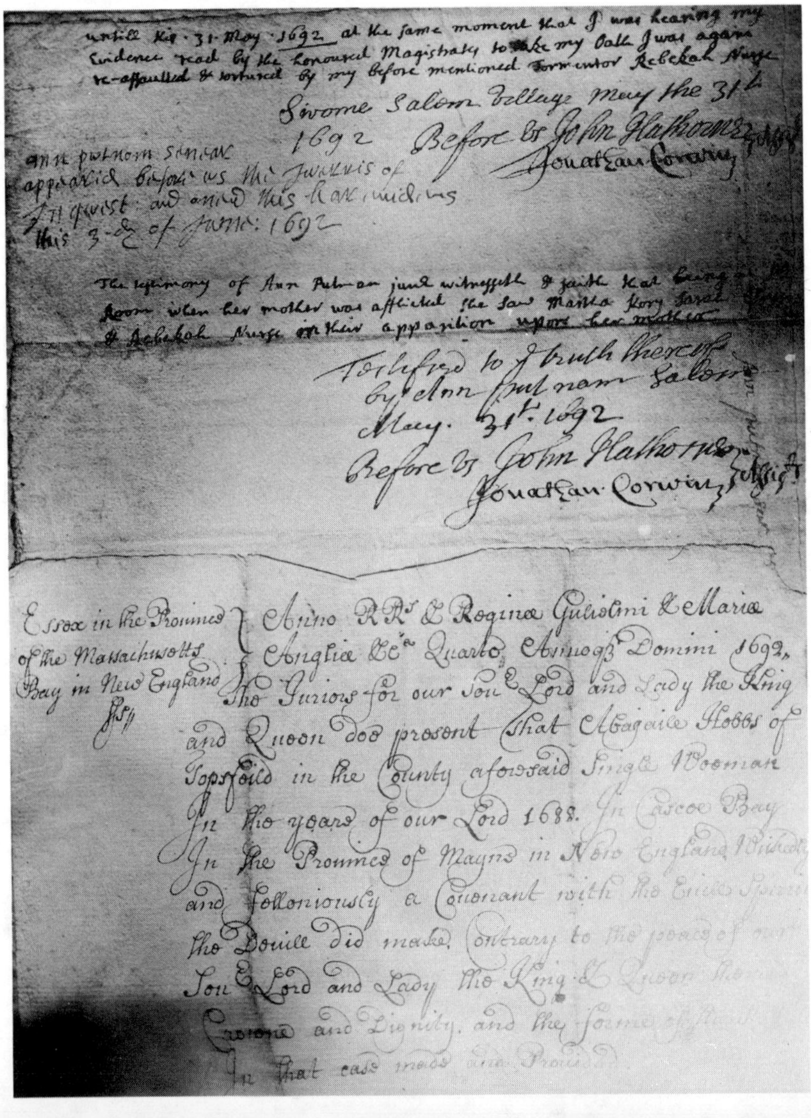

The top document contains the depositions of Mrs. Ann Putnam and her daughter, Ann, before Magistrates Hathorne and Corwin in Salem Village on May 31, 1692. The bottom document is the indictment against Abigail Hobbs "for covenanting with the Devil."
Essex Institute Collection

On the 18th of April warrants were issued against four more unfortunates: Giles Corey and Mary Warren (once one of the afflicted, now charged with being an afflicter), both of Salem Farms; Abigail Hobbs of Topsfield, and Bridget Bishop of Salem.

Mary Warren's questioning began on April 19 and continued until the middle of May. She put on an act of cunning and skill. Having visibly fought against the Devil for her soul, she ended by confessing she was a witch but had managed to escape from the Devil. Her subsequent repentence earned her her freedom. However, she never again joined the "afflicted" girls.

Giles Corey's examination took place on April 19, when the girls put on their usual act, charging him with having afflicted them. At each movement of his hands or head or body, all the girls mimicked him. Giles, at the time of his wife's examination, had believed that she might have been a witch and so testified against her. Seeing the unfairness of the questions now being put to him, he had a change of heart. To make restitution and to assure that his property went to his wife, if she escaped the gallows, and his two sons-in-law, he devised a clever plan to avoid being hanged as a witch but doing away with himself in such a manner that his property could not be confiscated for being a wizard. Henceforth, he refused to open his mouth to testify either for or against himself.

Bridget Bishop was an ideal scapegoat for the girls. She was the local tavern keeper and a flashy dresser. They must have envied her freedom and her opportunity for sexual promiscuity, while, frustrated, they were bound to a life of boredom, conforming to the strict morals of the community.

Abigail Hobbs was a wild creature who wandered about the woods at night and who, along with her children, took refuge in any house whose owners would give her shelter.

And so it went all during that April of 1692. A steady stream of victims of the girls' maliciousness came before the magistrates for questioning and were sent to jail. One of the strangest was the case of the Reverend George Burroughs.

In previous years Burroughs had been the pastor of Salem Village, but had left there and gone to Maine to live. Now married to his third wife, he had left behind a somewhat questionable reputation in the minds of the villagers, which undoubtedly became part of their folklore. Here then was grist for the fertile imagination of Ann Putnam, who lost no time in swearing under oath to a deposition, parts of which were as follows:

On the 8th of May, at evening, I saw the apparition of Mr. George Burroughs, who grievously tortured me, and urged me to write in his book, which I refused. He then told me that his two first wives would appear to me presently, and tell me a great many lies, but I should not believe them. Then immediately appeared to me the forms of two women in winding-sheets, and napkins about their heads, at which I was greatly affrighted; and they turned their faces toward Mr. Burroughs, and looked very red and angry, and told him that he had been a cruel man to them, and that their blood did cry for vengeance against him; and also told him that they should be clothed with white robes in heaven, when he should be cast into hell; and immediately he vanished away. And, as soon as he was gone, the two women turned their faces toward me, and looked as pale as a white wall; and told me that they were Mr. Burroughs' two first wives, and that he had murdered them.

Later, it was Giles Corey's turn to be accused of witchcraft by the girls. He refuses to declare himself either guilty or not guilty, and is sentenced to *peine forte et dure* until he pleads to the charge or dies.

The effect of these words from twelve-year-old Ann Putnam was devastating to the already overwrought community. Field Marshal Partridge was hastily dispatched to Maine to "kidnap" and bring the Reverend Burroughs posthaste back to Salem. They found him in his humble house, eating a frugal meal with his family. Without explanation they snatched him from the table and roughly hurried him off. On the 4th of May he was delivered to the Salem jailer.

On May 9 a special session of the magistracy was held behind closed doors, with William Stoughton coming from Dorchester and Samuel Sewall from Boston to sit with Hathorne and Corwin in Burroughs' interrogation. They questioned him mainly on his doctrine, and produced damaging evidence that he was not wholly sound in the matter of witchcraft. He could not recall when he had last served the Lord's Supper. Of all his children, only his oldest son had been baptized. Against Burroughs were two fatal charges: murder and heresy. He was forthwith committed for trial.

* * *

George Jacobs, Sr., was an infirm old man who walked with two staffs, yet his tall bearing was fearless and his speech strong, abrupt and decided. When the magistrates began, "Here are them that accuse you of acts of witchcraft," he replied, "Well, let us hear who are they and what are they." Sarah Churchill, his servant, accused him, saying, "Last night, I was afflicted at Deacon Ingersoll's; and Mary Walcot said it was a man with two staves: it was my master." She further accused him of hurting her twice. Jacobs retorted: "You tax me for a wizard: you may as well tax me for a buzzard. I have done no harm." Then Sarah said to him, "I know you lived a wicked life." Jacobs, turning to the magistrates, said, "Let her make it out." The magistrates asked her, "Doth he ever pray in his family?" She replied, "Not unless by himself." Upon being asked why not, Jacobs told the magistrates that he could not read, whereupon they said he should know the Lord's Prayer and asked him to recite it. According to the Reverend Parris, always overeager to uncover guilt in the accused, "He missed in several parts of it, and could not repeat it right after many trials."

* * *

By now the jails were overflowing with persons accused of witchcraft. It was high time for them to be brought to trial and their cases disposed of. Politically the colony of Massachusetts had undergone a change. On May 14, 1692, it was transformed into a royal province with the arrival in Boston of a new governor, Sir William Phips. William Stoughton became the deputy governor. The council remained much the same. For the moment the new government refrained from interfering with the witchcraft proceedings. The new governor's chief concern

was with the French to the north of him. He did not understand, nor did he wish to concern himself with, the witchcraft doings. He was perfectly satisfied to yield to the views of his council, and accordingly relegated all authority in these matters to William Stoughton, his deputy governor. It was decided to appoint a special court of oyer and terminer for the witchcraft trials. Stoughton was commissioned chief justice. Appointed associate judges were Nathaniel Saltonstall of Haverhill, Major John Richards of Boston, Major Bartholomew Gedney of Salem, Mr. Wait Winthrop, Captain Samuel Sewall, and Mr. Peter Sargent, all three of Boston. Saltonstall withdrew early in the trials, to be succeeded by Jonathan Corwin of Salem.

The court was opened at Salem in the first week of June, 1692. As there was no colony or province law against witchcraft in force when the trials began, the court proceeded under an act of James the First, passed in 1603, stating that convicted persons were to be sentenced to "the pains and penalties of death as felons." It is unfortunate that no record of the doings of this special court are now to be found. Some information, however, is available in contemporary writings.

Bridget Bishop was the only one to be tried on the first day of the court. As she was brought from the jail past the meetinghouse, Cotton Mather relates, "she gave a look toward the house; and immediately a demon, invisibly entering the meeting-house, tore down a part of it: so that, though there was no person to be seen there, yet the people, at the noise, running in, found a board, which was strongly fastened with several nails, transported into another quarter of the house."

In all probability some of the spectators were climbing around in the house, and dislodged a board. The court, however, judged it as conclusive proof that Bridget Bishop was guilty. At her trial she was accused of bewitching the son of Samuel Shattuck, the local hatter and dyer. Shattuck also condemned her for bringing in lace clothes too elaborate for an honest woman. Eighteen-year-old John Cook testified that about six years previous he had seen her form walking across their room and at that moment an apple which he had in his hand flew out of it and into his mother's lap. She then disappeared.

One after another the neighbors of Bridget Bishop charged her with all sorts of extraordinary "pranks." John Louder, a servant of John Gedney, Sr., had an argument with Bridget because her fowls used to come into their garden, and he now swore that "Some little time after which, I, going well to bed, about the dead of night, felt a great weight upon my breast, and awakening, looked; and, it being bright moonlight, did clearly see said Bridget Bishop, or her likeness, sitting upon my stomach; and putting my arms off the bed to free myself from the great oppression, she presently laid hold of my throat, and almost choked me, and I had no strength or power in my hands to resist, or help myself, and, in this condition, she held me to almost day."

Upon such evidence Bridget Bishop was condemned, and executed the next week. Her body, and probably the bodies of those who followed her on the gallows, were undoubtedly thrown into pits among the rocks by the officers having charge of the executions.

After the condemnation of Bridget Bishop the court took a recess. They consulted with the ministers of Boston and the neighboring towns regarding the prosecutions, who urged that they be vigorously carried out. Before adjourning, the court revived an old colony law making witchcraft a capital offense.

*   *   *

The court met again on Wednesday, the 29th of June and, after trial, sentenced to death Sarah Good, Sarah Wildes, Elizabeth How, Susanna Martin, and Rebecca Nurse, who were all hanged on July 19. At the time of her execution, a church elder, Noyes, pleaded with Sarah Good to confess because she knew she was a witch. "You are a liar," she said. "I am no more a witch than you are a wizard; and, if you take away my life, God will give you blood to drink." In due time her prophecy came true. A very corpulent man, he died of an internal hemorrhage, bleeding profusely at the mouth.

Evidence given at the trials themselves corroborated and added to the accusations previously brought against the accused at the time of their examinations. Witness after witness produced spectral evidence against the prisoners. Unfortunately for them, Chief Justice Stoughton was a firm believer in the matter of witches and wizards appearing, whether in their own guise or in other shapes, before those they would afflict. Thus, presentation of spectral evidence to the court of oyer and terminer was tantamount to a verdict of guilt.

It should be stated here that the court did not render the verdict. In each trial there was a jury who decided whether the defendant was "guilty" or "not guilty." In the case of Rebecca Nurse, so obvious was the injustice being done that the jury brought in a verdict of "not guilty."

Immediately, all the accusers in the court, as well as those outside, set up a hideous outcry, to the amazement not only of the spectators but also of the court, which seemed strangely surprised. One of the judges expressed himself as not satisfied with the verdict. The chief justice, "while not wishing to impose on the jury," gave reasons why he thought they had reached the wrong verdict. The jury redeliberated, and she was condemned, upon which the governor granted her a reprieve. But so loud was the clamor of certain "Salem gentlemen"

The execution of Mrs. Hibbens.
Essex Institute Collection

that he recalled the reprieve, and Rebecca Nurse was executed with the others. But not before, on July 3, 1692, the Reverend Parris had seen to it that she was excommunicated from the Church.

*   *   *

The court met again on August 5 and tried George Burroughs, John and Elizabeth Procter, George Jacobs, Sr., John Willard, and Martha Carrier. All were condemned, and, except for Elizabeth Procter, who was pregnant at the time, were executed on August 19.

The hanging of George Burroughs.

At his trial, George Burroughs, besides being accused by the "afflicted" girls, was charged with performing feats beyond the capability of giants, giving rise to the assumption that he was helped by the Devil. Even on the scaffold, when he was making a speech professing his innocence and eloquently reciting the Lord's Prayer, his accusers said a black man (the Devil) stood beside him and dictated it to him. At this point, immediately following Burroughs' execution, Cotton Mather, sensing a growing revulsion to the executions among the crowd of spectators, addressed them, saying that Burroughs was no ordained minister and that the Devil often appeared in the shape of an angel of light. The executions went on.

* * *

The next meeting of the court took place on September 9 and 17. The following were condemned and executed on September 22, 1692: Martha Corey, Mary Easty, Alice Parker, Ann Pudeator, Margaret Scott, Wilmot Reed, Samuel Wordwell, Mary Parker. All asserted their innocence on the scaffold.

* * *

Giles Corey met his death in quite another fashion. Having drawn up a deed bequeathing his property to his two sons-in-law, William Cleeves of Beverly and John Moulton of Salem, he refused to plead "guilty" or "not guilty" in answer to an indictment by the grand jury, but stood mute. The court found itself in a difficult position. Three times they called him before them and informed him of the penalty for standing mute on such occasions. It was known as *peine forte et dure*, and con-

sisted of being laid on his back, stripped mostly naked, and a weight of iron placed upon him, not quite enough to crush him. With little or no food given him, he would remain there until he died or until he answered. This punishment was carried out on Giles in an open field near the jail. To his executioners he called out to increase the weight, for he would never yield. For a man of eighty-one years of age, this was a heroic performance, and the manner of his death and his spirited deportment in dying profoundly affected the public mind. To counteract this reaction, Thomas Putnam sent a letter to Judge Sewall stating that his daughter Ann had been tormented by witches and told she would be pressed to death before Giles Corey but that God had saved her. A man in a winding sheet had then appeared to her and told her that Giles Corey had murdered him by pressing him to death with his feet but that Corey had made a pact with the Devil to prevent his being hanged for the deed. God hardened his heart so that he would not heed the advice of the court and die an easy death, but it must be the same manner of death Giles had brought upon the apparition. Cotton Mather took this vision as positive proof of a divine communication to Ann Putnam, since she could not have heard of this deed, which happened before she was born, and everybody else had long ago forgotten the affair. But of course she had heard about it, from her own father and others. Mather's statement was solely meant to offset the public sympathy that might threaten to arise in favor of Giles Corey.

* * *

"Giles Corey's Punishment and Awful Death" from *Witchcraft Illustrated*, George A. Kimball, Publisher. Giles refuses to answer and is crushed to death.
Essex Institute Collection

After the executions of September 22, 1692, the court fully expected to meet from month to month to continue to "supply new cart-loads of victims to the hangman." But they were destined never to meet again. A radical change was taking place. Men of prominence and ministers were beginning to have serious doubts on the validity of spectral evidence. Increase Mather, president of Harvard, was not so convinced of such as was his son, Cotton. "It is better that ten suspected witches should escape," he wrote, "than one innocent person should be condemned." The accusations of the "afflicted" girls were becoming embarrassing, especially when the wife of Sir William Phips, after sympathizing with those who suffered prosecution, was cried out upon by them. So, on October 29, the court of oyer and terminer was dismissed by the governor. What is more, he asked for petitions of release for the 150 accused witches still in jail. Those who had only spectral evidence against them he released on bond. Unfortunately, prisoners had to pay their jail costs before they could be released, so that not all succeeded in getting out of jail. However, new regulations were put into force, requiring the well-being of those prisoners who remained.

To complete the witchcraft trials still outstanding, the acts of the General Court of November 13 and December 16 created special sessions of the Supreme Court of Judicature. Stoughton still presided, but spectral evidence was eliminated as a basis of conviction, although now confessed witches were condemned. The court traveled around, and new juries were selected. On January 3, 1693, fifty-two witches were tried, but the cases against forty-nine of them evaporated into nothing. Stoughton signed death warrants for the other three and for five others who had been condemned previously. Governor Phips then issued reprieves for all eight, and in May, 1693, discharged all remaining witches. Thus ended the tragedy of the Salem Witch Trials of 1692. Never again was a witch to be condemned to death in the American Colonies.

To a world that no longer believes in witches, the Salem trial may seem to be one more example of the barbarism of yesteryear, which twentieth-century man has by now completely outgrown. There are many lessons to be learned from Salem, however; the most significant, perhaps, is the ease with which absurdities and falsehoods and unfounded charges can spread into a lynch spirit, can be believed in by intelligent and educated persons and by accusers themselves. Mass hysteria, fed by rumor, gossip, fear, imagination, speculation, fantasy, enmity, and other mechanisms, is still a potent force in the modern world. We have not seen the last of the witch-hunts.

The Wonders of the Invisible World:

Being an Account of the

TRYALS

OF

Several Witches,

Lately Executed in

NEW-ENGLAND:

And of several remarkable Curiosities therein Occurring.

Together with,

I. Observations upon the Nature, the Number, and the Operations of the Devils.

II. A short Narrative of a late outrage committed by a knot of Witches in *Swede-Land*, very much resembling, and so far explaining, that under which *New-England* has laboured.

III. Some Councels directing a due Improvement of the Terrible things lately done by the unusual and amazing Range of *Evil-Spirits* in *New-England*.

IV. A brief Discourse upon those *Temptations* which are the more ordinary Devices of Satan.

By *COTTON MATHER*.

Published by the Special Command of his EXCELLENCY the Governour of the Province of the *Massachusetts-Bay* in *New-England*.

Printed first, at *Boston* in *New-England*; and Reprinted at *London*, for *John Dunton*, at the *Raven* in the *Poultry*. 1693.

Title page of *The Wonders of the Invisible World* by Cotton Mather, in which he told of the trials and executions of the Salem witches in 1692.

"Witch House, Salem," a watercolor by S. Bartol. *Essex Institute Collection*

Andrew Hamilton, ignoring the two judges on the bench, turns to the jury and delivers his impassioned plea for freedom of the press to print the truth.
The New-York Historical Society, New York City

8

John Peter Zenger

[1735]

SHALL A NEWSPAPER BE PERMITTED TO MAKE DAMAGING statements about a person, blackening his reputation, charging him with acts for which the public has nothing but contempt—and then have its editors remain free from prosecution on the grounds that all the statements are true? Without such a right, without such immunity from prosecution, there is no freedom of the press, many will contend. For what does it avail a man to be able to write the truth about public officials if he can be arrested and charged with libel?

Yet the issue of the right to publish damaging statements, particularly about public officials, was not accepted in colonial America until the historic trial of an immigrant printer, John Peter Zenger, established one of the basic rights of the American people.

The year was 1735, a time of ferment in the rapidly growing city of New York, now teeming with its population of almost forty thousand. Dissatisfaction with British rulers ran high, but few of the colonists counted themselves other than Loyalists, and sentiment to secede or to declare independence was barely audible, if it existed at all.

In the old City Hall in New York, later to become the first Capitol of the United States under the Constitution, the trial of John Peter Zenger was held. The judges were appointees of the very forces that Zenger was accused of libeling, but trial by jury had been established in the colonies, and there was a hope that, the rulings of the judges notwithstanding, a jury might find Zenger not guilty.

For the background of the trial, one turns to the first years of the eighteenth century, when a shy and modest lad of thirteen, a native of Germany, arrived on the American shores. An indentured servant, the Zenger youth became apprenticed to a printer, and only in his mid-twenties did he become a free man, fulfilling the dream held by thousands of refugees who were leaving their native lands and traveling as pioneers and immigrants to the promise of the New World.

The British Crown Colony of New York was at this time under the rule of governors appointed directly by the king. In 1771, William S. Cosby was appointed to the post, a greedy, corrupt, and dictatorial figure who, once he assumed control, set out to exploit his position for his own financial gain. He stopped at nothing to get what he wanted. From 1725 to 1731 he had been governor of the island of Minorca in the Mediterranean, where he had confiscated property for his own private benefit, appropriated revenues, and had become intensely unpopular. He spent thirteen months carousing in London and on the Continent before he finally reached New York to take up his duties.

In his new post, Cosby lost no time in the effort to turn it into financial gain for himself. He inspired no loyalty in his subjects, and from the first days his administration was rocked by scandals. When his immediate predecessor, Rip Van Dam, refused to turn over to Cosby a portion of the wages that Van Dam had received while he had been acting governor, Cosby took the case to court. There, the Chief Justice of the New York Supreme Court, Lewis Morris, ruled against him, whereupon Cosby, in his anger, removed Morris from the court. Undaunted in his opposition to Cosby, Morris ran for the Assembly from the district of Eastchester and, in spite of Cosby's attempted trickery in the election, won handsomely.

"Sir William Cosby," miniature on enamel by
Christian F. Zincke. Governor Cosby became
angered at the critical attacks on him
by Zenger's weekly.
The New-York Historical Society, New York City

"Lewis Morris" by John Wollaston. A vociferous opponent
of Governor Cosby, Morris was one of the backers of
Zenger's weekly.
National Gallery of Art, Washington, D.C.

Facsimile of a front page
of Zenger's newspaper,
The New-York Weekly Journal.

Diorama of Zenger's printing shop.
*Zenger Memorial Room, Federal Hall,
New York City*

Numb. II.

THE

New-York Weekly JOURNAL.

Containing the freſheſt Advices, Foreign, and Domeſtick.

MUNDAY November 12, 1733.

Mr. Zenger.

INcert the following in your next, and you'll oblige your Friend,
CATO.

Mira temporum felicitas ubi ſentiri quæ velis, & quæ ſentias dicere licit.
Tacit.

THE Liberty of the Preſs is a Subject of the greateſt Importance, and in which every Individual is as much concern'd as he is in any other Part of Liberty : Therefore it will not be improper to communicate to the Publick the Sentiments of a late excellent Writer upon this Point. ſuch is the Elegance and Perſpicuity of his Writings, ſuch the inimitable Force of his Reaſoning, that it will be difficult to ſay any Thing new that he has not ſaid, or not to ſay that much worſe which he has ſaid.

There are two Sorts of Monarchies, an abſolute and a limited one. In the firſt, the Liberty of the Preſs can never be maintained, it is inconſiſtent with it ; for what abſolute Monarch would ſuffer any Subject to animadvert on his Actions, when it is in his Power to declare the Crime, and to nominate the Puniſhment ? This would make it very dangerous to exerciſe ſuch a Liberty   Beſides the Object againſt which thoſe Pens muſt be directed, is

their Sovereign, the ſole ſupream Magiſtrate ; for there being no Law in thoſe Monarchies, but the Will of the Prince, it makes it neceſſary for his Miniſters to conſult his Pleaſure, before any Thing can be undertaken : He is therefore properly chargeable with the Grievances of his Subjects, and what the Miniſter there acts being in Obedience to the Prince, he ought not to incur the Hatred of the People ; for it would be hard to impute that to him for a Crime, which is the Fruit of his Allegiance, and for refuſing which he might incur the Penalties of Treaſon. Beſides, in an abſolute Monarchy, the Will of the Prince being the Law, a Liberty of the Preſs to complain of Grievances would be complaining againſt the Law, and the Conſtitution, to which they have ſubmitted, or have been obliged to ſubmit; and therefore, in one Senſe, may be ſaid to deſerve Puniſhment. So that under an abſolute Monarchy, I ſay, ſuch a Liberty is inconſiſtent with the Conſtitution, having no proper Subject in Politics, on which it might be exercis'd, and if exercis'd would incur a certain Penalty.

But in a limited Monarchy, as *England* is, our Laws are known, fixed, and eſtabliſhed. They are the ſtreight Rule and ſure Guide to direct the King, the Miniſters, and other his Subjects : And therefore an Offence againſt the Laws is ſuch an Offence againſt the Conſtitution as ought to receive a proper adequate Puniſhment ; the ſevera.
Conſtil.

Zenger, representing at this time the *Weekly Gazette*, reported every detail of this election, including the story of how thirty-eight Quakers were illegally disqualified from voting because they would, according to their beliefs, only affirm rather than swear. He told of the intimidation of the voters by the king's sheriff and Cosby's attempt to stuff the ballot boxes. But its editor, Bradford, refused to print Zenger's unbiased report, and promptly dismissed him.

Morris now saw his chance to put his case, and those of others who had suffered injustices at the hands of Cosby and his henchmen, before the people. He would start and finance a rival newspaper to the *Gazette* and hire Zenger to publish it. Accordingly Morris, Van Dam, Alexander, and Smith set Zenger up in business, and on November 1, 1733, the first issue of the *New York Weekly Journal* made its appearance.

From its first issue, the paper spoke out forcefully against the Cosby administration. Most of the inflammatory articles were written by James Alexander, Lewis Morris, William Smith, Cadwallader Colden, and Lewis Morris, Jr. Despite typographical errors and poor grammar, Zenger's journal grew in popularity. Its only competition was the *New York Weekly Gazette*, the conservative and government-subsidized paper of William Bradford, to whom Zenger had been apprenticed. Zenger's paper lashed out against the colonial administration, held the governor and his coterie up to ridicule, and indulged in biting satire. Finally, it aroused the open condemnation of the governor's party when it printed the following two "scandalous songs":

A SONG MADE UPON THE ELECTION OF NEW MAGISTRATES
FOR THIS CITY
(To the tune of "To You fair Ladies now on land")

To you good lads that dare oppose
  all lawful power and might,
You are the theme that we have chose,
  and to your praise we write:
You dared to show your faces brave
  In spite of every abject slave;
          with a fa la la.

Your votes you gave for those brave men
  who feasting did dispise;
And never prostituted pen
  to certify the lies
That were drawn up to put in chains
  As well our nymphs as happy swains;
          with a fa la la.

And tho the great ones frown at this,
  what need have you to care?
Still let them fret and talk amiss,
  you'll show you boldly dare

Stand up to have your country dear,
  In spite of usquebaugh and beer;
          with a fa la la.

They beg'd and pray'd for one year more,
  but it was all in vain:
No wolawants you'd have, you swore;
  By jove you made it plain:
So sent them home to take their rest.
  And here's a health unto the best;
          with a fa la la.

A SONG MADE UPON THE FOREGOING OCCASION
(To the Tune of "Now, now, you Tories all shall stoop.")

Come on brave boys, let us be brave
  for liberty and law.
Boldly despise the haughty Knave,
  that would keep us in aw.
Let's scorn the tools bought by a sop
  and every cringing fool.
The man who basely bends a fop,
  a vile insipid tool.

Our Country's Rights we will defend,
  like brave and honest men;
We voted right and there's an end,
  and so we'll do again.
We vote all signers out of place
  As men who did amiss
Who sold us by a false address
  I'm sure we're right in this.

Exchequer courts, as void by law,
  great grievances we call;
The great men do assert no flaw
  is in them; they shall fall,
And be condemned by every man
  that's fond of liberty.
Let them withstand it all they can,
  Our laws we will stand by.

Tho' pettyfogging knaves deny
  us Rights of Englishmen;
We'll make the Scoundrel raskals fly,
  and ne'er return again.
Our Judges they would chop and change
  for those that serve their turn,
And will not surely think it strange
  if they for this should mourn.

Come fill a bumper, fill it up,
  unto our Aldermen;
For common-council fill the cup,
  and take it o'er again.
While they with us resolve to stand
  for liberty and law,
We'll drink their health with bat in hand,
  whoraa! whoraa! whoraa!

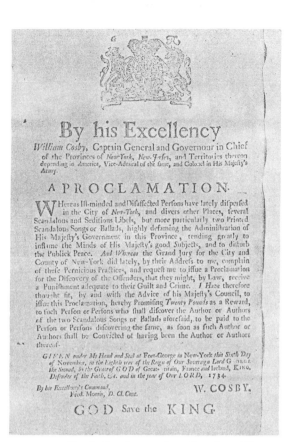

Facsimile of a proclamation, issued by Governor Cosby, offering twenty pounds reward for the names of the authors of the two scandalous songs then being circulated.

Upon orders from Governor Cosby, a Negro servant places in the fire one copy each of four issues (numbers 7, 47, 48, and 49) of Zenger's *The New-York Weekly Journal*.

Diorama of Anna Zenger bringing copies of Zenger's paper to him in prison. She continued to publish it during the nine months Zenger remained in jail awaiting trial.
Zenger Memorial Room, Federal Hall, New York City

By order of the governor, four issues of the *Journal,* Nos. 7, 47, 48, and 49, were condemned, and ordered to be publicly burned by the hangman. The aldermen refused to attend, but the ceremony was carried out, with a Negro servant stooping down to place into the fire one copy of each of the condemned papers. The lines of battle were thus drawn more tightly, and neither side was prepared for retreat.

On November 17, 1734, John Peter Zenger was arrested, upon issuance of a warrant that called upon the sheriff to take him into custody. The charge against Zenger was that he printed and published "several Seditious Libels throughout his Journals or News Papers, entitled, *The New-York Weekly Journal,* containing the freshest Advices, foreign and domestick; as having in them many Things, tending to raise Factions and Tumults, among the People of this Province, inflaming their Minds with Contempt of His Majesty's Government." Specifically the charge named the issues of January 28, 1734, and April 8, 1734.

An excessive bail of £800 was set for Zenger, so that he had no alternative to remaining in jail while awaiting trial. The people of New York were stunned. Zenger's arrest was wholly illegal. If, by it, Cosby hoped the *Journal* would cease publication, or would at least be more temperate in its criticism of the administration while its editor and printer was under arrest, he was doomed to disappointment. Support for the *Journal* grew during the nine months Zenger awaited trial. His wife, visiting him frequently in jail, talking to him, obtaining advice and information, hurried back to the printshop to publish the paper.

As the date of his trial approached, Zenger's position became even more precarious when the court took disbarment action against James Alexander and William Smith, the two attorneys who had come forward for the defense. But Zenger's friends and supporters were busy in his behalf, and quickly obtained the services of Andrew Hamilton, considered the outstanding member of the bar in Philadelphia, and perhaps the leading lawyer in the Colonies.

* * *

The trial was held on August 4, 1735, at City Hall on the corner of Nassau and Wall streets. Built in 1700, this was at the time the finest building in the city. The courtroom was crowded to capacity, with every class of people represented, most of whom resented the hardships and injustices that Governor Cosby heaped upon them. They hoped that an acquittal for Zenger would in some way result in their despicable governor being recalled.

Facsimile of decree of the court disbarring James Alexander and William Smith from acting as defense lawyers at Zenger's trial.

City Hall, where the trial of John Peter Zenger opened on August 4, 1735.
The New-York Historical Society, New York City

The jury of twelve headed by Thomas Hunt, Foreman, contained seven of Dutch ancestry who had no love for Cosby's arbitrary English authoritarianism. If a way could be found, they were most likely to vote according to the interests of the popular party.

Another setback for Cosby and his friends was the appearance of fifty-nine year old Andrew Hamilton to plead the cause of the defense. Hamilton had been carefully briefed on the facts of the case, including the truth of what Zenger had published against Cosby and his government, by Zenger's two previously barred lawyers, James Alexander and William Smith. Luckily, Hamilton was too famous a personage for the court to even contemplate barring him from the trial.

Zenger was being tried under an *Information* issued by Attorney General Richard Bradley, charging him with "printing and publishing parts of my *[New York Weekly]* Journal No. 13 and 23 as being *false, scandalous, malicious, and seditious.*" Zenger, of course, had not *written* these articles, the supposed authors being James Alexander and Lewis Morris. The presiding judge was James De Lancey, chief justice of the Supreme Court, and an old crony of Governor Cosby. He was assisted by Frederick Philipse, associate justice of the Supreme Court. While they could not defend Zenger, his two disbarred lawyers, James Alexander and William Smith, were present to assist Hamilton, as was John Chambers, originally designated by the court as counsel for the defense, but whom Hamilton soon overshadowed.

Diorama of the trial
of John Peter Zenger.
*Zenger Memorial Room,
Federal Hall,
New York City*

Andrew Hamilton, the famous
Philadelphia lawyer, heeded the
requests of Zenger's friends to
act as his chief defense counsel.
*Zenger Memorial Room,
Federal Hall, New York City*

The attorney general opened the proceedings:

May it please Your Honours, and you Gentlemen of the Jury: the Information now before the Court, and to which the Defendant Zenger has pleaded *Not Guilty*, is an Information for printing and publishing *a false, scandalous and seditious* Libel, in which his Excellency the Governor of this Province, who is the King's immediate Representative here, is greatly and unjustly scandalized, as a Person who has no Regard to Law nor Justice: with much more, as will appear upon reading the Information. This of Libelling is what has always been discouraged as a Thing that tends to create Differences among Men, ill Blood among the People, and oftentimes great Bloodshed between the Party Libelling and the Party Libelled. There can be no Doubt but you Gentlemen of the Jury will have the same ill Opinion of such Practices, as the Judges have always shewn upon such Occasions: but I shall say no more at the Time, until you hear the Information, which is as follows.

He then read the Information, which quoted from specific articles published in the *New York Weekly Journal* to the effect that many influential men were leaving New York because its governor arbitrarily removed judges, erected new courts without the consent of the legislature, took away jury trials as he pleased, denied certain men of influence their right to vote—all contrary to existing law.

Andrew Hamilton then rose and addressed the court with his opening remarks:

May it Please your Honour; I am concerned in this Cause on the Part of Mr. Zenger the Defendant. The Information against my Client was sent me a few Days before I left Home, with some Instructions to let me know how far I might rely upon the Truth of those Parts of the Papers set forth in the Information, and which are said to be libellous. And tho' I am perfectly of the Opinion with the gentleman who has just now spoke, on the same Side with me, as to the common Course of Proceedings, I mean in putting Mr. Attorney upon proving, that my Client printed and published those Papers mentioned in the Information; yet I cannot think it proper for me (without doing Violence to my own Principles) to deny the Publication of a Complaint, which I think is the Right of every free-born Subject to make, when the Matters so published can be supported with Truth; and therefore I'll save Mr. Attorney the Trouble of examining his Witnesses to that Point; and I do (for my Client) confess that he both printed and published the two News Papers set forth in the Information, and I hope in so doing he has committed no Crime.

"Frederick Philipse" by Henri Couturier. Philipse was an associate judge to Chief Justice James de Lancey at the Zenger trial. *The New-York Historical Society, New York City*

The witnesses, including Zenger's two sons, were released, and the chief justice ordered the trial to proceed. Attorney General Bradley sought to end the trial at that point: "Indeed, Sir, as Mr. Hamilton has confessed the Printing and Publishing these Libels, I think the Jury must find a Verdict for the King; for supposing they were true, the Law says that they are not the less libellous for that; nay indeed the Law says, their being true is an Aggravation of the Crime."

Hamilton at once remonstrated, and immediately stated the grounds on which he would conduct the defense: "Not so neither, Mr. Attorney, there are two Words to that Bargain. I hope it is not our bare Printing and Publishing a Paper, that will make it a Libel: You will have something more to do, before you make my Client a Libeller; for the Words themselves must be libellous, that is, *false, scandalous, and seditious,* or else we are not guilty." According to the law of the times, this was not strictly true, but Hamilton was relying on logic and perhaps the tenor of the people's feelings to argue against the existing common law of libel.

Bradley counteracted by citing numerous precedents and authorities to back his (and the court's) contention that it made no difference whether the libel was true or false. The government was a sacred body, and it was a crime to libel it. Hamilton rebutted by saying, "May it please Your Honour; I agree with Mr. Attorney, that Government is a sacred Thing, but I differ very widely from him when he would insinuate, that the just Complaints of a Number of Men, who suffer under a bad Administration, is libelling that Administration." He went on to suggest that the attorney general was attempting to set up a Star Chamber proceeding, now outlawed in England; that there was a wide difference between the authority of judges in Westminster Hall in England and that of provincial judges. He went on to ridicule the attorney general's doctrine: "That Truth makes a worse Libel than Falsehood." Then quoting the rule laid down by Lord Chief Justice Halt in a similar trial: "That he who would take upon him to write Things, it lies upon him to prove them at his Peril," Hamilton dramatically boomed out, "We are ready to prove them to be true, at *our* Peril." The court, however, refused to allow the defense to prove the truth to justify a libel, and admonished Hamilton to have the good manners to accept the ruling of the court.

Andrew Hamilton addresses the court and asserts that the bare printing and publishing of a paper does not make it a libel; the words themselves to be libelous must be false.

Hamilton then turned to the jury, and in one of court-room history's most dramatic moments said: "Then, Gentlemen of the Jury, it is to you we must now appeal, for Witness, to the Truth of the Facts we have offered, and are denied the Liberty to prove; and let it not seem strange, that I apply my self to you in this Manner, I am warranted so to do, both by Law and Reason." He then asked Bradley for a standard definition of libel, which Bradley gave according to the rule book.

Hamilton now pulled one of his famous courtroom tricks. He stated that words such as "scandalous," "scoffing," "ironical" had meaning only as they were *understood* by the persons judging them. Unwittingly the chief justice agreed. "Then," pursued Hamilton, "it follows that those twelve men [the jury] must understand the Words in the Information to be *scandalous,* that is to say *false;* and when they understand the Words to be so, they will say we are guilty of Publishing a false Libel, *and not otherwise.*"

The chief justice replied: "No, Mr. Hamilton, the jury may find that Zenger printed and published those Papers and leave it to the Court to judge whether they are libellous." To Hamilton—who eloquently made this clear to the jury—if this were the case, juries would in effect be rendered useless. Obviously no jury would accept such a status, and thus a defense of the rights of the jury was added to the defense of Peter Zenger.

Hamilton now launched into a lengthy and often digressive defense, punctuated with repeated interruptions by the court and the attorney general. He concluded:

The Question before the Court and you, Gentlemen of the Jury, is not of small nor private concern, it is not the Cause of a poor Printer, nor of New York alone, which you are now trying: No! It may in its Consequence, affect every Free man that lives under a British Government or the main of America. It is the best Cause. It is the Cause of Liberty; and I make no Doubt but your upright Conduct, this Day, will not only entitle you to the Love and Esteem of your Fellow-Citizens; but every Man who prefers Freedom to a Life of Slavery will bless and honour You, as Men who have baffled the Attempt of Tyranny; and by an impartial and uncorrupt Verdict, have laid a noble Foundation for securing to ourselves, our Posterity, and our Neighbours, That, to which Nature and the Laws of our Country have given us a Right—The Liberty—both of exposing and opposing arbitrary Power (in these Parts of the World, at least) by speaking and writing Truth.

Bradley made his closing comments for the prosecution, and the chief justice warned the jury to heed his charge that they were to decide only if the words set forth in the Information made a libel.

The jury withdrew. Spectacularly they were out only ten minutes, when they returned with a verdict of *not guilty.* The courtroom went wild, and demonstrated with many huzzas. Their cheers were taken up by the mob outside and spread down a street called Broadway. Freedom of the press had once for all been established in the American Colonies—a freedom that some years later was to be reaffirmed in the Constitution of the United States of America.

Facsimile of Zenger's letter of thanks to Andrew Hamilton.

John Peter Zenger was never called as witness and never uttered a word during his entire trial. It was a battle of legal minds, in which he was caught up as defendant; actually, they were trying an issue, or several of them, not a man. For this struggle, he spent almost ten months in jail, with severe personal hardships to himself and to his family, but emerged a hero in the community, a symbol of the right of subjects to stand up and criticize governmental authorities, and a never-to-be-forgotten figure in early American history.

The case of John Peter Zenger illustrates the oppressive nature of excessive bail, under which a man is held for a lengthy period awaiting trial. It provided the dramatics of two attorneys being disbarred for defending a client who was unpopular with the court; another attorney, one of exceptional prestige, ignoring the rulings of the court and then turning directly, over the heads of the court, to the jury; and finally a jury bringing in a verdict almost in direct contradiction to the instructions given it by the court. Furthermore, the Zenger case established, as no previous one had done, the concept of truth as a defense against libel.

But, most significant, no previous case made such a contribution to the right of freedom of the press. There could be no free press if governmental officials could have critics arrested, if their criticism were condemned as scandalous, if the truth of the criticism were considered irrelevant, and if the only issue in the libel case was whether the defendant was "guilty" of being the printer and publisher.

The Common Council of the City of New York honored Andrew Hamilton for his "learned and generous defense of the rights of mankind." Indeed, posterity, which has so often paid homage to Zenger, might give greater recognition to the mastermind of the case, who was not the defendant, but his learned counsel.

As for Zenger, after his trial, he continued quietly to publish books and periodicals until August 4, 1746, when he unobtrusively passed out of existence.

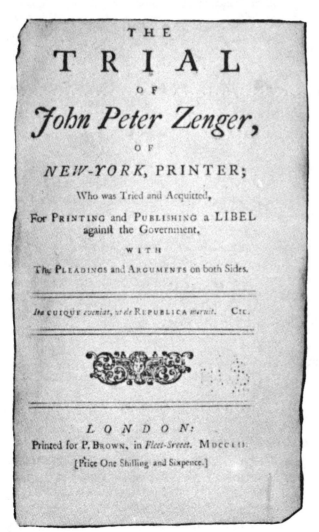

Title page of the report of the Zenger trial, published in London.

9

Louis XVI of France

[1793]

LOUIS XVI CAME TO THE THRONE OF FRANCE ON MAY 10, 1774, upon the death of his father Louis XV. He was twenty years old. The most serious problem faced by the new king was finances. In this respect he was fortunate in having first Turgot, then Necker, as his finance ministers. But in 1781 his wife, Marie Antoinette, whose love of lavish living was to be her undoing, succeeded in having Necker dismissed and her own choice, Calonne, put in charge of the finance ministry. Thus began the period of wild court extravagance that culminated in the French Revolution.

On July 14, 1789, the Bastille was taken by the Paris mob. But it was not until October 6 that they stormed Versailles, took the king and the royal family captive, and transferred them to the Tuileries. Strangely enough, the king was still popular, and on July 14, 1790, he swore to uphold the new constitution that was then being drawn up.

Fearful, however, for the safety of his family, he made the mistake of attempting to flee with them on June 20, 1791. Arrested at Varennes, he then agreed to rule as a constitutional monarch, and took his oath of office on September 13. But powerful opposition parties against Louis were growing. They forced him to declare a war against Emperor Francis II (nephew of Marie Antoinette), and, when he pursued it halfheartedly and lost, the popular hatred intensified against him and especially against the queen. On August 10, 1792, the people captured the Tuileries and suspended the power of the king. On September 21 the National Convention declared royalty in France abolished. In the following January it brought Louis XVI, former king of France, to trial for treason.

* * *

On Tuesday, January 11, 1793, at three o'clock, Louis Capet, surrounded by thirty municipal officers and large bodies of soldiers, arrived at the bar of the National Convention. President Barrère read the first charge, accusing him of suspending the assembly of the people's representatives on June 20, 1789. To which Louis answered, "There existed no laws which hindered me from doing so."

The president said, "You have caused an army to march against the citizens of Paris."

Louis replied, "I had then the power of marching my troops where I pleased."

The president then accused Louis of violating the many oaths he had taken to uphold the constitution, of attempting to flee from the Tuileries to Saint-Cloud ("That accusation is absurd," interposed Louis), of many military measures against the people, even after agreeing to rule as a constitutional monarch; of refusing to conscript enough men to fight a war against his "brothers," of destroying the French navy, and many other charges.

The president continued: "On January 26 the legislative body made a decree against the factious priests, the execution of which you have suspended."

Louis replied, "The constitution gave to me the free sanction of decrees."

The president then charged him with acts of counter-revolution, and named individuals who led them.

Louis answered: "I have no knowledge of the projects attributed to these men. Never did an idea of counter-revolution enter my head."

Louis continued in vehement denials of all the charges put to him by the president. He answered all questions assuredly and with such complete composure that he astonished all who were present. His examination lasted for two hours, at the end of which time he was allowed to choose Messieurs Target, Tronchet, and Desèze as counsel.

On Wednesday December 26, at ten o'clock, Louis and his counsel appeared before the Assembly to begin his defense.

M. Desèze spoke for him: "You have called Louis to your bar, and he appears before you with calmness and with dignity, fortified in the consciousness of his own innocence, and in the goodness of his intentions." He went on to review the events concerning the monarchy previous to its abolition, and the conduct of Louis afterward: "In 1789 the people of France demanded a monarchial form of government; now a monarchial government requires the inviolability of the chief, and

Louis XVI appearing before the Convention on December 26, 1792, to deny
the accusations that finally led him to the guillotine.

this inviolability was established, not in behalf of the king, but of the nation."

Louis's counsel was pointing out that the king had acted strictly according to the constitution, but now the Assembly was attempting to punish him under laws that never existed but were being made up for the occasion.

M. Desèze finished, and the new president, Fermont, after asking Louis a few questions, dismissed him. It was then moved that Louis's defense should be printed and distributed to the members of the Assembly within twenty-four hours and that meanwhile the Assembly should adjourn. At that, a terrific uproar took place in the galleries. The people swarmed down and in rage threatened the president unless he continued the trial until sentence had been passed. The crowd had its way, and the proceedings continued through Thursday, Friday, and Saturday. Arguments and debates became furious, with a majority disapproving of a death sentence for Louis.

On Thursday January 17, the convention voted. Of its members, 693 affirmed that "Louis is guilty of conspiring against the liberty of the nation, and of attempts against the safety of the state." On a second question, by a vote of 480 against and 282 for, they defeated the motion to put an appeal before the people.

The third and last question, "What punishment has Louis incurred?" was not answered until Friday, when the president, as the result of the *appel nominel*, declared that the punishment to be inflicted upon Louis was death. The majority vote was carried by only five members.

Desèze then asked that the sentence be appealed and that the execution of Louis be suspended. The next day a second vote was taken, and this time the death sentence was carried, not by a majority of five, but by twenty-seven votes. On the question of delaying the execution, 310 voted to do so; 380 were against delaying it.

On Monday, at ten minutes after ten in the morning, Louis Capet arrived at the guillotine, took three minutes getting out of his carriage, then mounted the scaffold. "His head was then severed from his body. The citizens dipped their pikes and handkerchiefs in his blood."

*   *   *

Louis XVI was not, as one member of the National Assembly referred to him, the *last king* of France. For a brief period in France's tumultuous political history, the monarchy did return. But, as with the death of Charles I in England, the days of the absolute monarchy in France were gone. The course of the path of history was clearly emerging, in which many peoples of the world would have the ultimate voice in who would lead their individual nations.

J. WILKES BOOTH.

THE

PAYNE

GEORGE E. ATZERODT.

DAVID E. HEROLD.

MRS. MARY E. SURRATT.

CONSPIRATORS.

SAMUEL ARNOLD.

MICHAEL O'LAUGHLIN.

EDWARD SPANGLER.

JOHN SURRATT.

10

Mary Surratt and
The Lincoln Conspirators

[1865]

AMERICA HAS FOUGHT MANY WARS DURING THE TWO centuries since the Colonies declared their independence from England, but none more bloody, none more filled with hatred, than the conflict that tore the country asunder in the midyears of the nineteenth century. From 1861, when the inauguration of Lincoln was followed by the secession of South Carolina, the attack on Fort Sumter, and the formation of the Confederate States of America, until April, 1865, when the surrender of Lee at Appomattox marked the end of all but token resistance, suffering reached new heights, and Union men and rebels alike were filled with rancor.

Lee's surrender to Grant took place on April 9, 1865, and although not at all unexpected, for the Confederate cause had been militarily deteriorating for some months, it brought joy and hope to millions in the North, and at the least the prospect of peace to those in the South. By telegraph and by courier, news of the victory of Grant's forces reached all parts of the country; in Chicago, 100,000 people poured out on the streets, perhaps the greatest demonstration that a huge city in the New World had ever witnessed.

A short time later, under less joyous conditions, Walt Whitman was to write:

The port is near, the bells, I hear, the people all exulting,
While follow eyes the steady keel, the vessel grim
    and daring . . .

The bells of victory could be heard, and the port of destination was indeed being neared. But the poet also heard the voice of tragedy:

But O heart! heart! heart!
O the bleeding drops of red,

Where on the deck my Captain lies
Fallen cold and dead.

On Good Friday, April 14, 1865, seated in a box at the Ford Theatre in Washington was the "Captain," President Abraham Lincoln. In the box were his wife, who had sent the guard away on an errand, and two young guests of the President, Clara Harris and her fiancé Major Henry Rathbone. At a moment that is today probably the best remembered cue in the history of drama, an actor stepped into the President's box and fired a shot. In his home a short distance away, the Secretary of State, William H. Seward, was attacked by an assailant, and seriously injured. By the next morning the President was dead. For this crime, four persons (including one woman, Mary Eugenia Jenkins Surratt) would go to the gallows after a trial that left many questions unanswered. The man who fired the shot (and that he did is one of the few undisputed facts in the matter) was to escape and probably be killed less than two weeks later, but rumors that he lived were to continue for half a century. One of the accused escaped from the country, allegedly with the aid of his coreligionists, finally to be compelled to return, stand for a trial in which there was a hung jury, and then be included in a highly controversial presidential amnesty. If the trial and execution of Mary Surratt are today all but forgotten and are granted only a few lines even in historical works dealing with the Civil War and Reconstruction, in 1865 they fanned imaginations, inflamed the spirits of America, and left in their wake bitterness and anger against President Andrew Johnson, the Catholic Church, the military tribunal, the radical Republicans, and other groups in the still-disunited states of America.

✻   ✻   ✻

President Abraham Lincoln.
Photograph by A. Gardner, April 10, 1865.
Library of Congress

The Booths were more than a family of actors; many considered them the first family of the stage in the United States. But like many others, the Booths were divided in their loyalties; some were supporters of the Blue, some of the Gray. Edwin Booth, generally considered the outstanding Shakespearean actor of the period, loved the Union and admired Lincoln; his brother John Wilkes Booth, somewhat less successful in their chosen career, was equally devoted to the Confederacy.

During the latter months of 1864 and early 1865, as Union victory seemed more and more imminent, John Wilkes Booth met with several other strong sympathizers of the cause of the South, including former Confederate soldiers and at least one courier or spy. Together they discussed plots, some so dramatic that they must be considered as the fantasies of an imaginative actor more than as the conspiracies of a realistic plotter. Most serious of their plans, and one that came closest to fruition,

was to kidnap the President of the United States, and hold him—but for what? Perhaps for the ransom of thousands of Confederate soldiers, prisoners of war in the North whose return to the Army of the South would immeasurably aid in the revival of the faltering Confederate war effort. A bold move, this kidnapping might throw the entire Union general staff into disarray, and with collapse of morale there might follow the collapse of the armed struggle.

But the kidnapping plan, laid out by Booth and many of his friends with great care, came to naught when the President's itinerary was changed and he did not appear in his carriage on a route on which he had been expected. And now, confronted with Appomattox and the surrender of Lee, Booth must act quickly and dramatically. It is said that he resolved that the man in the White House must be murdered when he heard a speech in whch Lincoln called for granting the right to vote to "intelligent" Negroes.

Abraham Lincoln reading his second inaugural speech. Booth and possibly other conspirators are in the crowd.
National Archives

John Wilkes Booth, Lincoln's assassin.
National Archives

Was this part of a conspiracy that had its roots in the highest echelons of the Confederacy or even of northern political power groups? Or was it the dramatic climax of an actor turned madman? That Booth had fellow conspirators, both in the kidnap plot and in the assassination, there can be no doubt; many of them, in fact, later confessed. But who they were, what connections (if any) they had with important figures in the Confederacy or in the Union, and what tasks each was to take for himself—these are questions that have never been clarified to the satisfaction of historians.

Deep in the kidnap plot was a Confederate spy (or a double agent?), young John Surratt, whose widowed mother had moved from Maryland to Washington and there opened a boardinghouse. Among the boarders was Louis Weichmann (or Wiechmann; many of the names are given alternate spellings, and several of the plotters adopted aliases on occasion). Weichmann and young Surratt had known each other in seminary school. Together they plotted, but Weichmann also seems to have been close to what is today called a "double agent," aiding Surratt on the one hand, and then sending news of the plans to the War Department. In the Surratt home there lived John's sister, Anna, a cousin, and a few boarders who seem not to have become involved. It was in this home that a motley crew of Confederate spies, some former Confederate soldiers, held conferences with John Wilkes Booth.

Perhaps no one in the Surratt home knew all that was being planned, not even John. On the other hand, it is difficult to believe that anyone in the home could have been innocent of knowledge that some poison was brewing in the witches' caldron. Finally, as the southern collapse became complete and time was itself escaping irretrievably from the hands of the plotters, Booth chose the night of April 14 for the execution of his plans. The President would be in his box at the Ford Theatre, where Booth had frequently acted and to which he had access. At a given cue, Booth would step into the President's box, draw a gun, and shoot. A young stagehand, holding a horse outside the theatre, would assist in the getaway, while a co-conspirator, David Herold, would meet Booth at a prearranged spot and join him in the escape. Several other high officers were supposedly slated for simultaneous assassination: the Vice-President, the Secretary of State, the Secretary of War, and the hero of the Union armies, General Ulysses S. Grant.

At the Ford Theatre, the bill that night was a comedy called *Our American Cousin* (probably, by tragic accident, the best-known nineteenth-century American drama). Like an actor who required little rehearsal and was confident that he could play his role flawlessly, at 10:10 P.M. Booth quietly entered the President's box from behind, and delivered the shot that was to prove fatal. The President of the United States slumped over in a chair. Booth himself was recognized by many in the audience as he stepped out of the box to jump onto the stage. During the jump, he evidently fell and broke a leg. He quickly arose, and limped hastily to the stage door, where Edward Spangler was awaiting him. He got on the horse as Spangler slammed a door in the face of a pursuer, and rode away.

Ford's Theatre, Washington, D.C., where Tom Taylor's comedy *Our American Cousin* was playing on the evening of April 14, 1865, when the Lincoln party attended.
National Park Service

Booth shoots Lincoln in his box at Ford's Theatre. Watching the play with Lincoln are Mrs. Lincoln, Miss Clara Harris, and Major Henry R. Rathbone.

The single-shot Deringer used by Booth in the shooting of Abraham Lincoln.
National Park Service

After firing the fatal shot, Booth leaped to the stage. In doing so, he caught the spur on his right heel in the fringe of the Treasury Guard's flag and fell on the stage, injuring his left leg.
Library of Congress

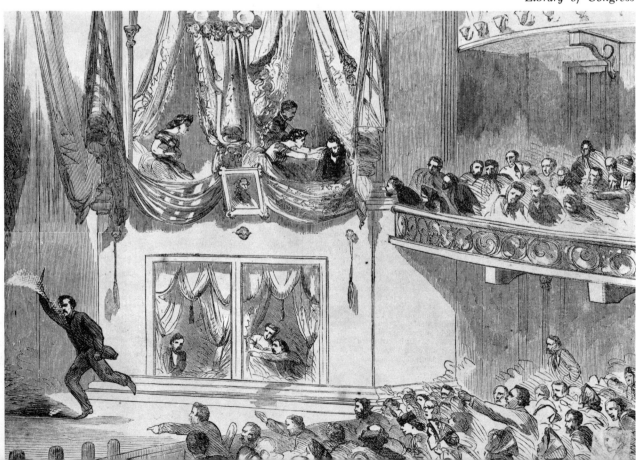

Booth turns to shout defiance at his pursuers, then dashes for the stage door.
National Park Service

Booth escapes on a horse a youth has waiting for him at the back of Ford's Theatre.

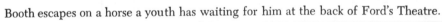

In an atmosphere of so many witnesses, and amid the confusion and pandemonium, an assassin stands an excellent opportunity of escaping, and this Booth did. He was off on his horse within minutes. On the same night, Secretary of State William Seward was attacked in his home, and left severely wounded and almost dead, while his assailant likewise fled. If there was a plot to include Johnson among the victims (as was charged in the trial, and for which a man went to the gallows), somewhere it misfired, for the Vice-President retired early, and was not disturbed until he was brought the news of the events of the evening of Good Friday. As for General Grant, he was out of town. All night Lincoln lay between life and death, and in the morning he expired. Some three hours later, Andrew Johnson took the oath of office, and War Secretary Edwin Stanton took command of the search for the criminals.

    ❊   ❊   ❊

John Wilkes Booth, already recognized and with a large reward having been offered for his capture, was in dire need of medical attention. He met David Herold in accordance with previous arrangements, and they made their way to Maryland, coming to the home of Dr. Samuel Mudd. Booth had met Mudd before, and had known him as a rebel sympathizer; now Booth was wearing a crude disguise, including whiskers that anyone could recognize as being store-bought. Booth and Herold gave false names, but it is difficult to believe that Dr. Mudd did not recognize them and did not suspect that they were fugitives, although news of the assassination had not yet reached him. Having received medical aid, Booth and Herold departed. Four days later, Mudd, now aware that Lincoln had been killed and that Booth was the most wanted man in America, became worried that he might become caught in the net and be accused of having harbored and aided the assassins of the President.

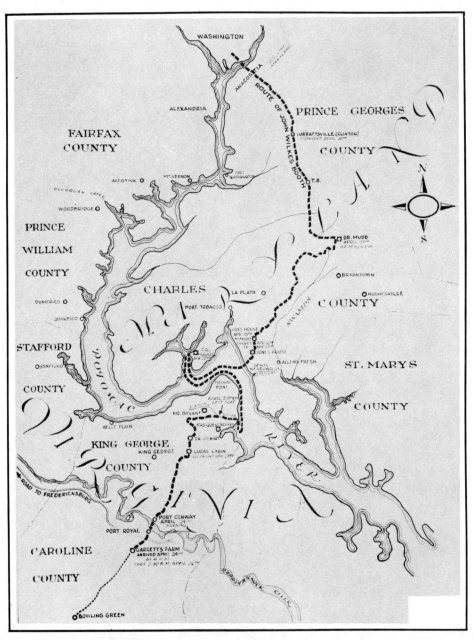

Map of Booth's flight.
National Park Service

He therefore told his brother about the two strangers who had come to him, and his brother promptly reported this to the authorities. Perhaps the conversation with his brother saved Dr. Samuel Mudd from dying with a rope around his neck.

Trailed by a huge number of federal police, Booth and Herold were traced to a farm in Virginia, where they had been hidden in a barn. By this time the names of the assassin and several of his accomplices were known, and large rewards were being offered for their capture. The federal agents were certain that Booth was being harbored at the Garrett farm—so certain that when the elder Garrett would not disclose the place of concealment, a rope was placed around his neck and he was threatened with being hanged on the spot. At this point, one of the younger Garretts volunteered information on the hideout.

Secretary of War Edwin M. Stanton, believed by some to have been involved in the conspiracy.
Library of Congress, Brady-Handy Collection

Kirkwood House, where both Vice-President Andrew Johnson and George Atzerodt stayed. Atzerodt reneged at the last moment at killing Johnson.
National Park Service

Secretary of State William H. Seward, who was also marked for assassination by the Lincoln conspirators. He was seriously injured, apparently by Lewis Paine.
Library of Congress, Brady-Handy Collection

David Herold surrendered soon after the police started shooting at the barn where they had hidden; but Booth refused to follow his accomplice into the hands of his enemy. Finally, the barn was set afire (later Edwin Booth was to compensate the Garretts for its loss), and the man who had been inside with Herold was shot. Shot by himself or by another is but one of the many unanswered mysteries, but far less a mystery than whether this man was indeed John Wilkes Booth. He died about an hour later, and his body was sent to Washington. Several years later, it was turned over to the Booth family for private interment.

Had John Surratt been assigned a role in the events of the assassination night? It is difficult to believe that he was not; if there was one person who had been the major conspirator with Booth in the kidnapping plans, it was young Surratt. But with a large reward for him, he was nowhere to be found; by the time the other prisoners came to trial, he was in Canada, safely watching the events in the United States from the sanctuary of the home of a priest. Conflicting evidence was later to be introduced as to his whereabouts at the time Lincoln was murdered. If, as was claimed, he was seen in Elmira, New York, the next day, then it would have been impossible for him to have been in Washington at the time of the murder. Furthermore, if the assassination was hastily planned only a day or two before Good Friday, it is entirely possible that he might have been omitted from any role, if only because he was not present.

It took but two weeks after the assassination to round up the men who had been known to be accomplices of Booth—all the men, that is, except John Surratt himself. The boardinghouse of Surratt's mother was under suspicion and constant surveillance. It was this house on H Street where, it was to be charged in court and repeated in the words of the new President, Andrew Johnson, Mrs. Surratt "kept the nest that hatched the egg." So the arrests began. Of the many taken into custody, eight were finally brought to trial. Of the eight, central attention was focused on John's mother, Mary Surratt. The remaining, lacking in luster, could hardly capture the imagination of the public. True, there was Jefferson Davis, but he had not been captured, and was being tried only *in absentia*. While he had led the rebellion, no one ever made out a strong case against him for complicity in the assassination plot. There were Booth, but he was presumably dead, and John Surratt, a fugitive. So the center of this huge stage was now being held by the fifty-year-old widow.

Booth was found hiding with David Herold in a barn on Garrett's Farm near Port Royal, Virginia, on April 26, 1865. A body, presumably that of Booth, is dragged from the burning barn.

War Department, Washington, April 20, 1865.

$100,000 REWARD!

THE MURDERER

Of our late beloved President, ABRAHAM LINCOLN,

IS STILL AT LARGE.

$50,000 REWARD!

will be paid by this Department for his apprehension, in addition to any reward offered by Municipal Authorities or State Executives.

$25,000 REWARD!

will be paid for the apprehension of JOHN H. SURRATT, one of Booth's accomplices.

$25,000 REWARD!

will be paid for the apprehension of DANIEL C. HARROLD, another of Booth's accomplices.

LIBERAL REWARDS will be paid for any information that shall conduce to the arrest of either of the above-named criminals, or their accomplices.

All persons harboring or secreting the said persons, or either of them, or aiding or assisting their concealment or escape, will be treated as accomplices in the murder of the President and the attempted assassination of the Secretary of State, and shall be subject to trial before a Military Commission and the punishment of DEATH.

Let the stain of innocent blood be removed from the land by the arrest and punishment of the murderers.

All good citizens are exhorted to aid public justice on this occasion. Every man should consider his own conscience charged with this solemn duty, and rest neither night nor day until it be accomplished.

EDWIN M. STANTON, Secretary of War.

DESCRIPTIONS.—BOOTH is 5 feet 7 or 8 inches high, slender build, high forehead, black hair, black eyes, and wears a heavy black moustache.

JOHN H. SURRATT is about 5 feet 9 inches. Hair rather thin and dark; eyes rather light; no beard. Would weigh 145 or 150 pounds. Complexion rather pale and clear, with color in his cheeks. Wore light clothes of fine quality. Shoulders square; cheek bones rather prominent; chin narrow; ears projecting at the top; forehead rather low and square, but broad. Parts his hair on the right side; neck rather long. His lips are firmly set. A slim man.

DANIEL C. HARROLD is 22 years of age, 5 feet 6 or 7 inches high, rather low foreheaded, otherwise light built; dark hair, dark eyes, Side (if any) moustache; dark eyes; weighs about 140 pounds.

GEO. F. NESBITT & CO., Printers and Stationers, cor. Pearl and Pine Streets, N. Y.

Poster offering rewards for the murderer of Abraham Lincoln and for the apprehension of John Surratt and David C. Herold.
Library of Congress

Poster offering a reward for the arrest of Jefferson Davis and other southern leaders.

Headquarters, United States Forces, Athens, Ga., May 9th, 1865.

$360,000 REWARD!

THE PRESIDENT OF THE UNITED STATES

HAS ISSUED HIS PROCLAMATION announcing that the Bureaus of Military Justice have reported upon indubitable evidence, that

JEFFERSON DAVIS,

Clement Clay. Jacob Thompson.

GEORGE N. SAUNDERS:

BEVERLEY TUCKER AND W. C. CLEARY,

incited and concerted the assassination of Mr. Lincoln and the attempt on Mr. Seward. He therefore offers for the arrest of Davis, Clay and Thompson, One Hundred Thousand Dollars each; for that of Saunders and Tucker, Twenty-Five Thousand Dollars each, and for that of Cleary, Ten Thousand Dollars.

By command of

Br'v't Brig Gen. WM. J PALMER, Com'd'g.

Henry Mc. Mister, Jr. Capt. & A. A. A. G.

The home of Mary Surratt at 541 Eighth Street, Washington, D.C., called by President Andrew Johnson the nest where the plot was hatched.
Library of Congress

The gallows were still widely used in America, but to hang a woman was an act likely to arouse sympathies that would not be forthcoming if the criminal were male. Mrs. Surratt's relationship with the plot was tenuous. Some evidence would be brought against her, but hardly enough to convict beyond a reasonable doubt and in reasonable times. But these were not reasonable times.

For Mary Surratt was arrested and brought to trial primarily for one reason: because her son John was a fugitive. With Booth presumably dead, John had become the most wanted man in the United States. Perhaps anger and revenge motivated the arrest and prosecution of the woman, and perhaps the hope that, with his mother held virtually as a hostage, John would return to Washington and stand trial himself.

If Mary Surratt was the central figure, it was not felt that she was the most likely to be doomed in the Greek-like tragedy that was being unfolded in the court. There was Lewis Paine (sometimes known as Payne, but also called by a variety of pseudonyms). Son of a Baptist preacher, Paine was accused of having assaulted Seward on the night of the assassination. Few thought the rope would not tighten around his neck.

Nor did anyone expect mercy for David Herold, who had assisted in the escape of Booth. One could plead his youth (he was but nineteen), but hardly his innocence.

An almost equally strong case was made out against George A. Atzerodt, accused of lying in wait for the Vice-President, "with the intent unlawfully and maliciously to kill and murder him, the said Andrew Johnson." That he knew of the plot and had participated in the planning stage there can be no doubt; the best that can be said of him is that he got drunk and lost his nerve. Or was it arranged from the very beginning that Johnson was to be spared?

Dr. Samuel Mudd was accused of being more than the physician who treated Booth at the time of his escape. The charge against him read that, on various days between March 6 and April 20, 1865, he did "advise, encourage, receive, entertain, harbor and conceal, aid and assist" John Wilkes Booth, the Surratts, and the other defendants, "with knowledge of the murderous and traitorous conspiracy aforesaid, and with the intent to aid, abet and assist them in the execution thereof and in escaping from justice after the murder of the said Abraham Lincoln."

If Mudd was to pay dearly for preparing a splint, Edward Spangler would do likewise for slamming a door. Against Samuel Arnold, there was a charge that he had been part of the conspiracy group that had planned the abduction; against Michael O'Laughlin, that he had not only been one of the conspirators but had also accepted the assignment to lie in wait for Ulysses S. Grant.

* * *

The trial of Herold, Surratt, and the other six opened in Washington on May 9, 1865, less than a month after the assassination, and from the first day it was marked by controversy and recrimination. The defendants were brought to the court, a large, gloomy, makeshift room in the same building in which they were imprisoned. In the words of Philip Van Doren Stern, "all except for Mrs. Surratt and Dr. Mudd had their hands fastened to thick iron bars ten inches long." The doctor was in ordinary handcuffs fastened to each other by chains, while the lady of the trial was being treated with decorum, her hands and feet both free. Steel anklets were on some of the defendants, iron weights on the feet of others.

Lewis Paine under arrest.
National Archives

The prisoners were allowed from one to three days to obtain counsel and prepare their cases; and for the first day the trial was held in secret court, a Star Chamber proceeding that was opened up to the press, by public demand, immediately thereafter.

From the first, the court was challenged, on the grounds that it had no jurisdiction, for it was a military tribunal. On May 1, President Johnson had issued an order, in which he cited an opinion of the Attorney General of the United States:

That the persons implicated in the murder of the late President, Abraham Lincoln, and the attempted assassination of the Honorable William H. Seward, Secretary of State, and in an alleged conspiracy to assassinate other officers of the Federal Government at Washington City, and their aiders and abettors, are subject to the jurisdiction of, and lawful triable before, a Military Commission.

The ruling was defended on the grounds that the United States was at war and that the President was commander in chief of the Armed Forces. In a longer opinion given by Attorney General James Speed to the President in July, the conclusion was reached that

if the persons who are charged with the assassination of the President committed the deed as public enemies, as I believe they did, and whether they did or not is a question to be decided by the tribunal before which they are tried, they not only can, but ought to be tried before a military tribunal. If the persons charged have offended against the laws of war, it would be as palpably wrong to hand them over to the civil courts, as it would be wrong in a civil court to convict a man of murder who had, in time of war, killed another in battle.

Lewis Paine in his cell awaiting his trial. The male prisoners were manacled and hooded, with only thin slots at the nose and mouth of the hood for breathing.

The old Penitentiary Building in Washington, D.C., where the conspirators were jailed and where the trial took place.

The defendants argued that the court did not have jurisdiction, on the grounds that the accused were not members of the Armed Forces (most of them had never been in the military service of the United States), and that "'loyal civil courts, in which all the offenses charged are triable, exist, and are in full and free operation." The military court, under the leadership of Judge Advocate General Joseph Holt, overruled the pleas. Thereupon the defendants asked that their cases be tried separately, each defendant stating that "he believes his defense will be greatly prejudiced by a joint trial," and this too was denied.

The trial then got under way. It was a strange trial by twentieth-century standards. For today, when the courts are so preciously guarding the right of a defendant not to be compelled to testify, at that time a defendant did not have the right to appear on the stand in his own behalf. Before the opening of the trial, not only were the prisoners kept in solitary confinement but also all the males had canvas hoods placed over their faces, with openings only for their mouths so that they might breathe and eat, a precaution allegedly taken to prevent suicide. For it is an irony of modern man that, even in instances in which the state will demand the life of a prisoner, the latter may never cheat the executioner of his prey.

The trial lasted for six weeks. By May 23 the prosecution had brought its array of witnesses; by June 10 the defense had completed its presentation and was resting. There was rebuttal on both sides, taking a total of four days. On the last two days of June, after the final presentation of the case against the prisoners by Special Judge Advocate John A. Bingham, the case went to the military judges, who deliberated for two days. But before that, let us take a look at the principal witnesses.

There was Louis J. Weichmann, of course. He had been a boarder in the Surratt house, and had been present at many conspiratorial meetings. He may have been a part of the plot and perhaps was turning state's evidence in order to save himself. He had shared a room and a bed with John Surratt, in a relationship that one modern author suggests may have been homosexual (both men remained unmarried); and he had driven Mrs. Surratt to Maryland on the afternoon of the assassination, under circumstances that threw considerable suspicion on her part in the murder. He was to link Mudd with Booth and Surratt, suggesting that Mudd may have mapped out an escape route on the back of an envelope. Louis J. Weichmann, a witness for the prosecution, being duly sworn, testified as follows:

The trial of the conspirators in
session in the courtroom of the
old Penitentiary.
Library of Congress

The full military court that tried
the Lincoln conspirators.
*National Archives,
Brady Collection*

JUDGE ADVOCATE. Will you state whether you know John H. Surratt?

A. I do.

Q. When did you first make his acquaintance?

A. My acquaintance with John H. Surratt commenced in the fall of 1859, at St. Charles's College, Maryland.

Q. How long were you together?

A. We left college in the summer of 1862, in July, together.

Q. When did you renew your acquaintance with him here in this city?

A. I renewed my acquaintance with him in 1863, in January in this city.

Q. State when you first made the acquaintance of the prisoner, Dr. Samuel A. Mudd?

A. It was about the 15th of January, 1865.

Q. State under what circumstances.

A. I was passing down Seventh Street, in company with Mr. Surratt; and, when opposite Odd Fellows' Hall, some one called, "Surratt, Surratt!" and, turning round, Mr. Surratt recognized an old acquaintance of his, Dr. Samuel A. Mudd, of Charles County, Maryland.

Q. The prisoner at the bar?

A. Yes, sir: that is the gentleman there (pointing to Samuel A. Mudd). Mr. Surratt introduced Dr. Mudd to me; and Dr. Mudd introduced Mr. Booth, who was in company with him, to both of us.

Q. He and Booth were walking together in the street?

A. Yes, sir. They were coming up Seventh Street, and we were going down.

Q. You mean J. Wilkes Booth?

A. Yes, sir: J. Wilkes Booth.

Q. Where did you go to from that, when you went?

A. Booth then invited us to his room at the National Hotel.

Q. What occurred there?

A. Booth told us to be seated; and he ordered cigars and wines to the room for four. Dr. Mudd then went out into the passage, and called Booth out, and had a private conversation with him. Booth and Dr. Mudd came in, and they then called Surratt out.

Q. Both of them called him out?

A. No, sir: Booth went out with Surratt; and then they came in, and all three went out together, and had a private conversation in the passage, leaving me alone.

Q. How long did that conversation last?

A. It must have been about fifteen or twenty minutes.

Q. You did not hear what it was?

A. No, sir: I do not know the nature of the conversation. I was seated on a lounge at the time, near the window. On returning to the room the last time, Dr. Mudd came to me, and seated himself by my side on the settee; and he apologized for his private conversation, stating that Booth and he had some private business; that Booth wished to purchase his farm.

Q. Did you see any maps or papers of that sort used?

A. No, sir. Booth at one time took out the back of an envelope, and made marks on it with a pencil. I should not consider it writing, but more in the direction of roads or lines. Surratt and Booth and Dr. Mudd were at that time seated round the table,—a centre-table,—in the centre of the room.

Q. Did you see the marks?

A. No, sir: I just saw the motion of the pencil. Booth also came to me, and stated that he wished to purchase Dr. Mudd's farm. Dr. Mudd had previously stated to me that he did not care about selling his farm to Booth, because Booth was not going to give him enough.

Sketches of the trial personalities by an eyewitness.

Continuing on the stand, Weichmann told of frequent calls of Booth on Mrs. Mary Surratt, of having seen the two together on the afternoon of the assassination, and of having driven Mrs. Surratt to the country immediately thereafter, where she delivered a package from the actor to one Mr. Lloyd. On this matter, Weichmann was cross-examined:

MR. JOHNSON.   I understood you to say on Saturday that you went with Mrs. Surratt the first time to Surrattsville, on the Tuesday before the assassination, in a buggy with her. Do you recollect whether you stopped on your way to Surrattsville?

A. Yes, sir.

Q. Where?

A. We stopped on two or three different occasions.

Q. Did you stop at Uniontown?

A. I do not know the name of the particular town. I do not know where Uniontown is.

Q. Did you stop at a village?

A. We stopped on the road: I do not remember any particular village that could be seen.

Q. Do you know Mr. Lloyd?

A. I have met him three times.

Q. Did you know him as the keeper of the hotel at Surrattsville?

A. I knew him as the man who had rented Mrs. Surratt's house from her, because I copied off the instrument.

Q. Do you recollect seeing him by the buggy at any time on your way between Washington and Surrattsville on that Tuesday?

A. Yes, sir: we met his carriage. His carriage drove past ours; and Mrs. Surratt called after Mr. Lloyd; and Mr. Lloyd got out and approached the buggy; and Mrs. Surratt put her head out, and had a conversation with him.

Q. From the buggy?

A. Yes, sir.

Q. Did you hear it?

A. No, sir.

Q. Did you hear any thing that was said?

A. No, sir.

Q. Any thing about shooting-irons?

A. There was nothing mentioned at all about shooting-irons. Mrs. Surratt spoke to Mr. Offutt about this man Howell. Mrs. Surratt was in the carriage: she said she was going to see him, and see if he would not take the oath of allegiance and get released, and that she was going to apply to General Augur and Judge Turner for the purpose.

Q. How long was the interview between Mr. Lloyd and Mrs. Surratt on that occasion?

A. That I could not say exactly: I do not think it was over five or eight minutes. I do not carry a watch myself, and I had no precise means of judging.

Perhaps the most damaging evidence against Mrs. Surratt was her reaction on the night of her arrest. While the arresting officers were at her home, Paine arrived, dressed as a workman. Sizing up the situation, he pretended that he had come to dig a gutter (at eleven thirty o'clock at night!). Mrs. Surratt denied that she knew the man at all. She is reported to have exclaimed: "Be-

fore God, I have not seen that man before; I have not hired him; I don't know anything about him." Later, her daughter and others were to claim that this denial was in no way a sign of her guilt, but rather simply a matter of a woman with poor eyesight not recognizing the visitor.

Anna E. Surratt, a witness called for the accused, Mary E. Surratt, being duly sworn, testified as follows:

MR. AIKEN.   State your full name to the Court.

A. Anna E. Surratt.

Q. Are you under arrest at the present time?

A. Yes, sir.

Q. When were you arrested? and where have you been confined since?

A. I was arrested on the 17th of April.

Q. State whether or not you are aware of frequent instances where your mother has failed to recognize her friends.

A. Yes, sir: her eyesight is very bad, and has been for some time past; and she often fails to recognize those whom she knows well.

Q. Is she able to read or sew by gaslight?

A. No, sir; not for some time past.

Q. Have you often plagued her about getting spectacles?

A. Yes, sir: I told her she was too young-looking to wear spectacles just yet. She said she could not do without them, that she could not sew or read, and very often she could not recognize those she knew best.

Q. Could she read or sew on a dark morning?

A. No, sir: she made out to read some, but she very seldom sewed, on a dark day.

Her mother's eyesight was not the only matter on which Anna Surratt was interrogated:

Q. Were you acquainted with J. Wilkes Booth?

A. Yes, sir: I have met him.

Q. Do you recollect the last time he was at your house?

A. Yes, sir; he was there on Friday or Monday—I do not know which day it was. I did not see him. I heard he had been there.

Q. Did your mother go to Surrattsville that day?

A. She went there on Friday, the day of the assassination.

Q. Was her carriage ordered, or not, and at the door to go to Surrattsville, at the time Mr. Booth called?

A. I think it was. I heard some one come up the steps just as ma was ready to start and the buggy was at the door. I had been out, and when I came in I found ma preparing to go to the country. She had been talking about it during the day, before Booth came, and perhaps the day before. She said she was obliged to go on business in regard to some land.

Q. How long did Mr. Booth remain there at that time?

A. But a very few minutes. He never staid very long when he came.

Of David Herold, the case was well-nigh airtight, the defense merely perfunctory. Character witnesses said that they considered him unreliable and boyish, but there was nothing objectionable in his character. "He was light and trifling in a great many things, more like a boy then a man . . . easily persuaded and led."

Edward Spangler was a minor figure in the affair. Against him, a prosecution witness, Jacob Ritterspaugh, a carpenter at Ford's Theatre, told of the door having been slammed by Spangler as he, Ritterspaugh, was in pursuit of the assassin. Employees of the theatre contradicted the testimony, described Spangler as a simple man who, at most, was used as a tool of Booth. That he was part of any great conspiracy no one seriously contended.

Nor was the case against Michael O'Laughlin and Samuel Arnold any stronger. Their landlady was Mrs. Van Tine, and she testified that John Wilkes Booth frequently came to her house to visit the two defendants, while another witness told of having delivered a letter from Booth to O'Laughlin, and a telegram with cryptic contents also came from the same source. In his defense, it was shown that Booth and O'Laughlin had been friends since early boyhood and that O'Laughlin had surrendered voluntarily when he knew he was wanted, and had protested his innocence from the moment of arrest.

Of O'Laughlin's roommate, the prosecution introduced a confession, in which he implicated not only several defendants but Booth and John Surratt, as well. In defense, it was claimed that O'Laughlin and Arnold had broken off their association with Booth several weeks before the assassination.

The case of Paine is particularly interesting, because some historians have claimed that the accused was an innocent stand-in for another person, by the name of Powell, who actually assaulted the Secretary of State on the night of Good Friday. But he was not only identified by a servant, nurse, and son of William H. Seward, but Paine's lawyer, Doster, admitted this part of the charge. Doster made Paine a victim of circumstances and environment, an impassioned fighter for the cause in which he fervently believed:

We now know that this Florida boy is not a fiend, but an object rather of compassion. We now know that slavery made him immoral, that war made him a murderer, and that necessity, revenge, and delusion made him an assassin. . . . We know that, from his point of view, he justified the murder of our Secretary of State; we know that, from our standpoint, we would gladly have seen, for four years, the death of the rebel Secretary of State.

It was a curious defense, arising from a note of utter hopelessness, and it could not have convinced a judge to bring in other than a guilty verdict.

Of George A. Atzerodt, the evidence that he was part of the conspiracy is overwhelming. In fact, his attorney attempted to introduce a confession, in which he would state the extent of his guilt and of his innocence. "He asks his statement to be placed on record," Mr. Doster stated for the defendant, "because he has been debarred from calling any other prisoners who might be witnesses, for the reason that they are co-defendants." To this the judge advocate sternly warned: "It is greatly to be deplored that the counsel for the accused will urge upon the Court proposals which they know to be contrary to law." In the direct examination of Samuel McAllister for the defense, the entire defense can be summed up in this colloquy:

Q. Do you know anything about his [Atzerodt's] reputation for courage.
ASSISTANT JUDGE ADVOCATE BINGHAM. I object to that; I do not think we are going to try his character for courage.
MR. DOSTER. May it please the Court, I intend to show that this man is a constitutional coward; that if he had been assigned the duty of assassinating the Vice-President, he never could have done it; and that, from his known cowardice, Booth probably did not assign him to any such duty.

Against Samuel Mudd, there were many statements of association with Booth and the Surratts, the mysterious writing on the envelope, and his aid to the stranger with the broken leg. In his favor, witnesses testified that his dealings with Booth concerned the sale of land, that he reported the visit of the two strangers to his brother, and that his reputation was above reproach.

This was the case against the conspirators.

Thus they paraded, character witnesses for the prisoners, damaging evidence that placed conspirators in the home of Mrs. Surratt but that failed definitely to link her with knowledge of the assassination. Whether she was an unwitting tool of Booth in delivery of field glasses when she went to Surrattsville with Weichmann, or whether she was an accessory before the fact, can probably not be ascertained with certainty today. That she would not, by the trial record, be adjudged guilty beyond a reasonable doubt in a twentieth-century American court, cannot be gainsaid, but this hardly establishes her innocence.

On the last day of June, 1865, at 10:00 A.M., the commission reached its verdict, separate for each defendant. As expected, Herold, Atzerodt, and Paine were given the death penalty. The case against Mudd, Arnold, and O'Laughlin was somewhat weaker; they were sentenced to life imprisonment. Spangler, who may have been another unwitting tool of Booth, was ordered to jail for six years. And Mrs. Surratt? Here, the court sentenced "her, the said Mary E. Surratt, to be hanged by the neck until she is dead, at such time and place as the President of the United States shall direct; two-thirds of the members of the commission concurring therein."

Nevertheless, the fight for Mrs. Surratt was not yet over. A plea for clemency was signed by five members of the commission; whether this plea ever reached the President, and if not who blocked it, became a matter of serious controversy years later.

The executions were set for Friday, July 7, exactly twelve weeks after the assassination. When it is considered that the verdict was not made public until two days earlier, it is seen with what rapidity it was carried out.

Hope for the three males sentenced to die was almost nil, but until the moment that she stepped upon the scaffold, the family and friends of Mrs. Surratt expected intervention. Her daughter, now freed from prison, made a desperate effort to see the President, but was denied entrance—denied by whom? This is only one of innumerable points in historical dispute. A writ of habeas corpus was granted, but just as rapidly it was declared lacking in validity. In the courtyard of the building where the prisoners had been housed these many long hot weeks, just outside the windows of the room where they had been tried, the gallows were erected. There, on a hot July day, with a huge crowd watching and approving, they marched to their deaths, three men and a woman.

Only one person could have saved Mary Surratt, and that was her son. From Canada, he made his way to England, and then to Italy, where he joined the Papal Zouaves, under another name. Whether anyone in the Vatican knew his identity is again unknown, but he was recognized by an American, his presence reported, was arrested, and escaped. Rearrested soon afterwards, he was brought back to America to stand trial, this time before a civilian court.

The hanging of Mary Surratt, Lewis Paine, George Atzerodt, and David Herold. Imprisoned were Michael O'Laughlin, Edward Spangler, Samuel Arnold, and Dr. Samuel Mudd. O'Laughlin died in prison. The rest were later pardoned.
National Archives

John Surratt, who refused to return from abroad to save his mother from the gallows. Apprehended in Italy, he escaped, was caught, and brought back to the U.S. His trial, in June, 1867, ended in a hung jury, and the case was declared *nolle prosse.*
Library of Congress, Brady-Handy Collection

The trial of John Harrison Surratt opened in Washington, on June 10, 1867, and in many ways it was the second trial of his mother. There were many of the same witnesses, such as John Lloyd for example, whom Mrs. Surratt had visited with Weichmann on the day of the assassination:

DISTRICT ATTORNEY. Where do you live?
A. On the Island, Washington city.
Q. How long have you been residing in the city?
A. I think I moved up from the country in October, 1865.
Q. Where had you been living previous to that?
A. I had been living at Surrattsville for a short time.
Q. You are a native of this city?
A. With the exception of an intermission of three years, I have been residing here for the past fifteen or twenty years.
Q. I believe you were a witness before the conspiracy trial, were you not?
A. Yes, sir; unfortunately.
Q. Will you state where you lived in the year 1865?
A. I moved to Surrattsville about the last of December, 1864. I resided at Surrattsville up to October, 1865.
Q. How far is that from this city?
A. I have always been told that it was about ten miles from the bridge.
Q. It is in Prince George's county, Maryland?
A. Yes, sir.
Q. Whose house did you occupy?

A. That of Mrs. Surratt.
Q. Mary E. Surratt?
A. Yes, sir.
Q. You saw her before the conspiracy trial?
A. Yes, sir.
Q. What was your business there?
A. That of hotel-keeping and farming.
Q. You kept the hotel at Surrattsville in Mrs. Surratt's house, and engaged in farming at the same time?
A. Yes, sir.
Q. State if you know the prisoner at the bar, John H. Surratt.
A. I do not see him. (Turning his eyes in the direction of the prisoner.) I believe that is Mr. Surratt.
(The prisoner was here requested to stand up. The witness then said:)
A. That is him; I know him; I had a short acquaintance with him.
Q. And you now recognize him?
A. Yes, sir.
Q. You knew Mrs. Mary E. Surratt?
A. Yes, sir; my acquaintance with them was very short the whole time.
Q. Did you rent this house of her?
A. Yes, sir.
Q. Now we have them all three [Atzerodt, Herold, John Surratt] at your house; state what they did.
A. There were several other persons besides them there at the time. I therefore paid no particular attention to them. They came in and took a drink, probably, and were playing cards, as well as I remember. After awhile Surratt called me into the front parlor, and said he wanted to speak to me. There I saw lying on the sofa what I supposed to be guns. They had covers on them. Besides these there were two or three other articles.
Q. State what the other articles were.
A. One was a rope—a bundle of rope as big around, I suppose, as my hat (a black felt hat of ordinary size). It was coiled rope. I should think from the size of the bundle that there was not more than 18 or 20 feet in it. I took it to be an inch and a quarter rope.
Q. What other articles do you think of?
A. There was a monkey-wrench.
Q. If you saw those things again would you be able to identify them?
A. I cannot say that I could.
Q. State what the prisoner said to you about those things after he had shown them to you.

A. He wished me to receive those things and to conceal the guns. I objected to it, and told him I did not wish to have such things in the house at all. He assured me positively that there should be no danger from them. I still persisted in refusing to receive them, but finally, by assuring me most positively that there would be no danger in taking them, he induced me to receive them. He did not say what sort of guns they were, as well as I remember.

Q. State what you did after you consented to receive and conceal them.

A. I told him there was no place about the premises to conceal such things at all, and that I did not wish to have them there. He told me then of a place where he knew it could be done. He then carried me up into a back room from the storeroom.

Q. Did you see her [Mrs. Surratt] any more from that time until the 14th of April, the day of the assassination?

A. She was there on the evening of the Friday of the assassination, I think.

Q. Not before?

A. I do not know how long before that, but not any day before it.

Q. Not between Tuesday and Friday?

A. No, sir.

Q. State if you then had any conversation with Mrs. Surratt [on Friday, April 14]; and if so, on what part of your premises, and what that conversation was.

A. When I drove up in my buggy to the back yard, Mrs. Surratt came out to meet me. She handed me a package, and told me, as well as I remember, to get the guns, or those things—I really forget now which, though my impression is that "guns" was the expression she made use of—and a couple of bottles of whiskey, and give them to whoever should call for them that night.

Q. What did you say to her?

A. I do not know that I made any reply to her at all. I was in liquor at the time, and being so, I did not want to have any conversation with her.

Q. How long did she stay there after this?

A. I do not remember. I went into my back room and threw myself on the lounge, when I immediately turned sick from the effect of the liquor. As I was raising up she came in and told me that her buggy spring was broken, and that I must do something to mend it. I told her, as well as I remember, that I had nothing to do it with, only to tie it with some rope yarn that I had.

Q. Do you recollect what time that was?

A. That was late in the evening after I got home.

Q. Before dark?

A. Yes sir.

Q. After you fixed up her buggy for her, how long did she stay?

A. She and Weichmann got in then and drove off.

Q. You speak of a package which she showed you at that time. What was it?

A. I did not notice the package until probably an hour later or more.

Q. When did you notice it?

A. I thought of it and carried it up stairs, and it feeling rather light, my curiosity led me to open it to see what it contained. I read in printed letters on the front-piece of it, "field glass." These letters were on a small part of it.

Q. Do you think you would know it if you were to see it?

A. I do not know that I should.

Q. You discovered that about an hour afterwards; what disposition did you make of it at that time?

A. I put it with the other things.

Q. You mean with the gun and cartridge-box?

A. Yes sir.

Q. Do you recollect of any of these parties to whom I have called your attention—Surratt, Atzerodt, or Herold—coming to your house that night, after this interview?

A. Herold was there about 12 o'clock that night.

Q. The same person who was at your house on Tuesday?

A. Yes sir.

Q. Who was in company with him at that time?

A. I do not know.

Q. Describe the man as well as you can, and whether there was anything the matter with him that attracted your attention?

A. The man—he was on horseback—looked to me to be about the size of Mr. Wilson, the assistant district attorney, with a big, heavy moustache. His moustache was the only thing noticeable about him, as far as I remember. He was on a large horse.

Q. Did he dismount?

A. No, sir.

Again, Weichmann came as a witness for the prosecution, essentially to repeat the story he had told at the trial of the present prisoner's mother.

Q. Do you remember a conversation with Mr. Lloyd on the subject of the interview between himself and Mrs. Surratt, at Uniontown, or near Uniontown?

A. No, sir; I had some conversation with him in 1865. He then felt astonished and angry on learning that I had not overheard the conversation between himself and Mrs. Surratt. I could not help that, however.

Q. Did you tell him you had sworn to the whisper?

A. He knew that; he had read it in the papers, and I think I told him.

MR. BRADLEY. I want to know what you said to him. Didn't you tell Mr. Lloyd on your examination below that you had sworn to a whisper?

A. I do not remember; I may have told him so; I believe that I did.

Q. Do you remember what his reply was?

A. No, sir.

Q. You were both in prison at that time?

A. Yes, sir; but in different rooms.

Q. Did not Mr. Lloyd tell you there, that if you had sworn to a whisper, you had sworn to what was not true?

A. I cannot remember what Mr. Lloyd said. I do not recall anything of that kind that he said. I am judge of my own conscience and Mr. Lloyd is not. I know what I heard, and he knows what he heard.

Q. I wish to know whether you have stated, at any time, that in your first interview with the Secretary of War you told him where John Surratt was?

A. No, sir; I never told the Secretary of War that, because I did not know.

MR. BRADLEY. I did not ask whether you had told the Secretary of War that. I want to know whether you did not tell Mr. John T. Ford that you had told the Secretary of War where John Surratt was at the time of the assassination?

A. No, sir.

Q. Did you repeat to him what passed at the interview with the Secretary of War?

A. I may have done so.

Q. If you did, you say you did not tell him that you had told the Secretary of War where John Surratt was at the time of the assassination?

A. I never said anything of the kind, because I did not know where he was. I told Mr. Ford that I had had an interview with the Secretary of War, and I believe I did state to him what passed at that interview.

Q. Did not you state to him that you had told the Secretary of War that John Surratt had left here a considerable time before the assassination, and that, from a letter which you had seen, he must have been in Montreal at that time?

A. I may have said that; I may have said that I had not seen John Surratt for a considerable time before the assassination, and that I had seen a letter from him dated April 12; but I did not state to the Secretary or to Mr. Ford that I knew where John Surratt was when the blow was struck, because I did not know.

Essentially, however, the defense of John Surratt was to rest on his alibi: that he was in Elmira, New York, and could not possibly have been in Washington, D.C., at the time of the assassination, and that he had disinterested and reputable witnesses, such as John Cass, among others, men sympathetic with the Union cause, who could establish this. John Cass was sworn and examined:

MR. BRADLEY.   Where do you reside?

A. At Elmira.

Q. What is your occupation?

A. Assessor of the city at present.

Q. Where were you residing in April, 1865?

A. In Elmira. I kept a clothing store at the corner of Water and Baldwin streets.

Q. Do you remember any particular incident which occurred the morning of the 15th of April, after the news of the assassination of the President was received in Elmira?

A. That morning I got the paper about half past seven o'clock with the news of the assassination. In consequence of the news in the paper, I staid at home probably longer than I would have done. I got down to the store about quarter to eight or perhaps eight o'clock. My store was directly opposite the telegraph office, and when I got down there I went over to the telegraph office and inquired the news of an operator who was a personal friend of mine. He told me they had received nothing since the news of the assassination, but as soon as they did he would let me know. I staid around there some time with other friends. Shortly after nine o'clock news came of the death of Abraham Lincoln. I immediately walked over to my store and told the clerks to close up.

Q. This was early in the morning, before any public order had been issued?

A. Yes, sir. They had received no public news of the death. I then went and stood at the front door of the store. By that time the bulletin had been placed on the side door. I at that time noticed a gentleman coming across the street whom I thought, from his dress, was a friend of mine from Canada. That was my first idea when I saw him coming across the street; but I soon saw it was not, and I then

turned and started to go back into the store. I had not, probably, got more than ten feet into the store, when this party whom I had observed, came in. He inquired for some white shirts. He asked me for a particular make, which make I did not keep, and told him so, but proceeded to show him some other descriptions of white shirts. He examined them, but said he would rather have those of the make which he had been accustomed to wearing. At that time I made a remark that we had received some very bad news. He asked, "What?" I said to him, "Of the death of Abraham Lincoln." The party made an answer to my remark which at the first commencement I took to be a little disrespectful, and I felt rather incensed, but before he concluded I was satisfied no disrespect was intended. My idea was that he was Canadian and had no sympathy with our people.

Q. What was the remark?

A. I cannot recall it, but I remember the feeling I had at the time.

Q. His explanation satisfied you that he meant no disrespect?

A. Yes, sir. I thought that he was a Canadian who had no sympathy with us, and who did not feel as we felt about the matter.

Q. Can you describe his dress?

A. He had on darkish pants; a kind of mixed blue coat—I should call it—pleated, with a belt around the waist. That was the first thing that caused my attention to be drawn to him.

Q. Have you ever seen that man since?

A. I have.

Q. Where have you seen him?

A. In the jail down here.

(The prisoner was requested to stand up.)

Q. Look at that man (pointing to the prisoner) and state if he is or not the man.

A. That is the man I saw there.

JUROR.   Was that on the 15th?

A. Yes, sir; while closing the store after seeing the news.

MR. PIERREPONT.   How did you get the first news of the assassination?

A. At home in the morning paper.

Q. What paper?

A. The *Elmira Advertiser*.

Q. At what time did you see the *Elmira Advertiser*?

A. Between 7 and 7½ in the morning.

Q. That was on Saturday morning, the 15th?

A. I do not remember the day.

Q. The next morning after the assassination?

A. Yes, sir.

Q. You think it was the 15th?

A. Yes, sir.

Q. That was the first you heard of it?

A. Yes, sir.

Q. What did you do when you heard of it?

A. I went into my dining room and took breakfast with my family; read the news, and felt very badly about it.

Q. When did you go to the telegraph office?

A. It must have been between eight and half past eight.

Q. Who did you see there?

A. Mr. Palmer.

Q. Did you get any more news?

A. I did not at that time. No other news had come.

Q. When did this man, who looked like a Canadian, cross the street?

A. I should say it was between the hours of nine and ten, probably half past nine.

Q. Was he dirty or was he clean?

A. Clean.

The trial of John Harrison Surratt ended in a hung jury. By that time, the sentiment of the public had changed; no longer was there a demand for vengeance against the plotters. The prosecution offered to enter a plea of *nolle prosse,* not an admission of innocence but a statement that the government no longer chooses to prosecute the case. Then the President issued a general amnesty, and included Surratt in it. The amnesty was one more controversial matter in which the President's opponents in Congress were rallying for a great battle— but that is another story, and we leave it for the next episode in the history of great trials.

So many questions are left unanswered by the historians of the death of Lincoln that shreds of suspicion will probably linger forever. At the time of the execution of Herold and company, many felt that Jefferson Davis and other leaders of the Confederacy were involved. In the years that followed, suspicion has fallen on Secretary of War Stanton or some members of his staff, on Vice-President Johnson, and even on Mrs. Lincoln!

Was there a third man in the Garrett barn who escaped, and if so, was this Booth? Why were there conflicting reports on the identification of Booth's body? Why were pages from Booth's diary torn out when the diary was turned over to the court? Why was the President unguarded at the moment when Booth was to step into the box and shoot him? Why did Robert Todd Lincoln burn Lincoln's papers, and what did he mean when he said, as he allegedly did, that these papers would have incriminated a member of his father's Cabinet? These are but a few, just a brief sampling, of hundreds of enigmatic questions that have challenged historians for decades.

It is common practice, in tying up the ends of a historical event, to trace what happened to the principals after the moment of crisis. Eventually, we follow them to death, the great leveler. But tragedy seems to have trailed many of those who played a major role in the Lincoln story. Mudd and the other three prisoners were sent to a prison off the coast of Florida, where O'Laughlin contracted yellow fever and died, and for his work during the yellow-fever epidemic Mudd was set free, as were the others. Two men who were allegedly responsible for preventing Anna Surratt from seeing President Johnson in a last-minute plea for mercy were Preston King and Senator James Lane. Within a year, King had drowned himself and Lane had shot himself. Clara Harris, who with her fiancé, Henry Rathbone, was in the box with the Lincolns when the President was assassinated, was herself shot and killed by the same Rathbone after she had married him, and Rathbone spent the rest of his life as an inmate of a mental hospital. Mrs. Lincoln, the President's widow, is said to have attempted suicide on at least one occasion; some have wondered whether her deep concern with money and fear of poverty (despite considerable funds at her disposal) may have been due to the fact that she was paying blackmail; at any rate, she spent a not inconsiderable amount of time in an insane asylum. These were only a few of the suicides, attempted and rumored suicides, insanity and alleged insanity, that dogged major and minor characters in this drama until their last days.

Not all the major and minor characters, however. For there was one who lived peacefully for many years, giving occasional lectures on the Lincoln story, then retiring into obscurity, sometimes teaching, never involved with violence. That was John Harrison Surratt. The world had forgiven his part in the conspiracy to kidnap the President, and had all but forgotten that he had been a Confederate spy. The Civil War had become garnished with heroic legends, in which both sides were being glorified in the American folklore, those who had been in the service of the South no less than those who had been dedicated to the North. So John Surratt's villainy was replaced by this aura of grandeur that came to surround the Civil War, but his record could never be completely free of blemish. For one might easily forgive a man who in his youth had plotted against the President. But one thing Americans could never forgive: that a son could let his mother go to the gallows while he hid in a Canadian sanctuary.

President Andrew Johnson.
Library of Congress

11

The Impeachment Trial of Andrew Johnson

[1868]

History has been kind to Andrew Johnson. During his lifetime, he was pilloried by many. However, from the end of the Reconstruction Era (the mid 1870's) until the inception of the modern civil rights revolution (the mid 1950's), President Andrew Johnson was a glorified figure in American history. Most biographers showed him as a victim of irresponsible radical Republicans out to pursue a policy of rule or ruin, to foist their views on the Presidency, to oust the Chief Executive so that they might themselves partake of a spoils system, to reduce the highest office in the land to one of puppetry to the will of Congress, and to crush the southern states that were seeking to reenter the Union. Johnson is depicted as carrying forward the banner of Lincoln, the fallen hero, while his opponents were greedy, avaricious, unscrupulous, ready to subjugate the white man to the will of the black, and who were saved from plunging the nation into irrevocable tragedy by the vote of one high-thinking and self-sacrificing man. It is a picture that today a few are beginning to challenge.

In 1864, in the midst of the Civil War, Andrew Johnson, a Union supporter from the secessionist state of Tennessee, was nominated as Lincoln's running mate, and was elected to the office of Vice-President of the United States. It is an office that is at best ambiguous, considered by many to be a political dead end, used to thwart the ambitious and silence the embarrassingly articulate; an office that makes a shadow figure out of one who was formerly proudly independent. In fact, one man in history considered it so unimportant that

he resigned to become a United States senator.

To many, however, the office of the Vice-Presidency has significance in one factor: that it is "one heartbeat away" from the White House. Eight Vice-Presidents have succeeded to the Presidency by the death of the man in office (four by assassination), and five of these eight— all in the twentieth century—went on to be elected in their own right after filling out the remainder of the predecessor's term. Of thirty-five men who have held the highest office in the land, eight have expired while serving; and not since Martin van Buren, Jackson's Vice-President, was elected in his own right in 1836, has a Vice-President won a promotion except through the black portal of death. So that the running mate of a successful presidential candidate can hardly look forward to rising higher on the road to Pennsylvania Avenue, except if the heartbeat should indeed be missed.

Few men have come into the land's highest office with so formidable a task before them as did Andrew Johnson. Born in North Carolina and bred in Tennessee, he had been a self-educated youth who had vigorously opposed powerful financial interests in his home state. Himself a Democrat, he was chosen as running mate for Lincoln, in the latter's struggle against George McClellan, in the hope of weaning away Democratic votes, presenting a national unity ticket, splitting some of the pro-southern sentiment, and assuring Lincoln's victory by adding Johnson's strength to the radical Republican and abolitionist votes that had nowhere else to go but to Lincoln.

In a victory that was closer in the popular than in the electoral columns (Lincoln received 55 percent of the popular, 91 percent of the electoral votes), Johnson became Vice-President. At the inauguration, two matters stand out and are often mentioned by historians. First, there was Lincoln's olive branch, which he held out to the secessionists, to whose early defeat he could now look forward: "With malice toward none, with charity for all . . ." It was the same Lincoln who had earlier preached "the Christian principle of forgiveness on terms of repentance," for which he was denounced by the abolitionist Thaddeus Stevens. And a second matter that is prominent in the details of the inauguration was the behavior of Andrew Johnson, who is said to have come to the ceremony in a state of intoxication. Johnson's apologists were later to insist that he was ill, and had merely taken an extra-strong shot of whiskey, but his behavior at the inauguration was to plague him for years. Like many other incidents in the drama that was unfolding, however, it was more of an excuse for those who were soon to be lining up as his enemies than as a factor in determining on which side of the battle lines individuals would be assuming their positions.

* * *

In three articles in the United States Constitution, impeachment is mentioned. It is provided that the President, Vice-President, and all civil officers of the United States "shall be removed from office on impeachment for and conviction of treason, bribery or other high crimes and misdemeanors," that their trials shall not be decided by jury, and that the House of Representatives shall have "the whole power of impeachment," while the Senate shall have the sole power to try *all* impeachments. Convictions shall be by two thirds of the members present, and if the President of the United States is being tried, the Chief Justice of the Supreme Court shall preside.

On about a dozen occasions in the years since the United States has existed, the House of Representatives has voted impeachment, and the Senate has tried the case. Almost all those indicted have been federal judges; many of the cases attracted only momentary interest, and are today merely footnotes in the history of this nation. But the trial of Andrew Johnson was quite different.

After the first shock of Lincoln's assassination, there was a general feeling of optimism in the camp of the radical Republicans in Congress. The dominant group was seeking not only to wipe out slavery but also to establish—if necessary by the force that had been used for military victory—some steps toward the education of the Negro and his preparation for participation in American life. The radicals worked out a program on the acceptance of which the return of the former secessionist states to the Union was conditioned. In the exciting days following his inauguration, Johnson had promised full cooperation to the radicals, and had pledged that there would be no truck with those who had committed treason against the Union. To Sumner, he stated that they were in agreement on the necessity of bringing about Negro suffrage; and to Thaddeus Stevens he is reported to have said: "To those who have deceived, to the conscious, influential traitor, who attempted to destroy the life of the nation—I would say, on you be inflicted the severest penalties of your crime."

But hardly had the honeymoon period begun, when the Congress and the man in the White House began to see the Reconstruction from divergent views. Eleven states had seceded from the Union, and the radicals feared that if the former secessionists were not barred from holding office, were not prevented from accession to power in their own states, and if these states returned to the Union in the hands of those who had led them out of it, the Republican program in Congress would be lost by the votes of the very people who had just been defeated. But Johnson, following the example set by Lincoln, favored the restoration of the states—they came to be known as the "Johnson states"—and demanded the seating of their delegations in Congress. More than that, the Thirteenth Amendment had been passed, calling for the abolition of slavery. Under the original Constitution, representation in Congress for slaveholding states was based on a population census that counted a slave as three fifths of a man. Now, under this amendment, the freedman was counted as a full man, strengthening the representation of the states that had just gone down to crushing defeat.

During the summer of 1865, Johnson and the radicals drew increasingly apart. Congress was not in session, and the President used the opportunity to implement his own program. He recognized a government in Virginia that the radicals considered a triumph of the old Confederacy. He offered liberal terms of amnesty, and laid down the conditions for the formation of state governments that would lead to the reestablishment of the Old South. For the radicals, in dismay, he had become "His Accidency the President."

When Congress came back into session, the Republicans were in an angry mood. Various measures, some of which were central to the entire Reconstruction program, were passed, vetoed, and then passed again over the President's veto. All the Presidents before Johnson, from Washington to Lincoln, had vetoed in all fewer acts of Congress than did President Johnson in his brief period in office. Between the executive and legislative sectors of the government, an unbending struggle for supremacy shaped up.

The Congress of the United States passed the Fourteenth Amendment to the Constitution (often considered the most important cornerstone of liberty in that document), and made ratification of the amendment a prerequisite for readmission to the Union. Johnson opposed the amendment, and urged the states not to ratify it. The President denounced the Freedmen's Bureau and vetoed an Act of Congress in 1866 extending its life. He issued amnesties and pardons wholesale to the men whom he had so recently denounced as traitors, vetoed a District of Columbia Negro suffrage bill, denounced Negroes as too ignorant to cast a ballot, and vetoed a whole series of Reconstruction bills as well as the historic Civil Rights Act of 1866. In the fall of 1866, the President went on a "swing around the circle," appearing in numerous northern cities to attack Congress, the Civil Rights Act, and even the proposed and as yet unratified Fourteenth Amendment. But popular sentiment was not with the President. He was literally driven off the platform at several points, and the November elections marked further victories for his opponents. During the course of his speeches, Johnson denounced his congressional opposition with angry words, in intemperate tones, and by unrestrained manners.

In an effort to humiliate the President, on the one hand, and reduce his office to one of impotence so that he could not carry out his program and would be forced to turn to Congress for militant Reconstruction, on the other, Congress passed a highly dubious, most controversial Tenure of Office Act. The bill provided that persons appointed to civil office by and with the advice and consent of the Senate shall be entitled "to hold such office until a successor shall have been in like manner appointed and duly qualified." The President could no longer remove from office, without the consent of the Senate, those whom he had appointed with that body's consent. Originally, in an early version of the bill, Cabinet members were excluded; later, in an ambiguous sentence, it was stated that the Cabinet members shall hold their offices "for and during the term of the President by whom they may have been appointed, and for one month thereafter, subject to removal by and with the advice and consent of the Senate." Early in March, 1867, the President sent the Congress his veto message, and the bill was passed over his veto.

President Andrew Johnson
portrayed as a tyrant.
Library of Congress

The lines were being drawn for a showdown. Johnson attempted to remove the Secretary of War, Stanton, and replace him first by Grant (who declined to play the President's game), and then by a weak adjutant general of the army, Lorenzo Thomas. Congressional leaders watched with glee as they succeeded in baiting the President into violation of a law; that is, into committing what they could label a "high crime and misdemeanor" as demanded by the Constitution as a prerequisite for removal. The hue and cry for impeachment could be heard in the nation's press, in the streets, in the halls of Congress.

The effort to impeach Johnson, which had failed to gain a sufficient number of adherents in the House on earlier occasions, received great impetus from the Thomas episode. The radicals felt that they had garnered the strength to remove the President, and in the House they debated an impeachment resolution from February 22 to 24, 1868. The resolution was probably as brief as anything so momentous in the history of Congress; it read, in full:

Resolved, That Andrew Johnson, President of the United States, be impeached of high crimes and misdemeanors in office.

With Thaddeus Stevens, fiery radical, summarizing and closing for the anti-Johnson forces, the vote was overwhelming: 126 for impeachment, 47 against (only a majority was required). A committee of two (Thaddeus Stevens and John A. Bingham) was authorized to communicate the House's action to the Senate, and a few days later the House elected a committee of "managers" to conduct the prosecution of the impeachment before the Senate. It was a powerful group, containing several of the most popular, most eloquent, most capable congressmen. The managers were John A. Bingham of Ohio, George S. Boutwell of Massachusetts, James F. Wilson of Iowa, Benjamin F. Butler of Massachusetts, John A. Logan of Illinois, Thomas Williams of Pennsylvania, and Thaddeus Stevens of Pennsylvania. Soon Butler emerged as the strongest figure in the group.

The impeachment trial of Andrew Johnson, President of the United States, opened before the Senate on March 5, 1868. Presiding, as provided for in the Constitution, was the Chief Justice of the United States, Salmon P. Chase, former Secretary of the Treasury in Lincoln's Cabinet. For the prosecution there appeared the committee of managers; for the defense, several of the most distinguished members of the bar, including Benjamin R. Curtis of Massachusetts and William M. Evarts of New York. But the decisive persons were the senators. There were 54 members who had been seated in the Senate: 42 Republicans, 4 Conservative Republicans (generally supporters of the President), and 8 Democrats. If the vote proceeded on party lines, the victory of the impeachers was to be expected.

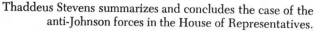

Thaddeus Stevens summarizes and concludes the case of the anti-Johnson forces in the House of Representatives.

Sketches of the Managers from the House of Representatives, elected to conduct the impeachment of President Johnson.

THE IMPEACHMENT TRIAL OF ANDREW JOHNSON 140

The managers presented an indictment in the form of eleven articles, which were largely repetitious, and essentially consisted of one general and three specific accusations against Johnson. The specific ones involved the deliberate violation of law in the attempted removal of Stanton; an alleged issuance of unlawful orders to General W. H. Emory, at a time when Congress and the President each feared military action against itself from the adversary; and statements reputed to have been made by Johnson in the whistlestop circuit tour, in which he was charged with having denied the legitimacy of Congress. In a more general sense, the articles accused the President of being "unmindful of the high duties of his office, and the dignities and proprieties thereof, and of the harmony and courtesies which ought to exist between the executive and legislative branches of the government." Johnson was charged with having attempted "to bring into disgrace, ridicule, contempt and reproach the Congress of the United States," activity that would not be likely to endear him to congressmen.

Most of the charges against the President were summarized in Article XI, which read as follows:

A committee of two, Thaddeus Stevens and John A. Bingham, informs the Senate of the House's resolution calling for the impeachment of President Johnson.

Photograph of the Managers. Back row:
James F. Wilson, Iowa; George Boutwell, Massachusetts; John A. Logan, Illinois:
Front row: Benjamin F. Butler, Massachusetts; Thaddeus Stevens, Pennsylvania;
Thomas Williams, Pennsylvania; John A. Bingham, Ohio.
Library of Congress

ARTICLE XI

That said Andrew Johnson, President of the United States, unmindful of the high duties of his office, and of his oath of office, and in disregard of the Constitution and laws of the United States, did, heretofore, to wit, on the eighteenth day of August, A. D. eighteen hundred and sixty-six, at the City of Washington, and the District of Columbia, by public speech declare and affirm, in substance, that the thirty-ninth Congress of the United States was not a Congress of the United States authorized by the Constitution to exercise legislative power under the same, but, on the contrary, was a Congress of only part of the States, thereby denying, and intending to deny, that the legislation of said Congress was valid or obligatory upon him, the said Andrew Johnson, except in so far as he saw fit to approve the same, and also thereby denying, and intending to deny, the power of the said thirty-ninth Congress to propose amendments to the Constitution of the United States; and, in pursuance of said declaration, the said Andrew Johnson, President of the United States, afterwards, towit, on the twenty-first day of February, A. D. eighteen hundred and sixty-eight, at the city of Washington, in the District of Columbia, did, unlawfully, and in disregard of the requirements of the Constitution that he should take care that the laws be faithfully executed, attempt to prevent the execution of an act entitled "An act regulating the tenure of certain civil offices," passed March second, eighteen hundred and sixty-seven, by unlawfully devising and contriving, and attempting to devise and contrive means by which he should prevent Edwin M. Stanton from forthwith resuming the functions of the office of Secretary for the Department of War, notwith-standing the refusal of the Senate to concur in the suspension theretofore made by said Andrew Johnson of said Edwin M. Stanton from said office of Secretary for the Department of War; and, also, by further unlawfully devising and contriving, and attempting to devise and contrive means, then and there, to prevent the execution of an act entitled "An act making appropriations for the support of the army for the fiscal year ending June thirtieth, eighteen hundred and sixty-eight, and for other purposes," approved March second, eighteen hundred and sixty-seven; and also, to prevent the execution of an act entitled "An act to provide for the more efficient government of the rebel States," passed March second, eighteen hundred and sixty-seven, whereby the said Andrew Johnson, President of the United States, did, then, to wit, on the twenty-first day of February, A. D. eighteen hundred and sixty-eight, at the city of Washington, commit, and was guilty of, a high misdemeanor in office.

SCHUYLER COLFAX,
Attest: Speaker of the House of Representatives.
EDWARD McPHERSON,
    Clerk of the House of Representatives.

Johnson, through his attorneys, sent an answer to the Senate on March 23, 1868. He defended his action on the Stanton matter, denied that he had said that Congress was not legally empowered to pass the legislation that it did, and stated that he exercised his right of freedom of opinion and freedom of speech to state his opinions on such matters.

President Johnson is served a summons to appear before the Senate by George T. Brown, Sergeant-at-Arms of the Senate.

President Johnson consulting with his attorneys. Through them, he sent his answer to the Senate on March 23, 1868.

On March 30, before a packed gallery for which special tickets were issued, the opening guns were fired. General Ben Butler made the initial speech for the managers:

Now, for the first time in the history of the world, has a nation brought before its highest tribunal its chief executive magistrate for trial and possible deposition from office, upon charges of maladministration of the powers and duties of that office. In other times, and in other lands, it has been found that despotisms could only be tempered by assassination, and nations living under constitutional governments even, have found no mode by which to rid themselves of a tyrannical, imbecile, or faithless ruler, save by overturning the very foundation and frame-work of the government itself. And, but recently, in one of the most civilized and powerful governments of the world, from which our own institutions have been largely modeled, we have seen a nation submit for years to the rule of an insane king, because its constitution contained no method for his removal.

Our fathers, more wisely, founding our government, have provided for such and all similar exigencies a conservative, effectual, and practical remedy by the constitutional provision that the "President, Vice-President, and all civil officers of the United States shall be removed from office on impeachment for and conviction of treason, bribery, or other high crimes and misdemeanors." The Constitution leaves nothing to implication, either as to the persons upon whom, or the body by whom, or the tribunal before which, or the offenses for which, or the manner in which this high power should be exercised; each and all are provided for by express words of imperative command.

The special ticket of admission to the impeachment trial.

The messengers of the Senate collect the tickets at the entrance to the Senate Chamber Galleries.

Members of the House of Representatives
proceeding to the Senate Chamber.

A full view of the Senate sitting as a court of impeachment for the trial of Andrew Johnson.
Library of Congress

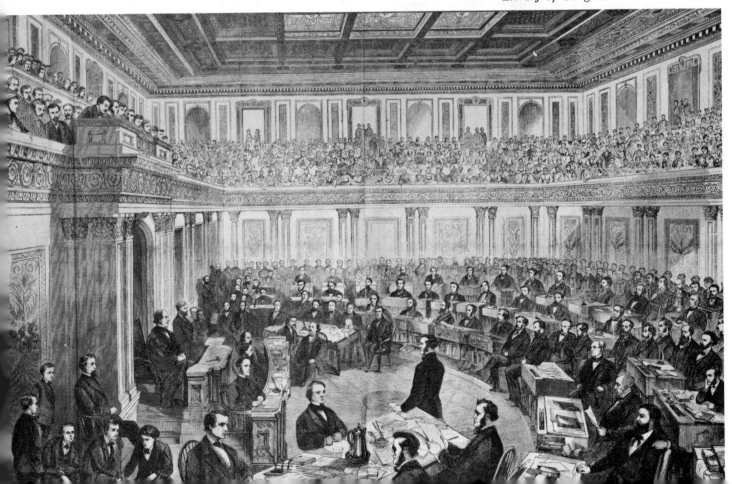

What is an impeachable high crime or misdemeanor? thundered Butler, and replied: It is

one in its nature or consequences subversive of some fundamental or essential principle of government, or highly prejudicial to the public interest, and this may consist of a violation of the Constitution, of law, of an official oath, or of duty, by an act committed or omitted, or, without violating a positive law, by the abuse of discretionary powers from improper motives, or for any improper purpose.

On the question of freedom of speech, Butler inveighed strongly against Johnson's defense.

Is it, indeed, to be seriously argued here that there is a constitutional right in the President of the United States, who, during his official life, can never lay aside his official character, to denounce, malign, abuse, ridicule, and condemn, openly and publicly, the Congress of the United States—a co-ordinate branch of the government?

It cannot fail to be observed that the President (shall I dare to say his counsel, or are they compelled by the exigencies of their defense,) have deceived themselves as to the gravamen of the charge in this article? It does not raise the question of freedom of speech, but of propriety and decency of speech and conduct in a high officer of the government.

Andrew Johnson, the private citizen, as I may reverently hope and trust he soon will be, has the full constitutional right to think and speak what he pleases, in the manner he pleases, and where he pleases, provided always he does not bring himself within the purview of the common law offences of being a common railer and brawler, or a common scold, which he may do, (if a male person is ever liable to commit that crime;) but the dignity of station, the proprietaries of position, the courtesies of office, all of which are a part of the common law of the land, require the President of the United States to observe that gravity of deportment, that fitness of conduct, that appropriateness of demeanor, and those amenities of behavior which are a part of his high official functions. He stands before the youth of the country the exemplar of all that is of worth in ambition, and all that is to be sought in aspiration; he stands before the men of the country as the grave magistrate who occupies, if he does not fill, the place once honored by Washington; nay, far higher and of greater consequence, he stands before the world as the representative of free institutions, as the type of man whom the suffrages of a free people have chosen as their chief. He should be the living evidence of how much better, higher, nobler, and more in the image of God, is the elected ruler of a free people than a hereditary monarch, coming into power by the accident of birth; and when he disappoints all these hopes and all these expectations, and becomes the ribald, scurrilous blasphemer, bandying epithets and taunts with a jeering mob, shall he be heard to say that such conduct is not a high misdemeanor in office? Nay, disappointing the hopes, causing the cheek to burn with shame, exposing to the taunts and ridicule of every nation the good name and fame of the chosen institutions of thirty million of people, is it not the highest possible crime and misdemeanor in office? and under the circumstances is the gravamen of these charges. The words are not alleged to be either false or defamatory, because it is not within the power of any man, however high his official position, in effect to slander the Congress of the United States, in the ordinary sense of that word, so as to call on Congress to answer as to the truth of the accusation. We do not go in, therefore, to any question of

truth or falsity. We rest upon the scandal of the scene. We would as soon think, in the trial of an indictment against a termagant as a common scold, of summoning witnesses to prove that what she said was not true. It is the noise and disturbance in the neighborhood that is the offence, and not a question of the provocation or irritation which causes the outbreak.

Butler's conclusions placed a heavy burden on the senators:

The responsibility is with you; the safeguards of the Constitution against usurpation are in your hands; the interests and hopes of free institutions wait upon your verdict. The House of Representatives has done its duty. We have presented the facts in the constitutional manner; we have brought the criminal to the bar, and demand judgment at your hands for his great crimes.

Never again, if Andrew Johnson go quit and free this day, can the people of this or any other country by constitutional checks or guards stay the usurpation of executive power.

I speak, therefore, not the language of exaggeration but the words of truth and soberness, that the political welfare and liberties of all men hang trembling on the decision of the hour.

The reply of the defense was more tempered. The attorneys argued both that the President had not violated the letter of the law, because Stanton had been appointed by Lincoln, not Johnson, and that Cabinet officers were meant to be advisers to the President, and therefore it was not intended that they stay in office when their services were no longer wanted.

Early in the trial, there was considerable jockeying for position and wrangling over the questions of procedure, as well as the ethical and legal propriety of certain senators acting as judge of their President. Particular attack was made against Benjamin Wade, Senator from Ohio, a vigorous proponent of a militant Reconstructionist policy. Wade was now president *pro tem* of the Senate, and in case of the removal of Johnson, Wade would succeed to the presidential office. The writers of the Constitution had not foreseen this conflict of interest, and had provided that all senators be eligible to vote; and the managers were not prone to relinquish one vote to which they were legally entitled, for they were seeking to hold every Republican in line. Those who accused Wade of conflict of interest could not reply to the charge that an equally great conflict existed in one of the Tennessee Democrats, who was in fact a member of the President's immediate family. So Wade did participate, and did indeed vote.

On procedural questions, when the judge attempted to make rulings of his own, the managers appealed to the Senate, where they were usually upheld, as they had a clear majority, and the two-thirds vote was not required except on the major problem of the innocence or guilt of the accused.

A view of the reporters' gallery at the trial.

Reporters racing for the
wireless to get their stories
to the newspapers.

Through many long weeks and many witnesses, the trial held the attention of the country. The popular sentiment in the North was clearly against Johnson, and toward the end of the trial, on May 11, a Republican from Maine who was supporting Johnson, and had broken party lines, took notice of the sentiment in the streets:

To the suggestion that popular opinion demands the conviction of the President on these charges, I reply that he is not now on trial before the people, but before the Senate. In the words of Lord Eldon, upon the trial of the queen, "I take no notice of what is passing out of doors, because I am supposed constitutionally not to be acquainted with it." . . . The people have not heard the evidence as we have heard it. The responsibility is not on them, but upon us. . . . And I should consider myself undeserving the confidence of that just and intelligent people who imposed upon you this great responsibility, an unworthy place among honorable men, if for any fear of public reprobation, and for the sake of securing popular favor, I should disregard the convictions of my judgment and my conscience.

Much of the debate at the trial centered upon what Johnson had said in his speeches, and whether newspaper reports were accurate or garbled. The managers read entire versions of these talks, particularly one given in Cleveland, into the trial record, and emphasized the sections dealing with Congress:

We have witnessed [Johnson is reported to have stated] in one department of the government every effort, as it were, to prevent the restoration of peace, harmony, and union; we have seen, as it were, hanging upon the verge of the government, as it were, a body, calling or assuming to be the Congress of the United States, when it was but a Congress of a part of the States; we have seen Congress assuming to be for the Union when every step they took was to perpetuate dissolution, and make disruption permanent. We have seen every step that has been taken, instead of bringing about reconciliation and harmony, has been legislation that took the character of penalties, retaliation, and revenge.

Another version of the same talk was not much different. In it, Johnson is reported to have said: "We have seen this Congress assume or pretend to be for the Union . . ." Now, did the President actually say what was attributed to him? The managers of the prosecution called William N. Hudson, an editor:

MR. MANAGER BUTLER.   What is your business?
A. I am a journalist by occupation.
Q. Where is your home?
A. In Cleveland, Ohio.
Q. What paper do you have charge of?
A. The *Cleveland Leader.*
Q. Where were you about the 3rd or 4th of September, 1866?
A. I was in Cleveland.
Q. What was your business then?
A. I was then one of the editors of the *Leader.*
Q. Did you hear the speech that President Johnson made there from the balcony of a hotel?
A. I did.

The gallery audience wildly applauds at the close of Manager Bingham's speech.

The ladies have their own gallery at the trial.

Q. Did you report it?
A. I did, with the assistance of another reporter.
Q. Who is he?
A. His name is Johnson.
Q. Was your report published in the paper the next day?
A. It was.
Q. Have you a copy?
A. I have.
Q. Will you produce it?
The witness produced a copy of the *Cleveland Leader* of September 4, 1866.
Q. Have you your original notes?
A. I have not.
Q. Where are they?
A. I cannot tell. They are probably destroyed.
Q. Have you the report in the paper of which you are the editor, which was published the next day?
A. I have the report which I have submitted.
Q. What can you say as to the accuracy of that report?
A. It is not a verbatim report, except in portions. There are parts of it which are verbatim, and parts are synopses.
Q. Does the report distinguish the parts which are not verbatim from those which are?
A. It does.

On cross-examination it was brought out that the speech was made by the President before a large crowd in Cleveland late in the evening, that Hudson had to take notes under uncomfortable conditions, and that his newspaper was unfriendly to the President.

But the accuracy of the reports could not be denied. Other witnesses likewise testified to the same effect; among them was Daniel C. McEwen:

MR. MANAGER BUTLER.   What is your profession?
A. Short-hand writer.
Q. How long has that been your profession?
A. For about four or five years, I should judge.
Q. Were you employed in September, 1866, in reporting for any paper?
A. I was.
Q. What paper?
A. The *New York World*.
Q. Did you accompany Mr. Johnson and the presidential party when they went to lay the cornerstone of a monument in honor of Mr. Douglas?
A. I did.
Q. Where did you join the party?
A. I joined the party at West Point, New York.
Q. How long did you continue with the party?
A. I continued with them till they arrived at Cincinnati on their return.
Q. Did you go professionally as a reporter?
A. I did.
Q. Had you accommodation on the train as such?
A. I had.
Q. The entrée of the President's car?
A. I had.
Q. Were you at Cleveland?
A. I was.
Q. Did you make a report of his speech at Cleveland from the balcony?
A. I did.
Q. How, phonographically or stenographically?

A. Stenographically.

Q. Have you your notes?

A. I have.

Q. Here?

A. Yes, sir.

Q. Produce them. (The witness produced a memorandum-book.) Have you, at my request, copied out those notes since you have been here?

A. I have.

Q. (Exhibiting a manuscript to the witness.) Is that the copy of them?

A. It appears to be.

Q. Is that an accurate copy of your notes?

A. It is.

Q. How accurate a report of the speech are your notes?

A. My notes are, I consider, very accurate so far as I took them. Some few sentences in the speech were interrupted by confusion in the crowd, which I have indicated in making the transcript, and the parts about which I am uncertain I enclose in brackets.

Q. Where you have not enclosed in brackets, how is the transcript?

A. Correct.

Q. Was your report published?

A. I cannot say. I took notes of the speech, but owing to the lateness of the hour—it was eleven o'clock or after—it was impossible for me to write out a report of the speech and send it to the paper which I represented. Therefore I went to the telegraph office after the speech was given, and dictated some of my notes to other reporters and correspondents, and we made a report which we gave to the agent of the Associated Press, Mr. Gobright.

Q. Did the agent of the Associated Press accompany the presidental party for a purpose?

A. Yes, sir.

Q. Was it his business and duty to forward reports of speeches?

A. I supposed it to be.

Q. Did you so deal with him?

A. I did.

Q. Have you put down the cheers and interruptions of the crowd or any portion of them?

A. I have put down a portion of them. It was impossible to take them all.

Q. State whether there was a good deal of confusion and noise there?

A. There was a great deal of it.

Q. Exhibition of ill-feeling and temper?

A. I thought there was.

Q. On the part of the crowd?

A. On the part of the crowd.

Q. How on the part of the President?

A. He seemed a little excited.

Q. Do you remember anything said there to him by the crowd about keeping his dignity?

A. I have not it in my notes.

Q. Do you remember it?

A. I do not remember it from hearing.

Q. Was anything said about not getting mad?

A. Yes, sir.

Q. Did the crowd caution him not to get mad?

A. The words used were, "Don't get mad, Andy."

Q. Was he then speaking in considerable excitement, or otherwise? Did he appear considerably excited at that moment when they told him not to get mad?

At this line of questioning, Mr. Evarts, counsel for the President, strenuously objected, and there followed a colloquy between the two adversaries:

MR. EVARTS.	That is not any part of the present inquiry, which is to verify these notes, to see whether they shall be in evidence or not.
MR. MANAGER BUTLER.	I understand; but I want to get as much as I can from memory, and as much as I can from notes, and both together will make a perfect transcript of the scene.
MR. EVARTS.	But the present inquiry, I understand, is a verification of notes. Whenever that is abandoned and you go by memory let us know it.
MR. MANAGER BUTLER.	The allegation is that it was a scandalous and disgraceful scene. The difference between us is that the counsel for the President claim the freedom of speech and we claim the decency of speech. We are now trying to show the indecency of the occasion. That is the point between us, and the surroundings are as much part of the occasion as what was said.
MR. EVARTS.	I understand you regard the freedom of speech in this country to be limited to the right of speaking properly and discreetly.
MR. MANAGER BUTLER.	Oh, no. I regard freedom of speech in this country the freedom to say anything by a private citizen in a decent manner.
MR. EVARTS.	That is the same thing.
MR. MANAGER BUTLER.	Oh, no.
MR. EVARTS.	And who is the judge of the decency?
MR. MANAGER BUTLER.	The court before whom the man is tried for breaking the laws of decency.
MR. EVARTS.	Did you ever hear of a man being tried for freedom of speech in this country?
MR. MANAGER BUTLER.	No; but I have seen two or three women tried; I never heard of a man being tried for it before (Laughter.) (To the witness.) I was asking you whether there was considerable excitement in the manner of the President at the time he was cautioned by the crowd not to get mad?

Despite their popular backing, the managers were fearful that there would be defections from the Republican ranks, sufficient to prevent the two-thirds majority necessary for conviction. On Monday, May 11, a conference was held, to obtain an indication of how the vote would go, and there it was found that the first article in the arraignment was weak and that the greatest strength might be marshaled to support the managers on Article XI. On the following Saturday, there was a debate on the order of the vote, and the order proposed by the impeachers was upheld, by a vote of 34 to 19, with one senator not voting, he being out of the room at the time. The vote on Article XI was taken, with 35 voting "guilty," 19 "not guilty." By one vote, impeachment had been defeated. There were still ten other articles, but the outlook was gloomy for the radicals; they needed time. There were motions and countermotions for adjournment, and by a vote of 32 to 21, the Senate adjourned until Tuesday, May 26, at noon.

In the ten-day period between their setback and the next scheduled vote, the managers worked desperately to obtain another vote. In the House of Representatives, they openly charged that members of the Senate were being bribed to vote in favor of the President, with $30,000 having been offered for the purchase of three votes. Butler made a report of the investigation of this charge to the House on the eve of the next scheduled Senate meeting. His committee had subpoenaed witnesses; here is a report of one interrogation: Representative Benjamin Butler is interrogating Thurlow Weed, who claimed to have information on the alleged bribery:

Q. Who was the man that talked with you about purchasing votes?
A. The subject was often talked about in New York.
Q. By whom to you?
A. I suppose, to answer your question in the spirit it was put, the next conversation I had was with Webster, Woolley, and Shook; they came to my room at the Astor House.
Q. When?
A. I think it was a week after Adams was there.
Q. Shook, Woolley, and Webster?
A. Yes, sir; and my impression is, though I am not very confident, that that was the first time I ever saw Woolley.

Q. What was there said about it?
A. Substantially what Adams said; it was said that there was a proposition made for votes and for money.
Q. What sum was mentioned?
A. $30,000, I think.
Q. For one vote or more?
A. For three votes. But three names were mentioned that I remember.

But it was to no avail, for even the scandal that hung over the defecting Republicans was not sufficient to save the managers from defeat.

The drama was ended, and Johnson's supporters rushed to congratulate him. By one vote, Andrew Johnson almost lost his job, and few have questioned the good fortune of American democracy that seven Republicans deserted their party and voted for the President. Within a year, several of the principal figures were dead: Thaddeus Stevens, perhaps the most dynamic of all the radicals and militant Reconstructionists; and two of the seven Republicans who voted with the Democrats. Of the other five dissident Republicans, all went down to defeat at the hands of their voters; they had committed political suicide, whether out of sincere conviction or because they were bribed (the latter an unproved charge to which historians give little credence, but then widely believed). Americans like to be told that it was out of sincerity—and in fact, John F. Kennedy was later to take one of these men and paint his story as a "profile in courage." It is a far prettier picture to make part of the American folklore than the one that Butler charged and that most of the country believed, in 1868.

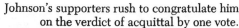

Johnson's supporters rush to congratulate him on the verdict of acquittal by one vote.

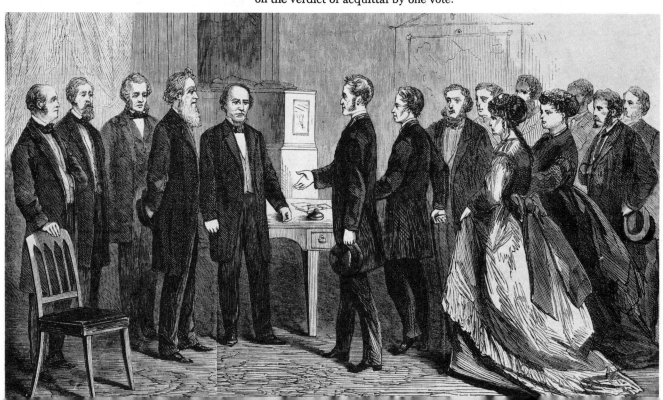

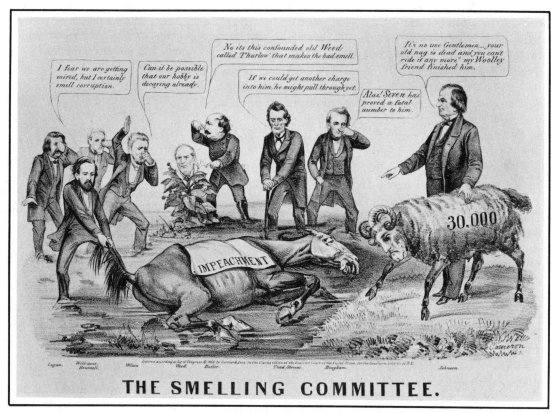

A cartoon, entitled "The Smelling Committee," depicting
President Andrew Johnson's victory over the Managers.
Library of Congress

A contemporary
magazine cartoon
entitled "Saved by a Doubt!"

There remained less than half a year between the failure of impeachment and the elections, and no one seriously considered the President as a candidate for reelection. He was succeeded by Ulysses S. Grant, and the war hero gave the country eight years of inefficiency and corruption often cited by Johnson supporters as evidence of the decline that had set in within the Republican ranks. Andrew Johnson returned to the United States Senate, where he had been tried for impeachment, returned triumphantly as Senator from Tennessee, amid the plaudits of his colleagues, in the body where he had so recently been pilloried. The nation was reunited, radical Reconstruction was defeated, and the efforts of the Republicans to impose a northern rule on the South were liquidated. America had been saved from folly— or had it?

For there is another side to the story. The historians who for decades have been vindicating Johnson were also indicting the Reconstructionists, accusing them of attempting to impose a rule of blackness and ignorance on the South. The nation went into a period of some eighty or ninety years during which the Negro was virtually completely disenfranchised in the South, shorn of all power in the economic, social, judicial, and political arenas, systematically robbed, cheated, and killed by mobs, often with the consent and connivance of government officials. The gains for which the war had been fought, except for the abolition of chattel slavery, were lost. The South had won the peace, new Black Codes were everywhere triumphant, and the Civil War was clothed in a nostalgic glory, while Reconstruction was vilified. For this view of history, Johnson is a hero, Butler a villain.

But in an era in which the struggle for civil rights is the paramount domestic problem of the land, when Negroes and whites are marching, shouting, and often being killed to obtain the rights that were encompassed among the aims of the Republicans, one might conjecture that the tragic history of the past hundred years —with the burning and mutilation of thousands of Negroes and the pursuit of democracy abroad while it was virtually unknown for one tenth of the nation at home—might have been different, had the aims of the 1960's been vigorously pursued in the 1860's. And this might possibly have occurred had the managers succeeded in obtaining just one more vote.

Read, then, what one modern historian has to say about Andrew Johnson. Kenneth Stampp, authority on the Civil War, writes: "A program that began with the dream of a new day for the southern yeomanry terminated with the landlords fashioning a new kind of bondage for their black laborers, and with Johnson their witting or unwitting ally." And again: "The truth is that, before the radical program began, the Johnson governments themselves had introduced the whole pattern of disenfranchisement, discrimination, and segregation into the postwar South. And there, quite possibly, matters might still stand, had Andrew Johnson had his way."

Finally, what would have been the effect of a different outcome of the impeachment proceedings, on the American political structure, and particularly on the office of the Presidency? Some have contended that, had impeachment been victorious, the Presidency would have been reduced to a puppet office, and the independent executive, in the American tripartite checks-and-balances system, would have been destroyed. Others have contended that a system closer to the European parliamentary one, in which the head of state who has lost the confidence of his legislators is removed, would have been introduced. American Presidents, thereafter, might have been answerable to Congress, and when the Chief Executive was no longer carrying out the will of Congress, resignation or removal would have been in order. Whether such a system of government would have been functional in the age of computers, jets, spaceships, atom bombs, and undeclared wars is highly debatable; that it would have had democratic safeguards can hardly be gainsaid.

Views of the wealthy Congressional Plymouth Church in Brooklyn Heights, whose beloved pastor was accused of adultery with Elizabeth Tilton, wife of his best friend, Theodore: (*a*) The historic meeting at which Beecher denounced such charges as false. (*b*) Exterior of Plymouth Church. (*c*) Its Navy Mission on Jay Street. (*d*) The Plymouth Bethel on Hicks Street.

12

Reverend Henry Ward Beecher

[1875]

TWO MILLION WORDS WERE SPOKEN OR INTRODUCED AS evidence at the Beecher-Tilton scandal trial that took place in Brooklyn City Court, beginning on January 11, 1875, and ending with the jury giving up in disagreement on July 2, 1875. Front-page newspapers headlines and by-lines on the trial appeared in major cities and minor hamlets all over the country. Even the foreign press followed and featured the trial in detail as it lumbered along day by day. How could a mere trial based on a charge of adultery have assumed such national and international importance? Why was there such a fervent interest in the fact that one man had or had not carried on an illicit affair with the wife of his best friend? Surely scandal for the sake of scandal was not the true answer.

No. The answer lay first of all in the leading individual in the case, the Reverend Henry Ward Beecher, known to forty million people for his writings, speeches, sermons, and his aggressive advocacy of the abolitionist cause. He was at the time the beloved minister of the highly fashionable and financially successful Congregational Plymouth Church, nestled among the finest homes of Brooklyn Heights. Second, the trial focused inevitably on the double-standard climate of morality that prevailed among America's wealthy upper middle classes. Whatever titillating parts the individuals concerned played in the proceedings, to the world at large it was not the Reverend Henry Ward Beecher who was on trial; the whole code of upper-class morals was at stake. If Beecher could be found guilty, then who among them could be safe in their moral smugness? Such things as adultery or sexual promiscuity just did not happen among polite society; or, if they did, it was no one's business but those vitally concerned; certainly *not* matters to be discussed or even admitted to. The Victorian code of behavior was very much in evidence in latter nineteenth-century America. Thus before the first of the two million words to be uttered at the trial was spoken, it was a foregone conclusion that no male jury (there were no females on juries) of his peers could possibly conclude that Beecher could have done such an "unheard-of act"—any more than any one of the individual jurors would admit to his own wife that he could possibly be unfaithful to her. To the "boys in the back room," perhaps; but not to the face of society at large. As one contemporary writer put it:

It is simply incredible that the man who thus wrote and lived, with the eyes of the world upon him, should be a liar, a sneak, a perjurer, a debauchee, and a confirmed, persistent hypocrite. The millions who during this long period (1868–1874) have been cheered and strengthened by his words cannot believe it. . . . Witless public—you who do not read or think or judge—you have done what the race has always done —struck the heart that loves you!

❋   ❋   ❋

Four and a half years passed from the fateful day, July 3, 1870, when Elizabeth Tilton confessed to her husband, Theodore, that since the fall of 1868 she had been committing adultery with her beloved pastor, the Reverend Henry Ward Beecher, until the matter came to trial. Fantastically, it would never have become a public matter were it not for the spite of a vociferous suffragist, social reformer, radical spiritualist, and advocate of free love, one Victoria C. Woodhull, co-editor with her sister, Tennie C. Claflin, of *Woodhull and Claflin's Weekly*, devoted to "progress, free thought and untrammeled lives." Having learned all the details of the affair from Elizabeth Cady Stanton, leader in the woman's rights movement, on May 3, 1871, and unable to stomach the hypocrisy of Beecher practicing what he so strongly opposed in his preaching, she finally broke the story in print with this card inserted in the May 20, 1871, edition of the *New York World* (in part):

The Reverend
Henry Ward Beecher.

Elizabeth Tilton.

Victoria C. Woodhull (left) and her sister,
Tennie C. Claflin, editors of *Woodhull
and Claflin's Weekly*. The former broke
the Beecher-Tilton scandal wide open
by the card she inserted in the
New York World on May 20, 1871.

I advocate free love in its highest, purest sense, as the only cure for the immorality, the deep damnation, by which men corrupt and disfigure God's most holy institution of sexual relation. My judges preach against "free love" openly, practice it secretly; their outward seeming is fair, inwardly they are full of "dead men's bones and all manner of uncleanliness." For example, I know of one man, a public teacher of eminence, who lives in concubinage with the wife of another public teacher of almost equal eminence. All three concur in denouncing offenses against morality. I shall make it my business to analyze some of these lives, and will take my chances in the matter of libel suits.°

Thus began the long-drawn-out public exposure of the affair between Elizabeth Tilton and Henry Ward Beecher that was to be kept under uneasy wraps, with many heartaches and much soul-searching, and culminating in an almost arrogant denial of the whole business, until the smoldering resentfulness of Theodore Tilton erupted in his swearing out a complaint against Beecher in City Court on August 20, 1874. In it he charged his former friend, whom he had loved and worshiped second only to his wife, with having alienated and destroyed Mrs. Tilton's affections for him. For having "wholly lost the comfort, society, aid and assistance of his said wife," Tilton demanded of Beecher $100,000. The charge specifically stated that Beecher had committed acts

on or about the tenth day of October 1868, and on diverse other days and times after that day and before the commencement of this action, at the house of the defendant, No. 124 Columbia Street, City of Brooklyn and at the house of the plaintiff, No. 174 Livingston Street, City of Brooklyn, wrongfully and wickedly and without the privity or connivance of the plaintiff, by means whereof the affection of the said Elizabeth for the said plaintiff was wholly alienated and destroyed.

° This card became "Exhibit No. 22" at the trial.

Lib Tilton was a quiet, shy little woman, given to reading and dreaming, for which she had plenty of time, since her husband, Theodore, was away from home a great deal of the time, making speeches, for which he was famous. As editor of Henry Bowen's two newspapers, the *Independent* and the *Union* (a position Beecher had urged his friend Bowen to give him), Tilton was a much-sought-after speaker. While he was away, it was not unusual for Beecher, making his round of calls on his parishioners, to drop in on this most devout follower and wife of his best friend. She adulated him; she went into raptures at his sermons, and was deeply flattered when he consulted her on a novel he was having difficulty writing. In contrast to the warm Elizabeth, Beecher's wife, Eunice, was a cold, sexless creature, about whom Beecher constantly complained as a cross he had to bear. There developed, then, the amorous and sexual liaison, an extramarital affair which was certainly not his first. Many years before, Henry Bowen's wife on her deathbed had whispered to him that she and the Reverend Henry Beecher had been sexually intimate. His knowledge of this past relationship was later to explain much of Bowen's vacillating tactics in the Beecher-Tilton affair.

In giving herself to Beecher, Lib Tilton reasoned that this was the right thing to do, that God himself had ordained it (for hadn't Beecher assured her this was so?), that it was in some way a consolation for the recent death of her son Paul. Since the love between the minister and herself was right and proper, any expression of that love was also proper, whether by the shake of a hand, a kiss, or even bodily intercourse. And so, for a year and a half they carried on their relationship until qualms of conscience and doubts as to the validity of her reasoning moved her to make the fateful confession to her husband.

From that day on, the events that transpired, the persons involving themselves in the great scandal, the under-the-sword-of-Damocles daily lives of the protagonists, the incredible letters, notes, confessions, apologies that were written, copied, and hidden away—all appear more like melodramatic fiction than like testimonial fact.

❋   ❋   ❋

Theodore Tilton.

Versöhnt!

H. W. B.: Ha, ha, ha! — Hi, hi, hi! — Ha, ha, ha! — Hi, hi, hi!

Caricature of the Reverend Beecher chortling as unsuspecting
Theodore Tilton and wife (who is shedding a tear at leaving
her beloved pastor) depart on a lecture tour.

Theodore Tilton reads his
statement on his version of
the affair to a skeptical
Committee of Investigation
of Plymouth Church.

The Committee of Investigation unanimously backed their pastor by acquitting the Reverend Henry Ward Beecher and denouncing Frank Moulton. Moulton, angered, shouts, "You're a liar!" at Professor Raymond, who has just read the committee's decision.

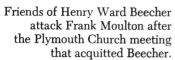

Friends of Henry Ward Beecher attack Frank Moulton after the Plymouth Church meeting that acquitted Beecher.

Chief Justice Joseph Neilson,
who presided at the trial.

Brooklyn City Court House,
where the civil trial of
the Reverend Henry Ward
Beecher opened on
January 11, 1875.

Chief Justice Joseph Neilson presided at the opening of the Beecher-Tilton trial on January 11, 1875. For Theodore Tilton, the plaintiff, William A. Beach headed a notable battery of lawyers. They were to present his case with simple directness, relying on the basic facts of the accusations and on Tilton's insistence that his wife was guiltless and the one who was sinned against. They would call but a dozen witnesses in contrast to some ninety-five for the defense.

To head his defense team Beecher had retained perhaps the ablest lawyer of his day, William M. Evarts, and six assistants. Out to save his own skin, Beecher no longer cared what he did to the reputation of Lib Tilton or anyone else. His lawyers set out to ruin the reputation of Theodore Tilton and to vilify all opposing witnesses. Beecher himself was to be his own worst witness, begging the question 894 times with answers of "I can't recollect" or "I don't know." In fact, only Evart's superb summation saved Beecher's moral hide.

The courtroom itself was unruly—far more like a circus than like a court of law. Opera glasses were sold in court with the spectators focusing on the principals as if they were actors on a stage.

From January 5 to January 10 the time was spent impaneling the jury. On January 11 Samuel D. Morris began the opening address for the plaintiff. It took three days, and set forth a chronology of events. Substantially the same events had been covered by Theodore Tilton in his statement before the committee of Plymouth Church hearing concerning the "alleged aspersions upon the character of the Reverend Beecher." Theodore Tilton and Elizabeth R. Richards were married on October 2, 1855, by the Reverend Henry Ward Beecher. For fifteen years an intimate friendship existed between the two men, until 1870, when Tilton became suspicious of the excess attentions of Beecher to his wife, and chided her for condoning them. This resulted in a short separation, and when she returned home on July 3, 1870, she "made a circumstantial confession to her husband of the criminal facts . . . but further stated that her sexual intercourse with Beecher had never proceeded from low or vulgar thoughts either on her part or his, but always from pure affection and a high religious love." In order to protect the family from shame, Tilton condoned the wrong. In December, 1870, differences between Tilton and his employer, Henry C. Bowen, arose, which were aggravated by the Reverend Henry and Mrs. Beecher.

Finally, Tilton in a pique wrote the following letter, which must have had a devastating effect on Beecher:

The judge and the lawyers as the trial begins (*top row, left to right*): Judge Neilson, the Honorable William M. Evarts, senior counsel for Beecher; William A. Beach, senior counsel for Tilton; ex-judge William Fullerton, counsel for Tilton; (*bottom row*) General B. F. Tracy, counsel for Beecher; S. D. Morris, counsel for Tilton; Thomas G. Shearman, counsel for Beecher; and General Roger A. Preyor, counsel for Tilton.

The opening scene. Mr. Morris, counsel for Tilton, presents the opening argument for the plaintiff to the jury on Monday, January 11, 1875.

Dec. 26, 1870, Brooklyn

HENRY WARD BEECHER,

Sir, I demand that, for reasons you explicitly understand, you immediately cease from the ministry of Plymouth Church, and that you quit the city of Brooklyn as a residence.

(*Signed*) THEODORE TILTON

Mrs. Tilton, wishing to restore harmony, wrote a note that she asked Francis D. Moulton, a mutual friend, to deliver to Beecher. This note referred to her confession and asked that, in spite of everything, friendly relations between the two men be once more established. Beecher at once rushed to Mrs. Tilton's house and coerced her into writing a note that would clear him of any blame if he should be questioned by a council of ministers.

Upon learning of this letter, Tilton had his wife write another, retracting the first. Moulton was dispatched to Beecher to retrieve Elizabeth's letter given to Beecher. Beecher then returned the letter to Moulton, and dictated to Moulton an apology asking Tilton's forgiveness.

These statements and letters were referred to or included in Mr. Morris's opening statement for the plaintiff and later brought into evidence as exhibits. They were damaging and destructive to the Beecher defense. Another incriminating letter was quoted, one written by Beecher to Francis Moulton somewhat later, on February 5, 1872, which read in part:

But I see you but seldom, and my personal relations, environments, necessities, limitations, dangers and perplexities you can not see or imagine. If I had not gone through this great year of sorrow, I would not have believed that any one could pass through my experience and be alive or sane.

During all this time you were literally my stay and comfort. I should have fallen on the way but for the courage which you inspired and the hope which you breathed. . . . I came back hoping that the bitterness of death was passed. But T.'s troubles brought back the cloud with even severer suffering. . . . No man can see the difficulties that environ me unless he stands where I do. To say that I have a church on my hands is simple enough, but to have the hundreds and thousands of men pressing me, each one with his keen suspicion or anxiety or zeal; to see tendencies which, if not stopped, would break out into ruinous defense of me; to stop them without seeming to do it; to prevent any one questioning me; to meet and allay prejudices against T. which had their beginning years before this; to keep serene as if I was not alarmed or disturbed; to be cheerful at home and among friends when I was suffering the torments of the damned; to pass sleepless nights, often, and yet to come up fresh and full for Sunday—all this may be talked about, but the real thing can not be understood from the outside, nor its wearing and grinding on the nervous system. God knows that I have put more thought and judgment and earnest desire into my efforts to prepare a way for Theodore and Elizabeth than ever I did for myself a hundred fold. . . . But chronic evils require chronic remedies. If my destruction would place him all right, that shall not stand in the way. I am willing to step down and out. No one can offer more than that. That I do

offer. Sacrifice me without hesitation, if you can clearly see your way to his safety and happiness thereby. I do not think that anything would be gained by it. I should be destroyed, but he would not be saved. Elizabeth and the children would have their future clouded. . . . Life would be pleasant if I could see that rebuilt which is shattered. But to live on the sharp and ragged edge of anxiety, remorse, fear, despair, and yet to put on all the appearance of serenity and happiness, can not be endured much longer.

Mr. Morris then brought up the story that appeared on November 2, 1872, in *Woodhull and Claflin's Weekly,*

a story in which Mr. Beecher was accused of adultery with Mrs. Elizabeth R. Tilton. . . . What did Mr. Beecher do in connection with that story, and with that publication; and what, if an innocent man, ought he have done, is the question that now concerns you. . . . And he, accused of adultery with the wife of a member of his church—what should he have done? What did he do? He did nothing. . . . I will state to you the fact—that after the publication of this story, there was a universal demand throughout the land—a universal call upon Mr. Beecher to speak but one reassuring word, and deny this charge. . . . But not a word, not a word.

Near the end of his address Mr. Morris referred to Beecher's reluctance to pursue further actions under the indictment secured the previous October 1 from the grand jury by Mr. Beecher charging Mr. Tilton with libel:

From that day until we came in court here with this case, we have been beseeching them, imploring them, making our appeals to them, making our appeals to the court, to bring on the indictment, but they would not, and there was no alternative left, and we brought our action here, and before you we will bring our evidence, before you we will bring our wrongs, the wrongs that we have suffered, to you we will present our broken home. Before your face we arraign the seducer.

Mr. Morris passionately concluded his opening address:

I call upon you to brand the seducer as his crime deserves to be branded. Let it be written on every door throughout the land: "Death, destruction to the seducer"; and when you have rendered that verdict you will receive the prayers and blessings of every virtuous mother and of every virtuous daughter in the land, and a peaceful conscience will follow you through life, will be with you in the last solemn scenes of earth, and console you when at last you stand with your life-record before the ever-living God.

How ironically worthy of the Reverend Henry Ward Beecher himself!

* * *

On the afternoon of January 13 Francis D. Moulton was called on behalf of the plaintiff. He recited the conversation that took place between himself and Beecher on the evening of December 31, 1870:

The packed courtroom listens to Frank Moulton,
the most important witness at the trial.

Francis (Frank) D. Moulton.

He [Beecher] said, "Of course, if this charge is made against me—if Theodore should make any charge against me—my defense would be the technical one of general denial; but with you, since you know the truth, I throw myself upon your friendship, and what I believe to be your desire to save me." And he told me there, he said to me in addition, that his intercourse, that he considered his sexual intercourse with Mrs. Tilton as natural, an expression of his love for her. He said he felt justified in it on account of the love that he held for her, and which he knew she held for him; and said he, at the close of the conversation, "My life is ended. When to me there should now come honor and rest, I find myself upon the brink of a moral Niagara, with no power to save myself, and I call upon you to save me."

Q. State, if you please, what degree of emotion he manifested, if any?

A. A very great degree of emotion.

Q. How did it manifest itself?

A. In excited conversation.

Q. In any other way?

A. Not that I know of.

Q. I did not know but what he wept on that occasion.

MR. EVARTS.   Well—

THE WITNESS.   Well, yes, he did weep.

Q. Look at the paper which I show you and say whether it is one of the three of which you have spoken in your testimony. (Handling witness a letter.)

A. Yes, sir; that is one of them.

Q. In whose handwriting is that letter?

A. Elizabeth Tilton's.

MR. FULLERTON.   I propose to read it in evidence (reading):

"Saturday Morning.

"MY DEAR FRIEND FRANK:

"I want you to do me the greatest possible favor. My letter which you have, and the one I gave Mr. Beecher at his dictation last evening, ought both to be destroyed. Please bring both to me, and I will burn them. Show this note to Theodore and Mr. Beecher. They will see the propriety of this request.

"Yours truly,
"E. R. TILTON."

(Letter marked "Exhibit No. 1.")

MR. EVARTS.   (To Mr. Fullerton) Did he say how he received it?

MR. FULLERTON.   How did you receive that note from her?

A. I think from Elizabeth Tilton direct.

Q. From whom?

A. From Elizabeth Tilton directly.

MR. EVARTS.   Not personally, do you mean?

A. Yes, sir.

Q. At her house?

A. Yes, sir.

Q. That is your recollection of it?

A. Yes, sir.

Then Moulton was questioned on Beecher's so-called "letter of attrition" that he had dictated to Moulton:

MOULTON.   Mr. Beecher said to me that he was in misery on account of the crime that he had committed against Theodore Tilton and his wife and family; he said that he would be willing to make any reparation that was within his power; he said that Mr. Tilton, he thought would have been a better man under the circumstances in which he had been placed than he had been; that he felt that he had done a great wrong, because he was Theodore Tilton's friend, he was his pastor, he was his wife's friend and pastor, and he wept bitterly; and I said to him, "Mr. Beecher, why don't you say that to Mr. Tilton; why don't you express to him the grief you feel, and the contrition for it? You can do no more than that, and I think I know Theodore Tilton well enough to know that he would be satisfied with that, for I know he loves his wife." Mr. Beecher

told me to take pen and paper, and to write at his dictation, and I did write at his dictation the letter of January 1st, 1871.

Q. What was done after you wrote that letter?

A. I read the letter to him, and he read it, and then he signed—

Q. Never mind, we will show that in a moment. You say you read it to him?

A. Yes, sir.

Q. Did you read it as it was?

A. Yes, sir; and as it is.

Q. Did he take it and read it?

A. Yes, sir.

Q. Do you mean to be understood that you read it to him, and that he read it afterwards for himself?

A. Yes, certainly.

Q. And did he write anything himself upon that paper or those —add anything to the letter?

A. Yes, sir.

Q. Is that the letter of which you speak?

A. Yes, sir, that is it.

Q. What part of it is in the handwriting, if any, of Mr. Beecher; the words at the foot of the last page?

A. Yes, sir.

MR. FULLERTON.   I propose to read it in evidence.

(Letter submitted to Mr. Evarts.)

Q. Before reading the letter I want to ask you if you wrote it down as he dictated it?

A. Word for word.

MR. FULLERTON.   (reading).

"BROOKLYN, Jan. 1, '71.
"In trust with F. D. Moulton.

"MY DEAR FRIEND MOULTON

"I ask through you Theodore Tilton's forgiveness, and I humble myself before him as I do before my God, he would have been a better man, in my circumstances than I have been —I can ask nothing except that he will remember all the other hearts that would ache—I will not plead for myself. I even wish that I were dead, but others must live and suffer. I will die before any one but myself shall be inculpated. All my thoughts are running towards my friends toward the poor child lying there and praying with her folded hands; She is guiltless, sinned against, bearing the transgressions of another. Her forgiveness I have, I humbly pray to God that he may put it into the heart of her husband to forgive me.

"I have trusted this to Moulton in confidence.
"H. W. BEECHER."

(Paper marked "Exhibit No. 2." The signature and preceding line were separated from the body of the writing.)

Now, let me ask you, if those words which I read last, to wit: "I have trusted this to Moulton in confidence. H. W. Beecher," is what he wrote upon that paper?

A. Yes, sir.

During the days of direct examination of Francis Moulton, fifty-seven letters were introduced as exhibits. How the protagonists in this human drama could have so stupidly conducted their affairs in print is almost unbelievable. It was, however, all grist for the courtroom drama.

Porter, counsel for the defendant, a former judge,
denounces Theodore Tilton, the plaintiff.

On the fourteenth day of the trial the plaintiff offered
Theodore Tilton himself as a surprise witness. Mr. Evarts
jumped up and interjected, "But stop a moment, we
object to him." Then he launched into a two-hour argument against the competency of Mr. Tilton to be a
witness. Judge Neilson finally declared that he *was* a
competent witness, and on the sixteenth day of the trial

Tilton took the stand. For some reason, Judge Neilson
now ruled out Elizabeth Tilton's letter of confession,
nor would he allow the plaintiff to have its contents
stated in court. The testimony tediously reviewed all the
facts and situations previously known from Tilton's angle.
Equally tedious was the testimony of the prosecution
witnesses that followed.

Mr. Beecher, in court with Mrs. Beecher,
shakes hands with Mrs. Tilton.

COURTROOM SKETCHES:

The Beecher family in court.

(a) Mr. Moulton
answers an easy question;

On the thirty-second day of the trial Mr. Tracy opened the argument for the defense. He immediately sought to tear apart the career of Theodore Tilton as one "who had fallen from an eminence seldom attained by men of his age to the very bottom of an abyss." Mr. Tracy said, "We propose to dissect him first in the interest of truth, and bury him afterward in the interest of decency." The defense would base their side of the case on "the most remarkable conspiracy of modern times." He would show that while Mr. Tilton was the editor of a religious newspaper, he was an advocate of free lust. He then launched into a "eulogy" of Henry Ward Beecher's past life and his contribution to humanity.

Turning once more to Tilton, he brought up his espousal of radicalism and woman's suffrage, his amours with women other than his wife, his advocacy of free love—against which he contrasted Elizabeth Tilton's charity, devotion, and piety. On Beecher's visits to Mrs. Tilton, he put the full responsibility for them on Tilton's constant urgings that Beecher call more frequently, even when he was not at home.

Mr. Tracy then went into the laws bearing upon the case. It was not for the defense to prove that he was not guilty, but for the complainant to prove that he was. "The plaintiff," stated Mr. Tracy, "accuses his wife now, and seeks to blast her character; but during all these years he is unable to lay his hand upon a single well authenticated fact which convicts this white-souled woman of the slightest impropriety of conduct in connection with her pastor." He accused Tilton of conspiring first with Henry C. Bowen and then with Francis D. Moulton against the reputation of Henry Ward Beecher, then had his associate cite authorities on the subject of conspiracy. He compared Moulton with Judas.

The most important point made by Mr. Tracy in his opening address for the defense was that Elizabeth Tilton's letter of confession was never produced, that she herself "now has no knowledge or conception of what was in that letter," and that on December 30, 1870, overwhelmed by the magnitude of the charges her husband had read into that letter, she wrote the following retraction:

DEC. 30, 1870.
Wearied with importunity, and weakened by sickness, I gave a letter inculpating my friend Henry Ward Beecher, under assurances that that would remove all difficulties between me and my husband. That letter I now revoke. I was persuaded to it almost forced when I was in a weakened state of mind. I regret it and recall all its statements.
(Signed)   E. R. TILTON.
I desire to say explicitly Mr. Beecher has never offered any improper solicitation, but has always treated me in a manner becoming a Christian and a gentleman.
(Signed)   ELIZABETH R. TILTON.

Thus the opening address continued, with Mr. Tracy taking up point by point the "incriminating" letters and circumstances and presenting each in a light and interpretation favorable to the defendant. In the case of the Tilton servant girl, Bessie Turner, Mr. Tracy brought up the reported two attempts of Tilton to have sexual relations with her, and pointed out that her letter of denial was obtained by Mr. Tilton under pressure.

(*b*) Mrs. Tilton gazes at her husband;

(*c*) Mr. Tilton catches a momentary glimpse of his wife;

(*d*) Mr. Moulton gets a puzzling question.

Now Mr. Tracy went into Theodore Tilton's relations with Victoria Woodhull, and accused him of conspiring with her to publish the scandal, as well as having sexual relations with her.

The opening for the defense went on until the thirty-fifth day of the trial. Mr. Tracy ended his eloquent plea for a verdict in favor of the defendant with the quotation, "Though hand join in hand, the wicked shall not be unpunished, but the seed of the righteous shall be delivered." There was a burst of applause from the spectators.

* * *

Several thick volumes of testimony for the defense and cross-examination account for the trial dragging into its ninety-second day, at which point Mr. Evarts rose to sum up for the defense. It was this brilliant oration of his (some compared him to Henry Clay) that was to end the trial in a hung jury. It lasted eight days. Mr. Beach then took ten days to sum up for the plaintiff. On Thursday, June 24, 1875, Judge Neilson made his charge to the jury. It required, in contrast to the two closing speeches, only one hour and twenty minutes.

Mr. Beach, who took ten days to sum up for the plaintiff.

Mrs. Tilton attempts to introduce some pertinent correspondence at the trial, but the judge refuses to hear her.

The foundation of the action, said Judge Neilson, was the charge of adultery. The burden of proving it rested on the plaintiff. The evidence bearing on this principal charge was treated under four divisions: the writings, the oral admissions, the tacit or implied admissions, and the conduct of the defendant. In a statement exceedingly valuable to the defense he said: "We are wont to say that all suitors are treated alike, and in most respects they are; but yet in a case of this character a man grown old in prayer and pious service has *prima facie* the benefit of a presumption which the mere man of the world has not."

On the matter of the statements of the witnesses, Judge Neilson pointed out (to the advantage of the defendant) several very glaring discrepancies in their testimony. "Mr. Moulton on various occasions, as he himself testifies, and as other witnesses state, declared that the defendant was not guilty of the sexual intercourse which he now says had been admitted. It is for you to consider how far the inconsistency in his statements goes to discredit him. . . . As to Mr. Tilton, you will consider whether his testimony to the confession of the defendant's guilt can be reconciled with his previous declarations that his wife was innocent."

At the conclusion of his charge, Judge Neilson asked both counsels if they were satisfied, to which both assented. He then ordered the jury to retire.

A week later, on Thursday, July 1, 1875, the jury sent a note to Judge Neilson:

May it please the Court: We think there is no possibility of our agreeing on a verdict, and we respectfully ask to be discharged.

Judge Neilson sent them back for further deliberations, but on Friday, July 2, because they were still unable to agree, Judge Neilson dismissed them.

* * *

For the ecclesiastical world, and especially Plymouth Church, a hung jury was tantamount to exoneration for the Reverend Henry Ward Beecher. Religious newspapers here and in England were quick to hail his vindication and denounce those who had any doubts. But the public at large was still divided over Beecher's guilt or innocence. The *New York Times* in its issue of July 3, 1875, neatly summed up public opinion:

The jury are unable to agree upon a verdict in the Beecher case. The division of opinion which prevails among twelve men who have had the advantage of hearing all the witnesses examined and cross-examined is shared by the public at large. But as we pass beyond the reach of those potent local influences which necessarily pressed heavily on the jury—for a man was under trial who in Brooklyn has been treated almost as a god—the divisions of opinion will be more strongly marked. There are many who will always hold that the plaintiff's case was fully proved. A second class will continue to believe Mr. Beecher innocent; while a third will consider that the Scotch verdict of "not proven" would have been the only just conclusion to have reached. And sensible men throughout the country will in their hearts be compelled to acknowledge that Mr. Beecher's management of his private friendships and affairs has been entirely unworthy of his name, position, and sacred calling.

If Beecher lived out the rest of his days under the shadow of the Great Scandal, he did his best to ignore it and brush aside any unpleasant reverberations that constantly confronted him. Unwilling to face further publicity on the matter, he quickly dropped his charge of criminal libel against Frank Moulton. But on his return to Plymouth Church he ousted from their roles everyone who had not backed him in the trial. Next, to repair the damage to his reputation, he went on a lecture tour, and no wonder the scandal-hungry audiences flocked to hear him. He turned to political issues with little success. He joined the cause of the downtrodden, and pleaded for reforms for the unemployed and underpaid. Briefly he delighted his Plymouth Church parishioners by denying the existence of Hell, but, predictably unpredictable, he soon recanted. He made many more enemies in the closing years of his life, but somehow he miraculously kept his following at a pitch of excitement—no more so than when, espousing the theories of Charles Darwin and Herbert Spencer, he threw Hell and damnation out the church window and questioned the infallibility of the Bible. His audiences devoured his teachings. In 1886 he made a lecture trip to England, preaching his new-found doctrine, which was financially and prestigiously one of his most successful ventures. On March 8, 1887, he died of a stroke. Theodore Tilton, who had long ago exiled himself to Paris, was shown a cable by a newspaper correspondent announcing Beecher's death. He made no comment, but sat for a while in silence at his table at the Café de la Régence. Then, ignoring the correspondent, he quietly returned to the chess game he had been playing.

And what of Lib Tilton? After the trial she lived quietly with her mother in Brooklyn and taught in a private school. But on April 13, 1878, she wrote a letter to her legal counselor that was immediately published in most of the newspapers in the country. In it she confessed that "the charge brought by my husband, of adultery between myself and the Reverend Henry Ward Beecher, was true." But by now, people had accepted the outcome of the trial and were inclined to give Beecher the benefit of the doubt, or at least were tired of hearing about the matter again. Lib Tilton, instead of causing a renewal of the scandal, faded into oblivion. She became a recluse, eventually lost her sight, and died in 1897. She was laid to rest in the same cemetery in which the Reverend Henry Ward Beecher was buried.

13

Ned Kelly

[1880]

IF AMERICA CAN BOAST OF ITS JESSE JAMES GANG OF OUT-laws, Australia can match them with her infamous Kelly gang of bushrangers. Whatever their crimes—and they were legion—the Jameses and the Kellys, viewed through romantically tinted glasses, today emerge as daring adventurers, instead of the horse thieves, bank bandits, and murderers that they were.

Ned Kelly was the leader of the notorious Kelly gang that for years terrorized the northeastern sector of Victoria. The Kelly home was in Greta. From the age of sixteen, Ned, along with his younger brother Dan, was in trouble with the police for horse and cattle stealing. In April 1878, when Ned was twenty-four, a Constable Fitzpatrick of Benalla came to the Kelly home to arrest Dan on a charge of cattle stealing. Only Mother Kelly and their sister were at home. Fitzpatrick was drunk, and made a pass at the young girl. Whereupon Mrs. Kelly bashed him over the head with a shovel. Dan came home about the same time these events were taking place, and insisted he was innocent of the constable's charge. When Ned arrived, not recognizing the constable, he shot him in the wrist. He then pried the bullet out of Fitzpatrick's wrist, and both agreed to forget the incident. However, Fitzpatrick, admittedly an unsavory character, reported that Ned and Dan had attacked him in the performance of his duty, with intent to kill. To avoid arrest the young men fled into the ranges. Meanwhile Mrs. Kelly was arrested for her part in the attack and, a few months later, was sentenced by Judge Redmond Barry to three years in jail. That she was imprisoned for trying to protect her daughter was indication of the extent to which the police would go to get the Kellys out of that part of the country.

Ned and Dan teamed up with two other young bush-rangers, Joe Byrne and Steve Hart. Informed that all four were hiding out in the Wombat Ranges, near Mansfield, four officers, Sergeant Kennedy and Constables Lonigan, Scanlon, and McIntyre, set out for Stringybark Creek. On October 25, 1878, Kennedy and Scanlon left their camp to patrol. Suddenly the other two were surprised by the Kelly gang. Ned killed Lonigan at once. When Kennedy and Scanlon returned, the gang was waiting for them. Ordered to surrender, Kennedy reached too late for his gun, and was killed. Scanlon's death followed. During the melee, McIntyre jumped on Kennedy's horse, and escaped. The government set a price of £1,000 for the capture of the four bandits.

Now the gang set about raiding and terrorizing the surrounding country. As they robbed banks, attempted to wreck a train, rifled stores and whole towns, tricked and locked up constables, the governments of Victoria and New South Wales together offered £8,000 for their apprehension. Though this was the largest reward ever offered in Australia for the capture of bushrangers, the gang was not seen by the police until June, 1880.

On June 26, 1880, a stoolpigeon, Aaron Sherrit, who had kept the police informed of the whereabouts of the Kelly gang, was shot by Byrne, accompanied by Dan. At the time of the shooting there were four constables in the house, and the chase was on. Early on Sunday morning the outlaws arrived at Jones's Hotel in Glenrowan. They locked all the guests in one large room, and then awaited a special train carrying police officers, which they planned to wreck and at the same time kill all of the officers. Since they had a long wait ahead of them, they permitted their captive hotel guests to dance

Ned Kelly.

and enjoy themselves. But now the gang blundered. They allowed a Mr. Curnon and his ailing wife to go home. He at once rode furiously toward the oncoming train to warn them. The gang had left the key to the hotel on the mantelpiece. Constable Bracken, one of the captives, secured it and let himself out. After the train, which had been intercepted by Curnon, arrived, the police, led by Bracken, immediately surrounded the hotel and reinforcements were quickly summoned. Throughout Sunday night the police waged a gun battle with the members of the gang in the hotel. Early Monday morning a tall figure appeared in back of the police line and began firing upon them. It was Ned Kelly, dressed in his suit of protective armor. For half an hour shots were exchanged, until finally Ned was shot in the leg, and captured.

Other events quickly followed. Byrne was killed at the bar. The captive guests broke out and ran for cover. The hotel was then set on fire. Later, the bodies of Dan Kelly and Hart were found in the ruins. They had either shot themselves or taken poison. Ned was the last member of the gang left alive to face a trial that could only end in his conviction for murder.

*   *   *

Five weeks after his capture, Ned Kelly's wounds had healed sufficiently for him to stand trial. On Saturday morning, July 30, he was charged at a hastily convened court in the jail with the murders of Constables Lonigan and Scanlon at Stringybark Creek on October 26, 1878. Constable McIntyre, the only eyewitness to the shootings, gave evidence. The presiding magistrate then ordered that the prisoner appear before the police court at Beechworth.

On Friday, August 6, 1880, the Beechworth Courthouse was packed with spectators. Mrs. Skillion, Ned's sister, had hired Mr. David Gauson of Melbourne to defend him. Henry Foster, police magistrate who was on the bench, immediately denied Gauson's application for adjournment for time to prepare the defense. The Crown called McIntyre, who gave an account of Lonigan's death. By cross-examination, Gauson revealed undue police persecution of the Kelly family. The final hearing took place on Monday without the defense being allowed to call a single witness. Gauson had failed to dent the case of the prosecution, nor had he laid any basis for a defense. Foster then sent Kelly back to jail to await trial for murder on October 14, the next session of the Beechworth Circuit Court.

Ned Kelly in one of the special
armored suits he designed for
his gang to wear in their battles
with the police. Though the
suits were bulletproof, the area
below the waist remained
unprotected. Ned Kelly was
finally captured when shots in
the leg brought him down.

Fearful, however, that a local jury might be favorable to Ned Kelly, there was now a change of venue. The trial would be held in Melbourne on October 28 at the Central Criminal Court. On the bench would be Mr. Justice Redmond Barry, the same judge who had sentenced Ned's mother to three years in jail and Ned *in absentia,* to fifteen years.

The trial got under way on Thursday, October 28, with Judge Barry refusing Mr. Bindon's (Ned's attorney, with Gauson instructing) application for further adjournment. Mr. C. A. Smyth opened the case for the prosecution by sketching the events leading up to the murder of Constable Thomas Lonigan, including warrants dated April, 1878, for the arrest of Edward and Dan Kelly on charges of horse stealing, and a warrant to arrest Ned for wounding with intent to murder Edward Fitzpatrick. Then McIntyre told of the events at Stringybark and of Lonigan's murder.

Following this, a long string of witnesses for the Crown testified that Ned had admitted to the murder and to his hatred of the police.

George Stevens, a groom, said that the prisoner had remarked in his hearing, "If there was any shooting at Stringybark, I did it."

James Gloster, a draper, said: "My impression was he took the shooting on himself to screen others. He said:

'My mother struggled up with a large family. I am very much incensed at the police. It is not murder to shoot one's enemies. The police are my natural enemies.'"

The next day, more witnesses appeared for the prosecution. Robert Scott, manager of the National Bank at Euroa, gave evidence that after his bank had been robbed of £2,300 by the Kelly gang, the prisoner had remarked, "Oh, I shot Lonigan."

J. W. Tarleton, manager of the Jerilderie branch of the Bank of New South Wales, which was held up by the Kelly gang, testified that while they were all held in the hotel bar, Ned Kelly made a speech, saying: "It is all very well to say that we shot the police in cold blood. We had to do it in self-defense." He also told his captives that he had been driven to being an outlaw, and, further, that he himself had shot Kennedy, Scanlon, and Lonigan.

Dr. S. Reynolds then declared that he had made the postmortem examination of the body of Thomas Lonigan and that he had died from a bullet which hit his eye and penetrated into the brain.

This closed the case for the Crown.

Early in the afternoon of October 29, Mr. Bindon opened the case for the defense. He called no witnesses, but asked that evidence he objected to be reviewed by the full court.

JUDGE BARRY.   What points do you allude to?

MR. BINDON.   All the transactions that took place after the death of Lonigan, which were detailed in evidence.

JUDGE BARRY.   I think the whole was put as part of the proceedings of the day.

MR. BINDON.   There was a period, after the death of Lonigan, when no further evidence was applicable.

JUDGE BARRY.   The way the evidence was put was that Lonigan was not killed by the prisoner in self-defense.

The request being overruled, Mr. Smyth summed up the evidence for the Crown. He presented a strong case: "When you find one man shooting down another in cold blood, you need not stop to enquire his motives. It was of malignant hatred against the police. The prisoner had been leading a wild, lawless life and was at war with society. I have proved abundantly by witnesses, who were scarcely cross-examined, that the murder of Lonigan was committed in cold blood."

It did not matter, went on the prosecutor, whose bullet killed Lonigan, because the whole gang was engaged in an illegal act. The murders that Ned Kelly and his gang committed were of a most bloodthirsty nature. They never appeared in the open except when they were fully armed, and therefore held a great advantage over their victims.

Mr. Bindon, summing up for the defense, deplored the introduction of evidence that had nothing to do with the present case, and asked the jury not to let such evidence influence their verdict. To refute McIntyre's evidence as to what had occurred in the Wombat Ranges, he pointed out that the police appeared in plainclothes, not in uniform, and that an unfortunate fracas occurred in which Lonigan was killed. McIntyre was the only witness, and a prejudiced one. So much was happening so fast that McIntyre could not possibly have distinguished correctly what took place that day. Only the prisoner and McIntyre knew what had happened, and the prisoner's lips were sealed. (At that time, Australian law did not permit the prisoner to testify.)

Judge Barry then summed up. He declared that if two or more men made preparations with malice aforethought to murder a man, even if two or three did not take part in the murder, they were principals in the first degree and equally guilty of the crime. . . . The fact that the police were in plainclothes had nothing whatever to do with the case. . . . It was not necessary to have McIntyre's evidence corroborated . . . the prisoner was not on trial for the murders of Kennedy and Scanlon; the object of introducing evidence subsequent to the shooting of Lonigan was to give the jury every opportunity to judge the conduct of the prisoner and his intentions during that particular day. . . . The judge held that the free confessions made by the prisoner at various times and in a spirit of vainglory could be accepted as evidence.

Judge Barry concluded by instructing the jury that they would have to regard the evidence as a whole, and accordingly say whether the murder had been committed. It could not be manslaughter. The verdict of the jury must either be guilty of murder or an acquittal.

The jury retired at ten minutes past five in the afternoon, and returned in a half hour with the verdict "guilty."

The judge and the prisoner then exchanged lengthy words, after which the judge passed the sentence of hanging, ending with the usual words "and may the Lord have mercy on your soul!"

"I will add something to that," answered Ned Kelly. "I will meet you there."

On Thursday morning, November 11, Ned Kelly was hanged from the prison gallows. His last words, as the trap was sprung, were, "Such is life." Two days later, Judge Barry was taken suddenly ill, and on November 23 he died. Ned Kelly's last words at his trial were indeed prophetic.

*   *   *

Sympathy in that part of Australia was clearly on the side of Ned Kelly. The people were becoming incensed at the arrogance of the police and at police brutality. For months afterward it was worth a constable's life to travel through "Kelly Land." The Kelly Reward Board, charged with distributing the £8,000 offered by Victoria and New South Wales for the apprehension of the gang, put off proceedings until March, 1881, when things quieted down a bit. The governor appointed a royal commission to look into the outbursts at Glenrowan and the efficiency of the police force. Constable Fitzpatrick was labeled a liar and dismissed from the force. It was estimated that the Kelly affair had cost the country £150,000.

Ned Kelly was the last and most famous of the Australian bushrangers. Like many another brigand band, he and his gang have left behind a romantic legend that will always be part of Australian folklore.

Lizzie Borden leans forward expectantly as her lawyer,
ex-governor Robinson, sums up in her defense at her trial for murder.

14

Lizzie Borden

[1893]

THE BUSTLING CITY OF FALL RIVER, MASSACHUSETTS, WAS sweltering in a heat wave on the morning of August 4, 1892. In the Andrew J. Borden household at 92 Second Street, the day's routine began much as on any other day. The servant girl, Bridget Sullivan, awoke and came downstairs to the kitchen from her attic room on the third floor at 6:15 A.M. She started the fire in the stove. The Borden's guest for the night, John V. Morse, the brother of Andrew's first wife, had risen a bit earlier and was in the sitting room by 6:00 A.M. At 6:30 A.M. Mrs. Abby Borden, Andrew's second wife, came downstairs, followed five minutes later by Andrew. He emptied his slop pitcher in the back yard, then went to the sitting room to chat with John Morse. From 7:00 to 7:30 A.M. Bridget served the three of them breakfast, during which time Morse noted that Mrs. Borden told Bridget to wash the windows that morning. With the family served, Bridget had her own breakfast and then, around 8:00 A.M., started on the dishes. As yet, Lizzie Borden had not come down. Her older sister, Emma, was away visiting friends in Fairhaven.

About 8:45 A.M. Mr. Borden saw Morse to the side door and invited him back for dinner, which was always served at midday. Soon after Morse left, Lizzie Borden came downstairs and ate a scant breakfast in the kitchen. Shortly after nine o'clock Mr. Borden left for the Union Savings Bank, of which he was president. Mrs. Borden went upstairs to tidy up the guest room. At 9:30 A.M. Mr. Borden arrived at the bank. *At just about that time Abby Borden was brutally beaten with an ax in the guest room of the Borden house.* Nineteen times the ax descended on her head, one blow penetrating as much as five inches into the skull.

At 10:40 A.M. Mrs. Caroline Kelly, the Borden's neighbor to the south, saw Mr. Borden, returning from town, go up the front steps of his house and try the front door. Bridget Sullivan, who had been washing the windows on the north side of the house, had just come inside. She heard Mr. Borden trying to unlock the door, and went to his aid. She had some trouble with the lock, and swore. Lizzie Borden, standing near the head of the stairs, heard her swearing, and laughed. Bridget opened the door and let Mr. Borden in. Lizzie had some conversation with her father. Bridget heard her tell him that Mrs. Borden had received a note saying someone was ill, and had gone out. After going upstairs, Mr. Borden returned, went into the sitting room, and lay down on the sofa, perhaps somewhat exhausted by the heat and his walk home. He was seventy years old. It was now some time between 10:50 and 10:56 A.M. During the few minutes, Lizzie supposedly left the house, went to the barn in the backyard, and up to the loft, where she searched for sinkers in a box on the workbench. Meanwhile Bridget Sullivan had gone up to her attic room to rest. She heard the City Hall clock strike eleven o'clock.

At about 11:08 A.M. Lizzie returned to the house and went to the sitting room, where her father was resting. *She found him with his head split open, covered with fresh blood.* Lizzie screamed, and Bridget ran to the head of the stairs and asked, "What's the matter?"

"Come down, quick; Father's dead; someone came in and killed him," Lizzie answered. Bridget rushed down and started to look into the sitting room, but Lizzie stopped her.

"No, Maggie, don't go in there; go for Dr. Bowen."

173

The residence of Andrew J. Borden at 92 Second Street, Fall River, Massachusetts,
where the murders were committed.
Fall River Historical Society

It was 11:12 A.M.

Bridget ran across the street to Dr. Bowen's house, but, finding him out, hurried back. From her house next door Mrs. Adelaide B. Churchill saw Bridget return. "Go for Miss Russell," said Lizzie, and Bridget went. Sensing something wrong, Mrs. Churchill called over and asked what was the matter.

Lizzie said, "Do come over. Someone has killed my father."

Mrs. Churchill rushed over. "Where's your father?" she asked.

"In the sitting room," Lizzie answered.

"Where were you when it happened?" asked Mrs. Churchill.

Lizzie said, "I went to the barn to get a piece of iron." She then told Mrs. Churchill she must have a doctor.

Mrs. Churchill ran over to Hall's stable and asked the man there to go for a doctor. John Cunningham, a newsdealer, overheard Mrs. Churchill's conversation. It was 11:15 A.M. when he phoned the police and reported a

row at the Borden house. Marshal Rufus B. Hilliard received the call and immediately dispatched Patrolman George W. Allen, who, four minutes later, was staring down at the body of Mr. Borden and at the same time noting there were no signs of a struggle. Allen deputized a painter, John S. Sawyer, to guard the side door and not let anyone in except the police or a doctor.

Meanwhile Mrs. Churchill, Dr. Bowen, Bridget, and Miss Russell returned to the Borden house. Dr. Bowen briefly examined the body. Blood was still flowing from the ten wounds in the head. All but two had gone through the skull.

At this point Lizzie said she wished someone would try to find Mrs. Borden. "I don't know but she is killed, too, for I thought I heard her come in," Lizzie remarked. Mrs. Churchill and Bridget started up the front stairs. Bridget, in front, suddenly paused, uttered an exclamation, and ran into the guest room. Mrs. Churchill reached the same step, saw what appeared to be a body, and raced downstairs to the kitchen.

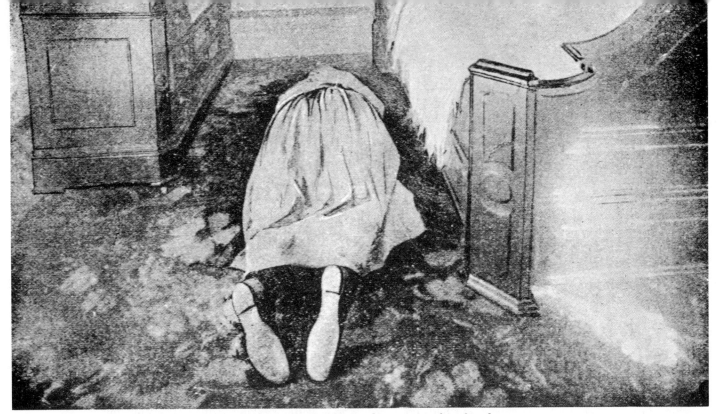

The bashed body of Abby Borden as it was found in the
guest room of the Borden house.

The mutilated body of Andrew Borden as it was found on the sofa
in the sitting room of the Borden house.

Noting her agitation Miss Russell asked, "What, another?"

Mrs. Churchill nodded. "Yes, she is up there." Bridget had followed her back to the kitchen. It was 11:30 A.M.

Dr. Bowen returned from the telegraph office, where he had sent a message to Emma in Fairhaven, telling her of the events and asking her to return at once. He went quickly to the guest room and found the body of Mrs. Borden lying face down. He noted that there was no sign of a struggle and that the coagulation of the blood indicated that she had been dead for some time. He was then joined by Medical Examiner Dr. William A. Dolan, who happened to be driving by, and stopped to inquire from the crowd outside the house what had happened. The two doctors found eighteen wounds in the skull. Later, another wound was found in her back. All were made by a sharp cutting instrument such as an ax or a hatchet.

A few moments earlier John Morse had returned from Weybosset Street, a distance of a mile and a quarter, where he had gone to see his niece. He had left there at about 12:30 P.M. and taken the horsecar back. He did not note the commotion in the street. He entered the north gate and went to a pear tree, picked two or three, and ate part of one. He then entered the side door, evidently being let in by Sawyer when he identified himself as Mr. Borden's brother-in-law. He looked at the body of Mr. Borden, then went upstairs far enough to see the body of Mrs. Borden, which he had been told was there. By then, several more police had arrived. Special Police Officer Patrick H. Doherty was the second policeman to reach the house, followed by Assistant Marshal John Fleet and officers Michael Mullaby, John Devine, and William H. Medley. They searched the house for evidence and made numerous inquiries covering the condition of things in the house before the murders. Bridget showed them to the cellar, where they found four hatchets—one with some suspicious stains on it—and removed them to the police station. All through the day the police searched the house, cellar, yard, and barn—but found not a thread of evidence that could be connected with the murders. As the police reporter for the *Fall River Globe*, Edwin H. Porter, put it:

A diagram of the property of Andrew Borden, showing the barn in the left rear to which Lizzie claimed to have gone just about the time Andrew Borden was murdered.

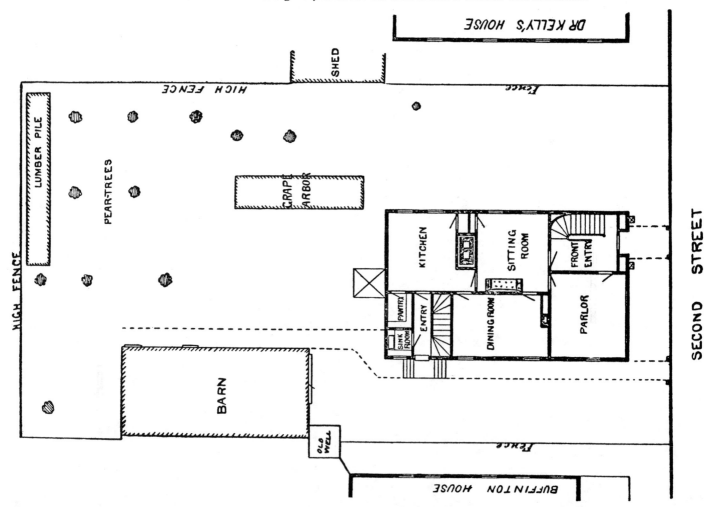

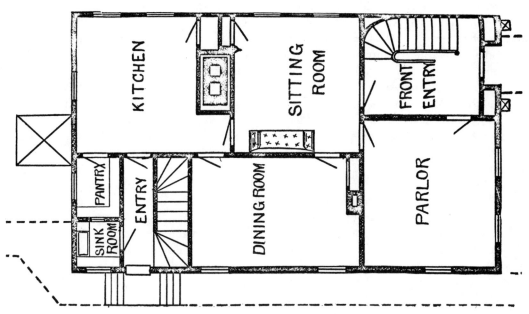

Ground plan of the Borden residence.

From cellar to attic the police and physicians delved into every nook and corner; every particle of hay in the barn loft and every blade of grass in the yard was turned over; and when the day was done the harvest had been nothing, except the discovery of the double murder of a peaceful old man and his harmless wife, struck down in their home like an ox in the stall. There was no assassin, no weapon, no motive; just the crime and veil of mystery surrounding which apparently time alone could lift.

Second-floor plan of the Borden house: (1) Mr. and Mrs. Borden's room, (2) chamber, (3) Emma Borden's bedroom, (4) Lizzie Borden's bedroom, (5) guest room where Mrs. Borden's body was found.

Andrew J. Borden was one of the wealthiest and most influential men in Fall River. He was president of one bank and a director of others, as well as of many of the city's prosperous manufacturing companies. He had made his initial fortune in the undertaking business and was now worth over a quarter of a million dollars. By his first wife, Sarah A. Morse, he had two children: Emma, the elder, now thirty-seven, and Lizzie Andrew Borden, now thirty-two. Sarah died when Lizzie was only two years old. Three years later, in June, 1865, Andrew married Abby Durfee Gray.

While much has been made in fiction and drama of hate that existed between the parents and the children, such did not seem to be so. True, Emma refused to call her stepmother "Mother," always referring to her as "Abby," while Lizzie as a child did call her "Mother," but stopped doing so in later years. Emma was the quiet one who preferred to stay at home. She had never been outside New England. Lizzie, on the other hand, was active in church matters, a member of numerous societies, and in 1890, made a grand tour of Europe with a party of young ladies. She was very close to her father, and had inherited much of his stubbornness and arrogance. He had taught her a great deal about business matters, perhaps looking forward to the day when someone would carry on his interests. She was exceedingly close to Miss Alice E. Russell, her best friend.

Thus the Borden household at the time of the murders consisted of Mr. and Mrs. Borden, Emma, Lizzie, and the servant girl, Bridget Sullivan, whom the sisters called "Maggie," and who had been with the family for two years and nine months. On the night before the murders those who slept in the house were Mr. and Mrs. Borden, Lizzie, Bridget, and the guest John V. Morse, who had arrived unexpectedly without even a toothbrush in his pocket. Emma was away in Fairhaven. At the exact times of the murders, beside the victims, there were only two people on the premises, Lizzie and Bridget. And at the time of Andrew Borden's murder, if one accepts Lizzie's contention that she was in the barn, only Bridget was in the house.

Could an unknown maniac have come unseen into the house, hacked to death Abby Borden around 9:30 A.M., hidden in a closet or somewhere until shortly after 11:00 A.M. when he similarly hacked Andrew Borden to death, then left without a soul seeing or hearing him? In a town like Fall River, on a narrow street where the houses were so close together, it hardly seemed possible. It did *not* seem *at all possible* to District Attorney Hosea M. Knowlton, who was called into the case by Mayor Coughlin. Egged on by public clamor for apprehension of a suspect, there seemed to him no choice but to arrest Lizzie Borden. Her cold and unemotional behavior at the time of the murders and at his long and searching examination of her at the inquest had convinced him that she was the murderer. He believed he had built up a good case of circumstantial evidence against her. Besides, who else was there to accuse?

The inquest had been held in secret before Judge Joseph C. Blaisdell. Not even Lizzie Borden's lawyer, Andrew J. Jennings, was allowed to be present. It was followed the next day with the arraignment of Lizzie Borden at the Second District Court, presided over by Judge Blaisdell on Friday, August 12. The court ordered the clerk to read the warrant. "'You needn't read it," said Mr. Jennings. "The prisoner pleads not guilty."

However, the warrant, drawn up by Marshall Hilliard, read as follows:

That Lizzie A. Borden of Fall River, in the county of Bristol, at Fall River, aforesaid, in the county aforesaid, on the fourth day of August, in the year of our Lord 1892, in and upon one Andrew J. Borden, then and there feloniously, willfully and of her malice aforethought, did strike, giving unto the said Andrew J. Borden, then and there, with the hatchet aforesaid, by the stroke aforesaid, in manner aforesaid, in and upon the head of the said Andrew J. Borden, one mortal wound, of which said mortal wound the said Andrew J. Borden then and there instantly died . . . and that the said Lizzie Borden, the said Andrew J. Borden, in manner and form aforesaid, then and there feloniously, wilfully and of her malice aforethought did kill and murder.

❀ ❀ ❀

Members of the Borden household who slept in the house the night before the fateful murders: Andrew J. Borden, Abby Borden, Lizzie Borden, Bridget Sullivan, and John V. Morse (Andrew's brother-in-law).

ANDREW J. BORDEN.

MRS. BORDEN.

The combination police station and courtroom in Fall River where Lizzie Borden was taken for her examination and questioning regarding the Borden murders. *Fall River Historical Society*

MISS LIZZIE BORDEN.

BRIDGET SULLIVAN.

JOHN V. MORSE.

Lizzie and her sister Emma (with hand covering her face)
sit dejectedly in the courtroom of the Fall River courthouse
at the examination of Lizzie before Judge Blaisdell.

Sketches of the court officers and witnesses at the examination of
Lizzie Borden (*from top, reading down and left to right*):
Judge Blaisdell, Clerk Leonard, Marshal Hilliard, Attorney Adams,
District Attorney Knowlton, Assistant Marshal Fleet,
and Officer Doherty.

More witnesses and scenes at the Borden examination (*from top to bottom, reading down and left to right*): Miss Lucy Collett, Miss Russell, uninterested spectator, Druggist Burle, Professor Wood, Miss Emma and Lizzie Borden, Joseph Desrosters and interpreter, Mrs. Churchill, and reporters. With suspicion pointing to Lizzie, Judge Blaisdell remands her to jail to await trial for murder.

On August 22nd a preliminary hearing was held before Judge Blaisdell to determine whether or not Lizzie Borden should be held for action by the grand jury. A great deal of conflicting evidence as to what was testified to at the inquest and what was stated under oath at the preliminary hearing convinced Judge Blaisdell that there was sufficient cause to hold her. He could not conceive that the body of Lizzie's stepmother had lain so exposed in the guest room all the time Lizzie was in the house and that she had neither seen it nor heard any commotion. Accordingly, she was returned to the Taunton Jail. She was "probably guilty."

✻　✻　✻

The grand jury of Bristol County met at Taunton on November 15, but it was not until December 2 that it finally returned three indictments against Lizzie Borden. One charged her with the murder of her father, Andrew J. Borden; another, with the murder of her stepmother, Abby D. Borden; and the third charged her jointly with the murder of both.

Lizzie Borden remained in the Taunton Jail until May 8, 1893, when she was taken to New Bedford, Massachusetts, and arraigned before Judge J. W. Hammond of the Superior Court to plead to the indictments. In each case she pleaded not guilty. The date of her trial was then set for June 5 to take place in New Bedford, and she was taken back to the Taunton Jail.

Meanwhile, former Governor George D. Robinson was retained to assist Andrew Jennings in her defense.

✻　✻　✻

The pail in which Lizzie Borden's meals were served to her in the Taunton jail.
Fall River Historical Society

The Taunton, Massachusetts, jail in which Lizzie Borden was held pending her trial.
Fall River Historical Society

Lizzie Borden at the time of the Borden murders.
Fall River Historical Society

The trial of Lizzie opened on the morning of June 5, 1893, before the Superior Court for the County of Bristol, Massachusetts. So important was it that it was presided over by three judges: Chief Justice Albert Mason and Associate Justice Caleb Blodgett and Justice Dewey. The first day, during which no spectators were allowed in court, was devoted to the selection of the jury. The court appointed Charles I. Richards of North Attleborough as the foreman.

On the second day the prosecution, represented by William H. Moody, made its opening statement. Mr. Moody addressed the jurors:

Upon the fourth day of August of the last year, an old man and woman, husband and wife, each without a known enemy in the world, in their own home, upon a frequented street in the most populous city in this County, under the light of day and in the midst of its activities, were, first one, then, after an interval of an hour, another, severely killed by unlawful human agency. Today a woman of good social position, of hitherto unquestioned character, a member of a Christian church and active in its good works, the own daughter of one of the victims, is at the bar of this Court, accused by the Grand Jury of this County of these crimes.

What were the major points of evidence the prosecution would seek to prove in the course of the trial? They were, as Mr. Moody stated in his opening speech, as follows:

1. That there was an unkindly feeling between the prisoner and her stepmother that came to light some five years previous during a controversy in the family over some property matters. At that time the defendant ceased to address her stepmother as "Mother."

2. That on Wednesday, the day before the murders, the prisoner went to a drug store in Fall River and attempted to buy ten-cents' worth of prussic acid, a deadly poison, to clean a sealskin cape. The druggist refused to sell it without a prescription.

3. That the prisoner had ample time to kill her stepmother while Bridget Sullivan, the servant girl, was outside the house washing the windows. That her stepmother was in the house at the time and had not gone out to visit a sick friend in response to a note that was undelivered. In fact, that there was no such note.

4. That at the time of the murder of Mr. Borden, the prisoner was *not* in the barn, as she contended, but in the house alone downstairs with her father while Bridget was resting in her attic room on the third floor.

5. That the clothes worn by the prisoner at the time of the murders which she turned over to the police were *not* the actual ones she had worn and that the true dress she had on, which must have been covered with bloodstains, she burned several days later in the presence of her best friend, Miss Alice Russell.

6. That the probable murder weapon was a handle-less ax that the defendant cleverly tried to camouflage; then she burned the freshly broken-off handle in the stove.

7. That when the bodies were discovered not a thing in the house had been disturbed, no property had been taken, no money and valuables were taken off the body of Mr. Borden, and there was not the slightest evidence of a struggle. That the assailant's approach aroused no suspicion in either of the victims. That the assailant, being the sole one present at the time of the murders, could only have been the defendant, Lizzie Borden.

Upon the conclusion of Mr. Moody's statement, the prosecution called its first witness, Thomas Kieran, an engineer, who testified as to various measurements in the Borden house. On cross-examination, the defense showed how a man might be hidden in the closet in the front hall and not be seen by anyone. That afternoon the jurymen visited the Borden house to acquaint themselves with the layout and arrangement of the property, which were to play so important a part in the trial.

On the third day of the trial John V. Morse, the defendant's uncle and guest in the house the night before the murders, was called to the stand. He had not seen Lizzie from the time he arrived on Wednesday until the murders on Thursday. He had been told she was in the house and upstairs in her room. He described in full his actions during this period. On cross-examination the defense made a telling point with regard to the lock on the front door. To refute the prosecution's charge that the house was always locked up tighter than a drum, Morse was asked:

Q. I will ask you whether you have observed anything in the use of the front door in regard to the spring lock, Mr. Morse?
A. Yes, sir.
Q. What is that?
A. Well, if you shut the door hard, the spring lock would catch; if you didn't, it would not.
Q. Then if it did not catch—
A. You could open it without any trouble.
(Morse also testified that the police who arrived after the murders made a thorough search of everything in the house.)
Q. To your observation, as they went about, they had free search?
A. They had free access to everything.

The afternoon of the third day of the trial was devoted entirely to the examination of Bridget Sullivan. She described her activities on the day of the trial. The prosecution tried to make the point that no note was delivered to Mrs. Borden:

Q. Let me ask you if anyone to your knowledge came to that house on the morning of August 4 with a message or a note for Mrs. Borden?
A. No, sir. I never seen nobody.

On cross-examination the defense's questions attempted to tear down the prosecution's contention of their ill-feeling between Lizzie and her stepmother. They asked Bridget:

Q. Did you have any trouble there in the family?
A. No, sir.
Q. You never saw anything out of the way?
A. No, sir.
Q. You never saw any conflict in the family?
A. No, sir.
A. Never saw the least—any quarreling or anything of that kind?
A. No, sir. I did not.

At another point Robinson queried Bridget about the possibility of an intruder entering the house while she was washing the windows. Bridget admitted that she had taken time out to go over to the corner of the yard to talk to Mrs. Kelly's girl and that anybody could have entered the side door and not be seen by her.

Q. Well, the coast was clear while you stood talking to the Kelly girl?
A. Yes, I could see the front door but I could not see the side door.

Dr. Seabury W. Bowen was the first witness as the trial went into its fourth day. The medical testimony having been duly gone through, the prosecution hammered away at the dress Lizzie had worn on the day of the murders. Dr. Bowen stood firm on his position that he hadn't noticed what the dress looked like.

Q. Did it appear to you to be a drab dress?
A. I did not pretend to describe a woman's dress and I do not intend to now.

On cross-examination of Dr. Bowen the defense sought to break down the prosecution's contention that Lizzie was cold, calculating, and unmoved at the time immediately following the murders. From the doctor, information was obtained that he had given her sedatives to calm her nerves for several days after the murders. The defense also hit at the prosecution's contention that Lizzie Borden had given conflicting testimony at the inquest and at the preliminary hearing. The attorneys for the accused asked Dr. Bowen:

Q. Does not morphine given in double doses to allay mental distress and nervous excitement somewhat affect the memory and change and alter the view of things and give people hallucinations?
A. Yes, sir.

Dr. Bowen was followed on the stand by Mrs. Adelaide B. Churchill. She described the events on the day of the murder as she saw them. The prosecution made a point when Mrs. Churchill testified the dress in evidence was not the one Lizzie had been wearing at the time of the murders.

But on cross-examination the defense scored heavily in an attempt to show that Mrs. Borden had received a note and that Bridget was lying when she said she knew nothing about a note. Mrs. Churchill testified that Bridget had said to her, "Mrs. Borden had a note to go to see someone that was sick."

With the taking of the stand by Miss Alice Russell, Lizzie's best friend, the question of the burning of a Bedford cord dress was paramount. Alice was considered the state's star witness. She had stayed in the Borden house to keep her friend company, and it was on Sunday morning that she came into the kitchen and saw Emma at the sink and Lizzie at the stove. Emma was saying to Lizzie, "What are you going to do?" and Lizzie replied, "I am going to burn this old thing up; it is covered with paint." Alice was emphatic that the dress Lizzie burned that day was a Bedford cord. Later in the trial, Lizzie's dressmaker testified she had made the Bedford cord dress for her and that the house was being painted at that time. Emma testified that Lizzie had got paint all over the dress and had not worn it since. Mrs. Churchill knocked the prosecution on its heels by denying she had ever seen the Bedford cord dress. And Alice Russell knocked the prosecution's case into a cocked hat when she testified she had seen it just twice: once when it was made for Lizzie and again when Lizzie burned it. Thus the prosecution contended that the almost certainly bloodstained dress worn by Lizzie when she supposedly committed the murders was the one Lizzie burned in the stove on that Sunday following the murders, while the defense sought to send the entire story up in smoke.

Late in the fourth day of the trial, Assistant Marshal John Fleet took the stand as the first of many police officials who were trying to bolster the case against Lizzie Borden. The actions of the police from the time they entered the murder case on August 4, 1892, and all through their testimony at the trial were a mockery of justice. They blatantly lied; each one's testimony conflicted with the other's; they slanted all their answers to incriminate Lizzie Borden and sew up the case against her. In the matter of the ax, Fleet's answers were intended to show that the suspected handleless ax was covered with ashes, while the other hatchets in the box in the basement were covered with dust. The prosecution was trying to prove that Lizzie had washed the bloodstains off both ax head and handle, then dipped them in ashes to simulate dust. He finally had to admit that there were so many bushels of ashes in the cellar that all the hatchets could be covered with them rather than dust.

Came the fifth day of the trial, and one police officer followed another on the stand. Philip Harrington told how he was in the kitchen, following the murders, and saw Dr. Bowen lift the cover of the stove and drop in a piece of paper. At that point he saw a roll of burned paper in the stove. He observed: "There had been some paper burned in there before, which was rolled up and still held a cylindrical form." The prosecution was contending that this was the handle of the murder weapon.

The following day, the most important evidence centered upon the loft in the barn. Lizzie Borden stated that she was in this loft at the time her father was murdered. The witness, Special Police Officer William H. Medley, testified that he had arrived at the Borden house about twenty minutes before noon on the day of the murders and, after talking with Lizzie, had gone up to the loft. He looked around the barn to see if anything had been disturbed. He put his hand on the loft floor and made an impression in the dust. He walked a few feet on the floor, and his feet made impressions in the dust. The prosecution then asked him:

Q. Did you see any other footsteps in that dust than those which you made yourself?
A. No, sir.
Q. Did you notice what the temperature was in the loft of the barn as you went up there?
A. Well, I know it was hot, that is all, very hot.
Q. Did you notice whether the windows or the hay door were open or closed?
A. Those were closed at the time.

Thus the prosecution tried to prove that Lizzie Borden never went to that loft in the barn to look for a sinker and that no one had been in the barn prior to Officer Medley's going up there shortly before noon. Yet later, on the tenth day of the trial, when the case for the defense was being heard, Mr. Jennings put witness after witness on the stand to testify they had been up in the loft of the barn long before Officer Medley had arrived.

Everett Brown, a youth who tried to enter the Borden home to see what all the excitement was about but was turned away by Sawyer, went up to the loft with his friend Thomas Barlow: "We went upstairs, looked out of the window on the west side, and went over to the hay, and was up in the barn about five minutes." They were in the barn when Officer Fleet came in the side gate. This would place them in the barn before Medley came to the Borden house.

The seventh day was given over mainly to medical witnesses. Dr. Dolan described the wounds from the blows. Dr. Edward Wood, the Harvard specialist, testified that he had examined the stomachs of the victims and had found no evidence of poison. He had examined the hatchet head, and there was no evidence of bloodstains. He affirmed that the killer would have to be bloodstained. Dr. Frank Draper agreed that the killer would have to be bloodstained. He produced the actual skulls of the victims, and at that point Lizzie Borden fainted.

Dr. David W. Cheever, Harvard professor of surgery, testified that Mrs. Borden was murdered first, followed within one or two hours by Mr. Borden. The medical testimony continued throughout the eighth day and a part of the ninth, at which point Mrs. Hannah Reagan took the stand.

Hannah Reagan was the matron at the Central Police Station who took care of Lizzie Borden during the preliminary trial. She stated:

On the 24th of August Emma came in to see Lizzie in the morning. I was in the room cleaning up; she spoke with her sister and I went into a toilet room and hearing loud talk, looked out and saw Lizzie lying on her side and Emma bending down over her. Lizzie said: "You have given me away, Emma, but I don't care, I won't give in one inch," measuring on her finger. Emma said: "Oh, Lizzie, I didn't"; at the same time sitting down; they sat there until 11 o'clock, when Mr. Jennings came, but Lizzie made no talk at all with her sister after; never opened her mouth to her; when I first heard the noise of loud talking I was about four feet away, in a closet; when Emma left that morning there was nothing said by either and no "good-bye" exchanged.

This testimony created a sensation, especially when cross-examination by Mr. Jennings failed to shake the witness.

On the tenth day of the trial Mr. Jennings opened the argument for the defense. So far the cross-examination of the prosecution's witnesses, except for Mrs. Reagen, had gone well for Lizzie Borden. There was, then, no need for them to put her on the stand in her own defense. Her attorneys were aware of their client's aloof, cold, and impatient character, and saw no need to jeopardize the case by the juror's reaction to possible angry retorts to Moody's or Knowlton's interrogation of Lizzie. In his statement Jennings made these points:

1. Every person accused of this crime is presumed to be innocent until they have been proved guilty beyond a reasonable doubt.

2. There are two kinds of evidence: direct and circumstantial. There is not one particle of direct evidence in this case, and the prosecution has not attempted to say there is. There is no blood, no weapon they have connected with her. Their case is based solely on circumstantial evidence. In a case based on circumstantial evidence, every single link in the chain must be proved. You can't tie a case together with weak links and strong links. Unless, with the links you have left, you tie the defendant to the murders of Andrew J. Borden and Abby Durfee Borden, you must acquit her.

3. You must decide on the facts. The facts might come under four heads:

a. *Motive:* There was no evidence of such.

b. *Weapon:* The prosecution has not produced any weapon that could possibly have done the deed.

c. *Exclusive opportunity:* There were opportunities for anyone to come into the house, do the deed, and escape. The prosecution's claim that Lizzie Borden did not go to the barn is false.

d. *Conduct and appearance of the defendant:* Lizzie Borden was upset, and cried when she discovered the murders. She loved her father, and this feeling was mutual. She was active in many religious and charitable groups.

The defense then put a number of witnesses on the stand who testified they were in the vicinity of the Borden house during the hours of the murders. Dr. Benjamin Handy was driving by the house and saw a young stranger nearby acting very queerly. Hyman Lubinsky, an ice-cream peddler, who knew Bridget Sullivan from having sold her ice cream, and therefore knew she was not the person he saw, and who passed by exactly at the time Lizzie said she left the barn, testified he saw a lady come out of the barn and walk to the side-door steps.

A contemporary print showing Lizzie Borden fainting when prosecution witness Dr. Frank Draper produced the skulls of the two victims. Sketch at top left is of the New Bedford Court House, in which the trial opened on June 5, 1893.
The New York Public Library

The star defense witness, of course, was Emma Borden. She testified that their father had worn a ring given him by Lizzie for ten or fifteen years, that they gave full cooperation with the police in their searches, that the Bedford cord dress was covered with paint, soiled and faded, and that this was the dress Lizzie burned the Sunday after the murders, that Lizzie and she never had any such quarrels as Mrs. Reagan testified, and that neither Lizzie nor she had made any such remarks attributed to them by Mrs. Reagan.

On cross-examination by Mr. Knowlton she stuck fast to her statements. When questioned about the relationship between Lizzie and her stepmother, she maintained it was cordial. She knew nothing about the hatchet that had no handle. There was nothing of the kind said as described by Mrs. Reagan. The jurors were deeply impressed at Emma's forthright, unevasive, and apparently truthful answers.

On the twelfth day of the trial George Robinson made the closing argument for the defense. It was a long one, and with Knowlton's closing argument for the Commonwealth took a day and a half. Robinson stressed the following points:

1. The ax blows were the work of an experienced hatchet man, not someone untrained, such as the defendant. She had no physical capacity for doing these foul deeds.

2. The police needed a murderer badly, and went all out to build up a case against Lizzie Borden.

3. The jurors must dismiss from their minds everything they had read in the press and proceed with their deliberations unbiased. It was not their job to unravel a mystery, but only to decide, "Did she do it?" It must be beyond a reasonable doubt, to convict her.

4. It was not proved that the defendant went to buy poison.

5. The defendant's actions on the murder day were not connected in any way with the murders.

6. There was no motive for Lizzie Borden to commit the murders.

7. There was no direct evidence against her: no blood, no murder ax.

8. The body of Abby Borden in the guest room could not have been seen by others, unless they specifically went into the guest room.

9. There were clear statements that there was a note delivered to Abby Borden.

10. The testimony of Mr. Lubinsky did prove that Lizzie Borden did go to the barn as she maintained, and stayed the time she said, since Lubinsky did not leave the stable until after eleven o'clock. Thus she was out of the house at the time Mr. Borden was murdered.

11. It was proved that Lizzie Borden did show grief and was extremely upset at the murders. But she was not one to express her personal feeling in public.

12. It would be impossible for her to keep changing blood-soaked dresses after each murder and do away with them without a trace.

13. It was perfectly possible for an intruder to enter the house and commit the deeds.

On these and many other points Robinson went into the details of the evidence, and in each case rebutted the prosecution's claims.

In his closing argument for the Commonwealth, Hosea Knowlton painted a picture of a murderess coming down the stairs after killing the stepmother she hated and not daring to face the stern old man who would know that it was she who had killed his beloved wife, and so with no choice but to ax him to death as well. He called on the jury to "rise to the altitude of your duty."

When Mr. Knowlton finished speaking, the chief justice asked Lizzie Borden if she wanted to say anything to the jury, to which she answered: "I am innocent. I leave it to my counsel to speak for me."

Mr. Justice Dewey then charged the jury. The charge was distinctly favorable to the defendant. He instructed the jury to take into account her fine character, her charitable works. He warned them that "failure to prove a fact essential to the conclusion of guilt, and without which that conclusion would not be reached, is fatal to the government's case." One must be satisfied she was in the house when the murder of her father was committed, he stated. Further: "However numerous may be the facts in the government's process of proof tending to show the defendant's guilt, yet if there is a fact established—whether in that line of proof or outside of it—which cannot reasonably be reconciled with her guilt, then guilt cannot be said to be established." He explained that a defendant in a murder trial is under no obligation to testify and that they should not be negatively influenced by her failure to take the stand. He warned against their having been influenced in any way by the lurid newspaper accounts of the murders, and directed them to use evidence only.

At the end of Justice Dewey's charge, the jury retired. In exactly one hour and ten minutes they returned with the verdict—*Not guilty.*

The trial had lasted just thirteen days.

* * *

After the trial, Lizzie returned for a brief period to the house on Second Street. Her father's considerable estate was divided equally between Emma and herself, all debts having been duly paid. The sisters then sold the narrow Second Street house and moved to the fashionable section of Fall River, into a house on French Street, which they named Maplecroft. They refused all contact with the press, who nevertheless continued to hound them for news.

In 1905 Lizzie and Emma had a quarrel that led to Emma's leaving the house. The year before, Lizzie had met the celebrated actress Nance O'Neil, and they had become close friends. When the road show starring her friend played Fall River, Lizzie gave a party for her at Maplecroft and invited the whole cast. Emma was shocked. In those days the "best people" did not consort with actresses. She soon moved away, and the sisters never saw each other again. However, in 1925, the sisters did have business dealings together. Emma asked the Probate Court at Taunton have the A. J. Borden building sold. Lizzie, not wanting to lose the building, raised the necessary funds and bought out Emma's interest in what turned out to be a very sound business deal.

Lizzie Borden continued to live in Maplecroft. In 1926 she underwent a serious operation from which she never recovered. On June 1, 1927, she died at the age of sixty-six.

Did she do it? The question will never be fully answered. Lizzie was emphatic in protesting her innocence over and over again to Emma, and Emma never doubted her, at least in public. Certainly the trial itself thoroughly exonerated her. In 1961 Edward D. Radin, one of America's leading mystery writers, wrote a startling book called *Lizzie Borden: The Untold Story.* In it he made a strong and logical case against the one person who might have been the real killer: Bridget Sullivan, the servant girl!

The case of Lizzie Borden is indeed one of the world's most famous trials. At its close, the leading periodical of the day, *Frank Leslie's Weekly*, commented:

"This *cause célèbre* will pass down into the annals of criminal jurisprudence as one of the most remarkable on record—in fact, taken in all its details and aspects it has no equal in the world's history of crime; and that is saying a great deal."

*   *   *

Why did the case of Lizzie Borden attract the attention of the public, capture the imagination as have only a few trials since, and come down to us in song, legend, myth, rumor, and gossip that has not abated to this day?

First, because of the wealth of the participants, their education and social class, their small-town New England propriety, which came into such sharp conflict with the American stereotype version of crime and violence. Those who, in their homes or on the streets, passed judgment on the accused were perhaps gaining satisfaction out of the knoweldge that the rich and the well-born are susceptible to the frailties of mankind, even as are the poor and the ignorant.

After her acquittal Lizzie Borden and her sister Emma bought this sumptuous house in the most fashionable section of Fall River. It was known as Maplecroft. Here they both lived until some time in 1905 when they quarreled, and Emma moved out.
Fall River Historical Society

Second, if violence has always fascinated us, then greater violence has held greater fascination. The manner in which the two people were murdered, the sadistic fury that seems to have gripped the murderer, exercises a magnetism for the law-abiding. Some will contend that violence takes on the form of epidemic and suggestion, and others that the potentially violent find vicarious satisfaction in the newspaper story. In either case, the Borden story had many blows and a great deal of blood, and that the latter flowed on the clean and prim appointments of an upper-class home in a New England town only added to the flavor.

Third, the deep suspicion that the murderer was a woman, and the accusation against her in court, heightened the interest because of its contrast with our version of the dainty and weaker sex. For men, who have been headhunters and warriors, as well as murderers in many societies, the ax-wielding woman makes good newspaper copy.

For students of criminal justice, the case has many interesting ramifications, including the right of a person not to testify, without this being used against a defendant in a prejudicial manner. Equally important is that the Lizzie Borden case constitutes an outstanding example of trial by newspaper, but in a manner somewhat different from that usually understood by such a phrase. For unlike Hauptmann, Sam Sheppard, and many others, Lizzie Borden found the newspapers entirely on her side, writing maudlin and sentimental stories about this poor little rich girl in her cell, and creating an atmosphere in the town so friendly to her that the trial at times was a mere formality.

The jury acquitted Lizzie Borden, and the most recent scholar looking at the case has affirmed the acquittal, but legend and popular memory and collective ideas have been less kind to her. Her guilt came to be taken for granted. Many anecdotes have come down to us about the case and the central figure in it; among others, there is a story that might be considered for first prize as the understatement of all time. A little child had wandered off to play in Lizzie's yard, and was called back by his mother. "Why can't I play there?" he asked, and the mother replied, "Because Miss Borden was not nice to her parents."

15

Oscar Wilde

[1895]

In 1895 Oscar Wilde was at the height of a dazzling literary career. His wit had gained him entry into the most restricted literary and political salons of London; his conversation was considered brilliant and without equal, and his comedies were playing to large and enthusiastic audiences. On the Continent as well as in England, the name of Wilde was widely known. In fact, Sarah Bernhardt herself was to produce *Salomé*. Art for art's sake and the cult of the aesthete and the dilettante were at their pinnacle, and they found in Wilde their hero.

But Wilde was not only brilliant; he was ostentatious, conceited, self-centered beyond exaggeration; and if he had many admirers, he was not lacking in enemies. Among the latter was the Marquess of Queensberry, eccentric and erratic, who might well have gone down in history for having given his name to the rules that governed the sport of pugilism had he not become even more famous as the adversary and persecutor, although not exactly the prosecutor, of Oscar Wilde.

That a man of Wilde's renown would be the center of a great deal of gossip was not at all unusual. But Wilde seemed to seek the gossip, relish in it, delight in being talked about. In Victorian England, many who heard about Wilde's escapades could not believe what came to their ears. They thought that perverse sexuality between men was extremely rare, something involving the criminal or the demented; little did they realize to what extent such practices were followed by members of all social classes and both sexes in Victorian England.

If rumors of such events concerning Oscar Wilde reached into many circles, people were prone to dismiss them more as the pose of the aesthete, than as the practice of the playwright.

For the Marquess of Queensberry, the pose was particularly troubling, for the companion of Wilde in his sorties through British society was his own son, Alfred Douglas, known to Wilde under the affectionate name of Bosie. Between the marquess and his children there was bitterness, even hatred, that kept London society excited as it watched denunciations, lawsuits, and even a public fistfight that resulted in an arrest.

Determined to compel Oscar Wilde to discontinue the friendship with his son—a determination that may have stemmed as much from bitterness toward the younger man as toward the older one—the marquess began to harass both of them. He would disown his son completely if the association with the notorious author were not terminated, he stated, and when this brought no result, he called on Wilde at the latter's home, from which he was thrown out.

On February 14, 1895, Oscar Wilde's greatest success, *The Importance of Being Earnest,* opened at the St. James's Theatre in London. Four days later, the marquess left a card for Wilde at the latter's social club, the Albermarle. The card read:

"To Oscar Wilde posing as a somdomite."

The misspelling has gone down in history, as have the events that followed.

Oscar Wilde and
Lord Alfred Douglas.

The Eighth Marquess
of Queensberry.

Ten days later, Wilde received the card at his club, and discussed the matter with attorneys and friends. To his attorney, he stated that the charge was untrue; he denied any homosexual activity. A few days later, Wilde obtained a warrant for the arrest of the marquess on a charge of criminal libel, and the trial opened at the Old Bailey in London on April 3. After an opening speech had been made on behalf of Wilde, the latter took the stand, and related some facts of his personal and literary life. Cross-examined by Edward Carson, an old schoolmate of his, Wilde held his own on literary matters. He defended the artistry in *The Picture of Dorian Gray*, and was examined on letters he had written to Lord Alfred Douglas:

Q. Is that not an exceptional letter?
A. It is unique, I should say.
Q. Was that the ordinary way in which you carried on your correspondence?
A. No; but I have often written to Lord Alfred Douglas, though I never wrote to another young man in the same way.

Q. Have you often written letters in the same style as this?
A. I don't repeat myself in style.
Q. Here is another letter which I believe you also wrote to Lord Alfred Douglas. Will you read it?
A. No; I decline. I don't see why I should.
Q. Then I will.

"Savoy Hotel,
"Victoria Embankment, London.

"DEAREST OF ALL BOYS,

"Your letter was delightful, red and yellow wine to me; but I am sad and out of sorts. Bosie, you must not make scenes with me. They kill me, they wreck the loveliness of life. I cannot see you, so Greek and gracious, distorted with passion. I cannot listen to your curved lips saying hideous things to me. I would sooner—than have you bitter, unjust, hating. . . . I must see you soon. You are the divine thing I want, the thing of grace and beauty; but I don't know how to do it. Shall I come to Salisbury? My bill here is £49 for a week. I have also got a new sitting-room. . . . Why are you not here, my dear, my wonderful boy? I fear I must leave—no money, no credit, and a heart of lead.

"Your own OSCAR."

Q. Is that an ordinary letter?
A. Everything I write is extraordinary. I do not pose as being ordinary, great heavens! Ask me any question you like about it.
Q. Is it the kind of letter a man writes to another?
A. It was a tender expression of my great admiration for Lord Alfred Douglas. It was not, like the other, a prose poem.

Wilde's case began to falter, however, when associations with lower-class youths, and particularly male prostitutes and blackmailers, began to be brought out by the defense.

On the stand, Wilde conducted his battle of wits. He seemed more concerned to impress than to win. When the lower-class status of a youth was emphasized, as casting suspicion on the relationship, he stated: "I recognize no social distinctions at all of any kind, and to me youth, the mere fact of youth, is so wonderful that I would sooner talk to a young man for half-an-hour than be—well, cross-examined in Court."

But his wit served as a trap into which Carson lured him. When asked if he had ever kissed a servant of Lord Alfred Douglas, he replied: "Oh, dear no! He was a peculiarly plain boy. He was, unfortunately, extremely ugly." So that was why he had not kissed him—not because he was a boy, but because he was ugly! Carson hammered away, and Wilde retreated, flustered, in anger. The episode is described by Frank Harris in his well-known biography of Wilde:

"Did you ever kiss him?" he [Carson] asked.
Oscar answered carelessly, "Oh, dear, no. He was a peculiarly plain boy. He was, unfortunately, extremely ugly. I pitied him for it."
"Was that the reason why you did not kiss him?"
"Oh, Mr. Carson, you are pertinently insolent."

"Did you say that in support of your statement that you never kissed him?"
"No. It is a childish question."
But Carson was not to be warded off; like a terrier he sprang again and again:
"Why, sir, did you mention that this boy was extremely ugly?"
"For this reason, If I were asked why I did not kiss a door-mat, I should say because I do not like to kiss door-mats."
"Why did you mention his ugliness?"
"It is ridiculous to imagine that any such thing could have occurred under any circumstances."
"Then why did you mention his ugliness, I ask you?"
"Because you insulted me by an insulting question."
"Was that a reason why you should say the boy was ugly?"
(Here the witness began several answers almost inarticulately and finished none of them. His efforts to collect his ideas were not aided by Mr. Carson's sharp staccato repetition: "Why? why? why did you add that?") At last the witness answered:
"You sting me and insult me and at times one says things flippantly."

The case was going poorly for Wilde. His own attorneys were amazed as the evidence accumulated. In reality, he had become the defendant, and he sought gracefully to withdraw. Justice Collins called for a directed verdict of not guilty against the marquess, "that it was true in substance and in fact that the prosecutor [Wilde] had 'posed' as a sodomite."

Edward Carson, Q.C., M.P.,
senior counsel for the
Marquess of Queensberry.

Mr. Justice Henn Collins,
before whom the first
trial took place.

Mr. Justice Charles,
before whom the second
trial took place.

Sir Edward Clarke, Q.C., M.P.,
senior counsel for Oscar
Wilde at all three trials.

Mr. Justice Wills,
before whom the third
trial took place.

Many of Wilde's friends urged him to flee to France before he was himself taken into custody, but he refused. There were delays of several hours before a warrant for his arrest was issued. It seemed as if some authorities wanted to avoid prosecution, but Wilde did not cooperate, and together with a younger man, Alfred Taylor, he was arrested and held without bail. The trial of the two defendants opened on April 26, 1895, and continued until the first of May. There was considerable evidence concerning Wilde's associations with young men, their being in hotel rooms together. On the witness stand, Wilde was strong on literary matters. Asked about a poem by Lord Alfred Douglas entitled "Two Loves," he was examined, particularly with regard to the line "I am the Love that dare not speak its name":

Q. Was that poem explained to you?
A. I think that is clear.
Q. Is it not clear that the love described relates to natural love and unnatural love?
A. No.
Q. What is the "Love that dare not speak its name"?
A. "The Love that dare not speak its name" in this century is such a great affection of an elder for a younger man as there was between David and Jonathan, such as Plato made the very basis of his philosophy, and such as you find in the sonnets of Michelangelo and Shakespeare. It is that deep, spiritual affection that is as pure as it is perfect. It dictates and pervades great works of art like those of Shakespeare and Michelangelo, and those two letters of mine, such as they are. It is in this century misunderstood, so much misunderstood that it may be described as the "Love that dare not speak its name," and on account of it I am placed where I am now. It is beautiful, it is fine, it is the noblest form of affection. There is nothing unnatural about it. It is intellectual, and it repeatedly exists between an elder and a younger man, when the elder man has intellect, and the younger man has all the joy, hope and glamour of life before him. That it should be so the world does not understand. The world mocks at it and sometimes puts one in the pillory for it. (Loud applause, mingled with some hisses.)

MR. JUSTICE CHARLES.   If there is the slightest manifestation of feeling I shall have the Court cleared. There must be complete silence preserved.

The defense made a strong case, impugning the character of witnesses who were blackmailers, showed inconsistencies in the testimony against him, and called for acquittal. The jury found the defendants not guilty on several counts, but disagreed on a number of others, and Wilde was now to be subjected to still another trial. Bail was applied for and set, and large sums were posted by a Reverend Stewart Headlam, who risked his position in the Church of England, and by Lord Douglas of Hawick, the oldest surviving son of the Marquess of Queensberry. Again, Wilde was urged to leave the country, but he adamantly refused, and on May 20, 1895, the third in the series of trials opened. The trials of Taylor and Wilde were separated, and over the stren-

uous objection of Wilde's attorneys, the Taylor case was heard first. Alfred Taylor was found guilty, and the Wilde verdict was now a well-nigh certainty.

Again, there were the procurers, the blackmailers, the seamy side of London life that the upper classes of England supposedly had little contact with. And again, there was cross-examination on Wilde's association with Douglas. After reading a letter written by Wilde to "Bosie," the prosecutor examined the defendant:

Q. Why did you choose the words, "My own Boy," as a mode of address?
A. I adopted them because Lord Alfred Douglas is so much younger than myself. The letter was a fantastic, extravagant way of writing to a young man. As I said at the first trial, it does not seem to me to be a question of whether a thing is right or proper, but of literary expression. It was like a little sonnet of Shakespeare.
Q. I did not use the word "proper" or "right." Was it decent?
A. Oh, decent? Of course; there is nothing indecent in it.
Q. Do you think that was a decent way for a man of your age to address a man of his?
A. It was a beautiful way for an artist to address a young man of culture and charm. Decency does not enter into it.
Q. Doesn't it? Do you understand the meaning of the word, sir?
A. Yes.
Q. "It is a marvel that those red rose-leaf lips of yours should have been made no less for music of song than for madness of kisses." And do you consider that decent?
A. It was an attempt to write a prose poem in beautiful phraseology.

Solicitor General
Sir Frank Lockwood, Q.C., M.P.,
who prosecuted the third
trial for the Crown.

Q. Did you consider it decent phraseology?
A. Oh, yes, yes.
Q. Then do you consider that a decent mode of addressing a young man?
A. I can only give you the same answer, that it is a literary mode of writing what is intended to be a prose poem.
Q. "Your slim gilt soul walks between passion and poetry . . . Hyacinthus, whom Apollo loved so madly, was you in Greek days." You were speaking of love between men?
A. What I meant by the phrase was that he was a poet, and Hyacinthus was a poet.
Q. "Always, with undying love"?
A. It was not a sensual love.

On the association with young men, Wilde was less poetic in his defense of his actions:

Q. How long had you known Taylor?
A. I met him first in September, 1892.
Q. Did you visit him?
A. Yes, I paid visits to his rooms, but I have not been there more than five or six times in my life.
Q. Was there any but male society there?
A. Oh, no; entirely male.
Q. What were their names?
A. I met Mavor and Schwabe there. I only went there to tea parties lasting half an hour or so, and I cannot after a lapse of three years remember whom I met. You ask me to remember whom I met at a tea party three years ago. It is childish. How can I?
Q. Did you meet Charles Hason there?
A. No, I met him at a dinner.
Q. The boys Wood, Mavor, and Parker, what was their occupation?
A. One doesn't ask people such questions at a tea party.
Q. Did Taylor strike you as being a pleasant companion?
A. Yes, I thought him very bright.
Q. Did you know what his occupation was?
A. No; I understood that he had none.
Q. Had any of these young men any occupation?
A. Oh, they were young men—singers—I did not ask.
Q. Did you see anything remarkable in the furnishing of Taylor's rooms?
A. No, nothing.
Q. The windows were curtained?
A. Yes, but not obscured.
Q. Did you know that Taylor's male friends stayed with him and shared his bed?
A. No, I know it now.
Q. Does that alter your opinion of Taylor?
A. No, I don't think so. I don't think it is necessary to conclude that there was anything criminal. It was unusual. I don't believe anything criminal took place between Taylor and these boys; and if they were poor and he shared his bed with them it may have been charity.
Q. Did it shock you that he should have done it?
A. No, I saw no necessity for being shocked.
Q. I must press you. Do you approve of his conduct?
A. I don't think I am called upon to express approval or disapproval of any person's conduct.
Q. Would the knowledge that they habitually shared his bed alter your opinion of Taylor?
A. No.

        *   *   *

Q. Did you ever sup alone with any young man at the Savoy Hotel about that time?
A. I could not remember. You are asking me of three years ago. Lord Alfred Douglas may have been with me.
Q. But he would be perfectly well known to the waiters at the Savoy?
A. Oh, yes.
Q. Wherever you are well known, he would be?
A. Oh, I don't know that.
Q. You have stayed together at the Savoy, at the Albemarle, at the Avondale, at St. James's Place, at the Metropole at Brighton, at Cromer, at Goring, at the Albion, at Worthing, and at Torquay?
A. Yes. He has not stayed with me at St. James's Place, but I have lent him my rooms there.
Q. Did Charles Parker ever visit you?
A. He might have visited me seven or eight times at St. James's Place, and on one occasion he dined with me at Kettner's, and we afterwards went to the Pavilion.
Q. When did you last see him?
A. In December last, in the street.

        *   *   *

Q. Do you remember a young man named Scarfe?
A. Yes. Taylor brought him to see me. Scarfe represented himself as a young man who had made money in Australia.
Q. Why was he brought to you?
A. Because many people at that time had great pleasure and interest in seeing me.
Q. Did he call you Oscar?
A. Yes.
Q. At once?
A. I had to ask him to. I have a passion for being called by my Christian name. It pleases me.
Q. Did you give him a cigarette case?
A. Yes.
Q. Has he dined alone with you?
A. Yes.
Q. Do you remember Alphonse Conway?
A. Yes. I met him on the beach at Worthing last year in August. He had an ambition to go to sea.
Q. Of what station in life is he?
A. Of no particular station.
Q. Did he not sell papers on the pier?
A. Oh, never while I was there.
Q. What was his mother?
A. She was a widow, and let lodgings.
Q. Did you buy him a suit?
A. Yes, of blue serge.
Q. And a stick?
A. Yes.
Q. And took him to Brighton?
A. Yes, we had twenty-four hours' trip to Brighton. That was a month afterwards.
Q. What rooms had you at Brighton?
A. Two bedrooms and a sitting room. We slept in adjoining rooms.

The jury was out about three hours, came in to ask one question, and then retired and brought its verdict a few minutes later. The verdict was guilty, and Wilde was given the maximum sentence:

Oscar Wilde and Alfred Taylor, the crime of which you have been convicted is so bad that one has to put stern restraint upon one's self to prevent one's self from describing, in language which I would rather not use, the sentiments which must rise to the breast of every man of honour who has heard the details of these two terrible trials. That the jury have arrived at a correct verdict in this case I cannot persuade myself to entertain the shadow of a doubt; and I hope, at all events, that those who sometimes imagine that a judge is half-hearted in the cause of decency and morality because he takes care no prejudice shall enter into the case, may see that that is consistent at least with the utmost sense of indignation at the horrible charges brought home to both of you.

It is no use for me to address you. People who can do these things must be dead to all sense of shame, and one cannot hope to produce any effect upon them. It is the worst case I have ever tried. That you, Taylor, kept a kind of male brothel it is impossible to doubt. And that you, Wilde, have been the centre of a circle of extensive corruption of the most hideous kind among young men, it is equally impossible to doubt.

I shall, under such circumstances, be expected to pass the severest sentence that the law allows. In my judgment it is totally inadequate for such a case as this. The sentence of the Court is that each of you be imprisoned and kept to hard labour for two years.

Oscar Wilde spent two years in jail for acts that had not been legally declared criminal until only a few years before his arrest. His imprisonment may have made a martyr of him, and may have contributed to the clamor that arose some years later for a change in the legal codes with regard to "perverse" or "immoral" sexual relations between consenting adults.

The Wilde case left bitterness among his friends, many of whom felt that he had been abandoned and betrayed by Alfred Douglas. That Wilde held this opinion himself is revealed in many passages in the long letter he wrote in prison, *De Profundis*. Many have contended that, had he not sought to protect Douglas, Wilde would not have himself been found guilty.

Out of his harsh imprisonment, there came demands for penal reform. Soon after his release he had published, at first without his signature although the authorship was almost public knowledge, *The Ballad of Reading Gaol*. Suffering in prison has seldom been expressed more forcefully:

> I know not whether Laws be right,
>   Or whether Laws be wrong;
> All that we know who lie in gaol
>   Is that the wall is strong:
> And that each day is like a year,
>   A year whose days are long.
>
> This too I know—and wise it were
>   If each could know the same—
> That every prison that men build
>   Is built with bricks of shame,
> And bound with bars lest Christ should see
>   How men their brothers maim.

Captain Alfred Dreyfus dramatically reasserts, "I am innocent!"
at his second court-martial at Rennes in 1899.

16

Captain Alfred Dreyfus

[1894 and 1899]

To the English-speaking world, the 1890's are remembered by many as the years of dilettantism and decadence, of Max Beerbohm and Oscar Wilde, of the world of aesthetes and pretenders. It was, for an American literary critic, the mauve decade. But for France, it was an era of turbulence and turmoil, when resentment and hatred of man against man rose to new heights, and when each Frenchman found it necessary to stand up and be counted. To be counted meant to be on one side or the other in a great internal battle that turned lifelong friends into lifelong enemies, that brought together unexpected and unlikely allies to become strange bedfellows, and that even split members of the same family into opposite camps. It was the era of Dreyfus, a man around whom a bitter struggle was raging, for whom trials were held, and duels took place; worldwide demonstrations bespoke the outrage of humanity; some persons killed and others committed suicide. Through much of this, Dreyfus incarcerated on an island in the Atlantic, sought to hold on to a semblance of hope and sanity, not even aware of the clamor surrounding his name and his exile.

Alfred Dreyfus was an unlikely candidate for the historic task of becoming the rallying point of lovers of justice throughout France and in many other parts of the world. An Alsatian Jew from a family of textile manufacturers, he spurned the wishes of his brothers who urged him to enter the family business, and instead chose a career in the army. In the army training school, he showed excellence of scholarship and eagerness in learning, but suffered from the anti-Semitic prejudice then gripping France as a whole and particularly her military. As a result he was graduated at a point in the class lower than his achievements warranted. He made few friends, was cold and emotionless, at least on an outward level, stoical, and absorbed in a patriotic dedi-cation to country and a zealous absorption in the military.

It is doubtful if Alfred Dreyfus was the victim of a conspiracy in which several people assembled to weave a sinister plot from which he would emerge as a rich Jewish traitor and a symbol of evil. Until his arrest, those most responsible for the events in which he was caught had probably never heard of him; and even then, many who became accomplices in an evil game did so because they were convinced that military honor, even French honor, was at stake. Against this, what mattered the innocence or guilt of one man, particularly a Jew?

Espionage was common in late nineteenth-century Europe, and it was not yet clothed in the techniques of modern sophistication and technology. It was an era of cloak-and-dagger spies, when codes were crude and easily broken, and when the cleaning woman would empty the basket in the embassy or consulate at the end of the day, carefully gather the torn and crumpled scraps of paper, and bring them to the military officials, who not infrequently found important guides to secret information that had been carelessly thrown away by a consular or embassy official.

On July 20, 1894, a French Army officer by the name of Marie Charles Ferdinand Walsin-Esterhazy (or just Esterhazy, as he came to be known) offered to sell documents and military secrets to the German military attaché in Paris, Lieutenant Colonel Max von Schwartzkoppen. At first repulsed by the German officer, Esterhazy was insistent, and in Germany Schwartzkoppen's superiors displayed interest. Some time later in the summer, Esterhazy left a note for Schwartzkoppen in the latter's mailbox. This note never reached its expected destination because a French agent purloined it, and delivered it to the counterespionage officials of the French military.

Written in pen and ink, and unsigned, it mentioned a list of items, of varying interest, that the writer would be delivering to Schwartzkoppen during the coming months. The note (which has gone down in history as the *bordereau*, usually translated as the memorandum, schedule, or list) excited considerable attention when examined by the French, for it meant that there was a traitor in the ranks. The writer promised an artillery manual, and spoke of going off to maneuvers. Obviously, this was a soldier who was writing, an officer, possibly a high one.

Thus the bordereau arrived in the hands of the French. To conceal that it had been stolen from a mailbox, it was torn into bits and then, unlike Humpty Dumpty, was put together again. Thus, it would appear that a German official had read it and thrown away the parts, unmindful of the curiosity of cleaning women. Ordinarily, an intercepted letter of this nature might have gone to Lieutenant Colonel Hubert Henry, a friend of Esterhazy and a man who, some historians conjecture, might have been a German agent as well, or perhaps a double agent. But Henry was on leave. Had he been in Paris and seen the bordereau, he might have recognized the handwriting, and history would have been different for years to come. In his absence, Colonel Sandherr received the item.

The famous bordereau, written by Esterhazy, became the basic evidence against Dreyfus in his trials for treason. Translated, it read:

Without having heard whether you wish to see me, I am now sending you some interesting information.

I. A note on the hydraulic brake, 120, and the way it worked.

II. A note concerning the covering forces. (Several modifications will be made by the new plan.)

III. A note concerning alterations in the formations of the artillery.

IV. A note relating to Madagascar.

V. The rough draft of a manual of artillery field practice.

This last document is very difficult to get, and I can have it at my disposal for a few days only. The War Office has sent a fixed number to the various regiments, and these regiments are responsible for them; each officer having one being obliged to return it after the maneuvers. If you would like to make extracts of the parts that interest you, and will keep the manual at my disposal, I will get one. Unless you would like me to make a copy of it *in extenso*, and to send you only the copy.

I am off to the maneuvers.

It was not the first indication of treason in the army that the French had had. A message to Schwartzkoppen from his Italian counterpart, the military attaché from Rome to Paris, Lieutenant Colonel Panizzardi, had been intercepted. It spoke of maps, and referred to a scoundrel by the initial *D*.

French officers with bordereau in hand ran to their files and examined the names of personnel starting with the letter *D*. At last they came to Dreyfus, and there they stopped. They had their man. The haughty, cold, pretentious Dreyfus, the Jew whose people recognized no national boundaries and loyalties and who, motivated only by an avaricious struggle for wealth, knew neither patriotism nor ethics.

Now there was the question of verification of the identity of the culprit by comparing the handwriting. The task was assigned to a major, the Marquis Du Paty de Clam, who was equivocal. He called in an expert from the Banque de France, who was equally unsure. The famed Bertillon was consulted, and in all likelihood forewarned that identification was desirable. Bertillon saw what he was asked to see: that the bordereau and specimens from the Dreyfus file were in the same handwriting. During the investigation, Colonel Henry returned from his leave, and apprised of the situation, immediately ordered that Dreyfus be arrested, but without any publicity.

Summoned to appear at headquarters on Monday, October 15, 1894, in civilian clothes, Alfred Dreyfus came, and was greeted by Du Paty, who showed him a bandaged thumb, and asked him to write a letter that would be dictated. At that point, he started to dictate from the bordereau, and Dreyfus wrote. At one point Du Paty demanded to know why Dreyfus was trembling, and as Dreyfus calmly explained that he was cold, and continued to write, Du Paty became enraged at the arrogant traitor. It was easy to see the similarities between the current writing of Dreyfus and the bordereau, and it was apparent that the calm was but a façade that not only concealed the guilt, but even demonstrated it. Finally, Du Paty shouted to Dreyfus that he was under arrest for treason. Dreyfus looked bewildered and protested his innocence. At this point Du Paty offered Dreyfus a gun, but the accused declined to commit suicide, and said that he would live to prove his innocence and vindicate his honor.

In prison, Dreyfus was held incommunicado. He was certain that the honorable army and its fine officers would not fabricate evidence and that he would be released as soon as the mistake was recognized. His wife was visited by Du Paty, who told her that her husband was under arrest, and demanded complete silence, lest any information make it impossible for him to be vindicated. The Dreyfus home was searched, the wife questioned, but no further evidence turned up.

At the War Department, General Auguste Mercier, Minister of War, recognized that the case against Dreyfus was a shaky one. Some of the information in the bordereau would not normally be coming into the hands of an officer like Dreyfus, and he was not at the time scheduled to go off on maneuvers. The case must rest on two matters: a confession or unassailable handwriting identification. But with all the pressure and threats, the confession was not forthcoming. And the handwriting experts were confused, divided among themselves, and quite unconvincing. It looked as if the wrong man was in jail, and it was best to rectify the error before the matter became public and the army became the recipient of unfavorable press.

Colonel Schwartzkoppen, German Military Attaché in Paris, to whom the bordereau was addressed.

Colonel Panizzardi, Italian Military Attaché in Paris whose message to Schwartzkoppen, speaking of maps and a French scoundrel by the initial D, was intercepted by French Intelligence.

It was a period of widespread and virulent anti-Semitism in France. Denunciation of the Jew reached even into respectable quarters. There was a National League of Anti-Semitism, financed by Royalists, Nationalists, and other Rightists, and in league with Jesuits and high officials of the Catholic Church. France was writhing under the defeat at the hands of the Germans in 1870, the loss of Alsace and Lorraine; and scapegoats were always useful in the period of national humiliation. The sentiment against Jews had deepened, owing to the Panama fiasco in which many small French investors lost their earnings when plans to build a canal ended in bankruptcy. Several of the leading personages in this ill-fated adventure were Jewish bankers.

While many of the French newspapers were openly anti-Semitic, none was more violently so than *La Libre Parole*, edited by Edouard Drumont. So it was natural that Lieutenant Colonel Henry, fearful that his friend Esterhazy might be apprehended as the true author of the bordereau, leaked the information to *La Libre Parole* that the Jew Dreyfus was being held as a traitor and that some people in the War Department, probably paid off by a syndicate of international Jewry, were preparing to let the dirty traitor go free. General Mercier read *La Libre Parole* of November 1, and immediately realized that, if Dreyfus were freed, his position as Minister of War would be in jeopardy. Worse, the government itself might topple.

Colonel Du Paty de Clam dictates a test letter to Captain Dreyfus in which he intersperses parts of the bordereau. Because Dreyfus's handwriting looked somewhat the same as that in the bordereau, M. Cochefert, Chief of the Detective Service, who is waiting in the hall, arrests Dreyfus immediately.

Mathieu Dreyfus, brother of the accused, apprised of the fate of Alfred, had at once rushed to his aid. He begged Charles Demange, venerable and prestigious attorney, to become Dreyfus's counsel. Demange consented, provided that, after interviewing the prisoner, he were convinced of his innocence. The interview took place in prison, and Demange, convinced that the evidence was so paltry that no court could convict, readily agreed to become Dreyfus's attorney. Demange, as much as Dreyfus, had confidence in the integrity of the military, and neither could believe that prejudice would overcome reason.

The court-martial of Captain Alfred Dreyfus opened in a great hall near the prison in Paris, on Wednesday, December 19, 1894. No crowd surrounded the court when the trial opened. No one expected that it would be open to the public. As reported by Joseph Reinach, ardent Dreyfusard and meticulous historian of the affair, "There were barely thirty people around the door."

It could, indeed, be said that the case was lost by Dreyfus in the first round, when the court voted to hold its sessions *in camera*. The public and press were barred. Only the seven military judges, the attorneys for the prosecution, attorneys for the defense, and the accused were present, together with a witness who happened at a particular time to be testifying. Such Star Chamber proceedings, so long held in disrepute in France as well as in other Western countries, could now be revived because of the military nature of the trial and the claims, entirely unfounded, that top-secret questions of national interest were involved.

At first, Demange and Mathieu Dreyfus saw in the trial nothing more than errors of experts in conflict. True, Demange stated that, if Dreyfus were not a Jew, he would not have been arrested. By the second day of the trial, the utter emptiness of the case against Dreyfus was becoming apparent. Henry testified for the prosecution, and with vehemence. He stated that as far back as the month of March, an honorable person—absolutely honorable—had notified the service that an officer was committing treason. Then in June the same person named the officer. "And this traitor," he shouted, "there he is!" Dreyfus jumped to his feet and demanded to know the name of the anonymous accuser. With a theatrical gesture, Henry tapped his cap and said, "There are secrets in an officer's head that even his cap must not know." He would not have to name the officer, but merely swear on his honor that he had told the truth. With dignity he assured the court, "I so swear!"

Then came the handwriting experts. On the third day of the trial, there was Bertillon. He spoke for three hours. He drew figures and made gestures, baffling everyone in the court. He even repudiated the burgeon-ing science of handwriting analysis, and compared it with astrology.

Within the court, the sentiment seemed to favor the accused, and at the War Department there was fear that with acquittal, the government would fall. Some suggested that a compromise be reached, that the guilt be declared as "not proven," but others were not to be deterred from their objective. During the trial, Du Paty approached the presiding judge, Colonel Maurel, and handed him an envelope, sealed. Du Paty claimed to have no knowledge of the contents; he simply said that there was another envelope inside, that he had been given this by a Cabinet member and that the contents should be made known to the judge of the court. There is a dispute as to whether this was the only such secret envelope given to Maurel during the trial. In this envelope, which came to be known as the "secret file" or *dossier secret*, were forgeries, irrelevancies, and hearsay, all implicating Dreyfus in this and other acts of treason. This, of course, was not unsealed and read in open court.

Lieutenant Colonel Hubert Henry, a close friend of Major Esterhazy, who finally committed suicide when he was arrested after his complicity in the plot against Dreyfus was unveiled.

Now, for three hours, Demange summed up. There was nothing to the trial, he declared, but the bordereau, which Dreyfus could not have written because it contained information unknown to him. There was no possible motive for the crime. The prosecution denied that it was its responsibility to offer a motive, contending that the similarity of handwriting was enough to condemn Dreyfus. The prisoner emphatically protested his innocence, and the judges retired to their own chambers. There, unknown to the defense, and in violation of French law, they opened the secret envelope and read the contents. The deliberations lasted one hour; the verdict was unanimous. Guilty! The judgment was read in open court. Only the defendant, in accordance with French military law, was absent. Demange sobbed.

Two weeks later the dreaded degradation took place. Alfred Dreyfus was publicly stripped of his uniform and compelled to walk the gauntlet of his former comrades, as they spat their condemnation on him. Shortly thereafter, he was placed on a ship that would take him to Devil's Island and years of imprisonment.

*　　*　　*

Found guilty at a trial behind closed doors, Dreyfus suffers a humiliating degradation following his conviction.

In the summer of 1895, some months after the exiling of Dreyfus, a new head of the Intelligence Bureau of the General Staff took his place in France, Lieutenant Colonel Georges Picquart. Among his subordinates was Henry. For several months Picquart was concerned with many matters other than Dreyfus; that affair was settled, and there was no question of the guilt of the condemned man. But in March, 1896, Colonel Schwartzkoppen—who had maintained close relations with Esterhazy and had not known that Dreyfus had been convicted on the basis of the authorship of a document by Esterhazy—sent the latter a postcard. The card, known as a *petit bleu,* was of a type widely used in France at the time. Schwartzkoppen had walked to a postal box, where he was seen dropping the card. It was retrieved and placed in the hands of Picquart, who in no way associated it with the Dreyfus case, but felt that Esterhazy bore watching. Nevertheless, the more Picquart looked into the Esterhazy matter, the clearer it became to him that there was grave doubt concerning Dreyfus's guilt. Finally he examined the secret dossier, and was astonished to discover that it was an envelope of rumors and forgeries.

| 1.—ILE ROYALE | A. Military Hospital
B. Convent
C. Chapel
D. Parade Ground | E. Sc.....
F. Eastern ....
G. Dockyard
H. Coal House | | 2.—ILE DU DIABLE | A. Dreyfus's Hut
B. Guard House
C. Dreyfus's Former Hut
D. Telephone | 3.—ILE SAINT JOSEPH | A. Stone Hut for Refractory Prisoners
B. Tanyard |

PANORAMIC VIEW OF THE ILES DU SALUT, SHOWING THE ILE DU DIABLE WHERE EX-CAPTAIN DREYFUS WAS IMPRISONED

Dreyfus was imprisoned at Devil's Island. His hut, surrounded by a barricade, is on the top of the center island.

Lieutenant Colonel Georges Picquart, who was appointed head of the Intelligence Bureau of the General Staff in 1895, was convinced a year later that Dreyfus was innocent, and tried to reopen the case.

During the summer of 1896, convinced by now that an innocent man had been condemned, Picquart brought the matter to the attention of his superiors. Everywhere he was told that the case was closed. "But an innocent man is in prison," he declared, and when he was informed that the matter could not be reopened, he stated, "You may be sure that I will not carry this message with me to my grave."

In spite of Picquart's concern, the case now seemed over. The prisoner was out of sight, adjudication of guilt was now a settled matter, and France could return to normalcy. The militarists were elated, as were the Royalists and the anti-Semites, while Socialists scoffed at the battle among the rich, and only a few intellectuals showed interest. Some Jews even ran for cover, finding greater security by dissociating themselves from the convict. After a year, Dreyfus was on the road to becoming a forgotten man.

*   *   *

Mathieu Dreyfus would not accept this fate for his brother. Desperately he sought to reopen the case and to discover new evidence that would definitely establish his brother's innocence. Mathieu despaired lest the matter be shrouded in silence. Public interest, which had begun to wane, was aroused again when a British newspaper published the sensational story of Dreyfus's escape from Devil's Island, a story that some historians attribute to Mathieu. As official denials were followed by details about the life in the prisons, the name of Dreyfus was once again on the lips of Frenchmen.

The crack in the solid front that Mathieu faced finally appeared when *Le Matin,* a liberal Parisian newspaper, obtained a copy of the bordereau and on November 10, 1896, prominently printed it for the first time. The entire case had rested on a supposed similarity of handwritings, and now it was clear, for all to see, that Alfred Dreyfus, in spite of the so-called expert handwriting analyst, could not have written the incriminating note. Who, then, was the author?

While almost one year was to pass before Mathieu learned the identity of Esterhazy and the part he played in the case, unknown to him, the center of attention in the affair was turning on Picquart. Just a few days before the publication of the bordereau, Picquart was sent on a mission far from Paris, so that he would be out of the way. With Picquart removed, Henry was free to continue to rearrange papers, make forgeries, and cover the trail that might lead to Esterhazy, Du Paty, and himself, and even to attempt to prepare a case against Picquart.

Why Picquart, after one year of struggle with his conscience, finally decided to reveal his secret is not clear. It is said that he fell from a horse and had a fore-boding of death. In April, 1897, he prepared a memorandum, to be handed to the President of France upon his death, in which all that he now knew about Dreyfus was revealed. In June, he confided his information to an attorney and friend, Louis Leblois, particularly citing the incriminating material of the *petit bleu.* Leblois in turn revealed the information to the vice-president of the French Senate and one of the most influential men in the political life of the nation, Auguste Scheurer-Kestner. With the espousal of the cause of Dreyfus by Scheurer-Kestner, the Revisionists (as the Dreyfusards came to be known) had won their most influential ally thus far.

In November, 1897, Mathieu learned the name of the author of the bordereau. A stockbroker of his acquaintance, who had seen a facsimile reproduction of the item, found the handwriting most familiar; then, going to his files, he pulled out a number of letters, and clearly had in front of him correspondence by the same person. He turned the evidence over to Mathieu Dreyfus, and named the author of the bordereau as Esterhazy.

With evidence in hand, Mathieu and Demange knocked on the doors at the War Department, but to no avail. They used every avenue to reach the Prime Minister and the President of France, but doors were closed. The Dreyfus case had been terminated, and no good could be served by reopening it. On November 15, 1897, Mathieu made public statements accusing Esterhazy of the writing of the bordereau, in the effort to goad him into a libel suit, and failing this, he printed and distributed two thousand copies of a pamphlet in which he named Esterhazy as the traitor. A new wave of agitation over the case began to rise. The anti-Semitic press eagerly awaited the answer of Esterhazy. Faced with increasing evidence that Esterhazy was the author of the bordereau, the War Department finally was forced to order his arrest. The finger that pointed to Esterhazy could no longer be ignored, and he was ordered to stand court-martial. The War Department, however, insisted that this had nothing to do with the Dreyfus case, that Esterhazy was being tried on an entirely different charge of passing on secrets. Dreyfus's guilt had long ago been established, not only on the basis of the handwriting in the bordereau but also on a great deal of other information: a mysterious confession that could neither be confirmed nor disconfirmed, and other data so secret that national security was involved and hence disclosure was impossible.

In this confused atmosphere, Esterhazy was given a two-day trial in January, 1898. Amid wild charges from the Anti-Semitic League to the effect that the Jewish Syndicate was spending millions to bribe the judges, the latter brought in a verdict of not guilty. Esterhazy was exonerated.

Major Esterhazy, finally suspected of being the real author of the bordereau, was exonerated at a two-day trial (January, 1898).

M. Mathieu Dreyfus, the brother of Captain Dreyfus, and Mrs. Alfred Dreyfus testify against Esterhazy at his trial and denounce him as the real author of the bordereau.

By now, however, many Frenchmen began to have serious doubts as to the guilt of Dreyfus. Elsewhere in the world the name of Dreyfus was becoming increasingly known, particularly among intellectuals, professors, writers, musicians, and others. Friendships were broken over the affair, never to be mended. Oscar Wilde, himself just out of prison and living in Paris under an assumed name, befriended Esterhazy. The youthful André Gide became a Dreyfusard, as did Marcel Proust. Wherever the intellectuals went, and particularly in the literary salons, the subject of Dreyfus dominated, and the debates became acrimonious until camps were so clearly divided that paths seldom crossed. Those who had not yet been drawn into the struggle were not long in taking sides. Among such people were France's leading Socialist, Jean Jaurès; a journalist and politician already known as The Tiger, Georges Clemenceau; and the acknowledged dean of French writers, prolific novelist, and world-famous member of the Academy, Emile Zola.

Jaurès attempted to interest his Socialist colleagues in the case, but many of them saw only an internal squabble among the military and the bourgeoisie, and spurned the matter because the cause of Dreyfus was not that of the working class. Clemenceau began to write columns and editorials on the case, trenchant criticism of the military, exposure of the entire matter as a shoddy frame-up. Zola, too, took up the cause, but again it was felt that something dramatic had to take place to make it utterly impossible to attempt to bury the matter in silence, something that would shake the foundations of the military and that would focus the eyes not only of France but of the entire world on the injustice. It was suggested to Zola (perhaps by Clemenceau—the commentaries are not in agreement) that he write a savage indictment of all those who had been involved, the judges in the first court-martial and the judges in the second, the members of the Ministry of War who had forged documents and framed evidence, up to the Cabinet members who must shoulder responsibility for what had occurred. The attack would be so libelous that it would be impossible to ignore, and the government would have to order the arrest of Zola, and place him on trial before the entire world. Zola complied. On the morning of January 13, 1898, only two days after the acquittal of Esterhazy, there appeared in *L'Aurore*, in blazing black letters across the front page, what has probably become the most famous headline in the history of journalism: J'ACCUSE. Within minutes, the entire edition had been sold out. The most damning indictment of French injustice had at last appeared in print.

The trap that the Revisionists had set for their enemies was obvious, and *La Libre Parole* urged the War Department not to become the victim by abetting Zola's wish to be arrested in order to cause the Dreyfus case to be reopened. After all, who was Zola? He was not even a Frenchman, they asserted, but a man born of an Italian father who still carried the foreign name; he was not a fine writer, this member of the Academy, but a cheap pornographer who portrayed all that was lowly in human life. But the clamor for a reply to Zola was too loud, his friends and enemies too numerous, and the eyes of the world now too clearly focused on the next episode in the Dreyfus drama for this to be ignored.

The problem was: How could Zola be arrested and charged with libel, without the entire Dreyfus case being reopened in court? The answer to this was found by the government: The libel charge would be based on the few words in *J'Accuse* where Zola charged the Ministry of War with ordering the judges to acquit Esterhazy. All the rest would be ignored in the case. Consequently, Zola and the editor of *L'Aurore*, A. Perrenx, were arrested.

Thus came a third trial in the Dreyfus drama that held France spellbound. Not only was French political life dominated by the case; it was almost paralyzed by it. Angry crowds surged through the streets, threatening to lynch Zola, his friends, his witnesses, his lawyers. For two weeks the court heard testimony, largely consisting of legal wrangling as Zola and his chief attorney, Fernand Labori, supported by Georges Clemenceau and his brother, sought to center the case upon Dreyfus.

The Zola trial lasted for little more than two weeks. For all the effort to exclude any mention of Dreyfus, for all the interruptions by the judge whenever the leading character's name was even whispered, the man on Devil's Island dominated the proceedings.

Dramatically to bring the Dreyfus case once again to the attention of the public, Emile Zola agreed to write a savage indictment of all those involved in convicting Dreyfus. On January 13, 1898, the front page of the newspaper *L'Aurore* blazes forth Zola's headline J'ACCUSE . . .!

At the height of the proceedings Zola himself addressed the jury, and none could silence him as he thundered the name of Alfred Dreyfus:

By my forty years of work, by the respect earned by the work of my life, I swear that Dreyfus is innocent. By all I have gained, by the name I have made, and my contribution to the growth of French literature, I swear that Dreyfus is innocent. May all of this perish, my work fail, if Dreyfus is not innocent. He is innocent!

The Zola trial was packed with drama. At one point Labori placed on the witness stand the chief counsel for Dreyfus, Demange. Over the strenuous objections of the judge, Demange planted a bombshell in court, before the public and before the world, when he announced that a secret and illegal document had been the main instrument in convicting Dreyfus.

Anatole France came to testify for Zola; army generals came to testify against him. General Pellieux swore to the existence of documentary proof against Dreyfus, and when the defense demanded that the documents be produced in court, the prosecution simply brought another general, Boisdeffre, to confirm the words of Pellieux.

Lieutenant Colonel Picquart, already under army discipline for having divulged information to Leblois, then dramatically denounced that same document to which Pellieux referred: "That document is a forgery."

Labori and Albert Clemenceau were merciless when interrogating the opposing witnesses. They ridiculed Du Paty, and caught Bertillon in a web of absurdities and contradictions. As for Esterhazy, the army had prepared him for the onslaught by instructing him not to answer any questions.

Brought to trial for libel, Zola was defended by Maître Labori. At the end of an unusually eloquent passage, which even his opponents applaud, Zola warmly embraces his counsel.

The trial resulted in an eight to four verdict (a French jury can convict by a majority) against Zola, who was thus found guilty of libel. Sentenced to jail and fined as well, he decided to go to England, from where he would direct his appeal. In such voluntary exile, he continued to arouse his countrymen to the wrong they had committed against an innocent man. His efforts were not in vain. It was now widely surmised that Esterhazy had written the bordereau.

In June, 1899, a new Minister of War, Eugène Cavaignac, took office. He made a careful study of the entire matter, and early in July, feeling he had conclusive proof of the guilt of Dreyfus, he presented his conclusions to the deputies. For the first time he disclosed the details of the correspondence between Schwartzkoppen and Panizzardi, including a document that actually named Dreyfus. His case against Dreyfus was forceful and convincing, and to the documentation Cavaignac added the fact that Dreyfus had confessed. When a vote was taken, the Chamber was unanimous in support of Cavaignac, with fifteen Socialist members abstaining. The supporters of Dreyfus were crushed. Not since the first days of the beginning of the movement was the outlook so bleak for Revision. So elated was the government with the Cavaignac statement that it was ordered to be printed and posted on bulletin boards in every city, town, and hamlet of France.

As Zola had risen to the occasion a year earlier, now it was Col. Picquart. He addressed an open letter to the Premier, in which he referred to the three documents mentioned by the Minister of War; two were dated 1894, and had no bearing on the Dreyfus case; and the third was a forgery! Before the posters arrived in the French towns, Cavaignac felt humiliated and betrayed, and Esterhazy and Picquart were both ordered arrested, the former for treason, the latter for revelation of secret army documents. Cavaignac assigned a subordinate, one Cuignet, to reexamine the documents, and Cuignet revealed that the Panizzardi document consisted of two sheets of paper, glued together and made to appear as if they were one. It was clear that the shabby forgerer was Henry, who in turn was immediately arrested.

On the night of Henry's arrest, Joseph Reinach, one of the most indefatigable Dreyfusards, and the man who was later to produce a remarkable seven-volume account of the case, predicted to Demange that on the next day they would read of Henry's suicide. The prophecy was fulfilled. All that remained now was for a new trial of Dreyfus to be ordered, and this was not long in coming. The trial was scheduled for the little-known town of Rennes.

Returned to France in July, 1889, for a second trial, Dreyfus, in overcoat and hat, lands at Port Haliguen at 1:35 a.m.

The announcement of the forthcoming new trial was met with elation in the ranks of the Dreyfusards, and an outburst of indignation by the nationalists. The latter denounced the political leaders who had ordered the trial as traitors in the pay of the Syndicate, but at the same time predicted success for the army at Rennes. For the anti-Dreyfusards, the issue was sharply drawn: Accused was France, on the one hand, and Dreyfus, on the other. If the latter was innocent, wrote a nationalist, then the generals were criminals. The judges at Rennes must be made to choose between the two.

In the Chamber of Deputies, the adherents of Dreyfus were crying for blood. If the judges at the first Dreyfus trial had illegally received evidence, and if there had been forgeries, then the man responsibile for this should now be arrested. This was General Mercier, who had been Minister of War in 1894.

Now it was Mercier versus Dreyfus, the honor of the army against the life of the Jew. Mercier let it be known that he would be present at Rennes, and there he would make available incontrovertible evidence against Dreyfus.

Meanwhile, within the Revisionist camp, despite the overflowing optimism as a new trial neared, there was growing dissension. The elderly, venerable, and prestigious attorney who had from the first defended the accused, Demange, was joined in the defense by the lawyer for Zola and later Picquart, the fiery Labori. This was more than a clash of personality and of political orientation; there was a chasm that separated the two men in their outlook on the case and in their strategy for Rennes. Demange essentially saw the affair as a tragic error that could be rectified by the presentation of evidence, particularly with regard to the authorship of the bordereau. For Labori, there were great social issues and moral questions that must be presented in the courtroom. Essentially, Demange had confidence in justice that must triumph in a French court; Labori had confidence in the workers and intellectuals who had imposed their conscience on the French courts.

Crowds came to Rennes, politicians and newspaper reporters and visitors from abroad, bringing to the shopkeepers an unexpected prosperity, and to the inhabitants an unwanted publicity. A military court of seven judges was set up, with a colonel, Albert Jouaust, as chief judge or president of the court-martial.

At six o'clock in the morning of August 7, 1899, just five weeks after Dreyfus's arrival from Devil's Island, the trial opened, and a sergeant led the accused into court. Alfred Dreyfus entered in the uniform to which he had been restored. As he entered there was a gasp from his family, his friends, and those who remembered him. Five terrible years had taken their toll. Barely forty years old, Dreyfus was gray, emaciated, aged. Only with the greatest effort could he stand erect in the military style in which he had been trained. Yet he walked in with hardly a show of emotion, saluted, and took the seat to which he was led.

For many of the great figures, Republicans, Socialists, Revisionists, writers, scientists, poets, the man who walked into the court was not only a pitiable figure, but a great disappointment. Despite himself, he had become their hero, not for any heroic qualities, but because of the events in which he had been entrapped. He was a man of the army, a lover of discipline, who at the time was hardly aware of the furor over his name, and certainly had no grasp of the great social forces that revolved around it. However, if this demeanor in court was for the most part less than heroic, he at least punctuated his stoical, emotionless state with several dramatic outbursts protesting his innocence.

Appointed public prosecutor for the Rennes trial was one Carrière, but behind him stood General Mercier, who at times conducted the case as if he were in Carrière's role. Whereas both Carrière and Mercier were treated with courtesy by Jouaust, not only Dreyfus but Demange and Labori as well were handled with curtness and rudeness. The battle lines were drawn. Only two major figures were absent: Henry, who was dead, and Esterhazy, safe in England.

Zola came from his exile across the Channel, confident that the air in France was safe for him to breathe again; and Picquart, who had spent almost eleven months in jail, was released (never to be tried, in fact) and came to the trial as observer and, later, as witness.

Again, as in 1894, Mercier demanded that the trial be held behind closed doors; again, the defense mildly objected, but not with the strenuous protest that might have proved successful. Mercier hinted that documents would be revealed so secret and explosive that, if they were to be seen in open court, the life of the country would be endangered. So again the public was excluded.

Inside the courtroom, one Colonel Chamoin, who had been selected to represent two cabinet members (the ministers of Foreign Affairs and of War), was caught by Labori as he sought to slip some new sheets into the secret file that was being presented to the judges. The colonel apologized, and explained that that morning, on the way to court, he had by chance met General Mercier, and the latter had asked him to kindly take along the extra papers so that the files would be more complete! There was a demand made on the Premier that Chamoin be arrested; but the Premier was at that point anxious only to keep his coalition government intact and to prevent the flames of civil war from being further fed. The Minister of War agreed to reprimand Chamoin.

Dreyfus and his senior counsel, Demange, during the first session of his second court-martial.

M. Bertillon confuses the court and everyone else with his expert handwriting analysis that still links Dreyfus with the writing of the bordereau.

Captain Lebrun-Renault alleges that Dreyfus confessed his guilt.

The judge allows witnesses to be interrupted by various officers whose evidence is entirely worthless.

And what had Mercier to say about this new situation? Only that he had received the material from Du Paty in Paris, and had not so much as read it.

There were almost a hundred witnesses at the Rennes trial, of whom about a score came for the defense. There were handwriting experts, and army colleagues of the accused, but all were overshadowed by a single figure: Mercier. Arrogantly, he unraveled a case against Dreyfus, repeating some old material, creating some new, offering opinion, hearsay, and crafty hints that there was more. Now Labori hammered away at the role of Mercier in the first trial and particularly at the secret documents, and the deliberate violation of the law by the general. The position of Mercier, under cross-examination, became more uncomfortable and untenable. The general again insisted that Dreyfus had written the bordereau; as for Esterhazy's confession, well, Esterhazy had lied. Mercier wiggled out of every corner.

General Mercier, now ex-Minister of War, imperturbably reiterates his stand that Dreyfus is guilty of writing the bordereau, and accuses Esterhazy of lying when he confessed to writing it.

Maître Labori, associate counsel for Dreyfus, is shot on his way to the court-martial at Rennes. His wife helps care for him.

Thus the trial continued for the first week. On August 14, Labori and Picquart were walking toward the court when the attorney was shot. While the would-be assassin escaped, another man, presumably an accomplice, grabbed the fallen attorney's briefcase. One can only conjecture that someone believed that the briefcase contained material that would incriminate Labori or Dreyfus, or at least that the Dreyfus defense would collapse with the disappearance of Labori and his briefcase. Rumor had it that the attorney had been killed; but the wound was not a grave one, and the enemies of Dreyfus were soon charging that the attempted assasination was all a frame-up, that the Syndicate had shot Labori to arouse sympathy for the Jewish defendant, and to solve the problem of the dissension within the ranks of the defense.

When the trial resumed, there were some dramatic confrontations. One came when Mercier protested that he was an honest man: "Had the slightest doubt stirred in my mind, I would have been the first to declare before you, and before Captain Dreyfus, 'I erred in good faith and I have come to acknowledge it in all honesty and do all that is humanly possible to right the terrible wrong that was done.'"

The accused lost no time in piercing the decorum of the courtroom with his cry: "That is what you should do! It is your duty!"

To which Mercier reiterated his belief in Dreyfus's guilt.

For the defense Demange summarized, appealing to the honor and humanity of the court, flattering the judges, even demeaning himself before them. Labori was silent, at the request of Mathieu Dreyfus. After the prosecution's summary, Dreyfus was asked if there was anything more that he wished to add, and took this opportunity again to affirm his innocence.

The trial lasted just over a month. The world expected a verdict of not guilty, perhaps worded in such a way as to save face for the military; the verdict might read, for example, not proven. The defense expected exoneration, Dreyfus and Demange because they had not lost faith in the integrity of the army; Labori because of worldwide pressures. But verdicts are often dictated by political considerations other than evidence. Again Dreyfus was found guilty of treason, this time by a vote of five to two. The verdict, however, stated that there were "extenuating circumstances," and the accused was sentenced to ten years.

The president of the court cries, "Silence!" as, in a dramatic moment, Generals Mercier, Billot, Roget, Maître Labori, and Captain Dreyfus all talk at once.

Extenuating circumstances! France and her military became the object of a campaign of ridicule. Who had ever heard of extenuating circumstances for treason by a high military officer? Meanwhile, the defendant faced the terrible prospect of five more years of imprisonment.

The French government had only one paramount wish at this time in the Dreyfus case: to put it to an end, and to bury it quietly, with little ado, reuniting the country and reducing the enmity that faced it within. Ten days after the conclusion of the trial at Rennes, Dreyfus was pardoned. That day, the elderly Dreyfusard, Senator Scheurer-Kestner, died. The following year, after bitter debate within the ranks of the Dreyfusards, the government issued a general amnesty, covering all pending cases relating to the affair. Some urged that the central figure reject the amnesty, and insist on another trial and exoneration. Others said that he had already suffered sufficiently. Picquart was especially embittered by the amnesty, and the relationship between the former "convict" from Devil's Island and the one man in the army who had stood by him deteriorated.

After Dreyfus was found guilty—but with extenuating circumstances—Demange sobs.

Convicted for a second time, Dreyfus leaves the court for the military prison.

In 1903, amid a greater calm, the Ministry of Justice unanimously accepted the request for an appeal of the Rennes verdict, but it was not until the summer of 1906 that the judgment of Rennes was set aside and the innocence of Dreyfus officially proclaimed. History was being replayed, but with a different script; and the degradation of 1895 became the restoration of 1906. On July 13 of that year, Dreyfus and Picquart were restored to the French Army and elevated to the ranks of major and brigadier general, respectively. One week later, to a wildly cheering crowd estimated at 200,000, Dreyfus was made a Chevalier of the French Legion of Honor. Even greater honor awaited Picquart, who was soon to become Minister of War in the Cabinet of that old Dreyfusard, Georges Clemenceau.

When war broke out between Germany and France in 1914, Alfred Dreyfus went on active duty. And among the many children of France who died in that war were the son and son-in-law of Mathieu Dreyfus, and the son of Hubert Henry. War so often mends the seams and reweaves the fabric of a society; the common enemy reunifies the divided country.

The Dreyfus affair inflamed anti-Semitism in France, but as it unrolled, it did much to discredit that movement. It was the last gasp of clericalism, monarchism, and militarism in their effort to obtain a stranglehold on French life, and it may have served the purpose of exposing these movements as dangers to the Republic.

Dreyfus died in 1935. He was survived by few of the principals in the case: Picquart, Zola, Anatole France, his brother Mathieu, Esterhazy, Mercier, Clemenceau, all had predeceased him. Only Alfred Dreyfus among them lived to see Léon Blum, a Jew and an early Dreyfusard, named Premier in France, facing a Germany that had adopted anti-Semitism as its official policy. It was apparent that the France that had once pilloried the Jew Dreyfus would now be threatened by the new rallying center for the extermination of Dreyfus's coreligionists. History has many ironies.

But history has many lessons, too, and one that stands out in this tragedy of courtroom drama is the danger that arises when a court, a nation, a military, a leader of a country, cannot admit an error and must proceed to compound it. When the question was posed—Dreyfus or the military?—and when many stated that even if the former were innocent, he must be condemned because the honor of the army and of France was at stake, then all ethical considerations were lost.

The judges enter into the Cour de Cassation to give their decision. It is for Revision.

Pardoned ten days after the end of his second court-martial, Captain Alfred Dreyfus
is reunited with his wife and children at their house at Carpentras.

17

Francisco Ferrer

[1909]

AT THE BEGINNING OF THE TWENTIETH CENTURY THE city of Barcelona in Spain had a population approaching the million mark. To administer to the religious needs of the diocese, there were more than five hundred religious houses, monasteries, and convents, plus some six thousand minor institutions of clerical propaganda and influence. All had to be financed out of the pockets of the people. Spain was completely dominated by the Catholic faith and a rich and powerful hierarchy, from the ruling monarchy down. Every school in the country was Catholic.

In protest against this situation strong forces of revolt began to rise. In 1901 a dedicated anarchist, Francisco Ferrer, having inherited $120,000, opened the first secular school in Spain, the Escuela Moderna, with the purpose of teaching children "to reflect upon the lies of religion, of government, of patriotism, of justice, of politics, and of militarism; and to prepare their minds for social revolution."

One of Ferrer's assistants, Mateo Morales, also an anarchist, threw a bomb at King Alphonso and his bride on the day of their wedding. The royal couple escaped injury, but fifteen people were killed. Without a shred of evidence against him, Ferrer was arrested for complicity in this outrage. For lack of evidence he was not immediately brought to trial but was kept in jail for one year. Finally, the case was brought to trial before a rigged special court without a jury. Out to get the blood of the only rich anticleric in Spain, the court still found the case so absurd that they were forced to acquit Ferrer.

After that, Ferrer was a marked man, and knew it. He went to great lengths to keep out of trouble. When the famous insurrection, accompanied by a general strike, riots, looting of churches, and the burning of several convents, broke out in Barcelona on July 26, 1909, Ferrer was nowhere to be found. But the police, who had been watching him closely since his last trial,

simply assumed he was connected with the flare-up, and finally arrested him at Alella, his birthplace, on September 1. Thereupon, Señor Ugarte, the public prosecutor, announced that he considered him an anarchist and the leading spirit behind the July insurrection.

On that opinion alone, without any supporting evidence, Ferrer was brought to trial for a second time. Meanwhile the police had searched his house and produced a document they claimed to have found there. It was a proclamation that read in part: "We are all agreed upon a revolution. All Revolutionaries must devote themselves to the cause, but we need to have three hundred comrades ready, as we are to risk their necks at Madrid to begin our movement. We await a favorable opportunity, such as after a general strike or on the Eve of Labor Day." Ferrer denied any knowledge of this document.

The trial on October 9, 1909, before the Council of War in the Model Prison of Barcelona, lasted only five hours. The court consisted of a lieutenant-colonel, as president, and six captains. The examining magistrate read the *procès verbal*, which gave the details of the prisoner's arrest and examination, listed the incriminating articles found in his possession, and the declarations of witnesses for both sides. The prosecutor then summarized the evidence in the *procès verbal* and stated that fifteen witnesses had seen Ferrer leading disturbances at Premía de Mar, Masnóu, and with armed groups in Barcelona. In the name of the king, he demanded that Ferrer be sentenced to death for the crime of rebellion, or to penal servitude for life.

Ferrer's defender, Captain Francisco Galcerán Ferrer, then made an eloquent plea, stating that Ferrer was a victim of political animosity and religious prejudice, that the evidence brought against his client consisted of old charges raked up for this occasion, and that they bore no reference to the present case.

Francisco Ferrer.
A drawing by F. Van Sloan.

Ferrer then spoke a few words in his own defense, ending with a statement that his only occupation of recent years had been in matters of education, instruction, and culture.

The president of the court then declared that the trial was at an end and that the council would arrive at their verdict in private.

The trial of Francisco Ferrer outdid in injustice anything that might have taken place in a Star Chamber proceeding. On the ground that there wasn't time, no witnesses were called, although Ferrer had many waiting who could vindicate him. Only hostile evidence had been admitted, anonymous denunciations given credence, and statements were accepted from unqualified witnesses. The sentence was death, which was ratified on October 12 by the Spanish Cabinet.

From all over Europe protests arose. Even the pope asked the papal nuncio in Spain to look into the matter. There were attempts by the governments of Great Britain and France to intervene to save him. Even King Alphonso indicated a willingness to reprieve Ferrer. But the king did not have the power to reverse a decision of the Cabinet, and Prime Minister Señor Maura was adamant that Ferrer should die. At nine o'clock on the morning of October 13 Francisco Ferrer was taken to one of the ditches of the foritification, blindfolded, and shot by a four-man firing squad.

The radical and democratic influence of Ferrer on Spain was great. His Escuelas Moderna branched out into all parts of Spain, a powerful force against clericalism and bureaucracy, and proof to people of all classes of the evil influence of clerical orders on the government of Spain. The world denounced the government that murdered Ferrer, as years later they were to denounce the Fascist regime that was victorious in the Spanish Civil War. It might well be said that Francisco Ferrer's trial laid the groundwork for the future Loyalist resistance against Spanish tyranny.

Madame Joseph Caillaux in the witness box to the extreme left listens while her husband, Joseph Caillaux, French Minister of Finance, testifies in her behalf at her trial for the murder of M. Gaston Calmette, managing editor of *Figaro*. Directly in front of Mme. Caillaux is her defense counsel, Maître Labori.

L'Illustration

18

Madame Joseph Caillaux

[1914]

ON THE AFTERNOON OF MARCH 16, 1914, MADAME JOSEPH Caillaux, wife of the Minister of Finance, and one of the darlings of Paris society, called at the offices of the newspaper *Figaro* and asked to see its distinguished managing editor, Monsieur Gaston Calmette. She waited impatiently for an hour before he returned to the office with his friend the well-known novelist Paul Bourget. Madame Caillaux sent in her card, and Bourget exclaimed, "Surely, you will not see her?"

"Oh, yes," replied Calmette, "she is a woman, and I must receive her." Bourget left. Madame Caillaux entered the room and, in her own words at her preliminary trial, related: "I had slipped my revolver, which was in my muff, out of its case. . . . I fired and fired again. The mouth of the revolver was pointed downwards." She then went on firing without any idea of what she was doing. Two of the bullets wounded Calmette fatally. He died a few hours later.

Joseph Caillaux, Finance Minister of France, had for some time been the target of Calmette's vitriolic campaign in *Figaro*. Calmette charged him with personally profiting from negotiations with Germany over Morocco, and sought in many other ways to libel his political career. He threatened to publish certain very personal letters that Caillaux had written to his present wife while still married to his former wife, now Mme. Gueydon. Caillaux went to President Raymond Poincaré and asked what could be done to prevent Calmette from publishing these letters. Poincaré could offer him no assurance that *Figaro* would not publish them, and Caillaux then shouted, "If Calmette publishes those letters, I will kill him." But it was his wife who committed the murder, on the very afternoon of this meeting.

* * *

In criminal cases, French justice differs considerably from American and English trials. The defendant is first interrogated informally and at length by an examining magistrate, who has almost unlimited authority over what evidence and what testimony from witnesses he wishes to take. He decides how long the preliminary trial will last. Each day he also reveals to the press exactly what the defendant and the witnesses have said. This is immediately published in next day's newspapers, and the case is tried and decided in the court of public opinion long before it comes to trial in a court of criminal jurisdiction. As the Caillaux case progressed through this preliminary trial, public opinion was decidedly against the defendant. Most of the Paris press agreed, but a few were critical of M. Calmette. *L'Aurore*, wondering at the temerity of the dead editor, concluded, "How could he suffer himself to be led on to undertake the violent campaign which provoked this terrible reprisal?"

* * *

The trial of Madame Caillaux began at the Seine Assizes in the Palace of Justice on July 20, 1914. She was defended by Zola's and Dreyfus's famous lawyer, Maître Fernand Labori. As is the case in a French trial, the defendant was the first witness. For an hour she recounted, amid sobs, the events of that fateful day, and insisted that she had shot M. Calmette without premeditation or intent to kill. She had simply wanted to frighten him into putting a stop to the *Figaro* campaign against her husband.

Labori then shifted the trial into political gear by calling Joseph Caillaux to the stand. For the better part of two days Caillaux defended himself against the libels Calmette tried to place upon him, and sought to justify his political career. He then recalled the strain and anxiety he and his wife had suffered at Calmette's threat to publish two more of his letters to his present wife (one had already been published). The disposition of President Poincaré regarding M. Caillaux's discussion with him of Calmette's intentions was then read to the court.

On the fourth day of the trial Mme. Berthe Gueydon, divorced wife of M. Caillaux, took the stand and handed an envelope containing five letters to M. Labori, saying he could read them to the court or not, as he saw fit. The courtrom went into an uproar. But it turned out to be a tempest in a teapot. The letters were finally read, but they contained nothing more than harmless love phrases and sentimentalities. Hardly justification for murder to suppress them!

The feeling of the spectators at the trial and those all over the world who avidly followed the proceedings in the newspapers was summed up by the American publication *The Independent:* "Because of the political turn the case has taken, especially when the prisoner is a woman, it is difficult to say what the outcome will be, but French papers predict either acquittal or a very light sentence."

On July 28 the case went to the jury, who returned in less than an hour with a verdict of acquittal. The verdict was exceedingly unpopular in France, and in a bitter editorial *Figaro* exclaimed: "It is the most enormous scandal of our epoch and covers the radical republic with mud and blood. It is an abominable parody of justice. Mme. Caillaux has torn an acquittal from a dazed jury, a terrified government and sold judges."

* * *

The trial of Madame Caillaux was remarkable in that the judgment of the jury went contrary to the verdict of the people and the press. In its recent decision on the appeal of Dr. Samuel Sheppard, accused of murdering his wife, the United States Supreme Court ordered a retrial on the grounds that the accused was denied a fair trial because he was simultaneously being tried in the press. In the case of the French jury, each member went home at night while the trial continued, read the newspaper accounts and editorials relating to it, discussed the merits of the case and the testimony with his family and friends—and still brought in a verdict of not guilty for Madame Caillaux.

19

Edith Cavell

[1915]

LONDON IS FILLED WITH MONUMENTS TO MANY BRITISH heroes, but few figures emerge in stone as dignified as the sculpture of Edith Cavell. There she stands, near Trafalgar Square, a majestic woman, with her long flowing robes accentuating the erect and dignified body, inspiring awe in the viewer. Above her head is chiseled one word: "Humanity." Below her name the inscription reads "Brussels," followed by the date: "Dawn October 12th, 1915," and then a brief statement: "Patriotism is not enough. I must have no hatred or bitterness for anyone." If the spirit of Edith Cavell is captured in these words, the same cannot be said for those who tried and executed her and for those who used her execution to arouse the hatred and bitterness that she denounced.

Born in England in 1865, Edith Cavell was trained in nursing, and became dedicated to alleviation of human suffering. In the early years of the twentieth century, she settled in Brussels, where she became director of an institution that has variously been described as a hospital, home for invalids, and institute for surgery. In August, 1914, with the outbreak of the First World War, she remained in Brussels, which soon fell to the advancing German Army. Orders were posted by the occupying authorities demanding that all French and British sodliers be reported to the Germans. False identification cards and false passports, however, were easily obtainable, making it simple for an underground railway system to be established to help those who wished to escape. Edith Cavell took an active part in setting up such a system, and her nursing home at 149 rue de la Culture became a beehive of activity.

On August 5, 1915, occupation authorities, having been tipped off, raided the nursing home. A letter incriminating the American consul in Brussels was found, and Miss Cavell and her chief assistant, Miss Wilkins, were arrested. After interrogation Miss Wilkins was released, but Edith Cavell was taken to prison.

Held for several weeks in her cell, during which time she was reported to have made a full statement of her activities, Miss Cavell was finally brought to trial on Thursday, October 7, 1915. There were thirty-four other defendants accused of various activities declared illegal under the occupation. Thirty-one were Belgian, three French, one, Edith Cavell, English. All were to be tried by a German military court, headed by a lieutenant colonel, and containing two captains and two lower officers. Five members of the Belgian bar appeared for the prisoners.

Miss Cavell sat through the entire proceedings stoically and impassively. There could be no defense for her, for her confession spelled out her guilt in unmistakable terms:

I acknowledge that between November, 1914, and July, 1915, I have received into my house, cared for and provided with funds to help them to reach the front and join the Allied Army:

1. French and English soldiers in civilian clothes, separated from the ranks, amongst whom was an English colonel.
2. The barrister, Libiez, of Mons.
3. Prince Reginald, of Croy, and one Mlle. Martin, who is one and the same person as the accused Thuliez, with whom I have just been confronted.

A lieutenant in the German Army testified that "the woman Cavell managed the headquarters in Brussels" of an organized effort to assist prisoners to reach Holland. A schoolboy was brought in to give evidence against his own mother. And then the trial adjourned until the following day.

Miss Edith Cavell.
Wide World Photos

On October 8, the recommendations of the prosecutor were made. "All this activity," he stated, "is akin to high treason and the law punishes it with the death sentence." Thus, he asked for death for the British nurse and four others, and for varying prison sentences for the remaining defendants. Of the British nurse, he charged:

Miss Cavell acknowledges that she received into her house between November 1914 and July 1915, French and English derelict soldiers in civilian clothes, amongst whom was an English colonel, and in addition Belgian and French men of military age wishing to reach the front, that she had cared for them and provided them with funds in order to facilitate their journey to the front and their entrance into the ranks of the Allies. She admits in addition, that she escorted most of the men who were brought to her at Brussels to certain spots previously arranged, to hand them over to guides known to her, who were waiting for her. She confesses also that she received news of the safe arrival in Holland of several of these men whom she had in this way conveyed into Holland. She is to be included amongst the chief organisers.

The lawyers for Edith Cavell made a last-minute plea, stating that she was dedicated to but one purpose in life: to help others. She thought that the soldiers would have been killed had they been apprehended in Brussels, and she wished, in her humanitarianism, only to save their lives. Was this not the culmination of her entire lifework? In fact, she had helped German soldiers in her lifetime, just as she had helped others. And now there was no proof that those she had aided had ever borne arms against Germany.

Asked by the court if she had anything to say, Miss Cavell answered, "Nothing."

Held over the weekend awaiting the sentencing, the prisoners were informed of the verdict on Monday October 11. In late afternoon of that dreary day, the prisoners were brought before the court, and there they heard: "The tribunal is of the opinion, partly on the strength of their own statements, and partly on the strength of the assertions of their fellow prisoners, that the following are the chief organizers" . . . and here were read the names of those sentenced to death, among them Edith Cavell. Eight of the accused were acquitted; the rest drew sentences up to fifteen years.

That night there was feverish, if somewhat inept, activity on the part of the American ambassador, Brand Whitlock, to gain postponement or clemency for Miss Cavell, but without success. Her fellow prisoners urged her to ask for mercy, but she refused. Before dawn the next morning, two of the prisoners, Philippe Baucq, a Belgian architect, and Edith Cavell, were executed by the firing squad.

When news of the execution reached her homeland, anger against the Germans rose to new levels, and enlistments of volunteers increased considerably. The Bishop of London called her death "the greatest crime in history," and American newspapers used it to fan the flames of the war spirit.

Following the end of the war, her body was brought to London, where she was given the burial of a war hero. Her courage and bravery, her refusal to ask for mercy, and her indomitable spirit became part of the myth that grew up around the name of Edith Cavell in the years that followed. Her name was put to many uses; often her followers recall her alleged last words (as reprinted in an eight-column headline by the *New York Herald*): "Happy to die for my country," and they forget the words chiseled on her memorial: "Patriotism is not enough."

Whether she had all the saintlike qualities attributed to her following her martyrdom is today difficult to say, but after her trial and execution made a martyr of her, her name was put to many uses far from the humanitarianism so often associated with it.

"Vanzetti and Sacco and Their Guards" by Ben Shahn (Gouache, 1932).
Downtown Gallery, Collection of Patricia M. Healy

Nicola Sacco and
Bartolomeo Vanzetti

[1921]

ON APRIL 15, 1920, IN THE LITTLE TOWNSHIP OF SOUTH Braintree, Massachusetts, not far from Plymouth where the Pilgrims had landed almost exactly three centuries earlier, two employees of a shoe factory were murdered and a payroll of slightly more than $15,000 seized by the escaping bandits. It was a perfectly planned crime, having all the earmarks of professional gangsters. It left in its wake two dead men: Frederick A. Parmenter and Alessandro Berardelli. Seven years later, Nicola Sacco and Bartolomeo Vanzetti were legally put to death by the Commonwealth of Massachusetts, having been found guilty of the double murder. Aside from these few facts, however, the partisans of the accused and their opponents agree on few points in a case that aroused millions of people to a pitch of anger that no criminal trial—not even that of Dreyfus—has before or since seen. The emotional involvement that the names of Sacco and Vanzetti bring forth have been passed down as their legacy; today millions who were not even alive at the time of the case, or were only little children, are strongly convinced that this was, if not a frame-up, then at least one of the gravest miscarriages of justice in all human history. While a few others, a minority but a vociferous one, maintain that the intellectuals were duped, that the men were guilty (or at least Sacco, so the story goes), and that they were given a fair trial under what was then Massachusetts law.

*   *   *

Following the first World War, aliens (and particularly alien radicals) were plagued by mass arrests, instigated by the Attorney General of the United States, A. Mitchell Palmer. Homes were entered without warning in what were known at the time as the Palmer raids; men were held for long periods without hearings or trials; there were thousands of deportations, and there were many suicides. Of the Palmer raids, Chief Justice Hughes stated:

> We cannot afford to ignore the indications that, perhaps to an extent unparalleled in our history, the essentials of liberty are being disregarded. Very recently information has been laid by responsible citizens at the bar of public opinion of violations of personal rights which savor of the worst practices of tyranny.

Nicola Sacco and Bartolomeo Vanzetti were Italian-born anarchists who had come to the United States, where they had continued their radical agitation, particularly among the Italian colony in eastern Massachusetts. In 1917, faced with universal conscription in a war that they opposed, they went to Mexico, an act that was to stigmatize them later as "slackers" and "draft dodgers."

On May 3, 1920, a close friend of both Sacco and Vanzetti, a compatriot named Andrea Salsedo, who was being held for deportation, met his death. In the language of the coroners, he "jumped or fell" from the fourteenth floor of his place of detention in New York City, plunging to death on the concrete pavement below. To the minds of many of his grieving comrades, he "jumped, fell, or was hurled." The death of Salsedo added to the aura of fear surrounding the Italian community, particularly its radical wing.

On May 5, Sacco and Vanzetti, together with two friends, went to pick up a car in a repair shop; following this visit, they were arrested on a streetcar returning to their own homes. At the time of their arrest, they were both carrying guns, and there is disputed testimony as to whether Vanzetti made an effort to reach for his gun. Taken into a police station and questioned, they behaved suspiciously, and told many lies concerning their own and their friends' whereabouts on various occasions. Their behavior under arrest became a major point of controversy. It added up, the prosecution contended, to a consciousness of guilt, and thus provided circumstantial evidence against them. For the defense, it was emphasized that they had not been notified of the nature of the charges, that they thought they were being held as part of the antiradical campaign, and that they were merely trying to protect themselves and their friends from deportation or worse.

Soon they were charged with two crimes: an unsuccessful holdup in Bridgewater, Massachusetts, on Christmas Eve, 1919, and the murder of Parmenter and Berardelli on April 15 in South Braintree. However, Sacco produced such an incontrovertible alibi for the Bridgewater occasion that the charge against him was dropped. At this point the entire Bridgewater case might have faded into insignificance were it not that Vanzetti was being tried on this charge before the murder case. On the matter of which of two charges a man is to be tried on first, the laws and customs are contradictory. Unless there are matters of availability of witnesses, competing venues, and the like, a defendant usually has the right to be tried on the more serious charge first, so that he does not come before the court in a murder case, for example, already stigmatized as a convicted criminal in a robbery case. It is charged by the defenders

of Sacco and Vanzetti that the prosecution reversed this procedure because the evidence against Vanzetti in the murder case was weaker than against Sacco (this is conceded almost universally), and in this way Sacco would be burdened by association with a convicted criminal, and Vanzetti by association with Sacco (who would be identified by numerous witnesses).

So the first trial opened at Plymouth before Judge Webster Thayer and lasted little more than a week, during which time Vanzetti did not take the stand in his own defense. While juries are repeatedly warned that this is not to be interpreted as a sign that a defendant is guilty, it is felt by many that such warnings are of little avail. The most important single fact about the trial with its guilty verdict and a sentence of twelve to fifteen years is that Vanzetti, almost immediately after its conclusion, charged that he had been double-crossed by his own lawyer. He claimed that John P. Vahey had sold him out to the prosecutor, Frederick Katzmann, and that it was on Vahey's insistence and advice that he had failed to take the stand to deny, emphatically and categorically, any connection with the crime. It is a serious charge of a defendant against an attorney, and against Vahey there is one important piece of circumstantial evidence: soon after the trial, he went into law practice as a partner of his erstwhile opponent Katzmann.

On September 11, Sacco and Vanzetti were indicted for the South Braintree killings, and on May 31, 1921, their trial opened in Dedham, before the same Judge Webster Thayer who had presided over the Plymouth trial and had already given Vanzetti, a first offender, the unheard-of sentence of twelve to fifteen years for the attempted holdup.

Courthouse at Dedham, Massachusetts, where the trial of Sacco and Vanzetti opened on May 31, 1921, before Judge Webster Thayer. *Dedham Historical Society*

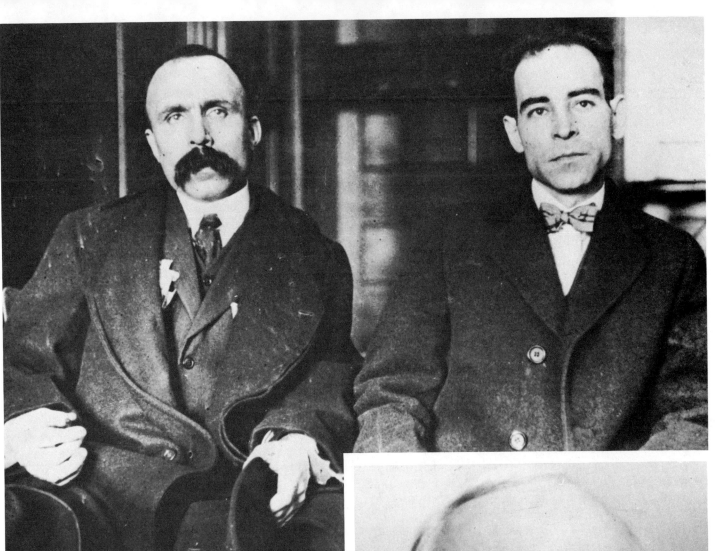

Nicola Sacco (*left*) and Bartolomeo Vanzetti (*right*) in court during their trial for murder.
United Press International

Judge Webster Thayer, who presided at the Sacco-Vanzetti trial.
United Press International

For the prosecution, Frederick Katzmann again took charge, assisted by Harold P. Williams; for the defense, chief counsel Fred Moore, aided by Jeremiah and Thomas McAnarney. Moore had long been associated with radical causes, although he too was to be repudiated by the defendants and their friends. Later, William G. Thompson became chief of the defense staff during the seven-year struggle to save the defendants from the chair. He came from a staid and reputable Boston law firm, and he was assisted by Herbert Ehrmann, who continues to this day to write on the case. A few years later Michael Musmanno, young and energetic, devoted himself to the cause.

The murder trial itself took more than six weeks. The transcript runs to thousands of pages, supplemented by more thousands of pages of hearings, reports, and documents. At Dedham, the prosecution's case rested on several points:

1. Eyewitnesses who claimed to have seen Sacco in South Braintree on the morning before the crime, at the scene of the crime, and leaving it.

2. A gun found in Sacco's possession, which was said to have been Berardelli's gun, and which he presumably picked up at the time of the murder.

3. At least one shell taken from the body of Parmenter, which was said by ballistics experts to have been fired from the gun in Sacco's possession.

4. Sacco's absence from work on the day of the crime.

5. The resemblance between the automobile belonging to Sacco's friends, and which he occasionally borrowed, and the murder car, found abandoned in the woods near the scene of the crime.

6. The behavior of the defendants at the time of their arrest and interrogation.

Against this, the defendants offered:

1. Evidence that many of the eyewitnesses could not have seen the crime or that they had given contradictory information at various times in the investigation and that their identification of Sacco took place in a prison, without a lineup, and with no one else there.

2. Testimony from people who had seen Vanzetti at various times in the day, on April 15, far from the scene of the murder.

3. Testimony from many people who had seen Sacco in Boston at the time of the crime.

4. Explanation of the behavior of the defendants in terms of their fear of deportation, and their memory of the Salsedo affair.

5. The vehement denials on the stand of the defendants themselves.   *   *   *

It is difficult to read the testimony without being convinced that both sides were trying to reach witnesses, and to use various inducements to have these witnesses change their stories; that both sides were deliberately suppressing information damaging to their case (such suppression is a much more serious charge in American law against a prosecutor than against a defense attorney); and that seldom has there been such an array of unreliable men and women who not only contradicted one another but also, in innumerable instances contradicted themselves and told unbelievable stories. A few highlights will give some idea of what went on in the courtroom.

Lola Andrews was a woman with a doubtful reputation. She changed her story many times during the course of the trial, retracted her entire testimony, then retracted her retraction. She was confronted with pictures that the defense attorneys had shown her during pretrial examination, and simply denied that she had seen them. Confronted with the stenographic record, she denied that she had said what the transcript stated. She claimed that she had been walking along the street of South Braintree on the morning of the murder, and was seeking employment. She needed directions so that she could locate the office of the Rice and Hutchins Company. She saw two men near an automobile; one was standing in the rear; the other had his head and shoulders under the car.

CROSS-EXAMINATION OF LOLA ANDREWS

Q. Now, do I understand, Mrs. Andrews, that the tall, slender, Swedish looking person was inside of the car as you went in?

Frederick G. Katzmann, the unrelenting prosecutor in the Sacco-Vanzetti trial.
Wide World Photos

A. The tall, slender man that you mean, he was sitting in the back of the car as I went into the Slater & Morrill factory.

Q. And when you came out, he was standing behind the car?

A. Yes, sir.

Q. You at no time spoke to him?

A. Meaning the man that was standing at the back of the car?

Q. Yes.

A. No, sir.

Q. The tall, slender man?

A. Yes, sir.

Q. And when you came back, the man that you did speak to was underneath the car, and had to come out from underneath the car to answer your inquiry?

A. Partly under the car, yes, sir.

Q. And before you reached the man that you did speak to, you passed the man that was standing up, the light complected man, at the rear of the car? You passed him before you reached the man at the front end of the car who was underneath the car, is that right?

A. You mean, that I passed the man that was standing at the back of the car?

Q. Yes.

A. Why, I didn't walk by him, Mr. Moore.

Q. Why, he was at the rear, you were beyond the rear of the car, and you had to pass him and the rear of the car going on up west on Pearl Street, didn't you?

A. Why, I don't understand that.

Mrs. Andrews had been interviewed in a pretrial examination, in the presence of a stenographer. Confronted with the record of her contradictions between that record and her identification of the man underneath the car as Sacco, the woman could do no better than deny that she had said what she had said:

Q. Did I show you any photograph that night that you thought looked at all like the man you saw?

A. You showed me a lot of photographs that night, and amongst them was one that I told you resembled the man that I saw.

Q. You remember that, don't you?

A. Yes, sir.

Q. Do you remember being asked this question: I called your attention to the group of photographs marked "22-36-C," and asked you if you have even seen any of those men. Answer: "I have never seen any of those men at all. The color of that man's hair and the face and the complexion looks like him." Do you remember so stating?

A. I don't remember so stating that answer to you in that way.

Q. Question: "But a larger man?" Answer: "Yes." Did you so state?

A. I did not, no, sir.

Q. Question: "An older man than he is?" Answer: "I don't know whether this man is 28 or 38." Did you so state?

A. Yes, sir, I did say that.

Q. Question: "But you would not by any means pretend to say that this is the man?" Answer: "No." Did you so state?

A. I did not make that answer.

Q. Question: "Would you say positively that it is not the man?" Answer: "That man there is not the man." Did you so state?

A. I said the man—

Q. Answer my question, please. Did you so state?

A. I don't remember.

Q. Will you say you did not?

A. I will say that I don't remember.

Q. Question: "You are positive?" Answer: "Yes." Did you so state?

A. I don't remember.

THE COURT: What is she speaking about? I don't know as the jury knows.

MR. MOORE: I am reading this, your Honor, in order to get to the picture, to which this is preliminary evidence. I have already asked with reference to a group of pictures.

THE COURT: That she says she has never seen.

MR. MOORE: Yes.

Q. Question: "Positive that is not the man?" Answer: "Yes." Did you so state?

A. I did not.

Q. Question: "You mean the man with the soft collar, standing, holding in his hand a derby hat is not the man you saw on April 15, 1920, in South Braintree?" Answer: "No, indeed." Did you so state?

A. I did not.

Q. Now, directing your attention to this list of pictures that I have just been referring to, "23-36-C." Now, running those over you find that there is only one man in that picture with a derby hat in his hand, don't you?

A. Yes, sir.

Q. Who is that the picture of now do you know?

A. It is the same picture that I pointed out to you at that time.

Q. Absolutely, isn't it?

A. Yes, sir.

Q. And at that time you answered me in this wise: Question: "You mean the man with the soft collar, standing, and holding in his hand a derby hat is not the man you saw on April 15, 1920 in South Braintree?" Answer: "No, indeed." Didn't you so answer?

A. I didn't answer you that way.

Q. My question was as I read it, wasn't it? I asked you that question did I not?

A. Yes, sir.

Q. You answered me in that wise, did you not?

A. I did not answer you the way—

Q. How did you answer me?

A. I told you that he resembled the man I saw at South Braintree.

Q. Question: "Why are you positive that he is not the man?" Answer: "The only way is that man does not look to me that his shoulders would hang down like." Did you so state?

A. I don't remember.

Q. Question: "He hasn't got that slouch?" Answer: "No, and the man I am speaking of even though dressed up would not be a man that looked like this man." Did you so state?

A. I did not.

Later, one witness after another impeached Lola Andrews; she was so shaken that at one point, as the official transcript reveals, she simply fainted. But this did not prevent the prosecutor Katzmann from stating to the jury that, in his eleven years in the service of the Commonwealth, he had never before "laid eye or given ear to so convincing a witness as Lola Andrews."

Some of the prosecution witnesses simply reversed their story on the stand and denied that they had ever identified the prisoners; others affirmed their identification, although they had denied this to defense representatives.

An important prosecution witness was William Proctor, captain in the Department of Public Safety of the Massachusetts State Police, in charge of the Division of State Police. He had been in the department for twenty-three years, a captain for sixteen. Proctor had received cartridge shells found at the scene of the shooting. After going through considerable testimony establishing his expert knowledge of ballistics, identifying bullets and Sacco's gun, Proctor was asked a series of questions, and gave answers which are among the most famous in the history of criminal jurisprudence:

Q. Have you an opinion as to whether bullet 3 was fired from the Colt Automatic which is in evidence?
A. I have.
Q. And what is your opinion?
A. My opinion is that it is consistent with being fired by that pistol.
Q. Is there anything different in the appearance of the other five bullets—
A. Yes.
Q. Just a minute, I had not completed. —the other five bullets to which I have just referred, which would indicate to you that they were fired from more than one weapon?
A. There is not.
Q. Are the appearance of those bullets consistent with being fired with the same weapon?
A. As far as I can see.
Q. Captain, did you understand my question when I asked you if you had an opinion as to whether the five bullets which you say were fired from an automatic type of pistol were fired from the same gun?
A. I would not say positively.
Q. Well, have you an opinion?
A. I have.
Q. Well, that is what I asked you before. I thought possibly you didn't understand. What is your opinion as to the gun from which those four were fired?
A. My opinion is, all five were fired from the same pistol.
Q. What is the basis of your opinion?
A. By looking the marks over on the bullets that were caused by the rifling of the gun. It didn't seem to cut a clear groove; they seemed to jump the lands, and seemed to make a different mark than the lands would make.

Later, after the trial was over, Proctor was to swear that he had repeatedly told Katzmann that it was his opinion that the bullets had not been fired from this gun and that Katzmann had elicited from him the information that, although in his opinion they were not so fired, it was consistent that they could have been. If this retraction was Proctor's genuine story, if he had so informed Katzmann and Katzmann permitted him to testify to a partial truth which was in fact misleading, even to the point of contributing to the doom of two

men, then the prosecution was guilty to an extent as great as was charged by any of the advocates of the defendants. Katzmann, in his answer to the Proctor affidavit, merely denied that the information Proctor had given to him had been told to him "repeatedly"! But soon afterward, Proctor died, while the case was still under appeal, and the defense was deprived of a valuable ally.

When the defense opened, it brought an array of witnesses who placed both Sacco and Vanzetti at points far removed from the scene of the murder. Sacco's whereabouts in Boston were traced for several hours; Vanzetti was at the home of close friends, where he delivered fish, and then was seen by a man who had been painting his boat at the shore during the entire day of the 15th. The difficulty, in the establishment of an alibi, is for anyone testifying to establish how he recalls that particular day. For the Boston incident, many of Sacco's friends were attending a luncheon in honor of a journalist, and there was documentary evidence that the luncheon did take place, and these people clearly recalled seeing Sacco just before and after. Their stories, furthermore, are consistent with one another (whereas it is impossible to believe some of the prosecution witnesses if one is to believe others). Sacco was in Boston on the 15th to go to the Italian consulate, a matter that was sworn to by deposition from a clerk who had since returned to Italy.

One of the upholders of the Vanzetti alibi knew the exact date because she connected it with her mother going to the hospital; another, with his wife's birthday.

Katzmann, however, was merciless on cross-examination, and he held the witnesses up to ridicule in a manner that has been widely criticized by almost every commentator on the case and that indicates not only his interest in conviction rather than in truth but also betrays the partiality of the court and its judge, a matter that was to become an international scandal.

For example, take the testimony of Melvin Corl, who testified that he was on the shore of the bay, painting his boat, when Vanzetti stopped by on April 15, 1920, and stayed and talked to him from about 2:00 P.M. to 3:30. On cross-examination by Katzmann:

Q. Mr. Vanzetti was a customer of yours, wasn't he?
A. Yes, sir.
Q. How long did you say he had been a customer?
A. Since about August, 1919.
Q. And did that, if you know, mark the commencement of his being in the fish business?
A. I do not think so.
Q. Had he been in the fish business before then?
A. I had seen him selling fish with another man, yes.
Q. How long before that?
A. Possibly a month or six weeks.
Q. Had he been a steady customer? Had he been a customer of yours from that time until his arrest?
A. He had bought fish from me up until I hauled my boat out in December.

This photo of Nicola Sacco and his family, showing a passport photograph presented to the Italian consul in Boston on the afternoon of the South Braintree murder, was offered as evidence that Sacco was not at the scene of the crime when it happened.
United Press International

Q. Yes.

A. And I do not know where he bought his fish then, but he was going to buy again from me after I put my boat in the water.

Q. What day did you start painting your boat?

A. I should say it was around probably the 12th or 13th of April.

Q. What day of the week did you start painting your boat?

A. On a Monday.

Q. Have you looked up the date to see what day the 12th came?

A. No, I haven't.

Q. How do you know it was not on the 5th of April?

A. Because I did not start my work until just before I put the boat in,—week before I put it in.

Q. Yes, but let us go back of that. Do you know the exact day you put your boat in?

A. Yes, sir.

Q. Is there any relationship between your wife's birthday and the date you put a boat in the water?

A. No, only by the remark she made.

Q. Some remark she made?

A. She made the remark I put it in on her birthday.

Q. Will you say you did not start on the week before that?

A. Yes.

Q. When was your attention first directed to any man that you had a conversation with during the week you were painting your boat?

A. Say that again please.

Q. When was your attention first directed to a conversation you had with any one man while you were painting your boat?

A. I could not say about that.

Q. Was there anybody down there talking with you while you were painting your boat on the 14th?

A. Mr. Jesse was there.

Q. Was he there every day?

A. Yes, sir. Right in his boat yard.

Q. Aside from Jesse,—was Jesse assisting you around your boat?

A. No.

Q. Is he a fisherman?

A. No. He runs a boat yard where my boat was hauled up in.

Q. You were down in his place?

A. Yes.

Q. So that he was there every day, wasn't he?

A. He was working in his shop.

Q. He was working in his shop; and did he have workmen there, too, working in the shop beside himself?

A. I could not say whether he had anybody at the time or not.

*   *   *

Q. Do you remember that Vanzetti was arrested on May 6th?

A. I read the account in the paper. I do not know just the date he was arrested, but I read about his being arrested.

Q. Do you know the date of the arrest of any other man in the past 2 years in North Plymouth?

A. No, not any fixed date.

Q. Where were you 21 days ago today?

A. I could not say just now. Probably I could figure it back.

Q. Where were you 20 days ago today?

A. Possibly on the water.

Q. No, not "possibly." Where were you?

MR. JEREMIAH MC ANARNEY.   You asked him.

THE COURT.   If he means by that that is his judgment, it may stand. If it is a mere guess, it is not evidence.

MR. JEREMIAH MC ANARNEY.   I submit if your Honor please, my brother can't cut the answer. He has to let the answer come.

MR. KATZMANN.   I let it come.

MR. JEREMIAH MC ANARNEY.   You said, "No, no." You tried to stop it.

MR. KATZMANN.   I did not stop it. I said, "No, no, where were you?"

THE COURT.   Go along with the next question.

Q. Where were you 20 days ago today?

A. I think on the water.

Q. Are you sure of it?

A. I am on the water most every day.

Q. Is that the way you fix it?

A. Yes, sir.

Q. What portion? Whereabouts on the water were you?

A. Possibly fishing off the Gurnetts.

Q. Do you fish off the Gurnett every day?

A. Every day that the weather is fine.

Q. Was the weather fine 20 days ago today?

A. I could not say now.

Q. That is the way you earn your livelihood, isn't it?

A. Yes.

Q. That is important to you, isn't it, Mr. Corl?

A. My fishing is, yes.

Q. Can't you tell this jury whether the day 20 days ago was a day you were fishing?

A. I could not tell unless I stopped to figure back.

Q. Where were you on the 19th day of June?

A. I can't place that date.

Q. What day of the week was it?

A. I do not just remember. I could not say the date.

Q. Don't know that. Do you fish on Sundays?

A. I carry fishing parties Sundays.

Q. Did you have a fishing party on the Sunday preceding the 19th of June?

A. No, sir.

Q. Have you had any fishing parties on any Sunday in June, 1921?

A. I had the second Sunday of June, I had a fishing party.

Q. What was that date?

A. I could not just say, but I know it was the second Sunday in June.

Q. Did you fish on the 19th day of June?

A. I do not know what day of the week that was.

Q. You don't. Do you know April 15, what day of the week it was?

A. No sir, not just now. I could figure it up.

Q. April 15, 1921. Could you figure that up?

A. Surely, to know what day of the week it was.

Q. What day of the week in April, 1920, did April 17th fall on?

A. Say that again.

Q. What day of the week did the 17th day of April, 1920, fall on?

A. On Saturday.

Q. Then what day of the week was the 15th?

A. Thursday.

Q. Yes. How do you remember it was the 17th that fell on a Saturday?

A. On account of my wife's birthday and going to Duxbury.

Q. On what day of the week did your wife's birthday fall, April 17, 1921?

A. Monday.

Q. What?

A. I think it was Monday.

*   *   *

Of the defendants, Bartolomeo Vanzetti came to the stand first, starting on the morning of Tuesday, July 5. He traced his doings on the day of the crime, told how he had been treated upon arrest and how he did not know the nature of the charge, and related the reasons for leaving the United States in 1917—because he opposed the war and wanted to avoid registration for the draft. In cross-examination, there was one point at which the prosecution hammered: that Vanzetti had told dozens of lies at the preliminary examination before the trial and at the time of his arrest, all purportedly to protect his friends and because he did not know the nature of the charges against him. Again, the alibi was questioned. How could he know so much about what he had done on April 15th, if he knew so little about so many other days:

Q. Mr. Vanzetti, do you remember this question and this answer at the Brockton police station that I made of you, which you gave in reply: " Q. Well, do you remember the holiday we had in April, the 19th of April, they call it Patriots' Day, the middle of April? A. Yes. I heard that before, but I did not remember that was in April." Do you remember saying that to me at Brockton?

A. What holiday?

Q. The 19th of April?

A. What holiday it is?

Q. Patriots' Day.

A. Patriot?

Q. Patriots' Day.

A. Oh, patriotics day.

Q. Yes, do you remember my asking you that question and your making that reply?

A. No, I don't; I don't remember.

Q. Will you say you did not make that reply to that question?

A. No, I don't say that I didn't.

Q. Do you remember the next question: "Q. This year it came on a Monday." You remember the answer: "A. I don't remember." Did you make that reply?

A. No, I don't remember.

Q. Will you say you did not make it?

A. Well, maybe I did. I might have, yes.

Q. Do you remember this question and this answer: "Q. You don't know where you were the Thursday before that Monday, do you? A. No." Do you remember that answer to that question?

A. Oh, yes, I answered some other thing no, that I don't remember in that time, but I remember it now, not only this.

Q. On May 6th, 1920?

A. Yes.

Q. You did not remember where you were on the 15th of April, did you?

A. More probable, yes.

Q. But after waiting months and months and months you then remembered, did you?

A. Not months and months and months, but three or four weeks after I see that I have to be careful and to remember well if I want to save my life.

History makes Sacco out to be a less majestic figure than his codefendant. Certainly he was less articulate, less able to handle the English language. On the witness stand, however, he held his own. He followed Vanzetti on the stand (except for a brief interruption when a former witness was recalled). In addition to denying participation in the crime, and explaining his own background and why he had lied upon arrest, Sacco described the manner in which he had been identified by witnesses in the jail: the lack of lineup, the forced posing before the witnesses, and other means used to obtain identification of him.

On cross-examination, the prosecution immediately took up the question of patriotism; the following is the opening of the cross-examination of Nicola Sacco:

MR. KATZMANN. Did you say yesterday you love a free country?

A. Yes, sir.

Q. Did you love this country in the month of May, 1917?

A. I did not say,—I don't want to say I did not love this country.

Q. Did you love this country in the month of 1917?

A. If you can, Mr. Katzmann, if you give me that,—I could explain—

Q. Do you understand that question?

A. Yes.

Q. Then will you please answer it?

A. I can't answer in one word.

Q. You can't say whether you loved the United States of America one week before the day you enlisted for the first draft?

A. I can't say in one word, Mr. Katzmann.

Q. You can't tell this jury whether you loved the country or not?

MR. MOORE. I object to that.

A. I could explain that, yes, if I loved—

Q. What?

A. I could explain that, yes, if I loved, if you give me a chance.

Q. I ask you first to answer that question. Did you love this United States of America in May, 1917?

A. I can't answer in one word.

Q. Don't you know whether you did or not?

MR. MOORE. I object your Honor.

THE COURT. What say?

MR. MOORE. I object to the repetition of this question without giving the young man an opportunity to explain his attitude.

THE COURT. That is not the usual method that prevails. Where the question can be categorically answered by yes or no, it should be answered. The explanation comes later. Then you can make any inquiry to the effect of giving the witness an opportunity of making whatever explanation at that time he sees fit to make, but under cross-examination counsel is entitled to get an answer either yes or no, when the question can be so answered. You may proceed, please.

Q. Did you love this country in the last week of May, 1917?

A. That is pretty hard for me to say in one word, Mr. Katzmann.

Q. There are two words you can use, Mr. Sacco, yes or no. Which one is it?

A. Yes.

Q. And in order to show your love for this United States of America when she was about to call upon you to become a soldier you ran away to Mexico?

MR. JEREMIAH MC ANARNEY. Wait.

THE COURT. Did you?

Q. Did you run away to Mexico?

THE COURT. He has not said he ran away to Mexico. Did you go?

Q. Did you go to Mexico to avoid being a soldier for this country that you loved?

A. Yes.

Q. You went under an assumed name?

A. No.

Q. Didn't you take the name of Mosmacotelli?

A. Yes.

Q. That is not your name, is it?

A. No.

Q. How long did you remain under the name of Mosmacotelli?

A. Until I got a job over to Mr. Kelley's.

Q. When was that?

A. The armistice.

Q. After the war was practically over?

A. Yes, sir.

Q. Then, for the first time, after May, 1917, did you become known as Sacco again?

A. Yes, sir.

Q. Was it for the reason that you desired to avoid service that when you came back in four months you went to Cambridge instead of to Milford?

A. For the reason for not to get in the army.

Q. So as to avoid getting in the army.

A. Another reason why, I did not want no chance to get arrested and one year in prison.

Q. Did you want to get arrested and spend one year in prison for dodging the draft. Is that it?

A. Yes.

Q. Did you love your country when you came back from Mexico?

A. The first time?

THE COURT: Which country did you say? You said—

Q. United States of America, your adopted country?

A. I did not say already.

Q. When you came back, I asked you. That was before you went.

A. I don't think I could change my opinion in three months.

Q. You still loved America, did you?

A. I should say yes.

Q. And is that your idea of showing your love for this Country?

A. (Witness hesitates.)

Q. Is that your idea of showing your love for America?

A. Yes.

Q. And would it be your idea of showing your love for your wife that when she needed you you ran away from her?

A. I did not run away from her.

MR. MOORE. I object.

THE WITNESS. I was going to come after if I need her.

THE COURT. He may answer. Simply on the question of credibility, that is all.

Q. Would it be your idea of love for your wife that you were to run away from her when she needed you?

MR. JEREMIAH MC ANARNEY. Pardon me. I ask for an exception on that.

THE COURT. Excluded. One may not run away. He has not admitted he ran away.

Q. Then I will ask you, didn't you run away from Milford so as to avoid being a soldier for the United States?

A. I did not run away.

Q. You mean you walked away?

A. Yes.

Q. You don't understand me when I say "run away," do you?

A. That is vulgar.

Sacco was adamant; he insisted on expressing his political philosophy:

The free idea gives any man a chance to profess his own idea, not the supreme idea, not to give any person, not to be like Spain in position, yes, about twenty centuries ago, but to give a chance to print and education, literature, free speech, that I see it was all wrong. I could see the best men, intelligent, education, they been arrested and sent to prison and died in prison for years and years without getting them out, and Debs, one of the great men in his country, he is in prison, still away in prison, because he is a Socialist. He wanted the laboring class to have better conditions and better living, more education, give a push his son if he could have a chance some day, but they put him in prison. Why? Because the capitalist class, they know, they are against that, because the capitalist class, they don't want our child to go to high school or to college or Harvard College. There would not be no chance, there would not be no,—they don't want the working class educationed; they want the working class to be a low all the times, be underfoot, and not to be up with the head. So, sometimes, you see, the Rockefellers, Morgans, they give fifty,—mean they give five hundred thousand dollars to Harvard College, they give a million dollars for another school. Everybody say, "Well, D. Rockefeller is a great man, the best in the country." I want to ask him who is going to Harvard College? What benefit the working class they will get by those million dollars they give by Rockefeller, D. Rockefellers. They won't get, the poor class, they won't have no chance to go to Harvard College because men who is getting $21 a week or $30 a week, I don't care if he gets $80 a week, if he gets a family of five children he can't live and send his child and go

to Harvard College if he wants to eat anything nature will give him. If he wants to eat like a cow, and that is the best thing, but I want men to live like men. I like men to get everything that nature will give best, because they belong,—we are not the friend of any other place, but we are belong to nations. So that is why my idea has been changed. So that is why I love people who labor and work and see better conditions every day develop, makes no more war. We no want fight by the gun, and we don't want to destroy young men. The mother been suffering for building the young man. Some day need a little more bread, so when the time the mother get some bread or profit out of that boy, the Rockefellers, Morgans, and some of the peoples, high class, they send to war. Why? What is war? The war is not shoots like Abraham Lincoln's and Abe Jefferson, to fight for the free country, for the better education, to give chance to any other peoples, not the white people but the black and the others, because they believe and know they are mens like the rest, but they are war for the great millionaire. No war for the civilization of men. They are war for business, million dollars come on the side. What right we have to kill each other? I been work for the Irish, I have been working with the German fellow, with the French, many other peoples. I love them people just as I could love my wife, and my people for that did receive me. Why should I go kill them men? What he done to me? He never done anything, so I don't believe in no war. I want to destroy those guns. All I can say, the Government put the literature, give us educations. I remember in Italy, a long time ago, about sixty years ago, I should say, yes, about sixty years ago, the Government they could not control very much these two,—devilment went on, and robbery, so one of the government in the cabinet he says, "If you want to destroy those devilments, if you want to take off all those criminals, you ought to give a chance to Socialist literature, education of people, emancipation. That is why I destroy governments, boys." That is why my idea I love Socialists. That is why I like people who want education and living, building, who is good, just as much as they could. That is all.

A great deal was made of the question of the cap picked up near the body of the murdered men. Sacco denied it was his, and Katzmann hammered away at the fact that there was a little hole in it, which the DA insisted was made when Sacco hung his cap on a nail in the shop, thus definitely establishing that Sacco was the owner of the cap and hence must have been at the scene of the murder.

Q. I call your attention to Exhibit 27 for identification, to that in the lining. What is it?

A. I never saw that before.

Q. What is it?

A. I don't know.

Q. Don't know what that is?

A. It is a hole.

Q. It is a hole?

A. Yes.

Q. And you never saw that before?

A. No.

Q. Still you say that is your hat?

A. Sure. Never say that before.

Q. Never saw that before. Was there any hole in your hat when you last saw it?

A. Hole, no.

Q. Sure of that?

A. Pretty sure.

Q. Where did you hang your hats up? If this is your hat, did you ever wear it to work?

A. Yes.

Q. What do you hang it up on?

A. On a wall.

Q. On what on the wall?

A. On the stake, on two stakes.

Q. Two stakes?

A. Yes, sticks.

Q. Sticks of wood?

A. One go across and put my jacket, my pants.

Q. Is there a hook here?

A. What do you mean, a hook?

Q. A hat hook, or clothes hook?

A. Yes, I made myself, for the purpose.

Q. What is it made of?

A. Sticks.

Q. That is wood?

A. Yes. Then there is a nail through.

Q. Is it on the nail you hang your hat?

A. Yes.

Q. That is something you put up for yourself in the Kelley shop, wasn't it?

A. Yes.

Later, a police officer was to state that he had made the hole in this cap when he was scratching it to see what was beneath the label.

* * *

It did not take the jury long to bring in verdicts of guilt, and reporters have stated that even Katzmann's assistant, Williams, wept when the verdict included Vanzetti, for he had grave doubt as to Vanzetti's relationship with the affair. Sacco shouted out: "They kill innocent men. They kill two innocent men."

On April 9, 1927, after many appeals and countless protests, the men were again brought before Judge Webster Thayer in his Dedham Courthouse, and they were sentenced. Each was given an opportunity to speak; each reiterated his innocence:

Nicola Sacco (in part):

You know it, Judge Thayer—you know all my life, you know why I have been here, and after seven years that you have been persecuting me and my poor wife, and you still today sentence us to death. I would like to tell all my life, but what is the use? You know all about what I say before, that is, my comrade, will be talking, because he is more familiar with the language, and I will give him a chance. My comrade, the kind man to all the children, you sentenced him two times, in the Bridgewater case and the Dedham case, connected with me, and you know he is innocent.

You forget all this population that has been with us for seven years, to sympathize and give us all their energy and all their kindness. You do not care for them. Among that peoples and the comrades and the working class there is a big legion of intellectual people which have been with us for seven years, to not commit the iniquitous sentence, but still the Court goes ahead. And I want to thank you all, you peoples, my comrades who have been with me for seven years,

with the Sacco-Vanzetti case, and I will give my friend a chance.

I forget one thing which my comrade remember me. As I said before, Judge Thayer know all my life, and he know that I am never guilty, never—not yesterday, nor today, nor forever.

Vanzetti's statement was long and eloquent. It opened on a simple note:

Yes. What I say is that I am innocent, not only of the Braintree crime, but also of the Bridgewater crime. That I am not only innocent of these two crimes, but in all my life I have never stolen and I have never killed and I have never spilled blood.

And it closed on a fiery one:

Well, I have already say that I not only am not guilty of these two crimes, but I never committed a crime in my life— I have never stolen and I have never killed and I have never spilt blood, and I have fought against crime, and I have fought and I have sacrificed myself even to eliminate the crimes that the law and the church legitimate and sanctify.

"Massachusetts—There She Stands!" a drawing by William Gropper for the Leftist press carries this subcaption quotation: "There is only one thing this court can do. Sentence Sacco and Vanzetti to the electric chair!"
—Judge Webster Thayer.
Manuscripts Collections, Carnegie Library, Syracuse University

This is what I say: I would not wish to a dog or to a snake, to the most low and misfortunate creature of the earth—I would not wish to any of them what I have had to suffer for things that I am not guilty of. I am suffering because I am a radical and indeed I am a radical; I have suffered because I was an Italian, and indeed I am an Italian; I have suffered more for my family and for my beloved than for myself; but I am so convinced to be right that you can only kill me once but if you could execute me two times, and if I could be reborn two other times, I would live again to do what I have done already.

I have finished. Thank you.

The court proceeded to sentence the men to death.

❖ ❖ ❖

Much of the tragedy and most of the drama in the case took place outside the courtroom. The bias of the trial judge, Webster Thayer, was widely attacked. It was rumored that, in many places outside the courtroom, he had made derogatory statements about the accused; finally, by a professor of unimpeachable integrity, he was accused of having referred to Sacco and Vanzetti, in the professor's presence, as "anarchist bastards." Thayer never specifically denied this accusation; the few apologists for him have claimed that he conducted the trial with fairness despite this apparent prejudice, and one commentator insisted that he was referring, not to the defendants, but to their lawyers!

Vanzetti, with moustache, and Sacco, handcuffed together, arrive at Boston Superior
Court to be sentenced to die in the electric chair the week of July 10, 1927.
Wide World Photos

As new evidence was turned up, and errors in the case became more and more glaring, appeals were made. But under Massachusetts law then in effect, these appeals for a new trial had to be heard by the original trial judge, and in one instance after another, he rejected the appeals. There were Lola Andrews' retraction; Proctor's accusation that the prosecution deliberately worded a question to receive what was known to be a seriously misleading answer; an affidavit from a friend of the foreman of the jury (who died shortly after the end of the trial) that before the trial began, the foreman had stated that the men should get what's coming to them, whether they had committed the crime or not; and there were confessions and mounting evidence that the crime was the work of other men.

Among the unanswered questions raised by the defense were: Who were the other three bandits in the automobile? What happened to the $15,000, and why was none of it ever traced to the accused or their families? How and when were Sacco and Vanzetti able to plan such a carefully timed and perfectly executed robbery?

Radicals and labor leaders took up the cudgels for the defendants in the death house; poets, novelists, artists, member of the intellectual community the world over; many of the members of the most aristocratic families in Massachusetts; and some of the most prestigious lawyers in the country. The names of these who joined the protest reads like a Who's Who of American and world intellectuals: Sherwood Anderson, Romain Rolland, H. G. Wells, Alfred Dreyfus, Edna St. Vincent Millay, John Dos Passos, Upton Sinclair, Sinclair Lewis, Maxwell Anderson, Albert Einstein, Thomas Mann, John Galsworthy, and many others.

It was only, however, when Felix Frankfurter, professor of law at Harvard and one of the most astute legal minds in America, decided to enter the controversy, that many neutrals became involved. In an article in the *Atlantic Monthly*, Frankfurter gave a cool appraisal of the case. Behind the legalisms, it was an indictment of American justice such as had never appeared from the pen of a legal mind in this country. He showed the prejudices and errors of Thayer, the absurdities and contradictions of the prosecution's case, the impossibility of the prosecution's story of the crime. It was an indictment that could not go unanswered, and the rejoinder came from Dean J. H. Wigmore, of the Northwestern University Law School. Wigmore made six points. The debate is summarized by an authoritative commentator:

1. Wigmore stated that Frankfurter should not have said that the men called for jury duty represented a selected element in the community; Frankfurter replied that he had made that observation only about part of the jury (the men called from their Masonic meeting), and that the record supported him; the rebuttal does not touch this point.

2. Wigmore asserted that Thayer did not say that the supreme court had "approved" the verdict; Frankfurter quotes Thayer's use of the word "approved" in the record; the rebuttal admits that Thayer did use the disputed word once, but indicates that satisfactory terminology occurs in eight other places.

3. Frankfurter was upbraided for not mentioning Sacco's imminent departure for Europe; Frankfurter quotes himself on this point; Wigmore admits the mention of the fact but says it was underemphasized. The whole argument on this element of testimony is very important because it is here that Wigmore relies chiefly upon the famous passage in Thayer's ruling which quotes completely nonexistent cross-examination.

4. Wigmore said Frankfurter did not mention Sacco's cap; Frankfurter quotes himself; the rebuttal is silent.

5. Wigmore emphasized the fact that the defense introduced the question of radicalism, and justified the cross-examination of Sacco as a test of sincerity; Frankfurter points out that the prosecution had full knowledge of Sacco's radicalism, and that one is therefore forced to conclude that the real purpose of the interrogation was to inflame the jury against the witness; the rebuttal merely states the finding of the supreme court to the effect that this was not Katzmann's purpose.

6. Wigmore contended that the Supreme Judicial Court did pass on the facts in the case when it upheld Thayer's denial of a directed verdict of innocence. He cites law and decisions to the effect that the high court can and does examine facts in such cases. Frankfurter replies by quoting the appellate decision: "only errors of law are before us. . . . As to findings of fact the trial judge's findings are final." The rebuttal asserts that this quoted phrase was applied only to the post-trial facts, and that one "question of law" is always the sufficiency of evidence. (Wigmore must have known that he was being indefensibly legalistic on this point; note the reform of Massachusetts appellate procedure in 1939.)*

---

* From Louis Joughin and Edward M. Morgan, *The Legacy of Sacco and Vanzetti*, pp. 260–261. Reprinted by permission.

This untitled drawing by William Gropper conveys the widespread feeling that the Sacco-Vanzetti trial was a travesty of justice.
Manuscripts Collections, Carnegie Library, Syracuse University

By WILLIAM GROPPER

William G. Thompson (*left*), counsel
for Sacco and Vanzetti, with
Herbert Ehrmann, associate counsel,
leave Boston State House after making
a plea for their clients.
United Press International

Massachusetts Governor Alvan Fuller, who appointed
a three-man Advisory Committee to review the case.
United Press International

"Raise Your Voice in Protest," a drawing
by William Gropper, depicts the rallies
against the verdict in leading cities
all over the world.
*Manuscripts Collections, Carnegie
Library, Syracuse University*

Among his many other accusations against Thayer, Frankfurter had pointed out that, in turning down the appeals, Thayer had referred to testimony that was not in the record!

*　　*　　*

In the last months of the long period of appeals, there were general strikes for Sacco and Vanzetti in South America; demonstrations in Milan, Turin, London, Berlin, and elsewhere; mass meetings in Asia and Africa. The United States embassies were stoned, and American prestige fell to a new level. The State Department sent a memorandum to its ambassadors on the case, but this did little to repair damage, particularly since the memo was itself replete with errors.

As protests mounted in intensity, the focus of attention was directed on Judge Thayer, Governor Alvan T. Fuller, a three-man Advisory Committee to review the case appointed by Fuller, the Supreme Court of the United States, and on the FBI. Two former employees of the Department of Justice stated that there was information in the FBI files on the case that had not been revealed, but all efforts to have these files opened were in vain; to this day, no one is certain of whether the files are still in existence, whether they ever existed, and if so, what they would have revealed. But there was at the time, and there remains to this day, a suspiciion that the government was suppressing information that would have aided the defendants.

The three-man commission was headed by A. Law-rence Lowell, the president of Harvard, and consisted, in addition to himself, of the president of the Massachusetts Institute of Technology, Samuel W. Stratton, and Robert A. Grant, a writer. Grant's supposed prejudice against Italians has been documented, particularly by Michael Musmanno, the young and energetic attorney who joined the defense during the last year and who was selfless in his devotion to the men and the case.

But to return to the commission. It was dominated by Lowell, and he seemed determined to bring in a verdict vindicating the trial judge and the integrity of Massachusetts justice. For example, when the alibi witnesses for Sacco insisted that they could place the time of their seeing Sacco because of the luncheon meeting in Boston that afternoon, Lowell shocked and frightened the defense with an announcement that he had information that the event had not taken place at the stipulated time. The very next day, the witnesses came back with copies of their Italian-language newspaper, in which the luncheon was announced. Lowell apologized to the witnesses for the defense, but the episode does not end here. So mortified was the Harvard president by this evidence of his error that he ordered the stenographer *to expunge* this entire section from the record. Later, when this was called to his attention, be avoided the question studiously; however, to a Harvard student who insisted on an answer, he wrote: "The charge of suppressing evidence in presence of counsel for the accused is an absurdity on its face to anyone who thinks about it." But the charge was not suppression of evidence; it was tampering with the official record of the hearings.

The Advisory Committee (*left to right*) consisted of Robert A. Grant, Samuel Stratton, president of M.I.T., and A. Lawrence Lowell, president of Harvard.
United Press International

In the end, it was not Sacco and Vanzetti who were any longer on trial; it was American justice, and particularly the justice of the Commonwealth of Massachusetts. Is this not the case in almost every significant trial? Socrates drank hemlock, but Athenian society stands forever indicted; religious dogma and superstition were on trial when Galileo appeared before his judges; and white justice, southern variety, was to be on trial years later in the Scottsboro case. With Massachusetts on trial, the sentiment began to rise that, even if the men were innocent, the Commonwealth could no longer back down; it could not give in to the rabble. And so their final pleas were rejected by the governor in the face of greater and greater evidence of the miscarriage of justice, and they went to their deaths.

Katzmann, Lowell, Thayer, and Fuller sank into ignominy and oblivion. For all practical purposes, their public careers were over; they were no longer useful to the society that they had served. Whatever political and intellectual acumen they had, all was to be forgotten, as they carried with them forever unto their graves the stigma of the role that they had played in what came to be known as the judicial murder of Sacco and Vanzetti. Fuller's name was mentioned as a vice-presidential candidate for 1928, but was quickly dropped. There was

a report that he would be named ambassador to France, but this too was denied, for in France he would be *persona non grata*. In November, 1927, when he traveled to France, the governor of Massachusetts chose to use a pseudonym. Thayer and Katzmann were thwarted in their political ambitions; they remained minor figures, and fell into obscurity. No political party wanted to be associated with either of them. Lowell retired, and to the end vigorously defended his actions, but was bitter and evasive when the facts of the case were called to his attention.

Although most commentators, reviewers, and historians have been convinced that the men were innocent, now and then a voice is raised that insists on the guilt of Sacco, and the possible guilt of Vanzetti. Their work, however, is one-sided and distorted; it ignores the overwhelming contradictions in the case; invents new and absurd explanations (as, for example, that the Italian-language newspaper announcing the luncheon was quickly forged one afternoon and brought back to Lowell the next day); and finally it bases its claim on ballistics tests made in 1962. These tests established, in the view of the experts, that the lethal bullet did indeed come from the Sacco gun. But the bullet was by that time over forty years old; an accumulation of rust on the gun

Following electrocutions of Sacco and Vanzetti at Charleston Prison, thousands of persons form a funeral procession for the eight-mile journey across Boston, while thousands of others look on.
Wide World Photos

had been scratched off and new markings made; and the bullet and gun had been in many hands, including those of people not connected with the government, over the decades.

History has found Sacco and Vanzetti innocent, and today they cannot be tried again, for, involuntarily *in absentia,* they cannot be given the fair trial denied them in the 1920's. Those who would alter this verdict cannot face the fact that American jurisprudence could have been so guilty of a crime against two innocent men; that America was victim of group prejudice and blinding hysteria such as would again raise its ugly head in the era of McCarthy. But there the record stands.

The involvement in the Sacco-Vanzetti case is perhaps without parallel, unless it was equaled by those involved in the Dreyfus case. And those who, insisting on Sacco's guilt, would reverse the verdict of history, do so as a warning to writers, artists, and professors not to meddle in the orderly process of government, a warning that could only have meaning today for citizens who become embroiled in the still continuing court struggles over civil disobedience and civil rights.

Among the legacy of Sacco and Vanzetti are twenty-three gouaches by Ben Shahn, two anthologies of poetry,

many other poems not in these anthologies, and plays, novels, short stories, and many works of art. The latter include a large bronze bas-relief by the world-famous sculptor Gutzon Borglum which a group of prominent citizens (Eleanor Roosevelt, Albert Einstein, Herbert Lehman, and others) sought to present to the Commonwealth of Massachusetts, with the request that it be placed on Boston Common, a recognition by the Commonwealth of the injustices of yesteryear. This offer was refused by Governor Hurley, who contended that there was still a division of public opinion on the matter.

But neither artist, nor poet nor novelist could ever equal in grandeur the words of Bartolomeo Vanzetti:

If it had not been for these thing, I might have live out my life talking at street corners to scorning men. I might have die, unmarked, unknown, a failure. Now we are not a failure. This is our career and our triumph. Never in our full life could we hope to do such work for tolerance, for joostice, for man's onderstanding of man as now we do by accident. Our words— our lives—our pains—nothing! The taking of our lives—lives of a good shoemaker and a poor fish-peddler—all! That last moment belongs to us—that agony is our triumph.

Memorial demonstrations for Sacco and Vanzetti were held all over the world. In London's Trafalgar Square over 10,000 gather in protest, and an American flag was torn down by one of the demonstrators.
Wide World Photos

This bronze bas-relief memorial by the sculptor Gutzon Borglum was presented to the Commonwealth of Massachusetts by a group of prominent Americans, including Eleanor Roosevelt, Albert Einstein, and Herbert Lehman. It was refused by the then Governor Charles F. Hurley.
Wide World Photos

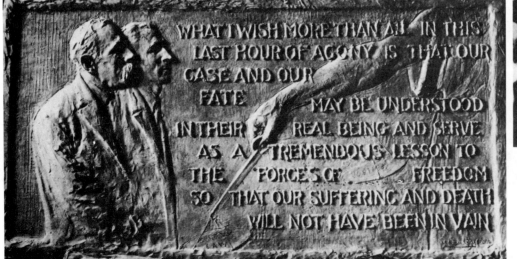

WHAT I WISH MORE THAN ALL IN THIS LAST HOUR OF AGONY IS THAT OUR CASE AND OUR FATE MAY BE UNDERSTOOD IN THEIR REAL BEING AND SERVE AS A TREMENDOUS LESSON TO THE FORCES OF FREEDOM SO THAT OUR SUFFERING AND DEATH WILL NOT HAVE BEEN IN VAIN

Clarence Darrow (*left*) and William Jennings Bryan, leading opponents
in the "Monkey Trial" of John T. Scopes at Dayton, Tennessee.
Wide World Photos

21

John Thomas Scopes

[1925]

DAYTON IS A SLEEPY LITTLE TOWN IN TENNESSEE, WITH A population that fluctuates between 1,500 and 2,000. Few people outside the state, and in fact not many within it, had heard of it before the summer of 1925. But in that year, for a period of about two weeks, it held the spotlight of world attention. An unassuming and modest young schoolteacher, charged with violating a state law prohibiting the teaching of evolution, was a defendant in a trial that brought two giants of American intellect into sharp collision, each a leading spokesman for warring antagonist forces. The repercussions were of a magnitude that could hardly have been foreseen when Scopes reluctantly consented to a technical arrest in order to make a test case challenging the constitutionality of the anti-evolution law.

Laws restricting the teaching of evolutionary theory, or for that matter any other theory that might conflict with the literal interpretation of the Bible, had been introduced into various state legislatures in the years following the First World War. The Fundamentalists, ridiculing those who placed the word of Darwin higher than that of God as they interpreted it, scoffing at opponents who admitted the possibility that they were descended from some kind of monkey, were deeply entrenched in rural areas, particularly in the South. The Fundamentalists joined hands with the Prohibitionists in the campaign against liquor, sin, and godlessness; they warned the people against Bolsheviks, scientists, intellectuals, atheists, agnostics, and drunkards, strange bedfellows, indeed! They defended the literalness of the Bible as the revealed truth of God against the onslaught of the Darwinian theory of evolution.

Laws forbidding the teaching of evolution in publicly supported schools had been passed in Florida and just missed passage in Kentucky and North Carolina. Even university professors were intimidated by their directors from speaking out against the legislation of the know-nothings. In Tennessee, an obscure legislator named John Washington Butler introduced such a bill in the spring of 1925. The lower house passed the bill, expecting it to be defeated by the more courageous senators. The Senate passed it, confident that it would be vetoed by the governor. The governor, hardly one to place himself on the firing line before the voters, signed the bill, making it a law, certain that it would not be enforced. In fact, unbelievably in his message to the legislature, he so stated. While the Butler law was short, it was not so simple as appeared at first glance!

Chapter 27, House Bill 185 (By Mr. Butler) Public Acts of Tennessee for 1925.

AN ACT prohibiting the teaching of the Evolution Theory in all the Universities, Normals and all other public schools of Tennessee, which are supported in whole or in part by the public school funds of the State, and to provide penalties for the violations thereof.

Section 1. BE IT ENACTED BY THE GENERAL ASSEMBLY OF THE STATE OF TENNESSEE, That it shall be unlawful for any teacher in any of the Universities, Normals and all other public schools of the State which are supported in whole or in part by the public school funds of the State, to teach any theory that denies the story of the Divine Creation of man as taught in the Bible, and to teach instead that man has descended from a lower order of animals.

Section 2. BE IT FURTHER ENACTED, That any teacher found guilty of the violation of this Act, shall be guilty of a misdemeanor and upon conviction, shall be fined not less than One Hundred ($100.00) Dollars nor more than Five Hundred ($500.00) Dollars for each offense.

Section 3. BE IT FURTHER ENACTED, That this Act take effect from and after its passage, the public welfare requiring it.
Passed March 13, 1925
  (W. F. Barry),
  Speaker of the House of Representatives.
  (L. D. Hill),
  Speaker of the Senate.
Approved March 21, 1925.
  (Austin Peay),
  Governor.

For all intent and purpose the Tennessee Anti-Evolution Act might have remained peacefully quiescent had a secretary in the National Office of the American Civil Liberties Union in New York not clipped a newspaper item announcing the passage of the Butler bill. She brought the item to the attention of the director of the ACLU, Roger Baldwin, and soon the organization issued press releases, stating that it would be willing to undertake to finance a test case challenging the constitutionality of the law.

In Tennessee, the ACLU offer came to the attention of George Rappelyea, a young businessman who had been born in New York. He might well have been motivated by a distaste for the restrictive legislation, combined with leanings more toward science than toward

revelation. With a nose for excitement, he also may have had an inkling that Dayton could possibly become the focal point of a little sideshow. So, in the cultural center of town, Robinson's Drug Store, Rappelyea spotted the likable John Scopes as a biology teacher who had all the possibilities for his test case. Inquiring just what he taught in his biology lessons, he was delighted to find that he readily admitted teaching evolution. At this point, Rappelyea pointed out to Scopes that he had been violating the law. He asked that Scopes voluntarily subject himself to arrest and consent to be the defendant in a test case. Scopes hesitated. Such an arrest for challenging of a law could seriously jeopardize his record as a teacher. But anticipating a quiet legal battle, a few legal briefs, arguments by counsel, and an obscure decision by a court, Scopes assented.

The trial began to assume gigantic proportions when the World Fundamentalist Association asked William Jennings Bryan to assist the prosecution. A three-time candidate for President on the Democratic ticket (and thrice defeated), a former Secretary of State under Wilson, the silver-tongued orator who had thundered against sinners and atheists from pulpits and in fields all over America, Bryan was in many ways a logical

William Jennings Bryan confers with John Washington Butler, author of Tennessee's Anti-Evolution bill.
Tennessee State Library and Archives, Nashville, Tennessee

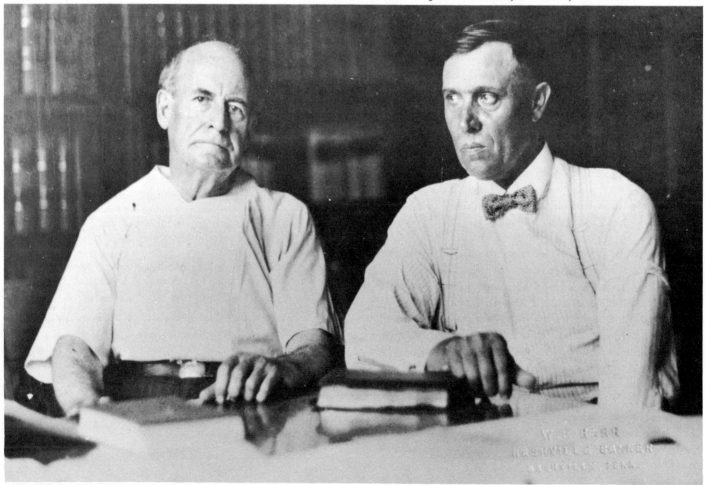

choice. That he had not practiced law for some thirty-five years, that he was an outsider as much as were the lawyers from New York, could be overlooked. For here was a man who would defend the right of the common people, the majority of the populace, to restrict their teachers to teaching only their own beliefs. Furthermore, Bryan was in agreement on legislative control of all educators.

Bryan's entrance into the struggle was a challenge that his opponents could not overlook. America's most famous criminal lawyer, Clarence Darrow, long an opponent not only of Fundamentalism but of all organized religion, an avowed agnostic, offered his services to the defense without charge—the first and only time in his career that he would serve without a fee. Strangely enough, at the ACLU there was less than unanimous enthusiasm at this offer. Many of the most eminent civil libertarians were opposed to the case becoming a forum for a clash between science and religion, between evolution and Genesis. It was, for them, a more basic issue: freedom to teach. Legislatures, they contended, could not be permitted to restrict teachers in the subject matters of their courses and how they were taught. They must not become censors of textbooks, overseers of curricula, and watchdogs of lecture halls.

While the ACLU discussed, debated, and argued the question as to whether Darrow would head the defense team, the decision was made by Scopes himself. Assisting Darrow were Dudley Field Malone, a liberal Catholic and a divorced man (two factors not likely to ingratiate him with the Tennessee population), and Arthur Garfield Hays, veteran lawyer of many civil-liberties battles. On Bryan's side were his son, William Jennings Bryan, Jr., and several local attorneys.

As the focus of attention turned on the case, Dayton found itself in a happy limelight. Into the town streamed itinerant preachers and evangelists, journalists from all over the nation and even from abroad, popcorn and hot-dog vendors. Soon the sleepy little hamlet was the center of the carnival of the decade. But Dayton came near to losing its leading role as the locale of the drama. Other Tennessee cities eyed the impending trial with envy, and when a technicality was discovered that would have postponed the case for about a month, Judge John T. Raulston hastily arranged a new indictment and proceeded with the case. Raulston was not going to lose the opportunity to preside at the circus and to have his picture on the front pages of the nation's newspapers.

Clarence Darrow, chief counsel for Scopes, addresses the jury.
United Press International Photo

Darrow shakes hands with
Judge John T. Raulston.
United Artists Corporation

Judge Raulston raises his gavel in the Dayton courthouse. Next to him are
Darrow, Scopes, and (*second from right*) Dudley Field Malone,
who is assisting Darrow in his defense of Scopes.
United Press International Photo

A jury was chosen (including one self-confessed illiterate), and the trial opened. There was argument over constitutional issues, with an effort on the part of the defense to quash the indictment and dismiss the case. It was during this argument that Clarence Darrow arose and, although the judge tried to quiet him and adjourn the court, continued his presentation. Raulston interrupted: "Sorry to interrupt your argument, but it is adjourning time." But Darrow was not to be interrupted:

Today it is the public school teachers, tomorrow the private. The next day the preachers and the lecturers, the magazines, the books, the newspapers. After a while, Your Honor, it is the setting of man against man and creed against creed until with flying banners and beating drums we are marching backward to the glorious age of the sixteenth century when bigots lighted faggots to burn the men who dared bring any intelligence and enlightenment and culture to the human mind.

The next day the defense shocked the community on two occasions: first, when it objected to opening the court each day with a prayer, and then when, owing to the sweltering heat, the trial was moved out on the lawn, the defense objected to a huge sign that proclaimed READ YOUR BIBLE. This, it contended, was definitely prejudicial to the defendant. Immediately the prosecution consented to its removal.

The trial then began in earnest. There was only one issue, the prosecution claimed: Did John Thomas Scopes violate the Butler Act or did he not? To prove that he did, a few youngsters were rounded up—with the aid of Scopes himself, who convinced them that they were not doing any harm to their teacher—who proceeded to testify as to what he had said in the classroom regarding evolution. This was sufficient to establish the case.

The defense, however, had no intention of limiting the scope of the trial to such an accusation. They marshaled many of America's most prestigious scientists to defend the theory of evolution. The prosecution, however, blocked all scientific testimony, claiming that the validity of evolution was not the issue. Only the violation of the law could be tried before the court. The judge so ruled, and it looked as if the trial would end almost before it began in a series of dull arguments. Many visitors packed their things and left Dayton.

The heavy guns for the defense that had been brought to Dayton were not to remain idle. At the end of a week of pretty dull arguments, Arthur Garfield Hays startled the court, the spectators, and the radio-listening audience by announcing that he was calling William Jennings Bryan as witness for the defense. The prosecutor, A. T. Stewart, local attorney general, jumped to his feet in vigorous objection. Bryan dramatically silenced him and grandly announced that he was ready to take the stand to defend the true faith against all agnostics and infidels.

Darrow could not have been more delighted. For several hours, he cross-examined Bryan, who attempted to defend the Bible as literal history. Time and time again Bryan showed his ignorance. Soon it was obvious the witness was losing the audience. Stewart attempted to put an end to the examination, but Bryan, a glutton for punishment, allowed the questioning to continue. At times he even admitted that the language of the Bible was not necessarily literal, but symbolic, such as a day that might be an age, not a period of twenty-four hours.

Darrow finally launched into his most devastating examination of Bryan:

DARROW: Mr. Bryan, do you believe that the first woman was Eve?

BRYAN: Yes.

D: Do you believe she was literally made out of Adam's rib?

B: I do.

D: Did you ever discover where Cain got his wife?

B: No, sir; I leave the agnostics to hunt for her.

D: You have never found out?

B: I have never tried to find out.

D: You have never tried to find out?

B: No.

D: The Bible says he got one, doesn't it? Were there other people on the earth at that time?

B: I cannot say.

D: You cannot say. Did that ever enter your consideration?

B: Never bothered me.

D: There were no others recorded, but Cain got a wife.

B: That is what the Bible says.

D: Where she came from you do not know. All right. Does the statement, "The morning and the evening were the first day," and "The morning and the evening were the second day," mean anything to you?

B: I do not think it necessarily means a twenty-four-hour day.

D: You do not?

B: No.

D: What do you consider it to be?

B: I have not attempted to explain it. If you will take the second chapter—let me have the book. (Examines the Bible.) The fourth verse of the second chapter says: "These are the generations of the heavens and of the earth, when they were created in the day that the Lord God made the earth and the heavens." The word "day" there in the very next chapter is used to describe a period. I do not see that there is any necessity for construing the words, "the evening and the morning," as meaning necessarily a twenty-four-hour day, "in the day when the Lord made the heaven and the earth."

D: Then, when the Bible said, for instance, "and God called the firmament heaven. And the evening and the morning were the second day," that does not necessarily mean twenty-four hours?

B: I do not think it necessarily does.

D: Do you think it does or does not?

B: I know a great many think so.

Owing to the heat, the trial moves outdoors, where Darrow startled
everyone by objecting to a sign urging the reading of the Bible.
United Press International Photo

D: What do you think?

B: I do not think it does.

D: You think those were not literal days?

B: I do not think they were twenty-four-hour days.

D: What do you think about it?

B: That is my opinion—I do not know that my opinion is better on that subject than those who think it does.

D: You do not think that?

B: No. But I think it would be just as easy for the kind of God we believe in to make the earth in six days as in six years or in 6,000,000 years or in 600,000,000 years. I do not think it important whether we believe one or the other.

D: Do you think those were literal days?

B: My impression is they were periods, but I would not attempt to argue as against anybody who wanted to believe it literal days.

D: Have you any idea of the length of the periods?

B: No; I don't.

D: Do you think the sun was made on the fourth day?

B: Yes.

D: And they had evening and morning without the sun?

B: I am simply saying it is a period.

D: They had evening and morning for four periods without the sun, do you think?

B: I believe in creation as there told, and if I am not able to explain it I will accept it. Then you can explain it to suit yourself.

D: Mr. Bryan, what I want to know is, do you believe the sun was made on the fourth day?

B: I believe just as it says there.

D: Do you believe the sun was made on the fourth day?

B: Read it.

D: I am very sorry; you have read it so many times you would know, but I will read it again:

"And God said, let there be lights in the firmament of the heaven, to divide the day from the night; and let them be for signs, and for seasons, and for days, and years. And let them be for lights in the firmament of the heaven, to give light upon the earth; and it was so. And God made two great lights; the greater light to rule the day, and the lesser light to rule the night; He made the stars also. And God set them in the firmament of the heaven, to give light upon the earth, and to rule over the day and over the night, and to divide the light from the darkness; and God saw that it was good. And the evening and the morning were the fourth day."

Do you believe, whether it was a literal day or a period, the sun and the moon were not made until the fourth day?

B: I believe they were made in the order in which they were given there, and I think in the dispute with Gladstone and Huxley on that point—

D: Cannot you answer my question?

B: I prefer to agree with Gladstone.

D: I do not care about Gladstone.

B: Then prefer to agree with whomever you please.

D: Cannot you answer my question?

B: I have answered it. I believe that it was made on the fourth day, in the fourth day.

D: And they had the evening and the morning before that time for three days or three periods. All right, that settles it. Now, if you call those periods, they may have been a very long time.

B: They might have been.

D: The creation might have been going on for a very long time.

B: It might have continued for millions of years.

D: Yes. All right. Do you believe the story of the temptation of Eve by the serpent?

B: I do.

D: Do you believe that after Eve ate the apple, or gave it to Adam, whichever way it was, that God cursed Eve, and at that time decreed that all womankind thenceforth and forever should suffer the pains of childbirth in the reproduction of the earth?

B: I believe what it says, and I believe the fact as fully—

D: That is what it says, doesn't it?

B: Yes.

D: And for that reason, every woman born of woman, who has to carry on the race, has childbirth pains because Eve tempted Adam in the Garden of Eden?

B: I will believe just what the Bible says. I ask to put that in the language of the Bible, for I prefer that to your language. Read the Bible and I will answer.

D: All right, I will do that: "And I will put enmity between thee and the woman"—that is referring to the serpent?

B: The serpent.

D: (reading) ". . . and between thy seed and her seed; it shall bruise thy head, and thou shalt bruise his heel. Unto the woman he said, I will greatly multiply thy sorrow and thy conception; in sorrow thou shalt bring forth children; and thy desire shall be to thy husband, and he shall rule over thee." That is right, is it?

B: I accept it as it is.

D: And you believe that came about because Eve tempted Adam to eat the fruit?

B: Just as it says.

D: And you believe that is the reason that God made the serpent to go on his belly after he tempted Eve?

B: I believe the Bible as it is, and I do not permit you to put your language in the place of the language of the Almighty. You read that Bible and ask me questions, and I will answer them. I will not answer your questions in your language.

D: I will read it to you from the Bible—in your language. "And the Lord God said unto the serpent, because thou hast done this, thou art cursed above all cattle, and above every beast of the field; upon thy belly shalt thou go and dust shalt thou eat all the days of thy life."

Do you think that is why the serpent is compelled to crawl upon his belly?

B: I believe that.

D: Have you any idea how the snake went before that time.

B: No, sir.

D: Do you know whether he walked on his tail or not?

B: No, sir. I have no way to know. (Laughter)

D: Now, you refer to the cloud that was put in the heaven after the flood as the rainbow. Do you believe in that?

B: Read it.

D: All right, Mr. Bryan, I will read it for you.

B: Your Honor, I think I can shorten this testimony. The only purpose Mr. Darrow has is to slur at the Bible, but I will answer his question. I will answer it all at once, and I have no objection in the world, I want the world to know that this man, who does not believe in a God, is trying to use a court in Tennessee—

D: I object to that.

B: (continuing)—to slur at it, and while it will require time, I am willing to take it.

D: I object to your statement. I am examining you on your fool ideas that no intelligent Christian on earth believes.

THE COURT: Court is adjourned until tomorrow morning.

✿ ✿ ✿

If Bryan left the witness stand shattered, Darrow hardly left the examination scene exultant. It was a pitiable sight to behold this leader of a segment of American life and thought squirming before the onslaught of reason.

The trial was all over but for the formality of a verdict. After nine minutes of deliberation, Scopes was found guilty, and the court fined him $100. Four days later, William Jennings Bryan lay down for a nap after a hearty meal, and never awoke. Was the humiliation at Dayton too much for one of the world's great orators?

✿ ✿ ✿

During the trial, Darrow had practically supplicated the judge to demand of the jury a directed verdict of guilt, so that the entire matter could be taken to a higher court, and preferably the United States Supreme Court, where the constitutionality of the law could be argued. Following the verdict, dissension again arose in the ranks of the ACLU. Darrow had fulfilled his role; he had drawn the attention of the world to the bigotry of the Fundamentalists and to their evil effects on education. Now, an attorney with greater respectability, some argued, would be more successful in the appellate courts. The name of Charles Evans Hughes was mentioned by some, and the 1924 unsuccessful Democratic candidate for President, John W. Davis, by others. As for the defendant, he was at first too busy with his graduate studies to be concerned about the choice of an attorney for his appeal; later, he reaffirmed his confidence in Darrow.

Defendant John T. Scopes stands before Judge Raulston as he is sentenced
after being found guilty by the jury.
United Press International Photo

Finally, briefs were filed, and Darrow did appear. He did nothing to make allies or to soft-pedal delicate issues; he was merciless in his handling of organized religion, and scoffed at many dearly held shibboleths. Many in the ACLU decided that, if the case were to go to the Supreme Court of the United States, Darrow must be removed. They appealed to Scopes. Again, as he had before, he expressed confidence in his controversial attorney.

But there was no need to be concerned over who would carry the appeal to Washington, for the case was neither won nor lost. On a technicality involving the error made by the judge in imposing a fine that could legally have been set only by the jury—some commentators believe the error was deliberately made, with connivance of the prosecution—the decision was reversed. No purpose would be served by a new trial, the higher court stated. As for the constitutionality of the Butler Act, four justices out of five (one was a new member of the court) issued their rulings. Two justices ruled that the Act was constitutional; one declared it completely invalid; a fourth found it constitutional, but declared that it banned, not the teaching of evolution as such, but only of materialistic and atheistic evolution.

There was no road to appeal, and thus the case of The State of Tennessee v. John Thomas Scopes came to an end.

*   *   *

John T. Scopes was not forgotten or abandoned by those who had made him a central figure in the drama. A scholarship for graduate work in geology was given to him, and he continued his studies at the University of Illinois, receiving an advanced degree. He married a Catholic girl and converted, maintaining, as did most of his new coreligionists, that science and religion, Bible and evolution, could be reconciled. He enjoyed a distinguished career as a geologist, in Venezuela and in Louisiana. In the latter years of his life, he wrote a book of reminiscences, which attracted little attention, although a play and movie based on his case, "Inherit the Wind," had remarkable success. Soon after the publication of his book, Scopes, the last and ironically the least of all the major characters in the case that bore his name, died.

The circus at Dayton could hardly be repeated today; it was like a last gasp of ignorance and bigotry. But in the 1970s, anti-evolutionists again made their appearance. They succeeded in placing laws on the books of many states, either making illegal the teaching of evolution, or mandatory that creationism be taught as at least an equally plausible view of how humanity arrived on this planet. If the creationists are not powerful in the colleges, they have been successful at lower levels of education, particularly in influencing textbook publishers to modify their publications so as to downgrade evolution to an unproven theory with little scientific basis for acceptance, and to suggest that their own view of the universe is equally plausible. Some schoolteachers in elementary and high schools, and even professors in state-controlled colleges, are reluctant to express their views not only on evolution but on many other subjects. Academic freedom in America is still not a clear-cut achievement, but the trial of Scopes went a long way to help make it a reality.

General William Mitchell,
much-decorated flying ace of World War I.

General Mitchell standing by plane.
U.S. Air Force Photo

22

General Billy Mitchell

[1925]

THE ARMY OFFICER STOOD IN A TENSE, CROWDED ROOM, surrounded by newspaper reporters. If he was nervous as he read from his prepared statement, it could not easily be discerned by the attentive listeners.

"I have been asked from all parts of the country to give my opinion about the reasons for the frightful disasters that have occurred during the last few days," he read. The disasters to which he referred did not require more explicit reference: among others there was the *Shenandoah,* a huge dirigible that had exploded on a peaceful mission, killing 14 of its crew of 28. Already, in the aftermath of the tragedy, it was being cited by military men as evidence that, contrary to the alarming contentions of Billy Mitchell, this was proof that aviation could not play a dependable and major role in warfare. And now Billy Mitchell, still in uniform, was stating to the press, and through it to the American people, his version of the tragedy.

"What business has the Navy over the mountains anyway? Their mission is out over the water." Then, laying one more brick in the wall of evidence he was building up for his own court-martial, he went on:

The impression is given to the public at large that the *Shenandoah* was a modern ship, properly constructed, properly operated and completely equipped. This was not the case. It shakes the faith of people in airship transportation because they are not given the exact facts on the subject. . . . This is a demand for the facts in the case, so that we will not be hindered in the commercial development of this splendid aircraft on account of the accident to an airship due to the incompetence of the Navy Department and the criminal negligence in ordering this trip.

(*Aviation* Magazine called this and subsequent remarks "The most daring indictment of the War and Navy Departments ever made by an officer.") With these words to the reporters, the officer turned and walked quietly from the room, while with more bustle and less dig-nity the reporters rushed to the nearest telephone and telegraph offices. As for Mitchell, he announced that he expected to be arrested, then packed his fishing tackle and went off for a relaxed weekend.

❂   ❂   ❂

The year was 1925: it was the decade of Prohibition, the Administration of the silent Calvin Coolidge who had followed the scandal-ridden era of Warren G. Harding. America was a nation where children still pointed upward when they saw an airplane in the sky, with its upper and lower wings looking more like a kite than like the powerful machine it was destined to become. Less than a quarter of a century had passed since the first successful flights of the Wright Brothers at Kitty Hawk, North Carolina. People were saying, "Wake up, the war's over!" by which they meant what later came to be named World War I. Many innovations had been tried out during this holocaust, among others, for part of the war, machines that fought in the air. One of the most daring flyers of the war was Colonel Billy Mitchell.

Technically the officer was only a colonel, but outside strictest formalized military protocol, William Mitchell was a general, and to many the only man carrying the rank who was not weighted down with brass. He had returned from the war convinced of the overwhelming significance of aviation in any new and future wars that might develop. America, he insisted, needed an air force independent of its army and navy, one that would be on a par with and recognized for its importance as much as these other branches of the military. Vehemently he called for research, for industry, for building until the American air force reached the strength of any in the world. Nay more, in his enthusiasm he had declared that a powerful bomb dropped from the air could sink any ship on the sea, even a battleship.

General Mitchell standing by
V.E. 7 at Bolling Field Air
Tournament, May, 1920.
U.S. Air Force Photo

For this, of course, no man, not even a member of the military, could be court-martialed. In what amounted, however, to a one-man campaign, Mitchell aroused the ire of West Pointers, and even more the men of Annapolis, by refusing to remain silenced in the face of what he considered their apathy and their negligence, their obstinate defiance of progress, and their unwillingness to relinquish their vested interests. First, it had brought demotion: from general to colonel, and with it exile, from Washington to Texas.

* * *

Up to the moment of his trial, Billy Mitchell's unshakable belief in air power and his unswerving fight to establish an independent United States Air Department alongside the War and Navy departments had often brought him into the limelight, but none of his bitter clashes with the higher brass were more dramatic and portentous than when he set out to prove that air power could indeed defeat sea power. In 1921, appearing before an Appropriations Committee in Congress, Mitchell had insisted that his airborne bombs could sink any seagoing vessels. When asked how much money he wanted to make such a demonstration, he scorned any funds and said all he needed were the targets. "You would recommend that a vessel be turned over to you to make such experiments?" the investigator inquired. To which he answered: "Yes, sir. Both armored and unarmored vessels."

Secretary of the Navy Josephus Daniels scoffed, and announced that he was prepared "to stand bareheaded on the deck of a battleship and let Brigadier General Mitchell take a crack at me with a bombing airplane."

Early in the spring of 1921, former German warships were allocated to the United States for the express purpose of being used as targets for bombing experiments. Billy Mitchell had succeeded in his request. But on the eve of the test demonstrations, Mitchell came close to being removed from his post, ostensibly because, scrawled on the bombs he and his flyers were about to drop, were the words "Regards to the Navy."

Public and congressional pressures, however, were high, and the tests took place, beginning with the arrival of summer, on June 20, 1921. For this test, Mitchell and his colleagues had come up with a revolutionary hypothesis: that a direct hit would be unnecessary, if not less than fatal; that for a big ship to be sunk, a near hit would create a series of powerful movements of thousands of tons of water with such force that the vessel would be devastated.

One by one, day after day, the flyers attacked the abandoned vessels, that lay there quiet and lonely, riding the ocean waves. And one by one the vessels were sunk by the bombers: first an old submarine, then an obsolete American battleship, to be followed by a destroyer and a cruiser. The finale was left for the most unsinkable of all ships, the German battleship *Ostfriesland*.

Champion of the efficacy of burgeoning air power, Billy Mitchell finally obtained the War Department's permission to prove his assertions. An old German battleship, the "unsinkable" *Ostfriesland,* and several other ships were put at his disposal as bombing targets. The first of the bombs dropped by Mitchell's planes explode just off the starboard bow of the battleship with force enough to split open the steel hull.
Library of Congress

The *Ostfriesland* begins to go down.
Library of Congress

The *Ostfriesland* takes the final plunge.
Library of Congress

If this drama was watched all over the world, its significance was not lost in America. Many new converts to the power of aviation were made. Yet, men trained in other schools of warfare were not ready to relinquish the battle. Secretary of War John W. Weeks said he would not be stampeded "by that circus performer," and added: "We'll stick to the army on the ground and the battleships on the sea." For many others, too, who made similar comments, Billy Mitchell was a marked man, their sitting duck, their main target, ready to be attacked the moment he gave them cause. And now, four years later, in his ringing indictment of his superiors for their culpability (as he saw it) in the *Shenandoah* disaster, his breaking of military discipline to make his statements about the crash, his use of intemperate language, his bitter accusations, Billy Mitchell gave his enemies this cause.

The news of the disaster reached a shocked public on the morning of September 4, 1925, when the *New York Times* carried a front-page headline:

SHENANDOAH WRECKED IN OHIO STORM
BREAKS IN THREE AND FALLS 7,000 FEET
14 DEAD, INCLUDING COMMANDER, 2 HURT

The Navy dirigible *Shenandoah,* whose silver beauty had been seen over many American cities, was ripped apart by a thunder squall . . .

On the day that newspapers announced the tragedy, three items appeared together with the main story. The widow of the commander, Lieutenant Commander Zachary Lansdowne, immediately charged "politics," and claimed that for a year her husband had tried to avoid the fatal flight. Secretary of the Navy Curtis D. Wilbur declared that, whereas the loss of the *Shenandoah* did not mean that such craft must be abandoned, it did show their limits. And on an inside page, there was a small item: one Colonel William Mitchell paid tribute to the fallen commander and his ship: "He was a man whose loss would be irreparable," and added, "America now lacks a dirigible for war."

General Mitchell in cockpit
of plane at Selfridge Field
for the Dayton Races, 1922.
U.S. Air Force Photo

The ill-fated dirigible *Shenandoah*, which became the basis of Mitchell's
savage indictment of the Navy Department, is shown here moored to her
landing tower at Camp Lewis, Tacoma, Washington, on October 19, 1924.
Library of Congress

On September 3, 1925, while in a storm over Ohio, the *Shenandoah* broke into three pieces
and crashed to the ground. Fourteen men died in the crash, including her chief officer, Lieutenant
Commander Zachary Lansdowne, who had long fought against the taking of the fatal flight.
United Press International

Immediately a board of inquiry was appointed to investigate the tragedy and draw lessons from it, but Mitchell was not waiting for the findings of such a court. Now was his opportunity to dramatize his struggle with the big brass and bring to the nation the change in attitude about air power for which he was dedicated. On Sunday, September 6, another front-page story, datelined San Antonio, Texas, hit the headlines in *The New York Times*:

MITCHELL CHARGES "GROSS NEGLIGENCE" IN SHENANDOAH LOSS

Colonel William Mitchell, Eighth Corps Air Officer, today launched a scathing denunciation of the practices and circumstances pertaining to the administration of national defense.

Referring to the *Shenandoah* and other tragedies, Mitchell accused his superiors: "These accidents are the direct result of incompetency, criminal negligence and almost treasonable administration by the War and Navy Departments." Then bitterly commenting on the conduct of these departments during the last few years, he angrily called it "so disgusting as to make any self-respecting person ashamed of the clothes he wears." It is hardly any wonder that the subhead of this *Times* article read: "Expects Arrest Monday."

* * *

The trial of Billy Mitchell opened on October 28, 1925, in a damp and dusty room of an outmoded building inexplicably chosen by the War Department for the court-martial. A few days previous, President Coolidge had made known the names of his judges; all officers of the army, as the rules of the situation called for. Many of these men were known for their outspoken opposition to Mitchell's campaign. The personnel of this court-martial was made up of the following: Major General Charles P. Summerall; Major General Robert L. Howze; Major General Fred W. Sladen; Major General Douglas MacArthur; Major General William S. Graves; Major General Benjamin A. Poore; Brigadier General Albert J. Bowley; Brigadier General Edward L. King; Brigadier General Frank R. McCoy; Brigadier General Edwin B. Winans; Brigadier General George LeR. Irwin; Brigadier General Ewing E. Booth; Colonel Blanton Winship, Law Member; Colonel Sherman Moreland, Judge Advocate; Lieutenant Colonel Joseph I. McMullen, Assistant Judge Advocate. A congressman from New York by the name of Fiorello La Guardia was sufficiently upset by this selection to state: "Billy Mitchell is not being tried by a board of his peers but by a pack of beribboned dog robbers of the General Staff."

The proceedings of the first day opened with a surprise move by Colonel Mitchell that succeeded in ousting three members of the court: its president, Major General Charles P. Summerall; Major General F. W. Sladen, Commandant of West Point; and Brigadier General Albert J. Bowley. As Assistant Chief of the Army Air Service, Mitchell had written an inspection report severely criticizing the air forces of Hawaii when Summerall was in command there, and calling Summerall himself "inefficient and ignorant." Summerall had violently disagreed with the report. And now this man was appointed president of the court to try him. Thus, Mitchell held, this was sufficient evidence of prejudice. A shocked Summerall immediately asked to be excused from serving, which was granted. The chair was then taken over by Major General Robert L. Howze. Sladen, as Commandant of West Point, where absolute deference to superior rank was rigidly taught, would surely be critical of Mitchell's language in the statements that formed the basis of the trial. Bowley was simply the one peremptory challenge allowed to the defense.

President Calvin Coolidge (center in light suit) immediately called together a special aviation board on September 17, 1925, to investigate the whole subject of military aviation.
Library of Congress

The outspoken Mitchell finally achieved his aim, a court-martial trial in which he could express his views on America's air power and his criticism of the War Department's opposition to a separate air force. On October 28, 1925, crowds line up around the courthouse where the trial is being held.
Library of Congress

Mitchell, in a surprise move, succeeds in ousting from the court, on the grounds of bias, its president, Major General Charles P. Summerall, and Major General F. W. Sloden, Commandant of West Point.
Library of Congress

The military tribunal to try Mitchell includes Major General Douglas MacArthur, fourth from the left.
Library of Congress

With this business out of the way, the formal trial began with the reading of the eight charges on which Mitchell was being tried. Each of the specifications was based on specific remarks and accusations against the War and Navy departments at stated times and places which "were conducive to the prejudice of good order and military discipline," including his tirade after the *Shenandoah* disaster.

No sooner had they been read than Mitchell denounced the proceedings. He pointed out that the charges avoided the questions raised by his public statements and reduced the entire matter to whether or not he had said certain things that might hold the War and Navy departments in disrepute. Indeed he had.

Mitchell's clever defense attorney, Representative Frank R. Reid of Illinois, then granted that libel was a punishable offense, but argued that it was impossible to libel the War Department because it was an intangible body and that Mitchell's statements had attacked a system only. He pointed out that President Coolidge at Annapolis on the previous June 3 had endorsed this right of expression when he said, "The officers of the Navy are given the fullest latitude in expressing their views before their fellow citizens, subject, of course, to the requirements of not betraying those confidential affairs which would be detrimental to the service." The trial day ended with the defense scoring heavily with this line of argument.

Mitchell stands as Lieutenant Colonel Joseph McMullen reads the charges.
Library of Congress

Colonel Sherman Moreland (*left, at table*) is the judge advocate.
Library of Congress

On the second day of the trial Reid nearly brought the court to dissolution. He claimed that while Mitchell was being tried on a charge, no accuser had been named, contrary to court-martial rules. Mitchell's commanding officer would have to bring the charge and appoint a disinterested officer to investigate the situation. The court admitted the failure but ingeniously maintained that such proceedings could be waived by simply holding that the President of the United States was the commanding officer and thus the sole accuser and prosecutor. The trial then continued, with the defense reading each of the eight specifications and Colonel Mitchell pleading not guilty to each one as it was read.

On the third day Reid threw another bombshell into the trial by threatening to call President Coolidge himself or, failing that, to put Secretary of War Davis on the witness stand to confront Mitchell with his accuser. The trial was adjourned to November 2.

The court reconvened on the appointed date and called to the stand the newspapermen from Texas, who testified that Colonel Mitchell had actually made the statements for which he stood accused. Since nobody denied his having made them, and since the defense had pointed out that on the basis of just these statements the President had called together a special aircraft board of investigation, this entire portion of the trial seemed pointless.

Having proved the already accepted fact that these statements had actually been made by Mitchell, the court proceeded to pull off the biggest surprise of the trial. *They moved to permit the defense to present evidence of the proof of these statements and establish the truth of the defendant's accusations against the War and Navy departments' air administrations.* In effect this put the defense in the unusual position of becoming the prosecution, if not literally in regard to the trial itself, at least as a forum from which to present Mitchell's' arguments to the country. Reid at once proposed to subpoena seventy-three witnesses and numerous official documents. The court then adjourned to allow time for the subpoenas to be served.

When the court reassembled on November 9, the defense announced that it would prove the truth and validity of Colonel Mitchell's accusations, and proceeded to read into the record a list of sixty-six, among them:

That the *Shenandoah* was designed for the use of hydrogen as a lifting gas and that when helium was substituted without changing the structure her safety factor was reduced.

That the authorities ordering and directing the fatal flight of the *Shenandoah* and the almost fatal flight of the *PN9-1* were wholly unacquainted with the subject of aviation and incompetent for their duties.

That the great bulk of airplanes in the possession of the army were designed and constructed at the time of the war and are antiquated, out of date and unsuited to perform the military mission for which they are used.

That Colonel Mitchell was demoted and transferred because he told the truth before the Aircraft Committee of the House of Representatives.

That the War Department was guilty of almost treasonable administration, due to the fact that up to 1923 there were in Hawaii no plans for the employment of the air service in the aeronautical protection of the islands.

That the War Department has spent a great deal of effort to lead the public to believe that antiaircraft cannon and machine guns constitute a defense against aircraft, lulling the public into a false sense of security against foreign invasion by enemy aircraft.

Mitchell is defended by the able Representative Frank R. Reid of Illinois, seated at his right, who contends that it is impossible to libel the War Department because it is an intangible body and that Mitchell's statements attacked a system only.

National Archives

That no adequate meteorological arrangements are available in the United States for operation of aircraft.

In the days that followed, witness after witness was called by both the prosecution and the defense to answer involved military and technical questions. Interrogating his defense witnesses, Reid hammered away at the deficiencies of the air service's men and equipment. Captain Robert Oldys testified that "personnel and equipment on hand in Hawaii, the Philippines and the Panama Canal departments bear the ratio of one to five between how many there are and how many there should be there."

The defense called Major Carl Spaatz, later to become the famous General "Touhy" Spaatz, who declared that the bulk of the air service equipment "is either obsolescent or obsolete," and pointed out that only 22 percent of the total aircraft in the army were fit for service. Major H. H. Arnold, later the renowned General "Hap" Arnold, bitterly attacked the use of obsolete planes, and produced a long list of figures showing casualties.

When Major General Frank W. Coe, Chief of the Coast Artillery, testified for the prosecution, Reid questioned him about a statement made to a committee of Congress by Brigadier General H. A. Drum that "with twelve antiaircraft guns of 3-inch calibre," he could keep any bomber that came within range from doing much harm. Could twelve antiaircraft 3-inch guns protect the city of Washington, Coe was asked. "I didn't say they could," he replied.

"Oh, didn't you," Mr. Reid asked. The congressman looked around for a copy of the report of the hearings, but before he could find them, General Coe continued: "Ten thousand antiaircraft guns can't protect the city of Washington." "That is all," said Mr. Reid, and with a smile he dismissed the witness.

Major General Summerall came to testify for the prosecution. He was smarting under the sharp criticism that Mitchell had directed at him, as well as the publicity given that criticism at the opening of the trial, and the humiliation when he had been compelled to step down from the court of which he was president. After testifying against Mitchell, Summerall was asked if he had been correctly quoted by newspapermen as saying that he and Mitchell were enemies.

SUMMERALL: I have no recollection of ever making that statement, and I am sure I never did.
REID: Are you now friendly toward the accused?
SUMMERALL: I am indifferent toward the accused.

A sensational witness appeared at the trial on November 12. The widow of the commander of the *Shenandoah*, Mrs. Zachary Lansdowne, came into court and declared under oath that on the evening before her appearance she had been handed by Mrs. George W. Steele, Jr., wife of Captain Steele, commander of the Lakehurst Air Station, a false story to narrate on the witness stand. Who had sent it? Captain Paul Foley of the Naval Board of Inquiry into the *Shenandoah* disaster! In a heated discussion the prosecution attempted to have Mrs. Lansdowne's testimony stricken from the record, but the defense won and it was left in.

Mrs. Douglas MacArthur arrives to attend the trial, escorted by Colonel Blanton Winship, one of the judges.
Library of Congress

The highlight of the defense came when it called to the stand the grand old man of the navy, Admiral Sims (retired). He bluntly stated that any invading fleet could be destroyed by a properly organized land-based air force. With every word he spoke, he shattered reactionary naval tradition. He charged that most admirals were uneducated; that the battleship was no longer a capital ship, having been replaced by the aircraft carrier. Coming from the most respected naval officer in the country, this was powerful ammunition for the cause of the defense.

* * *

Billy Mitchell was being tried under a "catch-all" clause in the Articles of War, the Ninety-sixth, which read in part: "Though not mentioned in these articles, all disorders and neglects to the prejudice of good order and military discipline, all conduct of a nature to bring discredit upon the military service . . . shall be taken cognizance of by a . . . court-martial and punished at the discretion of such court." Thus the prosecution was basing its case on *what* Mitchell had said, whereas the defense was basing its case on the *truth* of what Mitchell had said.

It is difficult to fight a war when the battle is not joined. Here was the Peter Zenger struggle all over again, with the defendant demanding the right to establish the truth of his "libel," and the prosecution contending that since truth was irrelevant, it was no defense.

But this was a military court and not a civilian one. The attorney for the defense could not turn away from the judges and appeal to a jury—except, one might say, the jury of public opinion.

The issue was not the substance of the charges; it was that Mitchell was a lawless person. In the words of Secretary of War Weeks, in a letter to President Coolidge that was read at the trial: "General Mitchell's whole course has been so lawless, so contrary to the building up of an efficient organization, so lacking in responsible team work, so indicative of a personal desire for publicity at the expense of every one with whom he is associated, that his actions tender him unfit for a high administration position such as he now occupies."

In summing up, the prosecution called Mitchell a loosetalking, imaginative megalomaniac, a charlatan seeking promotion, a demagogue seeking self-aggrandizement. In contrast was the decision of the defense. There would be no summing up. Instead, on December 17, Mitchell spoke for himself, and for only a few short minutes:

May it please the court: My trial before this court martial is the culmination of the efforts of the General Staff of the Army and the General Board of the Navy to deprecate the value of air power and keep it in an auxiliary position, which absolutely compromises our whole system of national defense.

These efforts to keep down our air power were begun as soon as the sound of the cannon had ceased on the Western front in 1919. When we sunk the battleships off the Virginia

Mrs. Zachary Lansdowne, wife of the deceased commander of the *Shenandoah*, testifies for the defense on November 12, 1925.
Library of Congress

Capes in 1921, and again in 1923, and proved to the world that air power had revolutionized all schemes of national defense, these efforts were redoubled and have continued to this day.

The truth of every statement which I have made, has been proved by good and sufficient evidence before this court, not by men who gained their knowledge of aviation by staying on the ground and having their statements prepared by numerous staffs to bolster up their predetermined ideas, but by actual fliers who have gained their knowledge first hand in war and in peace.

I wish to invite particular attention to the letter of former Secretary Weeks to the President of the United States, asking that I be not reappointed as Assistant Chief of the Air Service on account of evidence given by me to a Congressional committee.

I testified that the Air Service had only nine modern airplanes fit for war and that all others were obsolete and many dangerous. The evidence before this court bears out these facts in their entirety. It has been shown that at present we have only one standard plane in the service.

Secretary Weeks and, indirectly, the President of the United States, were wrongly and untruthfully informed as to the condition of our aviation and our national defense, by persons furnishing the data on which his letter was based.

This court has refrained from ruling whether the truth in this case constitutes an absolute defense or not. To proceed further with the case would serve no useful purpose. I have therefore directed my counsel to entirely close our part of the proceeding without argument.

Three hours later the judges brought in their verdict. It was read by Major General Robert L. Howze:

The court, upon secret written ballot, two-thirds of the members present at the time the vote was taken, concurring in each finding of guilty, finds the accused guilty of all specifications and of the charge.

Upon secret written ballot the court sentences the accused to be suspended from rank, command and duty, with forfeiture of all pay and allowances for five years.

The court is thus lenient because of the military record of the accused during the World War, two-thirds of the members present at the time the vote was taken, concurring.

Thus ended the longest court-martial in the history of America.

*   *   *

There is a folklore that grows up after an important trial, especially when the stenographic record has mysteriously disappeared. Myths and rumors mushroom, lies mingle with half-truths, historical facts are conveniently forgotten. When the course of history makes a patriotic hero out of the accused, the story of the trial is likely to be rewritten.

It is one of the minor myths that developed in later years that the verdict was roundly denounced by everyone except the star-wearing soldiers and their naval counterparts. The most influential newspaper in Ameri-

The venerable and much-respected Admiral Sims (retired), who bluntly shattered reactionary naval tradition when he testified for the defense. *National Archives*

ca, *The New York Times*, commented editorially the day following the trial that the verdict could not have been other than it was: "An army exists and functions by the enforcement of discipline. Colonel Mitchell broke the bonds of discipline defiantly. The effect upon the morale of the army would have been disastrous if he had not been convicted."

Mitchell on the stand as he testifies on November 23, 1925.
Library of Congress

The first Chief of the Army Air Corps, Major General Mason M. Patrick (*left*) with Billy Mitchell, whose fight for a separate air force was slowly coming to fruition.
U.S. Air Force Photo

History, however, gave quite another verdict. Perhaps, in a sense, Mitchell was gratified at both. For, as a good military man, he might well have believed and understood that military discipline cannot be flouted, that an army cannot exist if an officer goes unpunished for calling his superiors incompetent, criminally negligent, almost treacherous. But also that America could not go forward if someone did not make a dramatic appeal to the country on the question of air power. The trial, even the verdict, may have been his victory. He was both found guilty and vindicated. Even the verdict of guilt might have fitted into his master plan of vindication. In that sense, he might indeed have been disappointed that the punishment had been so lenient; a stronger sentence would surely have awakened America to his message more rapidly, more dramatically.

Colonel William Mitchell, stripped of his command and rank for five years, resigned from the service. Calvin Coolidge accepted his resignation, effective on February 1, 1926, a few days less than five months after the *Shenandoah* disaster.

*   *   *

After the verdict, Mitchell abandoned a plan for a hunting trip to Africa, and instead organized a tour of the United States. He lectured, wrote and continued to campaign for his cause. He spoke before lay audiences, groups of the American Legion, as well as appearing before Congressional committees. Undoubtedly he enjoyed the adulation he received. One authority said of him, "He has done more for the cause of aviation than any other man in the whole nation's history except the Wright Brothers."

Mitchell raised his voice in warning about what then was being termed the "shrinking world." He continued to call for a unified department of national defense, in which the air force would be a separate entity. Pictured often as a prophet as well as hero, not all his prophecies were accurate. For one, he down-played Russia as a potential world or even European power. But finally, in 1928, he had his moment of triumph; he obtained from the American Legion the vote he had long sought, favoring a unified air force. Even *The New York Times*, hardly his most consistent supporter, commented editorially that General Mitchell's "triumph is complete."

Now he retreated to Virginia, where he hunted, fished, gave press conferences, issued broadsides, and wrote articles. He found an ever-widening group of supporters, from the Hearst Press to the fiery Fiorello La Guardia. Although many urged that he be appointed Assistant Secretary of War for Aviation, he was bypassed. Even his rank was not restored. And he continued to make enemies. In a speech before the Foreign Policy Association he attacked the American aviation industry with such vehemence that one of the companies brought a $200,000 libel suit against him. He was accused of jingoism because he warned of a growing Japanese air power and the possibility of a surprise attack. By December, 1935, now only fifty-six years of age, he had given up any hope of reentering government service. However, his friends continued to fight for his reinstatement, and on January 16, 1936, the United States Senate voted in favor of it. Unfortunately, the bill was defeated in the House. On February 19, 1936, he died.

Almost every commentator on the Mitchell case, writing in the 1950's and 1960's, calls attention to the accuracy of his prophecies, as exemplified by World War II, with its blitzkrieg and air war over England and Germany, and with the destruction of a large part of the American fleet at Pearl Harbor. But, in an even greater long-range sense, Mitchell and his much vaunted air power may prove to be overrated in modern warfare. Intercontinental ballistic missiles, on the one hand, and guerrilla war, on the other, may combine to reduce air power to the secondary, or even tertiary, position it held when Mitchell was court-martialed. And if World War II proved Mitchell essentially correct, Vietnam may have proved him wrong.

Haywood Patterson, one of the nine Scottsboro boys to go on trial in Decatur, Alabama, on April 1, 1933, brings a good-luck sign into court in the form of a horseshoe and rabbit's foot. At left is Samuel Leibowitz of New York, and at right is Roscoe Chamlee of Chattanooga, defense counsel.

Wide World Photos

23

Scottsboro Boys

[1931 – 1950]

IN 1931, IN THE MIDST OF THE DEPRESSION, TENS OF thousands of Americans traveled from place to place, searching for an odd job, seeking to keep themselves alive, trying to find a way to beg, borrow, or steal enough to keep the body together from one day to the next. They were Negroes and whites, some hardly in their teens and many in the fifth or sixth decades of life; they were men and women, boys and girls, and they traveled by foot, hitched rides, or hopped freights. It was the army of the American hobo, wandering and rootless, usually too demoralized to be angry, but almost always hopeless, frightened, weary, and hungry.

In Alabama, on March 25, 1931, on a freight train crowded with these wanderers, a group of Negroes got into a fist fight with some white boys. Because the former outnumbered the latter, the whites were defeated and thrown bodily off the train. When the whites were seen on the railroad track, they anticipated being arrested on a charge of vagrancy, and told the authorities that the colored kids had fought with them and thrown them out. The authorities telephoned ahead, and at Paint Rock, Alabama, a sheriff's posse arrested nine Negro boys who had been on the train. Why nine? It is said that he had only rope enough to tie up nine of them.

The oldest of the nine was nineteen, the youngest, thirteen. One was almost blind, and others were suffering from many infirmities. They were the children of the depression and of the caste system in the South.

Two girls, Ruby Bates and Victoria Price, were found at the railroad tracks. Allegedly, both were prostitutes, Victoria an old hand, Ruby her protégée and apprentice.

It was a fine setting for an old-fashioned case of southern lynch justice; all that was needed was a statement from the girls that they had been raped, and southern womanhood would be protected. Each girl, it was claimed, had been raped in the freight car by six Negro boys; in all, nine Negroes were covered by the accusation.

Later, a Supreme Court justice was to describe the arrest: "Both girls and the Negroes were taken to Scottsboro, the county seat. Word of their coming and of the alleged assaults had preceded them, and they were met in Scottsboro by a large crowd. . . . The attitude of the community was one of great hostility."

Indeed, the judicial words are a remarkable understatement. In a city of 1,500 people, a crowd estimated at 10,000 gathered. A brass band played "There'll Be a Hot Time in the Old Town Tonight." The boys were quickly tried, and all but the youngest sentenced to death. The official transcript of the trial carries the final statement of the prosecutor to the white jury: "Guilty or not guilty, let's get rid of these niggers."

But Scottsboro did not reckon on the possibility that people—white people—might take an interest in these youths. The Communists discovered the case, and soon Socialists, liberals, churchmen, civil-liberties defenders— and just plain people—were deeply involved. "They shall not die" became the greatest rallying cry since Sacco and Vanzetti. All over the North and in many parts of the South, Alabama justice was on trial. In Rome, Moscow, Berlin, on every continent and in hundreds of languages, demonstrators demanded that the lives of these boys be saved.

In the Supreme Court of the United States, a new trial was granted, and more forcibly than ever before, fundamental issues were raised—the exclusion of Negroes from juries in the South, the right to adequate counsel, and others. In overturning the verdict, the Supreme Court stated:

In the light of the facts outlined in the forepart of this opinion—the ignorance and illiteracy of the defendants and their youth, the system of public hostility, the imprisonment and the close surveillance of the defendants by the military forces, the fact that their friends and families were all in other states and communication with them necessarily difficult, and above all that they stood in deadly peril of their lives—we think the failure of the trial court to give them reasonable time and opportunity to secure counsel was a clear denial of due process.

The new trial, with the spotlight of the entire world upon it, took place in the sleepy little town of Decatur, Alabama. Einstein had spoken up in defense of the Scottsboro nine, as had Thomas Mann and other leaders of the intellectual world from every corner of the globe. In Alabama, the white Southerners could not understand why people were making such a fuss about nine little colored boys.

Samuel Leibowitz now went to Alabama with powerful weapons at his disposal, above all, the repudiation of the rape story by Ruby Bates, and corroboration of the complete denial of the rape by her boyfriend who had accompanied her, Lester Carter. But the prosecutor, speaking to his all-white jury, also had a new weapon: "Show them," he shouted, "that Alabama justice can't be bought and sold with Jew money from New York!"

Again there was a verdict of guilty; again the cries against southern "justice" arose throughout America and the world. But this time the judge at the trial, James Horton, astonished his fellow Alabamans by overturning the verdict, stating that he could find no evidence in the trial record that would point to the guilt of the defendants. For this courageous act, Judge Horton was resoundingly defeated in the next election.

Now came the third trial, before a new judge, William Callahan, and again the boys were found guilty. A recent writer quotes this colloquy from that trial:

Victoria Price, who with Ruby Bates, accused the Negroes of rape. Ruby Bates later repudiated the entire rape story. *Wide World Photos*

Judge James E. Horton as he appears in court on March 28, 1933, just prior to the opening of the new trial for the Scottsboro boys, sentenced to die for the alleged rape of Victoria Price and Ruby Bates.
Wide World Photos

The prosecutors for the second Scottsboro trial (*left to right*): Attorney General Thomas E. Knight, Jackson County Solicitor H. G. Bailey, Wade Wright, and Assistant Attorney General T. L. Lawson.
Wide World Photos

Samuel Leibowitz (*second from left*), on May 1, 1935, confers with the defendants
just after he has asked the governor of Alabama to pardon them. Deputy Sheriff
Charles McComb is at his left. The Scottsboro boys (*from left to right*)
are Roy Wright, Olen Montgomery, Ozie Powell, Willie Roberson,
Eugene Williams, Charlie Weems, and Andy Wright.
Wide World Photos

PROSECUTOR: If we let this nigger go, it won't be safe for your mother, wife, or sweetheart to walk the streets of the South!

LEIBOWITZ: Your Honor, must we continue to try this case in a welter of such inflammatory appeals?

PROSECUTOR: (hurt): I ain't done nothin' wrong. Your Honor knows I always make the same speech in every nigger rape case.

JUDGE: Objection overruled.

The case again traveled to the Supreme Court, and again demonstrations were held, protests were loud, pressure was unrelenting. In the Supreme Court decision, which is frequently cited to this day, the court ruled for the first time that systematic exclusion of Negroes from juries was grounds for reversal. Many consider this as epoch-making in the history of the judicial fight for civil rights as the famed desegregation decision of two decades later.

Now came the fourth trial, and a behind-the-scenes deal was made, whereby four boys were freed, five were found guilty. The Northerners agreed to stop the protests, while the white southern officials agreed to have all the boys freed, quietly, within one year. The protests died down, but the Southerners betrayed their deal, and several of the boys remained in jail. Haywood Patterson escaped and, trailed by bloodhounds, plunged into a river, allowed the dogs to come after him, and then, with bare hands and brute strength, grabbed each dog around the neck and submerged it in water, choking and drowning the animals.

Not until 1950, nineteen years after the arrest, did the last of the Scottsboro boys, Andy Wright, emerge from prison. After the years in which they had been so unjustly confined, they did not find it easy to make new lives. Eight of the nine died early deaths. The ninth left Alabama to come North, in violation of his parole, and lived a quiet life. It was during this part of his life that he witnessed the revolution in race relations in the United States, the emergence of Dr. Martin Luther King, Jr., and the breakdown of the racist mores that had led to his victimization at the hands of the law. In 1976, Clarence Norris emerged from obscurity, and announced that he would return to Alabama. This he did, and was welcomed by the governor of that state!

Scottsboro was not the last miscarriage of justice in America, nor was it the last in which the victim was black. But the South was never quite the same after Scottsboro. For the case established that the humblest, the poorest, and the blackest of skin may quicken the sense of justice in their more fortunate fellowmen. A new freedom enters the courtroom when the spotlight of public attention is upon it. After Scottsboro, a southern court could never again be certain that the spotlight would not pierce its murky environment. And after King and the Mississippi summer, the Voting Rights Act and the election of black mayors in Atlanta and Birmingham, another Scottsboro would be unlikely.

The case also initiated a revolution in judicial history, although that would not be followed with full momentum for another decade or even more. It was the Scottsboro appeals to the U.S. Supreme Court that decided, for the first time, that the Bill of Rights and the protections that it offered to the accused could be applied to state and not merely federal cases, because any other interpretation violated the "due process" clause of the Fourteenth Amendment. This historic breakthrough, later to be extended to cases involving cruel and unusual punishment, self-incrimination, and others, is a historic though little recognized achievement of Scottsboro.

Bruno Richard Hauptmann in court in Flemington, New Jersey, on February 13, 1935, as Judge Thomas W. Trenchard begins his instructions to the jury.
Wide World Photos

24

Bruno Richard Hauptmann

[1935]

IT WAS AN AGE OF HEROES. IT WAS AN ERA WHEN MILLING crowds wildly cheered from sidewalks and bleacher seats, as they roared approval of those whom they so unreservedly adulated. Baseball was dominated by the figure of Babe Ruth, tennis by Bill Tilden, the silent screen by Rudolph Valentino and later John Gilbert, even royalty by a dapper young man who would one day give up a kingdom for his ladylove. But the super-hero who had captured the heart of his country, and in fact of millions throughout the world, was Charles A. Lindbergh. Tall and lean, and looking very much like a stereotype of a Scoutmaster, silent and modest with captivating humility, Lindbergh personified all that his countrymen sought in one they so unstintingly loved: individualism, perseverance, courage, achievement, and success in which all America might share. No wonder, then, that following his return from Paris, where he had been lionized by the French, he traveled up Broadway as the central figure of a ticker-tape parade the like of which New York had not seen before nor has it seen since.

Less than a quarter of a century after the flight of the Wright Brothers at Kitty Hawk, North Carolina, in which a heavier-than-air plane had stayed aloft for all of fifty-nine seconds, this handsome youth from St. Louis had flown from America to France, alone, spanning the ocean and uniting the continents. He had remained in the air more than thirty-three hours, with no aid from ground crews or automatic pilots; and if today we read of flying machines that encircle the globe in ninety minutes, and in which men travel at 19,000 miles an hour, it does not diminish the worship in which millions of Americans held the Lone Eagle as he returned triumphant to his homeland.

This was the man who, within a few years, was to become the victim of a crime that would shock the civilized world. That it was a crime crudely committed, perpetrated by an amateur entirely lacking in skill, who succeeded for many years in eluding police forces in what may have been the biggest manhunt in all history, only adds more unbelievable details to a story that taxes the credulity of any reader of fiction. It was a crime that was to leave in its wake not only the tragic-stricken family of Charles Lindbergh but was also to result in the suicide of one domestic servant (although she was most certainly innocent), the jailing of several men who tried to capitalize on the tragedy, the effort of a governor to tamper with state evidence, a second kidnapping for which gangsters and police officers were imprisoned, and the execution of Bruno Richard Hauptmann after one of the most publicized criminal trials in history.

Charles A. Lindbergh, Jr.
Wide World Photos

The facts of the case, up to the moment when the Lindbergh baby was kidnapped, can be summarized briefly. On May 27, 1929, almost on the second anniversary of his successful flight to France, Charles A. Lindbergh married Anne Morrow, daughter of a wealthy and politically prominent family. His popularity had not diminished; his success in the air had been followed by economic and political achievements. In the summer of 1930, Anne Lindbergh gave birth to a son, Charles A. Lindbergh, Jr. Soon afterward, the Lindberghs took up residence in Hopewell, New Jersey.

On the evening of March 1, 1932, Charles and Anne Lindbergh were sitting in the living room on the ground floor of their residence. In the house were several servants; in the nursery, one flight up, the baby was sleeping. As was brought out at the Hauptmann trial, in the direct examination of Colonel Lindbergh, during the course of the evening Lindbergh heard a noise:

Q. Well, some time during that night did you hear some sort of a noise or crash?
A. Yes, I did.
Q. About what time was it, and where were you?
A. Sitting on the sofa in the living room during the ten or fifteen minutes after we had come into the living room from the dining room. At that time, I heard a sound which seemed to me, at the time—the impression that entered my mind at the time vaguely was that it was like the top of—well, say, an orange crate, the top slats of an orange box, falling off a chair, which I assumed to be in the kitchen.
Q. That is, sort of like the falling of a crate, a wooden crate?
A. The slats of a crate.

Q. At any rate, what you felt was happening was that some piece of wood, like the slats of a crate, had fallen in the kitchen?
A. That is correct. I did not pay very much attention to it at the time, but enough to remark to my wife the words: "What is that?"
Q. And except for that, it went unnoticed?
A. Yes.
Q. About what time was that?
A. That would be about nine-ten or nine-fifteen.
Q. Was it the sort of a noise that would come with the falling of a ladder?
A. Yes, it was, if the ladder was outside.

Later that evening, probably just before ten o'clock, Betty Gow, the nursemaid, tiptoed into the baby's room to see that he was properly covered, and in the darkness she felt the blankets, but not the child. She turned to Mrs. Lindbergh's room, with the thought that the mother, who had retired, might have her son. Finding that Charles, Jr., was not with his mother, Betty hurried downstairs and told Colonel Lindbergh that the baby was missing. They hurried to the child's room, turned on the light, saw the empty crib, and an envelope on the windowsill. In the envelope was a note:

Dear Sir
Have 50000$ ready 25000$ in 20$ bills 15000 in 10$ bills and 10000$ in 5$ bills. After 2-4 days we will inform you were to deliver the mony We warn you for making anyding public or for notify the police. The child is in gut care. Instruction for the letters are singnature

At the bottom of the note were two overlapping circles, one in blue, one in red, with little holes punched in each one. Later that evening, about sixty feet from the house, a ladder and a chisel were found. Together with a single footprint, they constituted all the clues in the case.

Local and federal police were notified, and by early morning the Lindbergh estate was surrounded by reporters. Most of the events of the previous hours became public property; only the exact wording of the ransom note, some misspellings contained therein, and the unusual signature, remained a secret, confined to a few individuals. A few days later, a second ransom note arrived, and then a third; the ante was raised to $70,000. The authenticity of these notes could not be doubted: the handwriting, the misspellings, the cryptic signature all attested to their having one common author.

For many weeks after the baby was kidnapped, the belief that the child was alive dominated all efforts in the case. Exploitation of the family, and of its willing-

The nursery of the Lindbergh house in Hopewell, New Jersey, from which the baby was kidnapped on the evening of March 1, 1932. The original picture was part of the state's evidence at the Hauptmann trial.
Wide World Photos

A photograph of the ransom note pinned to the Lindbergh baby's crib by the kidnapper.
State Bureau of Identification Division,
State Police, Trenton, N.J.

ness to go to any lengths to recover the child knew few bounds. Al Capone, serving a jail sentence for income-tax evasion, stated with confidence that he knew the gang responsible for the abduction and that, if permitted to go free, he would be able to conduct negotiations and have the child returned safely. Lindbergh himself, through intermediaries, was put in contact with underworld figures from the Prohibition era, men with criminal records and whose present activities were not less shady than their past; he negotiated with them in the hope, as he was to state on the witness stand some years later, "that we might be able to learn through underworld channels what had happened to our son if the underworld knew anything about it." But the underworld knew less than it pretended, and if Capone did not convince anyone of his good faith, the same cannot be said of one Gaston B. Means, who milked a prominent socialite out of more than $100,000, to be used to pursue the kidnappers and lure them into returning the child. And in Norfolk, Virginia, a local citizen, one John Hughes Curtis, convinced a prominent clergyman and a retired rear admiral that he was in contact with the child's abductors, and as a result Curtis was empowered by Lindbergh to negotiate for the release of his son.

The kidnapper's third note designating
Dr. "Jafsie" Condon as go-between.
*State Bureau of Investigation Division,
State Police, Trenton, N.J.*

But no one who injected himself into the case was a more curious, more eccentric, and eventually a more significant figure, than Dr. John F. Condon, who came to be known by the single word made out of his initials, Jafsie. A former professor at Fordham, a religious man who lived frugally with his wife and children, he was deeply moved, to the point where he was willing to put up his entire life savings of $1,000 to bring back the missing child. He made this offer in a letter sent to an editor of the *Home News,* a minor newspaper then being published in the Bronx. The next day, on arriving home, Condon found a letter, purportedly from the kidnapper; shortly thereafter, he read it to Lindbergh over the telephone. Within this envelope was another one, addressed directly to Colonel Lindbergh, and after giving details of the ransom demand, the letter was signed with interlocking circles.

Following instructions in the correspondence, an advertisement was placed in the *New York American,* stating that the "money is ready." For the first time, the hopes of the Lindberghs ran high.

There followed many efforts to arrange a meeting. Finally, in a secluded spot at a cemetery in the Bronx, they met, Jafsie Condon with a box containing $50,000, whose serial numbers had been carefully recorded by the authorities, and a man who spoke to him in the dark.

Hopes soared for the baby's safety when **Dr. Condon**
received this note from the kidnapper stating the baby
was on the "Boad Nelly."
*State Bureau of Investigation Division,
State Police, Trenton, N.J.*

The meeting was later described by Condon at the Hauptmann trial:

Cross-examination of John F. Condon

Q. And what happened then?
A. He was crouching down under the hedge, and I said, "Come on, stand up like a man. I have the money here." I took the money and placed it on my forearm.
Q. You mean the box?
A. Yes sir, the box full of money. And then I said, "Give me the note." He put his hand down his coat pocket and said, "I got the note."
Q. Did he give you the note?
A. Not yet. He said, "Don't open it yet." I said, "I have never betrayed a confidence. I have carried out every order of both parties the best I could. I won't open it. I will take it up to Colonel Lindbergh." I then handed the money out with my left hand forward, and I could look down at him; he was crouched near the hedge. I said, "Stand up and look at me if you want to do that, and give me the note." He gave me the note and I handed him the box; the box therefore went on his right hand, and I took the note from his left hand and put it in my pocket.

Finally, the note was read by Colonel Lindbergh; it disclosed that the boy was "on the boad Nelly . . . between Horseneck Beach and Gay Head near Elizabeth Island." At last, the long quest seemed close to fruition: the ransom had been paid, and the whereabouts of the infant was known. All that was required now would be to rush to the boat and recover the kidnapped child.

Of course, there was no such boat. Soon the cruel hoax was exposed, and $50,000 in cash had been passed on, probably to the kidnapper, but possibly to an impostor, and the search for the baby was no nearer success; if anything, it might be further away, for if the kidnapper was indeed the person who had been paid the money, he would have no need to make further contact with the Lindberghs or with Condon.

The money was transferred on April 2, 1932. Several weeks later, on May 12, in a wooded section of the Lindbergh estate, a truck driver saw the partially decomposed body of an infant, identified by its clothing as the Lindbergh baby. In all probability, the child had been killed in the crib or had fallen from the ladder and been abandoned; certainly the baby had been dead since the night he had been stolen from his home. All through the negotiations, all through the payment of the ransom, the search in the bay for the boat, the discussions with publicity hounds, underworld figures, extortionists, Charles A. Lindbergh, Jr., had been dead.

In the days following the kidnapping, the members of the staff of the Lindbergh household were carefully questioned, their private lives investigated, their contacts with those outside the home pursued. Harassed by detectives and by reporters, members of the staff, themselves no doubt sharing the grief of the family and perhaps guilt-ridden over their own failures to use more care and prudence in protecting the child, became increasingly tense and even hysterical. Finally, on June 10, Violet Sharpe, a waitress in the Morrow household, committed suicide just as she was about to be questioned again by police; the suicide must have been planned, for it is improbable that any other explanation can be offered for the cyanide that she had in her room.

*   *   *

Seldom in the annals of crime has there been a manhunt for a criminal that occupied as much attention, and to which so many people devoted themselves, as the search for the kidnapper, and probably the murderer, of the Lindbergh baby. There was the ransom note with the hope that somewhere, somehow, a similar handwriting would turn up. Then there was the ransom money, in ten- and twenty-dollar bills, all with serial numbers recorded, and it was hoped that whoever it was who had them would start to spend the money, perhaps recklessly, and that the bills could be traced to him. Then there was the ladder, from which one rung had evidently been broken and had been replaced by a piece of wood that did not originally belong to it.

This ladder was to play a major role as trial evidence that would send Hauptmann to the chair. It was the impetus for a piece of scientific detection at which one can only marvel. A wood chemist and forester in Wisconsin, Arthur Koehler, dedicated himself to a study of the wood from which the ladder had been constructed. He studied the types of lumber used in the ladder, the exact nature of the machines used in cutting

and planing the lumber, the markings and defects in the wood. As one of the prosecution's most important witnesses, he established that, long before Hauptmann's arrest, he had traced the lumber in the ladder to a small company in the Bronx.

Direct testimony of Arthur Koehler

Q. Prior to September 1934 and before the day that Hauptmann was arrested, had you ascertained where some of the lumber that made up this ladder came from?

A. Yes.

Q. Where did it come from?

A. From the National Lumber & Millwork Company in the Bronx . . . I traced some of the lumber in the ladder to the planing mill that dressed it and from the planing mill to the National Lumber & Millwork Company.

Q. Now will you tell us how you traced it?

A. I traced it by means of the planer marks made on the lumber when it was planed at the planing mill.

Q. Where did you go?

A. I went to the M. G. and J. J. Dorn Company, McCormick, South Carolina.

Q. How many companies are there that manufacture these planing machines?

A. Two, in the eastern part of the United States.

Q. As a result of your investigation, did you find the machine that imposed these planer marks on this ladder?

A. I did.

Q. Where did you find the machine?

A. At the mill of the M. G. and J. J. Dorn Company, McCormick, South Carolina.

Q. Having found the planer machine that made these planer marks, did you then follow the lumber that came from that mill, made in the shipment when that planer was used?

A. Yes.

Q. How many loads of lumber did you follow?

A. About forty-two.

Q. And finally did you get to this lumber company in the Bronx?

A. Yes.

Q. Tell us what you found there.

A. I found one-by-four North Carolina pine in which the knife cuts made by the planer were exactly the same width as those on the ladder rail and also there was a defect in the planing on one edge and one side of the rail, which I found on the one-by-four North Carolina pine in the Bronx yard.

The trail had led to the National Lumber & Millwork Company in the Bronx, not very far from where Jafsie Condon had turned over the money to some nameless person. But sales records in the lumberyard were unavailable, and customers were numerous and anonymous, so that what looked like such a promising lead, and what was the culmination of years of scientific analysis, was a dead end. A dead end, and so near to the final victory: for what was not known at the time was that Bruno Richard Hauptmann had been an employee of this lumberyard just prior to the time of the kidnapping.

The serial numbers of the ransom money started showing up, in banks and at garages and in stores, sometimes in the Bronx and often elsewhere. But storekeepers and bank tellers could never identify the person who had brought the money; usually they could not recall a particular bill, one among many in the day's receipts.

It was hoped that somewhere the holder of the ransom money would become careless, would have a need to obtain quick negotiable cash, and would turn in several bills at one place. But he was careful and prudent, one man eluding an army.

In early April, 1933, President Franklin D. Roosevelt, still taking severe measures to fight the depression, directed all those in possession of more than a hundred dollars' worth of gold—whether in the form of bullion, coin, or certificates—to exchange the gold for other currency. Those engaged in the manhunt in the Lindbergh case hoped that now their task would be made easier, either because the holder of the "gold note" ransom money would be tempted to turn in large amounts or because his bills would become more conspicuous once most of the other "gold notes" were off the daily market. Actually, one large transaction of $3,000 of the ransom notes took place, but the bank teller had not spotted them as ransom bills at the time and could not recall the appearance of the person who had presented the money. After this exchange, the ransom money continued to appear here and there, a few bills a week but never traceable to any individual.

The case broke when a garage attendant, suspicious of a customer whom he had not seen before, jotted his license number on the ten-dollar gold note given him in payment for gasoline. By the morning, he had forgotten the incident, and the next day the money was deposited, with many other bills. At the bank it was spotted as a ransom bill, similar to many others that had appeared, except for a license-plate number, written neatly and legibly. Within a few hours, the authorities knew the owner of the car, had examined his writing on the license application, and had found it to resemble the writing in the ransom notes, and knew that the man they were seeking was Bruno Richard Hauptmann. In large numbers, they staked out his house, waited for him to leave in the morning, followed his car, which they brought to a stop, questioned him, and found a twenty-dollar ransom bill on his person. Yes, he had a few such bills at home. But the search of his home revealed much more than he had disclosed: a cache in the garage containing a buried treasure, with thousands of dollars of the ransom money, more in a shoe box in a closet, and written on a piece of wood in the same closet was a telephone number. It was the number of Jafsie Condon. This was only one of many pieces of highly incriminating evidence that Hauptmann, at his trial, could not satisfactorily explain:

Lindbergh ransom money, here being inspected by New York City police officials, was found in Hauptmann's home late in September, 1934.
Wide World Photos

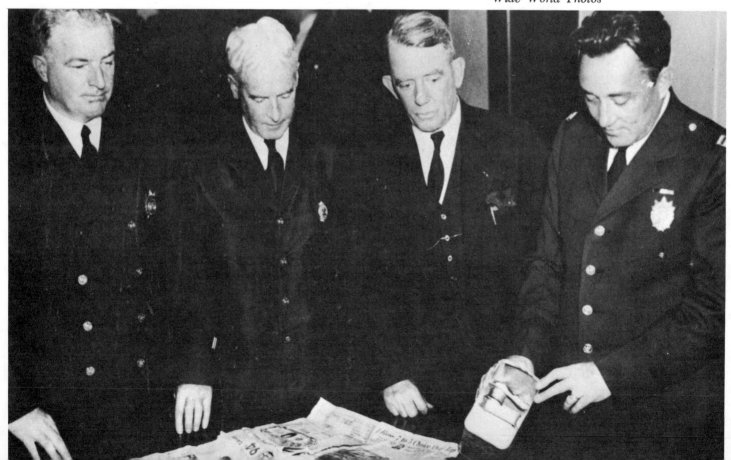

Q. Let me read you some of your answers then.* "How did you come to put the telephone number on there?" And your answer was, "I can't give you any explanation about the telephone number." Then your next question—I read to you a minute ago—"Your only explanation for writing Doctor Condon's address on this board and telephone number is that you were probably reading the paper in the closet and you probably marked it down?" And wasn't your answer as follows: "It is possible that a shelf or two shelfs in the closet and after a while I put new papers always on the closet, and we just got the paper where this case was in and I followed the story, of course, and I put the address on there"? Did you say that to Foley?

A. Yes.

Bruno Richard Hauptmann fought extradition to New Jersey, but in vain. On January 2, 1935, the murder trial opened in the town of Flemington, some sixty miles from New York, and not very far from where the body of the infant had been found. From every part of the United States and all over the world, reporters came; special radio and telephone installations were brought in; not since Leopold and Loeb had a murder trial attracted so much attention.

By the second day, the selection of the jury of eight men and four women was complete, and the case was ready for trial. Presiding in the case was a seventy-one-year-old judge, Thomas Whitaker Trenchard. Heading the prosecution was Attorney General David T. Wilentz, aided by the local prosecutor, Anthony Hauck, Jr. Against them the defense was headed by Edward J. Reilly, and assisted by C. Lloyd Fisher.

---

* The prosecutor is quoting from the testimony in the extradition trial.

In his opening statement, Wilentz summarized the most salient points against Hauptmann, and no sooner was he seated than Reilly, for the defense, called for a mistrial, on the grounds that the attorney general had made an impassioned appeal that was not a proper opening and that would inflame the minds of the jury. The motion having been denied, the first witness was called. He was a civil engineer, and served to introduce some floor plans and maps of the house and area. The court was silenced by sympathy as the next witness appeared, Anne Morrow Lindbergh, who told the story of the discovery of the kidnapping and identified some clothing as belonging to the baby. Mrs. Lindbergh was dismissed without cross-examination, the defense attorneys stating that they wished to spare her, but actually following a time-honored practice that victims (particularly grief-stricken women and innocent children), when subjected to cross-examination, tend to arouse hostility against the examining attorney and his client.

Mrs. Lindbergh was followed on the stand by her husband, who reviewed the events of the day and night of March 1, 1932. On cross-examination, the defense sought to cast doubt on the guilt of Hauptmann by focusing on three possibilities: that a member of the household may either have committed the crime or been an accomplice to it; that Lindbergh himself had believed that the Norfolk group (headed by John Hughes Curtis) was involved and had the infant; and that Jafsie Condon could hardly have been merely an innocent go-between.

After Bruno Richard Hauptmann was arrested, officials tear apart his garage, where $13,750 of the ransom money had been found, in the hope of discovering more of the bills. *Wide World Photos*

Justice Thomas W. Trenchard presiding
at the trial of Bruno Richard Hauptmann
in Hunterdon County Court, Flemington.
Wide World Photos

The Hauptmann jury in the box (*left to right, front row*):
Walton, Stockton, Charles Snyder, Mrs. Verna Snyder,
Mrs. Pill, Hockenburg; (*back row*): Cravatt, Smith,
Voorhees, Mrs. Brelsford, Case, and Biggs.
Wide World Photos

CROSS-EXAMINATION OF COLONEL LINDBERGH

Q. When did you first come in contact with Curtis?
A. Mr. Curtis came to our residence in East Amwell township either the latter part of March, or the first of April, I believe. My recollection now is that the first time he came there was the latter part of March. I am not certain of that.
Q. It was his idea that he should get in contact with the people that had your child by going out on a boat; is that correct.
A. That was one of the ideas.

After additional questioning about Curtis's role and arguments among attorneys, Lindbergh was permitted to state his opinion, that the defendant, Hauptmann, was guilty, and was then asked:

Q. Colonel, irrespective of the Curtis trial, did you ever have the belief that Curtis was connected directly or indirectly with the group of persons who had kidnapped your child?
A. I did, with reservations.

The remainder of Lindbergh's time on the stand was designed to show that at one time he might have suspected "the Purple Gang of Detroit" with having been implicated in the crime; that the innocence of Violet Sharpe, who had committed suicide, could not be assumed; and that suspicion might also fall on Red Johnson, a Scandinavian sailor who had since been deported and not recalled for the Hauptmann case and who had been friendly with one of the household employees at the time of the kidnapping.

Afer the Lindberghs, the prosecution called up some minor witnesses, and then followed with Bessie (or Betty) Gow, the nursemaid who had discovered the absence of the baby from his crib, who had been in contact with Red Johnson, and who had told him that the Lindberghs would be in Hopewell the night of the kidnapping. Miss Gow was taken through the events of the evening, until the identification by her of the body of the baby in the morgue. She was cross-examined by the defense on the payment of her expenses for her trip to the United States (she had returned to England following the kidnapping), on her relationships with Violet Sharpe, on whether she had a flashlight she might have used to signal to someone from within the Lindbergh home, and particularly on Red Johnson. But she was unshaken; efforts to implicate Johnson were, at best, weak.

Witnesses for the prosecution identified the ladder as the one that had been found on the premises; others gave details of the behavior of members of the police force during the investigation. Very damaging was the testimony of an elderly German-born man, one Amandus Hochmuth, who identified Hauptmann as the man he had seen in a car, containing a ladder, in the neighborhood of the Lindbergh home on the day before the kidnapping.

Chief attorney for the state, David T. Wilentz, at left, and Hauptmann's chief defense counsel, Edward J. Reilly, studying calendar to determine how long the trial might last.
Wide World Photos

Charles A. Lindbergh testifies
at the opening of the trial
as to the events that
transpired on the night of
the kidnapping.
Wide World Photos

The prosecution meets with its most important witness, John F. (Jafsie) Condon (in overcoat). On the left is Attorney General Wilentz, and behind him is Superintendent Schwarzkopf of the State Police. To the right of Jafsie is County Prosecutor Hauck.
Wide World Photos

When it was Dr. Condon's turn to testify, the attention of the world heightened. Here was the eccentric mystery man of the case, relating the story of how he had become involved in the search for the kidnapper. He went through the details of the negotiations, and identified the voice of Hauptmann as that of the man he had spoken to in the cemetery when he turned over the ransom money. The breakdown of Condon was a major aim of the cross-examination; first, because of his almost qualifying as an "eyewitness" that the defendant was, if not the kidnapper, then at least the recipient of the funds; and second, because if some question could be cast on the innocence of Condon, then this might constitute the reasonable doubt that, in an American court of law, is supposedly sufficient to demand a verdict of not guilty. In the cross-examination of Condon, the defense sought to cast doubt on both his credibility and his innocence:

Q. Now, when you decided after the kidnapping that you would like to do something in the way of aiding the colonel in the recovery of his child, that was how many days after the kidnapping?

A. As I recollect it, the first of March the baby was taken away; by the seventh of March I had determined to do something to help him and Mrs. Lindbergh to get the baby back, yes.

Q. That was six days after?

A. Yes.

Q. During those six days you had never seen the note left in the crib, had you?

A. I had not.

Q. During those six days the note, as far as you know, with the symbols left in the crib was in the possession of the authorities, right?

A. Colonel Lindbergh, I thought; in the possession of Colonel Lindbergh was my impression. I had not seen it.

Q. You had no knowledge of any signature up to the seventh of March?

A. I had not.

Then, without warning, the cross-examining counsel suddenly switched the line of questioning to the newspaper in which Condon placed his notice to the kidnapper:

Q. The little Bronx *News*.

A. The what—you mean the Bronx *Home News*? A hundred and fifty thousand circulation and over is a pretty good paper.

Q. Are you a stockholder?

A. No sir.

Q. But still, you have the circulation right at your finger tips?

A. No sir. It was the question such as you gave that had been brought since that made me recollect that I might have made a mistake in sending it to a little Bronx paper. I resent that—

Q. Well, whether you resent it or not, it is a fact that you knew there was such an association in the United States as the Associated Press, did you not, that reached every town and hamlet in the world?

A. I did.

Q. You knew also in the United States there was the United Press?

A. I did.

Q. You knew there were other press agencies?

A. Yes sir.

Why then, this obscure paper in the Bronx? Because, Dr. Condon insisted, all the other papers were pointing a finger at one miserable fellow whom Dr. Condon felt was innocent, Arthur, or Red, Johnson, the sailor who had spoken to Betty Gow, the nursemaid, the afternoon of the kidnapping. Condon insisted that he did not know Johnson, but sympathized with him, "because I always hated to see an underdog and always gave him a chance throughout my life, and I had heard that Arthur Johnson had nothing to do with it, from many people."

After Lindbergh and Condon, there came numerous other witnesses, among whom the handwriting and wood experts were the most important. If Arthur Koehler's testimony was damaging, even more so did it become when he returned to the stand late in the trial, further to illuminate the studies he had made. For Koehler had done more than trace the wood to the Bronx lumber yard; he had found that one board in the ladder (known as Rail 16) was from another source and that they contained nail holes, which he carefully measured. On direct examination, he linked this board and these nail holes to the defendant:

DIRECT EXAMINATION OF ARTHUR KOEHLER

Q. Now, what have you to say as to the size of the nails from the attic floor, whether eightpenny nails fit in the attic board, S-226?

A. Yes, I fitted eightpenny nails in there and they fit just right.

Q. Mr. Koehler, there has been testimony about nail holes, and prior to the arrest of Mr. Hauptmann, the defendant in this case, you examined this ladder on various occasions, did you not?

A. I did.

Q. Now, did you make any observations as to the nail holes in Rail 16 prior to his arrest?

A. I did.

Q. When did you make those observations, and what did those observations reveal in reference to nail holes in Rail 16 of the ladder?

A. When I first examined the ladder, which was the first week in March 1933, I noticed that there were four cut nail holes in Rail 16 and I so stated in my report, dated March 8, 1933.

Q. Now then, again, did you on another occasion prior to Mr. Hauptmann's arrest, did you again measure the distances between the nail holes and make a note of that?

A. Yes, in November 1933 I made a diagram of Rail 16, and on that diagram indicated the distances between the nail holes in the rail.

Q. And all of that, sir, before the arrest of the defendant Hauptmann?

A. It was.

Q. And did the nail holes, which you measured in 1934, prior to his arrest, and the nail holes which you observed in 1933, prior to his arrest—were those the nail holes which matched with the holes in the joists in Hauptmann's attic when you fitted it?

A. They were.

The defense ridiculed the idea that there was such a thing as a wood expert or that the witness was qualified, but they were dealing with a man whom they could not match in knowledge of the subject and who could not be ruffled under cross-examination.

CROSS-EXAMINATION OF MR. KOEHLER

Q. Now, when you studied and observed the plane marks on the ladder and when you undertook to duplicate them with the Hauptmann plane, if we may call it such, you tried to use the plane at the angle that you thought a man might have used it at in planing the rungs, didn't you?

A. I tried to use it at the angle the plane commonly is used. That is, you run it as nearly parallel to the edge as you can.

Q. Now, since you have not established, Mr. Koehler, what the dimensions of the nicks, or the spacings, are in the defendant's plane, and have not established what the dimensions of the nick ridges and the spaces on the ladder rungs are; in fact, having established no dimensions at all of the solids of the ridges on the board and the nicks in the plane, your whole premise fails, and your statement is merely an opinion, isn't it?

A. No. I can measure the distance between houses in a block without measuring the size of the houses.

Q. I believe you said that you examined the nail holes sometime in 1933, was it?

A. Yes.

Q. That was a year after the kidnapping.

A. Yes.

Q. And how do you account for the staggering of the nails in the one-by-six piece, in S-226?

A. That's because the joists underneath that board were spliced with the ends, one alongside the other, and one nail was driven into one joist and the other into the other joist.

Picking away at small points, the defense was no match for a scientist so sure of his every step, and most of whose work had been accomplished long before the arrest.

After seventeen days of trial, following some reexamination of Arthur Koehler, Mr. Wilentz arose and softly stated, "The prosecution rests." He had made out a strong case, indeed. A witness, albeit an elderly one, had seen Hauptmann in the area of the home; Condon had identified the voice; the ransom money had been passed by Hauptmann at a garage; more ransom money, much more, was found in his home and garage; several experts had identified the writing on the notes; and then there was the extraordinary link to the ladder.

The defense made the usual motions for a directed verdict of acquittal, basing this particularly on the lack of evidence that a murder had been committed in the county in which the trial was being held; after a brief argument, the motion was denied, and the trial proceeded. The defense, in the opening statement, pleaded poverty, accused the state of New Jersey of tieing up the Hauptmann funds, promised to account for Haupt-

One of the many handwriting experts, Albert D. Osborn, testifying for the state that Hauptmann had written the kidnap ransom notes.
Wide World Photos

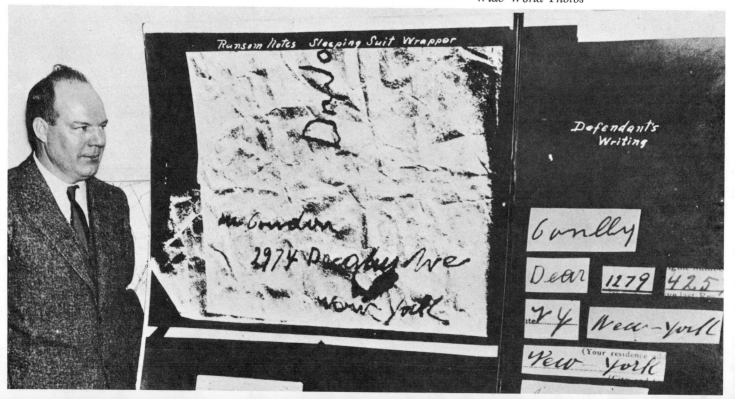

Wood expert Arthur Koehler testifies. Through painstaking research, he had linked up the kidnapper's ladder with a piece of flooring from Hauptmann's Bronx home. He had traced the wood used in the ladder from a South Carolina planing mill to the Bronx lumberyard where Hauptmann bought $10 worth of lumber shortly before the kidnapping.
Wide World Photos

mann's whereabouts on the night of the kidnapping and again on the night of the payment of the ransom, and placed the responsibility for possession of the ransom money squarely on the shoulders of one Isidor Fisch, a former acquaintance of Hauptmann's who was now dead.

The first witness was Bruno Richard Hauptmann. His testimony was interrupted by two friends of the Hauptmanns, who attempted to establish the alibi. Hauptmann then returned, and explained his financial dealings with Fisch, why Fisch left so much money with him, why he did not tell others about it. But the prosecution was merciless on cross-examination, tripping the defendant on his finances, on his handwriting, on what he had said at the time of his arrest.

Hauptmann's story, in the opinion of many, was most unconvincing. Peculiarities of spelling in the ransom note and in the further note giving "instructions" as to the whereabouts of the infant were identical with those found in other conceded samples of his writing. There was a serious contradiction in the story of when he met

Fisch. He stated that the ransom money belonged to Fisch, admitted that he had never told any of Fisch's relatives about it, and denied that his wife knew about it, although it was right in the house. He had been getting change, after small purchases with the ten- and twenty-dollar bills, and had been making large deposits of such change in the bank; he could explain only that there were errors on the bank slips, that this was not change. He could not explain how he had made purchases that could be traced to the period after the ransom money was passed but before Fisch was supposed to have left the funds with him. He had actually, in the midst of the depression, quit his job the day after the ransom money was turned over by Condon. His alibis explaining his whereabouts on the night of the kidnapping and again on the night when the ransom money was passed on by Condon at the cemetery were supported by his wife and some friends, but were hardly airtight.

Bitterness and acrimony marked the courtroom when Hauptmann was being examined by the prosecution:

CROSS-EXAMINATION OF BRUNO RICHARD HAUPTMANN

Q. You had on the door panel, that same door, some numbers of big bills, didn't you?

A. Yes.

Q. What were the size of those bills—$500 and $1,000, weren't they?

A. It was a thousand, I guess.

Q. Thousand-dollar bills?

A. Thousand-dollar bills.

Q. How many thousand-dollar bills did you have?

A. I can't remember now. When I put it on it was summertime, '32.

Q. Yes, sure, summertime, '32; after April 2, 1932.

A. No, summertime, '33; I wish to correct.

Q. Oh, I see.

A. I got $2,000 I should put in the stock market and I didn't put it in the stock market. I brought it to the bank, and I kept it home for a few days.

Q. Two one-thousand-dollar bills.

A. Yes.

Q. Tell me, where did you get those one-thousand-dollar bills?

A. That is Mr. Fisch brought it in my house to put it in the margin.

Q. Now do you remember being asked this: "Is there anything more you want to say about it or add to it?" You were asked that and your answer was this: "No. About them two numbers, I am sure it was five-hundred or thousand-dollar bills." Do you remember saying that?

A. I guess I did say so.

Q. You didn't even know whether it was a five-hundred- or a thousand-dollar bill; isn't that right? It was one or the other?

A. Yes, one or another.

Q. You mean to tell me that you sat in the Bronx courtroom talking to Foley about five-hundred-dollar bills and thousand-dollar bills and didn't know whether it was five hundreds you had or thousands?

A. That is true; I don't know if it was a five—

Q. You didn't know?

A. —hundred-dollar bill or a thousand-dollar bill.

Q. A man that had—the greatest amount of money you ever had in Europe was $100 and you couldn't remember in 1932 whether the bills laying around the house were thousand-dollar bills or five hundreds?

A. This time, '33, I get quite a lot of money to put in the market, put in force, so I really—I couldn't remember if it was five hundred or a thousand.

Q. You are having a lot of fun with me, aren't you?

Copy of a photograph, introduced as evidence by the state, showing broom closet in the Hauptmann home where the accused said he hid the box full of money given him by Isidor Fisch.
Wide World Photos

The closet door from the Hauptmann home on which was scribbled the telephone number of Dr. Condon. Also on the door was a serial number of one of the Lindbergh ransom bills.
Wide World Photos

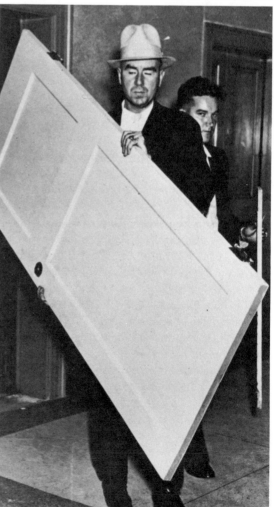

A. No.

Q. Well, you are doing very well. You are smiling at me every five minutes.

A. No.

Q. You think you are a big shot, don't you?

A. No. Should I cry?

Q. No, certainly you shouldn't. You think you are bigger than everybody, don't you?

A. No, but I know I am innocent.

Q. Yes, you are the man that has the will power; that is what you know, isn't it?

A. No.

Q. You wouldn't tell if they murdered you, would you?

A. No.

Q. Will power is everything with you, isn't it?

A. No, it is—I feel innocent and I am innocent and that keeps me the power to stand up.

Q. Lying, when you swear to God that you will tell the truth. Telling lies doesn't mean anything.

A. Stop that!

A. Didn't you swear to untruths in the Bronx courthouse?

A. Stop that!

Q. Didn't you lie under oath, time and time again? Didn't you?

A. No, I did not.

Q. When you were arrested with this Lindbergh ransom money, and you had a twenty-dollar bill, Lindbergh ransom money, did they ask you where you got it? Did they ask you?

A. They did.

Q. Did you lie to them or did you tell them the truth?

A. I said not the truth.

Q. You lied, didn't you?

A. Yes.

Q. Lies, lies, lies, about Lindbergh ransom money, isn't that right?

A. Well, you lied to me too.

Q. Yes? Where and when?

A. Right in this courtroom here.

Q. We will let the jury decide about that. In this courtroom. Did I ever ask you a question outside of this courtroom? Did I ever come into that jail to ask you anything?

A. No.

Q. You see you are not smiling any more, are you?

A. Smiling?

Q. It has gotten a little more serious, hasn't it?

A. I guess it isn't any place to smile here.

Q. "I am a carpenter."

A. I am.

Q. That was funny, wasn't it?

A. No sir, there was nothing funny about it.

Q. You had a good laugh, didn't you? Did you plan that in the jail there? Did someone tell you to give that answer when I asked you about the ladder, to stand in front of the jury and say, "I am a carpenter?"

A. No, sir.

Q. You thought that out yourself?

A. No, I didn't think anything about it.

Q. Let me ask you something. You have got a peculiar notion about will power, haven't you?

MR. POPE:* Well, I think this has gone just about far enough.

MR. WILENTZ:† I will withdraw the question. If it has, may

* Defense Attorney.
† Prosecuting Attorney.

we have a recess, if your Honor please?

MR. POPE: I think we ought to come back into a courtroom and see if we can't get down—

MR. WILENTZ: Now, I object to that. I think it is a reflection on the Court.

THE COURT: What do you mean by that, Mr. Pope?

MR. POPE: Well, I mean this patent abuse of the witness. It seems to me it is about time we protested against it. It has been going on for quite a while.

THE COURT: Whenever you have any occasion to protest, you make your protest to the Court, while the thing is going on, and the Court will deal with it. It always has and will continue to do so. We will now take a recess for five minutes.

What was the essence of the defense? That there was a man named Fisch to whom the ransom money really belonged (although there were contradictions in Hauptmann's story as to when he met the man); that there were alibi witnesses (although their ability to recall an evening months or years past is hardly credible evidence); that Hauptmann's spending sprees and his failure to work were accountable in terms of stock-market transactions and the Fisch money; that the entire story was based on circumstantial evidence with doubtful experts testifying on the ladder and on the handwriting; that there were no witnesses to place Hauptmann at the crime itself; and that the defendant denied, categorically denied, the charge.

After Hauptmann, all the witnesses were anticlimatic. Finally, on February 11, 1935, after rebuttal prosecution and rebuttal defense witnesses, both sides rested. It was the thirtieth day of the trial, and summations were in order. For the prosecution, Hauck spoke briefly, summarized the most salient points, reminded the jurors that "we are not required to have a picture of this man coming down the ladder with the Lindbergh baby," and insisted that the guilt of the prisoner had been proven "conclusively, overwhelmingly, beyond a reasonable doubt." For the defense, Reilly started with a quotation from St. Matthew: "Judge not, lest ye be judged." Reilly pointed out that only the members of the Lindbergh household knew the unexpected whereabouts of the Lindberghs and their baby on the night of the kidnapping; that Hauptmann could not have known. If the child did not cry out, he must have been "doped"—and this could have been done only as an inside job. As for the ladder, it was a plant. Hauptmann was innocent, absolutely innocent of murder, and even Colonel Lindbergh, who had Mr. Reilly's profound respect and sorrow, would not expect anything from the jury but their duty under the law. Following Reilly was David T. Wilentz, who in a final summation succinctly placed the entire case against Hauptmann before the jury, and sneered at the possibility of a recommendation of mercy as "a wishy-washy decision" that men and women of courage would not make.

On the following day Judge Trenchard made his charge to the jury, a charge to which the defense made many objections, but in vain. The judge instructed the jury that they alone must judge the evidence, decide where it had greater weight, but left little doubt about his own view. On the question of handwriting, he reminded the jury that a prosecution expert said that the conclusion that the notes were written by the defendant was "irresistible, unanswerable and overwhelming," and that the "defendant denies that he wrote them and a handwriting expert called by him so testified." On the question of Fisch, he said: "The defendant says that these ransom bills, moneys, were left with him by one Fisch, a man now dead. Do you believe that?" It was hardly an impartial charge. To the exceptions and objections of the defense, he turned a deaf ear.

On February 13, 1935, **three** years less a few days after the kidnapping, a jury found Hauptmann guilty. Mercy was not asked.

* * *

During the course of many appeals, Hauptmann steadfastly maintained his innocence. He died in the electric chair, on the night of April 3, 1936, still protesting that he had in no way been implicated in the crimes. But in the thirteen and a half months that elapsed between the verdict of guilty and the execution, a series of events took place in the case as dramatic as any in the courtroom itself.

Several months after the trial, the Lindberghs quietly slipped out of the country with their second-born son, Jon, and went to make their home in England, searching

Anna Hauptmann, the defendant's wife, discusses the case with defense counsel Frederick A. Pope during a lull in the court proceedings.
Wide World Photos

for the freedom from the spotlight of publicity that they had been unable to find in the United States, and leaving many Americans dismayed that the country that had idolized the Lone Eagle could not give him a feeling of protection and safety. Anna Hauptmann, standing by her convicted husband, went on a speaking tour to raise funds for the appeal. She pleaded poverty, and she received the support of a small but burgeoning Nazi movement in New York and other cities. Her appearances became the signal for anti-Semitic leaflets and other literature, and her husband was depicted as the victim of an international Jewish conspiracy. The defense, having internal conflicts of its own and problems with money, engaged the brilliant criminal lawyer, Samuel Leibowitz, who read the transcript of the trial, interviewed Hauptmann, and promised that he would leave no stone unturned to obtain a commutation of sentence if only Hauptmann would tell the truth, including a story of any accomplices he might have had. But Hauptmann insisted that there was no more to tell than had been said at the trial, that every word was the truth; and Leibowitz is reported to have expressed his utter disbelief, his amazement that anyone could continue to maintain innocence in the face of an overwhelming record, and then withdrew his offer to aid.

Many voices of doubt were raised, some of them people convinced of Hauptmann's guilt, but concerned that there were others, presumably much more significant, and as yet unapprehended. Some stressed that the trial was a far cry from impartial judicial procedure; others created fantasies that sought to explain the crime. H. L. Mencken, although affirming a belief in the prisoner's guilt, was certain that he had accomplices. Clarence Darrow, a lifelong foe of capital punishment, joined the voices of those asking for a new trial, as did Eleanor Roosevelt, first lady of the land. Some groups imputed the crime to international intrigue, some to world powers such as the Soviet Union or Japan.

But nothing that occurred in the posttrial period could match the efforts of Harold Hoffman, the new and young governor of New Jersey, to intervene in the case, ostensibly with the aim of discovering the truth, but actually on the side of Hauptmann. What was Hoffman's motive? As a young politician who had had a meteoric rise, who had become mayor of Perth Amboy while still in his twenties and then governor of New Jersey while not yet out of his thirties, Hoffman saw himself as a possible candidate for President or Vice-President on the Republican ticket. For this he required the spotlight of national attention; and if he could uncover the accomplices, or twist the case to show that an innocent man had been entrapped and that he, Hoffman, had gone to the rescue, his political stock might rise. He arranged an interview for himself in prison with Hauptmann, a secret rendez-

vous that the press heard of and that, as Hoffman surely must have known, was illegal. He obtained a special panel of experts to go with the broken rung of the ladder to the Hauptmann house, where they tried to fit the nails into the holes from which they had allegedly been taken. But the nails protruded, contrary to testimony at the trial. The prosecutor and his experts were taken aback, and Hoffman threatened to pursue charges of perjury. After heated exchange of angry words, the boards were taken to the laboratories of Columbia University, where microscopic examination disclosed that someone had placed some new filling material in the nail holes.

Finally, there were the kidnapping, confession, and repudiation of the confession of Paul Wendel. The role of Hoffman in this episode is not clear, but there is much to the possibility that he was, at the least, an accomplice-after-the-fact, if not an actual conspirator.

Paul Wendel was a former New Jersey lawyer who had been disbarred some years before. On the streets of New York, he was abducted by a group of gangsters and taken to a cellar in Brooklyn, where he was kept in chains, while being interrogated day after day by people who said that they knew that he had committed the Lindbergh kidnapping and murder. At first amazed, later he decided to confess the crime in order to obtain his freedom so that he could later repudiate the confession. Thinking ahead to the time when he would be pressing charges against his abductors, he carved his initials on a cellar floor, and later, after he had agreed to cooperate, he asked the men holding him to have his suit cleaned, and then carefully saved the cleaning tag. Upon signing the confession, he was brought back to New Jersey, where he was left at the home of Ellis Parker. Chief of detectives of Burlington County, New Jersey, Parker had a wide reputation for imaginative and unorthodox solution of crimes, and had been closely collaborating with Hoffman during the previous months. Wendel told the story of his own abduction to Parker, who offered to protect him from the gangsters by secreting him away into a mental institution, and Wendel readily agreed to having himself signed into the asylum. There he was carefully guarded by Parker's men, and visited by the Parkers, father and son, who likewise suggested that Wendel confess the crime, for which he would surely be able to go free on a plea of insanity, and then he would become rich and world famous as he wrote his memoirs. At first amazed by this turn, and resisting it, Wendel finally decided to repeat the game he had played in Brooklyn: he would confess and then, once free, would repudiate his own words. Having again confessed, Wendel was now turned over to the authorities, where he lost no time in telling the story to Attorney General Wilentz.

* * *

In addition to Hauptmann, who was executed, many persons went to jail for their part in the Lindbergh case. Gaston Means received a jail sentence of seventeen years for extortion; not content with his part in the early days of the investigation, and already in jail while Hauptmann awaited execution, Means also confessed that he was the actual kidnapper. But no one believed his story. John Curtis, the Norfolk man, was given a one-year suspended sentence. Five members of the gang that kidnapped Wendel were arrested and received sentences ranging up to twenty years in jail; with them, Ellis Parker was likewise indicted for kidnapping, but Hoffman refused to extradite him. Nevertheless, Parker and his son were not to remain free; they were arrested on a federal charge, and were tried, the young Parker receiving a three-year sentence, and his father, an elderly man, a six-year sentence. The older man died in jail. Hoffman, for whom many were demanding impeachment for the part that he played in the case, served out his term as governor, was given the political plum of an appointment that is usually accorded a party man, and few remembered the dubious role he attempted to play in the Hauptmann case. He died in 1954, and soon thereafter it was revealed that he had probably embezzled several million dollars from the government, all revealed in a note that he left to his daughter. Anna Hauptmann and her son disappeared from the public scene; it is believed that they returned to Germany.

*   *   *

Several questions are left unanswered by the trial record in the Hauptmann case, but they do not so much cast doubt on his guilt as they do on the question of whether he had accomplices, who they were, and on the court and police procedures that were used. How could Hauptmann have known so much about the layout of the Lindbergh home, the fact that the Lindberghs were to be in Hopewell on the particular Tuesday night (they were usually at the home of Mrs. Morrow, in Englewood, New Jersey, except for weekends), and just where the nursery room was and how it could be reached from the outside? Did he not have to have information passed on to him from the inside? Why did Violet Sharpe commit suicide just as she was about to be questioned again? Was it merely from nervous exhaustion and the despair of an innocent person who felt she was unable to face further interrogation and unwarranted suspicion? What was the role of Red Johnson, the Scandinavian seaman who did talk to Betty Gow, the nursemaid, on the afternoon before the crime; who knew that the Lindberghs were in Hopewell, and who so peculiarly aroused the sympathy of Dr. Condon, although they had presumably never met? Why was Johnson not recalled for the Hauptmann trial? Could Anna Hauptmann have been as inno-

cent and unsuspecting of the source of the money in her home as she contended (or pretended)? Was she the woman who was seen trying to change one of the ransom bills in the very first days after the money had been turned over? And if so, why did she flee from the store, if she did not know the taint of the funds? Was she the European *Hausfrau* who simply accepted everything her husband stated, asked no questions, and had no doubts, even to the point of not looking on the top shelf of the closet where he kept thousands of dollars in a shoebox?

What happened to about $35,000 of the ransom money? To this day it has not turned up. Was it given to another party or taken to Europe, and simply considered "too hot to handle," or was it put away, where it still lies buried, far from sight? And, finally, although Condon has always been considered a well-meaning and even innocent person (without whose intervention the case might never have been solved, for it was through him that the ransom money was given), none can read of his part in the matter without having second thoughts. Of all places, how is it a kidnapper would read an item in The Bronx *Home News?* Why The Bronx?

For criminologists and those concerned with the administration of justice and with trial procedure, the Hauptmann trial poses other knotty questions. If so many parts of the enigma were not solved at the time of Hauptmann's execution, is this not an excellent argument against the use of capital punishment? Surely there was greater chance that a lengthy jail sentence, with a guarantee that he serve at least thirty years, would have brought forth any new light that might have been shed—if Hauptmann had anything further to say about others.

Seldom has a man been tried and convicted in newspapers as surely as was Hauptmann. Information identifying the handwriting on the ransom note with the defendant was fed to the press, and published in *The New York Times* and other papers, when it was clearly debatable material that would be rebutted in court. A leading bar group stated that it was precisely in cases where the crime was reprehensible and the guilt clearly established that special care and caution must be taken to safeguard the rights of the accused.

The final statement of Hauptmann reiterated his innocence:

I am glad that my life in a world which has not understood me has ended. Soon I will be at home with my Lord, so I am dying an innocent man. Should, however, my death serve for the purpose of abolishing capital punishment—such a punishment being arrived at only by circumstantial evidence—I feel that my death has not been in vain. I am at peace with God. I repeat, I protest my innocence of the crime for which I was convicted. However, I die with no malice or hatred in my heart. The love of Christ has filled my soul and I am happy in Him.

Convicted murderer Bruno Richard Hauptmann in his cell at Flemington. *Wide World Photos*

The language is too obviously not Hauptmann's to be taken seriously; in fact, it is doubtful if the ideas are his, either.

*   *   *

Of Hauptmann's guilt, there can be no doubt. Many laymen look askance at the concept of "circumstantial evidence," particularly in a capital case. But if circumstantial evidence is meant to encompass everything but eyewitnesses and confessions, then it may contribute the strongest—not the weakest—links in a conviction. With all the unanswered questions, particularly on the question of accomplices (if any), the guilt of Hauptmann was established, in the classic words of law, beyond a reasonable doubt, and this by evidence that was almost entirely circumstantial.

In a case built on circumstantial evidence, it is the total impact that is important. Some of the aspects of the total case may not seem weighty by themselves; in isolation they may be weak, even incredible. In their total context, they take on greater importance. Even so simple a matter as the signature on the ransom notes, the interlocking circles, one blue, one red, both with holes in them, becomes important. In the opinion of the prosecution, they may have been symbols of the initials of the writer: blue was for *B*, which meant Bruno; red was for *R*, which meant Richard; and holes were for *H*, which meant Hauptmann. Would a criminal wish to leave such evidence behind? He might if, for example, he wanted to be apprehended (which is a farfetched interpretation of Hauptmann's life pattern). But, more likely, he may have wished to display to himself his power as the ignorant immigrant who could kidnap and kill the best-known baby in the country, receive ransom funds of tens of thousands of dollars, and then pass them on at will while a nationwide manhunt was in effect, although all the time he had arrogantly and egocentrically left behind the signature of the mastermind for his pursuers to behold.

Leon Trotsky in Mexico being interviewed on the Moscow Trials.
Wide World Photos

25

Leon Trotsky

[1937]

IN THE CITY OF COYOACÁN, MEXICO, IN THE SPRING OF 1937, an unusual event took place, perhaps unique in the history of courtroom procedures and trials. The defendants were Leon Trotsky and his son, Leon Sedov, but actually Stalin and the Russian regime were on trial. It was a court that had neither power nor jurisdiction, except the power to influence worldwide public opinion, and the jurisdiction that renowned intellectuals sometimes assume for themselves. It was not a usual trial, but hearings on the charges made against Leon Trotsky in the Moscow trials in August, 1936, and January, 1937.

The trials of the Old Bolsheviks in Moscow aroused wide skepticism and criticism. During those trials, many who confessed implicated Leon Trotsky in counterrevolutionary activities. Charges against Trotsky in the Moscow courts were abundant; he was accused of innumerable acts inimical to the Russian government and to the revolutionary movement that he had once led; and in addition, many specific acts were described by prosecutors and defendants. In Copenhagen, Trotsky was supposed to have given terrorist instructions to many of his followers; it was charged that there were conspiratorial letters from Trotsky to various defendants, some advising and advocating assassination. Today, years after Stalin's death and Khrushchev's famous denunciation of the Stalinist terror, and following the rehabilitation of many of the defendants in the Moscow trials, few consider that these charges have substance. In 1937, many of those who looked with hope to the Russian Revolution were not so certain of the innocence of the opponents of Stalin.

In the United States, a Preliminary Commission of Inquiry was set up to investigate the charges against Trotsky, and to offer the defendant an opportunity to obtain the hearing "in open court" that was impossible for him in the Soviet Union. The commission was headed by John Dewey, prestigious philosopher and sympathizer with Socialist causes, and its members included Carleton Beals, writer and specialist in Latin American affairs (who resigned while the commission was in session); Otto Ruehle, German Social Democratic leader and at the time a refugee from Hitler; and Benjamin Stolberg and Suzanne La Follette, labor editors. Later, a full Commission of Inquiry was established (similar committees and commissions were in existence in many parts of Europe), and the commission was to include, among others, Carlo Tresca, colorful anarchist; Professor E. A. Ross, sociologist; and John F. Finerty, counsel for the commission.

On April 10, 1937, the commission opened its hearings. The central witness, and the central figure in the entire drama, was, of course, Trotsky. He was examined by his attorney, Albert Goldman, at great length, on subjects ranging from the history of the Russian Revolution and the parts played in it by the principal figures to the events in Copenhagen and elsewhere, following exile. Some six hundred printed pages of testimony were taken; meanwhile the Stalinists were denouncing and ridiculing the kangaroo court, and the anti-Stalinists were pointing with pride and vindication to the corrections that were being made to the falsifications of history.

On the Moscow trials and on the confessions, Trotsky spoke what today seems both self-evident and yet prophetic:

GOLDMAN: Do you care to give us any opinion about any future trial involving Bukharin and others?

TROTSKY: I heard from private sources that Rykov refused to confess, and that is the reason why the promised trial cannot be materialized, Vyshinsky can accuse only people who confess.

GOLDMAN: Do you expect that Bukharin and Rykov also will be connected with you?

TROTSKY: Everything is possible. It is a witch's play, a very terrible one, but it is a combination of gunfire and what is necessary for Stalin. I could indicate that he eliminates for the moment Molotov as a national hero, from the list of victims. I could explain it because I knew the material. I can say now what it is about. It is the preparation for a new trial. I don't know the concrete circumstances. I know only that Bukharin was sent abroad in 1936, the beginning of 1936, for the factories. He was their agent. He was in Prague, a tourist. Now I ask myself if it was not with the purpose of preparing with him a new combination. He gave a lecture in Prague, totally in the official spirit. But it is possible they sent him in order to have the possibility to affirm that abroad he entered into communications with Trotskyites and German agents. I don't know, but it is quite possible. The same with Rakovsky. Immediately, he was sent to Japan. I was a bit astonished. What was the meaning of it? It was at the end of 1934, and the British friends of the Soviet Union—the friends of the Soviet Union are everywhere—they are directed by the agents of the G.P.U., without their knowing; the genuine direction is everywhere in the hands of the G.P.U. The friends in London declared: "You see, the repentance of Rakovsky is totally sincere. The Government sent him abroad." But his family remained in Moscow, the family of Rakovsky. At that time I was of the opinion that he was sent for demonstrative purposes in order to show the whole world that he was free, his repentance was sincere. Now, I ask myself if it did not have a second purpose, to frame him afterwards—that he was connected with the Japanese military chiefs in the Government, and so forth.

GOLDMAN: Your archives were stolen in France?

TROTSKY: Yes.

GOLDMAN: When?

TROTSKY: On the anniversary of the October Revolution, the 7th of November, 1936.

GOLDMAN: Have you any documents, reports, such as you want to give the Commission as to the possible perpetrators of the crime?

TROTSKY: Yes, I have the report of the French police, the testimony of my son to the examining judge, and my own testimony.

GOLDMAN: I will introduce it into evidence.

TROTSKY: It was sent to me by my French lawyer.

Much of the evidence in the hearings consisted of an elaboration of Russian revolutionary history; some of it was an expression and elucidation of the position of Trotsky, as compared with that of Stalin, with regard to the Spanish Civil War, the Chinese Revolution, and other issues that were then dividing the radical movement of the world. Much of the examination consisted of denials by Trotsky of the charges by Stalin:

GOLDMAN: Do you know a man by the name of Hess?

TROTSKY: Yes; I learned his name from the papers and from the Verbatim Report.

GOLDMAN: He is connected with the fascists in Germany.

TROTSKY: Rudolf Hess is one of the Ministers of Hitler.

GOLDMAN: Did you ever see him?

TROTSKY: Only in the photos.

GOLDMAN: Did you have connections with him?

TROTSKY: No; I only heard his voice on the radio.

GOLDMAN: Did you ever communicate with any official of the fascist régime of Hitler?

TROTSKY: Never.

GOLDMAN: Did you ever come to any agreement with them with reference to the surrender of Soviet territory?

TROTSKY: No.

GOLDMAN: I ask the same questions about the Japanese militarists.

TROTSKY: I give you the same answers.

GOLDMAN: Concretely speaking, you have no objection to the Soviet Union making an alliance with France, a military alliance, but at the same time you object to the Communist Party voting in favor of the war budget of the French militarists?

TROTSKY: Yes.

GOLDMAN: Now, a question has been asked many times in reference to this point. I would like to have you clear it up. Lenin accepted aid from the German Kaiser in the sense that he accepted permission of the Kaiser to go through Germany to Russia. Would you accept that aid?

TROTSKY: To go to Russia? Hitler would help me with pleasure in this direction—to go to Russia.

GOLDMAN: For the purpose of getting rid of you?

TROTSKY: Yes; I understand your question.

There was considerable delving into the charges that the Trotskyites (or Left Oppositionists) had engaged in terrorist activities inside the Soviet Union. This problem was investigated in the interrogation of Trotsky:

GOLDMAN: Now, Mr. Trotsky, you told us during the previous sessions what the methods were that were used by the Left Opposition after the expulsion. Will you repeat that answer briefly so that we can get it into the record at this time?

TROTSKY: During my sojourn in Siberia, the Left Opposition was permitted correspondence in Siberia. It was proposed to give to the G.P.U. the possibility to follow our inner life, and to see which one was inclined to capitulate, which one was opposed, et cetera. During the first eight or nine months our activity consisted of writing the principal political and theoretical theses, and so forth.

GOLDMAN: Have you any idea, approximately, how many Left Oppositionists were arrested and deported to Siberia at that time?

TROTSKY: At that time our appraisal was that there were about eleven thousand.

INTERPRETER: You mean estimate.

TROTSKY: We estimated about eleven thousand.

GOLDMAN: Subsequent to that, did you get any information—

TROTSKY: Excuse me, it was immediately after the Fifteenth Congress.

GOLDMAN: Eleven thousand were arrested in that short period after the Fifteenth Congress?

TROTSKY: During the same weeks.

GOLDMAN: From Moscow only or from the whole country?

TROTSKY: From the whole country.

GOLDMAN: Did you receive any information which would enable you to make an estimate as to how many Oppositionists were arrested after that?

TROTSKY: It is difficult to say. I quoted Victor Serge, who affirms in his very serious and cautious appreciation that from Leningrad alone in the last time, before the Zinoviev-Kamenev trial, they banished to Siberia between 60,000 and 100,000 women and children, families of people under suspicion. He had seen them at the railroad station, absolutely helpless, in crowded wagons.

GOLDMAN: Meaning trains.

DEWEY: What date?

TROTSKY: That was 1935 or 1936. Ciliga affirms the same.

GOLDMAN: From 1927, the end of 1927, when you were expelled, up to the present, did the Left Opposition ever use any other methods outside of education and propaganda to win over the masses?

TROTSKY: Not in the slightest degree. We warned in letters and conversations that we must be prepared to have provocations from certain elements to use violence. I warned them against that.

GOLDMAN: Will you prepare for the benefit of the Commission a list of those letters, articles, and documents wherein you predicted that violence would be used against the Left Opposition? Will you prepare such a list?

TROTSKY: Yes; it is only a question of translation. I hope we will succeed in translating it—all the quotations are in my hands. Only it is necessary to translate them into English. I hope to translate them before the Commission leaves for New York.

GOLDMAN: Do you claim that you anticipated the use of violence, the use of frame-ups by Stalin against you?

TROTSKY: I cannot say anticipation, because it was anticipation supported by some sketches from the bureaucracy, and I could appreciate the direction of the bureaucracy. I was sure that—in the session of the Central Committee in the Fall of 1927, I tried to picture it—I was absolutely sure that the next step would be better prepared by Stalin. That was my prediction. It would not be the last attempt. It was only a fi-asco, but that fiasco predicted a new attempt, better prepared.

GOLDMAN: Do you refer to that session of the Central Committee in which Stalin came out with the accusation about the Wrangel officer printing the Left Opposition program?

TROTSKY: Yes.

GOLDMAN: Now, will you briefly enumerate the trials that have been held in the Soviet Union since the Kirov assassination, involving you directly or indirectly? Give us in very summary form an idea of the accusations and the results.

TROTSKY: The first trial—before the trial, there were one hundred and four shot according to the Soviet press; they were supposed to be White Guards.

GOLDMAN: After the Kirov assassination?

TROTSKY: After the Kirov assassination.

GOLDMAN: And before the first trial?

TROTSKY: During the first sixteen days of December. They communicated themselves that there were one hundred and four shot without trial; that they came from abroad as agents of foreign powers, agents of diversion and terrorism and so on. Without appreciation—

GOLDMAN: Without what?

TROTSKY: Without appreciation. (Trotsky here spoke in French.)

FINERTY: Without defining the charges?

TROTSKY: Have you the word "precise"? They did not precise what connection there was between the people shot and the murder.

GOLDMAN: They did not give any definite charges?

TROTSKY: They were in a general formula connected with the murder of Kirov. Then, the first trial was the trial of Nikolayev, the genuine murderer of Kirov, and of his alleged accomplices, on the 28th and 29th of December, 1934; with fourteen condemned to be shot.

The commission continued and soon concluded its work, and in September, 1937, made public its report. After reviewing the conduct of the Moscow trials and the charges therein, the commission came to two conclusions: that the Moscow trials were frame-ups and that Trotsky and Sedov were not guilty. Aside from this, the hearings left two volumes rich for any student of modern Russian history.

*　　*　　*

A few years after the death of Stalin, his successor, Nikita Khrushchev, denounced the dictator for his crimes, and initiated a movement of cultural freedom and destalinization in the U.S.S.R. Some of those who had been executed were posthumously rehabilitated, and history books were again rewritten. Khrushchev himself was ousted, and retired to a quiet life. Although few today, inside the Soviet Union or out, believe in the truth of Stalin's charges against Trotsky and many other Old Guard leaders of the Revolution whom he had executed, Trotsky's name is ignored in official histories of the revolution when it is not denounced. Thus, history has with supreme irony imposed on both Stalin and Trotsky a similar fate: in Russia, they are seldom mentioned, and then only with comparable ignominy.

Twenty-one top Nazi defendants are in the prisoners' rows in the Palace of Justice at the first Nuremberg trial that began on November 20, 1945. All pleaded not guilty. Two others were absent. Robert Ley had committed suicide in his prison cell just prior to the trial. Martin Bormann, who was never found, was tried *in absentia*.

U.S. Army Photo

26

Nuremberg

[1945]

THEY WERE WARNED. HITLER AND HIS HENCHMEN WERE warned not to abrogate the terms of the Versailles Treaty that ended World War I and limited the German Army to a police force of 100,000; not to scuttle the Weimar Constitution that had brought democracy to Germany; not to collaborate with the German industrial moguls to set the mechanical wheels of rearmament in motion; not to violate international treaties and agreements. But what good were these warnings? Hadn't Adolf Hitler as early as 1923 exposed the groundwork of his grandiose plan for Germany's world conquest to the six million readers of his *Mein Kampf?* And hadn't the world laughed it off as the hallucinations of an insignificant Austrian housepainter writing from a prison cell?

But hallucinations began to take on the form of reality when Hitler and his National Socialists came to power in January, 1933. History tells us that great men (and Hitler was a diabolically great man) are thrust upon the world because the times are ripe for them. Germany was ripe for a hero who would deliver the Fatherland from the shackles of Versailles, from the smoldering resentment of the humiliations following World War I, from the territorial restrictions imposed by the victors of that war—a leader who would restore Germany to her "rightful" place as the leading nation of the world. Long before Hitler came to power, German Army Ordnance, as early as 1926, was acting in league with Germany's leading industrialists secretly to begin a program of rearmament. So effective were they over the subsequent years that they were able to place a ready-made military machine at the Fuehrer's disposal. It was all that Hitler could have wished, including, as it did, the full moral and financial support of the biggest manufacturers, headed by Krupp, and the wealthiest bankers, headed by Schacht. Of their own free will, at a time when they could have renounced Hitler, the financial and business wizards, for power and money, threw in their lot with him, with the full knowledge that they were breaking international law. At the Nuremberg Trials, this was to weigh heavily against them.

Thirty days after he had himself proclaimed Fuehrer, Hitler stepped up Germany's preparations for war by creating, on April 4, 1933, a Reich Defense Council to prepare plans for mobilization. The second meeting of the council was presided over by Wilhelm Keitel, who stressed that a war economy must be established at once and that any obstacle was to be summarily brushed aside.

War plans proceeded at an accelerated pace. In 1934, Alfred Jodl supervised the secret construction of U-boats. In March, 1935, Göring stated that Germany was building an air force. On March 7, 1936, Hitler ordered his troops into the Rhineland demilitarized zone, at the same time insisting that he had no territorial claims to make in Europe. He was not yet prepared for a general war.

But on November 5, 1937, at a meeting with his top political and military leaders, including Hermann Göring, Erich Raeder, and Konstantin von Neurath, he announced his intention to use force to gain his ends: "The aim of German policy is the security and preservation of the nation and its propagation. This is consequently a matter of space. . . . The German question can be solved only by way of force." The plan called for solving the space problem not later than 1943-1945. And yet the Nazi war criminals present at that meeting were to assert at Nuremberg that neither Hitler nor they had wanted war!

Hitler's first step in this territorial aggrandizement was to take over Austria. For this purpose he used Franz von Papen to prepare the political softening up, Artur von Seyss-Inquart to take over the chancellorsh'p of Austria and request Nazi troops to establish stability, Göring to engineer the military takeover, and Joachim von Ribbentrop to deceive the world as to the meaning of these acts. On March 13, 1938, Seyss-Inquart, now both chancellor and president of Austria, approved Anschluss—the incorporation of Austria into the German Reich.

German Fuehrer Adolf Hitler.
U.S. Army Photo

Czechoslovakia was next. With a brief respite at Munich, where Neville Chamberlain gave away the Sudetenland—the Czechs' natural geographical defense line against German attack—Hitler forced the aging President Emil Hácha to sign away his country at 4:30 A.M. on March 15, 1939, leaving Hácha no choice in view of Göring's threat to bomb the city of Prague off the map and the encroachment of the Czech frontiers by Hitler's army.

They were warned. On March 17th, two days after Hitler's takeover of Czechoslovakia, Sumner Welles, Acting United States Secretary of State, emphatically stated: "The position of the Government of the United States has been made consistently clear. It has emphasized the need for respect for the sanctity of treaties and of the pledged word, and for nonintervention by any nation in the domestic affairs of other nations; and has on repeated occasions expressed its condemnation of a policy of military aggression."

Hitler's nose-thumbing answer was to invade and take over Poland, under the pretense that Poland was adopting a threatening attitude toward Germany. On June 22, 1939, Hitler ordered a secret mobilization for the attack on Poland. To two urgent notes from President Roosevelt he did not deign to reply. On August 22nd Ribbentrop engineered a nonagression pact with Russia. On August 25th England and Poland signed a mutual-agreement pact. Wanting war, Hitler had now cleverly succeeded in limiting it for the time being to a one-front conflict.

On September 1, 1939, his troops crossed the Polish border, while his planes bombed Polish cities and towns. On September 3, at 11:00 A.M., Britain fulfilled her pledge to Poland and declared that a state of war existed between England and Germany. France followed England with a declaration of war almost immediately.

Warsaw fell on September 23. There now followed a few months of inactivity; then in quick succession Hitler's troops, violating all treaties and assurances, overran Luxembourg, Holland, and Belgium in May, 1940.

Meanwhile, by October, 1939, plans for invading Norway were already under way. The head of the Foreign Affairs Office, Alfred Rosenberg, had already made contact with the Norwegian traitor Vidkun Quisling. Others in the conspiracy to violate Norway's independence were Raeder, Karl Doenitz, Jodl, Keitel, and Ribbentrop. On April 9, 1940, disguised as British warships and merchantmen, ships of the German Navy sailed across the North Sea and attacked Norway. At the same time Hitler brought Denmark within his grip.

The Hitler octopus now had Western Europe firmly in its tentacles. In May the Low Countries were invaded, and the Maginot Line, the much-vaunted defense of France, collapsed. On June 21 the French signed an armistice, and Hitler danced his famous jig. There now remained only England and Russia. Hitler postponed his plans for invading England, and instead, against the advice of Raeder and his other military leaders, turned to a blitz campaign against Russia.

Never one to stint, Hitler had transferred a million and a half men from the West to the borders of the USSR with a minimum of detection and suspicion. Then, his preparations completed, on the morning of June 22, 1941, he sent wave after wave of German troops onto Russian soil. The Nazi leaders called it a defensive war, but at Nuremberg the prisoners were confronted with irrefutable evidence that Russia had not been planning to attack Germany. Now only two major nations remained neutral in this world holocaust: the United States and Japan.

But Ribbentrop had not been idle. He kept urging Japan to join Germany against Great Britain and establish herself in the Far East by seizing British territory and destroying British naval forces there. Japan was reluctant to bring the United States into the war, which she felt would happen if she declared war on the British. But when Germany invaded Russia and tied this age-old enemy of Japan down in that sector of the world, Japan saw her golden opportunity to realize her ambition of a Greater East Asia Co-Prosperity Sphere in the Orient. Ribbentrop fanned the flames, and on November 28, 1941, in a conversation with the Japanese ambassador in Berlin, urged that no time be lost, that now was the moment (with America virtually unprepared for war) to strike, and that Germany would enter the war against the United States immediately upon Japan engaging in war with the United States. On December 1 the negotiations between Japan and Washington to settle differences of opinion peacefully had broken down. On December 3 the Japanese ambassador to Rome asked Mussolini if he would honor the Tripartite Pact (September 27, 1940, between Germany, Italy, and Japan) in the event of Japan declaring war on the United States. The Duce gave his full assurances. Germany already had.

On Sunday, December 7, 1941—Pearl Harbor.

❖   ❖   ❖

They were warned. The Hague Convention of 1907 had outlawed the very war crimes the Nazis were so deliberately committing. But hadn't the Kaiser in World War I gone unpunished? Nor did the Nazis respect the Geneva Convention of 1929, which further defined "civilized warfare." Nor the fact that, in the year previous to Geneva, Germany had signed the Briand-Kellogg Treaty on August 27, 1928, which was finally approved by sixty-three nations—a convention and a treaty designed to put an end once for all to aggressive warfare. But the frustrated dreams of Hitler and the German industrialists were written in flames on the horizon, and the fine black print of treaties and conventions curled into oblivion.

Hitler and Franco cement an alliance and personal relationships on Hitler's visit to France, Spain, and Italy in October, 1940.
U.S. Army Photo

They were warned. On October 25, 1941, even before the United States entered the war, President Roosevelt, commenting on the Nazi murders of hostages in France, warned that they would bring on a "fearful retribution." On January 13, 1942, nine governments-in-exile declared in London that by means of judicial procedures they would punish the Nazi war criminals when the war was over. On October 7, 1942, England and the United States promised that a United Nations War Crimes Commission would be set up to ferret out such criminals and bring them to justice. On December 17, 1942, the Allied Powers notified the Nazis that they would punish all those responsible for persecuting and exterminating the Jews. The Moscow Conference in October, 1943, subscribed to by Roosevelt, Churchill, and Stalin, stated that the Allies would hold responsible all individuals who committed war crimes. Regarding the Nazi slaughter of the Jews, President Roosevelt said to the world on March 24, 1944, "None who participate in these acts of savagery shall go unpunished."

But such warnings fell on deaf ears. The barbarians who, for their own ends, totally ignored the Geneva Convention that established international rules for waging war—if war must be waged—gave no thought to such rules. Why should they? No one tries a victor. Let the victims fall where they may.

Robert Ley, former Reich Minister of Labor, is flushed from his hiding place by members of the U.S. 101st Airborne Division of the Seventh Army.
U.S. Army Photo

One guard is placed at each cell door, succeeding one guard for three cells after Ley's suicide. Prisoners were observed twenty-four hours a day.
National Archives

In spite of his initial successes and of apparent victory within his grasp, Hitler was soon to find that his dream of world domination was a mirage. With the landing of American troops in North Africa, the defeat of Rommel in the African deserts, the steady advance of Allied troops from Sicily up the Italian peninsula, then D-day and the steamroller advance through Normandy, across the Rhine, and the final assault on Berlin—Hitler and the Nazi empire were doomed. On April 30, 1945, Adolf Hitler committed suicide, together with his wife, Eva Braun. With him went Goebbels, who, after first poisoning his six children, with his wife walked out of the Berlin bunker and into death by gunfire. Before he died, Hitler had appointed Grand Admiral Doenitz to be his successor. It was Doenitz who signed Germany's surrender a few days later.

❊   ❊   ❊

True to their word, within a few months after the defeat of Germany the Allies set up the judicial machinery to try the major war criminals who had quickly been apprehended and put behind bars.

On August 8, 1945, in a document called the London Agreement, the governments of the United States, the United Kingdom, the Union of Soviet Socialist Republics, and the Provisional Government of the French Republic pledged to prosecute and punish the major war criminals of the European Axis. The Moscow Declaration of October 30, 1943, in regard to German atrocities in Occupied Europe, called for a return of those German officers, enlisted men, and members of the Nazi Party who were responsible for such atrocities for trial to the countries in which they had committed them. Now, in order to try war criminals whose offenses had no particular geographic location, the Agreement established an International Military Tribunal. The authority for such a court was contained in a charter to this Agreement.

This charter set up a constitution designating as judges four members (one from each of the signatory powers) and four alternate judges. It specified the following acts to be considered crimes coming under the jurisdiction of the IMT:

a. Crimes Against Peace: namely, planning, preparing, initiating or waging a war of aggression, or a war in violation of international treaties, agreements or assurances, or participating in a conspiracy to accomplish the foregoing.

b. War Crimes: namely, violation of the laws or customs of war, including (but not limited to) murder, ill-treatment or deportation to slave labor, ill-treatment of prisoners of war, killing hostages, plundering public or private property, wanton destruction of cities, towns, or villages or any other devastation not justified by military necessity.

c. Crimes Against Humanity: namely, murder, extermination, enslavement, deportation, and other inhumane acts committed against any urban population, before or during the war, or persecutions on political, racial, or religious grounds, whether such violated a domestic law of the country in which they were committed.

The opening session of the tribunal was held on October 18, 1945, at Berlin, which issued an indictment against the top twenty-four Nazi war criminals, and they were informed that they should be ready to stand trial within thirty days after the indictment was served on them. Also indicted were seven groups or organizations. The trials would take place at Nuremberg, Germany, with Lord Justice Lawrence presiding.

The indictment split the first charge of the charter into two parts:

The Common Plan or Conspiracy: covering the formation of the Nazi Party as the instrument of cohesion bringing the conspirators together; the aims and purposes of the Nazi Party to resort to war to overthrow the Treaty of Versailles, to avoid the restrictions on the military armament and activity of Germany, to acquire not only territories lost as a result of World War I but also the territories of other peoples, so that Germany could have "living space"; specific aggressive actions from the planning in 1936 to the actual invasion of Austria on March 12, 1938; and the collaboration with Italy and Japan, from November, 1936, to December, 1941, to wage aggressive war against the United States.

Crimes Against Peace: covering the violation of international treaties, agreements, and assurances.

The indictment listed pages and pages of specific charges under *War Crimes,* ghastly, gruesome, and unbelievable, except that documented proof showed that they had happened. Perhaps the most fantastic figures were atrocities committed in Russia: in the Lwow region the Germans exterminated about 700,000 Soviet people; in the Latvian S.S.R. 577,000 people were murdered. Prisoners of war were murdered or died as a result of hunger and forced marches; hostages were shot. Essential commodities and wealth in occupied countries were despoiled; raw materials, industrial equipment, agricultural products, currency were all plundered and sent to Germany to help further the war effort. Works of art were looted and destroyed. Cities, towns, and villages were laid waste. Civilian labor was conscripted. Occupied territory was "Germanized," with the children being forced to join the Hitler Youth Movement.

But the worst crimes of all were committed under Point Four: *Crimes Against Humanity.* Chief United States Prosecutor Robert H. Jackson, in his opening statement to the court, made the accusation that the lives of 6,000,000 Jews were extinguished by every conceivable diabolic means.

* * *

The Nuremberg Trials of the major German war criminals began on November 20, 1945, with pleas of "not guilty" by all defendants except Martin Bormann, Robert Ley, and Gustav Krupp von Bohlen und Halbach, the last of whom, it was agreed, was too physically and mentally sick to stand trial.

In the prisoner's dock sat twenty of the accused, the picture of innocence and hope.

Two of the defendants who were not in the prisoners' dock were Robert Ley, who hanged himself in his cell while awaiting trial, leader of the German Labor Front, and Martin Bormann *(in absentia),* Chief of Staff in the Office of Hitler's Deputy, Secretary of the Fuehrer, General in the SS. Indicted on counts 1, 3, and 4. (To this day, Bormann has never been apprehended, the most important person in the Nazi apparatus to have escaped—unless he were already dead.)

Herman Wilhelm Göring: President of the Reichstag, Reich Minister for Air, Commander in Chief of the Air Force, general in the SS, and top leader of the Nazi war effort next to Hitler. Indicted on all 4 counts.

Rudolf Hess: Until his abortive flight to England, deputy to Hitler and designated successor after Göring, Reich Minister Without Portfolio, general in the SS, and member of the Council of Ministers for the Defense of the Reich. Indicted on all 4 counts.

The defendants.
All individual portraits,
U.S. Army photos

Wilhelm Keitel: Field Marshal of the German Army, Chief of the High Command of the German Armed Forces, and a member of the Council of Ministers for the Defense of the Reich. Indicted on all 4 counts.

Joachim von Ribbentrop: Reich Minister for Foreign Affairs, general in the SS, and member of Hitler's political staff at General Headquarters. Indicted on all 4 counts.

Hans Frank: Governor General of the Occupied
Polish Territories, Reich Commissioner for the
Coordination of Justice, Reich Minister Without
Portfolio. Indicted on counts 1, 3, and 4.

Alfred Rosenberg: Reich leader in the
Nazi Party for ideology and foreign policy,
head of the Foreign Political Office of the
Nazi Party, Reich Minister for the Eastern
Occupied Territories. Indicted on all 4 counts.

Wilhelm Frick: Reich Minister of Interior,
Head of the Central Office for the
Incorporation of Sudetenland, Danzig, and the
other Eastern Incorporated Territories,
Director of the Central Office of All Occupied
Territories, and Reich Protector for Bohemia
and Moravia. Indicted on all 4 counts.

Julius Streicher: editor in chief of the anti-Semitic newspaper *Der Stürmer*, general in the SA, and gauleiter of Franconia. Indicted on counts 1 and 4.

Walter Funk: president of the Reichbank, Reich Minister of Economics, Plenipotentiary for War Economy, and member of the Council of Ministers for the Defense of the Reich. Indicted on all 4 counts.

Hjalmar Schacht: Reich Minister of Economics, Plenipotentiary for War Economy, and president of the Reichbank before Funk succeeded him in these posts. Indicted on counts 1 and 2.

Karl Doenitz: Commander in Chief of U-Boats, later Commander in Chief of the German Navy, and final successor to Hitler at the very end of the war. Indicted on counts 1, 2, and 3.

Erich Raeder: Commander in Chief of
the German Navy. Indicted on
counts 1, 2, and 3.

Baldur von Schirach: leader of
the German youth, Reich governor
and gauleiter of Vienna.
Indicted on counts 1 and 4.

Alfred Jodl: Chief of the Operations Staff
of the High Command of the German Armed
Forces, Chief of Staff to Keitel.
Indicted on all 4 counts.

Fritz Sauckel: Plenipotentiary for the
Employment of Labor, gauleiter and
Reich governor of Thuringia, general in
the SS. Indicted on all 4 counts.

Franz von Papen: Vice Chancellor
under Hitler, Ambassador to
Vienna and Turkey. Indicted on
counts 1 and 2.

Albert Speer: Reich Minister for Armaments and Munitions, Plenipotentiary for Armaments, and Chairman of the Armaments Council. Indicted on all 4 counts. (*left*)

Artur Seyss-Inquart: Chancellor of Austria, Deputy Governor General of the Polish Occupied Territory, and Reich Commissar for Occupied Netherlands. Indicted on all 4 counts. (*above right*)

Hans Fritzsche: Head of the Radio Division of the Propaganda Department of the Nazi Party, and before that head of the official German News Agency DNB. Indicted on counts 1, 3, and 4.

Ernst Kaltenbrunner (appeared later in the trial, as he was in the prison hospital suffering from a heart attack): Chief of the Security Police and Security Service, general in the SS. Indicted on counts 1, 3, and 4.

Constantin von Neurath: Reich Minister of Foreign Affairs before Ribbentrop, and Reich Protector for Occupied Czechoslovakia. Indicted on all 4 counts.

On the bench were four of the world's most distinguished jurists and their alternates. The president of the tribunal was Lord Justice Lawrence of the United Kingdom and North Ireland; for the United States, Mr. Francis Biddle; for the French Republic, M. Le Professeur Donnedieu de Vabres; for the Union of Soviet Socialist Republics, Major General I. T. Nikitchenko. It was their historic duty to weigh the prosecution's cases against the cases for the defendants and render for posterity a fair and just verdict. Against the criticism that judges from the victorious nations could not impartially try the Nazi defendants, the prosecution countered with the fact that judges everywhere impartially tried thieves and murderers without being connected with or condoning such themselves.

Some of the officiating judges of the International Military Tribunal (*left to right*):
Judge John Parker, United States; former Attorney General Francis Biddle, United
States; Henri Donnedieu de Vabre, France; Robert Falcon, France; A. F. Volchoff, USSR.
U.S. Army Photo

The judges take their places for the opening of the Nuremberg War Crimes Trial (*left to right*): A. F. Volchoff,
USSR alternate; Major General I. T. Nikitchenke, USSR; Justice Sir Norman Birkett, British alternate; Presiding
Judge Lord Justice Sir Geoffry Lawrence, Great Britain; former Attorney General Francis Biddle, United States;
Judge John J. Parker, United States alternate; Henri Donnedieu de Vabre, France; Robert Falcon, French alternate.
U.S. Army Photo

On November 21, 1945, Mr. Justice Robert H. Jackson of the United States made the opening address for the prosecution. It was a statement of historic importance because basic to it was the criminal charge against both individuals and organizations of plotting and carrying out international crimes of wiping out entire peoples and nations. Since no one man could engineer such atrocities on such a mammoth scale, it followed that thousands upon thousands of willing participants collaborated *of their own free, nay, enthusiastic, will,* to perpetrate the hideous crime of genocide. Thus the Nuremberg Trials laid the foundations for a new concept of international justice: that whole groups and organizations, as well as individuals, could be held criminally liable for committing crimes associated with aggressive war.

Said Mr. Justice Jackson at the beginning:

What makes this inquest significant is that these prisoners represent sinister influences that will lurk in the world long after their bodies have returned to dust. We will show them to be the living symbols of racial hatred, of terrorism and violence, and of the arrogance and cruelty of power. They are symbols of fierce nationalisms and militarism, of intrigue and warmaking which have embroiled Europe generation after generation, crushing its manhood, destroying its homes, and impoverishing its life. They have so identified themselves with the philosophies they conceived, and with the forces they have directed, that any tenderness to them is a victory and an encouragement to all the evils which are attached to their names. Civilization can afford no compromise with the social forces which would gain renewed strength if we deal ambiguously or indecisively with the men in whom those forces now precariously survive.

Justice Jackson then limited the scope of United States prosecution: "The case as presented by the United States will be concerned with the brains and authority behind all the crimes. These defendants were men of a station and rank which does not soil its own hands with blood. They were men who knew how to use lesser men as tools."

To forestall criticism of outside powers illegally interfering with the internal problems of a sovereign country, Jackson stated: "The purpose, as we have seen, of getting rid of the influence of free labor, the churches, and the Jews was to clear their obstruction to the precipitation of aggressive war. If aggressive warfare in violation of treaty obligation is a matter of international cognizance, the preparations for it must also be of concern to the international community." Thus the scope of the trials was enlarged to cover the growth of the Nazi Party and all the acts of their feverish pace to prepare for the launching of an aggressive war.

Continuing his opening statement, Jackson outlined the nature of crimes and torture against prisoners of the Nazis, then continued with the international events, now history, that accompanied the Nazis' aggressive buildup. It was his task to prove the charges made against the defendants in Point One of the indictment: The Common Plan or Conspiracy.

Justice Robert H. Jackson, chief United States prosecutor, prior to making the opening address for the prosecution, covering the Common Plan of Conspiracy.
U.S. Army Photo

To prove the charges in Point Two, Crimes Against Peace, was the task of H.M. Attorney General Sir Hartley Shawcross, Chief Prosecutor for the United Kingdom of Great Britian and Northern Ireland. On December 4, 1945, he began his opening statement by quoting Adolf Hitler: "I shall give a propagandist cause for starting the war, never mind whether it be true or not. The victor shall not be asked later on whether we tell the truth or not. In starting and making a war not the right is what matters but victory—the strongest has the right." He then outlined every illegal step that Germany made to take over the territories of other peoples in defiance of all treaties, covenants, and assurances.

On January 17, 1946, M. François de Menthon, Chief Prosecutor for the French Republic, opened the prosecution's case to prove counts Three and Four: War Crimes and Crimes Against Humanity as perpetrated by the defendants. On Hitler's fiendish race-myth concept he charged: "In the midst of the twentieth century Germany goes back, of her own free will, beyond Christianity and civilization to the primitive barbarity of ancient Germany. She makes a deliberate break with all the universal conceptions of modern nations. The National Socialist doctrine, which raised inhumanity to the level of a principle, constitutes, in fact, a doctrine of disintegration of modern society." He reviewed the war criminality of the Nazis' forced-labor policy (including forcing persons to work for the German war effort) in the countries they overran; the seizure of agricultural and industrial products from these countries; the debasement of their currencies by outrageous indemnities. Coming to the climax of his speech, he said: "The crime which will undoubtedly be remembered as the most horrible committed by the Germans against the civilian population of the occupied countries was that of deportation and internment in the concentration camps of Germany." Next, M. de Menthon stated: "Crimes committed against prisoners of war, although less known, bear ample testimony to the degree of inhumanity which Nazi Germany had attained." He gave specific policies and instances.

Sir Hartley Shawcross, chief prosecutor for the United Kingdom of Great Britain and Northern Ireland, presents to the court the charges in Point Two of the Indictment: Crimes Against Peace.
U.S. Army Photo

General R. A. Rudenko, chief prosecutor for the USSR, delivers the final argument for the prosecution.
U.S. Army Photo

François de Menthon, chief prosecutor for the French, pours out an impassioned address covering the charges under Points Three and Four of the Indictment: War Crimes and Crimes Against Humanity.
U.S. Army Photo

As a definition of crimes against persons and property, he offered:

The crimes against person and property, of which the defendants are guilty, are provided for by all national laws. They present an international character because they were committed in several different countries. . . . A crime of common law, the War Crime, is, nevertheless, not an ordinary infraction; it has a character peculiarly instrinsic—it is a crime committed on the occasion or under pretext of war. It must be punished because, even in time of war, attacks on the integrity of the physical being and of property are crimes if they are not justified by the laws and customs of war.

It was left to General R. A. Rudenko, Chief Prosecutor for the Union of Soviet Socialist Republics, starting on February 8, 1946, to review and sum up the entire charge of the prosecution. His presentation was more graphic, more descriptive of the tortures and terrible deaths than his colleagues had covered. In view of the far greater magnitude of crimes the Germans inflicted on Russian civilians and soldiers, this was understandable.

Addressing the judges directly, he said: "If your Honors please, I appear here as the representative of the Union of the Soviet Socialist Republics, which bore the main brunt of the blows of the fascist invaders and which vastly contributed to the smashing of Hitlerite Germany and its satellites. On behalf of the Soviet Union, I charge the defendants on all counts enumerated in Article VI of the Charter of the International Military Tribunal." He ended eloquently, if, in the light of today's world situation, with unintentional irony:

In the name of the sacred memory of millions of innocent victims of the fascist terror, for the sake of the consolidation of peace throughout the world, for the sake of the future security of nations, we are presenting the defendants with a just and complete account which must be settled. This is an account on behalf of all mankind, an account backed by the will and conscience of all freedom-loving nations.

May justice be done!

❊   ❊   ❊

These photographs from the book containing the report of the German commander responsible for clearing the ghetto in Warsaw, Poland, were presented as evidence against the Nazi defendants at Nuremberg.

U.S. Army Photos

It would be impossible to attempt to condense the more than forty-five large volumes of testimony and documents that encompassed the trial proceedings at Nuremberg. The prosecutors, their staffs, and all those who engaged in gathering evidence and witnesses to prove the guilt of the defendants had done their job well in the short time allotted them. In essence, the defendants' main defense was that they were merely carrying out orders from their superiors. Had they not, they would not now be on trial. In fact, as Göring remarked to a psychiatrist examining him in his cell, who asked if there were any "No men" at all in regard to the orders of the High Command: "Not aboveground!" And he laughed uproariously.

Each prisoner had his opportunity on the stand to state his case to the world. Each had a famous lawyer to offer his defense, then examine him on the stand in an attempt to show his innocence. But the mighty weight of documented evidence was too much for the defendants. After all of them had been given as long as they wanted to defend themselves, the four prose-cutors presented their closing arguments.

In the course of his closing address for the United States, Mr. Robert H. Jackson characterized the criminal activities of each of the defendants:

A glance over the dock will show that each defendant played a part that fitted in with every other, and that all advanced the common plan. It contradicts experience that men of such diverse backgrounds and talents should so forward each other's aims by coincidence.

The large and varied role of Göring was half militant and half gangster. He stuck a pudgy finger in every pie. He used his SA muscle-men to help bring the gang into power. In order to entrench that power he contrived to have the Reichstag burned, established the Gestapo, and created the concentration camps. He was equally adept at massacring opponents and at framing scandals to get rid of stubborn generals. He built up the Luftwaffe and hurled it at his defenseless neighbors. He was among the foremost in harrying the Jews out of the land. By mobilizing the total economic resources of Germany he made possible the waging of the war which he had taken a large part in planning. He was, next to Hitler, the man who tied the activities of all the defendants together in a common effort.

Reactions of some of the Nazi defendants in the dock at Nuremberg as the evidence piles up against them. *U.S. Army Photo*

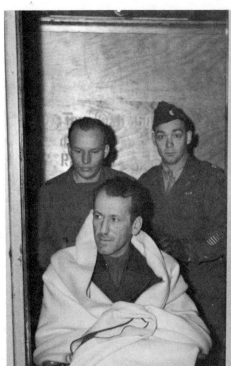

Ernst Kaltenbrunner, former
S.S. chief for Austria, being
wheeled into court after his
convalescence from a cranial
hemmorage, to take his place
in the defendant's row.
U.S. Army Photo

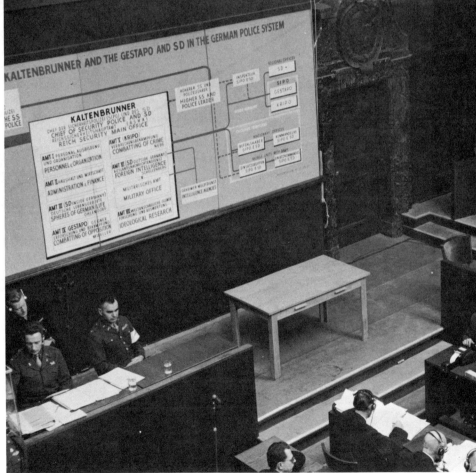

This chart illustrates the position of Kaltenbrunner in
the Nazi hierarchy, and fixes his responsibility for
issuing orders for his subordinates to follow.
U.S. Army Photo

The parts played by the other defendants, although less comprehensive and less spectacular than that of the Reichsmarshal, were nevertheless integral and necessary contributions to the joint undertaking, without any one of which the success of the common enterprise would have been in jeopardy. There are many specific deeds of which these men have been proven guilty. No purpose would be served—nor indeed is time available—to review all the crimes which the evidence has charged up to their names. Nevertheless, in viewing the conspiracy as a whole and as an operating mechanism it may be well to recall briefly the outstanding services which each of the men in the dock rendered to the common cause.

The zealot HESS, before succumbing to wanderlust, was the engineer tending the Party machinery, passing orders and propaganda down to the Leadership Corps, supervising every aspect of Party activities, and maintaining the organization as a loyal and ready instrument of power. When apprehensions abroad threatened the success of the Nazi scheme for conquest, it was the duplicitous RIBBENTROP, the salesman of deception, who was detailed to pour wine on the troubled waters of suspicion by preaching the gospel of limited and peaceful intentions. KEITEL, weak and willing tool, delivered the armed forces, the instrument of aggression, over to the Party and directed them in executing its felonious designs.

KALTENBRUNNER, the grand inquisitor, took up the bloody mantle of Heydrich to stifle opposition and terrorize compliance, and buttressed the power of National Socialism on a foundation of guiltless corpses. It was ROSENBERG, the intellectual high priest of the "master race," who provided the doctrine of hatred which gave the impetus for the annihilation of Jewry, and put his infidel theories into practice against the Eastern occupied territories. His wooly philosophy also added boredom to the long list of Nazi atrocities. The fanatical FRANK, who solidified Nazi control by establishing the new order of authority without law, so that the will of the Party was the only test of legality, proceeded to export his lawlessness to Poland, which he governed with the lash of Caesar and whose population he reduced to sorrowing remnants. FRICK, the ruthless organizer, helped the Party to seize power, supervised the police agencies to insure that it stayed in power, and chained the economy of Bohemia and Moravia to the German war machine.

STREICHER, the venomous vulgarian, manufactured and distributed obscene racial libels which incited the populace to accept and assist the progressively savage operations of "race purification." As Minister of Economics FUNK accelerated the pace of rearmament, and as Reichsbank president banked for the SS the gold teeth fillings of concentration camp victims—

M. Champetier de Ribes, French prosecutor at the Nuremberg Trial, makes his closing speech on July 29, 1946. *National Archives*

probably the most ghoulish collateral in banking history. It was SCHACHT, the facade of starched respectability, who in the early days provided the window dressing, the bait for the hesitant, and whose wizardry later made it possible for Hitler to finance the colossal rearmament program, and to do it secretly.

DOENITZ, Hitler's legatee of defeat, promoted the success of the Nazi aggressions by instructing his pack of submarine killers to conduct warfare at sea with the illegal ferocity of the jungle. RAEDER, the political admiral, stealthily built up the German navy in defiance of the Versailles Treaty, and then put it to use in a series of aggressions which he had taken a large part in planning. VON SCHIRACH, poisoner of a generation, initiated the German youth in Nazi doctrine, trained them in legions for service in the SS and Wehrmacht, and delivered them up to the Party as fanatic, unquestioning executors of its will.

SAUCKEL, the greatest and cruelest slaver since the Pharaohs of Egypt, produced desperately needed manpower by driving foreign people into the land of bondage on a scale unknown even in the ancient days of tyranny in the kingdom of the Nile. JODL, betrayer of the traditions of his profession, led the Wehrmacht in violating its own code of military honor in order to carry out the barbarous aims of Nazi policy. VON PAPEN, pious agent of an infidel regime, held the stirrup while Hitler vaulted into the saddle, lubricated the Austrian annexation, and devoted his diplomatic cunning to the service of Nazi objectives abroad.

SEYSS-INQUART, spearhead of the Austrian fifth-column, took over the government of his own country to make a present of it to Hitler, and then, moving north, brought terror and oppression to the Netherlands and pillaged its economy for the benefit of the German juggernaut. VON NEURATH, the old-school diplomat, who cast the pearls of his experience before the Nazis, guided Nazi diplomacy in the early years, soothed the fears of prospective victims, and as Reich Protector of Bohemia and Moravia, strengthened the German position for the coming attack on Poland. SPEER, as Minister of Armaments and War Production, joined in planning and executing the program to dragoon prisoners of war and foreign workers into German war industries which waxed in output while the laborers waned in starvation. FRITZSCHE, radio propaganda chief, by manipulation of the truth goaded German public opinion into frenzied support of the regime and anesthetized the independent judgment of the population so that they did without question their masters' bidding. And BORMANN, who has not accepted our invitation to this reunion, sat at the throttle of the vast and powerful engine of the Party, guiding it in the ruthless execution of Nazi policies, from the scourging of the Christian Church to the lynching of captive Allied airmen.

*　　*　　*

Now it was the judges' turn to render their verdict. It was a lengthy one, and took the two days of September 30, and October 1, 1946. On the former day, judgments were rendered against the groups and organizations on trial; on the latter date, against individuals. Each defendant was called before the judges separately and each given his judgment:

GÖRING: Guilty on all 4 counts: Death.

HESS: Guilty on counts 1 and 2: Life imprisonment.

VON RIBBENTROP: Guilty on all 4 counts: Death.

KEITEL: Guilty on all 4 counts: Death.

ROSENBERG: Guilty on all 4 counts: Death.

FRANK: Guilty on counts 3 and 4: Death.

FRICK: Guilty on counts 2, 3, and 4: Death.

STREICHER: Guilty on count 4: Death.

FUNK: Guilty on counts 2, 3, and 4: Life imprisonment.

SCHACHT: Not guilty.

DOENITZ: Guilty on counts 2 and 3: Ten years' imprisonment.

RAEDER: Guilty on counts 1, 2, and 3: Life imprisonment.

VON SCHIRACH: Guilty on count 4: Twenty years' imprisonment.

SAUCKEL: Guilty on counts 3 and 4: Death.

JODL: Guilty on all 4 counts: Death.

VON PAPEN: Not guilty.

SEYSS-INQUART: Guilty on counts 2, 3, and 4: Death.

SPEER: Guilty on counts 3 and 4: Twenty years' imprisonment.

VON NEURATH: Guilty on all 4 counts: Fifteen years' imprisonment.

FRITZSCHE: Not guilty.

KALTENBRUNNER: Guilty on counts 3 and 4: Death.

BORMANN (*in absentia*): Guilty on counts 3 and 4: Death.

Of the organizations on trial, the SS, the SD, the Gestapo, and the Leadership Corps of the Nazi Party were declared criminal organizations; acquitted were the Reich Cabinet, and the General Staff and High Command of the German Armed Forces.

Those who received the death sentence were executed at Nuremberg on October 16, 1946, with the exception of Göring, who managed to cheat the hangman's noose by taking poison in his cell the day before. Those who received prison sentences were put behind bars in the Spandau jail, under the administration of the four Allied Powers.

*　　*　　*

That the Nuremberg Trials established a historic and momentous precedent no nation would deny. Here in the case of the major war criminals, and later at the many trials of the lesser defendants, international justice against war criminals was carried out in fact, whereas after all previous wars it was carried out only by historical condemnation. Once for all, the political and military leaders of any nation starting an aggressive war, ordering mass exterminations, drafting others into slave labor, and killing and torturing prisoners of war in violation of the rules of war were put on notice that they would eventually be brought before a court of international justice to answer for these crimes.

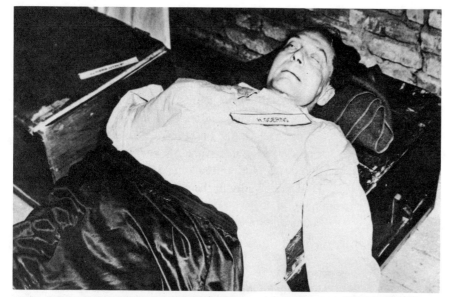

Hermann Göring cheats the hangman's noose by committing suicide with poison in his prison cell shortly before the scheduled time for his hanging.
U.S. Army Photo

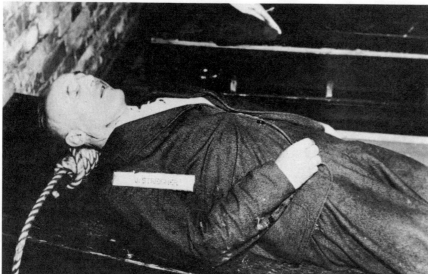

Julius Streicher, one of the twelve Nazi defendants sentenced to death by hanging.
U.S. Army Photo

Hjalmar Schacht, one of the three Nazi defendants who were acquitted.
U.S. Army Photo

Nuremberg, however, leaves basic international questions unanswered, and the answers will continue to be found in the realm of political reality rather than political morality. The victors will continue to decide what crimes have been committed, and the vanquished alone will have to pay for these acts. For some people, the crime in Vietnam was the bombing of the territory and the installations of the North, and they hold American political and military leaders responsible, as well as pilots and bombardiers. To others, it was the maltreatment of the pilots who were captured by the North, and the unwillingness of the northern regime to recognize them as prisoners of war, albeit an undeclared one. How well the common soldiers on the battlefield will heed their superiors is something else again, but such an order does further a vital principle. At last, nations are recognizing that moral wrongs have now become legal wrongs.

Along with a mandate to bring accused war criminals to trial, the charter of the International Military Tribunal clearly stated that each defendant would be given a fair trial, thus outlawing a drumhead court-martial of the leaders of a defeated country. The conduct of the trial itself could not have been more fair to the defendants than that of Nuremberg. They received their sentences after full opportunity to defend themselves, and each was judged on the evidence alone, and not on vague charges and suspicions.

All nations are now bound by the legal precedents established at Nuremberg. As Justice Jackson stated: "While this law is first applied against German aggressors, the law includes, and if it is to serve a useful purpose it must condemn aggression by any other nations, including those which sit here now in judgment." On December 11, 1946, the United Nations affirmed the principles of international law recognized by the charter of the Nuremberg Trials.

Among the aspects of the Nuremberg Trials that were precedent-making and that have disturbed some social thinkers is the one that the trials presumably involved ex post facto law. Many of the crimes for which the defendants were found guilty were not, in a narrow and legal sense, crimes in their own country at the time that the acts took place. In fact, the very opposite was the essence of the accusation: that the defendants, when in power, failed to define these acts against humanity as crimes. Nuremberg established, as would the Eichmann case later, that when behavior involves acts of such enormity that they are in conflict with the nature of civilization and the elementary standards of human existence, they are crimes for which the perpetrators are responsible, even though they may contravene no written national law.

It would be utopian to think that the new international law laid down at Nuremberg will put an end to wars. The United States was for many years engaged in a massive undeclared war in Vietnam, and although some European and American intellectuals held an "unofficial war crimes trial," there could be no serious talk of another Nuremberg, once the war was over. And the same could be said of the Soviet invasion of Afghanistan, and the continuing American war in Nicaragua, and the crimes of the South African government against the majority of the peoples under its rule.

Nonetheless, it is practical and expedient to hope that all those participating in such activities will be influenced by the Nuremberg precedent with regard to how each leadership conducts its part in national and international activities, how each nation conducts itself in a war and in relationship with its own people, how each treats captured civilians and prisoners of war, and how each is bound by the rules of modern warfare as laid down in the conventions and treaties formulated between 1907 and 1928.

Cardinal Joseph Mindszenty folds his arms and listens intently to
the final testimony at his trial in the Peoples' Court in Budapest.
Wide World Photos

Cardinal Joseph Mindszenty

[1949]

"ON THE MORNING OF FEBRUARY 3, 1949, THE SPECIAL Senate of the Budapest People's Court began hearing the case of Jozsef Mindszenty and his accomplices." Thus began the indictment against the leading Catholic prelate in Hungary, brought to trial by the Hungarian Communist State as the culmination of a gigantic power struggle between Church and State. The trial assumed international proportions when attempts were made to link the American Minister to Hungary, Arthur Schoenfeld, and later, his successor Selden Chapin, and Cardinal Spellman of New York, to an alleged plot by Mindszenty to enlist foreign aid in overthrowing the Hungarian Communist régime and reestablishing the monarchy of Otto Hapsburg.

From a strictly legal viewpoint, if what Cardinal Mindszenty admitted to at his trial were indeed true, then the court had no choice but to find him guilty of the charges in the indictment. But the big question was whether intense torture was inflicted on the cardinal prior to the trial and whether drugs were used to induce him to confess his "crimes." It was known that at one point he was interrogated for eighty-two hours, all the while standing on his feet, before he finally collapsed. When he appeared in court for trial, those who knew him hardly recognized the man.

The charges against Prince Primate Joseph Mindszenty were threefold: "Of having committed once continuously the crime of having directed an organization which aimed at the overthrow of the democratic order and of the Re-public; of having committed once continuously the crime of treason; of having committed once continuously the crime of failing to declare foreign currencies, and speculating."

These charges were based on the following: that after the enactment of Law VII, 1946, for the protection of the Hungarian Communist State, the cardinal took formal steps to contact Otto Hapsburg and set up a legitimist organization to overthrow the Communist régime, to which end he attempted to enlist American aid in an armed intervention; that he illegally brought into the country $141,000 and 15,000 Swiss francs, but declared only $4,800, then proceeded to convert much of it on the black market into Hungarian forint, gravely endangering the Hungarian economy.

After the indictment had been read, the president announced that Mindszenty had written a letter to the minister of justice, which was then read. It requested that his part in the trial be canceled, in order to remove himself as an obstacle to an agreement between the Church and the State. "Before the trial, which is soon to open," wrote the cardinal, "I voluntarily admit that I have committed the acts I am charged with according to the penal code of the State. In the future I shall always judge the external and internal affairs of the State on the basis of the full sovereignty of the Hungarian Republic." Thus he sought to resolve the foremost question of the moment that was vital to the peace and tranquillity of the Hungarian Communist State.

This capitulation, after years of Church-State struggle, offered for the good of his country and his people, was rejected, and the trial proceeded. It was conducted by the president, Dr. Vilmos Olti, a former Nazi who joined the Communist Party in 1945. In a Hungarian court it is the president who asks most of the questions, with an occasional yielding to the state prosecutor, in this case Guyla Alapi; to another member of the court, or, very rarely, to the counsel for the defense. The cards were well stacked, and all the defendants gave the expected answers. The questions followed the lines laid down in the charges, and easily proved that the charges were correct. There was no such thing as cross-examination by the defendant's counsel; no witnesses on either side were called; only the defendants were questioned, and this along court-approved lines. Each defendant was given his "hearing." This took less than two days. On the third day the prosecutor made his final speech. He pointed out that the trial had been completely open and fair, that no religious issues had even been mentioned, that it was not the cardinal who was on trial, but Joseph Mindszenty, Hungarian citizen, who had committed major crimes. "On the basis of the evidence produced," he declared, "there is no doubt that Mindszenty and his ac-

The friends and supporters of Cardinal Mindszenty were shocked at his physical appearance when he appeared in court after his ordeal of torture and interrogation in jail. The photo on the right shows the cardinal as he looked three years previous to his 1949 trial.
Wide World Photos

complices wanted to resurrect the kingdom in Hungary. . . . In order to attain their purposes, the main defendant and his accomplices got in touch with imperialist politicians, who hate popular democracies . . . to make them believe that there was a strong legitimist movement existing in Hungary . . . that Hungarian people would welcome the outbreak of a new war." He then covered the points brought out against the defendants on the second charge of political treason, and followed with the charge of illegal dealings in foreign currency. He ended: "Let the verdict of the People's Court be a salutary one; let it deal a heavy blow to the traitors, spies, and betrayers of the Hungarian people."

Dr. Kálman Kiczkó, Cardinal Mindszenty's counsel, summed up for the defense by simply agreeing that his client had harmed the state, and pointed out that the cardinal had admitted doing so. He appealed to the court for a lenient sentence.

The final words at a Hungarian trial are spoken by the defendants. In his final plea to the court, Cardinal Mindszenty reiterated his hope for a reconciliation of Church and State in Hungary: "I thank God that having strictly searched my mind, I cannot find myself guilty of being an enemy of peace. When the time came for the Church to make peace with the State, I was not against peace; I merely strictly outlined the preconditions therefore, and I sincerely meant that if we make peace, it should be a permanent one."

The court adjourned for two days; then returned and sentenced Cardinal Mindszenty to life imprisonment.

* * *

The Mindszenty trial shocked the world. It was natural that the Vatican should stoutly protest. But governments of most nations of the Western world denounced the proceedings and the verdict. The United States House of Representatives unanimously called for the United Nations to act against Hungary. The acting Hungarian consul general in New York resigned on the spot and sought asylum in the United States.

The trial itself was unfair in every respect on the questions of law and procedure as we, living under Anglo-Saxon law, know it. But could there not have been involved some *guilt with justification?* As in the case of Mary Queen of Scots, actions she vehemently denied at her trial could have been committed by her, and undoubtedly were, with justification in her devotion to the Catholic cause. Is it not equally plausible that Cardinal Mindszenty could have acted similarly in an equally just cause of dedicating himself to freeing his Hungarian people from what he considered the yoke of Hungarian Communist tyranny? Many Hungarian "Freedom Fighters" gave their lives for the same cause.

Cardinal Mindszenty in his Budapest residence on November 3, 1956. He had been freed five days earlier by Hungarian rebel forces. *Wide World Photos*

Morton Sobell, Julius Rosenberg, and Ethel Rosenberg leaving Federal Courthouse
on March 29 after the jury was locked up for the night by Judge Irving R. Kaufman.
Wide World Photos

Julius Rosenberg and his wife, Ethel, arriving at Federal Courthouse, New York.
Wide World Photos

28

Julius and Ethel Rosenberg and Morton Sobell

[1951]

WERE JULIUS AND ETHEL ROSENBERG EXECUTED ON THE night of June 19, 1953, and Morton Sobell sent to a living death of thirty years in prison, for a monstrous crime of treachery in which they sent the world into the Korean War, proliferated the atom bomb, gave away the greatest secrets of their country, and were responsible, as the sentencing judge declared, for a crime for which "millions of innocent people" might have to pay? Or were they the victims of the McCarthy era of hysteria, the fear that gripped the country in a Salem-like witch-hunt, convicted on flimsy, perjured, and framed-up evidence for a crime that may never have taken place? Or is there a point of truth between these two terrible extremes, where the accused may indeed have committed illegal acts far less monstrous than was charged, were found guilty despite many a reasonable and lingering doubt, and paid with a sentence unbelievably harsh and cruel? Somewhere the truth is to be found, and those who study the case are usually deeply partisan.

Called by the *Columbia Law Review* "the outstanding 'political' trial of this generation," the case of Julius and Ethel Rosenberg and Morton Sobell attracted worldwide attention that, although it has abated in its intensity, has never completely died.

The Second World War came to a quick end with the bombing of Hiroshima and Nagasaki. But if the atom bombs that wreaked havoc on these two Japanese cities brought in the aftermath of their tragedy a peace on earth, it was a troubled peace. For man had now fabricated a weapon so awesome in its powers of destruction that the planet itself was threatened. Although atomic energy was developed in the United States, it was the culmination of the work of scientists in England, France, Italy, Denmark, Germany, the Soviet Union, and else-

where, and the hope of some Americans that the secret of the atom could remain closeted within the confines of the United States was not widely shared in the world of science. Thus, the American monopoly became a marriage of atomic secret holders in the late summer of 1949, when the Soviet Union detonated its first atomic bomb, and the marriage in the years that followed was to become a not too exclusive club.

Soon after the end of World War II, with its shaky alliance between the Western powers and the Soviet Union, and with the outbreak of the undeclared yet bitter cold war, several British scientists were arrested as "atomic spies." They included Allan Nunn May, a Canadian who admitted his guilt and received ten years' imprisonment; May refused to divulge his accomplices, and seems to have been motivated by ideological considerations. And even more significant was Klaus Fuchs, head of the Theoretical Physics Division at a major British atomic-energy installation, who had traveled in the United States during the war, and who readily admitted his guilt.

Fuchs was arrested on February 2, 1950, and exactly one week later Joseph McCarthy inaugurated what came to be known as the McCarthy era with his talk in Wheeling, West Virginia.

Agents of the FBI were permitted to interview Fuchs, but how helpful he was to them is not certain, for he could offer no names and only the vaguest descriptions of his accomplices. Nevertheless, less than four months later, the first of these alleged accomplices was arrested: this was Harry Gold, a thirty-nine-year-old bachelor, a chemist who had held minor posts during the war in companies far removed from work on atomic bombs.

Following Gold, there were more arrests. The public was given an impression of a chain reaction, with one person leading to the next. The most sensational of the series, and the first involving atomic energy, came when a young machinist, David Greenglass, was arrested and held in $100,000 bail. Greenglass had been stationed at Los Alamos during the war, and was charged with having passed the secret of the bomb on to Harry Gold.

Greenglass was arraigned in early June, 1950, and in the middle of July the FBI announced that Greenglass had talked and had implicated his sister's husband, Julius Rosenberg. Now there was one more arrest, one more person held in bail of $100,000. Between the arrest of Greenglass and Rosenberg, McCarthy's influence rose to new heights, and America was facing the Communist world, for the first time, in a shooting war: Korea. On August 11, there came another arrest, that of Ethel Rosenberg, sister of David and wife of Julius. Finally, one week later, Morton Sobell was arrested in Texas, just across the border from Mexico. Why he had been in Mexico, and how he came to Texas, remain disputed points to this day.

The trial of the United States v. Julius Rosenberg, Ethel Rosenberg, and Morton Sobell opened in the Federal Courthouse in New York City on March 6, 1951. Anatoli Yakovlev, a former Soviet consular official, was named in the indictment, although he was now in the Soviet Union. David Greenglass, a co-conspirator, had pleaded guilty; also named as co-conspirators, not being tried, were Harry Gold and David's wife, Ruth Greenglass. Before the trial, the defendants had been called the "atom spies" in the press, often in statements that came from the FBI and from the prosecution.

In his opening statement, Irving Saypol, chief prosecutor, emphasized the Communist affiliations of the defendants, said that the defendants' "love of Communism and the Soviet Union soon led them into a Soviet espionage ring," and continued:

We will prove that the Rosenbergs devised and put into operation, with the aid of Soviet . . . agents in this country, an elaborate scheme which enabled them to steal through David Greenglass this one weapon, that might well hold the key to the survival of this nation and means the peace of the world, the atomic bomb.

Against Morton Sobell the prosecution presented one witness, Max Elitcher, who testified that Julius Rosenberg had admitted espionage to him and that Rosenberg, in an effort to induce Elitcher to be drawn into the ring, had implicated the latter's close friend and neighbor, Sobell. But Elitcher then went on to state that Sobell had denounced Rosenberg for mentioning his name. No connection was made between Sobell and atomic spying, and only the most tenuous between Sobell and spying. The defense countered by showing that Elitcher feared prosecution for perjury for having denied under oath his former membership in the Communist Party, and showed that he had never been indicted.

Sobell's Communist association was clear; his close association with the Rosenbergs threw a shadow over him. On advice of counsel he failed to take the stand; the counsel felt the case against him was so weak that his own testimony would be unnecessary and that he might prove vulnerable on cross-examination; juries, however, notoriously draw conclusions against defendants under such circumstances. And against Sobell was his Mexican trip, which had all the earmarks of flight and of panic, with inquiry about foreign ports, the use of numerous aliases, and other indications that he feared return to the United States. Despite the protestations over the years that he did indeed plan to return, he left many signs that such were not his intentions. Perhaps his defenders would be more convincing if they asserted that he was indeed in flight but that the flight could well have been motivated by fear rather than by guilt.

Such was the case against Morton Sobell, for which a jury found him guilty beyond a reasonable doubt, and for which a judge sentenced him to thirty years in jail.

Against Julius and Ethel Rosenberg, the case rested primarily on the testimony of her brother, David Greenglass. He claimed that Julius Rosenberg had induced him to write up secret information on the Los Alamos atomic bomb project, which Ethel typed. It was arranged that David, through his wife, Ruth, would pass other classified information on to an agent whom Julius would send to Albuquerque. One side of a Jello box was cut into two pieces, in an irregular fashion, David testified; and he was given one piece and Julius said that the messenger would come with the second. That messenger eventually arrived: he was Harry Gold, who said, "Julius sent me." And Gold had his half of the Jello box. When Gold left, he gave David $500, and the next day Ruth deposited $400 in her account. David Greenglass, corroborated by his wife, insisted that after the arrest of Fuchs, Julius had urged him to flee from the United States, offering him large sums of money and assistance to go abroad.

Next came Harry Gold to the witness stand. He neither mentioned nor implicated Sobell, and only in an indirect manner did he implicate the Rosenbergs. Mainly he recited the story of his own espionage and of his dealings with the Soviet official Yakovlev. But he did corroborate many parts of Greenglass's testimony: that he had been in Albuquerque, that he had met David, had turned money over to him, and had received from David an envelope, which the latter said contained "the secret of the atom bomb."

For the defense, Julius and Ethel Rosenberg each took the stand, and each made a complete denial. They recounted their dealings with the Greenglasses, their business difficulties and animosities. Much of the cross-examination of the defendants had nothing to do with spying; it involved their relations with Communist and even anti-Fascist organizations.

On Wednesday, March 28, 1951, the case went to the jury; and the following day a verdict was brought in of guilty against the three defendants. On April 5, they came before Judge Kaufman for sentencing: for the Rosenbergs, it was to be death; for Sobell, thirty years, to which the judge added: "While it may be gratuitous on my part, I at this point note my recommendation against parole."

In the two-year period that followed, there were appeals, motions for clemency, efforts to make a deal with the prisoners whereby they would be saved in return for a confession, and steadfast reiteration of their innocence on the part of the defendants. Throughout Europe and South America, demonstrations numbering thousands and tens of thousands called for the sparing of the lives of the Rosenbergs. "They shall not die"—the refrain that had been heard for two Italian immigrants and some poverty-stricken Negro youths—now reverberated on the streets of London, Paris, and other cities of the world. Nobel Prize winners cast their doubts on the proofs presented at the trial. Albert Einstein, the pope, the daughter of Alfred Dreyfus, and the sister of Bartolomeo Vanzetti all urged clemency. But in vain, and on Friday, June 19, 1953, early in the evening, so as to avoid a killing on the Sabbath, lest the Lord be insulted that His day of rest be violated, the Rosenbergs were put to death.

But a growing body of opinion in America has not put the case to rest. McCarthyism passed, and Sobell remained in jail, spending in fact several years at Alcatraz. While those who have confessed wartime treachery against the United States in the service of the enemy have since walked out of prison gates as free men, he remained behind bars, although a simple admission of his guilt would have unlocked the doors to his freedom. In the years since the trial, many highly placed Americans—professors, clergymen, jurists, and others—have denounced the manner in which Sobell was brought to the United States. That he was not "deported," as the American authorities contended, is apparent. He seems to have been kidnapped and brought illegally across the border, all in violation of the criminal laws of Mexico. It was a drama that was to be repeated some years later by Israel in the Eichmann case. But here the analogy ends, for if the many doubts in the Eichmann matter can be settled in favor of the Israeli government, it is only because of the unprecedented enormity of a crime against humanity.

Many aspects of the Rosenberg-Sobell case remain puzzling. They were convicted of wartime espionage, but it is generally admitted that the death penalty for espionage in wartime was meant to be directed exclusively against one's enemies, not one's allies.

The evidence against the three was meager, but it was not entirely absent. Yet, as the story continues to be studied, more questions arise, and fewer are settled. A tape recording of Gold's statement to his attorney, a highly prestigious Republican, reveals many discrepancies between this first statement and the testimony in court; not the least serious was his failure to mention the name "Julius" at any point in the tape. It may be but a slight oversight, but it is just about the only link that Gold made with Rosenberg.

Then there is the $400 that Ruth Greenglass deposited the day after Gold's visit. A study of her bank statements showed that this was only one of many mysterious cash deposits made at the time, deposits that in fact exceeded the income that the Greenglasses had. Yet this information was never presented in court. Where did the money come from? Was it from a black-market operation, for which David Greenglass felt himself vulnerable?

But nothing throws the entire case into doubt quite so much as the statements of some of the outstanding authorities on atomic energy that Greenglass was a poorly educated mechanic, with neither knowledge of nor access to scientific material, and that the high-secret information that he allegedly passed on to Gold, at the behest of Julius Rosenberg, was practically worthless. Dr. Philip Morrison, said to be co-holder of the patent on the Nagasaki bomb, called the Greenglass sketch "a caricature" of the bomb; while Dr. Henry Linschitz said that it was "too incomplete, ambiguous and even incorrect to be of any service or value to the Russians in shortening the time required to develop their nuclear bombs."

For this information, a judge said that "millions more of innocent people may pay the price of your treason. Indeed, by your betrayal, you have undoubtedly altered the course of history to the disadvantage of your country."

There is here a glaring and tragic inconsistency, for which two people gave their lives, and another person, protesting his innocence, was repeatedly denied parole after becoming eligible, and was denied release even after time served made his freedom mandatory. By court order, Morton Sobell was freed on January 14, 1969, after spending 18 years and 5 months in prison, and continues to devote his time to the vindication of the Rosenbergs and himself. The most recent studies have led many to the conclusion that there may have been some guilt on the part of Julius Rosenberg, little or none by the others, and that government wrongdoing in the course of the trial was so blatant that it exceeded the worst fears of the accused and their defenders.

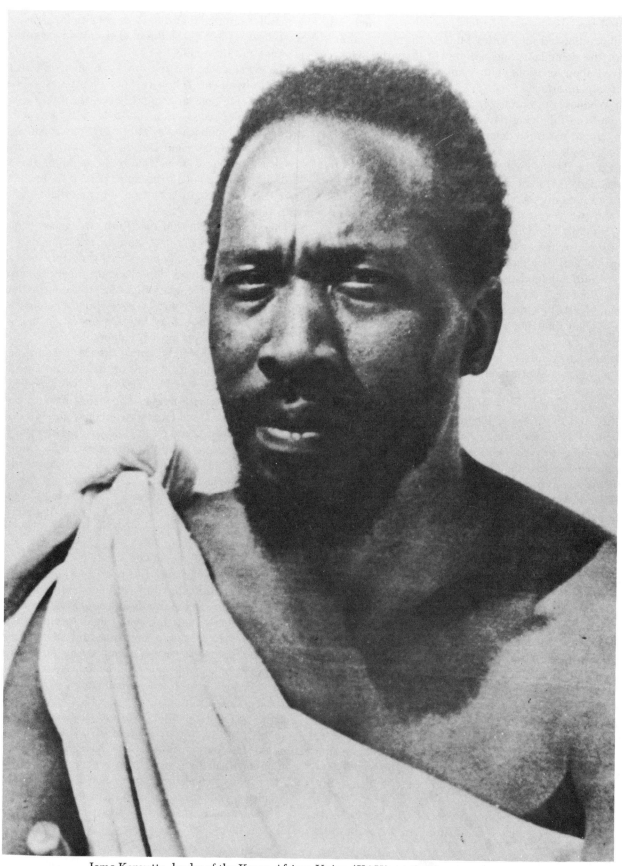

Jomo Kenyatta, leader of the Kenya African Union (KAU), at the time he was on trial in 1952 for managing a Mau Mau reign of terror in British East Africa.
Wide World Photos

29

Jomo Kenyatta

[1952]

MANY OF THE BEST-KNOWN FIGURES OF THE TWENTIETH century arose out of the struggles of colonial peoples for independence: Gandhi and Nehru in India, Sukarno in Indonesia, Luthuli in South Africa, Mboya in Kenya. But few figures among them emerge more majestic and noble than that of Jomo Kenyatta.

Kenya is a vast and rich land, sheltering many tribes, where numerous languages are spoken. As a country it takes its name from Mount Kenya, a volcanic mountain that rises some 17,000 feet above sea level, one of the highest points on the continent. And once—only a short time ago—it was part of the empire on which the sun never set; ruled by the Colonial Office, it was but one section of British East Africa.

The largest single group in Kenya are the Kikuyus, a tall, broad-shouldered people who tilled the soil, lived by the hunt, and produced, among their number, Jomo Kenyatta. Born in the latter part of the nineteenth century —perhaps in 1893, although the exact year is not known —Kenyatta in his youth became dedicated to righting the wrongs that he felt had been perpetrated by white settlers and colonialists against the natives.

In 1915, the Crown Land Ordinance had been passed by the British, which had the effect of expropriating "all land occupied by the African tribes of the Colony." The Kikuyus complained that they had become tenants on their own lands, and agitation for land reform became a major rallying cry of the natives.

Traveling to England to study as a young man, Kenyatta mastered anthropology under the great scholar Bronislaw Malinowski; he wrote *Facing Mount Kenya*, the story of his people, sometimes considered the best anthropological study of a primitive people written by one of their members. Kenyatta became active among African exiles and lovers of freedom; he spent some time in Mos-

cow; and then, in his mid-forties, returned to what was still British East Africa. He discovered that during the Second World War, the leading organization of his people, the Kikuyu Central Association, had been banned. Unable to have the ban lifted, he became prominent in the organization of a new group, the Kenya African Union (which came to be known as KAU, usually pronounced like the English word *cow*). As president of KAU, Kenyatta agitated for the short-range goal of the redistribution of land controlled by white settlers, for a greater share of power by the natives, and at the same time for the long-range goal of freedom for Kenya from Britain.

Freedom was a word that in dozens, perhaps hundreds, of languages was sweeping the once dark continent, and the freedom movement took on many forms: parliamentary demands, proposals at the UN, demonstrations, sabotage, and terror. Nowhere was the terroristic freedom movement more in evidence than in Kenya, where it came to be known as the Mau Mau. The terrorists struck suddenly; they struck at night, and put fear into the hearts of whites and noncooperating natives. Seldom were the terrorists apprehended. The Colonial Office, however, hoped to reveal a link between KAU and the Mau Mau, and to halt the growing freedom movement and remove and discredit its greatest leader, Jomo Kenyatta.

Meanwhile, Kenyatta had been speaking before huge gatherings throughout Kenya. In a country in which people traveled by foot, and information, by word of mouth, his meetings brought tens of thousands streaming in from the countryside. On October 21, 1952, Kenyatta and five of his confederates in the KAU were "detained" and charged with secret membership in the outlawed organization of the Mau Mau.

Was there such an organization as the Mau Mau? Or was the terror the unorganized or amorphously organized work of individuals and small groups, without central direction? And to the extent that the Mau Mau (and not merely the acts of individuals) had a real existence, was there a connection between it and KAU? These were the legal questions facing the court in the trial of Jomo Kenyatta. For, strange as it may sound, the colonial authorities had outlawed the Mau Mau without proof that the thing they were banning ever existed.

Once again, as in Rennes, France, and Dayton, Tennessee, a little town of which few had ever heard and of which the British Colonial Office did not know the existence became the center of a world-famous trial. But Kapenguria was not Dayton. The nearest hotel facilities were twenty-four miles away; but even there the counsel for the defense could not hold a meeting, because Asiatic and African lawyers were banned from such conferences with their European colleagues. Kapenguria was a town without a telephone. The nearest law library was in Nairobi, hundreds of miles and at best several days' travel away. And Kapenguria was off limits to Kikuyu who did not have passes; and a pass to come to town was not readily available for friends of Kenyatta.

Charged with management of the Mau Mau were Kenyatta and his five co-defendants: Kubai, Kaggia, Ngei, Karumba, and Oneko. The Mau Mau had been declared illegal on August 12, 1950, and since the defendants were not charged with any terrorist acts themselves, it seemed unlikely that a British court would hear evidence that they had managed the organization before it was outlawed. Furthermore, because the six were detained on October 21, 1952, the management would have had to exist during the intervening twenty-six-month period. Nevertheless, although twenty-one incidents purporting to demonstrate the involvement of the defendants in the management of Mau Mau were introduced at the trial, five occurred before the organization had been outlawed.

The prosecution contended that when the Kikuyu Central Association, which had been fighting for land reform, was declared illegal, it went underground and secretly became the Mau Mau. It was also contended that Kenyatta headed it, and used KAU as the legal arm and the Mau Mau as the illegal one of his movement.

The trial in the little schoolroom opened on November 24, 1952, and was postponed until December 3, to await the arrival of the chief counsel for the defense, D. N. Pritt. Aiding Mr. Pritt were attorneys from Nigeria, Jamaica, India, and elsewhere. Only one member of the defense team, H. O. Davies, was an African; although counsel came from many parts of Africa, they were prevented from joining the trial.

When the trial convened on December 3, after bail was refused, Deputy Public Prosecutor Somerhough made the opening statement. He said that the charge was that of managing an unlawful society, but added that he would be unable to establish a very strong link between the defendants and the Mau Mau:

I would ask Your Honour to take notice of the prohibition of this Society published in the *Gazette* of the Colony, and its effective date which is 12th August 1950. The dates between which the charges are set are 12th August 1950 and 21st October 1952 the date on which the accused, or at least five of them, ceased to be free agents.

The Crown cannot bind themselves to any particular place in the Colony where this society was managed. The Society is Mau Mau. It is a Society which has no records.

Arrested with Kenyatta (*on left*) were Jesse Kariuki (*center*) and Achieng Oneko (*right*). *Wide World Photos*

When the trial opened for the second week, the defense was able to welcome Chaman Lall, one of the most prestigious members of the Indian bar, a member of the Supreme Court of Delhi and of the High Court of the Punjab. With the arrival of Lall, the international significance of the trial became more apparent.

An African girl, Tabitha, testified that she had stood at a doorway and heard Kenyatta talk about the administering of an oath. The prosecution sought to bring in a police officer to establish that the witness had told the same story to the police, and this led to a bitter exchange between the Magistrate and Mr. Pritt:

MAGISTRATE. I was hoping—Mr. Pritt will forgive me for saying so, I am quite sure—I was hoping you would by now have ceased to ask for reservation of cross-examination. You do not want to put your clients to any prejudice, of course, but I at the same time wish—you would appreciate my task is a most difficult task, and with all these reservations of cross-examination they do not make my task any easier.

PRITT. May I say this? I have reserved no witness's cross-examination longer than overnight. This is the only case I have ever heard of in my life in which the defendants on charges—serious charges—to which they might be sentenced to a sentence of seven years' imprisonment—very serious charges—it is the only case I have ever heard of in my life in which they have been prosecuted with no particulars of any description being given—particulars even being refused; and as each thing comes up, as each new incident comes up, I hear a completely new story, that I have never heard in my life, I do not know until four o'clock in the afternoon whether my clients have ever heard of it in their lives. I do not know whether they are going to tell me it is true, or a distortion, or a complete invention; and until four o'clock every afternoon, sir, I am as ignorant of it as any beggar in the streets of Nairobi— perhaps more ignorant. Therefore, it is utterly —and, of course, the moment they tell me "Well, such and such a witness can put this right" I have set in train a series of efforts to get this witness from three hundred miles away. Consequently, sir, whilst anybody regrets any inconvenience to a Court, the gross, cruel, deliberate injustices worked upon me by the Government of Kenya in insisting on having this trial up here, and the most unfortunate procedure, whereby we are put in complete ignorance of the thing we have to answer until half a day before we have to answer it, makes it, of course, quite impossible for me to do any more than I am doing.

MAGISTRATE. There are many cases—of course, your experience of cases in England is much wider and greater than mine—but there must of course be many cases where charges are made where the Defence do not know the details of the allegation. They know the nature of the charge, but not the details—dates, meetings, names and places. They do not know that until the evidence comes out.

PRITT. But since we have had applause from the back of the superiority of Kenya over England, let me say that never has any man in the whole course of history stood his trial in England in a single criminal court on a charge involving a sentence of seven years' penal servitude, without every line and tittle of the evidence that is to be given against him on his trial being given beforehand in committal proceedings in police courts, with the express intention that he shall know, as the Government of Kenya is determined I shall not know, that he shall know the case before him in time for him to answer.

MAGISTRATE. I think the answer to that is that Kenya is unfortunately suffering at the present time from an Emergency.

PRITT. I know, sir, it is because of that; and the Emergency is being taken advantage of by the Government of Kenya to give my clients the minimum chance to defend themselves. I am employed by my clients to see that they shall get as much, and I have your co-operation with me in that, sir, I am happy to say.

The trial continued through the first half of December, until the magistrate read an item in the *East African Standard* of December 13, in which a cable that Mr. Pritt had sent to several Labour members of Parliament was quoted:

I am protesting continuously, first against the inconvenience of holding the hearing in a remote region where one must send 280 miles to Nairobi to look up authorities on the frequently arising points of law, or get documents or witnesses.

There are no facilities for research or study nearer than Nairobi and no means even of eating nearer than Kitale, 24 miles away.

Secondly, against the trial being in a closed district, virtually causing the exclusion of the public from the court.

Thirdly, against the inexcusable exclusion of some counsel from the Colony and others from the district where the trial is being held, although the accused have asked for them.

In ALL—
All this makes the proper preparation of the Defence case almost impossible, greatly increases expenses and wastes time. It amounts in all to a denial of justice.

I feel so strongly on this that I have undertaken to remain without further fee, however many weeks the case lasts.

The only point upon which I have expressed satisfaction is that the District Commissioner provided better facilities for interviewing the accused and secured the services of a Kenya African Union official which were essential to the Defence by granting him an Entry Permit which had previously been refused by the authorities in Nairobi.

My accommodation in Kitale is good and my colleagues are being accommodated by friendly private citizens, but under conditions making the work difficult. But they refuse to complain.

The honor of a British magistrate had been touched. The counsel for the defense argued that he had intended no slight on the presiding judge, but only on the conditions and facilities in Kapenguria. But so affected was the judge that he could not continue, and had to go home and think the matter over until the next morning, at which time he returned, and announced that the trial would be adjourned until a contempt case against Mr. Pritt could be settled. This was indeed settled at the end of December in Nairobi, when the Supreme Court of Kenya acquitted Pritt of the charge, and back he came to Kapenguria for a reconvening of the trial on January 2, 1953.

It was a bitter trial that lasted five months. The official interpreter, D. A. G. Leakey, walked out in a huff when his impartiality and ability as a translator was challenged. A hymnbook became the center of dispute, and charges were made that KAU oaths in the book were actually Mau Mau oaths in disguise. Finally, the prosecution concluded its case; the defense made the usual arguments for dismissal, the prosecution the usual rebuttal; the plea was rejected, and the case continued. The witness was Jomo Kenyatta, who testified in English.

Under direct examination, Kenyatta told of his career, his travels and studies in Europe, his return to Africa, and of his activities for schools, for land, and for freedom.

Under further examination, Kenyatta was asked about the policies of KAU:

Q. Is it a fact that the KAU has struggled for better working conditions, for freedom of assembly, press and movement, and for equal rights for all Africans on constitutional lines?

A. Yes, that is so.

Q. Does the KAU believe in violence?

A. No; we do not believe in violence at all: we believe in negotiation, that is, we ask for our rights through constitutional means—through discussion and representation. We feel that the racial barrier is one of the most diabolical things that we have in this Colony, because we see no reason why all races in this country cannot work harmoniously together without any discrimination. That is one thing, together with many others, that we have been fighting, and we believe that if people of goodwill can work together they can eliminate that evil. We say that God did not discriminate when he put the people into the country. He put everybody into this world to live happily and to enjoy the gifts of nature that God has bestowed upon mankind.

MAGISTRATE. I think these answers are becoming too long; they are tending to be speeches.

LALL. Could you give us approximately the membership of KAU to date?

KENYATTA. I have forgotten exactly but I know it is over 100,000 members.

Q. Is there any other organisation of the Africans in this country?

A. No, not as far as I know.

(Attorney Lall asked Kenyatta about the allegedly terrorist organization):

Q. When did you first hear about the word Mau Mau?

A. The word Mau Mau came into being in 1950, I think, where we found the expression used in *The East African Standard*, and everybody was surprised. What is this Mau Mau? The word Mau Mau is not, as far as I know, and I claim to know a few of our languages, it does not belong to any of the languages that I do know.

Lall led Kenyatta to the discussion of the public meeting in which he, Kenyatta, called upon an audience of between 30,000 and 50,000 for a public curse on Mau Mau. It was a highlight of the direct examination, and might well establish Kenyatta as being as free from any connection with the organization as an opponent of it:

LALL. Public curse on?

KENYATTA. Public curse on Mau Mau.

Q. I see.

A. And hear the strongest curse we could put in public in Kikuyu. I called on the people, and asked them to say in unison, that is in Kikuyu. I do not know how to say it in English, but I said, "All those people who want to get— who agree we should get rid of Mau Mau, put up your hands." Now all these people—I mean it is not in Barazi in this paper, but in some of the other papers, in the *East African Standard*—it shows the photograph while the people are holding up their hands. . . . Thousands of people holding up their hands. And after that I told them to repeat after me the Kikuyu curse: "Ngai Mau Mau, Irothie Na Miri Ya Mikongoe Yehere Bururi biui biui," which means to say, that is, "the Mau Mau may disappear in— abyss— or something—where you may not be recovered when you have gone, 'Irothie na miri ya Mikongoe,' You can never be recovered again."

There was here a bitter argument among Kenyatta, Lall, the magistrate, and the interpreter over the correct translation of "the curse." When the interpreter agreed to accept Kenyatta's translation, he was reprimanded by the magistrate.

Kenyatta handled himself skillfully on cross-examination, avoiding every trap that sought to link him with terror or the Mau Mau, and at the same time careful never to denounce the natives who were struggling for freedom, and never to lose an opportunity to denounce the colonialists. Had he stirred up racial enmity, he was asked, and when he denied that he had, the prosecutor continued:

Q. Would you say that consistently to represent one section of the community as robbers and thieves is to stir racial dislike?

A. I will not say that—if I represent African opinion no less than European leaders represent European opinion, I do represent African opinion.

The prosecution and defense battled over the relevancy of the questions and answers, and the interrogation continued:

Q. I will put it the other way round. Have you represented consistently that the Europeans are robbers and thieves?

A. No. But I have said in that connection, and I think I have been right in saying so, that Europeans have a better share in the land. They have better position. That is, if I am qualified in a certain thing, being an African—and this is why I attack the colour bar—no matter whatever qualifications an African may have he always has a lesser pay because of his color, not according to his qualifications. That does not mean that I represent Europeans as wicked people, but I say there has been injustice, and as such I cannot be assumed to say that Europeans are bad. I say the law—

Here Kenyatta was interrupted. He was interrogated on a report of a meeting where he claimed to have denounced the Mau Mau; the report omitted any such denunciation, and he characterized the report as incomplete, as any journalistic item must be. He was supplicated to say a kind word about the British in Africa. Had they not abolished slavery? He answered that they had taken part in abolishing slavery, only to grab the land and reduce the natives to serfdom. And then, on Mau Mau and the terror:

SOMERHOUGH. You know, do you not, that Mau Mau is anti-European?

KENYATTA. We cannot say it is anti any particular race. It is anti-people, many people, it has killed many Africans, Asians, Europeans, so I think it is anti-society, but not anti any particular—it would not be right to say it is anti only one particular group of people.

Q. Yes. But its principal object is to drive the European out, according to what we have heard about the oath.

A. What we have heard about the oath, yes, but in practice we do not find it so. . . . What I say, they have been anti African and in practice they have killed Africans, they have killed Europeans, they have killed Indians, and therefore I say it is anti-society, anti-people, as a whole, not anti a particular group, African, European or Asian.

Q. My question was, according to the oath, the principal object was to drive the Europeans out?

A. According to what we have heard.

Q. And do you not agree that the conditions for driving Europeans out would be considerably improved if Africans, ignorant Africans, could be persuaded that it was the English who made them slaves?

A. I do not think so, sir, unless you are anti-truth.

After seven days of cross-examination, the prosecution came up with a theory that Mau Mau was a continuation of the banned Kikuyu Central Association, all with the same objects: to drive out the Europeans, and that all of this was in the hands of Jomo Kenyatta.

Summaries by defense and by prosecution followed, and the defense stressed the weakness of the evidence linking the defendants to Mau Mau. When did the connection take place? Where? In the presence of whom? Could a man be convicted because he had failed to de-nounce the terrorist group at a meeting? Or because a newspaper had not reported his denunciation?

For the prosecution, there was a stronger link:

The Crown's contention, of course, is that Mau Mau, or a society like Mau Mau, can only flourish in an atmosphere of hatred between races. It is not good telling Africans to drive out Europeans if they like Europeans. . . . If you can get the idea into people's heads that they are victims of theft, the victims of ill usage, you prepare the ground, and the next step is, "Well, let us turn out the thieves, let us turn them out, let us, if necessary, kill them."

Finally, on April 8, 1953, the magistrate brought in his decision. He went briefly over the evidence, pointed out that at no time did any of the accused utilize the court to denounce the Mau Mau. He said that he felt these defendants had organized and developed Mau Mau, and had used KAU as a cover for the terrorist group. Kenyatta then addressed the court, on behalf of himself and his co-defendants:

We look forward to the day when peace shall come to this land and that the truth shall be known that we, as African leaders, have stood for peace. None of us would be happy or would condone the mutilation of human beings. We are humans and we have families and none of us will ever condone such activities as arson, etc.

Without taking up much more of your time, I will tell Your Honour that we as political bodies or political leaders stand constitutionally by our demands which no doubt are known to you and to the Government of this country, and in saying this I am asking for no mercy at all on behalf of my colleagues. We are asking that justice may be done and that the injustices that exist may be righted. No doubt we have grievances, and everybody in this country, high or low, knows perfectly well that there are such grievances, and it is those grievances which affect the African people that we have been fighting for. We will not ask to be excused for asking for those grievances to be righted.

I do not want to take up more of your time, Your Honour. All that I wish to tell you is that we feel strongly that at this time the Government of this country should try to strangle the only organisation, that is the Kenya African Union, of which we are the leaders, who have been working for the betterment of the African people and who are seeking harmonious relations between the races. To these few remarks, Your Honour, I may say that we do not accept your finding of guilty. It will be our duty to instruct our lawyer to take this matter up and we intend to appeal to a higher Court. We believe that the Supreme Court of Kenya will give us justice because we stand for peace; we stand for the rights of the African people, that Africans may find a place among the nations.

Now came the moment of sentencing, and the magistrate addressed himself to Kenyatta, the mastermind behind the plan of driving all Europeans from Kenya:

You have much to answer for and for that you will be punished.

The maximum sentences which this Court is empowered to pass are the sentences which I do pass, and I can only comment that in my opinion they are inadequate for what you have done.

The sentence was for seven years' imprisonment at hard labor, with recommendation that he be restricted for the remainder of his life thereafter:

Make no mistake about it, Mau Mau will be defeated, and although there may be more crimes of violence, more murders, more arson and more terror, the rule of law and the forces of law and order will prevail in the long run, even though the way may be hard and difficult.

The other defendants received the same sentence (although one was freed on appeal), and the London *Times* announced, some time later, that "Jomo Kenyatta will probably spend the rest of his life in the remote northern frontier district of Kenya."

Thus the defendants went off to jail, and some of the predictions proved true, and some quite false. There were more murders, more arson, more terror; the Mau Mau was not dead. The position of the British became increasingly difficult. A jailed martyr was now more revered than ever. And the terror continued. Among its victims were Dr. Leakey and his wife, perhaps murdered in reprisal for the position he took at the trial. At one time, there were at least 50,000 natives in detention camps, and the cost of the campaign against the Mau Mau became so burdensome that millions of pounds had to be poured into the colony.

In 1957, for the first time, the Kenya legislature had African and Asian members, and in the election of February 28, 1961, the Kenya African National Union won a majority of the seats. Tom Mboya, youthful leader of the party, had campaigned on the slogan, "Freedom and Kenyatta." In August, 1961, Kenyatta was freed, and at a meeting in Nairobi attended by some 30,000 Africans, unrestrained in their enthusiasm, Kenyatta was introduced as "a second god." Free, and the recognized leader of Kenya, president of its leading political party, and one of the most powerful and best-loved figures on the African continent, Kenyatta called for a land without discrimination, where citizens of all races and colors would be treated as equals. The man who had been sentenced to prison by the British magistrate, and who had been expected by the *Times* to spend the remainder of his life in virtual confinement, became the first prime minister of the Crown colony and protectorate on June 1, 1963, and was welcomed with ceremony and pomp by the Africans and the British as the first prime minister of the independent nation of Kenya on December 12, 1963. Like Dreyfus, he returned a hero; but to his own people, unlike Dreyfus, he had never ceased to be one.

Whether there was a formal connection between the Mau Mau and the KAU is difficult to establish today; that there seems to have been a division of labor, in which legal and illegal actions were developed side by side, seems apparent. That it proved effective in Kenya seems to be the verdict of history; whether nonviolence would have been equally successful will long be argued by those who followed the career and the trial of Jomo Kenyatta.

After nine years' detention imposed by the British authorities in the African colony, Jomo Kenyatta was released on August 14, 1961. Here he is surrounded by his followers and interviewers.
Wide World Photos

While the whites in Kenya feared him, the Africans revered him. Released from prison about a year before this picture was taken, Jomo Kenyatta campaigns for political power. When he mounted a speaking platform, in his black leather jacket and tribal cap, he flicked a fly whisk over his shoulder and shouted, "Uhuru," Swahili for "Freedom."
Wide World Photos

Victorious on May 27, 1963, in the Kenya parliamentary elections for the British East African Colony, Jomo Kenyatta (*right*) and Tom Mboya, Secretary General of the Kenya African National Union, join hands and wave plumes. Victory meant that former British prisoner Kenyatta would become Prime Minister of the colony.
Wide World Photos

Steven Truscott, fourteen, the
day after he was convicted
of murder in the rape-slaying
of Lynne Harper, twelve.
Wide World Photos

Steven Truscott, age twenty-
one, at the penitentiary at
Collins Bay, Ontario, where
he is serving his life sentence.
Wide World Photos

30

Steven Truscott

[1959]

It was a particularly hot and sultry day, that Tuesday, June 9, 1959. At the little town of Clinton in southwestern Ontario the temperature hovered near the 90-degree mark. Because the days were fast approaching the longest day of the year, most of the small populace remained outdoors in the evening to take full advantage of any breeze that might be stirring. The kids were down at the swimming hole, sauntering around the park, or riding their bikes up and down the roads. They gathered in small groups, bantering the usual nothings back and forth. Some gulped down their early dinners so they could be out of the house and away with their friends until bedtime.

Because a station of the Royal Canadian Air Force had been established in Clinton, many of the children were members of military families. Twelve-year-old Lynne Harper was one of them, the daughter of Flying Officer Leslie Harper. Having finished a rather large dinner about 5:45, she left the house and went to the park by the school. A while later, one of her schoolmates, fourteen-year-old Steven Truscott, rode into the park on his bicycle. She walked over to him and asked if he would give her a ride to King's Highway. She wanted to see the man with the ponies. Steven told her he had to be back home by 8:30 P.M. to baby-sit, but he still had plenty of time to give her a lift. They were seen leaving the park at 7:10. As they bicycled along, with Lynne on the handlebars, they passed and waved at several friends. One, twelve-year-old Douglas Oats, called out "Hi!" to them as they crossed the bridge over the river. It was about 7:25.

Steven claims that he then drove Lynne to the highway and came back to the bridge. Looking back from there, he saw Lynne hitch a ride in a new model Chev-

rolet with a yellow license plate. He then returned to the school yard, arriving, according to fourteen-year-old John Carew, slightly before 8:00. He joined a number of his friends and left them just in time to get home by 8:30 for his baby-sitting chore.

As dusk turned into twilight the lights in the houses at Clinton darkened, and the people of the village went to bed. All, that is, except little Lynne Harper.

* * *

Lynne Harper never returned home. As a result of a massive manhunt, her raped and strangled body was found at 1:50 P.M. on Thursday in a small wooded area called the Bush, halfway between the park and the highway on Country Road, over which Steven had ridden her two days before.

That night Dr. Penistan, with the assistance of Dr. Brooks, made an autopsy at the undertaker's parlor. According to the state of the contents of the girl's stomach, they fixed the time of death at between 7:15 and 7:45 P.M. of June 9, *exactly the time at which Steven had been with her and left her at the highway.* On Friday evening they picked up Steven for questioning by Inspector Graham who had been called from Toronto. He insisted on a medical examination of Steven. Dr. J. A. Addison of Clinton was called in and with Dr. Brooks examined the boy. They found two skin irritations, one on either side of the shank of his penis. Although neither had had any experience in a rape case, they stated that these irritations had been caused by the rape act. That was all the authorities needed. The crime was already solved. Steven Truscott was formally charged with raping and murdering Lynne Harper.

* * *

On Saturday, June 13, Steven appeared before Juvenile Court Judge Dudley Holmes. Mr. J. Frank Donnelly represented the youth. Against the serious objections of the defense counsel, Crown Prosecutor H. Glenn Hays obtained an order to remove the case from the Juvenile Court and try Steven as an adult. The High Court of Toronto turned down the defendant's application for appeal, and the trial of Steven Truscott began in the Goderich Courthouse on September 16, 1959, before Mr. Justice R. I. Ferguson.

If ever a trial ignored the most fundamental principle of American and Canadian justice, that a person is innocent until proven guilty, it was the trial of Steven Truscott. In her devastating book of the same name, Isabel LeBourdais has torn the prosecution's case wide apart. Based on five years' intensive research into every aspect of the case, she became convinced of Steven's innocence. But not so the people of Huron County at the time of the trial. As long as a suspect had been promptly apprehended, their fears of further such murders were put to rest, and now their appetite for vengeance was whetted. Steven must be found guilty—no matter what the evidence.

After Mr. Hays, the Crown attorney, made his opening address, in which he outlined the evidence the prosecution would present, the trial boiled down to a battle between the opposing doctors: Drs. Penistan and Brooks, the local police doctors for the prosecution, and Dr. Berkeley Brown for the defense. The entire case rested on the exact time that Lynne had died. If it were any time other than during the thirty-five minutes between 7:25 and 8:00 on the evening of June 9, Steven Truscott could not possibly have done it. Therefore, it was vital for the prosecution that the time-of-death estimate of Dr. Penistan and Dr. Brooks stand. They had based their conclusion on a two- to two-and-a-half-hour time lapse in which the contents of the stomach, such as Lynne's digestion of her dinner, emptied. Dr. Berkeley Brown disagreed. He claimed the stomach emptied in a minimum of three to three and a half hours. Many factors, such as bolting down food, fear, injury, could delay it much longer; one in Lynne's condition, up to five to five and a half hours. The jury had to decide which doctor was right. Many knew Dr. Penistan personally. They decided in his favor. But regardless of which doctor was closer to the actual time of death, was there not a clear case of *reasonable doubt* in this crucial part of the evidence?

The opposing doctors clashed again on a second crucial point of evidence: the condition of Steven's penis when examined during his questioning.

Dr. Brooks testified at length that in his opinion the skin wounds on either side of the penis could have been caused only by a rape. On the other hand, Dr. Berkeley Brown, having been a Canadian Army doctor on active duty during the war, was very familiar with genital troubles, as well as with rape cases. He testified that he had seen lesions similar to those on Steven's penis but that none of them were caused by rape: "It is interesting that the penis is rarely injured by rape. When it is injured, it is usually a tearing injury confined to the head of the organ which has a larger circumference, and when the hyman is ruptured by the head there may be a pulling that will tear this urinary opening of the foreskin, the frenum." Steven had no such injury.

The prosecution called many witnesses to establish that they had not seen Steven and Lynne on the fatal evening. Then the defense put on the stand many who swore that they had. Mr. Hays, on his cross-examination of these children, sought to brand them as little liars, a position that Judge Ferguson implied was correct in his summing up. But he could not shake them in their insistence that they had seen Steven and Lynne at the times and places to which they testified. Was there not here another case of *reasonable doubt?*

The prosecution insisted that the crime had been committed at the spot where the body was found. The defense sought to prove that this was impossible, that the rape and murder had occurred elsewhere and that the body had been brought to the Bush. The fact that there was very little blood from any of the wounds on Lynne's body (the body does not bleed after death) would seem to confirm this theory. If this were so, then Steven could not possibly have had time to commit the rape-murder, bring the body to the Bush, neatly fold the panties and place them with carefully rolled socks beside the body, wash from his own body and clothes all the blood that must have splattered all over him from the wounds, and return to the park completely unruffled and composed.

The trial ended with the usual presentations: Mr. Donnelly summarized the evidence of the defense witnesses, which pointed to the utter impossibility that Steven had committed the crime. Mr. Hays followed with his summation for the prosecution, in which he called all the witnesses for the defense liars. Yet he failed to reconstruct *how* Steven could have done the crime. Instead, he stated to the jurors, "You may be able to reconstruct the events to your own satisfaction, and really, gentlemen, if you are unable to reconstruct things, does it matter?"

Judge Ferguson followed Mr. Hays's speech with his charge to the jury. It was weighted so heavily in favor of the prosecution that Mr. Donnelly in his objections following the delivery of the charge said to the judge, "I submit that the jury listening to your charges could not help but get the impression that you consider a verdict of guilty was warranted on the evidence." To which Judge Ferguson replied, "What is wrong with that?"

When the case was given to the jury, the verdict was a foregone conclusion. The judge in his charge had drawn the jury's attention to all major evidence presented by the prosecution. But what had he done with that of the defense? The answer was inherent in the ten minutes the jury was out, after retiring for the last time and returning with the verdict: "We find the defendant guilty as charged with a plea for mercy."

The judge heard the verdict and ignored the plea for mercy. Judge Ferguson passed sentence on the fourteen-year-old defendant:

The sentence of this court upon you is that you be taken from here to the place from whence you came and there be kept in close confinement until Tuesday, the 8th day of December 1959, and upon that day and date you be taken to the place of execution, and that you there be hanged by the neck until you are dead, and may the Lord have mercy on your soul. Remove the prisoner.

❀   ❀   ❀

The Ontario Court of Appeals upheld the verdict on the grounds that Judge Ferguson had conducted the trial in approved fashion and had in his charge instructed the jury concerning reasonable doubt. But in Canada no one of Steven's age had been convicted of murder as an adult for eighty-four years, and Steven's death sentence was commuted to life imprisonment.

Today, at twenty-one, Steven is serving a life sentence in Collins Bay Penitentiary at Kingston, Ontario. But so great an impact on the people of Canada and the United States has Isabel LeBourdais's important book, *The Trial of Steven Truscott* (Lippincott), made, that Prime Minister Lester Pearson and former Prime Minister John G. Diefenbaker have now taken an active interest in the case. The Canadian Cabinet in April, 1966, ordered a review of the case of Steven Truscott by the Supreme Court of Canada. Perhaps now the principle of innocent until proved guilty without a reasonable doubt will triumph and in this case a wrong will be righted—a wrong, not based on whether Steven Truscott was guilty or innocent, but on whether his basic rights were summarily dismissed at a trial that so obviously required *him* to prove his innocence rather than the *prosecution* to prove his guilt.

Adolf Eichmann, in a drawing showing him haunted by the ghosts of millions of
Jews whose murders he is accused of masterminding in connection with the Nazi's
policy of genocide. His trial opened in Jerusalem on April 11, 1961.
Wide World Photos

31

Adolf Eichmann

[1961]

WHEN AN ACCUSED IS BROUGHT TO TRIAL IN A COURT OF criminal justice, the case is officially announced as the People (or sometimes the State) *vs.* the Defendant. Only in a remote sense, however, can the People be said to be prosecuting the case; that is, only in the sense that the prosecutor is speaking for them and is their representative. In the philosophy of criminal law, it has traditionally been contended that the victim of a crime is not merely the person who has been robbed, assaulted, or killed, but the entire community whose peaceful equilibrium is threatened by such activity.

In the trial of Adolf Eichmann, perhaps more than that of any defendant in the history of criminal trials, the People themselves were the accuser and the prosecutor was speaking for them; the People were the victims, and were demanding justice; and the People, an abstract collectivity, included the Israelis, the Jewish populations of Europe and America, and outraged and unbelieving humanity the world over. More than that, if ever it can be said that the voices of dead victims cried out for justice from their graves, this was such an instance.

Adolf Eichmann was one of the figures in the Nazi régime relatively little known to the public during the rise and fall of the Third Reich. Overshadowed by Ribbentrop, Goebbels, Göring, Heydrich, and many others, he remained in the background, careful to protect his obscurity. As if with a foreboding that Germany would lose the war and that, in the struggle to save himself he might have to go into hiding, Eichmann had been meticulous in his effort to leave behind not even a photograph.

An Austrian by birth (and with some Jewish relatives on his mother's side, a not uncommon experience for members and even leaders in the Nazi movement), Eichmann joined Hitler's party in 1932 and climbed rapidly during the following decade. From 1933 to 1939 he rose in the hierarchy, gradually becoming a specialist in what the Nazis euphemistically called "the Jewish problem." Then Germany invaded Poland, and the systematic anti-Semitism that the Nazi régime had officially introduced into their land, the illegal expropriation of the property of Jews, the discriminatory legislation against Jewish lawyers, doctors, and other professionals, turned into mass incitement of pogroms. Forced-labor camps, expulsions from territory on which Jews and their forebears had lived for centuries, and forcible separation of able-bodied men from their wives and children developed into the death camps of Buchenwald and Auschwitz. As the German war machine made its progress on the European continent, the leaders of the Third Reich set for themselves no less a task than genocide; the final solution of the Jewish problem, the extermination of ten millions of Jews, not to speak of gypsies, dissident Catholics, labor unionists, Communists, Socialists, and resistance fighters in many occupied and conquered lands.

No one man was the architect of the final solution of the Jewish problem, but central in its task was Adolf Eichmann. He headed the dreaded IV B 4 of the Reich Security Head Office, a new department dealing with deportation and emigration. First in Poland, later in Hungary, and then throughout Europe he pressed within the German hierarchy for a merciless policy of extermination. The crimes committed in the name of the German government tax the credulity even of men who have become inured to stories of atrocities: sadism and brutality, torture and murder, the tearing of children from their parents, the forcing of men to dig their own graves, even burial alive—and the authenticated stories know no end. At least six million lives were lost in the holocaust, and those that escaped carried the scars not only of their own memories but also the remembrance of those in their families who had been murdered.

Some of the leaders responsible died in the final days of the war. It is almost certain that Hitler was among them; a few, like Martin Bormann, escaped, and to this day have not been heard from; most were brought to trial, and were hanged for their war crimes or spent many years in jail. In the interrogation before and during the Nuremberg trials, the name of Adolf Eichmann arose with great frequency, and the belief, already widespread among Jewish leaders, that Eichmann was perhaps as responsible as any other single person for the tragedy that had befallen their community was confirmed and became known to wider circles.

But where was Eichmann? He had been interned by the Americans in a prisoner-of-war camp, where his identity was unknown. First he used the name Barth, and then later adopted the name Eckmann, in the belief that, if recognized and addressed as Eichmann, anyone within earshot might easily fail to detect his true name and identity.

Later, fearing identification and apprehension, he escaped from the American camp, made his way to Austria and then to Italy, and soon after the end of the war was befriended by a Franciscan priest in Rome (who evidently knew his identity) and by some people in the Vatican (who did not), and with their aid was able to obtain false papers and passage to Argentina, which he entered illegally in 1950. He traveled under the name of Ricardo Klement, and under that name settled near Buenos Aires, where he received a job and made contact with the German community.

As the story of Eichmann's crimes became better known, many Jews who had survived the holocaust dedicated themselves to his apprehension, as well as to that of other exterminators. They set up a historical bureau to record the story of the extermination and to bring to justice a maximum number of the war criminals. Their most wanted of all men was Adolf Eichmann. They sought out his former mistresses, and by befriending one of them were able to obtain (without her knowledge) an old photograph of their man. They obtained a job for a female spy as a maid in the home of the Eichmanns in Linz, Austria, to discover whether the family was in touch with him. The maid reported her conviction that the man was dead. In fact, it seems very likely that he was not in communication with his wife for several years, believing as he did that if she knew that he were alive, she would not be able to continue a pretense that he was dead.

The hunters often became discouraged, for no leads would turn up for a long time, and when a lead arose, the pursuers arrived only at another dead end. One by one, these men (unofficially to be known as The Avengers) gave up the struggle, and many migrated to Israel. Most had decided either that Eichmann was dead (in fact, years had passed, and he might have expired from natural causes) or that the pursuit was unlikely to bring results. Only Tuviah Friedman, who had escaped from Poland bearing the memory of his murdered mother, brother, and sister, could not rest. He had dedicated his life to a cause, and no other pursuit was possible.

While Friedman was publicly demanding the continued hunt for Eichmann, and keeping the name alive in Israeli and even in worldwide newspapers, others were working more quietly. Possibly—one may say probably—they were agents of the Israeli secret police, and perhaps for that reason the authentic story of the capture of Eichmann has not yet been told in all its details.

Of the conflicting stories, Moshe Pearlman's seems to be most authentic and believable; while Gideon Hausner, for Israeli security reasons, could disclose little of the capture of the man. The Avengers had almost given up by the time Eichmann, settled in Argentina, felt that it was almost safe to send for his wife and children. Nevertheless, in early 1951 he wrote to his wife under the name of Ricardo Klement, hoping that his handwriting would disclose his identity without his having to state it directly for anyone intercepting the mail to read. The children's other uncle, he wrote, would like to have the entire family come to Argentina. Mrs. Eichmann waited several months, obtained a passport in her own name, and in the spring of 1952 left Austria; several months later, she joined her husband in South America.

Arriving in Buenos Aires, Mrs. Eichmann soon took on a "second husband," became Mrs. Klement, and her children likewise changed their name, taking on the name of their stepfather. Her own identity became fairly well known in German circles in Argentina, but she adhered strongly to the fiction of a remarriage. From this second marriage, in fact, she eventually had another son, gratefully named Francisco Klement, after the priest who had aided the father.

The identification of Mrs. Eichmann and the discovery of her place of domicile did not prove difficult; but was the man with whom she was living Adolf Eichmann or was he a second husband, Ricardo Klement? Israeli agents, with telescopes and secret cameras, lodged themselves near the Klement home; they knew every step that he took on his daily routine, and they took pictures of him that were sent to Israel. But years had passed since anyone had seen Eichmann, and although Klement (supposedly seven years younger—for camouflage or vanity, one cannot be certain) was suspected of being the same person, recognition was difficult. A quarter of a century had passed since a camera had caught him for the old photograph that had been stolen from the house of a mistress, and identification was far from certain.

Eichmann was employed by the Mercedes-Benz factory in a suburb of Buenos Aires. From the moment that he left his house in the morning, walked to the bus, alighted from it, and walked to the factory, until he retraced his steps at night, every second of his daily routine was accounted for. It was known where he had lunch, what he would eat, how quickly he would walk. But if the routine was to facilitate his capture, the deviation from it was no less so. For one evening, after getting out of work, he did not make his way to the bus; instead he walked into a florist shop across the street, bought a bouquet of flowers, and then went from there to his home. That night the Israelis sent a cable: THE MAN IS THE MAN. For that day was the twenty-fifth anniversary of the wedding of Adolf Eichmann to Veronica Liebl.

They knew he was their man; now they had to arrest him. But here he was in Argentina, and the only road to justice seemed to be to bring him to Israel. Carefully studied and rehearsed plans were made to abduct Eichmann. After many alternative plans were studied, it was decided that he would be spirited out of Argentina on an Israeli plane. Thus, on May 11, 1960, Adolf Eichmann, alighting from his bus on a lonely road, was stopped the moment the bus took off, and in a matter of a few seconds spirited into an automobile, given drugs to keep him quiet, and taken to a house whose occupancy had been prearranged. There he was carefully guarded by armed men. The interrogation was brief:

"Who are you?" he was asked.

"Ich bin Adolf Eichmann," he admitted. To which he added a statement that he knew he was "in the hands of Israelis."

Twelve days later, to an Israeli Parliament (the Knesset) that was stunned into silence, David Ben-Gurion dramatically announced, that "the greatest of Nazi war criminals, Adolf Eichmann," had been found—note the careful choice of words—and "is already under arrest in Israel," where he would shortly be brought to trial under the Israeli Nazis and Nazi Collaboration Law.

While being held captive in Argentina, Eichmann had been presented with a statement, which he was asked to sign. It was not a confession of guilt, but rather a statement that he was proceeding to Israel of his own free will, to stand trial:

I, the undersigned, Adolf Eichmann, state herewith of my own free will: Since my true identity has now been revealed, I realize that there is no point in my continuing to try to evade justice. I declare myself willing to proceed to Israel and to stand trial there before a competent court.

It is understood that I will receive legal counsel and I shall try to give expression, without any embroidery, to the facts relating to my last years of service in Germany, so that a true

picture of the events may be transmitted to future generations. I am submitting this declaration of my own free will; I have not been promised anything and I have not been threatened. I want at last to achieve inner peace.

As I am unable to remember all the details and may also mix things up, I request that I be helped by the placing at my disposal of documents and testimonies to assist me in my endeavor to establish the truth.

ADOLF EICHMANN
Buenos Aires, May 1960.

❊   ❊   ❊

The announcement by Ben-Gurion was not accompanied by information about the capture of Eichmann. Where had he been found, by whom? Soon the air was filled with rumors, and the place of abduction became known. The violation of the territorial integrity of Argentina led to a sharp debate in the United Nations, and for a moment a demand, which no one expected would be honored, that Eichmann be returned to Argentina. After an apology by Israel and a reprimand of her by the Security Council of the UN, and following recall of ambassadors for a period of two months between the new Jewish nation and the Latin American sanctuary, the episode was closed.

Meanwhile, much of the criticism of Israel centered upon the kidnapping itself. Many friends of Israel, including some Jewish leaders, contended that it was an act so repulsive and so violent that it could not be condoned. The discovery of Eichmann in hiding should have been followed by exposure and by the demand that he be extradited, to Israel or to Germany, in order to stand a war-crimes trial, if not a trial in Argentina. But the Nuremberg courts had been disbanded; Germany did not ask that Eichmann be extradited; there was in existence no international tribunal of the UN set up for this purpose, and the task must fall on the new Middle Eastern nation, if it were to be carried out at all.

Eichmann had been promised a fair trial, and now Israel went to all lengths to assure him of one. He was offered an opportunity to obtain counsel from Germany or elsewhere, and when he chose as his chief defense counsel Dr. Robert Servatius, a counsel for the defense at the Nuremberg Trials, Israel agreed to pay a fee of $25,000 to the defense attorney. Every document available to the prosecution was placed at the disposal of the defense.

For many months, Eichmann was interrogated, and the material taped. He seemed almost anxious to talk about the past and his role in it, and was torn by a dual and self-contradictory ambition: to inflate his own figure in the history of the German Reich, and to depict himself as a minor cog in a machine so well oiled that it could have gone on without him.

Then came the trial. On April 11, 1961, in a special court that in many ways resembled a theatre, before three distinguished jurists, the courtroom scene unfolded. It was before a distinguished and learned court that Adolf Eichmann was tried. Dr. Benjamin Halevy, a graduate of Berlin University, was president of the Jerusalem District Court. Dr. Yitzhak Raveh, also from the same university, was a refugee who had fled from Germany in 1933. And presiding over the trial was Justice Moshe Landau, Danzig-born and London-educated.

In a bulletproof glass-enclosed cage sat the defendant, protected from the anger of survivors of the holocaust; on his sides were two guards, and on his ears were earphones that brought the proceedings to him, often after being translated from Hebrew into German. The court awaited his plea, but it did not come. Instead, Dr. Servatius arose to challenge the entire proceedings.

The grounds of the challenge were several. The defendant was before this court illegally, as a result of kidnapping, and hence this court lacked jurisdiction in the case. Against this, Gideon Hausner, chief prosecutor, cited numerous precedents, in America, England, Germany, and other countries, to justify the trial before this court in Jerusalem.

The Community Center in Jerusalem where the trial of Adolf Eichmann is about to take place.
Wide World Photos

Atrocity pictures being readied for an exhibit illustrating the Nazi persecution of Jews just prior to their execution. They are being examined by American newsmen who are in Jerusalem for the Eichmann trial.
Wide World Photos

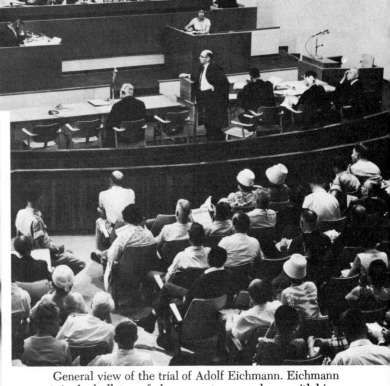

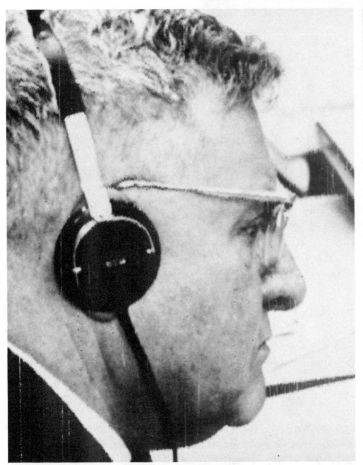

General view of the trial of Adolf Eichmann. Eichmann
is in the bulletproof glass cage; two guards are with him.
On the bench are Judges Benjamin Halevy, Moshe Landau,
and Yitzhak Raveh. Before them are Dr. Robert Servatius,
chief defense counsel (*seated*), and Gideon Hausner,
chief prosecutor (*standing*).
Wide World Photos

Robert Servatius, Eichmann's counsel, listens with
earphones to the proceedings during the
opening day of the trial on April 11.
Wide World Photos

State Attorney General,
Dr. Gideon Hausner,
cross-examines Eichmann.
Wide World Photos

The alleged crimes charged against the defendant, Dr. Servatius contended, had not been crimes in the land in which these acts were committed. This was all *ex post facto,* or retroactive, law. This had been the major argument of the defense at Nuremberg, and now Nuremberg was the precedent. It is one thing, the court stated, to hold a person responsible for an act that, at the time of its commission, was not only legal but moral and ethical; it is quite another when that act, although sanctioned by a constituted governmental authority, was inherently so abhorrent, immoral, and outrageous that the legality of the act itself was open to question.

But these acts were committed in another land, and hence the defendant could only have been tried in that country, the learned counsel for the defense argued. That country, the court ruled, had not asked for the defendant; did not want to put him on trial; and although the acts were in Germany, as well as in Hungary, Poland, and elsewhere, only Israel had made herself available for the purpose of this trial.

Against this, the German attorney argued that Israel could not be a party to the proceedings, since as a state she did not exist at the time that the alleged crimes were committed; therefore these could not have been crimes against the State of Israel. True, Israel as a state had not existed at that time, but as a people the Jews had had a continuing existence for thousands of years, and Israel was the continuation and embodiment of that people.

A fair trial was impossible, Dr. Servatius contended, because witnesses could not be obtained from the only land where they might be found, namely, Germany. These witnesses feared traveling to Israel, where they might suffer arrest on setting foot in the Jewish state or upon testifying for Eichmann. It was a delicate and convincing point, and in the effort to demonstrate to the world that Eichmann could and would receive a fair trial, the judges gave serious consideration to this matter. One method of handling it might have been to grant immunity to any witness coming to Israel for the purpose of testifying for Eichmann. But the survivors of the holocaust might have considered this the grossest betrayal that the state dedicated to the revival of the almost exterminated Jewish people could throw a mantle of protection around those who might have been involved in this extermination. Instead, it was agreed that testimony of the would-be witnesses would be taken before a court in Germany, or in whatever land wherein they resided, and that such persons would be subjected to cross-examination by deposition before foreign courts. Of six witnesses who eventually made deposition, two were granted immunity, while four were warned that in Israel they would be subject to arrest. However, all six refused to come to Israel. Actually, the problem here

raised was not so unique as might appear, for in ordinary criminal cases, involving no international matter, defendants are often unable to convince colleagues, friends, or co-conspirators to appear as witnesses because of the latters' fear of self-incrimination; and the fact that such fear acts to impede a defense could not seriously be considered a justification for granting immunity to a witness or for throwing out the entire trial as unfair.

One final argument against the procedure in the trial. Dr. Servatius declared that the judges were incompetent because they were prejudiced; they might themselves have suffered in the holocaust, or might have had relatives who suffered there, and since they were directly involved, they could not fairly and impartially sit in judgment on the defendant accused of a crime of which they were the victims. In a broader sense, this meant that no Jew should sit in judgment of Eichmann, and hence no Israeli court should try him.

To this last argument, Hausner rose up with indignation. It was true that the judges were not neutral with regard to the crimes; but it is not expected that in a robbery trial a judge would be impartial with regard to honesty. But the crimes themselves were not here on trial; if they were, no trial would be necessary. The only issue was whether the defendant committed them; at issue was the degree of his guilt.

In a sense, Hausner was affirming that every crime is one against the people, and that judges, as part of the community of people, are victims of such criminal acts; and Servatius was emphasizing that the three Israeli judges, more than in other cases, far more, personally were victims. If the crimes were not only against the Jewish people, but against humanity, who could sit in judgment, if not mortal human beings?

The arguments were over, and the contentions of the defense attorney had been rejected. A twelve-count indictment was submitted by the court. These twelve points have been summarized by Lord Russell, British barrister, as follows:

Collaborators (Punishment) Law, 1950, and (except for Counts 13–15 inclusive) under Section 23 of the Criminal Code Ordinance, 1936.

First Count

Committing a crime against the Jewish people.

This count alleged, *inter alia,* that Eichmann, together with others, caused the death of millions of Jews by gassing and other means in the extermination camps of Auschwitz, Chelmno, Belzec, Sobibor, Treblinka and Maidanek; and that he also co-operated with the four *Einsatzgruppen* A, B, C and D, which in Russia, between June 1941 and November 1942, exterminated not less than 363,000 Jews.

A story of pictures without words of the degradation to which the Jewish people were subjected before they were ruthlessly exterminated. Eichmann was tried as one of the leading architects and perpetrators of these crimes against humanity.
Yivo Institute for Jewish Research, New York

SECOND COUNT

Committing a crime against the Jewish people.

This count alleged that the accused, together with others, for the purpose of executing the final solution of the Jewish problem took steps to put millions of Jews to work in forced-labour camps, sent them to ghettos, transit camps and other concentration points, deporting them and conveying them by mass transportations under inhuman conditions.

THIRD COUNT

Committing a crime against the Jewish people.

This count contained allegations with regard to the organising of mass persecution of some 20,000 Jews on the night of 9-10 November 1938 (The Night of Broken Glass), the social and economic boycott of the Jews in Germany, the application of the Nuremberg Laws to them, and their mass arrest and deportation to camps like Dachau and Buchenwald.

FOURTH COUNT

Committing a crime against the Jewish people.

This count dealt with the measures which the accused was alleged to have taken in Theresienstadt and certain other ghettos in the East, with regard to the sterilisation of Jews and gypsies, and the forced interruption of their pregnancy by artificial abortion with the intention of destroying the Jewish people.

FIFTH COUNT

Committing a crime against humanity.

Namely, between 1931–45, causing the murder, extermination, enslavement, starvation and deportation of the civilian Jewish population in Germany and other Axis countries.

SIXTH COUNT

Committing a crime against humanity.

Namely persecuting the Jews, as described in Counts 1–5 above, on national, racial, religious and political grounds.

SEVENTH COUNT

Committing a crime against humanity.

In Germany and other Axis countries he established various organisations for the purpose of robbing Jews in those countries of their property, depriving them of their livelihood and even robbing the dead and those about to die of their hair, gold teeth, clothing, artificial limbs, etc., and sending them to Germany. The extent of the success of such robbery is reflected by the fact that when the Germans, at the time of their retreat in January 1945, burned 29 stores of personal effects and valuables, out of 35 such stores which had been erected in the extermination camp at Auschwitz, the 6 stores saved from the fire were found to contain *inter alia*: 348,820 men's suits; 836,255 women's dresses; 38,000 men's shoes.

EIGHTH COUNT

Commiting a war crime.

During the period of the Second World War, in Germany and other Axis States and in the countries occupied by them, caused the ill-treatment, deportation and murder of the Jewish inhabitants of such areas.

NINTH COUNT

Committing a crime against humanity.

Caused the deportation of over half a million Polish civilians from their places of residence with intent to settle German families in those places.

TENTH COUNT

Committing a crime against humanity.

Committing a similar offence, as alleged in Count 9, in respect of the inhabitants of Yugoslavia.

ELEVENTH COUNT

Committing a crime against humanity.

Causing the deportation of tens of thousands of gypsies to extermination camps for the purpose of their being murdered.

TWELFTH COUNT

Committing a crime against humanity.

In 1942 caused the deportation of approximately 100 children from Lidice in Czechoslovakia to Poland and their murder there.

The last three counts of the indictment (13, 14 and 15) alleged that during the period of the Nazi régime in Germany, the Accused had served in various capacities in the SS, SD and the Gestapo, all of which were declared criminal organisations by the International Military Tribunal at Nuremberg on 1 October 1946, in accordance with Article 9 of the Nuremberg Charter.

Up to the moment of the indictment, some believed, as his pretrial statements indicated, that the accused would admit his guilt, perhaps attempt to diminish the extent of involvement, state that he deserved any punishment, and throw himself on the mercy of a forgiving court. Just the opposite took place. Eichmann pleaded not guilty, and tenaciously clung to the story of his innocence throughout the trial.

The volunteers for the witness stand on behalf of the prosecution were numerous. Most of them, however, were people who had suffered at the hands of the Nazis; few had had any contact with Eichmann, or could place specific guilt upon this man. And although, in a broad sense, naziism was on trial, even Christianity was on trial, even civilization itself, the court had before it a specific individual defendant, and testimony not pertinent to his role in the crimes must be excluded.

Nevertheless, scores of witnesses came forth for the prosecution. For those who had been in Germany or German-occupied countries during the war, their sufferings were hardly believable. Many were asked (as was one learned witness) how it was possible for the Jews to have faced brutality, hardship, and certain death, with so little struggle, rebellion, sabotage, or insurrection? Perhaps a more terrible question might have been: How was it possible for the human race, after centuries of civilization, after almost two millenniums of Christianity, to have fallen into patterns so barbaric and sadistic that they tax the imagination?

A woman told of being lined up and shot at with other victims and of being thrown into a mass grave, only to find herself breathing; then rising up from the grave in which she was surrounded by corpses, and making her way, stealthily, to freedom. A novelist who as a young man had been interned in Auschwitz became so involved on the witness stand that he fell into a faint as he was telling his story. From America came Judge Michael Musmanno, who thirty-five years earlier had defended Sacco and Vanzetti, and who had sat as a judge in some of the Nuremberg cases. Musmanno testified to Eichmann's involvement, his responsibility, his personal guilt, as he had learned it in the Nuremberg Trials. And if most of the testimony showed a ruthless and brutal bureaucrat who sent literally millions to their death, and who opposed at every step any compromise, any softening of the Nazi line toward the Jews, at least one witness, Abraham Gordon, placed the man as a personal murderer. In Hungary, he had been present when Eichmann and one of his henchmen had walked into the woodshed behind the house with a Jewish boy; he had heard screams, and then had seen the two men walk out, blood on their shirts, dragging a newly slain corpse.

The direct examination of Gordon included:

BACH. Do you remember 19th March 1944?

GORDON. Yes. It was a Sunday, the day when the German Army occupied Hungary, and entered Budapest. . . .

Q. Were you, shortly after the German occupation, taken away from school with a lot of other young Jews and made to work?

A. Yes, we were arranged in groups for various types of work. Tunnels were being dug, one across the street from the Majestic Hotel to the Eden Hotel. We did not know what the purpose of these tunnels was; we thought that perhaps they were being made as air-raid shelters or munition dumps for the German Army.

Q. How long did you work on these tunnels?

A. I was employed there for about one month.

Q. And during that time did you work in the same place?

A. We went to other jobs as well. Once or twice I was sent to work at the headquarters of the Hungarian police.

Q. During your work did you ever see Adolf Eichmann?

A. Yes . . . after we had finished work on the tunnels we were taken to a villa which, I found out later, was Adolf Eichmann's private residence. Before the war it belonged to a Jewish industrialist by the name of Asher.

Q. What work were you supposed to do?

A. When we arrived we were met by a German who led us to a toolshed, issued us with tools and told us to go into the backyard and dig some trenches.

Q. When you say "told us," how many were you?

A. There were fifteen of us.

Witness Abraham Lindwasser testifies on Treblinka. In the background is a large photo of a model of this death camp.
Wide World Photos

While giving testimony against Eichmann, Polish-born Yehiel Dinur faints. The trial was suspended while he was given assistance.
Wide World Photos

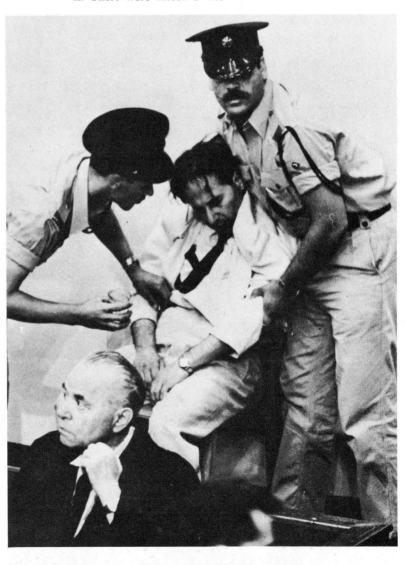

Q. Who was this German?

A. We did not know who he was but we thought that he was Eichmann's bodyguard.

Q. How did you know that the villa was Eichmann's residence?

A. In the first place the engineer in charge told us that a Gestapo Commander by the name of Adolf Eichmann lived there.

Q. Did you ever see Eichmann himself?

A. I saw him a few times.

Q. You see the accused in Court? Can you say with certainty that this is the man?

A. I must say that he has changed. I saw his picture in the press.

(Witness was handed some photographs.)

Q. Look at these photographs.

A. I am sure, without a shadow of doubt, that this is Eichmann. (The photograph which the witness identified was a photograph of Eichmann which had previously been shown to Eichmann and he had acknowledged it as being a photograph of him by signing it.)

Q. When you first saw Eichmann where was he?

A. The first time I saw him he was sitting on the balcony sipping a drink. The second time I saw him was during an air-raid and he was then walking about the courtyard. We went on working and he screamed at us and said, "Get into the trenches."

Q. How many times in all did you see Eichmann?

A. The next time I saw him was when I was in one of the trenches and, all of a sudden, I heard screams. Eichmann's chauffeur, whose name was Teitl, went up to one of the Jewish boys who was working with me, whom I knew as Solomon, and who was not more than seventeen years old.

Q. Will you tell the Court in your own words what happened then?

A. I saw Teitl walk up to the boy and shout at him. Then Eichmann's bodyguard, whose name was Slavic, joined them and I heard them shout at the boy, "You stole cherries from the tree." I then saw that Eichmann was standing on the balcony having some kind of conversation with Slavic who was down below. The boy began screaming, "I didn't do it, I am innocent." I then saw Slavic and Teitl leading the boy away in the direction of the tool-shed. He resisted and had to be forced. They pushed him into the toolshed and locked the door and then I saw the driver, Teitl, walk away and I never saw him [the boy] again that day. Then I saw Slavic return. He went round the back of the toolshed and shortly afterwards he re-appeared with Eichmann. Both entered the toolshed.

Q. What did you see or hear after that?

A. I saw Slavic and Eichmann enter the toolshed and the door was closed behind them. Then I heard frightful screams and beatings, thuds and weeping.

Q. Could you identify the voice?

A. It was the voice of the boy Solomon. The screams lasted for about ten or fifteen minutes, and then for the first time they stopped. The door then opened and Eichmann came out of the toolshed. He was rather dishevelled. His shirt was sticking out. I saw stains which I thought were blood-stains. When he had entered the shed he was dressed properly. When he came out, as I have said, he was dishevelled and looked exhausted. A few minutes after Eichmann had left the toolshed Slavic came out and shouted for the driver. Teitl arrived and together they entered the toolshed and dragged out the body of the boy. They dragged him by his feet and he gave no signs of life.

Q. Can you describe what you saw?

A. Well, I could not see his eyes but his face was swollen and bleeding. It is very difficult for me to describe what I saw. The driver went away and came back with a car.

Q. Did the car belong to Eichmann?

A. We saw it every day. It was always parked at the villa.

Q. What happened then?

A. After the car arrived I saw the body of the boy being placed in the back seat. I could not see exactly but I thought that they put it under the back seat. Then the car was driven off but returned about half an hour later. In the meantime we had been ordered to carry on with our work. The driver of the car was a Hungarian, but he also spoke German. He said, "I threw the stinking corpse into the Danube and your fate will be the same as that of the boy, so beware."

With all this, there were documents: Documents that the Nazis had not succeeded in destroying, and no trace of which was supposed to have been left by the Nazi bureaucracy. Documents carrying Eichmann's name, carrying remarks by him and signature, giving orders, always for a cruel and relentless final solution: extermination of the Jews.

Through six weeks of such testimony, the defendant, in his bulletproof cage, sat; his face twitching, occasionally he would whisper to his attorney. Then came the defense.

Yes, Dr. Servatius had obtained depositions, six of them, from people in Germany. For the most part they exonerated Eichmann, told that he had actually played only a small part and had no authority, although one deposition, ironically, stated the very reverse. Finally, the defendant was placed, figuratively speaking, on the stand. Actually, he was examined and cross-examined in his cage; Israel did not wish to risk the possibility that he would be killed by an Avenger while the trial was still in session. He would not take an oath on the Bible (although offered the New Testament for this purpose), but he was sworn without benefit of Scriptures.

For day after day, hour after hour, Eichmann was examined by Dr. Servatius. He traced his entire career and his life, from the time that he had been a young man until his apprehension in Argentina. He had joined the Nazi Party because it was against Versailles, the cause of all the trouble, and not because it was anti-Jewish. In fact, he himself had never been anti-Jewish. He had always, throughout his career, during the heyday of Nazi victories and in the period of extermination, been a friend of the Jewish people. He had been almost a Zionist; he had wanted to see the Jews get some solid ground under them; he had planned to make a Jewish colony in Madagascar.

The incident of the boy in the shed was a lie; it could not have happened and did not. As for the trains that had been sent filled with Jews, packed in like cattle, to their deaths in Europe—he was only the transportation clerk, nothing more. He was taking orders, had nothing to do with policy, often opposed it; he was only doing his small part in the job. One of the questions that Dr. Servatius asked his witness concerned a statement that Eichmann had made during interrogation by the Israeli police:

DR. SERVATIUS.   You said during the police interrogation that you carried a burden of guilt. Could you tell the Court how you now regard this question of guilt?

EICHMANN.   Some sixteen to twenty-four years have elapsed since all these events took place: what existed then exists no longer. It is difficult to say what constitutes guilt, and I must make the distinction between guilt from the legal point of view and from the human aspect. The facts in respect of which I am answerable to this Court concern the role which I played in connection with the deportations. When they took place they were in pursuance of an order given by the Head of the State and the guilt must be borne by those who were responsible for political decisions: when there is no responsibility there can be no guilt or blame. The responsibility must be examined from the legal point of view, and as long as human beings go on living together in society, no global solution can be found except the Government of a State based on law and order and abiding by these orders. . . . In order to safeguard the security of a State, it must find means to bind the individual, and this was done in Germany by making him take the oath. The question of conscience is a matter for the Head of State. One must trust and be loyal to the sovereign power. He who is led by a good Head of State is lucky. I had no luck. The Head of State ordered the deportations, and the part I played in them emanated from the master at the top, the Chief of the SS and the police. He was the man who passed on the orders to the Chief of the SIPO and SD, and he, in his turn, passed them on to Müller, my immediate superior, who passed them on to my department. . . . In the criminal code of the SS, it was laid down that the punishment for disobedience or insubordination would be death. I did all I could by legal means to

obtain a transfer to other duties, but I did not succeed, and when in the autumn of 1939 I was transferred to the SIPO and SD this was done against my will and by order from above. I had to obey. I was in uniform at the time and there was a war on. When I went abroad in 1950 it was not because I was afraid of being brought to justice, but for political and family reasons.

My position was similar to that of millions who had to obey. The difference lies only in that my assignment was the most difficult and I had to carry it. All those who say here that it was easy and did not require an effort to disobey orders give no reasons, and do not say what they would themselves have done. It is said that one could have feigned illness. This may have been a way for generals, but not for their subordinates. If it had transpired that the illness was simulated the result would have been extremely serious, and the binding chains of one's oath should be borne in mind.

Himmler said in his famous speech at Poznan that SS generals could ask to be transferred, but that applied only to generals. The small man could not have followed that course, especially when he was the recipient of secret orders. He could have shot himself, but he could not protest. Ethically I condemn myself and try to argue with myself. I wish to say, in conclusion, that I have regret and condemnation for the extermination of the Jewish people which was ordered by the German rulers, but I myself could not have done anything to prevent it. I was a tool in the hands of the strong and the powerful and in the hands of fate itself. That is what I have to say in answer to your question.

Testifying at his trial, Eichmann claims he had been concerned only with "emigration and evacuation" of the Jews. *Wide World Photos*

Gideon Hausner pointed an accusing finger when he rose to cross-examine Eichmann; it was the finger of all the victims and all their suffering survivors. He presented Eichmann with document after document, witness after witness, event after event, who had placed Eichmann in conferences, making policy, demanding stronger anti-Jewish action, rejecting compromise. For two weeks, the defendant nervously twitched and answered: "I don't remember." "I can't recall." "This is not so."

Hausner quoted Eichmann's statement to the police: " 'I am aware that I shall be found guilty as an accomplice to murder. I am aware that I face the death penalty and I am not asking for mercy because I don't deserve it.' " He interrogated the accused further on it: "You said that you were ready to hang yourself in public as an atonement for these terrible crimes, and this has been recorded, from your own mouth, on page 360 of your statement."

ATTORNEY-GENERAL.   Are you ready to repeat those words now, here in Court?

EICHMANN.   I confirm what I said during my interrogation and again this morning, in answer to my Counsel's last question. I have read what I said again and I do not deny it.

ATTORNEY-GENERAL.   So you confess to being an accomplice to the murder of millions of Jews?

EICHMANN.   That I cannot admit. So far as my own participation is concerned, I must point out that I do not consider myself guilty from the legal point of view. I was only receiving orders and carrying out orders. . . .

ATTORNEY-GENERAL.   Please answer my question. Answer briefly "Yes" or "No." If an explanation is required you can give it afterwards. My question is not a legal question. In your heart do you feel yourself guilty as an accomplice in the murder of millions of Jews?

EICHMANN.   Yes, from the human point of view, because I was guilty of carrying out the deportations.

Adolf Eichmann takes the stand (inside his bulletproof cage) in his own defense.
Wide World Photos

Documents had been found in which Eichmann himself had ordered the execution of Jews, with compulsory attendance at the executions of their co-religionists. The defendant was cross-examined on why these hangings were cleared through him. Anticipating such questioning, he had already stated, on direct examination, that he was nothing more than a cog in the machine, passing on orders that came from Himmler. To this, Hausner asked: "Why should the order have gone through Eichmann? Did not Himmler have more direct channels to the places where the executions were carried out?"

A. The local police stations would contact me on such matters.

Q. What did these Jews do to warrant hanging?

A. I cannot say. And there is no point in trying to imagine a reason.

Q. But surely you can remember. There you were, ordering people to be hanged in the presence of fellow Jews in the ghetto. Why?

A. I had to pass on Himmler's order.

JUDGE LANDAU: That is not an answer. You were asked: Do you remember what crimes these Jews committed?

A. No, not now.

HAUSNER: How many execution orders went through you?

A. I do not know.

Q. Try to remember. Tens, hundreds, thousands?

A. Only individual cases went through me.

Q. How many?

A. I do not know. I refuse to state an exact figure or even a guess.

Q. If you were just the channel for transmitting the orders, why did a report of each execution have to be sent to Department IV B 4?

A. This was just routine.

Q. But you were the recognized authority through whom Himmler issued orders for execution and it was from you that he received confirmation that the hangings had been carried out?

A. Not in every case. I even remember an instance which was handled by Müller. It concerned Jews involved in sabotage.

Q. That is possible. Müller handled cases of sabotage, but when it came to the ordinary murder of Jews, you were the one who dealt with it!

A. No, actually it was the function of another department.

Q. Then why were you involved?

A. I don't know. The requests used to arrive with the incoming mail. That is how they reached me. I have no idea why.

And there was the documented statement that Eichmann had made, that he would "jump laughing into his grave" because he had dragged millions of Jews with him. Not Jews, the defendant nervously explained, but enemies of the Reich!

In his summation, Mr. Hausner painted Eichmann as one of the worst examples of evil incarnate, and he concluded on a majestic but tragic note:

Multitudes of the Jewish nation are gone and they cannot be brought back to life. To lament their death and their suffering, and to bewail that part of the nation which has been struck down, a new writer of *Lamentations* must arise. But there must be justice for the crime that was perpetrated. I am proud of the fact that the day has come when a man of Israel can speak the language of justice to a captured evildoer. Here in this state, we do not speak to him with pleading and importunity. There is no need to beg for his mercy, no need to bribe him. We do not flee from him, or have to wander in terror from one country to another. Here law and justice prevail. In this period of the return of the exiles of Judea and Jerusalem, justice is being done here; the trial is taking place here for the blood of the righteous that was spilled, as the Prophet Joel foretold. And again I ask you, Judges of Israel, render a just and truthful verdict.

On the other hand, for Servatius the accused was but a minor bureaucrat:

All those who dealt with these problems were of higher rank than the defendant. They received the political directives directly from the political authorities. The accused's department would only deal with police measures and would also prepare certain technical matters with regard to the implementation of the purely technical aspect of these orders.

The accused had no influence whatsoever on these problems. The concentration of ghettos in the East was only the concern of the local authorities where the ghettos were situated. The accused took part in the meeting deciding on the liquidation of the Lódz ghetto, but he was there only as a representative of Himmler. Therefore it is absolutely impossible to draw any conclusion with regard to his personal competence and authority there.

On December 15, 1961, Eichman was found guilty, a verdict expected by all. For unless his guilt had been firmly established in the Israeli minds before the event this defendant could not have been apprehended without arousing international repercussions far beyond those that actually did take place. Only the enormity of the crimes, and the indisputable evidence of his complicity, mollified the voices of protest that sought to label the Israeli action one of gangsterism.

But what would happen to the man? Some had suggested that he be made to work the Israeli soil, to spend his remaining years at hard labor helping in some small way to build the land of the people whom he had almost destroyed. He would not have survived long in such a task; Israel would have had to expend great labor to guard him; most important, such a sentence would have given no satisfaction to the still suffering survivors of the holocaust.

Some suggested that Eichmann be spared, that he should not die only to demonstrate that within the heart of newborn Israel there is a magnanimity, a forgiveness, that stands in sharp contrast to the cruel barbarism of the man in the dock and his countrymen. Such a voice as that of Martin Buber, the verenerable philosopher, spoke out against the proposed execution of Eichmann.

But just as this was a case of a crime against a people, it was necessary that the people had to speak out for justice. And justice could not be satisfied by anything less than the death penalty. It is noteworthy that in the eight years that had passed since the proclamation of the State of Israel, capital punishment had been legal, but never invoked. Eichmann, however, was a unique defendant.

Servatius pleaded for mercy; Hausner for the death penalty; and in sentencing Eichmann to be hanged, the court declared:

Even had we found that the Accused acted out of blind obedience, as he alleges, we would still have said that one who had participated in crimes of such dimensions, for years on end, must undergo the greatest punishment known to the Law, and no order given to him could be a ground even for mitigating his punishment. But in fact we have found that in acting as he did, the Accused identified himself in his heart with the orders received by him and he was actuated by an ardent desire to attain the criminal objective. The Court sentences Adolf Eichmann to death for the crimes against the Jewish people, the crimes against humanity, and the war crimes of which he has been found guilty.

*　*　*

Hannah Arendt, in her controversial book on the trial, and one in which she is critical of the court and prosecution and often views the defendant as being a puppet in a system of evil rather than a creator and instigator of it, nevertheless finds that the death penalty was necessary, and suggests that the court might have stated, upon passing such a sentence:

Let us assume, for the sake of argument, that is was nothing more than misfortune that made you a willing instrument in the organization of mass murder; there still remains the fact that you have carried out, and therefore actively supported, a policy of mass murder. For politics is not like the nursery; in politics obedience and support are the same. And just as you supported and carried out a policy of not wanting to share the earth with the Jewish people and the people of a number of other nations—as though you and your superiors had any right to determine who should and who should not inhabit the world—we find that no one, that is, no member of the human race, can be expected to want to share the earth with you. This is the reason, and the only reason, you must hang.

Adolf Eichmann listens tight-lipped in the
Jerusalem courtroom on May 29 as Israel's
Supreme Court rejects his appeal from the death
sentence.
Wide World Photos

*   *   *

After appeals had been denied, Eichmann went to the gallows on May 31, 1962. He saw his wife on the last day and said goodbye, refused the solace of a Protestant minister, and to the end would not admit what he had so readily admitted in Argentina: his guilt and his sorrow for the untold tragedy that he had inflicted upon humanity. Instead, with arrogance, he hurled his final words: "Long live Germany. Long live Argentina. Long live Austria. These are the countries with which I have been most closely associated, and I shall not forget them. I greet my wife, my family and my friends. I had to obey the rules of war and my flag."

Following execution, the corpse was cremated, and the ashes were taken out to sea, beyond the territory of Israel, and there scattered in the waters, for even the soil of the Jewish State must not be sullied by the ashes of this mass murderer.

The capture, trial, and execution of Adolf Eichmann stand as more than a grim reminder of the evil of a not too distant past; as more than a historic documentation of mass murder for their murderers and their children to know, and from which they cannot turn away in pretended ignorance; as more than a heroic story of the determination of wronged people not to forget their victims and their victimizers. More than all these, it was a great act of catharsis and redemption for the Jewish people and their friends and allies in every corner of the globe. With Eichmann, captured, tried, and executed, many Jews felt that they had in some small way repaid a debt to their buried and tortured parents, brothers and sisters, friends and children; and if with this feeling, they could now breathe a little easier and happier, if the air was now purer and life was sweeter, then it was a good and necessary act for which the Israelis deserve the congratulations of freedom-loving people.

Richard Loeb, the eighteen-year-old killer whose fantasies led him to commit murder.
Newspaper Enterprise Association Photos

32

Leopold and Loeb

[1924]

ON A VERY WARM MAY 21, 1924, ABOUT FOUR O'CLOCK IN THE afternoon, a sedan car was driving slowly down the street near the exclusive Harvard Preparatory School, located in the wealthy section of Chicago's swank South Shore. In the driver's seat was Nathan F. Leopold, Jr., age nineteen. His father was retired from a lucrative box-manufacturing business that had made him one of Chicago's richest millionaires. In the back seat sat Richard Loeb, one year his junior, whose father was the vice-president of Sears, Roebuck and Company and a multimillionaire. It was not a scene to incite any special interest in passersby. Sons of very rich families all had cars to use, money to spend, and time on their hands to do whatever they pleased. The only strange aspect of this particular situation was that Leopold, who had a car of his own, was driving a *rented* car.

Stopping in front of the school, by chance they spotted little Bobby Franks, a fourteen-year-old distant cousin of Richard Loeb. They hailed him, saying they wanted to discuss the merits of a new tennis racket. Bobby willingly got into the back seat of the car with Richard. Loeb suddenly pushed him onto the floor and with terrific force brought a chisel down on his head. Blood spurted all over the back seat. Three more times Loeb smashed the chisel into the boy's head, until there was no doubt he was dead. Then he calmly wrapped the body in Leopold's lap robe.

With little concern, they drove the car past the Loeb house and the Franks house, through Jackson Park, and along many miles of crowded streets. It was too early in the afternoon for them to dispose of the body, so they went into a restaurant for a sandwich. When darkness fell, they drove toward Hammond. Reaching a deserted spot, they parked the car near a culvert next to the Pennsylvania Railroad tracks. After stripping Bobby's body naked, Leopold pushed it into the culvert. They thought there was little chance of anyone's discovering it for many years—if ever.

Picking up Bobby's clothes, they drove toward town and stopped for dinner. There Leopold thoughtfully called his family to say he would not be home for dinner, and not to worry. Later, on the way to Loeb's house, where they burned the clothing in the furnace, they stopped in the country to bury Bobby's shoes, belt buckle, jewelry, and the bloodstained lap robe. Finally, they went to Leopold's house and spent some time washing the bloodstains off the floor of the rented car. At midnight they mailed a special-delivery ransom note to Mr. Franks, demanding ten thousand dollars in old twenty- and fifty-dollar bills for the safe return of his son. At the same time Leopold telephoned the Franks house to announce the kidnapping saying that instructions would follow and that his son was safe.

They had planned to have Mr. Franks, carrying the ransom money, catch an Illinois Central train and at a designated spot near the Champion factory throw the package from the train's observation platform. Leopold had instructed Mr. Franks to take a yellow cab, which they had ordered to pick him up, to a specific drugstore, where final instructions would be given him. But although Leopold and Loeb called the drugstore three times to contact Mr. Franks, he never arrived. By now it was getting too late for Bobby's father to catch the train. Baffled as to what to do next, they left the drugstore. At a nearby newsstand they were confronted with banner headlines of newspaper extras announcing that Bobby Franks's body had been discovered.

Within a week of the murder of Bobby Franks the police were hot on their trail. After a workman on the maintenance crew of the railroad had come upon a lone foot sticking out of a culvert and called the police, another worker found a pair of horn-rimmed eyeglasses nearby. Astute police work traced them through the manufacturer and distributor to just three people who had purchased such glasses. One was a woman who was still wearing hers, the second a man who was in Europe at the time. The third was Nathan Leopold, Jr. He readily admitted that he had owned such a pair, but he could easily have lost them near the culvert on one of his bird-watching trips to the area

The next day both the suspects were taken to the state's attorney's office, where the questioning continued. It was there that Loeb broke. The boys had agreed on a time limit for sticking to their alibi, and Richard was under the impression that that time had elapsed. Therefore, confronted with the fact that Leopold was still adhering to the old story, he concluded that Leopold had broken his word and betrayed him. In anger Loeb confessed everything.

Crowe moved in for the kill. He threw facts at Leopold that only Loeb could have known. Leopold was stunned, his world shattered. There was nothing left to him but to confess all. Later that morning the two confessions, duly typed, were read to each of them. They admitted they had killed Bobby Franks for the sake of a thrill. Stated Robert E. Crowe: "I have a hanging case. The state is ready to go to trial immediately."

*   *   *

Nathan F. Leopold, Jr., the nineteen-year-old killer, who was a slave to Richard Loeb's commands. *Wide World Photos*

with his class from the university. Where was he on May 21? He had been bird-watching with his friend Richard Loeb in Lincoln Park. In the evening they had gone for an automobile ride around Lincoln Park and picked up two girls.

The police soon shattered this alibi. Upon questioning, the Leopold's chauffeur, Sven Englund, told them Leopold had never taken his car from the garage, since the chauffeur had been repairing it most of the day. Also, that evening he had seen the two boys washing red stains off the floor of a strange car.

Now the police turned their attention to the ransom note. In addition to the eyeglasses, a battered Underwood typewriter had been retrieved from Jackson Park Harbor, and it was quickly established as the one on which the ransom note had been written. While Leopold claimed he owned a Hammond typewriter, two cub reporters on the *Chicago Daily News*, interviewing Leopold's classmates, found that several of them had borrowed Leopold's typewriter to do their term papers. It was an Underwood.

At this point State's Attorney Robert E. Crowe had both Leopold and Loeb brought to the La Salle Hotel for questioning. For hours on end they questioned Leopold without breaking him. He stuck resolutely to the story that he and Richard had concocted. Now he waited for Richard to corroborate it.

Bobby Franks, the fourteen-year-old victim of the thrill killing. *Wide World Photos*

Leopold (*right*) and Loeb (*left*), just after they confessed the crime. State's Attorney Robert E. Crowe is seated in the center.
Wide World Photos

When America's most famous criminal lawyer, Clarence Darrow, agreed to defend Nathan Leopold, Jr., and Richard Loeb, it was for a very specific reason. Dissatisfied with a number of labor leaders' cases he had handled, Darrow had turned to the defense of accused criminals. He had saved the lives of two hundred two accused men. He had carried on a passionate crusade against capital punishment, with an eye to seeing it abolished forever. He had recently written *Crime, Its Cause and Treatment,* his most valuable and revolutionary book to date, but it had fallen on deaf ears. If he defended Leopold and Loeb, he knew he could reach people everywhere and bring them his message. So what if all the evidence pointed to the boys' guilt and they seemed indefensible? If he could save them from the gallows, when the world was howling for their deaths, he could indeed deal a death blow to capital punishment.

In spite of State's Attorney Crowe's attempts to keep the defendants from being put in the county jail until he had finished questioning them, Darrow insisted that they be moved there, and Judge John R. Caverly agreed. Within an hour Darrow and his two clients were conferring in the county jail.

By now Leopold and Loeb were quarreling heatedly with each other. Knowing that such actions would injure his defense efforts, Darrow spoke convincingly to them for several hours. Finally, Leopold looked at Loeb and said: "Yes, Dickie, we have quarreled before and made up; now we are at the homestretch of the greatest gauntlet we will ever have to run. It is right that we should go along to-

gether." Darrow then asked them to relate every detail of the murder, leaving out nothing. Leopold and Loeb told him the full story.

*　　*　　*

Clarence Darrow realized there was only one way to save Nathan Leopold and Richard Loeb from the gallows, and that was to prove beyond a doubt that they were both mentally ill, yet he could not plead not guilty because of insanity. In that case he would have to defend them before a jury. With the temper of the country at white heat, no jury would hesitate to convict them.

On Monday morning, July 23, 1924, at 9:30 A.M., the trial of Nathan Leopold and Richard Loeb for the murder of Robert Franks opened before Chief Justice John R. Caverly. For the prosecution, State's Attorney Robert Crowe had four assistants: Joseph P. Savage, John Sbarbaro, Thomas Marshall, and Milton Smith. Assisting Clarence Darrow for the defense were the brothers Benjamin and Walter Bachrach. The two defendants were brought into the courtroom. Judge Caverly ordered the case to proceed.

Dressed in his usual baggy clothing, Darrow took only a few minutes to drop his bombshell. First he stated: "We want to state frankly here that no one in this case believes that these defendants should be released. We believe they should be permanently isolated from society." Then he turned to Judge Caverly and said: "After long reflection and thorough discussion, we have determined to make a motion in this court for each of the defendants in each of

Attorney for the defense Clarence Darrow with defendants Loeb and Leopold (*far right*) before the bar.
Wide World Photos

the cases to withdraw our plea of not guilty and enter pleas of guilty to both indictments."

The prosecution was stunned. With just a few words Darrow had taken the case away from a jury trial and the possibility of being tried separately on the murder and the kidnapping-for-ransom charges. If Judge Caverly accepted his change of plea, the case would be continued only before him.

Upon agreeing, the judge asked each defendant separately if he understood that under the guilty plea to murder, the "Court has the authority to sentence you to a term of years in the penitentiary, not less than fourteen, or to life imprisonment, or to death by hanging"? And similarly on the charge of kidnapping for ransom, except that the minimum term in the penitentiary was five years instead of fourteen. Both defendants acknowledged their understanding and persisted in their pleas.

Darrow then addressed Judge Caverly: "We dislike to throw this burden upon the court or any court, but we feel that we must. We ask that the court permit us to offer evidence as to the mental condition of these young men to show the degree of responsibility that they had. We wish to offer this evidence in mitigation of punishment."

Over the prosecution's violent objections, Judge Caverly agreed to hear evidence of mitigation. "I want to give you all the leeway I can. I want to get all the doctors' testi-

mony about the boys if I can. There is no jury here, and I'd like to be advised as fully as possible."

Clarence Darrow had won a big first round for the defense.

* * *

The plea for mitigation of the punishment in this trial developed into a battle between opposing alienists. At the time State's Attorney Crowe first brought in the defendants for questioning, he had engaged Chicago's best-known psychiatrists to interview Leopold and Loeb: Drs. Hugh Patrick, Harold D. Singer, and William O. Krohn.

This posed a problem for Darrow and his staff, since they could not afford to rely on second best. Walter Bachrach went to Atlantic City, where the annual meeting of the American Psychiatric Association was being held. He persuaded the biggest men at that convention to join the defense team: Dr. William Alanson White, dean of American psychiatrists, head of the largest mental institution in the country (St. Elizabeth's in Washington), and President of the American Psychiatric Association; Dr. William Healy, currently co-head of the Judge Baker Foundation of Boston, a pioneer in criminal psychiatry; and Dr. Bernard Glueck, supervisor of the psychiatry clinic at Sing Sing Prison at Ossining, New York. In addition, Darrow engaged Drs. Karl Bowman of Boston and

Harold S. Hulbert of Chicago to do the in-depth inquiries into the boys' family backgrounds, interview their friends, and develop exhaustive profiles on each to uncover any fact or thought that had any conceivable bearing on their mental instability. The Bowman-Hulbert report, covering several thousand pages, was the basis of the defense's case. It had probed deeply into the defendants' confused personalities. It included physical, neurological, educational, social, and mental studies of the two boys. It analyzed their glandular makeup and their physical chemistry. Several thousand more pages were submitted by the other psychiatrists. With this evidence Clarence Darrow planned to show why Leopold and Loeb were mentally ill and should not be hanged. The report was exhaustive.

RICHARD LOEB

When he was four and a half years old his governess was Miss Struthers, a Canadian. She was excessively strict, so much so that to fool her Richard formed a habit of lying. This habit increased as he grew up and "persisted up to the present time."

Miss Struthers, being a very repressed person, would never discuss the subject of sex with him. "As a result, the patient was eleven years old before he appreciated there was any real difference between the two sexes, learning the facts of life at that time from their chauffeur. His first sex experience was at fifteen.

"Her influence upon the patient has been very great and has had an unfortunate effect. She was too ambitious to have him become an ideal boy. She effeminized him and would not allow him to mix with other boys." She left the household when the patient was fifteen years old.

Loeb graduated from the University of Michigan at eighteen, the youngest graduate the university had ever had.

When he was about ten or eleven Loeb developed important fantasies, several of which kept repeating themselves. "He would picture himself in jail. He would imagine he was being stripped of his clothing, being shoved around and being whipped. There was a great feeling of self-pity in this, but no feeling of fear. 'I was abused, but it was a very pleasant thought. The punishment inflicted on me in jail was pleasant. I enjoyed being looked at through the bars, because I was a famous criminal.' He would particularly imagine himself as the 'Master Mind' directing others.

"In his fantasies about crimes the patient gradually commenced to imagine himself doing all sorts of crimes. He derived intense pleasure from such fantasy, and particularly had a feeling of being superior to others, in that they didn't know who was connected with the crimes and he knew the truth about it while they did not.

"It is important to note, that a number of his actual crimes were the direct result of a great deal of pleasurable fantasy in regard to a particular type or form.

"One particular point connected with all this fantasy was the idea that he was the 'Master Mind' and was so clever at planning crimes that he could escape detection from the greatest detectives in the world. That he would be in truth, the 'Master Criminal Mind of the Century' and would work out a wonderful plan for a crime which would stir the country, and which would never be solved. In all his fantasies of crime he always had one or a few more associates with him, and he was always the leader.

Loeb carried his propensity for lying to an extreme, lying to everyone, including his parents and friends. "The patient was deceitful in other ways. He would cheat at cards, and perfected an elaborate system of signals with his companion for doing this." Loeb carried his petty crimes further. He stole small sums of money. He shoplifted from stores—things he never needed, but it gave him a thrill to get away with it. Caught several times, he had no feelings of remorse, only fury at himself for being caught. At fifteen he was stealing cars. From a moving car he threw bricks through store windows. At sixteen he stole several bottles of liquor from his cousin. At eighteen he planned to rob a wine cellar, preparing ropes to tie up the maid and two loaded revolvers to use if needed.

"In November of 1923 the patient planned to return to Ann Arbor to rob his own fraternity house with the assistance of his companion [Leopold]. They arrived at three o'clock Sunday morning. They wore masks, carried flashlights, two loaded revolvers, rope to tie anyone who might interfere with them and the patient carried a chisel wrapped with tape, to knock anyone over the head. The robbery went through as planned. They secured about seventy-four dollars, several watches, knives, fountain pens, a typewriter, etc."

In November, 1923, Loeb and Leopold had a bitter argument and thought of dissolving their friendship, but realized they needed each other more than ever. It was then agreed that Loeb would have complete domination over Leopold and could call on him for exacting obedience in any important, not trivial, demands.

"On the way back from Ann Arbor the patient first broached the plan of kidnapping a boy coupled with the idea of ransom." In March they discussed various plans for getting the ransom money and planned the kidnapping in detail. "They decided to get any young boy whom they knew to be of a wealthy family, to knock him unconscious, then to take him to a certain culvert, then to strangle him, then pour hydrochloric acid over his face, penis, and any identifying scars to retard identification, and to strip off all his clothes for the same purpose and dispose of them, to push the body deep into this funnel-shape culvert, through which the water flowed, expecting the body to entirely decompose and never be found."

In its psychiatric interpretation of Loeb, the report stated numerous facts. Loeb always felt inferior. Until the age of nine, he was physically inferior. He avidly read detective stories, which made lasting impressions on him. He translated his fantasies into action at an early age. He never felt any remorse or guilt for his actions. To cover up his lack of sexual potency, he used other ways to show his superiority, such as boasting of high marks (never achieved) in school and convincing his friends his was the "greatest mind of the century." However, many of his friends thought he was crazy. The report found that "the total lack of appropriate emotional response to situations is one of the most striking features of his present condition." It went on: "From this evidence it must be concluded that the patient is markedly different from the average individual; that he has gradually fallen off in his efficiency, contacts and interests with the world of reality; that he has gradually projected a world of fantasy, which was satisfactory to him, over into the world of reality, and at times even confused the two. There is a definite splitting between the emotional and intellectual faculties. There has been a great deal of abnormal mood reaction, and a total lack of appropriate mood to certain situations.

"His crime is to be explained by his peculiar fantasies, which have grown to such an extent that they now dominate him and control his actual behavior."

NATHAN LEOPOLD, JR.

Leopold's third governess, Mathilda Mantz, or "Sweetie," had a profound effect on his maturation. She was a woman ignorant of the English language. She was homely, suspicious, irritable, not tactful, jealous, oversexual in unusual ways, scheming, and very immature in her judgment. She trained her charge to love and respect her more than he loved and respected his mother. She exposed herself indecently to the youth. She had encouraged the boy to steal some stamps from another boy's stamp collection, and then intended to blackmail him, threatening to tell on him.

"The psychiatric importance is that this woman, of very peculiar mentality, was so close to the boys, especially the younger one, they took her abnormal ideas as normal. She gave him the wrong original conception about sex, about theft, about right or wrong, about selfishness, and about secrecy. He was so constituted that he was never able to emancipate himself from her erroneous teachings and mistakes."

That Leopold was an exceptionally brilliant student was shown by his rapid advancement in his academic career. He attended the University of Chicago for one year at age sixteen, then the University of Michigan at Ann Arbor for a year, returning the following year to the University of Chicago while living at home. He received a Bachelor of Philosophy degree and Phi Beta Kappa at nineteen. After one term in postgraduate work he began studying law at the University of Chicago. Leopold spoke German as well as he did English. He took Greek at the university and majored in languages. He took further correspondence courses in French, Latin, Sanskrit, Umbrian, Russian, Spanish, Modern Greek, and Oscan. His friends called him the "Great Nathan" and recognized his superiority in languages, birding, and psychology. Without working hard to achieve them, he made very high grades.

One of Leopold's slightly older social acquaintances was

Dr. Bernheimer of Chicago, known to his friends as "Murph," whom he consulted medically and with whom he discussed his own philosophy. Leopold believed "that selfishness was the ideal life, that each man was a law unto himself, and that conventions were not binding on those of superior intellect." He found in Richard Loeb the perfect friend, one whose friendship he could not live without. His affection went so deep that he agreed to be Loeb's slave and join him in any delinquency Loeb might suggest as the price of keeping up the friendship.

Leopold's life was crowded with fantasies, the most prevalent being that of king and slave. Sometimes he was the king, but more often he was the slave who saved the life of the king. For this the king offered to free him, but the slave refused. At age twelve, while at summer camp, he fantasized that the eighteen-year-old, good-looking counselor was his slave. "These fantasies continued up until about a year ago and during that time the patient would add other good-looking boys to his list of slaves.

"During the past two or three years he has fitted his closest companion [Loeb] into his king-slave fantasy." He came to feel that Loeb was much more brilliant and intellectual than he was.

"His sex urge has been very strong. He realized this, but he has felt that his mental superiority gave him the right to do as he wished sexually without the ordinary convention of right and wrong applying to himself.

"While the patient does not believe there is any such thing as intrinsic right and wrong, he feels that the general ideas of right or wrong are good enough for the average person, but that the person who is superior intellectually is also superior to convention.

"He has never been greatly attracted towards the opposite sex, nor has he ever had a true love affair leading to an engagement."

Leopold's life in petty crime essentially followed that of Loeb. He stole his brother's necktie, some fruit from a Greek restaurant, some pipes from a Chicago department store. He cheated at cards, with Loeb as his accomplice. He joined Loeb in robbing the fraternity house, setting fire to several buildings, smashing store windows with bricks hurled from a car, and planned other robberies. And finally he joined in the kidnapping and murder.

The kidnapping and murder went off basically as planned, but several aspects went wrong. "The body was put in a funnel-shaped culvert, but unfortunately, not pushed in far enough, so that a foot protruded, and it was visible in daylight the next day and was seen. It was at this time the patient dropped his glasses, but he didn't notice it. They returned home, washed the car, and continued their every-day life that night . . . the ransom plans did not work out exactly as they anticipated."

The report gave Leopold's reaction to the crime. "He got no pleasure from the crime. With him it was purely an intellectual affair, devoid of any emotion.

"His reason for going into the crime was his pact of friendship with his companion, and his companion's desire to do it. Once they started into the plan he had no feeling of guilt or remorse."

In its psychological assessment of Leopold the report stated: "In judgment he is quite immature. He has never developed to the healthy adult levels, where the individual's emotions are harnessed and directed by his intellectual processes for his own well-being and without sacrifice to an individual in his environment. He has used his intelligence rather to rationalize his behavior, and his explanations have been satisfactory to himself. He lacks a proper sense of proportion, and has assigned very high emotional values to certain topics and very low emotional values to other topics."

* * *

Nathan Leopold, Jr. was in love with Richard Loeb. When they were fifteen and fourteen respectively, Leopold accompanied Loeb to the latter's summer home in Charlevoix, Michigan, a vast estate of hundreds of wooded acres. They had their first homosexual liaison on the train in a Pullman berth. Leopold worshipped Loeb as his superman: "I can illustrate it to you by saying that I felt myself less than the dust beneath his feet. I am jealous of the food and drink he takes because I cannot come as close to him as does his food and drink." They entered into a pact: If Dickie Loeb would have sexual relations with him, then Babe Leopold would agree to carry out whatever criminal acts Loeb demanded of him. It was a relationship that culminated in the murder of Bobby Franks.

* * *

The trial opened on July 23, a sultry, hot day. State's Attorney Crowe rose and made an opening statement that lasted an hour and forty-five minutes. Most of it he spent asking sarcastically, "Just how insane can a sane man be without being so insane that he needs a jury to determine how insane he is?"

Clarence Darrow then put his defense psychiatrists on the stand. Dr. Bernard Glueck of Sing Sing characterized Loeb as being without any evidence of normal feelings and suffering from a disordered personality. Dr. William Healy contended there was no reason why Leopold should not have committed the crime, given his "abnormal mental trends with typical feelings and ideas of a paranoiac personality." Dr. William A. White described Leopold and Loeb as having infantile emotional personalities that were not normal. However, each alone could not have carried out the crime. It was the fusion of their beings into one that caused the deed to be done. The testimony of these three defense psychiatrists took days to present.

It was now the prosecution's turn to show why all the evidence pointed to deliberate murder that could only call for hanging. The prosecution's psychiatrists, Drs. Patrick, Singer, and Krohn, insisted that the two boys were perfectly sane, that there was no evidence of mental disease, that their health was excellent, and that they had led a perfectly normal social life. Darrow took every opportunity to angrily refute them, and spent days cross-examining them. He sought to show that mental instability was not the same thing as insanity.

Crowe charged Leopold and Loeb with kidnapping Bobby Franks solely for money to pay their gambling debts. This was seen by the court as somewhat ridiculous, in view of all the spending money and infinite financial resources of the young men's families. Another tactic Crowe employed was to accuse them of having sexually assaulted Bobby and then killed him to hide their actions. The autopsy on the victim proved otherwise. Crowe accused Darrow of taking on the case only for the enormous fee he would be getting. Darrow had already refuted that charge.

On August 19 the state concluded its rebuttal and began its summation, with Marshall quoting ancient legal authorities, Blackstone, and others, showing legal precedents for the execution of young convicted murderers, ages fourteen to nineteen. Savage then recounted every detail of the crime, stressing its premeditation and cold-blooded execution. The prosecution called on Judge Caverly to ignore Darrow's anarchism and to sentence the defendants to death.

The defense then presented their summation. Walter Bachrach stressed the length of time and the many opportunities the defense alienists had used to thoroughly examine Leopold and Loeb, as opposed to very superficial examinations and findings of the alienists for the prosecution. He then brilliantly summed up the entire psychiatric testimony.

His brother, Benjamin Bachrach, then spoke briefly and ended with: "Your Honor, in this case there is only one point at issue. The physical facts are uncontested. The legal sanity of both defendants is undisputed. There remains only one question, that of punishment. Your Honor, permit me to introduce one of the greatest experts in the world on the question of punishment, my colleague, Clarence Darrow."

At that point the court recessed for the day.

* * *

On August 22 Clarence Darrow opened his plea for mitigation of sentence. He spoke for twelve hours. He argued that Leopold and Loeb's crime had been one of compulsion, that there was no way they could have helped themselves. At the start he dismissed the ransom as a reason for the crime.

At that time Richard Loeb had a three-thousand-dollar checking account in the bank. He had three Liberty Bonds, one of which was past due, and the interest on each of them had not been collected for three years. I said, had not been collected; not a penny's interest had been collected—and the coupons were there for three years. And yet they would ask to hang him on the theory that he committed this murder because he needed money.

In addition to that we brought his father's private secretary here, who swears that whenever he asked for it, he got a check,

Clarence Darrow making his famous twelve-hour plea for mitigation of sentence before Judge John R. Caverly in the crowded Chicago courtroom. *Wide World Photos*

without ever consulting the father. She had an open order to give him a check whenever he wanted it, and she had sent him a check in February, and he had lost it and had not cashed it. So he got another in March.

Your Honor, how far would this kind of an excuse go on the part of the defense? Anything is good enough to dump into a pot where the public are clamoring, and where the stage is set and where loud-voiced young attorneys are talking about the sanctity of the law, which means killing people; anything is enough to justify a demand for hanging.

How about Leopold?

Leopold was in regular receipt of one hundred and twenty-five dollars a month; he had an automobile; paid nothing for board and clothes and expenses; he got money whenever he wanted it, and he had arranged to go to Europe and had bought his ticket and was going to leave about the time he was arrested in this case.

He passed his examination for the Harvard Law School, and was going to take a short trip to Europe before it was time for him to attend the fall term. His ticket had been bought, and his father was to give him three thousand dollars to make the trip.

Your Honor, jurors sometimes make mistakes, and courts do, too. If on this evidence the court is to construe a motive out of this case, then I insist that human liberty is not safe and human life is not safe. A motive could be construed out of any set of circumstances and facts that might be imagined.

In addition to that, these boys' families were extremely wealthy. The boys had been reared in luxury, they had never been denied anything; no want or desire left unsatisfied; no debts; no need of money; nothing.

And yet they murdered a little boy against whom they had nothing in the world, without malice, without reason, to get

five thousand dollars each. All right. All right, Your Honor, if the court believes it, if anyone believes it—I can't help it.

That is what this case rests on. It could not stand up a minute without motive. Without it, it was the senseless act of immature and diseased children, as it was; a senseless act of children, wandering around in the dark and moved by some emotion that we still perhaps have not the knowledge or the insight into life to understand thoroughly.

Darrow then asked the reason for the boys' actions, and proceeded to answer his own question.

Why did they kill little Bobby Franks?

Not for money, not for spite, not for hate. They killed him as they might kill a spider or a fly, for the experience. They killed him because they were made that way. Because somewhere in the infinite processes that go to the making up of the boy or the man something slipped, and those unfortunate lads sit here hated, despised, outcasts, with the community shouting for their blood.

Are they to blame for it? There is no man on earth who can mention any purpose for it all or any reason for it all. It is one of those things that happened; that happened, and it calls not for hate but for kindness, for charity, for consideration.

Darrow then reconstructed the crime by describing each of the events in order of occurrence and asked again and again if these acts were those of a sane person and what reason there could be for committing them. "For what? For nothing! The mad act of the fool in *King Lear* is the only thing I know of that compares with it. And yet doctors will swear that this is a sane act. They know better."

Having finished his presentation of the details of the murder, Darrow expressed his incredulity that anyone could ask for the death of these boys.

. . . You may search the annals of crime, and you can find no parallel. It is utterly at variance with every motive and every act and every part of conduct that influences normal people in the commission of crime. There is not a sane thing in all of this from the beginning to the end. There was not a normal act in any of it, from its inception in a diseased brain, until today, when they sit here awaiting their doom.

But we are told that they planned. Well, what does that mean? A maniac plans, an idiot plans, an animal plans, any brain that functions may plan; but their plans were the diseased plans of the diseased mind. Do I need to argue it? Does anybody need more than to glance at it? Is there any man with a fair intellect and a decent regard for human life and the slightest bit of heart that does not understand this situation?

And still, Your Honor, on account of its weirdness and its strangeness and its advertising, we are forced to fight. For what? Forced to plead to this court that two boys, one eighteen and the other nineteen, may be permitted to live in silence and solitude and disgrace and spend all their days in the penitentiary, asking this court and the state's attorney to be merciful enough to let these two boys be locked up in a prison until they die.

In all of the many times he asked for mercy and for an understanding of his well-known aversion to capital punishment, Darrow appealed directly to Judge Caverly.

How many times has mercy come even from the state's attorney's office? I am not criticizing. It should come and I am telling this court what this court knows. And yet forsooth, for some reason, here is a case of two immature boys of diseased mind, as plain as the light of day, and they say you can get justice only by shedding their last drop of blood!

Why? I can ask the question easier than I can answer it. Why? It is unheard of, unprecedented in this court, unknown among civilized men. And yet this court is to make an example or civilization will fail. I suppose civilization will survive if Your Honor hangs them. But it will be a terrible blow that you shall deal. Your Honor will be turning back over the long, long road we have traveled. You will be turning back from the protection of youth and infancy. Your Honor would be turning back from the treatment of children. Your Honor would be turning back to the barbarous days which Brother Marshall seems to love, when they burned people thirteen years of age. You would be dealing a staggering blow to all that has been done in the city of Chicago in the last twenty years for the protection of infancy and childhood and youth.

Basing his statement on the findings of the Hulbert-Bowman report, Darrow then proceeded to analyze each of the defendants and show that, as a product of their environment and education, they were inevitably led into the crime. He especially stressed Leopold's infatuation with the philosophy of Nietzsche.

At seventeen, at sixteen, at eighteen, while healthy boys were playing baseball or working on the farm or doing odd jobs, he was reading Nietzsche, a boy who never should have seen it at that early age. Babe was obsessed of it, and here are some of the things which Nietzsche taught:

"Why so soft, oh, my brethren? Why so soft, so unresisting and yielding? Why is there so much disavowal and abnegation in your heart? Why is there so little fate in your looks? For all creators are hard, and it must seem blessedness unto you to press your hand upon millenniums and upon wax. This new table, oh, my brethren, I put over you: Become hard. To be obsessed by moral consideration presupposes a very low grade of intellect. We should substitute for morality the will to our own end, and consequently to the means to accomplish that."

Of course the books are full of statements that the fact that a man believes in committing a crime does not excuse him.

That is not this case, and counsel must know that it is not this case. Here is a boy at sixteen or seventeen becoming obsessed with these doctrines. There isn't any question about the facts. Their own witnesses tell it and every one of our witnesses tell it. It was not a casual bit of philosophy with him; it was his life. He believed in a superman. He and Dickie Loeb were the supermen. There might have been others, but they were two, and two chums. The ordinary commands of society were not for him.

Many of us read this philosophy but know that it has no actual application to life; but not he. It became a part of his being. It was his philosophy. He lived it and practiced it; he thought it applied to him, and he could not have believed it excepting that it either caused a diseased mind or was the result of a diseased mind.

Darrow then referred to the age of the defendants.

Your Honor, if in this court a boy of eighteen and a boy of nineteen should be hanged on a plea of Guilty, in violation of every precedent of the past, in violation of the policy of the law to take care of the young, in violation of all the progress that has been made and of the humanity that has been shown in the care of the young, in violation of the law that places boys in reformatories instead of prisons—if Your Honor, in violation of all that and in the face of all the past, should stand here in Chicago alone to hang a boy on a plea of Guilty, then we are turning our faces backward toward the barbarism which once possessed the world. If Your Honor can hang a boy of eighteen, some other judge can hang him at seventeen, or sixteen, or fourteen. Some day, if there is any such thing as progress in the world, if there is any spirit of humanity that is working in the hearts of men, someday men would look back upon this as a barbarous age which deliberately set itself in the way of progress, humanity and sympathy, and committed an unforgivable act.

As he came to the end of his plea, Darrow asked that Leopold and Loeb be sentenced to prison for life.

I do not know much salvage there is in these two boys. I hate to say it in their presence, but what is there to look forward to? I do not know but that Your Honor would be merciful if you tied a rope around their necks and let them die; merciful to them, but not merciful to civilization, and not merciful to those who would be left behind. To spend the balance of their lives in prison is mighty little to look forward to, if anything. Is it anything? They may have the hope that as the years roll around they might be released. I do not know. I do not know. I will be honest with this court as I have tried to be from the beginning. I know that these boys are not fit to be at large. I believe they will not be until they pass through the next stage of life, at forty-five or fifty. Whether they will be then, I cannot tell. I am sure of this; that I will not be here to help them. So far as I am concerned, it is over.

I would not tell this court that I do not hope that some time, when life and age have changed their bodies, as it does, and has changed their emotions, as it does—that they may once more return to life. I would be the last person on earth to close the door to any human being that lives, and least of all to my clients. But what have they to look forward to? Nothing. And I think here of the stanza of Housman:

Now hollow fires burn out to black,
And lights are fluttering low:
Square your shoulders, lift your pack
And leave your friends and go.
O never fear, lads, naught's to dread,
Look not left nor right:
In all the endless road you tread
There's nothing but the night.

Now Clarence Darrow pleaded for the lives of Nathan Leopold and Richard Loeb.

Now, I must say a word and then I will leave this with you where I should have left it long ago. None of us are unmindful of the public; courts are not, and juries are not. We placed our fate in the hands of a trained court, thinking that he would be more mindful and considerate than a jury. I cannot say how people feel. I have stood here for three months as one might stand at the ocean trying to sweep back the tide. I hope the seas are subsiding and the wind is falling, and I believe they are, but I wish to make no false pretense to this court. The easy thing and the popular thing to do is to hang my clients. I know it. Men and women who do not think will applaud. The cruel and thoughtless will approve. It will be easy today; but in Chicago, and reaching out over the length and breadth of the land, more and more fathers and mothers, the kind and the humane, the kind and the hopeful, who are gaining an understanding and asking questions not only about these poor boys, but about their own— these will join in no acclaim at the death of my clients. They would ask that the shedding of blood be stopped, and that the normal feelings of man resume their sway. And as the days and the months and the years go on, they will ask it more and more. But, Your Honor, what they shall ask may not count. I know the easy way. I know Your Honor stands between the future and the past. I know the future is with me, and what I stand for here; not merely for the lives of these two unfortunate lads, but for all boys and all girls; for all of the young, and, as far as possible, for all of the old. I am pleading for life, understanding, charity, kindness, and the infinite mercy that considers all. I am pleading that we overcome cruelty with kindness, and hatred with love. I know the future is on my side.
Your Honor stands between the past and the future. You may hang these boys; you may hang them by the neck until they are dead. But in doing it you will turn your face toward the past. In doing it you are making it harder for every other boy who, in ignorance and darkness, must grope his way through the mazes which only childhood knows. In doing it you will make it harder for unborn children. You may save them and make it easier for every child that sometime may stand where these boys stand. You will make it easier for every human being with an aspiration and a vision and a hope and a fate.
I am pleading for the future; I am pleading for a time when hatred and cruelty will not control the hearts of men, when we can learn by reason and judgment and understanding and faith that all life is worth saving, and that mercy is the highest attribute of man.
I feel that I should apologize for the length of time I have taken. This case may not be as important as I think it is, and I

am sure I do not need to tell this court, or to tell my friends that I would fight just as hard for the poor as for the rich. If I should succeed in saving these boys' lives and do nothing for the progress of the law, I should feel sad, indeed. If I can succeed, my greatest reward and my greatest hope will be that I have done something for the tens of thousands of other boys, for the countless unfortunates who must tread the same road in blind childhood that these poor boys have trod; that I have done something to help human understanding, to temper justice with mercy, to overcome hate with love.
I was reading last night of the aspiration of the old Persian poet, Omar Khayyam. It appealed to me as the highest that I can vision. I wish it was in my heart, and I wish it was in the hearts of all.

So I be written in the Book of Love,
I do not care about that Book above;
Erase my name or write it as you will,
So I be written in the Book of Love.

Clarence Darrow finished. There was not a sound in the courtroom. Tears streamed down Judge Caverly's face.

* * *

Following Darrow's plea State's Attorney Crowe presented the final summing up of the State's case. It took him nearly two days. It was "unrestrained, sarcastic, and vituperative." It referred to the defendant Leopold acting as if he had, in this case, "a friendly judge." Judge Caverly bristled but let the remark be entered in the record. Crowe then ended his case demanding the death penalty as the only answer to the crime. As he finished speaking, Judge Caverly ordered Crowe's "friendly judge" remark stricken from the record: "the closing remarks of the State's Attorney as being a cowardly and dastardly assault upon the integrity of the court."

* * *

On September 10 at 9:30 A.M. Judge Caverly entered the courtroom to deliver his verdict. The prosecution and defense teams were there. Leopold and Loeb were led in. Each replied in the negative when asked if he had anything to say before sentence was pronounced. Judge Caverly then calmly and in a low voice outlined the law, the circumstances of the case, the penalties, and how he had now arrived at a decision. "In choosing imprisonment instead of death, the court is moved chiefly by the consideration of the age of the defendants, boys of eighteen and nineteen years."
He then sentenced each of the defendants to life for murder, plus ninety-nine years for kidnapping. And he added: "In the case of such atrocious crimes it is entirely within discretion of the department of public welfare never to admit these defendants to parole. To such a policy the court urges them strictly to adhere."
Shortly thereafter Leopold and Loeb were taken to the Illinois State Prison at Joliet, Illinois, to serve their life sentences for the murder and kidnapping of little Bobby Franks.

* * *

More than six decades after the murder, the slaying of Bobby Franks remains the only case that was not highly politicized (as were those of Dreyfus, Sacco and Vanzetti, and the Rosenbergs) that still remains well known to public and professionals. Few people are now alive who remember the trial, but the killing is still called, and very accurately, "the crime of the century" (as was a title of a book about it). It was clear from the judge's remarks at the time of the sentencing that these two young men should never walk free again; that they must live out the remainder of their lives behind prison bars. For Richard Loeb, the ukase was true: less than a decade after he was sentenced, he was killed by a fellow-prisoner in a brawl, the details of which are still in dispute.

For Nathan Lepold, the future was quite different. He served a third of a century in prison, was said to have been a model prisoner, to have studied and mastered many languages, to have initiated and run a correspondence course for convicts that gave education to many who had not been exposed to it before. The death of Loeb, some commentators believe, freed Leopold from the strange tie between the two; others felt it enabled Leopold, and a small group of people who were convinced of his rehabilitation and of

the full payment of his debt to society, to make Loeb the greater culprit in the planning and carrying out of the crime.

Despite the admonition of the sentencing judge and despite some legal technicalities, Leopold became eligible for parole when Governor Adlai Stevenson reduced his original sentence, citing as a reason particularly his contribution to malaria testing during the World War II. Leopold applied for parole several times and was regularly rejected, until it was granted on the fifth application, permitting him to walk out of prison, a free man, on March 13, 1958.

Given permission to migrate to Puerto Rico, Nathan Leopold went to the island, where he worked in hospitals and church missions for as little as ten dollars a month. He married, received a master's degree at the University of Puerto Rico, and taught mathematics. On rare occasions he would grant interviews to criminologists and journalists, and rumor has it that he wrote at least one article on crime and prison life under a pseudonym.

On August 29, 1971, Nathan Leopold died, unforgiven by some still-living members of his own family and of that of the victim, but probably an example of expiation, atonement, redemption, and rehabilitation unparalleled in the annals of American crime.

33

Angela Davis

[1972]

ANGELA DAVIS WAS A PHILOSOPHY TEACHER AT THE UNIVERsity of California in Los Angeles who leaped into prominence during the last months of the 1960s, when a movement arose to dismiss her from her professional post. She was black, articulate, highly educated, extremely militant, and a member of the Communist party of the United States. In California a law had long been on the books prohibiting the state college system from employing a Communist. Using this law, a sharply divided board of regents dismissed the assistant professor, setting off widespread protests that included voices beyond those of young radicals and outraged blacks. The American Association of University Professors threatened legal action. The director of the Afro-American Studies Center at UCLA asked for permission to discuss the case with the regents, and was refused.

It did not take long for Angela Davis to become a heroine. A lecture she gave at UCLA was attended by two thousand cheering students, and a faculty movement was started to withhold all grades as a form of protest. In her first round in court she was victorious. The court ordered UCLA to accept enrollment in her classes for credit, and a short time later a higher court ruled that the 1950 ban on Communist teachers was unconstitutional, Faced with this judicial defeat, the regents changed tactics, upholding the dismissal on the basis of what they claimed to be her poor teaching. To many it looked as if Ronald Reagan and the conservative majority on his board of regents would face a setback, since Davis received the support opf her department, her faculty, professional associations, the student body, and blacks of all political persuasions throughout the country. Then, in August 1970, the case took a new and unexpected turn.

❀   ❀   ❀

California has a vast prison system. Large numbers of prisoners are black and Mexican-American. They charge that a racist society pushes them toward crime, and that racism in prison keeps them in confinement while whites are released. The prisoners also charge the guards with racism. In 1969, in a struggle between a white guard and black prisoners at San Quentin, one of the world's largest prisons, the guard had been killed.

On August 7, 1970, James D. McClain was on trial for the murder of the prison guard. The trial was being held in the Marin County Courthouse at San Rafael, five or six miles from San Quentin. While the trial was going on, a young man entered the courtroom, drew a gun, and freed McClain and a convict witness, William Arthur Christmas. Taking several hostages, including three women jurors and the judge, the young man drove away. At a roadblock a shootout ensued. Judge Harold J. Haley, McClain, Christmas, and Jonathan Jackson, the youth who had apparently led the entire plot, were killed.

At the funeral of Jonathan Jackson, Panther leader Huey Newton said Jackson had died heroically in the effort to bring freedom to others. For the Jackson family, the tragedy was particularly acute, for Jonathan's older brother, George, was a prisoner at San Quentin, having spent twelve years in captivity, serving an indeterminate one-day-to-life sentence for armed robbery. Denied parole year after year, he had won the admiration of a small coterie; his letters from prison were about to be published in book form (*Soledad Brother*) and he was already receiving national attention.

There were recriminations among officials after the shootout. Some declared that the killing of the judge had been unnecessary, and, in an effort to forestall criticism, police declared that the first shooting had come from the getaway car.

About a week after the courtroom event, a newspaper reported what was probably a leak from an official investigator. One of the guns used by Jackson belonged to Angela Davis. By the time the story appeared, the philosophy teacher was not to be found. Under California law, anyone who aids and abets in the commission of a major crime is equally guilty as the perpetrator. On the basis of the report

Angela Davis demonstrators gather in a parking lot across the street from the Santa Clara County Courthouse in San Jose.
United Press International

about the gun's ownership, warrants were issued for the arrest of Angela Davis, charging her with murder and kidnapping. In fact it was said that not one gun but two used in the shootout had been purchased in her name, with a hint that a third gun might have been bought by her. More than that, the purchases had apparently been made only one or two days before the killing.

One other prisoner had been in the courtroom, as a witness in the McClain case. This was Ruchell Magee, one of the men who came to be known as the Soledad Brothers, after the name of the prison. Although he had been present in court, and a sheriff or other police officer had apparently freed him when so ordered at gunpoint, Magee either had not gone or was not taken into the getaway car. Eventually he was charged, like Davis, with murder and kidnapping, under the aiding and abetting provisions of the law. But since most of the attention was on Angela Davis, Ruchell Magee was an obscure figure. Those who knew him said that he was an outstanding jailhouse lawyer, a prisoner who spends his time studying criminal law, and often becomes extremely knowledgeable in the field.

For two months law enforcement officials sought Angela Davis. She was finally apprehended in a New York motel. Her hairstyle had changed, but otherwise she looked much the same as she had in California. Held without bail and charged with unlawful interstate flight to avoid prosecution, she fought extradition, and almost immediately became a focal point for protest. A demonstration was held, and for the first time the cry was heard that would be repeated during the next year, "Free Angela Davis." Black intellectuals rallied to her side, and any hope by governmental authorities that she would be seen as an accessory to a brutal and nonpolitical murder was quickly abandoned. In New York she went on a hunger strike, started a suit to be released from solitary confinement, and watched as her cause gained wide support. Even the YWCA spoke out in her favor.

Throughout the world, the name of Angela Davis became known. Petitions were circulated in Italy in her behalf. Rumors had it that kidnapping and hijacking plots were being hatched to secure her freedom. A wildcat strike broke out in Pittsburgh because a bus driver was not permitted to wear his "Free Angela Davis" button. A demonstration for her freedom was held in Bonn, Germany. In America, an explosion in an oil refinery immediately set off rumors that it was caused by her partisans. In the Soviet Union, fourteen leading scientists expressed their concern over her safety, lauded her as a selfless fighter for social ideals, and appealed to American courts to judge her with "full impartiality and humanity." Perhaps the most dramatic protest took place in front of American military headquarters in Saigon, a demonstration of about forty American soldiers demanding freedom for Angela Davis.

The American government was acutely sensitive to all of this. It invited the Soviet scientists to come to this country to watch the trial (and expressed hope that a reciprocal arrangement could be worked out for trials in the Soviet Union of international interest), and the State Department and the U.S. Information Agency sent frequent lengthy reports to its outposts all over the world, giving them the government's perspective on the case.

Just before Christmas of 1970, Angela Davis finally lost her battle against extradition and was returned to California, where she was immediately visited by her family. She announced the appointment of a prominent militant black attorney from Atlanta, Howard R. Moore, Jr., as chief counsel for the defense, and asked for permission to act as her own co-counsel. The prosecution objected, but her plea was granted with warnings that the rules of the court would have to be followed. This meant that she could address the court and jury without being placed on the witness stand and therefore would not be subject to cross-examination.

The other defendant, Magee, was brought to the courtroom during pretrial motions and hearings literally in chains. He was bound to his seat, and when he demanded to be heard, he was ordered removed from the court. At one point in the preliminary skirmishes Magee produced an affidavit in which he charged that an attorney appointed to defend him had come to him in prison and, purportedly speaking on behalf of two California judges, offered him immunity if he would perjure himself by testifying against his codefendant. The attorney denied the charge, and asked for the right to withdraw from the case.

The generally conservative NAACP stated that it would watch the trial with great care, and warned that Angela Davis was not being given the benefit of a presumption of innocence. The Urban League expressed its fear that she would not be given a fair trial. She received visits in jail and expressions of support from the young Irish Catholic leader Bernadette Devlin and the American antiwar activist and actress Jane Fonda.

In August 1971, just about a year after the shootout in which his brother had died, George Jackson was killed in prison, under conditions that have never been satisfactorily explained. The authorities charged that he was making an effort to escape, but many observers felt that this was an unlikely story. His death came at a time when he had achieved a national reputation for his prison writings, and during the pretrial jailing of Angela Davis it left widespread fear concerning the atmosphere in which she was to be tried.

The case being prepared against Angela Davis began to become public knowledge, in the manner that American prosecutors so often permit evidence to become known before a jury has been selected and a trial has begun. It became known that a charge would be filed that she had been seen the day before the shootout near the Marin County courthouse with a young man later identified as Jonathan Jackson, and that she would be named as the person who had purchased the guns.

Magee was not cooperating in all respects with the more prominent defendant; and probably without forewarning her attorneys, he made a charge in open court that Judge

McMurray was prejudiced against him. He called upon the judge to step aside, and to everyone's astonishment, McMurray did. Moore and the other attorneys for Davis appeared to be unhappy with the judge's self-disqualification, and when a new judge was named, it was Davis's turn to charge prejudice.

In New York City a minor portion of the trial in the Davis case was being held. The man who had been apprehended with Angela Davis at the time of her arrest was David Poindexter, a mysterious, wealthy, and apparently radical black, charged with harboring a fugitive. It might appear that this would be self-evident, but there was an important technicality. One had to prove beyond a reasonable doubt that Poindexter knew that a *federal* warrant had been issued for the futitive's arrest, and not merely that she was wanted in California. After a trial that lasted a little less than two weeks, Poindexter was acquitted, and immediately announced his intention of going on a barnstorming tour of all the United States to demand freedom, at least on bail, for Angela Davis.

With the Poindexter case disposed of, attention shifted again to the West Coast. There Magee expressed his contempt for the defense lawyers who had been assigned to him, called the judge a Klansman in disguise, contended that the case should be tried in a federal and not a state court, and asked that his trial be separated from that of Davis. As for her, there was a constant demand for her release on bail. The probation department of California recommended that she be freed on the posting of one hundred thousand dollars, but this was rejected. Together with the fight for bail there was a motion for change of venue, as the climate in San Marin County was said to be inimical to a fair trial. One might say the request was granted in part. Although San Marin would no longer be the seat of the trial, it was not going to be heard in San Francisco or Los Angeles, as the defense lawyers had requested, but in San Jose, a move that was loudly denounced.

By the end of 1971, with the trial not yet underway, the government said that it had already incurred expenses amounting to a third of a million dollars in the matter of Angela Davis. She had spent a year in California in jail, and it appeared that she would continue to be confined during the trial itself, but this suddenly changed when the California Supreme Court ruled that capital punishment was unconstitutional in that state. The question of bail was reopened on the grounds that Angela Davis was no longer charged with a capital crime. Judge Arnason, now in charge of the case, ordered her release, and a wealthy farmer put up the money, for which he and his family were threatened, ostracized, and subjected to many forms of harassment. Suddenly, without enough advance warning for the word to pass around, Angela walked out of jail. She was cheered joyously by about one hundred persons who had gathered to greet her, and she smiled.

❄   ❄   ❄

In a small courtroom in San Jose, California, with the strictest of security measures, the trial of Angela Davis, severed from that of Magee, finally opened on February 18, 1972. During the jury selection, a *New York Times* reporter was arrested on a marijuana charge and his press credentials were removed, only to be restored after a short time. Later, when he refused to plead guilty even to a minor offense, he was given a trial and acquitted. Many interpreted the incident as a sign that an effort would be made to intimidate the press.

A protracted struggle over jury selection was anticipated, but after a panel of eleven whites and one black was temporarily seated, the defense took the other side completely by surprise and announced that the panel was acceptable. The prosecution was jockeyed into the position of either renouncing its unstated objectives of having an all-white jury, or raising an objection that would quite obviously appear to be racially motivated. The latter path was taken, and the lone black was removed, leaving anger among spectators and a definite impression that color alone had caused the exclusion. The defendant used the occasion to reiterate her pessimism about the possibility of obtaining a fair trial in Santa Clara County.

In an opening statement the prosecution revealed the nature of its case. Not only would it be shown that the guns used in the shootout had been purchased by and belonged to Angela Davis, but that her motive had not been political. She was in love, it was contended, with George Jackson, and was motivated in her effort to free him in exchange for the hostages in order to fulfill that love.

As co-counsel, Angela Davis was able to speak for herself. In an opening statement she admitted that the guns were hers, pointed out that she needed them for protection, and that her love for George Jackson was one of political admiration. She had indeed been struggling for the freedom of the Soledad Brothers, but she believed in obtaining that freedom through the courts, not through violence. She reminded her audience that she had been brought up in Birmingham, where guns were traditionally needed by black people to protect themselves against violence, not to perpetrate violence.

The witnesses produced little that was unexpected. Those who had been jurors at the time of the shootout testified as to what had occurred, and particularly what had been said by those now dead. Jonathan Jackson seemed to have made it clear, they declared, that the hostages were going to be exchanged for the freedom of the Soledad Brothers, and that his own brother George would be among those freed.

On April 6, after the trial had been plodding along for several weeks, out-of-court activity again attracted attention when James Carr, a former cellmate of George Jackson, was killed in an ambush. There was speculation that the killing was connected with the case, that he was going to be a witness—for which side was not clear—and that he had been murdered to prevent his testimony. The matter was never cleared up, but in court the question arose as to whether the jury had heard of the event, and whether it

Angela Davis outside Santa Clara Superior Court on the first day of her trial.
United Press International

had prejudiced their ability to hear the case. The prosecution had spoken to reporters about the Carr murder, and following vigorous protests from the defense about these statements, the court warned both sides to refrain from discussing the trial with newsmen.

In the trial itself, witnesses recounted the events of the San Rafael shootout. One gun that had been used was identified as having been purchased by the accused only two days before the killings. The love element was proven to exist by letters sent by Angela Davis to George Jackson, and after a vigorous struggle the letters were read in court. "All my efforts have gone into one direction—free George Jackson and the Soledad Brothers," she had written, and the prosecution was prone to read sinister connotations into those words.

Thus far, the involvement of Angela Davis had been only weakly developed. It depended mainly on the guns and her alleged love. However, prison guards identified her as a person who had accompanied Jonathan Jackson when he visited his brother in August 1970. The date of the visit was placed as two days before the shootout. An effort was made to link the defendant to a car driven to the

courthouse on the day of the shootings. An attendant at a gas station remembered seeing her the day before in that car in that area. A former convict said that Davis had visited the prison, but did not enter it, on the day before the events in which Jonathan lost his life. Some of the witnesses were vague as to how they were able to recall such details and identify people with such certainty, and the defense did its best to confuse them by having a woman with a strong resemblance to Angela Davis sit next to her during a part of the trial.

Such was the case against Angela Davis, except for her flight, with whatever suggestion of guilt one wished to draw from it. For the defense, witnesses told of her whereabouts at the time of the shootout and before, of her surprise in hearing of it and her distress to learn that her guns were missing. An expert challenged the credibility of the prosecution eyewitnesses. And, in a poignant and tragic drama, Lester Jackson, the father of the slain youths, Jonathan and George, was called as witness for the prosecution's rebuttal. He refused to testify and was held in contempt. The judge was in a dilemma. Obviously, to jail the man would arouse widespread sympathies for the defendant, for this was the man who had lost two sons in the tragedy that had unfolded. But on the other hand, permitting him to refuse with impunity to take the stand would violate elementary principles of law. The matter was solved by fining the elder Jackson one hundred dollars. The fine was paid, and he left the court without testifying.

The state called for a conviction of murder in the first degree. The defense scoffed and said the entire case against the defendant was absurd. After three days of deliberation, the jury brought in its verdict. Angela Davis was found not guilty.

It was a victory for the militant and all of her supporters, but an effort was made to turn it into a victory for the American government as well. The acting director of the FBI said that he was satisfied with the verdict as an example of American democracy at work. But asked if there had been a fair trial, Angela Davis replied negatively. A fair trial would have been no trial.

Thus she emerged, martyr yet free. She was a symbol of courage, strength, and defiance of the most powerful forces in the nation. Her trial is not a record of the testimony itself, of what went on inside the court and on the stand, but of the marches, the slogans, the millions of words written about it, and the bringing of her message to people she might otherwise never have been able to reach. This was a manifestation of the new politics in America and, in fact, in many other parts of the world.

As for the verdict, it could not have been otherwise under the rule that guilt must be established beyond a reasonable doubt. The links the prosecution made of the defendant to the planning of the murder were tenuous at best, though not nonexistent. Certainly they were insufficient to sustain a conviction. And then again, it was a jury of all-whites, not working in the obscurity of a little Southern town, but sensitive to worldwide publicity, and to the charge of racism that would inevitably come with a verdict other than exoneration. Thus, there was a constituency—youthful, disaffected, militant—of blacks and whites marching in the streets, powerless to make decisions, yet constituting a force contrary to the decision-making powers, and placing judges and juries on the defensive and the alert.

Dr. Herman Tarnower, shot by Jean Harris. *Wide World Photos*

34

Jean Harris

[1980]

LOVE, ONCE PASSIONATE, FAITHFUL, AND SEEMINGLY ETER-nal, has so often turned to envy, jealousy, hatred, violence, and abandonment that suicide and murder, either or both, arising out of such deteriorating relationships are not at all rare. William Congreve, major English poet, had stated this in what are, perhaps, his most immortal lines:

> Heav'n has no rage, like love to hatred turn'd,
> Nor Hell a fury, like a woman scorn'd.

What is less well known is the title of the piece from which these lines are taken: *The Mourning Bride.* Congreve would today be faulted for making his statement so gender-specific. A man scorned, like a woman, has turned to beating unto death his beloved girlfriend or wife, or killing the man who had replaced him in the heart and bed of this woman, and ending his own life in despair. But it is the woman, more often than the man, who lives by a code of fidelity, who combines her sexuality with deep affection and love, and who is used and discarded by a man, only to find herself lonely, depressed, frustrated, angry, and to find swelling within her the fury so succinctly described in the poetry of Congreve.

The brutal assault on lover or spouse, the murder or attempted murder of a husband or wife by the mate, or suicide on the part of the scorned one, because of despondency, hopelessness, abandonment, and rejection, all are not at all rare in American society, and in some societies are so common that they are almost normative, particularly if the assulter is the male.

It may seem unusual, then, that the death of a physician in a wealthy suburb of New York, and the arrest and trial of a woman with whom he had been intimately involved for fourteen years, should have developed into one of the most interesting and sensational trials of the early 1980s. But the dead man, Dr. Herman Tarnower, was not an ordinary physician; on the contrary, he was a national celebrity. And the facts that came to light about his private life,

as well as that of his former mistress and convicted killer and the peculiarities of their relationship, whetted the appetite of readers who might be tiring of the latest news about wars abroad and weapons that could kill an ever greater percentage of the earth's inhabitants. Furthermore, with so much crime, particularly "ordinary crime" or "street crime," the public often derives some kind of satisfaction in the knowledge that this type of violence is not unknown in middle-class, and even upper-class, circles.

Dr. Herman Tarnower, at the time of his death in 1980, was sixty-nine years old. He was a bachelor, the type once known as a rake, and now called, in a more euphemistic if not adulatory manner, a womanizer. Financially successful, quite possibly a millionaire, he had become known as "the diet doctor," a phrase that he apparently found distasteful, although his work on diets had turned him into a man of great wealth. His book *The Complete Scarsdale Medical Diet* had become a best-seller, and at the time of his death his name was probably better known that that of most physicians in America, although his scientific standing in the profession was not of the same dimensions. That he was several pounds overweight for a man of his age and height, judged by the information in his own book, and that he could not follow with success the diet prescribed by him for others, is only one of the smallest ironies of this case, and certainly not his greatest secret.

Fourteen years earlier, he had met Mrs. Jean Struven Harris, then forty-three years of age, a divorcée with two children. For fourteen years, they had gone on trips together to many parts of the world; he had given her clothes and other valuables; and once, in what might have been a rash moment, he had proposed marriage and given her a valuable engagement ring. Although he had reneged on the question of marriage, the relationship continued.

That there were other women in his life must have been apparent, but none of them seemed important, and in the early years of their romance other affairs were not more than ephemeral, so that there was a sense of ongoing security betwen Mrs. Harris and the physician. How much she helped him with the editorial work on the book that made him world-famous is in dispute, but whether it was for this help or other reasons, Herman Tarnower remembered Jean Harris in his will, leaving her almost a quarter of a million dollars. He took a deep interest in the welfare of her two sons, and in fact made a lavish wedding party for one of them, but whether that was at his suggestion or hers is still unknown, for it came at a time when the relationship was no longer at its zenith, and another woman had entered Tarnower's life.

In the period before the crucial events of March 10, 1980, when Tarnower died from gunshot wounds inflicted in her presence but in a manner that would be disputed, Mrs. Harris had obtained a position as headmistress of the Madeira School, a private school for middle- and upper-class girls in Virginia, a position for which she did not seem to be well suited, either by experience or by temperament. She ran into many problems in the school, found that considerable numbers of students were violating her strict rules, expelled (just before graduation) some who confessed and left unscathed others equally guilty, and became the subject of a great deal of dissension. She was under great strain not only in the school, but in what once would have been called her love life, and while she still made every effort to see Hi Tarnower, sometimes with success, she was increasingly aware that she had been replaced as his favorite by another woman. That she was taking drugs, legally prescribed, sometimes by Dr. Tarnower, does not seem to be in dispute. Life was on the way down for Jean Harris. Trouble on the job, trouble with her lover, who appeared to be abandoning her for a much younger woman, and psychological depression that may have been aggravated by the drugs could have made her suicidal. Her distress was apparent to her colleagues at the school. One day she drew up a will, got people at school to witness her signature, and got in her car and went north to New York. She had a loaded gun with her, and some extra bullets.

Jean Harris's story is that she intended to kill herself that day, but would do so only on the premises, if not in the very presence, of the man who was abandoning her. Such suicides, carried out not in private but before the eyes of the person held responsible, are not at all unknown. A suicide-prone person is not acting according to the rules that govern the rest of society; the would-be suicide is what the rest of us would call irrational. And that such irrationality can and does lead to the performance of the act before another would not be unheard of; suicide experts agree, in fact, that suicide is an act of revenge against the living.

Only Jean Harris can know whether she drove north with that gun intending to carry out, or merely threatening to carry out, the act of ultimate self-destruction in the presence of Hi Tarnower; and even of that, one cannot be certain, for in her depressed and distraught state, she could not be clear as to what her own plans might be. But this we know: she did drive to Purchase, New York, to the Tarnower estate, with a loaded gun.

Both that day and the day before, she had tried to reach Tarnower by telephone. Apparently she finally got through to him while he was with a patient. He took the call and left the receiver off the cradle while he went into another room to talk to Jean, but the patient later testified that she had heard parts of the conversation, and what she heard was damaging to Jean's story. But even that loud, often angry discussion has some element of dispute about it, for present in the building at the time was Tarnower's other woman, Lynne Tryforos, twenty years younger than Jean and apparently now his favorite.

Since Lynne never took the stand, and remained the background woman, in complete obscurity, throughout the trial, it is not certain that she was not the one who heard what was being said on the telephone. At any rate, it was later to be described as an angry exchange of words, a plea from the physician to Mrs. Harris not to come but to leave him alone, and a word to placate her, not to forget that he had put her in his will, and that she would be coming into a large sum of money. Actually, almost half a million dollars was divided in the will between the two women, Jean and Lynne, with the latter receiving a little more, and the division would remind some people of the way the doctor shared his bed and quarters with the women, as was later described by the housekeeper, a key witness at the trial.

Notwithstanding this telephone plea asking her not to come (if we are to accept this evidence), Jean did arrive at the estate on the night of March 10, 1980. She knew her way around the house; she went directly to Tarnower's room without checking in with the groundskeeper and his wife, and there found the physician in bed, alone, probably sleeping, or perhaps awakened by her entrance.

There is only one living witness to what transpired in that room during the period that followed, and she was the defendant in the case, so her testimony was frequently challenged, and eventually was not accepted as truth by the jury. Harris claimed that after an exchange of words, she put the gun to her temple, and that Tarnower tried to stop her by grabbing her hand before she had a chance to pull the trigger. A struggle ensued, she was later to state, and during that struggle he was shot several times. Leaving a seriously wounded man, and taking with her the gun with which she might have carried out the classic act of murder followed by suicide (for she had more bullets in her pocket), she stalked out of the house. Her sole purpose, she claimed, was to obtain aid for the injured man. She could not use the telephone in the physician's room because it was not connected; she saw no reason to alert the groundskeeper and his wife, who might have called for help. Instead, she hopped into her car and was about to make her way to the nearby town of Purchase, where she would make a call from a booth, saying that a man in the Tarnower estate was in need of urgent medical assistance. It is not clear from Harris's story whether she would then have returned to the estate itself, to discover the condition of the wounded man. In the meanwhile, the groundskeeper heard the shots, ran up to the room, saw Dr. Tarnower bleeding but apparently alive, and called for help. When Jean Harris reached her car and started to drive away, the bloodstained lethal weapon with her, she was stopped by the police.

Jean Harris returned to the scene of the shooting with the police. There they waited for the ambulance that would arrive a few minutes later to take Tarnower to the local hospital, where he died almost immediately after arrival. During the trial, prosecution witnesses would testify that, had an ambulance been called the moment Tarnower had been shot—by accident during a struggle, as Mrs. Harris contended—there was a good chance that he might have lived. His death was attributed to an enormous loss of blood, not to the damage to a vital organ.

Let us leave Mrs. Harris and the police and detectives in the room where Tarnover lay dying, and go back for a moment to an event that had occurred earlier that weekend. Jean had written a very long letter to the doctor, which came to be known as the "Scarsdale letter" (reprinted in full on page 383), and had mailed it to him by certified mail, which meant that he personally would have to sign

for it. Aside from the contents and tone of that letter, which became points of serious argument as the trial proceeded, a curious issue, perhaps unique in the history of murder defenses, was raised. Would a woman who intended to murder a man that day have sent him a letter, which she knew (or at least assumed) would arrive after his death? Would she send him a certified letter when she knew he would be dead and unable to sign for it, and thus it would only be returned to her?

It is a puzzling question, and one is tempted to reply that the letter itself is evidence,—particularly when taken with the doctor's will, the distress, the setbacks—that she set out on her journey with the intent to kill herself. Otherwise, is one to assume an astute and Machiavellian plot—that she was already laying the basis for a defense by a series of actions on the day of the death, that she would one day present in court in case she were ever to be accused of murder? This is the stuff of which second-rate movies, lacking in verisimilitude, are based. But there is still another possible key to unraveling the mystery: that on the day of the death (or murder, as it eventually was

Jean Harris, seated in the center, discusses her defense with her lawyer, Joel Aurnou (*right*). Other members of the defense team (*standing left*): Barbara York, Victor Grossman, and Bonnie Steingart. *Wide World Photos*

termed) Jean Harris was in such a state of emotional confusion, inner turmoil, and mental anguish that her various acts were themselves irreconcilable by the standards of rationality.

At the scene of the shooting, she made some damaging statements, according to detectives and police who were on the scene—some made to the detectives themselves, others to a lawyer whom she called in their presence. She immediately obtained the assistance of an attorney, Joel Aurnou—not the man she had called in the presence of the police—and an arraignment took place without delay. Harris was released the next day on bail of forty thousand dollars, on the condition that she not leave the county.

An examination revealed that five bullets had evidently been fired. Three of them were removed from the body of the victim, one had gone through his hand, and a fifth was missing. But all that was of little interest compared to the fact that the victim was the author of a book that had sold some three million copies. The murder did not hurt sales. Buyers now flocked to the stores to obtain it, more interested in the slain man than in his prescriptions for losing weight. One of the sons of the woman who would now stand trial for murder was quoted as saying to a reporter, "This is a very sad thing. Perhaps your paper should write a good story on gun control."

There were several possible defenses for the woman who had brought the deadly weapon to the scene and who had been alone with the physician when he suffered the severe gunshot wounds from which he died. Joel Aurnou, Harris's chief attorney, could have pleaded insanity, or at least temporary insanity, and inasmuch as this is technically a not-guilty plea, it would have entitled Jean Harris to apply for freedom from a mental institution or a psychiatric center after a short period of time, and would furthermore not have deprived her of the more than two hundred thousand dollars in the doctor's will, which, under the law, she could not receive if found guilty of murder.

Aurnou might have tried to cop a plea, to allow Harris to plead guilty to a lesser charge of manslaughter, negotiate a sentence that some have contended would have resulted in her incarceration for not more than three years, but again would probably have removed her from the will. Or he could have insisted on the truth of the story that she told: she had come there with the intention of killing herself, desperate and despondent, under the influence of depressant drugs, and in the effort to take her own life right in front of the man whose actions were to such an extent responsible for her state, a struggle ensued, and the gun's deadly bullets hit him instead of her. Thus, he could have argued, there was no intent to kill, and death came as an accident, Harris's only crime being that she had illegally taken a gun into the State of New York, and she should be acquitted of all other charges. It was Aurnou's gamble, no doubt with the consent and urging of the defendant, that he should fight for acquittal, and that he would attain it. That there might still have been another defense is something that we will suggest a little later.

There were many important pretrial hearings that were to prove vital in the case. One dealt with the accused's statements, both to the lawyer over the telephone and to the detectives and police on duty, that were so damaging; Aurnou insisted that she had not been given her *Miranda* warnings (warnings to a suspect that he or she has the right to remain silent, may have an attorney present, and any statement made can be used against the accused in court), hence the apparent admission that she had killed him could not legally be admitted into evidence once the trial began.

The second involved the Scarsdale letter—to whom did it belong, what did it say? Aurnou now had the letter in his possession, and argued with tenacity that he should not have to show it to the judge or prosecution, that it belonged to the sender inasmuch as the recipient was dead and could not sign for it, and on the grounds that it might be self-incriminating he should not be compelled to let the judge see it. During the pretrial hearings, Aurnou won some minor skirmishes, but he lost these two major battles. A challenge to the indictment was made on a technical point, and again the prosecution was victorious.

Some laymen, unversed in the law, might wonder why Aurnou did not destroy the letter. The deliberate destruction of evidence is probably not rare, but it is a serious crime, and could not be contemplated by any lawyer—neither one who is of the highest integrity nor one who believes that everything is fair to get a client free—when that evidence is known by the courts to exist. Destruction of this letter would have led to criminal prosecution of the attorney and possible disbarment.

The summer wore on, and with the trial expected to start in the fall, there was increasing speculation that a plea of insanity, or at least temporary insanity, would be entered, but finally the attorney for Mrs. Harris rejected that possibility. He was seeking complete acquittal, and feared that a jury, not being convinced on the question of insanity, might well bring in a compromise verdict of guilt on a lesser charge of manslaughter.

In October of 1980, with the trial approaching, the defense asked that the press be barred from pretrial hearings, a request denied by the judge, Russell Leggett. The defense feared that statements were coming out in the hearings that might be barred at the trial, that they would be prejudicial to the defendant, and that this would make more difficult the selection of an impartial jury. But the judge ruled that such a matter could be handled by a careful screening of potential jurors.

Among the most damaging of the pretrial testimony was that of Detective Arthur Siciliano, who had arrived at the scene and was with Mrs. Harris when, according to him, the following conversation took place:

HARRIS: The doctor has been shot.
SICILIANO: Where is he?
HARRIS: Upstairs.
SICILIANO: Who did it?
HARRIS: I did it.

Jean Harris (*left*) listening to the testimony of Suzanne van der Vreken (*right*) at her murder trial in White Plains, New York.
Wide World Photos (*Drawing by Libby Dengrove*)

She sat and listened, showing a great deal of anger at the testimony, ready to deny that it had ever taken place, or at least in that form. To add to the case that she had been told of her rights under *Miranda*, Siciliano even testified that she had signed a card stating that she had been so informed.

A married Belgian couple, Henri and Suzanne van der Vreken, were groundskeepers, cooks, and homemakers for Dr. Tarnower. That they knew many details about the life of their employer was apparent, and there was some hint during the trial that there was less than devotion—in fact, some resentment and possibly hatred—toward him, that might have emanated from their vision of his lifestyle, of which they certainly did not approve. Suzanne verified Si-

ciliano's version of the events: that she had immediately said that "his girlfriend" was the one who had done the shooting, and that she had passed on this information to another police officer.

Again there was warning that she should not make statements, but Mrs. Harris was in a state of agitation as officers, ambulance attendants, servants, and others gathered. The warnings were even coming from lawyers who were her friends. A patrolman testified that he had overheard a conversation with her lawyer friend, Leslie Jacobson, in which she said: "Oh, my God, I think I've killed him." Did she use these words? Did she know that a patrolman was listening? Was it privileged communication to her attorney (it turned out that Jacobson did not become her attorney)? These were questions that were best handled in the pretrial investigation, out of hearing of a jury, and without prejudicing a jury if the statements should not be admitted.

The pretrial hearings had dragged on for four weeks. The last witness was Suzanne van der Vreken, and she testified that she had heard Mrs. Harris say, "Hi, why didn't you kill me?" It was an ambiguous statement, open to diverse interpretations, and might well have supported the contention of the defense that Jean had come for the purpose of killing herself, but the witness did not agree. At any rate, the main purposes of the pretrial hearings seemed to be twofold: to keep out of the trial certain incriminating material, and to establish that the defendant had made statements implicating herself without being warned of her rights. On both points, Aurnou had lost, although he was laying the basis for an appeal, in case he ended up losing the case.

On November 22, 1980, the trial opened, and few expected that it would last nearly until the end of February. The jury was selected without great difficulty; that it consisted of eight women and four men (aside from the alternates), and contained several blacks, seemed to indicate that Aurnou felt women would be more sympathetic to the defense he was about to mount, and that women and blacks would be more likely to lean in the direction of sentimentality for the woman on trial, surely the victim and underdog in this case. George Bolen, the lawyer chosen by the prosecution to handle the case, was less flamboyant than his opponent. Sometimes he allowed himself to be drawn into a trap during cross-examination, but he had prepared his case meticulously and handled it calmly and convincingly. Perhaps he had the easier of the two tasks. After all, the woman on trial was mounting an almost incredible defense: that she had traveled with gun several hundred miles for the purpose of killing herself in front of her lover; that as she was about to do so, he struggled to save her, and in the course of that struggle the bullets hit him, not her; that she did not realize the severity of the wounds, and was leaving the scene of the accident without notifying people in the house, so that she could ride away, gun in car, to reach a telephone booth to alert someone that a wounded man was in need. If anyone saw this as a match of wits of Aurnou against Bolen, such a person should have taken note of the handicap: Bolen had been given about 150 points in a 300-point bowling match.

During the weeks that followed, there were many witnesses, and the story unfolded of what might have been Tarnower's increased interest in Lynne Tryforos over Jean Harris, or a neat little juggling act in which the doctor saw to it that they did not share his bed on the same nights. This situation was an additional burden for Suzanne van der Vreken, it turned out, because she had to hurriedly hide Lynne's clothing when Jean was to be the guest, and then turn the tables the next day, returning Lynne's dresses and negligees and carefully hiding Jean's things, each time leaving the clothing exactly as if it had not been touched.

Aside from the testimony of police officers and the van der Vrekens, who repeated before the court what was already well known, and some character witnesses for Mrs. Harris, who told of a serenity and satisfaction with her at Madeira that undoubtedly had an element of exaggeration, a major portion of the weeks ahead concerned pathological studies of Herman Tarnower's body, autopsy reports that had sometimes been modified by further study. It all added up to a dispute concerning the events in the room at the time of the shooting. Much of the testimony was highly technical, and primarily involved the crucial question of whether the shot that hit Tarnower's palm had left palmar tissue in such manner that it could be determined that he was holding his hand in front of his chest to protect himself from a deliberate murder. In America expert testimony is usually easily obtained by both sides; that the experts contradict each other with such ease and frequency is enough to make one wonder about their scientific knowledge as well as their integrity. So it was in this case, with experts on both sides absolutely certain about their testimony, and if the case had been decided on this issue alone, it would appear that there was at least reasonable doubt as to Jean Harris's guilt, and that Aurnou's witnesses came off a little better than Bolen's.

Despite the testimony of detectives who were at the scene so soon after the shooting, Aurnou might have made a decision not to put the defendant on the stand. If he had not shown the prosecution's witnesses to have fabricated or exaggerated or even misunderstood what Harris had said when they arrived at the scene, if he could not exclude their testimony because of the *Miranda*-rights issue, he had at least shown that the local police were incredibly inept at the handling of a violent death. Fingerprints had not been taken, vital elements had been touched and moved, notice was not taken of some of the most potentially significant details. It all added up to a significant side issue, for it cast considerable doubt on the efficiency of the local police, and, by extension, on their credibility. What was left were the pathologists' contradictory statements, and Harris's own story of her intention to commit suicide and not to kill the man she loved. The decision to have Mrs. Harris take the stand was thus a hard one, and might have been made at her own insistence, especially hard because Aurnou had seen her behavior in court—angry, cutting, contentious. She had the sort of personality that one might easily associate with a woman who had the capacity to kill, or to turn intended suicide into intent to kill. It is difficult to know what the jury might have done had the case ended at this point.

But it did not end. On January 27, 1981, Harris did take the stand, and on direct examination, treated gently by Aurnou, she told of her great love for the doctor. From time to time she cried, and then brought herself back to composure. She had bought the gun in 1978, for protection. But she was not an easy client even for her own lawyer. Sometimes she interrupted him. She brought up her rivalry with Lynne Tryforos, although Aurnou had not wanted her to do so. Her first day on the stand was nicely described by a headline in the *New York Times:* "Sad, Humorous, Cutting."

The next day she was on the stand again, and the audience settled down for what was going to be a long examination, not to speak of the length and anticipated fireworks of the cross-examination. Now the references to Lynne were becoming more numerous. A letter Harris had written to Tarnower about a month before his death had a remarkably humorous line, even if it was not so intended: "Not only are you the man I have loved for 14 years, I think you are unconstitutional."

AURNOU: And when you said you loved him for 14 years, did you love him then, on the 10th of March, as you always had?

HARRIS: Yes.

A little later:

AURNOU: Were you aware at the end of 1979 and the beginning of 1980 that the doctor was seeing another woman?

HARRIS: Yes.

AURNOU: More than one woman?

HARRIS: I didn't have first hand knowledge of it. I didn't see him with them.

And taking up the theme again:

AURNOU: Were you aware that he was seeing Lynne?

HARRIS: Yes, indeed, I knew.

AURNOU: But did you always have the same feelings for Dr. Tarnower that you had since 1966 and 1967?

HARRIS: They never changed.

It was a grueling direct examination. On February 2, Harris had her first full day of cross-examination, and she did nothing to conceal her anger and contempt for Lynne Tryforos, or for her cross-examiner, George Bolen. When Bolen asked if Tarnower had taken her on a vacation, she replied: "I don't like your saying he took me. We went together. I sound like a piece of baggage." Everyone laughed, including the woman on the stand, but if she had made her point that she was equal to the cross-examiner in wit and repartee, if not his superior, she had also shown the turmoil and anger within her.

And then there came the day, on cross-examination, when the Scarsdale letter was to be introduced. All of the valiant efforts of Joel Aurnou to prevent the jury from hearing it had failed.

BOLEN: May I have that letter, please, Mr. Aurnou? Mrs. Harris, is that the letter you wrote to Dr. Tarnower, parts of it on Saturday, March 8, 1980, and the rest of it on March 9, 1980?

HARRIS: I believe so, yes.

BOLEN: And is that the letter that you mailed on the morning of March 10, 1980?

HARRIS: Yes.

Aurnou made a last-ditch effort to place the onus for reading what he knew would be a damaging letter on Bolen. "I am consenting that you read it, Mr. Bolen," remarked Harris's lawyer, although he had no choice, and the consent was hardly voluntary. "If that is what you want to do in a public courtroom, go ahead." And the letter was read. There was a deliberate lack of emotionalism in the reading, as if Bolen were searching to avoid any charge that his tone of voice, his emphasis, even his pauses, had given greater meaning to the words than were put there by the writer.

THE SCARSDALE LETTER

Hi

I will send this by registered mail only because so many of my letters seem not to reach you—or at least they are never acknowledged so I presume they didn't arrive.

I am distraught as I write this—your phone call to tell me you preferred the company of a vicious, adulterous psychotic was topped by a call from the Dean of Students ten minutes later and has kept me awake for almost 36 hours. I had to expel four seniors just two months from graduation and suspend others. What I say will ramble but it will be the truth—and I have to do something besides shriek with pain.

Let me say first that I will be with you on the 19th of April because it is right that I should be. To accuse me of calling Dan to beg for an invitation is all the more invidious since it is indeed what Lynne does all the time. I am told this repeatedly, "She keeps calling and fawning over us. It drives us crazy." I have and never would do this—you seem to be able to expiate Lynne's sins by dumping them on me. I knew of the honor being bestowed on you before I was ever asked to speak at Columbia on the 18th. Frankly I thought you were waiting for Dan's invitation to surprise me—false modesty or something. I called Dan to tell him I wanted to send a contribution to be part of those honoring you, and I assured him I would be there. He said, "Lee and I want you at our table." I thanked him and assured him I would be there "even if the slut comes—indeed, I don't care if she pops naked out of a cake with her tits frosted with chocolate!" Dan laughed and said, "And you should be there and we want you with us." I haven't played the slave for you—I would never have committed adultery for you—but I have added a dimension to your life and given you pleasure and dignity, as you have me. As Jackie says, "Hi was always a marvelous snob. What happened?" I suppose my check to Dan falls into the "signs of masochistic love" department, having just, not four weeks before, received a copy of your will, with my name vigorously scratched out, and Lynne's name in your handwriting written in three places, leaving her a quarter of a million dollars and her children $25,000 apiece—and the boys and me nothing. It is the sort of thing I have grown almost accustomed to from Lynne—that you didn't respond to my note when I returned it leaves me wondering if you sent it together. It isn't your style—but then Lynne has changed your style. Is it the culmination of years of broken promises, Hi—I hope not. "I want to buy you a whole new wardrobe, darling." "I want you to get your teeth fixed at my expense, darling." "My home is your home, darling." "Welcome home, darling." "The ring is yours forever, darling. If you leave it with me now I will leave it to you in my will." "You have, of course, been well taken care of in my will, darling." "Let me buy an apartment with you in New York, darling."

It didn't matter all that much, really—all I ever asked for was to be with you—and when I left you to know when we would see each other again so there was something in life to look forward to. Now you are taking that away from me too and I am unable to cope—I can hear you saying, "Look, Jean, it's your problem—I don't want to hear about it."

I have watched you grow rich in the years we have been together, and I have watched me go through moments when I was almost destitute. I have twice borrowed fifty cents from Henri to make two of the payments on the Garden State Parkway during those five years you casually left me on my hands and knees in Philadelphia. And now—almost ten years later—now that a thieving slut has the run of your home, you accuse me of stealing money and books, and calling your friend to beg for an invitation. The very things your whore does openly and obviously (to your friends and your *servants!* sadly not to you) you now have the cruelty to accuse me of.

My father-in-law left me a library of over 5,000 books. I have given away in the past ten years more books than you own. I have thanked you most sincerely and gratefully for books you have given me. Ninety percent of them have been given to a school library and on at least four different occasions I have asked you if you wouldn't like a letter on school stationery that you could use as a tax deduction. Each time you have airily refused and *now,* for God's sake, you accuse me of stealing your books. It borders on libel. Any time you wish to examine my home or the school library, you are certainly welcome to do so—a surprise raid might be most convincing for you.

Twice I have taken money from your wallet—each time to pay for sick damage done to my property by your psychotic whore. I don't have the money to afford a sick playmate—you do. She took a brand new nightgown that I paid $40 for and covered it with bright orange stains. You paid to replace it—and since you had already made it clear you simply didn't care about the obscene phone calls she made, it was obviously pointless to tell you about the nightgown. The second thing you paid for (I never replaced it) was a yellow silk dress. I bought it to wear at Lyford Cay several years ago. Unfortunately I forgot to pack it because it was new and still in a box in the downstairs closet. When I returned it was still in the box rolled up, not folded now, and smeared and vile with feces. I told you once it was something "brown and sticky." It was, quite simply, Herman Tarnower, human shit! I decided, and rightly so, that this was your expense, not mine. As for stealing from you, the day I put my ring on your dresser my income before *taxes* was $12,000 per year. I had two children in private school. They had been on a fairly sizable scholarship until I told the school I wouldn't need it because we were moving to Scarsdale. It was two years before we got it back. That more than anything else is the reason David went to Penn State instead of the University of Pa. He loathed every minute of it—and there is no question that it changed his life. That you should feel justified and comfortable suggesting that I steal from you is something I have no adjective to describe. I desperately needed money all those years. I couldn't have sold that ring. It was tangible proof of your love and it meant more to me than life itself. That you sold it the summer your adulterous slut finally got her divorce and needed money is a kind of sick, cynical act that left me old and bitter and sick. Your only comment when you told me you had sold it (and less than two months before, you had assured me you would get it from the safe so I could wear it again!) was "Look, if you're going to make a fuss about it you can't come here anymore. I don't need to have anyone spoil my weekend." Too bad Somerset Maugham didn't get hold of us before he died. He could have come up with something to top the *Magnificent Obsession.*

You have never once suggested that you would meet me in Virginia at *your* expense, so seeing you has been at my expense—and if you lived in California, I would borrow money to come there, too, if you would let me. All our conversations are my nickels, not yours—and obviously rightly so because it is I,

not you, who needs to hear your voice. I have indeed grown poor loving you, while a self-serving, ignorant slut has grown very rich—and yet you accuse me of stealing from you. How in the name of Christ does that make sense?

I have, and most proudly so—and with an occasional "Right on" from Lee and others—ripped up or destroyed anything I saw that your slut had touched and written her cutesie name on—including several books that I gave you and she had the tasteless, unmitigated gall to write in. I have refrained from throwing away the cheap little book of epigrams lying on your bed one day so I would be *absolutely sure* to see it, with a paper clip on the page about how an old man should have a young wife. It made me feel like a piece of old discarded garbage—but at least it solved for me what had been a mystery—what had suddenly possessed you to start your tasteless diatribes at dinner parties about how every man should have a wife half his age plus seven years. Since you never mentioned it to anyone under 65, it made the wives at the table feel about as attractive and wanted as I did. Tasteless behavior is the only kind Lynne knows—though to her credit she is clever and devious enough to hide it at times. Unfortunately it seems to be catching.

The things I know or profess to know about Lynne—except for what I have experienced first hand—I have been told by your friends and your servants, mostly the latter. I was interested to hear from Vivian and Arthur's next door neighbor in Florida—I don't remember her name though I am sure Lynne does: "I took her to lunch, she seemed so pathetic"—that you sat at table while I was there and discussed Lynne and her "wonderful family—brother a Ph.D." I can't imagine going out to dinner with you and telling my dinner partner how grand another lover is. I told the woman to ask you sometime why if her family is so fine, Lynne decided to sell her kids to the highest bidder and make you and your family the guardian of her children if she should die before they do. It must go down as a "first" for a splendid family to do. My phone tells me this—that "mysterious" caller. I hope to God you don't know who it is! Who pays him?

When my clothes were ripped to shreds Suzanne said, "Madam, there is only one person who could have done it. You must tell him." In my masochistic way I tried to downplay it in my note to you, although in all honesty it was so obvious you would know who did it. Instead you ignored it and went happily off to Florida with the perpetrator. Suzanne told me—and I would think would say so in court.

1. The clothes were not torn when she went into the closet to find something of Henri's on "Wednesday or Thursday" while we were away.

2. On the Sunday morning before we came home Henri and Suzanne both saw Lynne drive hurriedly up to your house. They were outside and she did not see them. They saw her go in but not out.

3. Lynne knew you were coming home that evening and she would see you by 8:00 the next morning. What business did she have at your home that morning?

4. When I discovered the clothes destroyed, Suzanne was sitting in the dining room at the wooden table right next to the door. I said, "My God—Suzanne, come look," and she was right there. When I called your slut to talk to her about it and see what she was going to do about it, she said, "You cut them up yourself and blamed it on me." That was the first time it occurred to me they had been "cut," not ripped. Only someone with a thoroughly warped mind would decide that a woman with no money would ruin about ⅓ of her wardrobe for kicks. Suzanne still believes Lynne did it and I most certainly do, too. I think there is enough evidence to prove it in court.

The stealing of my jewelry I can't prove at all. I just know I left some things in the white ashtray on your dresser, as I have for many years. When I thought of it later and called, Lynne answered the phone. When I called again and asked Suzanne to take them and put them away, they were gone. I only hope if she hocked them you got something nice as a "gift." Maybe I gave you some gold cuff links after all and didn't know it. I didn't for one instant think Henri or Suzanne took them. I had *never* called Lynne at the office anonymously as you have accused me that grim November day in 1977. I had in fact called her at the office before I left and said, since I did not have her number and could not get it, I would call her at the office every time I got an anonymous phone call if she did not immediately stop them. Within two weeks my "mysterious" caller told me her number. I have had it ever since then. Every single time she changes it I get it. And yet *though I was the one being wronged,* you refused to let me come see you that month because a lying slut had told you *I* was calling her. The thought of it had never crossed my mind. Her voice is vomitous to me. The next month I called her virtually every single night *only* because of your rotten accusation while she sat simperingly by, letting you make it. Not *once,* not *once* did Lynne answer the phone. At one, two, or three in the morning it was her children who answered, very quickly, TV playing. Where does mumsie spend her nights? That she "totally neglects her children" is something Henri and Suzanne have told me. That you admire her for it is sad. She uses them to write "super doctor" cute notes. With that kind of training Electra is going to be ready to earn her own color television any day now. I hope to God you're not the one who buys it for her. I don't think [she] would mind too much as long as you didn't change your will. "Stupid" is certainly not the word for Lynne. In that I was totally wrong. "Dishonest, ignorant and tasteless," but God knows not stupid.

It would have been heartbreaking for me to have to see less and less of you even if it had been a decent woman who took my place. Going through the hell of the past few years has been bearable only because you were still there and I could be with you whenever I could get away from work, which seemed to be less and less. To be jeered at, and called "old and pathetic" made me seriously consider borrowing $5,000 just before I left New York and telling a doctor to make me young again—to do anything but make me not feel like discarded trash. I lost my nerve because there was always the chance I'd end up uglier than before.

You have been what you very carefully set out to be, Hi—the most important thing in my life, the most important human being in my life, and that will never change. You keep me in control by threatening me with banishment—an easy threat which you know I couldn't live with—and so I stay home alone while you make love to someone who has almost totally destroyed me. I have been publicly humiliated again and again but not on the 19th of April. It is the apex of your career and I believe I have earned the right to watch it—if only from a dark corner near the kitchen. If you wish to insist that Lee and Dan invite Lynne, so be it—whatever they may tell you, they tell me and others that they dislike being with her. Dan whispers it to me each time we meet. "Why weren't you here? Lee hates it when it's Lynne." I always thought that taking me out of your will would be the final threat. On that I believed you would be completely honest. I have every intention of dying before you do, but sweet Jesus, darling. I didn't think you would ever be dishonest about that. The gulf between us seems wide on the phone but the moment I see you it's as though we had been together forever. You were so absolutely perfect over David's wedding and I will always be grateful. I wish 14 years of making love to one another and sharing so much happiness had left enough of a mark that you couldn't have casually scratched my name out of a will and written in Lynne's instead. But for God's sake don't translate that into begging for money. I would far rather be saved the trial of living without you than have the option of living with your money. Give her all the money she wants, Hi—but give me time with you and the privilege of sharing with you April 19th. There were a lot of ways to have money—I very consciously picked working hard, supporting myself, and being with you. Please, darling, don't tell me now it was all for nothing. She has you every single moment in March. For Christ sake give me April. T. S. Eliot said it's the cruelest month. Don't let it be, Hi. I want to spend every minute of it with you on weekends. In all these years you've never spent my birthday with me. There aren't a lot left—it goes so quickly. I give you my word if you just aren't cruel I won't make you wretched. I never did until you were cruel—and then I just wasn't ready for it.

After the letter there was a little more cross-examination, but everything else was anticlimactic. The letter itself belied, if not in specific words, then at least in tone, the picture that Harris had drawn of the state of the relationship on the day of the shooting. But more than that, it painted the writer as a woman filled with such rage that she might have been capable of driving to New York with gun in car, and with the intent to kill.

And the letter did more than that. Feminists had been following the trial, some present in the courtroom taking notes. If Jean Harris had never become their heroine, they at least could think of her as a victim of the dominant males in our society, a woman who had taken revenge on a man who had wooed her, used her, and wronged her. The vituperation in the letter left them bereft of the sanctity and integrity of a woman who might have been their martyr and a symbol of their cause.

There was a summing up by both sides, and careful instructions were given to the jury about the possible verdicts and about their task as judges of the facts of the case, but not of the law.

The jury was out eight days, and during that time it came back on occasion to hear testimony reread (sometimes at great length). It was rumored (but only after the fact) that the first vote was eight to four for acquittal, but one by one the acquittal people were won over, and finally the jury returned with a verdict that was the most severe of the choices before them: guilty of murder in the second degree. The verdict brought with it a mandatory sentence of not less than fifteen years in jail, during which the defendant would be ineligible for parole; the actual sentence was fifteen years to life.

All appeals have thus far been denied. (A case can never be said to be closed; it is always within the realm of imagination or fantasy that some new evidence can be turned up, or a new angle brought out, and that even after many years there will be a new trial, or some other outcome.) At this time, about one-fourth of the mandatory minimum sentence has been served, and the likelihood of a successful appeal is slim. Jean Harris is serving her sentence in a women's prison in New York State, and it would appear that only extremely ill health would convince a governor to commute the term to time served.

Aurnou and Harris, she more than he, had lost a case that under no circumstances would have been difficult to win. In retrospect, one might ask what went wrong, what

Jean Harris (*fourth from left*) being sentenced by Judge Russell R. Leggett. She is flanked by prosecutor George Baker (*left*) and defense lawyer Joel Aurnou (*third from left*). *Wide World Photos* (*Drawing by Libby Dengrove*)

could have turned out better? After all, Harris did make the trip from Virginia with a gun, and Tarnower was killed in her presence. If she had wanted to commit suicide, she did not have to do so at his bedside. But against this, there was a woman taking large doses of medication prescribed by the now-dead doctor, there was bungled police work that cast some doubt on her supposed confession, a great deal of conflicting testimony by the pathologists that even leaned slightly in her favor, and a portrait of a woman both depressed and distraught.

An insanity defense might have worked, but it would have meant admitting that the act was murder, and not an accidental killing. The insanity defense, in the end, comes down to a confession, and if the jury had not accepted it, it would have had to find Harris guilty (which of course it did anyway). After the fact, it is indisputable that putting Harris on the witness stand was a grave mistake, and word of mouth in legal circles has it that it was her insistence, not her lawyer's, that made her a witness.

Aurnou knew two things: that Harris would show herself to be the type of angry and contentious woman who could have killed, and that once she was on the stand, the Scarsdale letter, with whose contents he was so familiar, would be read in court and would be damaging to her. There was no way that the jury could have learned of the contents of that letter except through cross-examination of Mrs. Harris. So Aurnou might have rested his case without

Harris's testimony, with the judge charging the jury that no inference as to guilt or innocence could be drawn from that, and he might have tried in his summation to suggest that she was too emotionally distraught to face the task of examination and giving evidence. His case would have rested on reasonable doubt, and some such reasonable doubt he had created through the testimony of pathologists, police officers produced by his adversary, the will that she had just written, and other factors. Whether a jury would have found sufficient reasonable doubt as not to warrant a guilty verdict is only a matter of speculation.

Had Harris not taken the stand, had her jealous rages not been betrayed by her own written words, there is still another defense that might have been available. That would have been the defense of woman as victim, fighting back against an evil man who had used, abused, and discarded her. There are no precedents, for such a defense—the judge might have charged the jury that that is not the law—but juries are known to disregard such charges and make their verdict on the basis of what the law ought to be. If such a plea had failed, the result might have been the same: second-degree murder, or perhaps a compromise with a manslaughter conviction or criminally negligent homicide. Had Harris been acquitted after such a trial, she would not only be free today, she also might be the new heroine of the feminist movement and a new symbol of justice for wronged women everywhere.

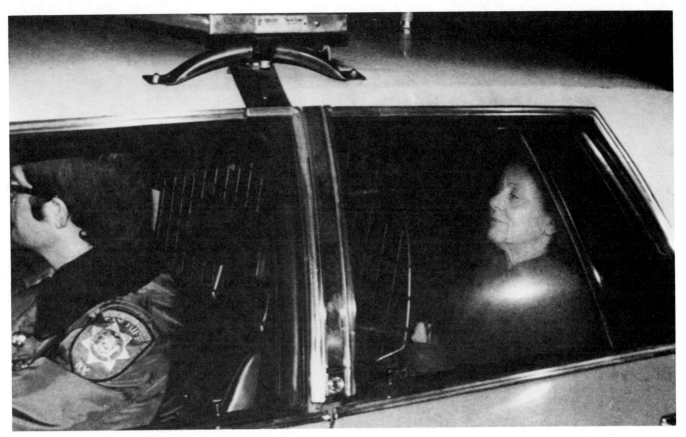

After being sentenced for the murder of Dr. Herman Tarnower, Jean Harris is driven away from the Westchester County Courthouse.
Gannett-Westchester Newspapers/Michael De Chillo

BIBLIOGRAPHIES

and

INDEX

Bibliographies

1. SOCRATES

CHURCH, F. J. *The Trial and Death of Socrates: Being the Euthyphron, Apology, Crito and Phaedo of Plato.* London: Macmillan and Company, 1880.

GROTE, GEORGE. *Life Teachings, and Death of Socrates.* New York: Stanford & Delisser, 1858.

PHILLIPSON, COLEMAN. *The Trial of Socrates.* London: Stevens and Sons, Limited, 1928.

PLATO. *Collected Works: The Apology of Socrates, Phaedo, Crito.* A version by Henry Cary. London: George Bell & Sons, 1890.

PLATO. *Socrates: A Translation of the Apology, Crito and Parts of the Phaedo.* ed. by W. W. Goodwin. New York: Charles Scribner's Sons, 1878.

ROBINSON, C. E. *The Days of Alkibiades.* New York: Longmans, Green and Company, 1916.

TAYLOR, A. E. *Socrates.* Boston: Beacon Press, 1951.

2. JOAN OF ARC

BANGS, MARY ROGERS. *Jeanne d'Arc: The Maid of France.* Boston: Houghton Mifflin Company, 1910.

BARRETT, W. P. *The Trial of Joan of Arc.* Translated into English from the Original Latin and French Documents. New York: Gotham House, Inc., 1932.

DENIS, LÉON. *The Mystery of Joan of Arc.* Translated by Arthur Conan Doyle. London: John Murray, 1924.

FABRE, LUCIEN. *Joan of Arc.* Translated from the French by Gerard Hopkins; made and printed in Great Britain: Odhams (Watford) Press, Ltd., Watford, Herts. New York: McGraw-Hill Book Company, Inc., 1954.

GOWER, LORD RONALD. *Joan of Arc.* London: John Nimmo, 1893.

IRELAND, W. H., ed. *Memoirs of Jeanne d'Arc.* 2 volumes. London: Robert Triphook, 1824.

LESCURE, M. F. ADOLPHE DE. *Jeanne d'Arc: L'Héroïne de la France.* Paris: Libraire Ducrocq, 187?.

PAINE, ALBERT BIGELOW. *Joan of Arc: Maid of France.* 2 volumes. New York: The Macmillan Company, 1925.

SEPET, MARIUS. *Jeanne d'Arc.* Tours: Alfred Mame et Fils, Editeurs, 1895.

The Trial of Joan of Arc. A translation by W. S. SCOTT, of the verbatim report of the proceedings from the Orléans Manuscript. London: The Folio Society, 1956.

3. MARY QUEEN OF SCOTS

HENDERSON, T. F. *Mary Queen of Scots.* 2 volumes. London: Hutchinson and Company, 1905.

HOSACK, JOHN. *Mary Queen of Scots and Her Accusers.* 2 volumes. Edinburgh and London: William Blackwood and Sons, 1874.

JENKINS, ELIZABETH. "Mary (Mary Stuart)," *Encyclopaedia Britannica*, 14th Ed., Vol. 14, pp. 994-997.

LANG, ANDREW. *The Mystery of Mary Stuart.* New York: Longmans, Green and Company, 1902 (3rd ed.).

MACCUNN, FLORENCE A. *Mary Stuart.* New York: E. P. Dutton and Company, 1905.

MACKIE, CHARLES. *Castles, Palaces and Prisons of Mary of Scotland.* London: 1850.

MAXWELL-SCOTT, THE HON. MRS. *The Tragedy of Fotheringay.* Founded on the Journal of D. Burgoing, Physician to Mary Queen of Scots, and on Unpublished MS. Documents. London: Adam and Charles Black, 1895.

PETIT, JOSEPH ADOLPHE. *History of Mary Stuart, Queen of Scots.* Volume 2. Translated from the Original and Unpublished MS. of Professor Petit by Charles de Flandre. London: Longmans, Green and Company, 1874.

"The Real Trial of Mary Queen of Scots."—*Juridical Review*, Vol. 40, pp. 341-360, Dec. 1, 1928.

SHOEMAKER, MICHAEL MYERS. *Palaces and Prisons of Mary Queen of Scots.* New York: G. P. Putnam's Sons, 1903.

WILLIAMS, HENRY SMITH, ed. *The Historians' History of the World.* Volume 19. New York: The Outlook Company, 1904.

4. GUY FAWKES

AINSWORTH, WILLIAM HARRISON. *Pictorial Life and Adventures of Guy Fawkes.* Philadelphia: T. B. Peterson & Brothers, 184?.

ANONYMOUS. *Guy Fawkes: A Legend of the Tower of London.* London: John Williams, 1840.

BARLOW, THOMAS. *The Gunpowder-Treason with a Discourse of the Manner of Its Discovery.* London: T. Newcomb & H. Hills, 1679.

CARSWELL, DONALD, ed. *Trial of Guy Fawkes and Others (the Gunpowder Plot).* London: W. Hodge & Company, 1934.

GARNETT, HENRY. *Portrait of Guy Fawkes.* London: R. Hale, 1962.

SPINK, HENRY H. *The Gunpowder Plot and Lord Mounteagle's Letter.* London: Simpkin, Marshall & Company, 1902.

5. GALILEO GALILEI

FAHRIE, J. J. *Memorials of Galileo Galilei: 1564–1642.* Leamington and London: The Courier Press, 1929.

GALILEO, GALILEI. *Dialogue on the Great World Systems.* In the Salusbury Translation, revised, annotated, and with an introduction by George de Santillana. Chicago: University of Chicago Press, 1953.

HOLDEN, EDWARD S. "GALILEO." A series of articles in *The Popular Science Monthly*, 1905.

NAMER, ÉMILE. *Galileo, Searcher of the Heavens.* Translated and adapted from the French by Sibyl Harris. New York: Robert M. McBride Company, 1931.

OWEN, ROBERT DALE. "Galileo and the Inquisition." Extracts from the *Free Enquirer*, New York, 1830.

SANTILLANA, GEORGE DE. *The Crime of Galileo.* Chicago: University of Chicago Press, 1955.

STERNE, CARUS. "Copernicus, Tycho Brahe and Kepler." An article in *Open Court*, July, 1900.

WEGG-PROSSER, F. R. *Galileo and His Judges.* London: Chapman and Hall, 1889.

6. CHARLES I OF ENGLAND

ABBOTT, JACOB. *History of King Charles the First of England.* New York: Harper & Brothers, 1848.

BELLOC, HILAIRE. *Charles the First—King of England.* Philadelphia: J. B. Lippincott Company, 1933.

————. *Cromwell.* London: Cassell and Company, Ltd., 1934.

COIT, CHARLES WHEELER. *The Life of Charles the First: The Royal Martyr.* Boston: Houghton Mifflin Company, 1926.

FELLOWES, W. D. *Historical Sketches of Charles I, Cromwell, etc.* London: J. Murray, 1828.

GUIZOT, FRANÇOIS PIERRE GUILLAUME, translated by Andrew R. Scoble. *History of Charles the First and the English Revolution.* London: Richard Bentley. 1854. 2 volumes.

HERBERT, SIR THOMAS, Groom of the Chambers to His Majesty. *Memoirs of the Last Two Years of Charles I.* London: Shakespeare Press, 1839.

LOCKYER, ROGER, ed. *The Trial of Charles I.* A Contemporary Account Taken from the Memoirs of Sir Thomas Herbert and John Rushworth. London: The Folio Society, 1959.

NALSON, J. *The Trial of Charles the First, King of England, Before the High Court of Justice for High-Treason.* London: J. Nalson, Booksellers, 1740.

WEDGWOOD, C. V. *A Coffin for King Charles.* New York: The Macmillan Company, 1964.

WILLIAMSON, HUGH ROSS. *The Day They Killed the King.* London: Frederick Muller, Ltd., 1957.

7. SALEM WITCHCRAFT

BEARD, GEORGE M. *The Psychology of the Salem Witchcraft Excitement of 1692.* New York: G. P. Putnam's Sons, 1882.

KIMBALL, HENRIETTA D. *Witchcraft Illustrated.* Boston: George A. Kimball, 1892.

LEVIN, DAVID. *What Happened in Salem?* New York: Harcourt, Brace, and World, Inc., 1960.

MATHER, COTTON. *Wonders of the Invisible World.* London: John Russell Smith, 1862.

PERLEY, M. V. B. *A Short History of the Salem Witchcraft Trials.* Salem, Mass.: M. V. B. Perley, 1911.

Records of Salem Witchcraft. Copied from the original documents and privately printed for W. Elliot Woodward, Roxbury, Mass.: 1864.

ROBBINS, ROSSELL HOPE. *The Encyclopedia of Witchcraft and Demonology.* New York: Crown Publishers, Inc., 1959.

STARKEY, MARION L. *The Devil in Massachusetts.* New York: Alfred A. Knopf, Inc., 1949.

UPHAM, CHARLES W. *Salem Witchcraft*, 4 volumes. Boston: Wiggin and Lunt, 1867.

8. JOHN PETER ZENGER

BROWN, JAMES WRIGHT. *Life and Times of John Peter Zenger.* A Statement of Facts Chronologically Arranged—as gathered from Rutherford, Konkle, Cheslaw, Sheehan, Cooper and Robb. New York: *Editor and Publisher*, March 14, 21, 28; April 4 and 11, 1953.

BURANELLI, VINCENT, ed. *The Trial of Peter Zenger.* New York: New York University Press, 1957.

HART, CHARLES SPENCE. "The Freedom of the Press," in *St. Paul's Church, Eastchester: 1665–1940.* Mount Vernon, New York: 1953.

RUTHERFURD, LIVINGSTON. *John Peter Zenger: His Press, His Trial and a Bibliography of Zenger Imprints, also a Reprint of the First Edition of the Trial.* New York: Dodd, Mead and Company, 1904.

The Story of John Peter Zenger. John Peter Zenger Memorial, Federal Hall Memorial, New York: 1953.

9. LOUIS XVI

BORROW, GEORGE. *Celebrated Trials.* Volume 5. London: Knight and Lacey, 1825.

CLÉRY, JEAN-BAPTISTE. *A Journal of the Terror, Being an Account of the Occurrences in the Temple During the Confinement of Louis XVI.* Ed. by Sidney Scott. London: Folio Society, 1955.

DESÈZE, RAYMOND. *The Defense of Louis.* Translated from the French by Cézar Dubuc. Paris: National Press, 1792.

LAMBALLE, MARIE-THÉRÈSE. *The Royal Family of France During the Revolution.* 2 volumes. Philadelphia: The Rittenhouse Press, n.d.

TATE, GERALD A. *Louis XVI: The Last Phase.* London: Methuen & Company, 1929.

TURBAT (DU MANS). *Procès de Louis XVI, Roi de France . . .* Paris: Lerouge, 1814, 3rd ed.

10. MARY SURRATT AND THE LINCOLN CONSPIRATORS

BISHOP, JIM. *The Day Lincoln Was Shot.* New York: Harper & Brothers, 1955.

DE WITT, DAVID M. *The Assassination of Abraham Lincoln and Its Expiation.* New York: The Macmillan Company, 1909.

EISENSCHIML, OTTO. *Why Was Lincoln Murdered?* Boston: Little, Brown and Company, 1937.

MC LOUGHLIN, EMMETT. *An Inquiry into the Assassination of Abraham Lincoln.* New York: Lyle Stuart, 1963.

MOORE, GUY W. *The Case of Mrs. Surratt: Her Controversial Trial and Execution for Conspiracy in the Lincoln Assassination.* Norman, Okla.: University of Oklahoma Press, 1954.

OLDROYD, OSBORN H. *The Assassination of Abraham Lincoln: Flight, Pursuit, Capture and Punishment of the Conspirators.* Washington, D.C.: O. H. Oldroyd, 1901.

PITMAN, BENN. *The Assassination of President Lincoln and the Trial of the Conspirators.* The Courtroom Testimony as Originally Compiled by Benn Pitman, with an introduction by Philip Van Doren Stern. Facsimile Edition. New York: Funk and Wagnalls, 1954. Originally published by Moore, Wilstach, & Baldwin, Cincinnati and New York, 1865.

ROSCOE, THEODORE. *The Web of Conspiracy.* Englewood Cliffs, N.J.: Prentice-Hall, 1960.

SHELTON, VAUGHAN. *Mask for Treason: The Lincoln Murder Trial.* Harrisburg, Pa.: Stackpole Books, 1965.

Trial of the Alleged Assassins and Conspirators at Washington, D.C., May and June 1865, for the Murder of President Abraham Lincoln. Verbatim report. Philadelphia: T. B. Peterson & Brothers, 1865.

Trial of John H. Surratt in the Criminal Court for the District of Columbia, Hon. G. P. Fisher, presiding. Washington, D.C.: Government Printing Office, 1867.

11. PRESIDENT ANDREW JOHNSON'S IMPEACHMENT

CLEMENCEAU, GEORGES. *American Reconstruction 1865–1870 and the Impeachment of President Johnson.* New York: Lincoln MacVeagh and Dial Press, 1928.

DE WITT, DAVID M. *The Impeachment and Trial of Andrew Johnson, Seventeenth President of the United States: A History.* New York: The Macmillan Company, 1903.

FRANKLIN, JOHN HOPE. *Reconstruction: After the Civil War.* Chicago: University of Chicago Press, 1961.

LOMASK, MILTON. *Andrew Johnson: President on Trial.* New York: Farrar, Straus and Cudahy, 1960.

ROSS, EDMUND G. *History of the Impeachment of Andrew Johnson, President of the United States, by the House of Representatives, and His Trial by the Senate for High Crimes and Misdemeanors in Office, 1868.* Santa Fe, N. M.: New Mexican Printing Company, 1896.

STAMPP, KENNETH M. *The Era of Reconstruction, 1865–1877.* New York: Alfred A. Knopf, 1965.

STRYKER, LLOYD PAUL. *Andrew Johnson: A Study in Courage.* New York: The Macmillan Company, 1929.

TREFOUSSE, HANS LOUIS. *Ben Butler: The South Called Him BEAST!* New York: Twayne Publishers, 1957.

———. *Benjamin Franklin Wade: Radical Republican from Ohio.* New York: Twayne Publishers, 1963.

Trial of Andrew Johnson, President of the United States, Before the Senate of the United States, on Impeachment by the House of Representatives for High Crimes and Misdemeanors. Published by order of the Senate. 3 volumes. Washington, D.C.: Government Printing Office, 1868.

12. REVEREND HENRY WARD BEECHER

BEECHER, WM. C., AND THE REV. SAMUEL SCOVILLE. *A Biography of Rev. Henry Ward Beecher.* New York: Charles L. Webster & Company, 1888.

HIBBEN, PAXTON. *Henry Ward Beecher: An American Portrait.* New York: George H. Doran Company, 1927.

Independent, The. Scrapbooks of clippings relating to the Beecher-Tilton Trial. New York: New York Public Library, 1875.

Official Report of the Trial of Henry Ward Beecher. 2 volumes.

SHAPLEN, ROBERT. *Free Love and Heavenly Sinners: The Story of the Great Henry Ward Beecher Scandal.* New York: Alfred A. Knopf, 1954.

Theodore Tilton Against Henry Ward Beecher. Verbatim Report of the Trial by the Official Stenographer. New York: McDivitt, Campbell and Company, 1875.

WILLIAMSON, FRANCIS P. *Beecher and His Accusers: A Complete History of the Great Controversy.* Philadelphia: Flint & Company, 1874.

13. NED KELLY

BOND, GEOFFREY. *Ned Kelly: The Armoured Outlaw.* London: Arco Publications, 1961.

BROWN, MAX. *Australian Son: The Story of Ned Kelly.* Melbourne: Georgian House, 1948.

CLUNE, FRANK. *The Kelly Hunters.* Sydney: Angus and Robertson, 1954.

HARE, FRANCIS AUGUSTUS. *The Last of the Bushrangers.* London: Messrs. Hurst and Blackett, 1895.

JACOBS, PHILIP A. *Famous Australian Trials.* Melbourne: Robertson and Mullens, Ltd., 1943.

KENNEALLY, J. J. *The Complete Inner History of the Kelly Gang and Their Pursuers.* Melbourne: J. Roy Stevens, 1945.

A Noose for Ned. Reprint of a very rare pamphlet, with Foreword by Frank Clune. Melbourne: Hawthorn Press, 1948(?).

SECCOMBE, THOMAS. *The Lives of Twelve Bad Men.* New York: G. P. Putnam's Sons, 1894.

14. LIZZIE BORDEN

Frank Leslie's Weekly, August, 1892, to July, 1893.

PEARSON, EDMUND. *Trial of Lizzie Borden.* New York: Doubleday, Doran & Company, 1937.

Police Gazette, June, 1893.

PORTER, EDWIN H. *The Fall River Tragedy—A History of the Borden Murders.* Fall River, Mass.: G. R. H. Buffinton, Publisher, 1893.

RADIN, EDWARD D. *Lizzie Borden—The Untold Story.* New York: Simon and Schuster, 1961.

15. OSCAR WILDE

BRASOL, BORIS. *Oscar Wilde: The Man, the Artist, the Martyr.* New York: Charles Scribner's Sons, 1938.

BROAD, LEWIS. *The Friendships and Follies of Oscar Wilde.* London, Hutchinson & Company, 1954.

CROFT-COOKE, RUPERT. *Bosie: The Story of Lord Alfred Douglas, His Friends and His Enemies.* London: Witt, 1963.

DOUGLAS, LORD ALFRED. *The Autobiography of Lord Alfred Douglas.* London: M. Secker, 1929. (Published in USA under title *My Friendships with Oscar Wilde,* New York: Coventry House, 1932.)

———. *Without Apology.* London: M. Secker, 1938.

HARRIS, FRANK. *Oscar Wilde: His Life and Confessions.* New York: Covici, Friede, 1930.

HOLLAND, VYVYAN. *Son of Oscar Wilde.* London: Hart-Davis, Ltd., 1954, and New York: E. P. Dutton & Company, 1954.

HYDE, H. MONTGOMERY. *Oscar Wilde: The Aftermath.* New York: Farrar, Straus & Company, 1963.

HYDE, H. MONTGOMERY, ed. *The Trials of Oscar Wilde.* London: William Hodge and Company, 1948.

QUEENSBERRY, THE MARQUESS OF, AND PERCY COLSON. *Oscar Wilde and the Black Douglas.* London: Hutchinson & Company, 1949.

SHERARD, ROBERT H. *The Life of Oscar Wilde.* New York: M. Kennerly, 1907.

WINWAR, FRANCES. *Oscar Wilde and the Yellow Nineties.* New York: Harper & Brothers, 1940.

16. CAPTAIN ALFRED DREYFUS

BYRNES, ROBERT F. *Antisemitism in Modern France.* Vol. 1: *The Prologue to the Dreyfus Affair.* New Brunswick, N.J.: Rutgers University Press, 1950.

DERFLER, LESLIE, ed. *The Dreyfus Affair: Tragedy of Errors?* Boston: D. C. Heath and Company, 1963.

HALASZ, NICHOLAS. *Captain Dreyfus: The Story of a Mass Hysteria.* New York: Grove Press, Inc., 1957.

KAYSER, JACQUES. *The Dreyfus Affair.* New York: Covici, Friede, 1931.

PALÉOLOGUE, MAURICE. *An Intimate Journal of the Dreyfus Case.* New York: Criterion Books, 1957.

REINACH, JOSEPH. *Histoire de L'Affaire Dreyfus.* 7 volumes, *Le Procès de 1894.* Paris: Editions de la Revue Blanche, 1901–1911.

SCHWARTZKOPPEN, MAX VON. *The Truth About Dreyfus.* From the Schwartzkoppen Papers. New York: G. P. Putnam's Sons, 1931.

TUCHMAN, BARBARA. *The Proud Tower.* New York: The Macmillan Company, 1965.

ZOLA, ÉMILE. *L'Affaire Dreyfus: La Vérité en Marche*. Paris: Bibliothèque-Charpentier, 1901.

17. FRANCISCO FERRER

ARCHER, WILLIAM. *The Life, Trial and Death of Francisco Ferrer*. London: Chapman and Hall, Ltd., 1911.
DE ANGULO, JAIME. *The "Trial" of Ferrer*. New York: New York Labor News Company, 1911.
GIBBON, PERCEVAL. "The Ferrer Trial," *McClure's Magazine*, January, 1910.
RABY, R. CORNELIUS. *Fifty Famous Trials*. Washington, D.C.: Washington Law Book Co. 1937.

18. MADAME JOSEPH CAILLAUX

The Independent, August 3, 1914. New York.
The Literary Digest, April 11, 1914. New York.
RABY, R. CORNELIUS. *Fifty Famous Trials*. Washington, D.C.: Washington Law Book Co., 1937.
RAPHAEL, JOHN N. *The Caillaux Drama*. London: Max Goschen, Ltd., 1914.

19. EDITH CAVELL

GOT, AMBROISE. *The Case of Miss Cavell: From the Unpublished Documents of the Trial: The Property of a Former Commissioner of the German Government*. London: Hodder and Stoughton, 1920.
HOEHLING, A. A. *A Whisper of Eternity: The Mystery of Edith Cavell*. New York: Thomas Yoseloff, Inc., 1957.
WHITTON, LT. COL. F. E. *Service Trials and Tragedies*. London: Hutchinson & Company, 1930.

20. NICOLA SACCO AND BARTOLOMEO VANZETTI

EHRMANN, HERBERT B. *The Untried Case: The Sacco-Vanzetti Case and the Morelli Gang*. New York: Vanguard Press, 1933.
FELIX, DAVID. *Protest: Sacco-Vanzetti and the Intellectuals*. Bloomington: Indiana University Press, 1965.
FRANKFURTER, FELIX. "Case of Sacco and Vanzetti," *Atlantic Monthly*, March, 1927.
————. *The Case of Sacco and Vanzetti: A Critical Analysis for Lawyers and Laymen*. Boston: Little, Brown & Company, 1927.
JOUGHIN, LOUIS, AND EDMUND M. MORGAN. *The Legacy of Sacco and Vanzetti*. New York: Harcourt, Brace, 1948.
MUSMANNO, MICHAEL A. *After Twelve Years*. New York: Alfred A. Knopf, 1939.
RUSSELL, FRANCIS: *Tragedy at Dedham*. New York: McGraw-Hill Book Company, Inc., 1962.
SACCO, NICOLA, AND BARTOLOMEO VANZETTI. *The Letters of Sacco and Vanzetti*. Edited by Marion D. Frankfurter and Gardner Jackson. New York: Viking Press, 1928.
The Sacco-Vanzetti Case. Transcript of the Record of the Trial of Nicola Sacco and Bartolomeo Vanzetti in the Courts of Massachusetts and Subsequent Proceedings 1920–7. 6 volumes. New York: Henry Holt & Company, 1928.

21. JOHN THOMAS SCOPES

ALLEN, LESLIE H., ed. *Bryan and Darrow at Dayton: The Record and Documents of the "Bible-Evolution Trial."* New York: Arthur Lee, 1925.
DARROW, CLARENCE. *The Story of My Life*. New York: Grosset & Dunlap, 1932.
GINGER, RAYMOND. *Six Days or Forever? Tennessee v. John Thomas Scopes*. Boston: Beacon Press, 1958.

LEVINE, LAWRENCE W. *Defender of the Faith: William Jennings Bryan: The Last Decade, 1915–1925*. New York: Oxford University Press, 1965.
STONE, IRVING. *Clarence Darrow for the Defense*. Garden City, N.Y.: Doubleday & Company, 1941.
TOMPKINS, JERRY R., ed. *D-Days at Dayton*. Baton Rouge, La.: Louisiana State University Press, 1965.
WEINBERG, ARTHUR, ed. *Attorney for the Damned*. New York: Simon & Schuster, 1957.
The World's Most Famous Court Trial: Tennessee Evolution Case. Cincinnati: National Book Company, 1925.

22. GENERAL "BILLY" MITCHELL

Aviation Magazine, September 14, November 23, December 28, 1925.
BURLINGAME, ROGER. *General Billy Mitchell: Champion of Air Defense*. New York: McGraw-Hill Book Company, 1952.
LEVINE, ISAAC DON. *Mitchell: Pioneer of Air Power*. Revised edition. New York: Duell, Sloane and Pearce, 1958.
MITCHELL, RUTH. *My Brother Bill: The Life of General "Billy" Mitchell*. New York: Harcourt, Brace, 1953.
MITCHELL, WILLIAM. Unpublished diary. Library of Congress.
New York Times, October 29 to December 19, 1925.

23. SCOTTSBORO BOYS

AMERICAN CIVIL LIBERTIES UNION. *Report on the Scottsboro, Alabama, Case*. New York, 1931.
BELFRAGE, SALLY. "The Scottsboro Boys Today." *Fact*, Vol. 3, No. 6, November-December, 1966, pp. 58-64.
CARTER DAN T. *Scottsboro: A Tragedy of the American South*. New York: Oxford University Press, 1971.
CHALMERS, ALLAN K. *They Shall Be Free*. Garden City, N.Y.: Doubleday & Company, 1951.
ENDORE, GUY. *The Crime at Scottsboro*. Hollywood, Calif.: Hollywood Scottsboro Committee, 1938.
Four Free, Five in Prison—on the Same Evidence. What the Nation's Press Says About the Scottsboro Case. New York: Scottsboro Defense Committee, 1937.
FRAENKEL, OSMOND K. *Ozie Powell (and Others), Petitioners vs. The State of Alabama . . .* New York: Court Press, 1933.
LEIBOWITZ, SAMUEL. *Haywood Patterson, petitioner, against State of Alabama . . .* New York: Ackerman Press, 1937.
————. *(Brief for) Haywood Patterson, Appellant*. 1937.
PATTERSON, HAYWOOD, petitioner. *Transcript of record*. Supreme Court of the United States . . . Washington, D.C.: Judd & Detweiler, Inc., 1937.
———— (with Earl Conrad). *Scottsboro Boy*. Garden City, N.Y.: Doubleday & Company, 1950.
Scottsboro: A Record of a Broken Promise. New York: Scottsboro Defense Committee, 1939.
Scottsboro: The Shame of America: The True Story and the True Meaning of the Famous Case. New York: Scottsboro Defense Committee, 1936.

24. BRUNO RICHARD HAUPTMANN

Bruno Richard Hauptmann, Petitioner, vs. State of New Jersey, Respondent. On Certiorari. Respondent's brief . . . Trenton, N.J.: MacCrellish & Quigley Company, 1935.
HALDEMAN-JULIUS, ANNA MARCET. *The Lindbergh-Hauptmann Kidnap-Murder Case*. Girard, Kan.: Haldeman-Julius, n.d.
HARING, JOHN VREELAND. *The Hand of Hauptmann: The Handwriting Expert Tells the Story of the Lindbergh Case*. Plainfield, N.J.: Hamer Publishing Company, 1937.
O'BRIEN, PATRICK JOSEPH. *The Lindberghs: The Story of a Distinguished Family*. Philadelphia: International Press, 1935.

PEASE, FRANK. *The "Hole" in the Hauptmann Case?* New York: Published by the author, 1936.

SCHOENFELD, DUDLEY D. *The Crime and the Criminal: A Psychiatric Study of the Lindbergh Case.* New York: Covici, Friede, 1936.

The State of New Jersey, Defendant in Error, vs. Bruno Richard Hauptmann, Plaintiff in Error. Somerville, N.J.: Somerset Press, Inc., 1935.

WALLER, GEORGE. *Kidnap: The Story of the Lindbergh Case.* New York: Dial Press, 1961.

WENDEL, PAUL H. *The Lindbergh-Hauptmann Aftermath.* Brooklyn, N.Y.: Loft Publishing Company, 1940.

WHIPPLE, SIDNEY B. *The Lindbergh Crime.* New York: Blue Ribbon Books, 1935.

———. *The Trial of Bruno Richard Hauptmann,* edited with a history of the case. Garden City, N.Y.: Doubleday, Doran & Company, Inc., 1937.

25. LEON TROTSKY

The Case of Leon Trotsky. Report of Hearings on the charges made against him in the Moscow Trials, by the Preliminary Commission of Inquiry, John Dewey, Chairman (and others). New York: Harper & Brothers, 1937.

DEWEY, JOHN. *Truth Is on the March.* New York: American Committee for the Defense of Leon Trotsky, 1937.

HALLGREN, MAURITZ A. *Why I Resigned from the Trotsky Defense Committee.* New York: International Publishers, 1937.

KATZ, M. *The Assassination of Kirov: Proletarian Justice Versus White-Guard Terror.* New York: Workers Library Publishers, 1935.

Not Guilty. Report of the Commission of Inquiry into the charges made against Leon Trotsky in the Moscow Trials. John Dewey, Chairman (and others). New York: Harper & Brothers, 1938.

SCHACHTMAN, MAX. *Behind the Moscow Trial.* New York: Pioneer Publishers, 1936.

TROTSKY, LEON. *I Stake My Life.* New York: Pioneer Publishers, 1937.

———. *The Stalinist Bureaucracy and the Assassination of Kirov.* London: I. L. P. Marxist Group, 1934.

WOLFE, BERTRAM D. *Three Who Made a Revolution.* New York: Dial Press, 1948.

26. NUREMBERG

ALEXANDER, CHARLES W., AND ANNE KEESHAN. *Justice at Nuernberg: As Pictured by the Camera of Charles W. Alexander.* 1946.

BERNSTEIN, VICTOR H. *Final Judgment: The Story of Nuremberg.* New York: Boni and Gaer, 1947.

GILBERT, G. M. *Nuremberg Diary.* New York: Farrar, Straus and Cudahy, Inc., 1947.

HARRIS, WHITNEY R. *Tyranny on Trial: The Evidence at Nuremberg.* Dallas: Southern Methodist University Press, 1954.

International Military Tribunal. *Trial of the Major War Criminals Before the International Military Tribunal: Nuremberg, 14 November 1945–1 October 1946. Official Record of the Proceedings.* Volume 1. Germany: published at Nuremberg, 1947.

———. *The Trial of German Major War Criminals: Opening Speeches of the Chief Prosecutors.* London: His Majesty's Stationery Office, 1946.

JACKSON, ROBERT H. *The Case Against the Nazi War Criminals: Opening Statements for the United States of America.* New York: Alfred A. Knopf, 1946.

KELLEY, DOUGLAS M. *22 Cells in Nuremberg: A Psychiatrist Examines the Nazi Criminals.* New York: Greenberg Publisher, 1947.

MUSMANNO, MICHAEL A. *The Eichmann Kommandos.* Philadelphia: Macrae Smith, 1961.

WECHSLER, HERBERT. *Principles, Politics, and Fundamental Law.* Cambridge, Mass.: Harvard University Press, 1961.

WOERZEL, ROBERT K. *The Nuremberg Trials in International Law.* New York: Frederick A. Praeger, Inc., 1960.

27. CARDINAL JOSEPH MINDSZENTY

BAER, NICHOLAS. *Cardinal Mindszenty and the Implacable War of Communism Against Religion and the Spirit.* London: B.U.E. Ltd., 1949.

FABIAN, BELA. *Cardinal Mindszenty: The Story of a Modern Martyr.* New York: Charles Scribner's Sons, 1949.

SHUSTER, GEORGE N. *In Silence I Speak.* New York: Farrar, Straus and Cudahy, 1956.

SWIFT, STEPHEN K. *The Cardinal's Story.* New York: The Macmillan Company, 1949.

The Trial of Jozsef Mindszenty. Budapest: Hungarian State Publishing House, 1949.

28. JULIUS AND ETHEL ROSENBERG AND MARTIN SOBELL

MEEREPOL, ROBERT AND MICHAEL. *We Are Your Sons: The Legacy of Julius and Ethel Rosenberg.* Boston: Houghton Mifflin, 1975.

NIZER, LOUIS. *The Implosion Conspiracy.* Garden City: Doubleday, 1973.

RADOSH, RONALD and JOYCE MILTON. *The Rosenberg File: A Search for the Truth.* New York: Holt, Rinehart and Winston, 1973.

RUBEN, WILLIAM. *The Atom Spy Hoax.* New York: Action Books, 1954.

SHARP, MALCOLM. *Was Justice Done? The Rosenberg-Sobell Case.* New York: Monthly Review Press, 1956.

The Testament of Ethel and Julius Rosenberg. New York: Cameron & Kahn, 1954.

U.S. vs. Rosenbergs, Sobell, Yakovlev, and David Greenglass. Transcript of trial, published by Committee to Secure Justice for Morton Sobell, New York.

SOBELL, MORTON. *On Doing Time.* New York: Charles Scribner's Sons, 1974.

WEXLEY, JOHN. *The Judgment of Julius and Ethel Rosenberg.* New York: Cameron & Kahn, 1955.

29. JOMO KENYATTA

BALDWIN, WILLIAM W. *Mau Mau Man-Hunt: The Adventures of the Only American Who Has Fought the Terrorists in Kenya.* New York: E. P. Dutton & Company, 1957.

BENNETT, GEORGE. *Kenya: A Political History: The Colonial Period.* London: Oxford University Press, 1963.

COX, RICHARD. *Kenyatta's Country.* New York: Frederick A. Praeger, 1966.

DELF, GEORGE. *Jomo Kenyatta: Towards Truth About "The Light of Kenya."* New York: Doubleday & Company, 1961.

HOLMAN, DENNIS. *Bwana Drum.* New York: W. W. Norton, 1964.

MBOYA, TOM. *Freedom and After.* Boston: Little, Brown and Company, 1963.

SLATER, MONTAGU. *The Trial of Jomo Kenyatta.* London: Secker and Warburg, 1955.

30. STEVEN TRUSCOTT

LEBOURDAIS, ISABEL. *The Trial of Steven Truscott.* Philadelphia: J. B. Lippincott Company, 1966.

31. ADOLF EICHMANN

ARENDT, HANNAH. *Eichmann in Jerusalem: A Report on the Banality of Evil.* New York: Viking Press, 1963.

FRIEDMAN, TUVIAH. *The Hunter.* Garden City, N.Y.: Doubleday and Company, 1961.

HAUSNER, GIDEON. *Justice in Jerusalem.* New York: Harper & Row, 1966.

PANETH, PHILIP. *Eichmann: Technician of Death.* New York: Robert Speller & Sons, 1960.

PEARLMAN, MOSHE. *The Capture and Trial of Adolf Eichmann.* New York: Simon and Schuster, 1963.

REYNOLDS, QUENTIN, WITH EPHRAIM KATZ AND ZWY ALDOUBY. *Minister of Death: The Adolf Eichmann Story.* New York: Viking Press, 1960.

ROBINSON, JACOB. *And the Crooked Shall Be Made Straight: The Eichmann Trial, the Jewish Catastrophe, and Hannah Arendt's Narrative.* New York: The Macmillan Company, 1965.

RUSSELL, LORD, OF LIVERPOOL. *The Record: The Trial of Adolf Eichmann for His Crimes Against the Jewish People and Against Humanity.* New York: Alfred A. Knopf, 1963.

32. LEOPOLD AND LOEB

BUSCH, FRANCIS X. *Prisoners at the Bar.* New York and Indianapolis: The Bobbs-Merrill Company, Inc., 1952.

HIGDON, HAL. *The Crime of the Century: The Leopold and Loeb Case.* New York: G. P. Putnam's Sons, 1975.

LEOPOLD, NATHAN F., JR. *Life Plus 99 Years.* Garden City, N.Y.: Doubleday & Company, 1958.

MAC KENZIE, FREDERICK ARTHUR. *Twentieth-Century Crimes.* Boston: Little, Brown and Company, 1927.

MC KERNAN, MAUREEN. *The Amazing Crime and Trial of Leopold and Loeb.* Chicago: The Plymouth Court Press, 1924.

STONE, IRVING. *Clarence Darrow for the Defense.* Garden City, N.Y.: Doubleday & Company, 1941.

SYMONS, JULIAN. *A Pictorial History of Crime.* New York: Crown Publishers, Inc., 1966.

WEINBERG, ARTHUR, ed. *Attorney for the Damned.* New York: Simon and Schuster, Inc., 1957.

————AND LILA. *Clarence Darrow: A Sentimental Rebel.* New York: G. P. Putnam's Sons, 1980.

33. ANGELA DAVIS

DAVIS, ANGELA, ET AL. *If They Come in the Morning: Voices of Resistance.* Foreword by Julian Bond. New York: Third Press, Joseph Opaku Publishing Company, 1971.

JACKSON, GEORGE. *Blood in My Eye.* New York: Random House, 1972.

————. *Soledad Brother: The Prison Letters of George Jackson.* New York: Coward, McCann and Geoghegan, 1971.

NADELSON, REGINA. *Angela Davis.* New York: Peter H. Wyden, 1972.

34. JEAN HARRIS

ALEXANDER, SHANA. *Very Much a Lady: The Untold Story of Jean Harris and Dr. Herman Tarnower.* Boston: Little, Brown, 1983.

SPENCER, DUNCAN. *Love Gone Wrong: The Jean Harris Scarsdale Murder Case.* New York: New American Library, 1981.

TRILLING, DIANA. *Mrs. Harris: The Death of the Scarsdale Diet Doctor.* New York: Harcourt Brace Jovanovich, 1981.

Index